Censorship and Student Communication in Online and Offline Settings

Joseph O. Oluwole
Montclair State University, USA

Preston C. Green III
University of Connecticut, USA

A volume in the Advances in Educational Marketing, Administration, and Leadership (AEMAL) Book Series

Managing Director:	Lindsay Johnston
Managing Editor:	Keith Greenberg
Director of Intellectual Property & Contracts:	Jan Travers
Acquisitions Editor:	Kayla Wolfe
Production Editor:	Christina Henning
Cover Design:	Jason Mull

Published in the United States of America by
Information Science Reference (an imprint of IGI Global)
701 E. Chocolate Avenue
Hershey PA, USA 17033
Tel: 717-533-8845
Fax: 717-533-8661
E-mail: cust@igi-global.com
Web site: http://www.igi-global.com

Copyright © 2016 by IGI Global. All rights reserved. No part of this publication may be reproduced, stored or distributed in any form or by any means, electronic or mechanical, including photocopying, without written permission from the publisher. Product or company names used in this set are for identification purposes only. Inclusion of the names of the products or companies does not indicate a claim of ownership by IGI Global of the trademark or registered trademark.
        Library of Congress Cataloging-in-Publication Data

Oluwole, Joseph, author.
  Censorship and student communication in online and offline settings / by Joseph O. Oluwole and Preston C. Green, III.
  pages cm
  Includes bibliographical references and index.
  ISBN 978-1-4666-9519-1 (hardcover) -- ISBN 978-1-4666-9520-7 (ebook) 1. Freedom of speech--United States. 2. Students--Legal status, laws, etc.--United States. 3. Censorship--United States. 4. Internet--Censorship--United States. 5. Intellectual freedom--United States. I. Green, Preston C., III (Preston Cary) II. Title.
  KF4772.O48 2016
  342.7308'53--dc23
        2015032761

This book is published in the IGI Global book series Advances in Educational Marketing, Administration, and Leadership (AEMAL) (ISSN: 2326-9022; eISSN: 2326-9030)

British Cataloguing in Publication Data
A Cataloguing in Publication record for this book is available from the British Library.

All work contributed to this book is new, previously-unpublished material. The views expressed in this book are those of the authors, but not necessarily of the publisher.

For electronic access to this publication, please contact: eresources@igi-global.com.

Advances in Educational Marketing, Administration, and Leadership (AEMAL) Book Series

Siran Mukerji
IGNOU, India
Purnendu Tripathi
IGNOU, India

ISSN: 2326-9022
EISSN: 2326-9030

Mission

With more educational institutions entering into public, higher, and professional education, the educational environment has grown increasingly competitive. With this increase in competitiveness has come the need for a greater focus on leadership within the institutions, on administrative handling of educational matters, and on the marketing of the services offered.

The **Advances in Educational Marketing, Administration, & Leadership (AEMAL) Book Series** strives to provide publications that address all these areas and present trending, current research to assist professionals, administrators, and others involved in the education sector in making their decisions.

Coverage

- Academic Administration
- Direct marketing of educational programs
- Academic Pricing
- Enrollment Management
- Faculty Administration and Management
- Advertising and Promotion of Academic Programs and Institutions
- Educational Marketing Campaigns
- Educational Management
- Governance in P-12 and Higher Education
- Educational Leadership

IGI Global is currently accepting manuscripts for publication within this series. To submit a proposal for a volume in this series, please contact our Acquisition Editors at Acquisitions@igi-global.com or visit: http://www.igi-global.com/publish/.

The Advances in Educational Marketing, Administration, and Leadership (AEMAL) Book Series (ISSN 2326-9022) is published by IGI Global, 701 E. Chocolate Avenue, Hershey, PA 17033-1240, USA, www.igi-global.com. This series is composed of titles available for purchase individually; each title is edited to be contextually exclusive from any other title within the series. For pricing and ordering information please visit http://www.igi-global.com/book-series/advances-educational-marketing-administration-leadership/73677. Postmaster: Send all address changes to above address. Copyright © 2016 IGI Global. All rights, including translation in other languages reserved by the publisher. No part of this series may be reproduced or used in any form or by any means – graphics, electronic, or mechanical, including photocopying, recording, taping, or information and retrieval systems – without written permission from the publisher, except for non commercial, educational use, including classroom teaching purposes. The views expressed in this series are those of the authors, but not necessarily of IGI Global.

Titles in this Series

For a list of additional titles in this series, please visit: www.igi-global.com

Open Learning and Formal Credentialing in Higher Education Curriculum Models and Institutional Policies
Shirley Reushle (University of Southern Queensland, Australia) Amy Antonio (University of Southern Queensland, Australia) and Mike Keppell (Swinburne University of Technology, Australia)
Information Science Reference • copyright 2016 • 344pp • H/C (ISBN: 9781466688568) • US $195.00 (our price)

Examining the Impact of Community Colleges on the Global Workforce
Stephanie J. Jones (Texas Tech University, USA) and Dimitra Jackson Smith (Texas Tech University, USA)
Information Science Reference • copyright 2015 • 295pp • H/C (ISBN: 9781466684812) • US $185.00 (our price)

Cases on Leadership in Adult Education
Oitshepile MmaB Modise (University of Botswana, Botswana)
Information Science Reference • copyright 2015 • 327pp • H/C (ISBN: 9781466685895) • US $175.00 (our price)

Supporting Multiculturalism and Gender Diversity in University Settings
Molly Y. Zhou (Dalton State College, USA)
Information Science Reference • copyright 2015 • 270pp • H/C (ISBN: 9781466683211) • US $175.00 (our price)

Promoting Trait Emotional Intelligence in Leadership and Education
Shelly R. Roy (University of Charleston, USA & Fairmont State University/Pierpont Community and Technical College, USA)
Information Science Reference • copyright 2015 • 341pp • H/C (ISBN: 9781466683273) • US $210.00 (our price)

Multidimensional Perspectives on Principal Leadership Effectiveness
Kadir Beycioglu (Dokuz Eylul University, Turkey) and Petros Pashiardis (Open University of Cyprus, Cyprus)
Information Science Reference • copyright 2015 • 480pp • H/C (ISBN: 9781466665910) • US $205.00 (our price)

Marketing the Green School Form, Function, and the Future
Tak C. Chan (Kennesaw State University, USA) Evan G. Mense (Southeastern Louisiana University, USA) Kenneth E. Lane (Southeastern Louisiana University, USA) and Michael D. Richardson (Columbus State University, USA)
Information Science Reference • copyright 2015 • 400pp • H/C (ISBN: 9781466663121) • US $205.00 (our price)

Handbook of Research on Teaching and Learning in K-20 Education
Victor C.X. Wang (Florida Atlantic University, USA)
Information Science Reference • copyright 2013 • 1180pp • H/C (ISBN: 9781466642492) • US $525.00 (our price)

www.igi-global.com

701 E. Chocolate Ave., Hershey, PA 17033
Order online at www.igi-global.com or call 717-533-8845 x100
To place a standing order for titles released in this series, contact: cust@igi-global.com
Mon-Fri 8:00 am - 5:00 pm (est) or fax 24 hours a day 717-533-8661

Table of Contents

Foreword viii

Preface xi

Acknowledgment xix

Section 1
Context

Chapter 1
Background 1
    INTRODUCTION 1
    MAIN FOCUS OF THE CHAPTER 2
    CONCLUSION 12

Section 2
Unprotected Speech

Chapter 2
True Threat 20
    INTRODUCTION 20
    MAIN FOCUS OF THE CHAPTER 20
    CONCLUSION 32

Chapter 3
Fighting Words 36
    INTRODUCTION 36
    MAIN FOCUS OF THE CHAPTER 36
    CONCLUSION 42

Chapter 4
Defamatory Speech 44
    INTRODUCTION 44
    MAIN FOCUS OF THE CHAPTER 44
    CONCLUSION 48

Chapter 5
Obscene Speech 50
- INTRODUCTION 50
- MAIN FOCUS OF THE CHAPTER 50
- CONCLUSION 53

Chapter 6
Child Pornography 55
- INTRODUCTION 55
- MAIN FOCUS OF THE CHAPTER 55
- CONCLUSION 59

Section 3
Student Free Speech and the United States Supreme Court

Chapter 7
Material and Substantial Disruption/Infringement of Rights 62
- INTRODUCTION 62
- BACKGROUND 63
- MAIN FOCUS OF THE CHAPTER 64
- CONCLUSION 80

Chapter 8
Lewd, Vulgar, Plainly-Offensive, and Obscene Speech 84
- INTRODUCTION 84
- MAIN FOCUS OF THE CHAPTER 85
- CONCLUSION 95

Chapter 9
School-Sponsored Speech 97
- INTRODUCTION 97
- MAIN FOCUS OF THE CHAPTER 98
- CONCLUSION 105

Chapter 10
Advocacy of Illegal Drug Use 108
- INTRODUCTION 108
- MAIN FOCUS OF THE CHAPTER 109
- CONCLUSION 120

Section 4
Lower Courts and Off-Campus Speech

Chapter 11
Their Stories: Offline Off-Campus Speech 123
- INTRODUCTION 123
- MAIN FOCUS OF THE CHAPTER 124

    SPEECH DIRECTED AT OR AGAINST SCHOOL OFFICIALS OR THE SCHOOL 124
    SPEECH DIRECTED AT OR AGAINST STUDENTS 178
    HYBRID SPEECH: SPEECH DIRECTED AT OR AGAINST SCHOOL OFFICIALS AS WELL AS NON-
        SCHOOL ENTITIES 195
    CONCLUSION 198

Chapter 12
Their Stories: Online Off-Campus Speech 208
    INTRODUCTION 208
    MAIN FOCUS OF THE CHAPTER 209
    SPEECH DIRECTED AT OR AGAINST SCHOOL OFFICIALS OR THE SCHOOL 209
    SPEECH DIRECTED AT OR AGAINST STUDENTS 268
    CONCLUSION 299

Section 5
Reflections

Chapter 13
Assessing the Current Jurisprudence 304
    INTRODUCTION 304
    MAIN FOCUS OF THE CHAPTER 305
    CONCLUSION 346

Chapter 14
Acceptable Use Policies 352
    INTRODUCTION 352
    MAIN FOCUS OF THE CHAPTER 353
    CONCLUSION 357

Chapter 15
State Anti-Bullying Statutes and Student Speech 359
    INTRODUCTION 359
    MAIN FOCUS OF THE CHAPTER 360
    CONCLUSION 379

Chapter 16
Forging the Path Forward from Censorship 590
    INTRODUCTION 590
    MAIN FOCUS OF THE CHAPTER 591
    CONCLUSION 603

Compilation of References 606

About the Contributors 619

Index 620

Foreword

Being involved in public education for over forty years has presented me with varying perspectives on one of the most challenging issues – student speech – that impacts teacher and administrative decisions regarding what is in the best interests of students and student safety within public school settings. As a teacher, supervisor, and building and district administrator, I took seriously the doctrine of in loco parentis to define my responsibilities and guide my decision-making. Complimenting that doctrine was my informed judgment of whether the behavior or speech that was brought to my attention caused a substantial disruption of the school day. With those two standards in hand, I had angst over decisions and played them over in my head to bring resolution to disciplinary actions that could lead to censorship of protected speech. I took advice from lawyers and administrators, and read and reread court cases. In the end, it was my decision, and I had to own it even though there were naysayers and irresolute conclusions from others in the same situations. The decisions about student speech occurring during the school day within the schoolhouse gate offered opportunities for more expeditious resolutions because I had the United States Supreme Court precedents to rely on. These precedents – Tinker v. Des Moines Independent Community School District (1969); Bethel School District No. 403 v. Fraser (1986); Hazelwood v. Kuhlmeier (1988) – determined in the context of on-campus student speech identified situations where school officials could censor student speech without violating the First Amendment. For on-campus speech, it was also easier to more readily ascertain what had happened, who was involved, and other facts surrounding the speech in question. Decisions about off-campus speech brought greater anguish, however. If the speech in question was outside the schoolhouse gate, it conjured up many conflicting issues and at times competing rights of students and schools that were convoluted.

Administrative responses to off-campus student speech has resulted in various disciplinary actions including student suspensions from school as well as school-sponsored activities and expulsion from school. Administrators must balance the First Amendment right to free speech with student safety when making disciplinary decisions. This balancing has become complicated in modern times with the presence of the internet. This global system of interconnectedness is redefining educators' authority over students' right to free speech off-campus. Identifying exactly where the line is drawn is somewhat abstruse. Educators trying to find the balance when presented with the power and expansiveness of the internet, and looking to the courts' contradictory conclusions, find themselves sinking in the deep sea of decisionmaking without a well-inflated life preserver.

The phrase that has helped to bring guidance and define the line, since the United States Supreme Court decision in Tinker v. Des Moines Independent Community School District (1969), is the "schoolhouse gate." Technology has, however, clouded that vision. The beguiling vastness and openness of the

Foreword

internet for all forms of communications has ushered into schools a new arena that enables school officials and students to access electronic speech in any place and at any time. With a click of a mouse or a press of a button, we are able to see and hear conversations like never before whether on a cell phone, computer, or tablet; and on Instagram, Twitter, or Facebook. Yet the juxtaposition of the vast information on cyberspace and the lack of clear and concise legal guidelines on school authority over cyberspeech is haunting many educators and districts with a need for greater direction and consistency. The searing question is, how do we maneuver through such an undulating current of information when the lines of our authority are in such grave question? At times like this, we seek to lean on directional oversight, good case law, and policies; yet those only offer us inconsistencies.

As administrators, educators, judges, legal scholars and others look for guidance in finding the right balance, this book is a must. The expertise of Oluwole and Green, once again, as they did for us in *SextEd: Obscenity versus Free Speech in Our School (2013),* brings a well-inflated life preserver to help navigate the muddy waters. They bring greater clarity to the student-speech jurisprudence, case law, past practice, and the all-encompassing issues surrounding district authority over off-campus student speech. This dynamic duo provide educators, administrators, judges and legal scholars what we need to make the most informed decisions; and to help districts have the difficult conversations necessary for establishing better internal guidelines for the respect of students' speech rights. They carefully walk us through the intricacies of precise tests from landmark cases to bring us as close as possible to the right balance between free speech and school authority in order to ensure the safety and well-being of students.

A burning question is whether school officials overreach in exercising censorship authority beyond what the courts refer to as the "schoolhouse gate"? Is our authority limited only to the school day when students are with us? Or should we view what students say outside of school as impacting what happens in school? If so, then does this premise bestow on school officials the authority to discipline students for their speech off-campus? As Oluwole and Green note, the answers to these questions remain clouded in the courts. Schools and students may have to stage a grassroots movement pressuring the courts to bring greater clarity and consistency to cases that guide districts and school decisions. This is important in order to delimit the scope of school-censorship authority over off-campus speech and to provide greater discernment for all constituencies. With the current lack of clarity, school administrators are in a real conundrum of trying to balance student discipline with First Amendment rights with blurry vision about what is constitutionally permissible amidst the inconsistency in the case law. With so much confusion and sometimes indirection in the courts, there is need for a comprehensive source that brings some much-needed clarity to the state of the law. Oluwole and Green – top scholars in their field – provide that in this book. At times, the book will challenge the status quo and raise more questions than answers. But that is necessary and partly a consequence of the very uncertain state of the jurisprudence. They have compiled in one book all the necessary information to explain and guide us to accomplish the balance we seek with students' First Amendment rights and the professional standard of creating a safe environment for all children. Their in-depth research presents the reader with the knowledge to inform decisions about school censorship of off-campus speech under the Free Speech Clause.

Eunice A. Grippaldi
Livingston Public Schools, USA

Eunice Grippaldi *has 40 years of public education experience as a classroom teacher, district supervisor, building principal, assistant superintendent and deputy superintendent. She is an acclaimed mentor to many school administrators who she has developed into great leaders in a variety of districts. She is currently the program coordinator for the Educational Leadership program at Montclair State University. In that role, she has conceptualized and overseen the development of several innovative programs including the Fast Track Program, the Online Program, the Offsite Programs and the integration of hybrid instructional delivery into the traditional face-to-face programs.*

Preface

When a person tweets on Twitter to his or her friends, that person takes the risk that the friend will turn the information over to the government, (Roasio v. Clark County School District, 2013, p. 6).

This is the first comprehensive book to address students' constitutional rights to free speech while off-campus in an offline setting and an online setting. The book is legal scholarship that pertains to a practically very important issue – the scope of the censorship authority of school officials over student speech when students are off-campus. It tells the stories of the students whose off-campus speech was muzzled by their schools. In particular, it covers students who challenged the jurisdiction of schools to censor their speech under the First Amendment. It describes the current state of the law on off-campus student speech in the United States and in so doing reveals that the jurisprudence is unsettled with courts coming to differing conclusions. It is important to explore all available cases in the jurisprudence as we did in order to show the struggles courts face in deciding cases in the off-campus student speech jurisprudence. As noted in our discussions throughout the book, this uncertainty exists due to the United States Supreme Court's failure to rule on off-campus student speech. Our goal for the book is to present the jurisprudence and to show that there are currently no conclusive and uniform answers for students and school officials on the issue of school censorship of off-campus student speech.

The book discusses the legal decisions in the various cases we found in our extensive research of off-campus speech jurisprudence using a variety of legal research databases. We have no access to documents on settled cases and judicial decisions that were not published in the legal research databases, so those are not included. The book uses legal research methodology – the significant examination of legal precedent (Russo, 2006). Legal research involves and demands investigation into case law in order to "locate authority that will govern the disposition of the question under investigation" (Russo, 2006, p. 7).

Our research of the case law reveals confusion in the lower courts regarding how to address school censorship of off-campus student speech. As West (2008) keenly observed, the power of schools to punish students for speech is fraught with uncertainty and the legal standard governing off-campus speech is unsettled. Questions remain as to whether schools can even muzzle student speech off-campus. Indeed, for both offline and online off-campus speech, "the lower courts are in complete disarray, handing down ad hoc decisions that, even when they reach an instinctively correct conclusion, lack consistent, controlling legal principles" (Pike, 2008, p. 990). Courts also find it challenging to distinguish between off-campus and on-campus speech when students communicate digitally; particularly because online speech is omnipresent even when the speech is created in the privacy of the student's home. There is the added challenge that online speakers lose control of their speech once they speak. Even when a student-speaker sends out an online message such as a tweet only to friends, with an expectation of privacy, there is a real risk that the message would be turned over to school officials without the knowledge or prodding of the speaker (Roasio v. Clark County School District, 2013). Since the speech is digital and therefore accessible by anyone on school grounds, there is a real possibility that the speech would get on school grounds. Courts disagree over whether digital off-campus student speech brought on-campus by someone other than the speaker mutates into on-campus speech. Courts also disagree over whether digital off-campus speech needs to be accessed on school grounds before it is censorable. School officials would become omnipotent over students and the First Amendment would be reduced to hokum if digital communications created in students' bedrooms can be censored simply because of their digital and thus omnipresent nature.

We believe that there must be a limit to the reach of school-censorship authority, particularly when speech occurs outside the schoolhouse gate. As the United States Supreme Court has stated, "the parents' claim to authority in their own household to direct the rearing of their children is basic in the structure of our society" (Reno v. American Civil Liberties Union, 1997, quoting Ginsberg v. New York, 1968, p. 639). Even when students are not at home, school officials need to respect parental authority to direct and discipline their own children and to make choices about their permissible speech. To allow school officials, as agents of the state, to exercise coterminous authority with parents over students' off-campus speech undercuts the parental authority so basic to our societal structure.

Some courts have advocated or limited the censorship authority of schools over off-campus speech. On the United States Court of Appeals for The Third Circuit, for instance, Judge Fisher advocates limiting school-censorship authority to speech that targets school officials and is reasonably forecast to cause material and substantial disruption at the school (J.S. ex rel. Snyder v. Blue Mountain School District, 2011, p. 939). In some other cases, courts such as the United States Court of Appeals for the Fourth Circuit and the United States Court of Appeals for the Eighth Circuit, require proof that the speech targeted a member of the school community and that the speech is reasonably foreseeable to reach the school (Kowalski v. Berkeley County Schools, 2011; S.J.W. v. Lee's Summit R–7 School District, 2012). Unfortunately, despite these different limitations, the current off-campus student-speech jurisprudence has not clearly defined the gate separating off-campus speech from on-campus speech. It remains unresolved whether the off-campus versus on-campus distinction for student speech should "turn solely on where the speaker was sitting when the speech was originally uttered" (J.S. ex rel. Snyder v. Blue Mountain School District, p. 940). As the United States District Court for the District of Connecticut rightly observed, the unsettled nature of the current jurisprudence has created confusion for school officials:

If courts and legal scholars cannot discern the contours of First Amendment protections for student internet speech, then it is certainly unreasonable to expect school administrators, such as Defendants, to predict where the line between on-and off-campus speech will be drawn in this new digital era (Doninger v. Niehoff, 2009, p. 224).

Even the United States Supreme Court has acknowledged the uncertainty in the student free speech jurisprudence (Papandrea, 2008).

The United States Supreme Court has excluded certain categories of speech from First Amendment protection. These categories include obscenity, defamation, true threats and fighting words (R.A.V. v. City of St. Paul, 1992). Since the federal and state governments can censor adult and student speech

Preface

that falls under any of these categories, it stands to reason that school officials should be able to censor such speech as well. Our research shows, however, that only a few cases have analyzed off-campus student speech using these categories. This implies that courts do not necessarily view the off-campus rights of adults as coextensive with the off-campus rights of students. There is nothing in the Supreme Court's student-speech jurisprudence endorsing such a view, however. Given that the Supreme Court has not considered student speech under any of the unprotected speech categories, there is uncertainty as to whether school officials can rely on those categories to censor off-campus student speech. Because students have no First Amendment recourse for unprotected speech, we believe that school officials can rely on these categories to censor off-campus speech. This book discusses the various categories of unprotected speech as possible avenues for valid school censorship of student speech.

While the Supreme Court has not yet accepted for review any case involving off-campus speech, it has decided cases involving students' on-campus speech. These Supreme Court cases, discussed herein, are Tinker v. Des Moines Independent Community School District (1969); Bethel School District No. 403 v. Fraser (1986); Hazelwood v. Kuhlmeier (1988); and Morse v. Frederick (2007). In those cases, the Supreme Court created tests for determining when school officials can censor student speech. In Tinker v. Des Moines Independent Community School District, the Supreme Court created the material and substantial disruption test which authorizes censorship of student speech that materially and substantially disrupts the school. A few lower courts also believe that case created the infringement-of-rights test which allows school officials to censor speech that impinges on the rights of others. Since the Supreme Court has never applied the infringement-of-rights test, we cannot definitively confirm that it is a test that the Supreme Court actually recognizes. The Bethel School District No. 403 v. Fraser (1986) case authorized school officials to censor vulgar, lewd, plainly-offensive and obscene speech. Hazelwood v. Kuhlmeier (1988) empowered school officials to censor school-sponsored speech while Morse v. Frederick (2007) authorized school censorship of speech that advocates illegal drug use. Even though the language of these tests seems pretty straightforward, as will be seen in this book, their scope is not. Specifically, the lower courts are divided and uncertain as to whether these tests can be extended from their on-campus speech contexts to off-campus speech. Since the Supreme Court is the highest court in the land, other courts look to it for guidance on how to approach students' constitutional rights. And without clarity from the Supreme Court, conflicting rulings will continue to emerge in the lower courts.

While the most applied of the Supreme Court tests to off-campus speech is the material and substantial disruption test, Judge Smith of the United States Court of Appeals for The Third Circuit cautions against such application because of the potential chilling effect on student speech:

Applying Tinker to off-campus speech would create a precedent with ominous implications. Doing so would empower schools to regulate students' expressive activity no matter where it takes place, when it occurs, or what subject matter it involves—so long as it causes a substantial disruption at school. Tinker, for example, authorizes schools to suppress political speech—speech 'at the core of what the First Amendment is designed to protect,'—if it substantially disrupts school activities. Suppose a high school student, while at home after school hours, were to write a blog entry defending gay marriage. Suppose further that several of the student's classmates got wind of the entry, took issue with it, and caused a significant disturbance at school. While the school could clearly punish the students who acted disruptively, if Tinker were held to apply to off-campus speech, the school could also punish the student whose blog entry brought about the disruption. That cannot be, nor is it, the law (J.S. ex rel. Snyder v. Blue Mountain School District, 2011, p. 939, citing Morse v. Frederick, 2007, p. 403).

Judge Smith actually called it "absurd" to take the "antecedent step of extending *Tinker* beyond the public-school setting to which it is so firmly moored" when reviewing off-campus speech cases (J.S. ex rel. Snyder v. Blue Mountain School District, 2011, p. 940). As will be axiomatic in this book, however, a number of courts and judges do not agree with Judge Smith. Even on the United States Court of Appeals for The Third Circuit, there is no consensus about the reach of the material and substantial disruption test. This was evident in Layshock ex rel. Layshock v. Hermitage School District (2011), for instance, where Judge Jordan vigorously argued that the material and substantial disruption test applies to off-campus speech because property lines have become insignificant in the digital age:

We cannot sidestep the central tension between good order and expressive rights by leaning on property lines. With the tools of modern technology, a student could, with malice aforethought, engineer egregiously disruptive events and, if the trouble-maker were savvy enough to tweet the organizing communications from his or her cellphone while standing one foot outside school property, the school administrators might succeed in heading off the actual disruption in the building but would be left powerless to discipline the student. Perhaps all of us participating in these en banc decisions would agree on that being problematic. It is, after all, a given that '[t]he most stringent protection of free speech would not protect a man in falsely shouting fire in a theatre and causing a panic' and no one supposes that the rule would be different if the man were standing outside the theater, shouting in. Thus it is hard to see how words that may cause pandemonium in a public school would be protected by the First Amendment simply because technology now allows the timing and distribution of a shout to be controlled by someone beyond the campus boundary. If it is accepted that the First Amendment would not protect such a deliberate disturbance, we should acknowledge that we are weighing competing interests and do so in the straightforward though sometimes challenging way directed by Tinker (Layshock ex rel. Layshock v. Hermitage School District, 2011, pp. 221-22, citing Schenck v. United States, 1919, p. 52).

These opposing views of Judge Smith and Judge Jordan illustrate the ongoing division and uncertainty playing out in courts around the country over the scope of the Supreme Court's student-speech precedents; and concomitantly the First Amendment rights of students to speak off-campus. This book seeks to reveal the uncertainty in the off-campus student-speech jurisprudence so that legal scholars and the judiciary will appreciate the importance of bringing clarity to the current state of the law. This is especially important because a jurisprudence with "inconsistent and conflicting standards will chill more speech than would a single, clear, and predictable national standard" (Rothman, 2001, p. 302). The book assesses the off-campus jurisprudence and concludes with guidance for students and schools on how to navigate the jurisprudence in compliance with the Free Speech Clause.

ORGANIZATION OF THE BOOK

The book is divided into five sections with a total of sixteen chapters. A brief description of each chapter follows:

Section 1 is titled "Context" and includes the first chapter of the book. This chapter is designed to provide some background and context for the book.

Preface

Section 2 is titled "Unprotected Speech" and includes Chapters 2 through 6. This section covers pertinent categories of speech that the United States Supreme Court has categorically excluded from First Amendment protection. We explore these categories because if students have rights outside the schoolhouse gate, as with adults, those rights should be protected for all speech except the categories of unprotected speech. As a federal district court noted, the analysis must start "with the basic rule that speech, whether written or oral, is protected under the First Amendment unless it falls within one of the exceptions delineated by the Supreme Court, in which case the speech may be limited by the respective governmental entity" (D.G. v. Independent School District No. 11 of Tulsa County, Oklahoma, 2000, p. 9). However, "[i]f the speech does not fall within one of the limited exceptions to the rule, it is protected speech and cannot be censored or punished" (p. 9).

Chapter 2 defines true threat and discusses true threat as unprotected speech. It also reviews the true-threat doctrine and the two perspectives used by the judiciary in true-threat analysis: reasonable-speaker perspective and the reasonable-listener perspective. The goal of the chapter is to describe true threat – one of the few categories of speech for which students, like adults, are not entitled to First Amendment protection.

Chapter 3 describes the fighting-words jurisprudence. It explains why fighting words are unprotected speech. It reviews the Chaplinsky v. New Hampshire (1942) case in which the Supreme Court first excluded fighting words from First Amendment protection. The chapter aims to show that, since fighting words are unprotected speech, school officials can censor such speech outside the schoolhouse gate without violating the First Amendment. However, school officials must establish that the speech qualifies as fighting words pursuant to *Chaplinsky* – a challenging task.

Chapter 4 examines defamatory speech. It describes the elements that must be established in order for speech to constitute defamation. It also discusses slander and libel – two forms of defamatory speech. We point out that defamatory speech by students off-campus is speech that school officials can censor with impunity under the First Amendment.

Chapter 5 focuses on obscene speech. The chapter reviews various cases on obscene speech. It sets forth the criteria that must be satisfied before speech will be classified as obscene. The chapter concludes that school officials can regulate the obscene speech of students created off-campus without violating the First Amendment.

Chapter 6 examines child pornography speech. We review Supreme Court precedent for determining when speech can be excluded from First Amendment protection as child pornography. We conclude that, under child pornography precedent, school officials can constitutionally censor student speech created off-campus if it features child pornography.

Section 3 is titled "Student Free Speech and the United States Supreme Court." It encompasses Chapters 7 through 10. The section examines the United States Supreme Court's decisions on student free speech. It discusses the various tests the Supreme Court has established for determining when student speech is protected. These tests constitute the jurisprudential and "historical framework of student First Amendment rights" (Roberts, 2008, p. 1179). The tests are important because they provide "an understanding of where the law began, where the law currently is, and where the law is moving" (p. 1179).

Chapter 7 focuses on the Tinker v. Des Moines Independent Community School District (1969) case – the first Supreme Court decision on student free speech. It examines the two tests established in *Tinker* for determining the scope of school authority over student speech. These tests are the "material and substantial disruption" test and the "infringement of rights" test. We analyze the *Tinker* case to determine if it authorizes school officials to censor off-campus student speech.

Chapter 8 reviews the Bethel School District No. 403 v. Fraser (1986) case – the second Supreme Court decision on student free speech. It discusses the test established in that case which empowers schools to punish students for speech that is vulgar, lewd, obscene or plainly offensive. The chapter explores this case in order to determine if school officials can find within this case authority to regulate off-campus student speech that is lewd, vulgar, plainly offensive or obscene.

Chapter 9 examines the United States Supreme Court's decision in Hazelwood v. Kuhlmeier (1988). This case set the precedent for school regulation of school-sponsored speech. In this chapter, we analyze the *Hazelwood* case and explore whether school officials can censor student off-campus speech pursuant to *Hazelwood*.

Chapter 10 discusses the last Supreme Court case to rule on student free speech rights. That case – Morse v. Frederick (2007) – established that schools can regulate student speech that advocates illegal drug use. We examine the case to determine if it gives school officials any authority to regulate off-campus speech.

Section 4 focuses on lower court decisions about off-campus speech. This section encompasses Chapters 11 and 12. In this section, we tell the story of students whose speeches have been muzzled by schools across the country. The section also highlights the uncertainty in the lower courts about the authority of schools over student off-campus speech. As evident in the various cases covered in this section, there is dissensus in the lower courts about the application of the United States Supreme Court's on-campus student-speech precedents to off-campus student speech.

Chapter 11 explores lower court cases on student speech that occurs off-campus but offline. The chapter discusses these cases in three categories: speech directed at or against school officials (including teachers and school administrators) or the school; speech directed at or against students; and finally, student speech directed at or against persons not affiliated with the school.

Chapter 12 explores lower court cases on student online off-campus speech. The lower court cases we found dealing with online off-campus student fall into two categories: speech directed at or against school officials or the school; and speech directed at or against students. We discuss the cases under each of these categories, highlighting the lack of uniformity in the lower courts about how to address offline off-campus student speech.

Section 5 presents our reflections on the student off-campus speech jurisprudence. This section encompasses Chapters 13 through 16.

Chapter 13 assesses the current state of the off-campus student free speech jurisprudence. As Tuneski (2003) rightly pointed out, "existing precedents provide little guidance to school officials faced with the challenge of determining whether their sanctions are constitutionally permissible" (p. 158). Without an understanding of the current state of the jurisprudence, "schools run the risk of abridging protected student speech that lies beyond the scope of their authority" (Tuneski, p. 158). In this chapter, we try to bring some clarity to the muddled jurisprudence.

Chapter 14 examines critical state and federal requirements for the development of acceptable use policies. It also reviews the role of acceptable use policies in shaping the approach of schools toward student off-campus speech. It highlights components that should be included in acceptable use policies. It also reveals that school districts are increasingly adopting responsible use policies in order to address the student use of personal electronic devices.

Preface

Chapter 15 explores the role of state anti-bullying statutes in censorship of student off-campus speech. These statutes were enacted to reduce bullying incidents in schools. However, they have been expanded to include off-campus speech. We examine the details of a representative and comprehensive anti-bullying statute. We also discuss the relationship of the law to off-campus speech.

Chapter 16 presents our conclusions to the book. It discusses ideas for the future of the off-campus student-speech jurisprudence. In this chapter, we also present recommendations for schools and students on how they should navigate the jurisprudence.

REFERENCES

Bethel School District No. 403 v. Fraser (1986). 478 U.S. 675, 682.

Chaplinsky v. New Hampshire (1942). 315 U.S. 568, 572.

D.G. v. Independent School District No. 11 of Tulsa County, Oklahoma (2000). 2000 U.S. Dist. LEXIS 12197 *1-15.

Doninger v. Niehoff (2009). 594 F.Supp.2d 211 (affirmed in part, reversed in part on other grounds by Doninger v. Niehoff (2011) 642 F.3d 334).

Ginsberg v. New York (1968). 390 U.S. 629, 639.

J.S. ex rel. Snyder v. Blue Mountain School District (2011). 650 F.3d 915.

Kowalski v. Berkeley County Schools (2011). 652 F.3d 565.

Layshock ex rel. Layshock v. Hermitage School District (2011). 650 F.3d 205.

Morse v. Frederick (2007). 551 U.S. 393.

Papandrea, M. (2008). Student speech rights in the digital age. *Florida Law Review*, *60*, 1027–1102.

Pike, K. R. (2008). Locating the mislaid gate: Revitalizing tinker by repairing judicial overgeneralizations of technologically enabled student speech. *Brigham Young University Law Review*, *2008*, 990.

R.A.V. v. City of St. Paul (1992). 505 U.S. 377.

Reno v. American Civil Liberties Union (1997). 521 U.S. 844.

Roasio v. Clark County School District (2013). 2013 WL 3679375.

Roberts, C. E. (2008). Is Myspace their space? Protecting student cyberspeech in a post-Morse v. Frederick world. *UMKC Law Review*, *76*, 1177–1192.

Rothman, J. E. (2001). Freedom of speech and true threats. *Harvard Journal of Law & Public Policy*, *25*, 283–367.

Russo, C. J. (2006). Legal research: The "traditional" method. In S. Permuth & R. D. Mawdsley (Eds.), *Research methods for studying legal issues in education* (pp. 5–24). Dayton, OH: Education Law Association.

Schenck v. United States (1919). 249 U.S. 47, 52.

S.J.W. v. Lee's Summit R–7 School District (2012). 696 F.3d 771.

Tinker v. Des Moines Independent Community School District (1969). 393 U.S. 503.

Tuneski (2003). Online, not on grounds: Protecting student internet speech. *Virginia Law Review, 89*, 139-87.

West, S. R. (2008). Sanctionable conduct: How the Supreme Court stealthily opened the schoolhouse gate. *Lewis and Clark Law Review, 12*, 27–44.

Wynar v. Douglas County School District (2013). 728 F.3d 1062, 1071-72.

Acknowledgment

It is never easy writing a book. It involves taking time away from family for long hours of research and writing. Our families have made great sacrifices to support the successful completion of this book. We could not have done it without their unwavering support, encouragement and care. We dedicate this book to them. We also dedicate it to the voices for the First Amendment rights of students.

Our thanks to Srividhya Sundaram and David Lennox for their invaluable research support for this book. Thanks to Gina Doane who has sacrificed time with her precious miracle boy James Doane and her husband Forrest to help with presentations and lectures on harassing, intimidating and bullying off-campus speech. We would also like to thank the IGI Global staff and teams; Kayla Wolfe (Acquisitions Editor); Lindsay Johnston (Managing Director); Erin O'Dea (Editorial Assistant); Austin DeMarco (Managing Editor); Paige Anderson (Acquisitions Editorial Assistant); Deanna Jo Zombro (Multi-Volume Book Production Specialist); Taylor Brainard (Marketing Assistant); and Jan Travers (Director of Intellectual Property and Contracts) for their first-rate support throughout the process of publishing this book.

Section 1
Context

Chapter 1
Background

ABSTRACT

This chapter provides some background on the existing uncertainty in the student free speech jurisprudence. It reveals the origins of the "schoolhouse gate" phrase that is a staple of the student free speech jurisprudence. It examines the case law on schools' power over student behavior while they are off-campus. This power over conduct was a forerunner to power over speech. Power over speech, however, implicates the First Amendment's Free Speech Clause guarantee of the right to free speech. The chapter underscores the presence of uncertainty in the courts as to whether the free speech guarantee covers students while they are off-campus. The goal of the chapter is to provide context for the others chapters in the book by highlighting the uncertainty evident in the lower court decisions on students' off-campus speech.

INTRODUCTION

This chapter provides context for the later chapters of the book. It presents some background, through case law, on the judicial view of school authority over students' off-campus behavior. While schools have long exercised power to regulate students' behaviors off-campus, such regulatory powers are not unbridled. The Free Speech Clause of the First Amendment to the United States Constitution guarantees the right of free speech to all Americans. This Amendment provides in pertinent part: "Congress shall make no law ... abridging the freedom of speech." While the language starts with the word "Congress", the United States Supreme Court has interpreted the Amendment as applicable to the states and school districts via the Fourteenth Amendment (Gitlow v. New York, 1925; Engel v. Vitale, 1962). The question becomes whether the First Amendment protects students from school censorship of speech when they speak off-campus. The chapter discusses the origins of the idea of a schoolhouse gate – a phrase the United States Supreme Court introduced into First Amendment jurisprudence in 1969. The failure of the United States Supreme Court to define this phrase and to specifically address the constitutional right of students to free speech off-campus has created uncertainty in the lower courts – as evidenced in later chapters of this book. The chapter per the authors highlights the incertitude in the lower courts about the reach of schools' censorship power when students are off-campus. As a consequence of this

DOI: 10.4018/978-1-4666-9519-1.ch001

uncertainty, schools have taken great liberties with censoring students' off-campus speech by imposing several forms of discipline for speech. The objective is to create an awareness of the need for judicial action to resolve the uncertainty in the student-speech jurisprudence so as to limit the incidents of school censorship of protected off-campus student speech.

MAIN FOCUS OF THE CHAPTER

Regulation of Off-Campus Student Conduct

From time immemorial, schools have disciplined students for off-campus conduct such as alcohol consumption, violation of traffic laws, fighting, assault, drug use and property destruction (Erb, 2008). In 1908, for example, a school district punished a student for violating a school rule that required all students to stay in their homes between the hours of 7 and 9 p.m. to study (Hobbs v. Germany, 1909). Sixteen-year old Henry Germany accompanied his father to a religious service between 7 and 9 pm. When the student returned to school, as punishment, the teachers offered him the choice of a 40-minute school room confinement for a week or corporal punishment. When the student refused to accept either punishment, school officials forced him to leave the school. The student's father filed suit against the school, claiming that the school acted ultra vires. The Supreme Court of Mississippi agreed, noting that "[i]n the home the parental authority is and should be supreme, and it is a misguided zeal that attempts to wrest it from them" (p. 517). Additionally, the court expressed hope that, as long as there is liberty in the state of Mississippi, no law that supersedes the sanctity of parental authority around the parent's hearthstone would ever be passed. In his concurring opinion in Dritt v. Snodgrass (1877), Judge Norton of the Supreme Court of Missouri expressed a similar view that school authority over students' conduct should remain within the school:

When the school room is entered by the pupil, the authority of the parent ceases, and that of the teacher begins; when sent to his home, the authority of the teacher ends, and that of the parent is resumed. For his conduct when at school, he may be punished or even expelled, under proper circumstances; for his conduct when at home, he is subject to domestic control (Dritt v. Snodgrass, 1877, p. 291).

Not all courts, however, support restraining schools' exercise of power over students while they are off-campus. This was evident in Bush By and Through Bush v. Dassel-Cokato Board of Education (1990), for example. In that case, student-athlete Keri Bush challenged the school's decision to discipline her for simply attending an off-campus party where alcohol was served. The school suspended Keri from interscholastic swim, even though the county sheriff's deputy explained to the school that Keri did not possess or drink alcohol at the party. A federal district court in Minnesota upheld the school's suspension of Keri, reasoning that the discipline was a reasonable way to deter students' consumption of alcohol. The court ruled that schools have authority to pass regulations designed to deter students' consumption of alcohol, "even if the activity regulated occurs off school grounds" (p. 573). A federal court in Illinois ruled similarly about the power of schools to discipline students present at off-campus parties where alcohol is served or consumed (Clements by Clements v. Board of Education of Decatur Public School District No. 61, 1985). That court held that discipline was not "sufficiently egregious" to qualify for the "narrow concept of arbitrary or capricious official conduct which justifies the extraor-

Background

dinary intervention by the court in the operation of the public schools of the state" (p. 537). In R.R. v. Board of Education of the Shore Regional High School District (1970), R.R., a 15-year old student, was suspended from classes and all school-sponsored activities after he got into a fight with his five-year old neighbor. R.R. was also required to undergo evaluations conducted by the school psychologist and school psychiatrist. The fight occurred at the neighbor's house after school hours. The Superior Court of New Jersey ruled that school officials have the authority to suspend or expel students for off-campus conduct if the discipline is "reasonably necessary" for the emotional or physical well-being or safety of the disciplined student or his peers.

Chief Judge Lay of the United States Court of Appeals of the Eighth Circuit has expressed displeasure that some judges, as in the cases discussed above, rubber-stamp school discipline for off-campus conduct. Specifically, he chastised such judges for acting as a "super school board" (Felton v. Fayette School District, 1989, p. 195). Other courts and students need to rally around Chief Judge Lay's displeasure. The United States Supreme Court needs to rein in overeager school censorship as well as "super school board" courts; otherwise students will effectively become serfs of the state.

Origins of the Insouciance, Recognition, and Subsequent Constriction of Students' Constitutional Right to Free Speech

It is one thing for courts to defer to school regulation of students' conduct off-campus; but quite another for schools to censor students' speech off-campus. Free speech is a precious right granted under the United States Constitution. Nevertheless, schools have failed to adequately respect or recognize this right, particularly when students speak off-campus. An example from Wheeler II (2004), involving a seventh-grade student, illustrates this point. The seventh grader, while off-campus, used a free website to anonymously post a discussion topic called "gRiMmEr SuCKS!" (p. 24). The student distributed handwritten slips at the school advertising the site and posted the following on the slam site: "Hey dudes and dudettes! Hope ya'll brace your self for some mad s***t!!! Hehe! Have funnn" (p. 24). A student appearing under the name "Dark Jedi" responded with sexually-suggestive comments about other students and comments that personally attacked students with special needs. Other students responded with critical comments about the school, teachers and their fellow students. Students posted many comments about their teachers, including the following: "Omg did u no dat he checks out gurls! He is a f***** pervert!"; "Is mr. black gay or wut?? Hes wears those skin tight pants and those pink and purple shirts ewwwww!" (p. 24). Examples of comments on the slam site that attacked fellow students are: "d.v. she a slut and all her slutty f***** paddid bras shes so damn flat"; and "I don't want ur s*** d.v. so shut up and grow some f***** boobs!!!!" (p. 24). The school suspended the students who posted the various sophomoric comments. The speech-censorship incident, like many others discussed in this book, raised questions about the right of students to free speech, prompting the Indiana Civil Liberties Union to intervene on behalf of the students (Wheeler II, 2004). Incidents like this force us to confront questions such as: Do students have a right to free speech? Do students retain the right to free speech while off-campus? More importantly, as relates to the thesis of this book, do schools have the right to censor students' speech while they are off-campus?

Prior to the 1960s, the United States Supreme Court "rarely" accorded First Amendment protection to the speech of anyone (Moss, 2011, p. 1418). The Supreme Court upheld criminal sanctions for a variety of minority views, including opposition to a war draft, advocacy of industrial strikes and membership in the communist party (Moss, 2011). Amidst the rarity of First Amendment protection for any speech, public schools wielded unbridled power over student speech. The United States Supreme Court, however, offered a glimmer of hope for students in 1943 and then again in 1969 when it recognized students as persons under the United States Constitution (West Virginia State Board of Education v. Barnette, 1943; Tinker v. Des Moines Independent Community School District, 1969). While this was not an explicit recognition that students have a right to free speech, it was an acknowledgment that the United States Constitution protects students and not just adults. The recognition of students as persons under the United States Constitution was a condition precedent to First Amendment rights for students. It meant that, as with adults, it was conceivable for the first time that students have a right to free speech under the Free Speech Clause of the First Amendment to the United States Constitution. The Free Speech Clause provides that "Congress shall make no law ... abridging the freedom of speech" (United States Constitution Amendment I). This Amendment is made applicable to the states and school districts through the Due Process Clause of the Fourteenth Amendment (United States Constitution Amendment XIV; Pisciotta, 2000). As part of its recognition of students as persons under the Constitution, in West Virginia State Board of Education v. Barnette (1943), the Supreme Court warned schools not to "strangle the free mind at its source" in their efforts to censor students (p. 637). As evident in this book, however, it appears that schools (and courts) have failed to heed the Supreme Court's warning over the years.

Even after West Virginia State Board of Education v. Barnette (1943), schools continued to strangle the minds of students with regulations of student speech originating off-campus. Further, as Papandrea (2008) observed, despite the strangling of student speech, courts struggled for many decades "to determine when, if ever, public schools should have the power to restrict student expression that does not occur on school grounds during school hours" (p. 1028). Even when courts initially acknowledged broad off-campus speech rights for students, subsequently they "considerably eroded speech rights" (Salgado, 2005, p. 1377). A significant reason for the erosion was the decision of courts to examine censored speech to determine if it could be "construed as potentially causing a substantial disruption on campus–an elastic concept than can be stretched to include virtually any unpopular speech" (p. 1377). The fluidity of the "substantial disruption" concept, effectively enables schools to characterize almost any off-campus speech as on-campus speech (Salgado, 2005).

In Tinker v. Des Moines Independent Community School District (1969), the United States Supreme Court, for the first time, explicitly recognized the right of students to free speech under the Free Speech Clause of the First Amendment. The Supreme Court also stated that "[i]t can hardly be argued that either students or teachers shed their constitutional rights to freedom of speech or expression at the schoolhouse gate" (p. 506). This was the first use of the phrase "schoolhouse gate" in the Supreme Court's free speech jurisprudence. It was an acknowledgment that students' rights need to be adjusted inside the "context of the school environment" (Papandrea, 2008, p. 1038). The phrase implies that students have a right to free speech when they arrive at the schoolhouse gate. In essence, students bring free speech rights to the schoolhouse gate – rights they do not lose simply by crossing the schoolhouse gate. Put another way, Harpaz (2000) believes that one can infer from the phrase that the authority of the school over student speech "ends as the student leaves the schoolhouse" (p. 142).

Despite the United States Supreme Court's statement in Tinker v. Des Moines Independent Community School District (1969), schools have continued to push the boundaries of their reach over student speech. In fact, in this age where more and more student speech is occurring off-campus, schools are extending their power outside the schoolhouse gate. Power without authority, however, is overreaching.

Background

The Supreme Court has never given explicit authority to schools to regulate off-campus student speech. In fact, the Court has never addressed an off-campus speech case. As discussed later in this book, the Supreme Court's "schoolhouse gate" statement in the *Tinker* case was made in the context of on-campus speech. Thus, it is not surprising that school district efforts to muzzle student speech off-campus or discipline students for speech off school premises have fueled litigation. Since the Supreme Court has never specifically addressed the authority of schools to regulate off-campus speech, the lower courts have struggled to interpret the scope of Supreme Court precedent on student free speech. Some lower courts "extrapolate" from Supreme Court precedent that off-campus speech is "subject to the domain of the school" while other lower courts conclude to the contrary (Tuneski, 2003, p. 159). Amidst this struggle, schools try to find ways to link the off-campus speech to the school so that they can censor the speech. Schools make such a link by, for instance, highlighting the effect of the off-campus speech on the school or the sometimes tenuous presence of the speech on the school campus (Harpaz, 2000).

Delimiting Off-Campus Speech

For purposes of this book, off-campus speech refers to speech that occurs outside school hours and away from the school premises. It also includes student speech away from the school bus and school-sponsored events such as school trips. On-campus speech, on the other hand, refers to speech on school grounds or on the school bus or at school-sponsored events. These are the typical definitions of off-campus speech and on-campus speech as evident in the discussions of cases later in this book. However, in order to account for the blurred lines digital media has created between speech on school grounds or school events (on-campus speech) and off-campus speech, some courts have extended the definition of on-campus speech to include speech "aimed at a specific school and/or its personnel [that] is brought onto the school campus or accessed at school by its originator" (J.S. ex rel. H.S. v. Bethlehem, 2002, p. 865; Evans v. Bayer, 2010, pp. 1371-72).

Some courts, however, appear to see no distinction between on-campus and off-campus speech. For example, according to a federal court in California, "the geographic origin of the speech is not material" (J.C. ex rel. R.C. v. Beverly Hills Unified School District, 2010, p. 1108). That court went on to rule that the same legal standard applies to on-campus and off-campus speech. As evident in the book, other courts even fail to distinguish on-campus from off-campus speech before beginning their legal analysis of whether schools have authority to regulate the student speech in question. Instead, those courts simply implicitly assume that the speech is off-campus speech (Beussink v. Woodland R-IV School District, 1998). However, the "question of whether the student is truly 'at school' is an important one, because the Court has emphasized that the rights of students at school are not 'coextensive with the rights of adults in other settings.'" (West, 2008, citing Bethel School District No. 403 v. Fraser, 1986, p. 682; Wheeler II, 2004). Further, the wrong classification of off-campus speech as on-campus speech strips speech of First Amendment protection that it should otherwise be entitled to (Salgado, 2005, p. 1400-01).

The Extant Status of Students' Online and Offline Off-Campus Speech

Professor Sonja R. West of the University of Georgia Law School highlighted the uncertainty in the student-speech jurisprudence in the article "Sanctionable conduct: How the Supreme Court stealthily opened the schoolhouse gate":

The Supreme Court's few cases addressing student speech have answered only a handful of questions regarding school officials' ability to censor their students while in the classroom, during a school assembly or when participating in a school sponsored, non-public forum. These cases, however, have left open a number of scenarios where it remains unclear how courts should balance students' free speech rights against school officials' authority (West, 2008, p. 28).

As noted earlier, the United States Supreme Court's use of the phrase "schoolhouse gate" suggests that the gate is the defining border between on-campus speech and off-campus speech. The problem is that the border has not been clearly defined. The absence of a clear definition is particularly notable in the age of digital-media student communications. As Roberts (2008) observed, "[t]raditional restrictions of student speech were limited to the physical borders of the school, whereas the Internet has no borders or territorially-defined limits" (p. 1178). A further challenge arises from the fact that "[t]he unique characteristics of the Internet pose trying questions to many areas of the law, including the First Amendment rights of students" (Roberts, p. 1178). Justice Cappy of the Supreme Court of Pennsylvania acknowledged as much in J.S. v. Bethlehem Area School District (2002) when he stated that the "advent of the Internet has complicated analysis of restrictions on speech" (p. 863). This is particularly because digital media allows students to create speech virtually anywhere off-campus. Twitter, Facebook, Myspace, Friendster, IM (Instant Messaging), YouTube and Instagram have become staples of student communication (Madden, et al., 2013). In fact, the "most avid users of social-networking websites" are teenagers (Emrick, 2009, p. 787). Further, students communicate through various modes on the internet such as emails, newsgroups, telephony, video broadcasting, audio broadcasting, listservs and the World Wide Web (Swartz, 2000).

Even though students have always communicated with and about their peers while offline and off-campus in their homes, at the mall and other public places, the internet has created another forum for students to communicate. This forum enables students to communicate before a broader audience anonymously or in their actual names. The internet not only allows students to connect with other students outside school, it also empowers them to "challenge the status quo", express frustrations and criticize their school, administrators, teachers, students and policies (Tuneski, 2003). The internet provides a forum for students to, at times, flip a "virtual finger" through vulgar or obscene speech (Emrick, 2009, p. 805). The internet has become "today's restroom wall" (Carvin, 2006). Additionally, it is a forum for students to gossip, find support, offer support to others, and provide insights and opinions on issues confronting teenagers. For example, Papandrea (2008) pointed out that "[o]ftentimes students who have difficulty finding a community at school seek a community on the Web. Self-proclaimed 'nerds' have discussed the importance of having a forum to deal with the often demoralizing experience of school" (p. 1034).

Students also create magazines online to share political and other ideas with other students and the public at large (Papandrea, 2008). They create web logs (blogs) in the form of a diary to share information about their day-to-day activities, pictures and other interesting revelations about themselves. Internet forums offer students the "opportunity to engage in autobiographical expression and cathartic storytelling that can promote self-realization and self-reflection" (Papandrea, p. 1034). Students also use satire and impersonate teachers and fellow students online, posting parody profiles (Verga, 2007). Sometimes, student speech online can be highly controversial and deeply offensive. However, as the United States Supreme Court acknowledged in Terminiello v. City of Chicago (1949), "[s]peech is often provocative and challenging. It may strike at prejudices and preconceptions and have profound unsettling effects as it presses for acceptance of an idea" (p. 4). The First Amendment is designed to protect such speech de-

Background

spite its controversial, hurtful, offensive or unsettling nature (Tuneski, 2003). Additionally, the Supreme Court has ruled that "a function of free speech under our system of government is to invite dispute. It may indeed best serve its high purpose when it induces a condition of unrest, creates dissatisfaction with conditions as they are, or even stirs people to anger" (Terminiello v. City of Chicago, p. 4).

With offline speech, schools had no access to or knowledge of student off-campus speech unless they searched through a student's personal diary unwittingly brought on-campus, seized underground student newspapers or relied on tattling by other students (Papandrea, 2008). For online speech, however, even if a student might not intend online speech to get to school, the ubiquity of the internet increases the possibility that the speech might be accessed at school (Roberts, 2008). School access is made even more likely because at least 95% of schools are connected to the internet (Swartz, 2000). "In cases involving student cyberspeech, however, it is rarely clear that the speech at issue occurs within the gates. A student who comes to school the morning after creating a website on her home computer does not bring the site with her, attached to her person" (Brenton, 2008, p. 1224). As Wheeler II (2004) pointed out, "cyberspeech is simply cast out into the ether with no primary locus" (p. 29). Students who post messages on social media, even when using the site's settings to keep the message private, are assuming a legal risk that a recipient of the message could become a school witness and turn the private message over to the school (Roasio v. Clark County School District, 2013). Even with the ability to control school-internet access, schools must not forget that the United States Supreme Court has ruled that the internet is a protected medium of communication under the First Amendment (Reno v. American Civil Liberties Union, 1997).

The concomitant expansion of school censorship of students' speech beyond the schoolhouse gate with the growth of digital media is driven by a variety of reasons. According to Papandrea (2008), the effort to wield power over student speech reflects the inclination of adults to fear the unknown and the lack of control over the cultural change that is digital communication. Furthermore, a lot of school officials appear to "fear that the Internet is some dark force of evil that corrupts students" (Hudson, Jr. 2000, p. 200). Schools also seem to believe that, because students are on the school premises for about nine hours each week day, it is of no consequence that the speech originated during the time of the day when the student is away from the school premises (Calvert, 2001). Thus, schools have disciplined students, for example, for comments made off-campus online in the privacy of their homes outside of school hours. This threatens to make schools 24-hour/7-day enforcers and policemen in students' homes and cyber police of student internet use. This would effectively deprive students of any forum for personal and confidential expression free of school reins off-campus and on-campus (Salgado, 2005). The fact that students are bound by "compulsory attendance laws for part of the week" should not override the rights of students to free speech while they are in private or public locations off-campus (Caplan, 2003, p. 140). As one court noted, "[i]t would be an unseemly and dangerous precedent to allow the state in the guise of school authorities to reach into a child's home and control his/her actions there to the same extent that they can control that child when he/she participates in school sponsored activities" (Layshock ex rel. Layshock v. Hermitage School District, 2010, p. 260). Society and the constitution would find it absurd if schools dictated what students wore while they were off-campus, including in the privacy of their homes (Salgado, 2005). Yet, schools are aggressively exercising extensive power over students' speech off-campus. In Texas, for example, a principal reportedly went to great lengths simply to prevent a student from writing letters to the editor of the local newspaper while off-campus (Hudson, Jr., 2002). Such overreaching, we believe, is particularly unfortunate when students use no school time or school resources in creating the speech.

Schools sometimes claim that they need to censor off-campus student speech in order to protect students from speech. Schools argue that they should be able to punish students for their off-campus speech if the speech is offensive, disruptive, vulgar or distasteful. However, such reasoning is "largely a modern conceit" that presumes a "childhood–a prolonged period of innocence–that was rare in premodern times and continues to be rare in many parts of the world" (Garfield, 2005, p. 567). Garfield (2005) pointed out that, in the Middle Ages, children often slept in the same bed as their parents and married around puberty. In essence, even in premodern times, students did not need the school to protect them from sexually-explicit speech. Additionally, "contemporary children living in war-torn countries like Congo-where war has shuttered their schools, left them lame and hungry, [and] killed their parents before their eyes-need more than limited access to violent video games to learn peaceful conflict resolution" (Garfield, p. 567). The Constitution also does not require schools to protect students from political speech that the school finds objectionable. According to the American Civil Liberties Union (ACLU), people in authority need to respect students' free speech rights so that they do not develop into "disillusioned adults" who are intolerant of opposing viewpoints (Pisciotta, 2000).

Free speech is critical to students' appreciation of self-autonomy and democratic self-government (Papandrea, 2008). As a federal circuit court of appeals noted, "it is obvious that they must be allowed the freedom to form their political views on the basis of uncensored speech *before* they turn eighteen, so that their minds are not a blank when they first exercise the franchise" (American Amusement Machine Association v. Kendrick, 2001). Therefore, it should take more than a desire to protect children from speech for schools to censor a First Amendment right to speech off-campus. The Supreme Court needs to make this very clear. Censorship is a danger to freedom of speech, particularly if schools are allowed to regulate what students say off-campus. Even if courts overturn discipline and academic sanctions imposed by "overzealous or misinformed administrators" or the cases are settled, such judicial decisions come months or years after the censorship, with "significant damage" already done to the student's right to free expression (Verga, 2007, p. 729). As such, it is crucial and urgent that courts "methodically police this censorship to ensure that the threat it poses to First Amendment values is kept to an absolute minimum" (Garfield, p. 650).

The Disquietude of Overzealous School Censorship of Students' Off-Campus Online Speech

Incredibly, some schools are actually searching through students' private emails and Facebook accounts. In Minnesota, for example, school officials forced R.S., a 12-year old student, to reveal her password so they could search through her personal communications (CNN, 2012). She was punished for writing on her Facebook page that she hated a school hall monitor who she felt picked on her. She wrote this while off-campus and without using school resources. The ACLU's court complaint against the school punishment pointed out that R.S. was "intimidated, frightened, humiliated and sobbing" as school officials searched through her personal communications (CNN, 2012). The school claimed it did nothing wrong. Such censorship of off-campus speech should be unacceptable.

Schools continue to find innovative ways to censor student speech. Some schools actually hire internet-monitoring contractors to track student speech online. For example, A.S. Popkin, Deputy Editor of Technology and Science at NBC News, recently reported that a school district in Los Angeles paid Geo Listening $40,500 to monitor the postings of approximately 13,000 students in eight schools with daily reports sent to the schools (A.S. Popkin, 2013; Klein, 2013). As author Nate Anderson aptly noted,

Background

internet-monitoring systems can be subject to abuse: "Used less than well, it can be a bit creepy, sort of on par with having a kid's uncle listen outside her bedroom during a slumber party. And used badly, it can make a nice tool for keeping an eye on critics/dissenters" (A.S. Popkin, 2013).

The borderless nature of cyberspace elevates the concerns about schools overreaching in their efforts to censor student speech. Roberts (2008) emphasizes that courts must create a test for cyberspeech that accounts for two "competing concerns so that neither students nor teachers use the Internet to abuse First Amendment rights in the school context" (p. 1182). One concern is that cyberspace gives students the opportunity to "circumvent any restrictions school officials impose on their speech by simply claiming that cyberspace is not on school grounds" (p. 1182). A second concern is that, since the internet enables easy transmission of messages even without the consent or intent of the original speaker, schools may consequently be able to access and chill a significant volume of student speech (Roberts, 2008).

Courts must require schools to embrace a marketplace of ideas that allows students to experiment with ideas as Justice Holmes admonished in Abrams v. United States (1919). The marketplace of ideas embraces a "multitude of tongues" rather than an "authoritative selection of ideas" (Li, 2005). Unfortunately, schools often fail to appreciate the importance of a marketplace of ideas, even opting for punishment of students who help identify true threats to the school – an unprotected speech category – as evident in this example:

Three high school students from the suburbs of Seattle created their own little marketplace of ideas: a website on the Internet where friends and classmates could post messages on an electronic bulletin board and chat room, sharing with each other–and the world–their thoughts, opinions, wishes, speculations, and fears. This uncensored forum featured discussions of school work, extracurricular activities, politics, popular culture, and teenage angst, along with forays into gossip, coarse language, insults, and boasts about alcohol, drugs, and sex. School administrators became alarmed by the website, which they considered both offensive and a distraction from coursework. The student webmasters shut down their creation after an unknown person in the chat room intimated that the next day would be "doomsday," prompting the Administration to close the building as a precaution. Instead of rewarding the student webmasters for their cooperation, the school initially decided to suspend them. Operating an uncensored marketplace of ideas on the Internet was, the school believed, a form of misconduct (Caplan, 2003, pp. 94-95).

School Disciplinary Actions against Off-Campus Student Speech

Schools have imposed a wide range of discipline on students for their off-campus speech in order to censor the speech. Examples include a school official whipping a student with rawhide (Lander v. Seaver, 1859); a three-day suspension coupled with a transfer from advanced placement (AP) class to lesser-weighted honors courses (Evans v. Bayer, 2010); a three-day suspension plus a loss of all grades during suspension (Neal et al. v. Efurd, 2005); and a ten-day suspension that included suspension from all extra-curricular activities (Killion v. Franklin Regional School District, 2001). A student was given a five-day suspension that was later increased to full-semester suspension (Wisniewski v. Board of Education of the Weedsport Central School District, 2007). Further, because of the hostility in the school and the community, the family was forced to move out of the community. Another school suspended a student for ten days and placed her at an alternative education program as punishment for her off-campus speech that the school found objectionable (Layshock ex rel. Layshock v. Hermitage School District, 2011). This student was also banned from graduation ceremony and all extra-curricular activities.

In Doninger v. Niehoff (2007), as discipline for off-campus speech, a student was barred from running for senior class secretary, required to show a copy of the off-campus speech to her mother and issue a written apology to the superintendent. In another case, a student was punished with in-school suspension along with placement on a zero-tolerance policy for the remainder of the school year (Barnett ex rel. Barnett v. Tipton County Board of Education, 2009). In Requa v. Kent School District No. 415 (2007), a student was given a 40-day suspension that was later changed to a 20-day suspension with the stipulation that the student write a research paper during the suspension. The school also threatened to exclude the student from the graduation ceremony.

In D.J.M. ex rel. D.M. v. Hannibal Public School District No. 60, 2011, a student was suspended for the rest of the school year and ended up in juvenile detention and psychiatric hospital consequent to the student's speech. Another school punished a student with a full-calendar year suspension from extracurricular and co-curricular activities; this suspension was later reduced to 25% of the student's fall extracurricular activities with the stipulation that the student visit a counselor thrice and apologize (T.V. ex rel. B.V. v. Smith-Green Community School Corporation, 2011).

As an Indiana court aptly stated, "[i]t is beyond dispute that matters of student discipline and their impact upon the education of the children of our state are questions of great public importance" (Board of School Trustees of the Muncie Community School v. Barnell, 1997, p. 802). The deprival of an education and impact on students' reputations that attends discipline are not constitutionally insignificant (Riggan v. Midland Independent School District, 2000). The discipline of students, as censorship of speech, for any length of time has a significant impact on First Amendment rights. As a plurality of the United States Supreme Court warned in Elrod v. Burns (1976), "the loss of First Amendment freedoms, for even minimal periods of time, unquestionably constitutes irreparable injury" (p. 373). It is, therefore, incumbent upon courts to exercise a "special solicitude for claims that the protections afforded by the First Amendment have been unduly abridged" (Planned Parenthood Association v. Chicago Transit Authority, 1985, p. 1229).

Students' Recourse against School Censorship

Students often have little to no recourse when schools infringe their free speech rights because lawyers do not find it profitable to litigate student speech cases (Moss, 2011). Even when pro bono attorneys pursue student speech cases, they tend to do so at a loss. Consequently, "there is essentially no private bar of school speech lawyers" (Moss, p. 1435). Nonprofit organizations such as the Student Press Law Center (SPLC) and the ACLU often serve as the only avenues to pursue claims against schools. Even then, those organizations are not able to take all the cases. With the limited avenues for recourse, schools effectively get away with censorship. The sad reality is that, as noted by the executive director of SPLC, most of the complaints to SPLC are "well-founded" (Moss, p. 1435). Besides, it is "a pretty big step for a 16-year-old to call a lawyer" (Moss, 2011, p. 1435, citing Rogers, 2011).

SPLC's executive director estimates that, even if SPLC accepts 1,000 complaints about school censorship from students each year, the actual number of complaints received must be 10 times that (Moss, 2011, p. 1435, citing Rogers, 2011). Moreover, as a federal district court stated, it is rare for courts to overturn a school's discipline of its students (Barnett ex rel. Barnett v. Tipton County Board of Education, 2009). This makes it even more important for the First Amendment to serve as an impenetrable

Background

wall against extension of school-censorship authority over student off-campus speech. Otherwise, once the school disciplines a student for off-campus speech, the student will face a virtually impossible task of overturning the discipline in court.

In some cases where students pursue a legal claim against a school district, the lack of clarity on student rights could subject the district to significant litigation fees and monetary damages. For example, Sean O'Brien, sued his school for $500,000 after he was suspended and threatened with expulsion for describing his teacher as "an overweight middle-aged man who doesn't like to get haircuts" on his website (Pisciotta, 2000; Swartz, 2000). The school eventually settled the case for $30,000 and an apology.

Karl Beidler was awarded $10,000 in monetary damages and $52,000 in attorney fees after he was suspended for creating a website that ridiculed his assistant principal (Student Press Law Center, 2001). In another case, a student received $60,000 from his school district as partial settlement of a First Amendment claim. The student had been expelled from his volleyball team after he posted online messages from his home computer taunting an opposing basketball team and an opponent's mother (Simonich, 2002). In yet another case, a court awarded a student legal fees of $52,000 and an additional $10,000 as damages after the student put his assistant principal in a Viagra commercial, and as a cartoon character engaged in a sexual act, posted on the student's website created off-campus (Tuneski, 2003). In these examples, as in most, the school and the students were not certain of their rights and responsibilities; this gray area in the law exposes districts to tremendous liability. Therefore, it behooves the courts to clearly define the scope of students' free speech rights for both students and school districts.

Judicial Diffidence, Incertitude, and Off-Campus Student Speech

While the lower courts know from the United States Supreme Court's use of the phrase "schoolhouse gate" that there is a gate that delimits the reach of school power over student speech, courts sometimes shy away from precisely defining the limits of the gate. For instance, a federal court of appeals recently stated that "[t]here is surely a limit to the scope of a high school's interest in the order, safety, and well-being of its students when the speech at issue originates outside the schoolhouse gate. But we need not fully define that limit here" (Kowalski v. Berkeley County Schools, 2011). Additionally, in 2013, a federal district court in Oregon pointed out that the United States Court of Appeals for the Ninth Circuit has never ruled on whether schools can constitutionally censor students' off-campus speech on social media after school hours (Roasio v. Clark County School District, 2013). Thus, the federal district courts in that circuit lack clarity on how to proceed with censorship of off-campus student speech. Due to the reticence of courts, the "current state of the law threatens to chill student speech that would otherwise be protected outside the context of schools" (Tuneski, 2003, p. 158).

The lack of judicial clarity on the boundaries of the schoolhouse gate might encourage legislatures to extend the power of schools over students while off-campus. The National School Boards Association reported that the Indiana House of Representatives approved a bill that would extend the authority of schools to punish students outside the schoolhouse gate (National School Boards Association, 2012a). The bill was designed to authorize schools to punish students for any conduct or speech off-campus that interferes with the school, regardless of whether the conduct or speech is lawful or unlawful. Executive Director of the Student Press Law Center Frank LoMonte expressed trepidation that other states might follow in Indiana's footsteps, noting that "[t]his could be like a bad cold that gets passed from state to state" (National School Boards Association, 2012a).

LoMonte's concern extended to the fact that schools could manipulate such laws in furtherance of "image control" (National School Boards Association, 2012a). Schools would however, be mistaken to use censorship in furtherance of image control; particularly where such actions are based on the notion that readers would view uncensored student messages as school endorsed. Certainly, the "proposition that schools do not endorse everything they fail to censor is not complicated" (West, 2008, p. 38, citing Board of Education of Westside Community School v. Mergens, 1990, p. 250). As the United States Supreme Court has indicated, the perspective of the law is that students and other observers "are likely to understand that a school does not endorse or support student speech that it merely permits on a non-discriminatory basis" (Board of Education of Westside Community School v. Mergens, p. 250).

Even when the Supreme Court has been presented with opportunities to review student off-campus speech cases, it has refused to do so. For example, in 2012, the Supreme Court refused to review three off-campus online student speech cases that revealed confusion in the lower courts about the jurisprudence. This refusal prompted Francisco M. Negrón Jr., general counsel of the National School Boards Association, to express frustration as did counsel for the various parties in the case. Negrón Jr. stated that "[w]e've missed an opportunity to really clarify for school districts what their responsibility and authority is. ... This is one of those cases where the law is simply lagging behind the times" (National School Boards Association, 2012b). The unsettled nature of the law complicates the ability of school officials to understand the "intricacies of First Amendment jurisprudence" (Nixon v. Northern Local School District Board of Education, 2005, p. 966).

With the Supreme Court failing to provide clarity, lower courts will continue to interpret the student-speech jurisprudence in muddled and conflicting ways. It also means that schools and legal scholars can only continue to speculate about the scope of school power outside the schoolhouse gate until there is a decisive ruling by the Supreme Court. Consequent to the lack of judicial clarity and specific guidance, schools will continue to take liberties with censoring student off-campus speech. One of the things we can interpret from Supreme Court precedent is that, if students bring free speech rights to the schoolhouse gate, outside the schoolhouse gate they should be entitled to the same speech rights as persons free from school control. The speech rights accorded persons under the United States Constitution are broad and protected from censorship. In R.A.V. v. City of St. Paul, Minnesota (1992), the United States Supreme Court made this clear, ruling that "[t]he First Amendment generally prevents government from proscribing speech or even expressive conduct because of disapproval of the ideas expressed" (p. 382). Additionally, schools may not regulate speech based on "hostility-or favoritism-towards the underlying message expressed" (p. 386). Instead, the "school's proper response is to educate the audience rather than squelch the speaker when students express view of which school authorities disapprove" (West, 2008, pp. 38-39, citing Hedges v. Wauconda Community Unit No. 118, 1993, p. 1299). The school must not simply "throw up its hands, declaring that because misconceptions are possible it may silence its pupils, that the best defense against misunderstanding is censorship" (Hedges v. Wauconda Community Unit No. 118, p. 1299).

CONCLUSION

In this chapter, we presented critical context for subsequent chapters. We discussed how schools have exercised disciplinary power over students' off-campus conduct. We then discussed how schools are increasingly extending disciplinary power to off-campus student speech. We also discussed the origins

Background

of the "schoolhouse gate" phrase that often plays a vital role in determining where the campus ends and off-campus begins. We noted that courts have struggled to define the borders of school, especially in the digital age with the ubiquity of the internet. The failure of the Supreme Court to speak on the subject has created uncertainty in the student free speech jurisprudence. Subsequent chapters in this book will further highlight this uncertainty.

Despite the uncertainty in the jurisprudence, we must remember that the First Amendment right to free speech is so precious that it should not be taken for granted. Indeed, because the First Amendment jealously guards free speech rights, since 1791, the United States Supreme Court has only excluded "few limited areas" of speech from First Amendment protection (R.A.V. v. City of St. Paul, Minnesota, 1992, pp. 382-83). The Supreme Court has emphasized that "a limited categorical approach has remained an important part of our First Amendment jurisprudence" (p. 383). These limited categories include true threats, obscenity, child pornography, fighting words and defamation (Oluwole, Green, & Stackpole, 2013; Watts v. United States, 1969; Roth v. United States, 1957; Miller v. California, 1973; Chaplinsky v. New Hampshire, 1942; New York v. Ferber, 1982; Osborne v. Ohio, 1990; New York Times Co. v. Sullivan, 1964; Gertz v. Robert Welch, Inc., 1974; Salgado, 2005). According to the Supreme Court, these categories are excluded from First Amendment protection because they have "such slight social value as a step to truth that any benefit that may be derived from them is clearly outweighed by the social interest in order and morality" (R.A.V. v. City of St. Paul, Minnesota 1992, p. 383; Chaplinsky v. New Hampshire, 1942, p. 572). As long as the limitation is reasonable and content-neutral, the Constitution also allows the government to limit the time, place and manner of speech if the limitation is narrowly tailored to further a significant government purpose and leaves open to the speaker sufficient alternate communication channels (Brenton, 2008; Perry Education Association v. Perry Local Educators' Association, 1983). Beyond these categories and limitations, any content-based effort to censor speech should face a very stringent judicial scrutiny (Brenton, 2008). The Constitution generally "allows people to utter words that risk a great deal of substantial and material disruption to daily life. They can hurt each other's feelings, impugn their motives, misquote them, level mistaken allegations of fact against them, even advocate breaking the law or overthrowing the government" (Caplan, p. 140). As Supreme Court Justice Brandeis cautioned, "[i]f there be time to expose through discussion the falsehood and fallacies, to avert the evil by the processes of education, the remedy to be applied is more speech, not enforced silence. Only an emergency can justify repression. Such must be the rule if authority is to be reconciled with freedom" (Whitney v. California, 1927, p. 377).

REFERENCES

Abrams v. United States (1919). 250 U.S. 616, 630.

American Amusement Machine Association v. Kendrick (2001). 244 F.3d 572.

Barnett ex rel. Barnett v. Tipton County Board of Education (2009). 601 F.Supp.2d 980, 983.

Bethel School District No. 403 v. Fraser (1986). 478 U.S. 675, 682.

Beussink v. Woodland R-IV School District (1998). 30 F. Supp. 2d 1175.

Board of Education of Westside Community School v. Mergens (1990). 496 U.S. 226, 250.

Board of School Trustees of the Muncie Community School v. Barnell (1997). 678 N.E.2d 799, 802.

Brenton, K. W. (2008). Bonghits4jesus.com? Scrutinizing public school authority over student cyber-speech through the lens of personal jurisdiction. *Minnesota Law Review, 92*, 1206–1245.

Bush By and Through Bush v. Dassel-Cokato Board of Education (1990). 745 F.Supp. 562.

Calvert, C. (2001). Off-campus speech, on-campus punishment: Censorship of the emerging internet underground. *Boston University Journal of Science and Technology Law, 7*, 243–287.

Caplan, A. H. (2003). Public school discipline for creating uncensored anonymous internet forums. *Willamette Law Review, 39*, 93–194.

Carvin, A. (2006). *Is MySpace your space as well?* Retrieved December 12, 2013, from http://www.pbs.org/teachers/learning.now/2006/10/is_myspace_your_space_as_well.html

Chaplinsky v. New Hampshire (1942). 315 U.S. 568, 572.

Clements by Clements v. Board of Education of Decatur Public School District No. 61 (1985). 478 N.E.2d 1209.

CNN. (2012, March 10). Minnesota girl alleges school privacy invasion. *CNN*. Retrieved November 29, 2013, from http://www.cnn.com/2012/03/10/us/minnesota-student-privacy/index.html

D.G. v. Independent School District No. 11 of Tulsa County, Oklahoma (2000). 2000 U.S. Dist. LEXIS 12197 *1-15.

D.J.M. ex rel. D.M. v. Hannibal Public School District No. 60 (2011). 647 F.3d 754, 759.

Doninger v. Niehoff (2007). 514 F.Supp.2d 199.

Dritt v. Snodgrass (1877). 66 Mo. 286.

Elrod v. Burns (1976). 427 U.S. 347, 373.

Emrick, T. (2009). When Myspace crosses the school gates: The implications of cyberspeech on students' free-speech rights. *University of Toledo Law Review. University of Toledo. College of Law, 40*, 785–818.

Engel v. Vitale (1962). 370 U.S. 421.

Erb, T. D. (2008). A case for strengthening school district jurisdiction to punish off-campus incidents of cyberbullying. *Arizona State Law Journal, 40*, 257–287.

Evans v. Bayer (2010). 684 F. Supp. 2d 1365, 1368, 1371–72.

Felton v. Fayette School District (1989). 875 F.2d 191.

Garfield, A. E. (2005). Protecting children from speech. *Florida Law Review, 57*, 565–651.

Gertz v. Robert Welch, Inc. (1974). 418 U.S. 323.

Gitlow v. New York (1925). 268 U.S. 652.

Harpaz, L. (2000). Internet speech and the First Amendment rights of public school students. *Brigham Young University Education and Law Journal, 123*, 142–143.

Hazelwood v. Kuhlmeier (1988). 484 U.S. 260.

Hedges v. Wauconda Community Unit No. 118 (1993). 9 F.3d 1295, 1299.

Hobbs v. Germany (1909). 49 So. 515.

Hudson, D. L. Jr. (2000). Censorship of student internet speech: The effect of diminishing student rights, fear of the internet and columbine. *Law Review of Michigan State University Detroit College of Law, 2000*, 199–222.

Hudson, D. L., Jr. (2002). Underground papers and off-campus speech. *First Amendment Center*. Retrieved November 29, 2013, from http://www.firstamendmentcenter.org/underground-papers-off-campus-speech

J.C. ex rel. R.C. v. Beverly Hills Unified School District (2010). 711 F.Supp.2d 1094, 1108.

J.S. ex rel. H.S. v. Bethlehem (2002). 807 A.2d 847, 865.

Killion v. Franklin Regional School District (2001). 136 F.Supp.2d 446, 449.

Klein, R. (2013). California district hires company to monitor students' online activity. *Huffington Post*. Retrieved November 29, 2013, from http://legalclips.nsba.org/2013/08/29/california-district-hires-company-to-monitor-students-online-activity/#sthash.4iCISc7b.dpuf

Kowalski v. Berkeley County Schools (2011). 652 F.3d 565, 573.

Lander v. Seaver (1859). 32 Vt. 114, 115.

Layshock ex rel. Layshock v. Hermitage School District (2010). 593 F.3d 249 (rehearing en banc, opinion vacated by Layshock ex rel. Layshock v. Hermitage School District (2010) 650 F.3d 205).

Layshock ex rel. Layshock v. Hermitage School District (2011). 650 F.3d 205, 210.

Li, S. (2005). The need for a new, uniform standard: The continued threat to internet-related student speech. *Loyola of Los Angeles Entertainment Law Review, 26*, 65–106.

Madden, M., et al. (2013). *Teens, Social Media, and Privacy*. Pew Internet and American Life Project. Washington, DC: Pew Research Center. Retrieved November 29, 2013, from pewinternet.org/~/media//Files/Reports/2013/PIP_TeensSocialMediaandPrivacy.pdf.

Miller v. California (1973). 413 U.S. 15.

Morse v. Frederick (2007). 551 U.S. 393.

Moss, S. A. (2011). The overhyped path from Tinker to Morse: How the student speech cases show the limits of Supreme Court decisions–for the law and for the litigants. *Florida Law Review, 63*, 1407–1457.

National School Boards Association. (2012a). Indiana legislature considers proposal that would allow schools to discipline students for off-campus behavior, including online speech. *Legal Clips*. Retrieved November 29, 2013, from http://legalclips.nsba.org/2012/02/08/indiana-legislature-considers-proposal-that-would-allow-schools-to-discipline-students-for-off-campus-behavior-including-online-speech/#sthash.Lt2bSJtr.dpuf

National School Boards Association. (2012b). Supreme Court declines to hear student internet speech cases. *Legal Clips*. Retrieved November 29, 2013, from http://legalclips.nsba.org/2012/01/19/breaking-news-supreme-court-denies-cert-in-student-internet-speech-cases/

Neal et al. v. Efurd (2005). No. 04-2195.

New York Times Co. v. Sullivan (1964). 376 U.S. 254.

New York v. Ferber (1982). 458 U.S. 747.

Nixon v. Northern Local School District Board of Education (2005). 383 F.Supp.2d 965.

Oluwole, J., Green, P., & Stackpole, M. (2013). *SextEd: Obscenity versus free speech in our schools*. Santa Barbara, CA: Praeger Publishers.

Osborne v. Ohio (1990). 495 U.S. 103.

Papandrea, M. (2008). Student speech rights in the digital age. *Florida Law Review, 60*, 1027–1102.

Perry Education Association v. Perry Local Educators' Association (1983). 460 U.S. 37.

Pike, K. R. (2008). Locating the mislaid gate: Revitalizing tinker by repairing judicial overgeneralizations of technologically enabled student speech. *Brigham Young University Law Review, 2008*, 990.

Pisciotta, L. M. (2000). Beyond sticks & stones: A First Amendment framework for educators who seek to punish student threats. *Seton Hall Law Review, 30*, 635–670.

Planned Parenthood Association v. Chicago Transit Authority (1985). 767 F.2d 1225, 1229.

Popkin, A. S. H. (2013, October 6). Careful what you tweet: Police, schools tap social media to track behavior. *NBC News*. Retrieved November 29, 2013, from http://www.nbcnews.com/technology/careful-what-you-tweet-police-schools-tap-social-media-track-4B11215908

R. R. v. Board of Education of the Shore Regional High School District (1970). 263 A.2d 180.

R.A.V. v. City of St. Paul, Minnesota (1992). 505 U.S. 377, 382–90.

Reno v. American Civil Liberties Union (1997). 521 U.S. 844.

Requa v. Kent School District No. 415 (2007). 492 F.Supp.2d 1272, 1275, 1282.

Riggan v. Midland Independent School District (2000). 86 F.Supp.2d 647, 656.

Roasio v. Clark County School District (2013). 2013 WL 3679375.

Roberts, C. E. (2008). Is Myspace their space? Protecting student cyberspeech in a post-Morse v. Frederick world. *UMKC Law Review, 76*, 1177–1192.

Background

Rogers, T. (n.d.). Faculty advisers increasingly face the ax for not censoring high school papers. *About.com*. Retrieved December 7, 2013, from http://journalism.about.com/od/schoolsinternships/a/student-censorship.htm

Roth v. United States (1957). 354 U.S. 476.

Russo, C. J. (2006). Legal research: The "traditional" method. In S. Permuth & R. D. Mawdsley (Eds.), *Research methods for studying legal issues in education* (pp. 5–24). Dayton, OH: Education Law Association.

Salgado, R. (2005). Protecting student speech rights while increasing school safety: School jurisdiction and the search for warning signs in a post-Columbine/Red Lake environment. *Brigham Young University Law Review*, *2005*, 1371–1414.

Simonich, M. (2002, December 2). Newsmaker: Jack Flaherty Jr. / Teen fought school district in court, won. *Pittsburgh Post-Gazette*. Retrieved March 11, 2014, from http://old.post-gazette.com/localnews/20021202newsmakerreg5p5.asp

Student Press Law Center. (2001). District pays $62,000 in damages after losing suit filed by student suspended for web site. *SPLC.org*. Retrieved November 29, 2013, from http://www.splc.org/news/report_detail.asp?id=673&edition=18

Swartz, J. K. (2000). Beyond the schoolhouse gates: Do students shed their constitutional rights when communicating to a cyber-audience? *Drake Law Review*, *48*, 587–604.

Terminiello v. City of Chicago (1949). 337 U.S. 1.

Tinker v. Des Moines Independent Community School District (1969). 393 U.S. 503.

Tuneski (2003). Online, not on grounds: Protecting student internet speech. *Virginia Law Review*, 89, 139–87.

T.V. ex rel. B.V. v. Smith-Green Community School Corporation (2011). 807 F.Supp.2d 767, 773-74.

United States Constitution Amendment I. (n.d.). Retrieved online May 1, 2015, from https://www.law.cornell.edu/constitution/overview

United States Constitution Amendment XIV. (n.d.). Retrieved online May 1, 2015, from https://www.law.cornell.edu/constitution/overview

Verga, R. J. (2007). Policing their space: The First Amendment parameters of school discipline of student cyberspeech. *Santa Clara Computer and High-Technology Law Journal*, *23*, 727–748.

Watts v. United States (1969). 394 U.S. 705.

West, S. R. (2008). Sanctionable conduct: How the Supreme Court stealthily opened the schoolhouse gate. *Lewis and Clark Law Review*, *12*, 27–44.

West Virginia State Board of Education v. Barnette (1943). 319 U.S. 624.

Wheeler, T. E. II. (2004). Slamming in cyberspace: The boundaries of student First Amendment rights. *Res Gestae, 47,* 24–32.

Whitney v. California (1927). 274 U.S. 357, 377.

Wisniewski v. Board of Education of the Weedsport Central School District (2007). 494 F.3d 34, 37.

KEY TERMS AND DEFINITIONS

Censorship: The suppression of speech by an agent of the government such as a public school official or a government agency such as a public school.

First Amendment: This is the first right listed within the bill of rights added to the United States Constitution in 1791 to guarantee Americans certain rights free from government infringement. It covers the right to free speech, the right to free exercise of religion, right against government establishment of religion, the right to a free press, the right to peaceable assembly and the right to petition for redress of grievances.

Free Speech Clause: The clause in the First Amendment to the United States Constitution which prohibits the government from denying citizens the right to free speech.

Jurisprudence: The body of case law governing a particular area of American life.

Lower Court: Any court in America other than the United States Supreme Court which is the highest court in the United States.

Off-Campus Speech: Speech that occurs in any locale outside the borders or premises of a school and outside school hours. It includes student speech away from the school bus and school-sponsored events such as school trips.

Offline Speech: Speech that occurs in any non-digital setting.

On-Campus Speech: Speech that occurs in any area inside the school or on school premises. It includes speech on the school bus or at school-sponsored events.

Online Speech: Speech in online communication forums, including Twitter, Facebook, Myspace, Friendster, IM (Instant Messaging), YouTube, and Instagram.

Schoolhouse Gate: The United States Supreme Court's terminology for the borderline separating a school and its premises from locales outside the school.

Section 2
Unprotected Speech

Chapter 2
True Threat

ABSTRACT

This chapter discusses one of the categories within which schools can constitutionally exert power over student speech while students are off-campus. The goal of the chapter is to describe true threat – one of the few categories of speech for which students, like adults, cannot claim a right to free speech against censorship. The chapter begins with a definition of true threats. It also discusses the two perspectives the judiciary uses in analyzing the existence of a true threat: (a) the reasonable-speaker perspective; and (b) the reasonable-listener perspective.

INTRODUCTION

This chapter provides an overview of the jurisprudence on true threat. It discusses the origin of true threat as an unprotected speech category in Watts v. United States (1969). This chapter also provides the United States Supreme Court's definition of true threat which was first outlined in 2003, almost four decades after the true-threat doctrine was first introduced. Since only a few courts have applied the true-threat doctrine in the school context, the chapter per the authors discusses some non-school cases that illuminate the application of the doctrine to speech. The chapter then considers examples of school cases that further shed light on the operation of the doctrine. The objective is to facilitate an understanding of the true-threat doctrine. If school officials have an understanding of the true-threat doctrine, they will be less likely to censor protected off-campus student speech.

MAIN FOCUS OF THE CHAPTER

The Jurisprudential Background and Framework of the True-Threat Doctrine

Speech that qualifies as a true threat (also referred to as a genuine threat) is not protected under the First Amendment. In other words, any person who communicates a true threat cannot claim the threat is protected speech immunized from punishment under the Free Speech Clause of the First Amendment.

DOI: 10.4018/978-1-4666-9519-1.ch002

Consequently, schools have constitutional latitude to censor such speech, regardless of whether the student-speaker is on-campus or off-campus at the time of the speech. This latitude extends to students' communications in cyberspace (Verga, 2007).

Especially after the school massacres at Columbine High School in 1999 and more recently the Sandy Hook Elementary School in 2012, the increased threats to schools, school shootings and other violence on school campuses (Centers for Disease Control and Prevention, 2012), it is very important for schools to understand what the judiciary considers as true threats. Such an understanding will enable schools to remain proactive with respect to school safety without infringement of students' free speech rights under the First Amendment. Post-Columbine, school officials are increasingly paying attention to threatening speech in cyberspace in particular (Erb, 2008). If school officials do not have an adequate grasp of what constitutes true threats, they risk overreaching, classifying a vast amount of speech viewed as menacing or threatening in any way as a true threat (Salgado, 2005). The censorship of threatening student speech that is not a true threat under the law could chill student speech for a long period of time. Even if the student is able to pursue remedies through litigation, the case could span years and extend even beyond the student's time at the school. In essence, litigation is an "inadequate remedy" for students (p. 1392). Inappropriately censoring protected speech as a true threat could also ensnare schools in protracted litigation, at taxpayers' expense, defending the censorship (Salgado, 2005).

The United States Supreme Court has identified the following rationales for excluding true threats from First Amendment protection: (a) the need to protect people from living in fear of violence; (b) the importance of protecting people from the disruption that results from the fear of violence; and (c) the need to foreclose the possibility that the violence threatened in the speech will be carried out (R.A.V. v. City of St. Paul, Minnesota, 1992). The fear of violence threatened in a true threat can be highly disruptive, debilitating psychologically and even lead to physical problems, including insomnia, heart problems and appetite loss (Rothman, 2001). Rothman identified a fourth rationale as the need to guard against coercing people to act contrary to their will and interest. However, the Supreme Court has ruled that the coercive nature of speech is not necessarily a justification for excluding the speech from First Amendment protection (NAACP v. Claiborne Hardware Company, 1982, p. 910; Rothman, 2001).

The "seminal" United States Supreme Court case on the true-threat doctrine is Watts v. United States (1969) (Pisciotta, 2000, p. 642). While that case did not define a true threat, it created the true-threat doctrine (Pisciotta, 2000). In that case, the Supreme Court was confronted with the speech of an 18-year old man, Robert Watts, at a public rally about police brutality. After an attendee stated that young people needed to get educated before voicing their opinion, Robert retorted:

They always holler at us to get an education. And now I have already received my draft classification as 1-A and I have got to report for my physical this Monday coming. I am not going. If they ever make me carry a rifle the first man I want to get in my sights is L.B.J.' 'They are not going to make me kill my black brothers.' (Watts v. United States, 1969, p. 1401).

The Supreme Court identified three factors for determining whether a statement making a threat constitutes a true threat (Watts v. United States, 1969). First, a threat must be assessed within the context in which it was made. Despite the fact that the speech on its face appeared to be a threat against the president [L.B.J.] of the United States, the Supreme Court ruled that the speech was not a true threat but rather constitutionally-protected speech. The Court reasoned that Robert's speech was merely "political hyperbole" that must be protected, given the American commitment to robust, uninhibited and wide-open commentary on public issues (p. 1401). While the Court acknowledged that Robert's speech was "very crude" and "offensive", this fact alone was not sufficient to take the speech outside the realm of First Amendment protection (p. 1401). This is not surprising because discussions of issues of public concern sometimes entail "vehement, caustic, and sometimes unpleasantly sharp attacks on government and public officials" (p. 1401). Besides, such attacks are political speech – the context of Robert's speech – and thus entitled to First Amendment protection. As the Supreme Court emphasized, protected political speech is, by nature, "often vituperative, abusive, and inexact" (p. 1402).

Secondly, the Supreme Court ruled that before a threat can be deemed a true threat, the content of the speech must be analyzed to determine if the threat is explicitly conditional (Watts v. United States, 1969). If the threat is explicitly conditional, then it cannot qualify as a true threat. Robert's threat was explicitly conditional as evident in his use of the word "if" ("If they ever make me carry a rifle the first man I want to get in my sights is L.B.J.") (pp. 1401-02). Additionally, Robert set forth another express condition to his threat against the president: he stated that he would not report to the physical for the draft on Monday – a precondition to getting the rifle he threatened to use. Accordingly, the Court found that Robert's threat was not a true threat. Instead, he was merely clumsily stating his opposition to the president politically.

Thirdly, the Supreme Court stated that true-threat analysis requires examination of the reaction of the listeners to the threat (Watts v. United States, 1969). If the listeners perceived the threat as serious, then it is more likely to be deemed a true threat. After Robert's threatening statement about the president, he laughed as did the crowd. Consequently, the Court reasoned that since the listeners did not take his threat seriously, it did not constitute a true threat.

In NAACP v. Claiborne Hardware Company (1982), the United States Supreme Court provided some additional insights into the nature of true threats. In that case, Charles Evers, field secretary of the National Association for the Advancement of Colored People (NAACP), spoke at a public rally advocating boycott of white merchants. During that speech, he warned that any black person who violated the boycott would be "disciplined" by other blacks (p. 902). He also warned them that they should not expect protection from law enforcement because the sheriff would not be sleeping with boycott violators at night. Two days later, at another public rally, Charles gave another speech during which he stated that, "[I]f we catch any of you going in any of them racist stores, we're gonna break your damn neck" (p. 902). In its analysis of the speech, the Supreme Court stated that "violence has no sanctuary in the First Amendment, and the use of weapons, gunpowder, and gasoline may not constitutionally masquerade under the guise of advocacy" (p. 916). Despite Charles' reference to violence, the Supreme Court ruled that his speech was merely an "emotional and persuasive" plea for unity in the boycott effort and his "threats of vilification or social ostracism" were constitutionally-protected speech (p. 926). The Court reasoned that his speech, primarily, was "highly charged political rhetoric lying at the core of the First Amendment" (pp. 926-27). The Court emphasized that "[s]trong and effective extemporaneous rhetoric cannot be nicely channeled in purely dulcet phrases" (p. 928). Furthermore, an "advocate must be free to stimulate his audience with spontaneous and emotional appeals for unity and action in a common cause" (p. 928).

Even after recognizing true threats as an unprotected category of speech in 1969, and identifying the three factors for a true-threat analysis, the United States Supreme Court failed to provide a comprehensive definition for true threats for almost four decades (Salgado, 2005). The absence of a clear definition made it challenging to describe the parameters of this unprotected speech category. Finally, in 2003, in Virginia v. Black, the Supreme Court defined true threats, characterizing them as "statements where the speaker means to communicate a serious expression of an intent to commit an act of unlawful violence to a particular individual or group of individuals" (p. 359). This definition introduced the following factors into the true-threat analysis: (a) the speaker must have communicated an intent to commit an unlawful violence in the statement (Virginia v. Black, 2003). According to the Federal Bureau of Investigation (FBI), if intent is not part of the evaluation of a threat, the student making the threat might actually feel that the school is treating him arbitrarily or unfairly. This feeling could in turn trigger and escalate an actual intent to commit violence where there was none before (O'toole, 1999); (b) the communication must be a serious expression of intent (Virginia v. Black, 2003); (c) the speaker must have meant to communicate the serious expression of intent. In other words, the communication cannot be accidental or unintentional; and (d) the threatened unlawful violence can be against an individual or a group. Additionally, the Court ruled that in order for speech to qualify as a true threat, it is not necessary to prove that the speaker actually intended to execute the threat or that the speaker had the ability to execute the threat (Virginia v. Black, 2003; see also United States v. Viefhaus, 1999).

In Virginia v. Black (2003), the Supreme Court considered whether cross burning that is done with an intent to intimidate can be prohibited without violating the First Amendment. During a Ku Klux Klan rally in Carroll County, Virginia, members of the Klan discussed their views of Mexicans and blacks and then burned a cross approximately 350 yards from the road. Barry Black, the head of the rally, was arrested and convicted of burning a cross with intent to intimidate a person or group of persons. In the same year, two other individuals unaffiliated with the Klan were convicted for burning a cross in the yard of James Jubilee, an African-American man. They claimed that the cross burning was retaliation for James' complaints that the backyard was being used as a firing range. On appeal, the cases of these two men as well as Barry Black's case were consolidated.

In its First Amendment review, the Supreme Court described cross burning as symbolic speech designed to convey its message of hate in a dramatic and effective way (Virginia v. Black, 2003). The Court associated cross burning with the Klan's history of violence, stating that anyone "who burns a cross directed at a particular person often is making a serious threat, meant to coerce the victim to comply with the Klan's wishes unless the victim is willing to risk the wrath of the Klan" (p. 357). The Court stated that even those not affiliated with the Klan rely on the threatening, intimidating and menacing nature of cross burning to coerce victims into acting against their will or at the very least to create fear in victims. Additionally, intimidation that is constitutionally proscribable is "a type of true threat, where a speaker directs a threat to a person or group of persons with the intent of placing the victim in fear of bodily harm or death" (p. 360). Since cross burning is intimidating and because injury or death is a real possibility (rather than a mere hypothetical) with cross burning, it can be constitutionally proscribed (pp. 357, 360).

The Reasonable-Recipient and Reasonable-Speaker Views

Courts use an objective rather than subjective standard in determining whose perspective should govern in the determination of whether a threat is genuine. The United States Court of Appeals for the Ninth Circuit is the only federal court of appeals to require proof of subjective intent in order for speech to constitute a true threat: "speech may be deemed unprotected by the First Amendment as a 'true threat' only upon proof that the speaker subjectively intended the speech as a threat" (United States v. Cassel, 2005, p. 633; United States v. Elonis, 2013). The subjective-intent requirement focuses on the actual speaker's view of the threatening statement rather than that of a reasonable person.

The objective standard looks at whether a reasonable person would view the threat as a true threat under the Supreme Court definition of true threat set forth in Virginia v. Black (2003). There is, however, a disagreement in the courts "as to the person from whose viewpoint the statement should be interpreted: a reasonable person standing in the shoes of the speaker, or a reasonable person standing in the shoes of the recipient" (Salgado, 2005, p. 1388). Even though an objective standard is used, since both the reasonable-recipient view and the reasonable-speaker view consider the reaction of the listener, the risk of "incorporating the reaction of a potentially overly sensitive listener" into the true-threat analysis introduces some subjectivity, undermining the objectivity of the test (Rothman, 2001, pp. 319-20). Table 1 identifies the federal circuit court of appeals that use the reasonable-recipient view and those that use the reasonable-speaker view. Table 2 identifies the states in the jurisdiction of each federal circuit court of appeals.

In order to determine if speech constitutes a true threat, the reasonable-recipient view (also known as the reasonable-listener view) examines "whether an objectively reasonable recipient would view the message as a threat" (United States v. J.H.H., 1994, pp. 827-28; United States v. Adams, 1999, p. 3; United States v. Daugenbaugh, 1995, pp. 173-74; United States v. Dinwiddie, 1996, p. 925; United States v. Malik, 1994, p. 49; United States v. Roberts, 1990, p. 891). Under the reasonable-recipient view, "a threat is not a state of mind in the threatener; it is an appearance to the victim" (United States v. Schneider, 1990, p. 1570). Under this view, "[t]he fact that the victim acts as if he believed the threat is evidence that he did believe it, and the fact that he believed it is evidence that it could reasonably be believed and therefore that it is a threat" (United States v. Schneider, p. 1571). If hypersensitivity of the recipient overtakes the analysis of true threats, then subjects such as death which are staples of literature and art will be censored (Salgado, 2005). If students have to fear the reaction of school officials to their speech on such subjects, students will be forced to exercise prior restraint in their speech, chilling the constitutional right to free speech. It is also very difficult for students to predict how sensitive their teacher or other school officials will be to their speech. If students find it difficult to predict the sensitivity of school officials who they have some relative familiarity with at the school, it would be

Table 1. Table created from information compiled from Rothman (2001) and United States v. Fulmer (1997)

United States Circuit Court of Appeals	Reasonable-Speaker View	Reasonable-Recipient View
First Circuit Court of Appeals	X	
Second Circuit Court of Appeals		X
Third Circuit Court of Appeals	X	
Fourth Circuit Court of Appeals		X
Fifth Circuit Court of Appeals		X
Sixth Circuit Court of Appeals	X	
Seventh Circuit Court of Appeals	X	
Eighth Circuit Court of Appeals		X
Ninth Circuit Court of Appeals	X	
Tenth Circuit Court of Appeals		X
Eleventh Circuit Court of Appeals		X
District of Columbia Circuit Court of Appeals		X

Table 2. Table created from information compiled from the Administrative Office of the United States Courts (2013)

United States Circuit Court of Appeals	States in the Court's Jurisdiction
First Circuit Court of Appeals	Maine, Massachusetts, New Hampshire and Rhode Island
Second Circuit Court of Appeals	Connecticut, New York and Vermont
Third Circuit Court of Appeals	Delaware, New Jersey and Pennsylvania
Fourth Circuit Court of Appeals	Maryland, North Carolina, South Carolina, Virginia and West Virginia
Fifth Circuit Court of Appeals	Louisiana, Mississippi and Texas
Sixth Circuit Court of Appeals	Kentucky, Michigan, Ohio and Tennessee
Seventh Circuit Court of Appeals	Illinois, Indiana and Wisconsin
Eighth Circuit Court of Appeals	Arkansas, Iowa, Minnesota, Missouri, Nebraska, North Dakota and South Dakota
Ninth Circuit Court of Appeals	Alaska, Arizona, California, Hawaii, Idaho, Montana, Nevada, Oregon and Washington
Tenth Circuit Court of Appeals	Colorado, Kansas, New Mexico, Oklahoma, Utah and Wyoming
Eleventh Circuit Court of Appeals	Alabama, Florida and Georgia
District of Columbia Circuit Court of Appeals	District of Columbia

even more of an impossible ordeal for students to anticipate how a judge or jury will view the student's speech. Moreover, if the student-speaker is not even aware or is negligent that the recipient would view the speech as a genuine threat, the deterrence of speech that constitutes true threats will be undermined (Rothman, 2001). The reasonable-recipient view fails to adequately protect the student-speaker because it empowers schools to punish students who clumsily communicate, even though they "do not speak with the purpose, knowledge, or reckless disregard of making a threat" (p. 317). Additionally, students who unwittingly use words that can be misinterpreted, or interpreted in multiple ways, are at heightened risk of censorship because the reasonable-recipient view disregards the intent of the student-speaker. The reasonable-recipient view effectively allows schools to censor students for their "lack of oratorical skills" (Rothman, p. 317).

In order to determine if speech constitutes a true threat, the reasonable-speaker view examines whether "a reasonable person would foresee that the statement would be interpreted by those to whom the maker communicates the statement as a serious expression of intent to harm or assault" (United States v. Orozco–Santillan, 1990, p. 1265; J.S. v. Bethlehem Area School District, 2002, pp. 857-58; Mahaffey ex rel. Mahaffey v. Aldrich, 2002, p. 785; Planned Parenthood of the Columbia/Willamette, Inc. v. American Coalition of Life Activists, 2002, p. 1075; Roy v. United States, 1969, pp. 877-78; United States v. Glover, 1988, p. 344; United States v. Khorrami, 1990, p. 1192). In other words, the government must show that the "defendant knowingly and willfully uttered the words alleged to constitute the threat, that he understood the meaning of the words to be an apparent threat" (United States v. Callahan, 1983, p. 965). The reasonable-speaker view appears preferable to the reasonable-recipient view in protecting speech because it accounts for the intent of the speaker. According to the United States Court of Appeals for the First Circuit, the reasonable-speaker view is preferable because it prevents jurors from considering the recipient's unique sensitivity (United States v. Fulmer, 1997). The court stated that, unlike the reasonable-recipient view, the reasonable-speaker view does not expose the speaker to punishment for uttering an "ambiguous statement that the recipient may find threatening because of events not within the knowledge of the defendant" (p. 1491). Interestingly, however, courts that embrace the reasonable-speaker view take into account the reaction of the recipient (the reasonable-recipient view) in determining whether the speaker should have reasonably expected the recipient to view the speech as a genuine threat. Even though the United States Court of Appeals for the First Circuit indicated a preference for the reasonable-speaker view, it likewise considers the reasonable-recipient view. In fact, the court noted that the "actual recipient's reaction to the statement shows that the recipient did perceive the message as a threat. This reaction is probative of whether one who makes such a statement might reasonably foresee that such a statement would be taken as a threat" (United States v. Fulmer, p. 1500).

The Totality of the Circumstances of the Speech

In determining whether speech qualifies as true threat, courts will analyze the content of the speech in light of the totality of the circumstances surrounding the speech (State v. Perkins, 2001). Consideration of the totality of the circumstances entails the judge or jury considering the "full context of the statement, including all relevant factors that might affect how the statement could reasonably be interpreted" (State v. Perkins, pp. 770-71). The goal is to resolve if the speaker is serious about the expressed intent to harm or if the speaker was simply communicating in jest, hyperbole, innocuous speech, political speech or other protected speech. If it is ambiguous, it is the role of the jury to interpret the speech in order to determine if the speech is serious as opposed to "just the rhetoric of hyperbole that comes so easily to the lips of angry Americans" (United States v. Schneider, 1990, p. 1570). Ambiguous or conditional language can still constitute a true threat (United States v. Fulmer, 1997). In fact, "[m]ost threats are conditional; they are designed to accomplish something; the threatener hopes that they will accomplish it, so that he won't have to carry out the threats. They are threats nonetheless" (United States v. Schneider, p. 1570). Even subtle language conveying a threat can be deemed a threat (United States v. Orozco–Santillan, 1990).

The trier of fact must ensure that the threat is not protected speech that is merely a "harmless expression of frustration or anger" (Salgado, 2005, p. 1386). In examining the totality of the circumstances in order to determine if speech constitutes a true threat as opposed to a mere expression of frustration, courts review several factors, including:

1. Whether the threat was conditional;
2. Whether the threat was equivocal;
3. Whether the threat was communicated directly to the target or a third party;
4. Whether the speech was intentionally communicated;
5. Whether the person making the threat had made similar statements to the target on prior occasions;
6. Whether the recipient had reasonable grounds to believe that the person making the threat is prone to violence (i.e. does the person making the threat have a history of violence?);
7. How the recipient/target of the speech reacted to the speech;
8. How other listeners reacted to the speech (Doe v. Pulaski County Special School District, 2002; United States v. Dinwiddie, 1996; United States v. Hart, 2000);
9. Whether the statement communicated a serious expression of intent to intimidate or inflict bodily or other harm (In re A.S., 2001; see also State v. Perkins, p. 270);
10. Whether the threat is realistic (Salgado, 2005);

True Threat

11. Whether the threat is immediate. In other words, it must be determined whether the threat has an "imminent prospect of execution" (United States v. Kelner, 1976, p. 1027);
12. Whether the threat is specific with respect to the person threatened; and
13. Whether the threat "conveys a gravity of purpose" (United States v. Kelner, p. 1027).

These factors apply to the reasonable-recipient standard as well as the reasonable-speaker standard (State v. Perkins, 2001).

True Threat in the Courts

United States v. Kelner (1976) is a case often cited in cases involving the true-threat doctrine as it illustrates the judicial analysis of true threats using some of the factors discussed earlier. In that case, Russell Kelner, a member of the Jewish Defense League (JDL), conducted a television interview with reporter John Miller while dressed in military fatigue and holding a .38 caliber pistol. Seated next to him was another male in military fatigue. The interview occurred shortly before Yasser Arafat, the leader of the Palestine Liberation Organization, was scheduled to visit New York. During the interview, the following exchange occurred between Kelner and Miller:

Kelner: *We have people who have been trained and who are out now and who intend to make sure that Arafat and his lieutenants do not leave this country alive.*
Miller: *How do you plan to do that? You're going to kill him?*
Kelner: *I'm talking about justice. I'm talking about equal rights under the law, a law that may not exist, but should exist.*
Miller: *Are you saying that you plan to kill them?*
Kelner: *We are planning to assassinate Mr. Arafat. Just as if any other mur [sic] just the way any other murderer is treated.*
Miller: *Do you have the people picked out for this? Have you planned it out? Have you started this operation?*
Kelner: *Everything is planned in detail.*
Miller: *Do you think it will come off?*
Kelner: *It's going to come off.*
Miller: *Can you elaborate on where or when or how you plan to take care of this?*
Kelner: *If I elaborate it might be a problem in bringing it off (United States v. Kelner, 1976, p. 1021).*

The United States Court of Appeals for the Second Circuit ruled that the speech was not made in jest because Kelner and the other male were in military fatigues and because Kelner had a .38 caliber pistol during the speech (United States v. Kelner, 1976). The court applied four of the factors identified above for true-threat analysis. First, the court concluded that the threat was unconditional because, during the interview, Kelner stated: "We are planning to assassinate Mr. Arafat" (p. 1028). Second, this same statement made the threat unequivocal. Third, the threat specifically identified a target, when Kelner mentioned "Arafat and his lieutenants" at the beginning of his speech (p. 1028). Fourth, the threat was immediate as evident in Kelner's statement that "We have people who have been trained and who are out now ..." (p. 1028). Based on these four factors, Kelner's speech constituted a true threat.

While only a few courts have used the true-threat doctrine in determining whether schools can punish students for their speech, more courts are recognizing the importance of the doctrine to such determination. The first case to apply the true-threat doctrine in the context of a Free Speech Clause challenge to school censorship of student speech is Lovell By and Through Lovell v. Poway Unified School District (1996) (Wheeler II, 2004). In that case, Sarah Lovell, a tenth-grade student, approached school administrators and the guidance counselor to request a change to her school schedule. For several hours, however, she was sent to various offices as she sought a resolution. When she finally returned to the guidance counselor's office later in the day, the guidance counselor told her that the schedule could not be changed because Sarah had been incorrectly approved for overloaded classes. Sarah was apparently frustrated and muttered some words under her breath which the guidance counselor nonetheless heard. The guidance counselor claimed that Sarah threatened to shoot her when she whispered, "If you don't give me this schedule change, I'm going to shoot you!" (Lovell By and Through Lovell v. Poway Unified School District, 1996, p. 369). The guidance counselor claimed she felt threatened by Sarah's comment. Sarah claimed, however, that she never made that statement and did not threaten the guidance counselor. According to Sarah, she simply muttered, "I'm so angry, I could just shoot someone" (p. 369). Even though Sarah promptly apologized, the school opted to suspend her from school for three days and a disciplinary report was placed in her school file. The disciplinary report read:

Sarah stated, "... if you don't give me this schedule change, I'm going to shoot you!" I believe that the tone and manner conveyed by Sarah Lovell demonstrates possible future danger. I have witnessed Sarah's volatile nature, poor and lack of impulse control, and possible violent verbal tendencies. I am extremely concerned about Sarah's potentially explosive behavior (Lovell By and Through Lovell v. Poway Unified School District, 1996, p. 369).

Sarah and her parents filed suit against the school challenging the censorship of her speech under the First Amendment.

Even though Sarah's speech was on campus, the United States Court of Appeals for the Ninth Circuit pointed out that students have a greater right to free speech off-campus than they do on-campus (Lovell By and Through Lovell v. Poway Unified School District, 1996). That distinction was, however, irrelevant to Sarah's case (not only because she spoke on-campus but also because her speech was a true threat): "we hold that threats such as Lovell's are not entitled to First Amendment protection in any forum, it does not matter that the statement was made by a student in the school context" (p. 371). The court ruled that Sarah failed to meet the burden of proof needed to show that her version of the speech was more credible than the guidance counselor's version. It analyzed Sarah's speech based on the reasonable-speaker test and relied on some of the factors it identified from United States v. Kelner (1976), discussed earlier. The court concluded that the school had the authority to censor the speech. The reaction of the listener and the circumstances surrounding the speech were critical to the analysis though not singularly dispositive. In this case, the guidance counselor indicated that she felt threatened by Sarah's speech (Lovell By and Through Lovell v. Poway Unified School District, 1996). Besides, any reasonable person who heard the speech from "an angry teenager" would interpret it as a "serious expression of intent to harm or assault" (p. 372). This showed that Sarah's speech could be censored under the reasonable-speaker test. Even though Sarah's speech was muttered, she should have foreseen that the guidance counselor would interpret it as a genuine threat. Sarah's statement was also specific, unconditional and unequivocal. It communicated a "gravity of purpose and imminent prospect of execution" given the context of increased violence in various schools around the country (pp. 372, 373). The guidance counselor's failure to seek immediate help, once she heard the speech, did not in itself undermine the true-threat nature of the speech. The court ruled that the guidance counselor's display of "fortitude and stoicism in the interim does not vitiate the threatening nature of Lovell's conduct, or Suokko's [guidance counselor] belief that Lovell threatened her" (p. 373).

Another case in which the true-threat doctrine was used to analyze the constitutionality of a school's censorship of a student's speech is D.G. v. Independent School District No. 11 of Tulsa County, Oklahoma (2000). In that case, an eleventh-grade student wrote a poem to express her frustration and anger at her teacher after she felt the teacher wrongly accused her of speaking during a class movie. Although this case involved on-campus student speech, it highlights how the true-threat doctrine has been applied in a school context. The poem read as follows:

Killing Mrs. [Teacher]
I hate this class it is hell
Every day I can't wait for the bell,
I bitch and whine until it is time,
For me to get in the hall.
Back in the day,
I would sit and pray
to see if I may
Run away (from this hell)
Now as the days get longer
My yearning gets stronger
To kill the bitcher.
One day when I get out of jail
Cuz my friends paid my bail.
And people will ask why.
I'll say because the Bitch had to die!
By [Student] (D.G. v. Independent School District No. 11 of Tulsa County, Oklahoma, 2000, p. 3).

Even though the speech clearly referenced killing the teacher, and despite acknowledging that there is a prevalence of violence in schools today, the federal district court ruled that the speech did not constitute a true threat. The court used the reasonable-speaker view, inquiring into the "state of mind" and intent of the student in writing the poem (D.G. v. Independent School District No. 11 of Tulsa County, Oklahoma, 2000, p. 13). In its analysis, the court used five of the factors identified above for true-threat analysis. First, the court pointed out that the student did not intend to communicate the poem to the teacher. In fact, the poem was accidentally discovered on the floor of another teacher's class. The only person to whom the student showed the poem was her friend who laughed off the poem. Second, the court examined the reaction of the listeners as evidence of the student's intent. The court found that the school officials who saw the poem did not view the threat as a genuine threat against the teacher's life. Additionally, school officials failed to take action against the student for six days after the poem was discovered. The student was permitted to return to the class after she admitted writing the poem. The school psychologist evaluated the student after reading the poem and concluded that the student was merely expressing anger and frustration rather than a genuine threat.

Third, the failure of the school to take prompt action against the student and the decision to allow her back into the target-teacher's class after the poem's discovery, highlight the fact that the threat was not immediate and consequently not a genuine threat (D.G. v. Independent School District No. 11 of Tulsa County, Oklahoma, 2000). This appears contrary to the ruling of the United States Court of Appeals for the Ninth Circuit in Lovell By and Through Lovell v. Poway Unified School District (1996), discussed earlier, that a failure to seek immediate help after learning of a threat does not vitiate the nature of the threat as a true threat. However, the Ninth Circuit Court of Appeals simply held that the failure to promptly seek help does not per se preclude a threat from qualifying as a true threat. The federal district court in D.G. v. Independent School District No. 11 of Tulsa County, Oklahoma (2000) likewise did not suggest that this third factor was dispositive; it was just one of five factors it considered. Fourth, the federal district court observed that the targeted teacher did not fear for her life after she read the poem (D.G. v. Independent School District No. 11 of Tulsa County, Oklahoma, 2000). Fifth, the court relied on the school psychologist's finding that the student had no history of violence that would suggest that the student was communicating a true threat. The court noted that if the student "intended this poem to convey a genuine threat, or even if she wrote the poem with the intent of putting teachers in fear by making them think it was a genuine threat, the school district could appropriately punish her" (p. 13).

Boim v. Fulton County School District (2007) was another case in which a court applied the true-threat doctrine in analysis of student speech. While this is another on-campus speech case, it further illustrates how courts use the true-threat doctrine. In this case, a teacher seized high schooler Rachel Boim's notebook after he observed another student writing in Rachel's notebook during art class. The teacher searched the notebook and found the following speech by Rachel in a section of the notebook titled "Dream":

As I walk to school from my sisters [sic] car my stomach ties itself in nots. [sic] I have nervousness tingeling [sic] up and down my spine and my heart races. No one knows what is going to happen. I have the gun hidden in my pocket. I cross the lawn and hed [sic] to my locker on A hall. Smiling sweetly to my friends hoping they dont [sic] notice the cold sweat that has developed on my forhead [sic]. Im [sic] walking up to the front office when the bell rings for class to start. So afraid that I think I might pass out. I ask if my mother dropped off a book I need. No. My first to [sic] classes pass by my heart thumping so hard Im [sic] afraid every one can hear it. Constantly I can feel the gun in my pocket. 3rd peroid [sic], 4th, 5th then 6th peroid [sic] my time is comming [sic]. I enter the class room my face pale. My stomach has tied itself in so many knots its [sic] doubtful I will ever be able to untie them. Then he starts taking role [sic]. Yes, my math teacher. I lothe [sic] him with every bone in my body. Why? I dont [sic] know. This is it. I stand up and pull the gun from my pocket. BANG the force blows him back and every one in the class sits there in shock. BANG he falls to the floor and some one [sic] lets out an ear piercing scream. Shaking I put the gun in my pocket and run from the room. By now the school police officer is running after me. Easy I can out run him. Out the doors, almost to the car. I can get away. BANG this time a shot was fired at me. I turn just in time to see the bullet rushing at me, almost like its [sic] in slow motion. Then, the bell rings, I pick my head off my desk, shake my head and gather up my books off to my next class (Boim v. Fulton County School District, 2007, pp. 980-91).

Concerned that Rachel might be planning a violent attack at the school, under the pretext of a dream, the school official in charge of student discipline discussed Rachel's speech with the school resource officer – a police officer (Boim v. Fulton County School District, 2007). The officer agreed that Rachel's speech was troubling and could forebode violence against her math teacher. The math teacher who was the target of the speech expressed shock at the writing and indicated that he "felt threatened" (p. 981). The teacher also stated that it would be unsettling to send Rachel back to his class. Rachel and her parents, however, insisted that the speech was simply creative fiction. Nonetheless, the principal decided to suspend Rachel for ten days and recommended her expulsion to an independent arbiter who approved the expulsion. The shootings at Columbine High School and a local high school in Conyers, Georgia heightened the principal's concern about the speech. The county board of education reversed the expulsion but upheld the suspension. Rachel's parents challenged the school's censorship of Rachel as a violation of her First Amendment right to free speech and sought the removal of the discipline from her school record.

In its review of Rachel's appeal, the federal circuit court of appeals for the eleventh circuit ruled in favor of the school district (Boim v. Fulton County School District, 2007). Specifically, the court ruled that there is "no First Amendment right allowing a student to knowingly make comments, whether oral or written, that reasonably could be perceived as a threat of school violence, whether general or specific, while on school property during the school day" (p. 984). The court implied that the reason Rachel's speech was a true threat was that it was on-campus speech. The court further chastised her for bringing the speech on-campus. Her failure to "exercise strict control over the notebook in which it was written" exposed Rachel to the risk that school officials or students would find the speech (p. 985). The court implied that if Rachel's speech was discovered in a non-school context, the speech might be constitutionally protected: "We admit that in many places and in ordinary times [Rachel] in saying all that was said ... would have been within [her] constitutional rights. But the character of every act depends upon the circumstances in which it is done" (p. 984, quoting Schenck v. United States, 1919, p. 52). Based on the reasonable-recipient view, the court concluded that, even if Rachel's speech was a literary work, as she had argued, the speech could still be reasonably interpreted as a true threat of violence (Boim v. Fulton County School District, 2007). Consequently, Rachel could be disciplined for the speech.

Interestingly, the speech in D.G. v. Independent School District No. 11 of Tulsa County, Oklahoma (2000) and that in Boim v. Fulton County School District (2007) were interpreted as threats to kill a teacher. Yet both came to different conclusions. The court in D.G. v. Independent School District No. 11 of Tulsa County, Oklahoma ruled for the student while the court in Boim v. Fulton County School District ruled for the district. A critical difference in the rulings was the vantage point of the reasonable person used. In D.G. v. Independent School District No. 11 of Tulsa County, Oklahoma, the court used a reasonable-speaker view which allowed the court to account for the student's intent. In Boim v. Fulton County School District, the court used the reasonable-recipient view, with the court disregarding Rachel's insistence that her speech was merely fictional writing. These two cases highlight how a court's choice of reasonable-person view could impact whether the student's speech is constitutionally protected or vulnerable to censorship. Before censoring student speech as a true threat, schools therefore must determine which of the reasonable-person views courts use in the jurisdiction in which the school is located (see Tables 1 and 2). Further, D.G. v. Independent School District No. 11 of Tulsa County, Oklahoma and Boim v. Fulton County School District reveal that the schools cannot solely rely on the words used in a student's speech to make a true-threat determination; after all, in both cases, the students explicitly spoke of a teacher being killed.

Indeed, with the increased levels of school shootings, school officials need to be very vigilance. However, vigilance must not trample free speech rights. Our Constitution affords people the right to make use of threatening or violent language in advocacy. Even Martin Luther King, Jr., the great civil rights leader who advocated non-violence, used violent rhetoric that was protected speech under the First Amendment. Specifically, he wrote:

[I]f our white brothers dismiss as 'rabble-rousers' and 'outside agitators' those of us who employ nonviolent direct action, and if they refuse to support our nonviolent efforts, millions of Negroes will, out of frustration and despair, seek solace and security in black-nationalist ideologies, a development that would inevitably lead to a frightening racial nightmare .... The Negro has many pent-up resentments and latent frustrations, and he must release them. So let him march; let him make prayer pilgrimages to the city hall; let him go on freedom rides ... If his repressed emotions are not released in nonviolent ways, they will seek expression through violence; this is not a threat but a fact of history (Rothman, 2001, p. 322).

If a student writes this same speech off-campus, some school officials might overreact, deeming it as censorable speech simply because of the rhetoric. However, if school officials carefully conduct a true-threat analysis, they should conclude that the speech is not a true threat.

CONCLUSION

In this chapter, we discussed the true-threat doctrine as an unprotected speech category. Since this speech is unprotected under the First Amendment, it is subject to censorship on-campus as well as off-campus. We also discussed the role of the reasonable-recipient view and the reasonable-speaker view in determining the outcome of true-threat cases. In June 2015, the United States Supreme Court ruled that in order to be convicted for making a true threat, it must be shown that the defendant:

1. Communicated with the purpose of making a threat; or
2. Had knowledge that the speech would be viewed as a threat (Elonis v. United States, 2015).

It is yet unclear whether or how the reasonable-recipient view and the reasonable-speaker view will impact the lower courts' analysis of the defendant's knowledge of whether the speech would be viewed as a threat. It is important for courts to clarify this quickly, however. With a better understanding of the true-threat doctrine, school officials will be less likely to overreach, censoring protected off-campus student speech. Instead, they will be able to focus on censorship of speech that presents a genuine threat. They will be able to better distinguish true threats from jokes, hyperbole, political speech or other protected speech, considering the totality of the circumstances.

As the Eighth Circuit Court of Appeals warned, the "First Amendment does not permit the government to punish speech merely because the speech is forceful or aggressive. What is offensive to some is passionate to others" (United States v. Dinwiddie, 1996, p. 925). The United States Supreme Court is "willing to accept violent rhetoric, even against a backdrop of violence, in order to preserve robust and unfettered debate" (Rothman, 2001, p. 322). The Supreme Court is yet to exclude off-campus student speech from this general rule. Schools must focus on identifying, as best they can, what constitutes true threats so that they do not infringe upon protected speech merely because it contains violent rhetoric.

REFERENCES

Administrative Office of the United States Courts. (2013). United States Courts: Court Locator. *Administrative Office of the United States Courts*. Retrieved December 18, 2013, from http://www.uscourts.gov/court_locator.aspx

Boim v. Fulton County School District (2007). 494 F.3d 978.

Centers for Disease Control and Prevention. (2012). Understanding school violence: Fact sheet. *CDC*. Retrieved November 29, 2013, from http://www.cdc.gov/ViolencePrevention/pdf/SchoolViolence_FactSheet-a.pdf

D.G. v. Independent School District No. 11 of Tulsa County, Oklahoma (2000). 2000 U.S. Dist. LEXIS 12197 *1-15.

Doe v. Pulaski County Special School District (2002). 306 F.3d 616.

Elonis v. United States (2015). 135 S.Ct. 2001.

Erb, T. D. (2008). A case for strengthening school district jurisdiction to punish off-campus incidents of cyberbullying. *Arizona State Law Journal*, 40, 257–287.

J.S. v. Bethlehem Area School District (2002). 807 A.2d 847, 857-58.

Lovell By and Through Lovell v. Poway Unified School District (1996). 90 F.3d 367.

Mahaffey ex rel. Mahaffey v. Aldrich (2002). 236 F.Supp.2d 779, 785.

NAACP v. Claiborne Hardware Company (1982). 458 U.S. 886.

O'toole, M. E., ... (1999). The School Shooter: A Threat Assessment Perspective. *Federal Bureau of Investigation Office of the Attorney General*. Retrieved November 29, 2013, from http://www.fbi.gov/stats-services/publications/school-shooter

Pisciotta, L. M. (2000). Beyond sticks and stones: A First Amendment framework for educators who seek to punish student threats. *Seton Hall Law Review*, 30, 635–670.

Planned Parenthood of the Columbia/Willamette, Inc. v. American Coalition of Life Activists (2002). 290 F.3d 1058, 1075.

R.A.V. v. City of St. Paul, Minnesota (1992). 505 U.S. 377.

Rothman, J. E. (2001). Freedom of speech and true threats. *Harvard Journal of Law & Public Policy*, 25, 283–367.

Roy v. United States (1969). 416 F.2d 874, 877-78.

Salgado, R. (2005). Protecting student speech rights while increasing school safety: School jurisdiction and the search for warning signs in a post-Columbine/Red Lake environment. *Brigham Young University Law Review*, 2005, 1371–1414.

Schenck v. United States (1919). 249 U.S. 47, 52.

State v. Perkins (2001). 626 N.W.2d 762.

United States v. Adams (1999). 73 F. Supp. 2d 2, 3.

United States v. Callahan (1983). 702 F.2d 964, 965.

United States v. Cassel (2005). 408 F.3d 622, 633.

United States v. Daugenbaugh (1995). 49 F.3d 171, 173-74.

United States v. Dinwiddie (1996). 76 F.3d 913, 925.

United States v. Elonis (2013). 730 F.3d 321.

United States v. Fulmer (1997). 108 F.3d 1486.

United States v. Glover (1988). 846 F.2d 339, 344.

United States v. Hart (2000). 212 F.3d 1067, 1071.

United States v. J.H.H. (1994). 22 F.3d 821, 827-28.

United States v. Kelner (1976). 534 F.2d 1020, 1027.

United States v. Khorrami (1990). 895 F.2d 1186, 1192.

United States v. Malik (1994). 16 F.3d 45, 49.

United States v. Orozco–Santillan (1990). 903 F.2d 1262, 1265.

United States v. Roberts (1990). 915 F.2d 889, 891.

United States v. Schneider (1990). 910 F.2d 1569, 1570.

United States v. Viefhaus (1999). 168 F.3d 392, 396.

Verga, R. J. (2007). Policing their space: The First Amendment parameters of school discipline of student cyberspeech. *Santa Clara Computer and High-Technology Law Journal, 23*, 727–748.

Virginia v. Black (2003). 538 U.S. 343.

Wheeler, T. E. II. (2004). Slamming in cyberspace: The boundaries of student First Amendment rights. *Res Gestae, 47*, 24–32.

KEY TERMS AND DEFINITIONS

First Amendment: This is the first right listed within the bill of rights added to the United States Constitution in 1791 to guarantee Americans certain rights free from government infringement. It covers the right to free speech, the right to free exercise of religion, right against government establishment of religion, the right to a free press, the right to peaceable assembly and the right to petition for redress of grievances.

Free Speech Clause: The clause in the First Amendment to the United States Constitution which prohibits the government from denying citizens the right to free speech.

Objective Standard: The judicial standard that requires consideration of incidents from the point of view of the reasonable person rather than that of the specific person(s) in the pertinent case under consideration.

Off-Campus Speech: Speech that occurs in any locale outside the borders or premises of a school and outside school hours. It includes student speech away from the school bus and school-sponsored events such as school trips.

Reasonable-Recipient View: The judicial standard that determines if speech constitutes a true threat based on whether a reasonable recipient of the threat would view it as expressing a genuine intent to cause harm.

Reasonable-Speaker View: The judicial standard that determines if speech constitutes a true threat based on whether a reasonable speaker of the threat would view it as expressing a genuine intent to cause harm.

Subjective Standard: The judicial standard that requires consideration of events from the viewpoint of the person(s) in the pertinent case under consideration.

Totality of the Circumstances: The judicial standard that entails review of all the circumstances involved in a situation before making a judgment.

Trier of Fact: The judge or jury that makes determinations of fact in a case.

True Threat: Speech that expresses a genuine intent to cause harm.

Chapter 3
Fighting Words

ABSTRACT

This chapter describes the fighting-words jurisprudence. It explains why fighting words are unprotected speech. It reviews the Chaplinsky v. New Hampshire (1942) case in which the United States Supreme Court first excluded fighting words from First Amendment protection. The chapter aims to show that, since fighting words are unprotected speech, school officials can censor such speech outside the schoolhouse gate without violating the First Amendment. However, school officials must establish that the speech qualifies as fighting words – a challenging task.

INTRODUCTION

Although the First Amendment generally guards against government censorship of speech, there are categories of speech that are not afforded constitutional protection. One of these categories is "fighting words." This chapter analyzes the fighting words and examines its application to public-school censorship of student speech. The first part of this chapter discusses the United States Supreme Court's decisions related to the fighting-words doctrine. The second examines examples of online communications in the K-12 and higher education contexts. The third part discusses cases in which courts have applied the fighting-words doctrine to student communications. The final part of this chapter analyzes whether public schools can justify the restriction of online student communication through the fighting-words doctrine.

MAIN FOCUS OF THE CHAPTER

United States Supreme Court Decisions

The United States Supreme Court established the fighting-words doctrine in Chaplinsky v. New Hampshire (1942). Members of the Rochester, New Hampshire community accused Walter Chaplinsky of making derogatory statements about religion in a public square. After a police officer had warned Chaplinsky to stop making such proclamations, Chaplinsky called the officer "a God damned racketeer" and "a damned Fascist" (p. 570). He also declared that "the whole government of Rochester are Fascists or agents of Fascists" (p. 570). Chaplinsky was then convicted of violating a state statute, which provided that:

No person shall address any offensive, derisive or annoying word to any other person who is lawfully in any street or other public place, nor call him by any offensive or derisive name, nor make any noise or exclamation in his presence and hearing with intent to deride, offend or annoy him, or to prevent him from pursuing his lawful business or occupation (Chaplinsky v. New Hampshire, 1942, p. 569).

The Supreme Court of New Hampshire found that the statute included two severable provisions – the first relating to words uttered to another in a public place, while the second addressed noise and exclamations. Assuming that the second provision was unconstitutional, the New Hampshire court ruled that the first provision was constitutional because its purpose was to keep the peace by prohibiting words that had a "direct tendency to cause acts of violence by the person to whom, individually, the remark is addressed" (p. 573). The court went on to state that the provision did "no more than prohibit the face-to-face words plainly likely to cause a breach of the peace … including 'classical fighting words'" (p. 573). The test for whether an utterance could be classified as "fighting words" was articulated as "what men of common intelligence would understand would be words likely to cause an average addressee to fight" (p. 573).

Chaplinksy then appealed to the United States Supreme Court. The Court upheld the conviction. It found that the First Amendment did not protect certain statements. Such statements included fighting words – "those which by their very utterance inflict injury or tend to incite an immediate breach of the peace" (Chaplinsky v. New Hampshire, 1942, p. 572). The Court then agreed with the state high court's analysis that the statute, as construed, was narrowly drawn to limit speech that would cause a breach of the peace.

Subsequent to Chaplinsky v. New Hampshire (1942), in a series of cases, beginning with Terminiello v. City of Chicago (1949), the United States Supreme Court limited the scope of the fighting-words doctrine. In Terminiello v. City of Chicago, Arthur Terminiello was a speaker at a meeting sponsored by the Christian Veterans of America. Outside of the auditorium where the meeting was held, about one thousand persons protested against the meeting. Several skirmishes occurred despite the efforts of the police to maintain order. Terminiello responded to the protest by "condemn[ing] the conduct of the crowd outside and vigorously, if not viciously, criticiz[ing] various political and racial groups whose activities he denounced as inimical to the nation's welfare" (p. 895). The city of Chicago found him guilty of breaching the peace in violation of a city ordinance and fined him. A state trial court charged the jury that "breach of the peace" applied to speech that "stirs the public to anger, invites dispute, brings about a condition of unrest, or creates a disturbance" (p. 895).

After the state appellate and supreme courts upheld the conviction, Terminiello appealed to the United States Supreme Court. The Court reversed the conviction. The Court found that the trial court's instructions defining "breach of the peace" was a ruling of state law, and therefore, was as binding on the Supreme Court as the actual words of the ordinance. The Court then noted that one of the functions of speech in this country's system of government was to invite dispute. Further, free speech "may indeed best serve its high purpose when it induces a condition of unrest, creates dissatisfaction with conditions as they are, or even stirs people to anger" (p. 896). Because speech was "often provocative and challenging, ... [i]t may strike at prejudices and preconceptions and have profound unsettling effects" (p. 896). The trial court's construction of the statute violated the First Amendment because it permitted conviction for the carrying out of constitutional speech.

Several years after Terminiello v. City of Chicago (1949), in Cohen v. California (1971), the United States Supreme Court found that the fighting-words doctrine applied to particularized encounters rather than generalized provocations. Paul Cohen was convicted of violating a California statute, which prohibited "maliciously and willfully disturbing the peace and quiet of any neighborhood or person ... by offensive conduct" (p. 16). Cohen was seen in a municipal courthouse corridor wearing a jacket with the words "Fuck the Draft" in protest of the Vietnam War, which was plainly visible to women and children (p. 16). Cohen did not engage in any threatening behavior or conduct. A state appellate court affirmed the conviction, interpreting the statutory provision to mean behavior that tended "to provoke *others* to acts of violence or to in turn disturb the peace" (p. 17). The court found that the state had proven its case because it was foreseeable that Cohen's wearing of the jacket might provoke others to commit a violent act against him or forcibly to remove his jacket.

The Supreme Court reversed the lower court's decision. Because Cohen was arrested and convicted because of his speech, as opposed to his conduct, the Court limited its analysis to whether the government unconstitutionally restricted Cohen's speech. The Court ruled in the affirmative, in part, because the restraint of speech did not fall under the fighting-words doctrine. The Court reached this conclusion because the four-letter invective was not directed at any particular person. Indeed, "[n]o individual actually or likely to be present could have regarded the words on [Cohen's] jacket as a direct personal insult" (Cohen v. California, 1971, p. 20).

In Gooding v. Wilson (1972), the United States Supreme Court held that a Georgia statute, which provided that "[a]ny person who shall, without provocation, use to or of another, and in this presence ... opprobrious words or language, tending to cause a breach of the peace ... shall be guilty of a misdemeanor" was facially unconstitutional because it was vague and overbroad (p. 519). Unlike the *Chaplinsky* case, the Georgia courts had not interpreted the language of Georgia's breach of the peace statute. Therefore, the Supreme Court examined the wording of the statute for overbreadth because "persons whose expression is constitutionally protected may well refrain from exercising their rights for fear of criminal sanctions provided by a statute susceptible of application to protected expression" (p. 521). The Court then concluded that the statute was unconstitutionally vague and overbroad. The common dictionary definition of "opprobrious" was "conveying or intended to convey disgrace" (p. 525). The definition of the term "abusive" included "harsh, insulting" language (p. 525). These terms went beyond the scope of "fighting words."

In Lewis v. City of New Orleans (1974), the United States Supreme Court invalidated a city ordinance that made it unlawful "to curse or revile or to use obscene or opprobrious language toward or with reference to" a police officer in the performance of his duty, on the ground that it was unconstitutionally vague and broad (p. 132). In light of the *Gooding* case, the Supreme Court had remanded a conviction based upon this language to Louisiana's highest court. On remand, the Louisiana Supreme Court did not attempt to narrowly define "opprobrious or any other term, but concluded that the statute as written fit within the fighting-words doctrine. The United States Supreme Court reversed because nothing in the lower court's opinion prevented the possibility that the terms could be used to limit constitutionally-

Fighting Words

protected speech. In a concurring opinion, Justice Lewis Powell suggested that the fighting-words doctrine might require a more narrow application because "a properly trained police officer may reasonably be expected to 'exercise a higher degree of restraint' than the average citizen, and thus be less likely to respond belligerently to 'fighting words'" (p. 135).

In City of Houston v. Hill (1987), the United States Supreme Court struck down as constitutionally overbroad a municipal ordinance that made it "unlawful for any person to assault, strike or in any manner oppose, molest, abuse or interrupt any policeman in the execution of his duty" (p. 455). The Court reasoned that the Houston ordinance was even more sweeping than the one declared unconstitutional in *Lewis* because "[i]t is not limited to fighting words nor even to obscene or opprobrious language, but prohibits speech that 'in any manner...interrupts' an officer" (p. 462). As a consequence, the police could regularly use the ordinance to prohibit protected expression.

In Texas v. Johnson (1989), the United States Supreme Court held that the state of Texas could not justify the conviction of a person for burning the American flag under the fighting-words doctrine. Gregory Lee Johnson participated in a demonstration against the 1984 Republican National Convention, which was being held in Dallas. During a demonstration in front of Dallas City Hall, Johnson set an American flag on fire while protesters chanted: "America, the red, white, and blue, we spit on you" (p. 399). Johnson was arrested and convicted of the crime of desecration of a venerated object under the state penal code.

Because Johnson was convicted for conduct instead of speech, the Court had to determine whether his burning of the flag constituted expressive conduct, which would avail him of First Amendment protection (Texas v. Johnson, 1989). The Court concluded that the burning of the flag was indeed expressive conduct because of its "overtly political nature" (p. 406). The Court then had to determine whether the government's restriction of the expressive conduct was justified. The government had more latitude in restricting expressive conduct than speech, so long as the governmental interest was unconnected to expression. On the other hand, the government had a greater burden to overcome if the law was directed at the communicative nature of the conduct. The Court rejected the state's claim that Johnson's speech fell under the fighting-words doctrine because "[n]o reasonable onlooker would have regarded Johnson's generalized expression of dissatisfaction with the policies of the Federal Government as a direct personal insult or an invitation to exchange fisticuffs" (p. 409).

In R.A.V. v. St. Paul, Minnesota (1992), the Supreme Court held as facially invalid a municipal ordinance that prohibited bias-motivated crimes, which provided:

Whoever places on public or private property a symbol, object, appellation, characterization or graffiti, including, but not limited to, a burning cross or Nazi swastika, which one knows or has reasonable grounds to know arises anger, alarm or resentment in others on the basis of race, color, creed, religion or gender commits disorderly conduct and shall be guilty of a misdemeanor (p. 380).

The municipality had convicted several teenagers under the ordinance for burning a cross inside the yard of a black family (R.A.V. v. St. Paul, Minnesota, 1992). One of the teenagers challenged the constitutionality of the ordinance. A state trial court dismissed the count on the ground that the ordinance was constitutionally overbroad. The Minnesota Supreme Court reversed because in previous cases, it had limited the reach of the phrase "arouses anger, alarm or resentment in others" to conduct amounting to fighting words (p. 380). The state high court further held that the ordinance was not unconstitutional conduct because it was narrowly tailored to achieving the compelling governmental interest of defending the community against bias-motivated threats to breaches of the peace.

The United States Supreme Court reversed the state high court's decision (R.A.V. v. St. Paul, Minnesota, 1992). It accepted the lower court's authoritative statement that the statute prohibited only fighting words. The Supreme Court still found that the ordinance was unconstitutional. Writing for the majority, Justice Antonin Scalia explained that while the government could regulate speech, such as fighting words, obscenity, and libel because of their proscribable content, it could not further regulate such speech based upon whether it was more hostile to certain content over others. The Court went on to conclude that the ordinance "goes even beyond mere content discrimination, to actual viewpoint discrimination" (R.A.V. v. St. Paul, Minnesota, p. 391). The statute allowed proponents of racial tolerance to use fighting words that did not invoke race, color, creed, or religion, while at the same time prohibiting their opponents from responding in kind.

Finally, the Court rejected the municipality's claim that the ordinance was still constitutional because it was narrowly tailored to satisfy a compelling governmental interest (R.A.V. v. St. Paul, Minnesota, 1992). Protecting the basic human rights of members of groups who had been historically subjected to discrimination was a compelling interest. The ordinance failed the narrow tailoring consideration because "[a]n ordinance not limited to the favored topics, for example, would have precisely the same beneficial effect" (p. 396).

Application of the Fighting-Words Doctrine to Student Online Communications

In this section, we examine two cases that have applied the fighting-words doctrine to student online communications. In Layshock v. Hermitage School District (2007), a federal district court ruled on the application of the doctrine to a high school senior's series of unflattering profiles, created off-campus, of his principal on Myspace. The school district responded by:

1. Suspending the student for 10 days;
2. Placing him in an alternative curriculum program for the remainder of the school year;
3. Banning him from participating in or attending school district events; and
4. Prohibiting him from participating in the high school graduation ceremony.

The district court found that the disciplinary measures violated the First Amendment. The court rejected the district's claim that the student's speech constituted fighting words. As the court explained: "A "Myspace" internet page is not outside of the protections of the First Amendment under the fighting-words doctrine because there is simply no in-person confrontation in cyberspace such that physical violence is likely to be instigated" (p. 602).

In the higher education context, one published opinion addressed whether the electronic correspondences were subject to the fighting-words doctrine. In State v. Drahota (2010), the Supreme Court of Nebraska addressed the question of whether a student could be convicted for breaching the peace because of two emails that he sent to a former professor, who was also running for state office at the time. These emails were the culmination of an increasingly intense electronic exchange between the two men over issues of politics and patriotism. The first e-mail stated in pertinent part:

Fighting Words

Does that make you sad that the al-queda leader in Iraq will not be around to behead people and undermine our efforts in Iraq? I would guess that a joyous day for you would be Iran getting nukes? You, Michael Moore, Ted Kennedy, John Murtha, and the ACLU should have a token funeral to say goodbye to a dear friend of your anti-american sentiments (State v. Drahota, 2010, p. 800).

The second email, which contained the subject line "traitor," stated:

I have a friend in Iraq that I told all about you and he referred to you as a Benedict Arnold. I told him that fit you very well. GO ACLU!!!!!!!!!!!!!!! GO MICHAEL MOORE, GO JOHN MURTHA!!!!!!!!!!!! By the way, I am assuming you are a big fan of Murtha's, and anti-marine like him, but being a big liberal, don't you support those Marines that are being jailed without charges at Camp Pendleton. Oh, I forgot, they are not Al Queda members so you and the ACLU will not rush to their defense. I'd like to puke all over you. People like you should be forced out of this country. Hey, I have a great idea!!!!!!!!!!!!!!!!!! Let's do nothing to Iran, let them get nukes, and then let them bomb U.S. cities and after that, we will just keep turning the other cheek. Remember that Libs like yourself are the lowest form of life on this planet (State v. Drahota, 2010, p. 800).

A trial court convicted the student for breaching the peace. A state appellate court upheld the conviction under the fighting-words doctrine, holding that *Chaplinsky* defined fighting words as either:

1. Inflicting injury; or
2. Tending to cause an immediate breach of peace.

The Supreme Court of Nebraska reversed the conviction. The state high court observed that the *Chaplinsky* had "only upheld the statute's constitutionality as limited by the state court" (State v. Drahota, 2010, pp. 801-02). "Specifically," the court explained, *Chaplinsky* "held that a state may constitutionally regulate epithets likely to provoke the average person to retaliate and thereby cause a breach of peace" (p. 802).

Further, while *Chaplinsky* had never been overruled, "the Supreme Court has never held that the government may, consistent with the First Amendment, regulate or punish speech that causes emotional injury but does *not* have a tendency to provoke an immediate breach of peace" (State v. Drahota, 2010, p. 802). Indeed, the justification for placing fighting words outside of the scope of the First Amendment was not their capability for inflicting injury, but their tendency to provoke a breach of peace.

Applying this understanding of the fighting-words doctrine, the Supreme Court of Nebraska found that the student's statements did not constitute fighting words. The court cited the content and context of the speech in reaching this conclusion. The emails were part of an ongoing political debate, in which both persons had made several provocative statements without incident. Also, at the time that the emails were sent, the recipient was running for statewide office. In the context of political dialogue, speech could be prohibited under the fighting-words doctrine only if they provoked immediate breach of peace. Holding otherwise would restrict the free exchange of ideas.

While the state Supreme Court cautioned that there were situations in which political speech could have triggered the fighting-words doctrine, such was not the case here because the recipient could not have immediately retaliated. In fact, he "did not know who sent the emails, let alone where to find the author" (State v. Drahota, 2010, p. 804). Thus, the court concluded that the student's speech did not constitute fighting words.

As the *Drahota* and *Layshock* cases make clear, students will also make as-applied challenges to student discipline for their emails, tweets, and websites based on the fighting-words doctrine. School districts will have a difficult time justifying such discipline because the fighting-words doctrine generally applies in situations where there is face-to-face confrontation and the ability of the recipient to immediately retaliate (Calvert, 2010). Calvert (2010) suggests that courts might consider modifying the fighting-words doctrine in instances of cyberbulling of minors if three variables are present:

1. "[T]he electronic message must be conveyed…directly to the target recipient … in a one-to-one fashion";
2. "[T]he … sender and the target recipient must be in such a close geographic proximity that a physical response by the target could occur within a matter of a few minutes"; and
3. "The content of the texted, IM'ed or e-mailed message … must be so personally abusive … that responsive violence … is likely to occur" (p. 44).

CONCLUSION

Although the First Amendment does not protect fighting words, this chapter has shown that school districts might have a difficult time defending censorship of off-campus online student speech on the basis of the fighting-words doctrine. The reason for this conclusion is that the fighting-words doctrine generally applies to face-to-face confrontations (Calvert, 2010). In order for the fighting-words doctrine to broadly apply to off-campus electronic statements from students, courts might have to modify their application of the fighting-words doctrine. The doctrine, however, will allow school censorship of off-campus offline student speech without any modification.

REFERENCES

Calvert, C. (2010). Fighting words in the era of texts, IM's and e-mails: Can a disparaged doctrine be resuscitated to punish cyber-bullies? *DePaul Journal of Art, Technology, and Intellectual Property Law*, *21*, 1–48.

Chaplinsky v. New Hampshire (1942). 315 U.S. 568.

City of Houston v. Hill (1987). 482 U.S. 450.

Cohen v. California (1971). 403 U.S. 16.

Gooding v. Wilson (1972). 405 U.S. 518.

Layshock v. Hermitage School District (2007). 496 F.Supp.2d 587.

Lewis v. City of New Orleans (1974). 415 U.S. 123.

State v. Drahota (2011). 788 N.W.2d 796.

Terminiello v. City of Chicago (1949). 337 U.S. 1.

Texas v. Johnson (1989). 491 U.S. 397.

KEY TERMS AND DEFINITIONS

Compelling Interest: A strong constitutionally-recognized justification for certain government action.

Fighting Words: Speech which inflicts injury simply from being uttered or speech with the tendency to incite a disturbance.

Fighting-Words Jurisprudence: The body of case law governing the censorship of fighting words under the First Amendment.

Narrowly Tailored: The constitutional requirement that laws, policies and government actions must be have a precise means-end fit. It requires the government to use the least restrictive means to accomplish its intended end.

Obscene Speech: Speech that satisfies the three-part *Miller* test, consequently qualifying as obscene under the First Amendment.

Online Speech: Speech in online communication forums, including Twitter, Facebook, Myspace, Friendster, IM (Instant Messaging), YouTube, and Instagram.

Overbroad: This describes when a law or government action censors constitutionally-protected speech while censoring speech that is constitutionally censorable.

United States Supreme Court: The highest court in the United States. The decisions of this court are binding on all federal, state and local governments and the entire citizenry.

Vague: A law or policy that is so ambiguous that it is challenging for a person of ordinary intelligence to comprehend its meaning or its scope.

Chapter 4
Defamatory Speech

ABSTRACT

This chapter discusses defamatory speech which includes slander and libel. It covers various cases, including United States Supreme Court precedent on defamation. It also discusses the applicability of the defamation jurisprudence to student speech. The chapter also describes the Communication Decency Act (CDA). The chapter concludes that even though the CDA has limited online defamation lawsuits by protecting social networking sites from defamation suits, students are vulnerable to defamation challenges, and can also sue for defamation.

INTRODUCTION

Defamation is an area of tort law that makes it illegal for an individual to make a false statement that tends to harm another individual's reputation (Schimmel, Stellman & Fischer, 2010). A statement can be defamatory only if it is communicated to a third person (Schimmel, Stellman, & Fischer, 2010). There are two types of defamation. Slander applies to oral statements, while libel applies to written statements. Because emails, tweets and instant messaging are written statements, they fall under the category of libel (Burke, 2011). This chapter provides an overview of the law of defamation and its application to off-campus utterances by students. The first part discusses United States Supreme Court cases that define the modern parameters of defamation law. The second part discusses the Communication Decency Act (CDA) and the definitive case on CDA, Zeran v. American Online Inc. (1997). The final part discusses cases that have addressed defamation with respect to student online communications.

MAIN FOCUS OF THE CHAPTER

United States Supreme Court Case Law on Defamation

Prior to the United States Supreme Court's decision in New York Times v. Sullivan (1964), courts consistently held that the First Amendment provided no protection against defamatory statements (Gertz

DOI: 10.4018/978-1-4666-9519-1.ch004

Defamatory Speech

v. Robert Welch, Inc., 1974). In the *New York Times* decision, the Court held that the First Amendment protected the media from civil libel actions brought by public officials with respect to their official duties. Montgomery County (Alabama) Police Commissioner L.B. Sullivan brought a civil libel action against the *New York Times* and several black clergymen for a political advertisement that allegedly libeled him for his actions during a series of voting rights protests by university students.

A state trial court entered a judgment on a jury verdict awarding the commissioner $500,000 in damages, which the state supreme court affirmed (New York Times v. Sullivan, 1964). Both courts found that the statements in the advertisements were libelous *per se*: that is, the damages to the person's reputation were presumed. They reached this conclusion on the ground that it was common knowledge that the statements in the advertisements would damage the reputation of the public official. Thus, the only defense available to the defendants was that the statements were indeed true. Because the newspaper had already averred that some of the statements were false, the courts found that the newspaper had committed libel.

The defendants appealed to the United States Supreme Court, which reversed and remanded the case (New York Times v. Sullivan, 1964). The Court held that a finding of libel *per se* was unfounded because such a finding would have a chilling effect on public debate and discussion. Rather, the correct standard for public officials was whether the statements were made with "actual malice": in other words, that the statements were made "with knowledge that it was false or with reckless disregard of whether it was false or not" (p. 279).

In Garrison v. Louisiana (1964), the United States Supreme Court extended the actual malice standard to criminal defamation statutes designed to protect public officials in the performance of their duties. In this case, a district attorney was convicted under a state criminal defamation statute for criticisms made about the conduct of judges. The statute authorized punishment for statements made with malice without regard to whether the statements were actually true. The Supreme Court found that the considerations raised in the *New York Times* case also applied to criminal defamation statutes: the concerns for public discussion or debate outweighed concerns for one's reputation. Therefore, the statute was unconstitutionally overbroad in that it did not allow for the defenses of truth or reasonable belief of the truth.

In Curtis Publishing Company v. Butts (1967), the Supreme Court extended the actual malice standard to "public figures." *Butts* was a consolidation of two cases. In one case, an athletic director of a state university brought a civil libel action alleging that a newspaper had wrongfully claimed that he had fixed a football game. A private corporation, not the state, employed the athletic director. The second case arose from a news report of an eyewitness account of a riot that occurred at the University of Mississippi after federal marshals had attempted to enroll a black student. The dispatch declared that the respondent, who was a private citizen, "had taken command of the violent crowd and had personally led a charge against federal marshals sent there to effectuate the court's decree and to assist in preserving order" (p. 140).

The Supreme Court observed that both cases were different from the *New York Times* case in that the persons bringing charges were private individuals, rather than public officials (Curtis Publishing Company v. Butts, 1967). Nevertheless, the Court held that the *New York Times* "actual malice" standard should apply in cases were the persons were "public figures." Because of their fame, public figures could shape events in such a way as to have a major impact on an area of public concern. Also, similarly to public officials, public figures could effectively rebut challenges to their reputation through the media.

Applying this standard, the Court found that the standard of "actual malice" was established in the first case, but not in the second (Curtis Publishing Company v. Butts, 1967). With respect to the first case, the Court found that the story was not "hot news," the editors recognized that more investigation was necessary, and elementary precautions had not been followed. For instance, the person who had allegedly heard the conversation setting up the "fix" had been accused of check bouncing charges and was thus not a trustworthy figure. The reporter who had been assigned the story was not a football reporter and there had been no attempt to corroborate the information by someone knowledgeable of the sport. By contrast in the second case, the person sending the dispatch was known as a responsible journalist, and the news that was gathered required immediate dissemination.

In Rosenbloom v. Metromedia, Inc. (1971), a plurality of the Court concluded that the *New York Times* standard applied to civil libel suits brought by private individuals. In *Rosenbloom*, a magazine distributor who was a private individual brought a defamation action against a radio station for allegations that he had distributed obscene material. The plurality found that the determining factor was not whether the defamed individual was a private or public figure, but "whether the utterance involved concerns an issue of public or general concern" (p. 44).

In Gertz v. Robert Welch, Inc. (1974), the Supreme Court articulated a different test for defamatory statements made regarding private individuals. In *Gertz*, a policeman in Chicago had been convicted of murder. The victim's family hired an attorney to represent it in a civil case against the policeman. A magazine article claimed that the policeman was a communist sympathizer with a criminal record, who was involved in a "frame-up" against the policeman. The attorney brought a libel action against the magazine. After a jury ruled in favor of the attorney, a federal district court entered a judgment notwithstanding the verdict for the magazine. Even though the district court concluded that the attorney was not a public figure, it found that the *Sullivan* standard should apply to any matter of public discussion regardless of the status of defamed individual.

The United States Court of Appeals for the Seventh Circuit agreed that the *Sullivan* standard applied even though it disagreed with the lower court's finding that the individual was not a public figure (Gertz v. Robert Welch, Inc., 1974). In reaching this conclusion, the Seventh Circuit interpreted the *Rosenbloom* case to require that the *New York Times* standard should apply to any publication involving a matter of significant public interest.

The Supreme Court reversed the decisions of the lower courts (Gertz v. Robert Welch, Inc., 1974). In reaching its conclusion, the Court found that the attorney was not a public official or figure, but rather a private individual. The Court then made a distinction between the rules that applied for public officials and figures and private individuals. The Court held that publishers of allegedly defamatory statements could avail themselves of the *New York Times* protections when they were made with respect to public officials or public figures.

By contrast, broadcasters of allegedly defamatory materials could not obtain protection under the *New York Times* standard when their statements were made with regard to private individuals (Gertz v. Robert Welch, Inc., 1974). The Court made this distinction because "[p]ublic officials and public figures usually enjoy significantly greater access to the channels of effective communication and hence have a more realistic opportunity to counteract false statements than private individuals normally enjoy" (p. 342). The Court went to find that the attorney was neither a "public official" nor a "public figure." While the attorney was well known in some circles, "he had achieved no general fame or notoriety in the community" (p. 351). The Court then held that as long as the state does not impose strict liability on defamation suits, "the States may define for themselves the appropriate standard of liability for a publisher or broadcaster of defamatory falsehood injurious to a private individual" (p. 347).

Section 230 of the Communications Decency Act ("CDA")

In the early 1990's, it appeared as though the courts would analyze defamation over the internet in the same fashion as they had traditional print decisions (Burke, 2011). Congress became concerned that such an approach would prevent the internet from becoming a viable medium for encouraging debate and discussion (Burke, 2011). To encourage the development of the internet, Congress passed the Communications Decency Act of 1996 (CDA). Section 230(c)(1) provides that "[n]o provider or user of an interactive computer service shall be treated as the publisher or speaker of any information provided by another information content provider (Communications Decency Act of 1996, 2014).

In an important case on the application of the CDA, Zeran v. America Online, Inc. (1997), the United States Court of Appeal for the Fourth Circuit made it difficult for victims of online defamation to obtain a legal remedy. Kenneth Zeran sued America Online (AOL) for unreasonable delay in removing defamatory messages that were posted on its message boards. Specifically, these messages claimed that Zeran had been selling t-shirts with offensive slogans connected to the 1995 bombing of the Alfred P. Murrah Building in Oklahoma City. Consequently, Zeran was bombarded with abusive and threatening telephone calls. AOL moved for judgment on the pleadings and interposed section 230 of the CDA as an affirmative defense. After a federal district court granted AOL's motion, Zeran appealed to the Fourth Circuit.

The Fourth Circuit upheld the lower court's ruling (Zeran v. America Online, Inc., 1997). It found that the plain language of section 230 of the CDA "create[d] a federal immunity to any cause of action that would make service providers liable to information originating with a third-party user of the service" (p. 330). The court observed that Congress created such immunity to preserve the internet as a means for maintaining robust communication, which should be subject to minimal government regulation. Congress further enacted section 230 "to encourage service providers to self-regulate the dissemination of offensive material over their services" (p. 330).

Application to Students and Schools

While the CDA protects social networking sites from defamation challenges, it does not protect persons who have made derogatory statements through social media from defamation challenges. Two published cases have addressed online communication at the K-12 level. In I.M.L. v. State (2002), the Utah Supreme Court examined the applicability of criminal libel statutes to derogatory statements made on the internet by a student against his school's administration and faculty. In this case, a high school student called the principal a "town drunk," who was having a sexual relationship with a secretary at the school. Other posts alleged that a faculty member was secretly a homosexual, and that another teacher was addicted to drugs. The student was charged with criminal libel under a Utah statute, which provided: "A person is guilty of libel if he intentionally and with a malicious intent to injure another punishes or procures to be published any libel" (p. 1043). The statute defined libel as "a malicious defamation" (p. 1044). The statute further provided that "malice may be presumed from the act of making the libel" (p. 1044).

The student moved to dismiss the criminal libel charge on the ground that the statute was facially unconstitutional (I.M.L. v. State, 2002). The Supreme Court of Utah agreed with the student. It found that the statute contravened the *New York Times* and *Garrison* decisions by punishing statements concerning public figures regardless of whether the statements were made with actual malice. The court also found that the statute was unconstitutionally overbroad because it provided no immunity for truthful statements.

In Draker v. Schreiber (2008), a vice-principal at a Texas high school sued two students for defamation for creating a website profile of her on Myspace, which "contained her name, photo, and place of employment, as well as explicit and graphic sexual references" (p. 320). A state trial court granted summary judgment to the students on the defamation claim because the "'exaggerated and derogatory statements' included on the Myspace website in question were not assertions of fact that could be objectively verified, they were not defamatory as a matter of law" (p. 321). The administrator then tried to mount a cause of action based on intentional infliction of emotional distress. The trial court also granted summary judgment to the students with respect to this claim. On appeal, the Texas Court of Appeals upheld the lower court's granting of summary judgment on the intentional infliction of emotional distress because the administrator had failed to allege facts independent of her defamation claim.

Two cases in the higher education context have applied defamation law to electronic utterances made by students. In Retzlaff v. de la Viña (2009), a male former business school student, Tom Retzlaff, brought a cause of action for defamation based on an email that the dean of the school distributed to eight other school officials. In this case, a female student had alleged that Retzlaff had harassed her. An investigation of the complaint exposed numerous violations, which resulted in the student's expulsion from the university. Retzlaff brought a defamation cause of action based on an email that the dean of the business school sent to university administrators and law enforcement personnel. The email relayed a report from the harassed student that Retzlaff carried a gun in his car, which she had seen. The district court granted summary judgment to the university on this claim because Retzlaff had provided no evidence that the dean had acted negligently. Also, the court found that the e-mail communication was protected by qualified privilege under state law because it was sent only to administrators and law enforcement personnel. Finally, the e-mail was privileged because "it was a discretionary duty within the scope of her authority and was performed in good faith" (p. 657).

In Wagner v. Miskin (2003), a college physics professor sued a University of North Dakota student, who was a Minnesota resident, for defamatory statements that she made about him over the internet. A jury awarded the professor $3 million in damages. She appealed the decision, arguing in part that the state did not have personal jurisdiction over her. The Supreme Court of North Dakota rejected this assertion because the student's internet activity was directed at the state and the resident professor. Further, the court observed that:

1. The student's website contained articles that were linked to university issues and staff; and
2. The primary topics of the articles were the professor, his trial attorney, and the litigation.

CONCLUSION

In a series of decisions starting with New York Times v. Sullivan (1964), the Supreme Court held that the First Amendment applies to defamation challenges by public officials, and public figures, while holding that First Amendment protection does not apply to challenges made by private individuals. While the Communications Decency Act (CDA) has limited online defamation lawsuits by protecting social networking sites from defamation suits, the cases discussed herein show that students can bring defamation challenges, or be subjected to such challenges for their online communication.

REFERENCES

Burke, M. (2011). Cracks in the armor?: The future of the Communications Decency Act and potential challenges to the protections of Section 230 to gossip web sites. *Boston University Journal of Science and Technology Law*, *17*, 232–257.

Communications Decency Act of 1996, Section 230(c)(1) (2014).

Curtis Publishing Co. v. Butts (1967). 388 U.S. 130.

Draker v. Schreiber (2008). 271 S.W.3d 318.

Garrison v. Louisiana (1964). 379 U.S. 64.

Gertz v. Robert Welch, Inc. (1974). 418 U.S. 323.

New York Times v. Sullivan (1964). 376 U.S. 254.

Retzlaff v. de la Viña (2009). 606 F.Supp.2d 654.

Rosenbloom v. Metromedia, Inc. (1971). 403 U.S. 29.

Schimmel, D., Stellman, L., & Fischer, L. (2010). Teachers and the law (8th ed.). Academic Press.

I.M.L. v. State (2002). 61 P.3d 1038.

Wagner v. Miskin (2003). 660 N.W.2d 593.

Zeran v. American Online, Inc. (1997). 129 F.3d 227.

KEY TERMS AND DEFINITIONS

Communications Decency Act (CDA): Federal law enacted to promote decency in online communications so as to ensure student safety.
Defamation: An area of tort law that prohibits making a false statement that could damage another's reputation.
Libel: A written false statement that could damage a person's reputation.
Libelous *Per Se*: A libel case where the damages to the plaintiff's reputation are presumed.
Malice: Making a statement with knowledge of its falsity or with reckless disregard of its falsity or truth.
Off-Campus: Any locale outside the borders or premises of a school.
Online Speech: Speech in online communication forums, including Twitter, Facebook, Myspace, Friendster, IM (Instant Messaging), YouTube and Instagram.
Public Figures: A person in the public spotlight.
Public Official: A federal, state or local government official.
Slander: An oral false statement that could damage a person's reputation.

Chapter 5
Obscene Speech

ABSTRACT

This chapter discusses obscene speech – a category of speech that the United States Supreme Court has excluded from First Amendment protection. The lack of constitutional protection for obscene speech provides an avenue for school officials to censor such student speech off-campus. The goal of the chapter is to provide an overview of the obscenity jurisprudence. The chapter also discusses examples of cases applying Supreme Court precedent on obscenity to censorship of off-campus student speech.

INTRODUCTION

In Miller v. California (1973), the Supreme Court affirmed its holding in Roth v. United States (1957) that obscenity was not protected by the First Amendment. In Rosario v. Clark County School District (2013), a school district attempted to justify the sanctions for off-campus student speech under *Miller*. This chapter first discusses pertinent Supreme Court cases relating to obscenity, culminating with the *Miller* case. Next, this chapter discusses how a school district attempted to censor off-campus student speech as obscenity in the *Rosario* case.

MAIN FOCUS OF THE CHAPTER

United States Supreme Court Case Law on Obscenity

The United States Supreme Court first addressed whether the First Amendment protected obscenity in Roth v. United States (1957). *Roth* was a consolidation of two cases:

1. Roth v. United States challenged the constitutionality of a federal statute;
2. Alberts v. California challenged a state obscenity law.

DOI: 10.4018/978-1-4666-9519-1.ch005

Obscene Speech

In both cases, a jury had convicted the appellants for selling obscene books. The Supreme Court upheld both convictions. It found that the First Amendment did not protect obscenity because "such utterances are no essential part of any exposition of ideas, and are of such slight social value as a step to truth that any benefit that may be derived from them is clearly outweighed by the social interest in order and morality" (p. 485).

The Supreme Court also rejected the common law rule for obscenity, articulated in the English case Hicklin v. Regina (1868), that material could be judged obscene "merely by the effect of an isolated excerpt upon particularly susceptible persons" (Roth v. United States, 1957, pp. 488-89). Instead, the *Roth* court adopted the following standard for determining obscenity: "whether to the average person, applying contemporary community standards, the dominant theme of the material taken as a whole appeals to prurient interest" (p. 489).

The United States Supreme Court again addressed the issue of obscenity in Jacobellis v. Ohio (1964). In this case, an Ohio trial court convicted and fined a movie manager for obscenity for showing a French film, *Les Amants* ("*The Lovers*"). The state supreme court upheld the conviction. Although the United States Supreme Court reversed the conviction, the Justices failed to agree on the appropriate standard for analyzing the case. Indeed, *Jacobellis* is famous for Justice Potter Stewart's concurrence, which contains the following quip: "I shall not today attempt further to define the kinds of material I understand to be embraced within that shorthand description; and perhaps I could never succeed in intelligibly doing so. But *I know it when I see it*, and the motion picture involved in this case is not that" (p. 197, emphasis supplied).

The Supreme Court would again rule on obscenity in A Book Named "John Cleland's Memoirs of a Woman of Pleasure" v. Attorney General of Massachusetts (1966). In this case, the Massachusetts courts ruled that the book *John Cleland's Memoirs of a Woman of Pleasure* (also known as *Fanny Hill*), which recounted the life of a prostitute, was obscene. The Supreme Court reversed. The plurality opinion elaborated on the *Roth* test by noting that:

... three elements must coalesce: it must be established that (a) the dominant theme of the material taken as a whole appeals to a prurient interest in sex; (b) the material is patently offensive because it affronts contemporary community standards relating to the description or representation of sexual matters; and (c) the material is utterly without redeeming social value (A Book Named "John Cleland's Memoirs of a Woman of Pleasure" v. Attorney General of Massachusetts, 1966, p. 418).

The dissenting Justices in the *Memoirs* case emphatically criticized the plurality opinion's final prong for determining whether obscenity had occurred. For instance, Justice Harlan criticized the requirement that the material must be utterly without social value as having no meaning at all.

In Ginsberg v. New York (1968), the Supreme Court addressed the question of whether a New York statute that criminalized the sale of obscene material to persons under the age of 17 was unconstitutional. The statute based its definition of obscenity on whether the material appealed to minors, regardless of whether it would have been obscene to adults. A luncheonette owner was convicted under this statute for selling "girlie magazines" to a 16-year-old boy. A state trial court judge found that the magazines displayed "nudity," which was defined as "female ... buttocks with less than a full opaque covering, or ... the female breast with less than a fully opaque covering of any portion thereof below the top of the nipple" (p. 432). The judge also found that the magazine pictures were "harmful to minors" because they displayed nudity that

1. *Predominantly appeals to the prurient, shameful, or morbid interest of minors, and*
2. *Is patently offensive to prevailing standards in the adult community as a whole with respect to what is suitable material for minors, and*
3. *Is utterly without redeeming social importance for minors (p. 433).*

On appeal, the United States Supreme Court upheld the constitutionality of the statute (Ginsberg v. New York, 1968). The luncheonette owner contended that a person's First Amendment right to view sexual material could constitutionally depend on whether the person was an adult or a minor. The Court countered that the state had the constitutional authority to ensure the well-being of children. The Court identified two reasons for the legislature to limit minors' access to obscene material. First, the state could pass laws designed to aid parents in the raising of their children. Second, the state had an independent interest in protecting the welfare of children. The Court further found that the age restriction was rationally related to these goals.

In Stanley v. Georgia (1969), the Supreme Court addressed whether an "obscenity statute, insofar as it punishes private possession of obscene matter, violates the First Amendment" (p. 559). In this case, a person was arrested and convicted of possessing obscene films at home in violation of Georgia statute. The Court held that the state could not make mere possession of obscene material a crime. The Court maintained that the Constitution protected the right of individuals to receive information and ideas: "This right to receive information and ideas, regardless of their social worth…is fundamental to our society" (p. 564). The Court rejected the state's claim that it had the right to protect a person's mind from the effects of obscenity because that amounted to the unacceptable notion that "the State has the right to control the moral content of a person's thoughts" (p 565).

In Miller v. California (1973), the United States Supreme Court developed a new standard for determining whether obscenity had occurred. In this case, the appellant conducted a mass mailing campaign advertising the sale of adult material. The brochures primarily "consist[ed] of pictures and drawings very explicitly depicting men and women in groups of two or more engaging in a variety of sexual activities, with genitals often primarily displayed" (p. 18). After a recipient of one of these brochures had complained to the authorities, the appellant was convicted of violating a California statute, which made it a misdemeanor to distribute obscene material. While the statute incorporated the obscenity test developed by the Supreme Court in the *Memoirs* case, the trial court employed the community standards test formulated in the *Roth* case. A state appellate court affirmed the conviction.

The Supreme Court agreed to hear the case on appeal to clear the confusion that it had created in the *Roth* and *Memoirs* cases (Miller v. California, 1973). The Court vacated and remanded the state appellate court decision. The Court affirmed its holding in *Roth* that the First Amendment did not protect obscenity. However, the Court limited the scope of obscenity regulations to works depicting or describing sexual conduct. The Court explicitly rejected the constitutional standard developed in the *Memoirs* case that the material must be utterly without redeeming social value. Instead, the Court articulated the following basic guidelines (known as the *Miller* test) for triers of fact regarding obscenity cases:

… (a) whether the "average person, applying contemporary community standards" would find that the work, taken as a whole, appeals to the prurient interest … (b) whether the work depicts or describes in a patently offensive way, sexual conduct specifically defined by the applicable state law; and (c) whether the work, taken as a whole, lacks serious literary, artistic, political, or scientific value (Miller v. California, 1973, p. 24).

Student Speech Case Applying Supreme Court Obscenity Case Law

The *Miller* test has been applied in the student speech context to determine whether school districts can justify their censorship of students. In Rosario v. Clark County School District (2013), a former Nevada school high school student was disciplined for a series of tweets that he posted from a restaurant at the end of basketball season. The unedited tweets were as follows:

1. "Mr. Isaacs is a b*tch too"
2. "I hope Coach brown gets f*ck*d in tha *ss by 10 black d*cks"
3. "Now I can tweet whatever I want and I hope one of y'all m*ther f*ck*rs snitch on me"
4. "F*ck coach browns b*tch *ss"
5. "Finally this b*tch *ss season is over"
6. "Aiight I'm done y'all can go snitch now like before"
7. "Oh yeah and Mr. Dinkel's square *ss"
8. "AND Ms. Evans b*tch *ss boyfriend [this is referring to defendant Gygatz] too He a p*ssy *ss n*gg* tryna talk sh*t while walking away" (Rosario v. Clark County School District, 2013, p. 3).

The student filed suit in federal court, alleging that the district's punishment of him violated the First Amendment (Rosario v. Clark County School District, 2013). The defendants moved to dismiss the plaintiff's complaint for failure to state a claim. The court ruled that the second tweet could not survive the motion to dismiss because it was obscene as a matter of law under the *Miller* test. Thus, the plaintiff could not receive First Amendment protection for this tweet. The court refused to find that the other tweets were obscene. While many of the tweets contained "racist, violent, offensive, and hateful" language, they were not obscene (p. 4). The court then found that the remaining tweets satisfied the motion to dismiss stage in part because the courts disagreed as to whether schools could discipline students for off-campus speech.

CONCLUSION

In Miller v. California (1973), the Supreme Court affirmed its holding in prior cases that obscenity was not protected by the First Amendment. In Rosario v. Clark County School District (2013), a school district relied on the *Miller* test to justify punishing a student for off-campus speech. As with *Rosario*, other school districts may in the future attempt to justify their sanctions of children for off-campus online behavior on obscenity grounds.

REFERENCES

A Book Named "John Cleland's Memoirs of a Woman of Pleasure" v. Attorney General of Massachusetts (1966). 383 U.S. 413.

Ginsberg v. United States (1968). 390 U.S. 629.

Jacobellis v. Ohio (1964). 378 U.S. 184.

Miller v. California (1973). 413 U.S. 15.

Regina v. Hicklin (1868). L.R. 3 Q.B. 360.

Roasio v. Clark County School District (2013). 2013 WL 3679375.

Roth v. United States (1957). 354 U.S. 476.

Stanley v. Georgia (1969). 394 U.S. 557.

KEY TERMS AND DEFINITIONS

Common Law: The body of laws and rules governing the English-speaking world that is developed primarily through judicial interpretations and precedents.

Contemporary Community Standards: Prevailing community standards at the time of speech that is being censored as obscene.

First Amendment: This is the first right listed within the bill of rights added to the United States Constitution in 1791 to guarantee Americans certain rights free from government infringement. It covers the right to free speech, the right to free exercise of religion, right against government establishment of religion, the right to a free press, the right to peaceable assembly and the right to petition for redress of grievances.

Miller **Test:** The three-part test the United States Supreme Court created in Miller v. California (1973) for determining whether the government can censor speech as obscenity. Under this test, courts inquire into: (a) whether, under contemporary community standards, the average person would deem the speech as a whole as appealing to a prurient interest; (b) whether the speech describes or shows sexual conduct defined by state law in a manifestly offensive way; and (c) whether the speech as a whole has no serious political, scientific, literary or artistic value (Miller v. California, 1973).

Obscene Speech: This is constitutionally unprotected speech that satisfies the three-part *Miller* test.

Off-Campus: Any locale outside the borders or premises of a school.

Roth **Test:** The three-part test that was a predecessor to the *Miller* test. The test, created by the Supreme Court in Roth v. United States (1957), that required proof of the following before censorship could be deemed constitutional: (a) the speech has a principal theme that, as a whole, appealed to a prurient interest; (b) the speech is manifestly offensive in contravention of contemporary community standards about sexual issues; and (c) the speech has utterly no redeeming social value (A Book Named "John Cleland's Memoirs of a Woman of Pleasure" v. Attorney General of Massachusetts, 1966).

Sexual Material: Material that appeals to prurient interests.

Chapter 6
Child Pornography

ABSTRACT

This chapter discusses child pornography speech which the United States Supreme Court first categorically excluded from First Amendment protection in New York v. Ferber (1982). The goal of the chapter is to provide an overview of the child-pornography jurisprudence. The chapter also highlights a case applying the Supreme Court precedent on child pornography to student speech. The chapter concludes that, due to its unprotected nature, students censored for child pornography speech have no First Amendment recourse.

INTRODUCTION

In New York v. Ferber (1982), the United States Supreme Court held that the First Amendment does not protect child pornography. Thus, students who are punished by school districts for accessing or distributing child pornography cannot challenge these sanctions on free speech grounds. Yet, as T.V. ex rel. B.V. v. Smith-Green Community School Corporation (2011) illustrates, school districts must demonstrate that the alleged internet activity fits within the standards established in case law as well as state and federal statutes. The first part of this chapter provides an overview of Supreme Court case law on child pornography. The remainder of the chapter discusses the T.V. ex rel. B.V. v. Smith-Green Community School Corporation (2011) case, in which a court ruled that a school district could not punish students on child pornography grounds for sexually-risqué photographs that the students took of themselves during slumber parties and posted on social media websites.

MAIN FOCUS OF THE CHAPTER

United States Supreme Court Case Law

The United States Supreme Court first addressed the constitutionality of child pornography in New York v. Ferber (1982). In *Ferber*, a book proprietor of sexually-oriented products sold two films depict-

DOI: 10.4018/978-1-4666-9519-1.ch006

ing young boys masturbating to an undercover police officer. He was indicted and found guilty of a New York criminal statute, which forbade "persons from knowingly promoting sexual performances by children under the age of 16 by distributing material which depicts such performances" (New York v. Ferber, 1982, p. 749). This statute did not require the materials to be legally obscene. A state appellate court upheld the conviction.

The state supreme court reversed, finding that the statute violated the First Amendment by being underinclusive and overbroad (New York v. Ferber, 1982). The state appealed to the United States Supreme Court, which reversed and remanded the lower court's decision. The Court acknowledged that, in Miller v. California (1973), it had articulated the following standard for determining whether material was obscene (and thus falling under the state's power to regulate): "'a state offense must also be limited to works, which taken as a whole, appeal to the prurient interest in sex, which portray sexual conduct in a patently offensive way, and which, taken as a whole, do not have serious literary, artistic, political or social value'" (New York v. Ferber, 1982, p. 755, quoting Miller v. California, 1973, p. 24).

However, the Court reasoned that states had greater latitude to regulate child pornography (New York v. Ferber, 1982). First, states had a compelling interest in protecting the physical and psychological well-being of minors. The Court noted that it had recognized the importance of protecting the well-being of children in Ginsberg v. New York (1968), a case in which it had upheld a state statute protecting minors from exposure of obscene material. Second, the distribution of photographs and films depicting children engaged in sexual activity was intrinsically related to the sexual abuse of children in two ways (New York v. Ferber, 1982). The depictions served as a permanent reminder of the child's participation, and the government needed to close the network for child pornography to effectively control the sexual exploitation of children. Third, the advertising and selling of child pornography provided an economic motive for this illegal activity. Fourth, the value of permitting the performance of child pornography was *de minimus*. Finally, the Court observed that classifying child pornography as outside of the scope of First Amendment protection was consistent with its earlier decisions.

The Court articulated several limitations on state child pornography restrictions (New York v. Ferber, 1982). For instance, child pornography prohibitions must be clearly defined in the language of the state law and through authoritative interpretations of the written law. The state must limit the offense to "works that *visually* depict sexual conduct by children below a specified age" (p. 764, emphasis in the original). In other words, "the distribution of descriptions or other depictions of sexual conduct, not otherwise obscene, which do not involve live performance or photographic or other visual reproduction or live performance, retains First Amendment protection" (pp. 764-65). Further, there must be an element of scienter: that is, intent or knowledge of wrongdoing.

Applying this standard, the Court held that the state's child obscenity statute was not constitutionally underinclusive (New York v. Ferber, 1982). The statute depicted the prohibited acts – "actual or simulated sexual intercourse, sexual bestiality, masturbation, sado-masochistic abuse or lewd exhibition of the genitals" – which was not entitled to First Amendment protection (p. 747). Further, the Court noted that in Miller v. California (1973), it had given the term "lewd exhibition of the genitals" as an example of a valid regulation. Moreover, the statute contained a scienter requirement.

The Court also rejected the claim that the statute was unconstitutionally overbroad because it would have forbidden the distribution of material that had serious literary, scientific, or educational value (New York v. Ferber, 1982). The Court applied the overbreadth rule that it had developed in Broadrick v. Oklahoma (1973) for statutes regulating expressive conduct: it would find a statute facially unconstitutional only if the overbreadth was substantial (New York v. Ferber, 1982, p. 769). The Court then concluded that the statute was not substantially overbroad. Indeed, the Court "consider[ed] this the paradigmatic case of a state statute whose legitimate reach dwarfs its arguably permissible applications" (p. 773).

In Osborne v. Ohio (1990), the Court analyzed whether a statute that criminalized the mere possession of child pornography violated the First Amendment. The petitioner was convicted and sentenced to six months in prison for possessing four photographs depicting adolescent boys in sexually-explicit positions. An Ohio appellate court and the state supreme court affirmed the conviction.

On appeal, the United States Supreme Court upheld the constitutionality of the statute under the First Amendment (Osborne v. Ohio, 1990). The Court rejected the petitioner's claim that its prior decision in Stanley v. Georgia (1969) required a finding of unconstitutionality. In *Stanley*, the Court invalidated a statute that prohibited the private possession of obscene material. The Court refused to extend its ruling in *Stanley* "because the interests underlying child pornography prohibitions far exceed the interests justifying the Georgia law at issue in *Stanley*" (Osborne v. Ohio, 1990, p. 108). The *Stanley* Court found that the state did not have a compelling interest in controlling the private thoughts of the viewers of obscene material. By contrast, the state of Ohio had a compelling interest in protecting the physical and psychological well-being of children, and in destroying the market for child pornography.

The petitioner also asserted that the statute was facially overbroad because it criminalized the possession of "nude" photographs of minors (Osborne v. Ohio, 1990). The Court rejected this claim in light of the fact that the Ohio Supreme Court's interpretation of the statute prohibited nudity constituting "a lewd exhibition or involv[ing] a graphic focus on the genitals" (p. 113). This interpretation avoided the imposition of penalties for innocuous photographs of children. Further, this interpretation was constituent with the Court's finding in *Ferber* that the "lewd exhibition of genitals" was an example of a valid regulation.

In Ashcroft v. Free Speech Coalition (2002), the Supreme Court examined the constitutionality of the Child Pornography Prevention Act (CPPA). The CPPA was a federal statute that expanded the prohibition of child pornography to include computer-imaging technology that depicted minors engaging in child pornography. The CPPA also forbade the distribution of images that conveyed the impression of minors engaged in child pornography.

An adult-entertainment trade association and others claimed that the CPPA violated the First Amendment (Ashcroft v. Free Speech Coalition, 2002). A federal district court disagreed and granted summary judgment to the federal government. The United States Court of Appeals for the Ninth Circuit, on the other hand, held that the statute was facially invalid.

On appeal, the Supreme Court held that the CPPA was unconstitutionally overbroad in violation of the First Amendment (Ashcroft v. Free Speech Coalition, 2002). The Court rejected the government's assertion that the speech was indistinguishable from *Ferber*. In *Ferber*, the Court had found that the ban on prohibiting and selling child pornography was "inextricably related" to sexual abuse in two ways. First, the continued circulation of child pornography would harm the child who had been involved in child pornography. Second, the state had an interest in shutting down the distribution network because of the economic incentive in producing child pornography. By contrast, there was no intrinsic link between virtual child pornography and sexual abuse of minors. The Court characterized the government's claim that virtual imagery could lead to sexual abuse as indirect. The harm did not flow from the speech but on the possibility of subsequent criminal acts.

The federal government argued that *Ferber* justified the protection against indirect harm because that case acknowledged that child pornography was rarely valuable speech (Ashcroft v. Free Speech

Coalition, 2002). The Court rejected this assertion because *Ferber*'s reasoning was based upon how the speech was made, not how it was communicated. In *Ferber*, the Court held that speech that was neither obscene nor the product of sexual abuse was permissible under the First Amendment.

Moreover, the Court rejected the government's assertion that the CPPA was justified because it was difficult to differentiate between actual depictions of child pornography and those produced by computer imaging (Ashcroft v. Free Speech Coalition, 2002). The Court observed that this justification ran afoul of the overbreadth doctrine established in the *Broderick* case in that the statute banned a substantial amount of protected speech. Further, the Court held that the statutory provision prohibiting images that conveyed the impression of child pornography was substantially overbroad. For instance, a film containing no sexually-explicit scenes involving children could still violated the statute if the title and trailer indicated that the film contained child pornography.

Case Law Dealing with Online Child Pornography in the School Context

While school districts may sanction children for possessing or distributing child pornography online while outside of the schoolhouse gate, T.V. ex rel. B.V. v. Smith-Green Community School Corporation (2011) suggests that courts might not readily or necessarily justify punishments for racy pictures on child pornography grounds. In this case, two Indiana high school students, M.K. and T.V., had taken several pictures of themselves during several sleepovers. In a number of photographs, the girls were sucking on lollipops. One picture contained the caption: "Wanna suck my cock." In another photograph, one of the girls, who was fully clothed, was sucking on a lollipop, while another lollipop was positioned between her legs. The other girl, who was also fully clothed, was pretending to suck on the lollipop. In another picture, the girls were pretending to kiss each other. In the final slumber, the girls took photographs detailing the following activity:

One of the pictures shows M.K. standing talking on the phone while another girl, holds one of her legs up in the air, with T.V. holding a toy trident as if protruding from her crotch and pointing between M.K.'s legs. In another, T.V. is shown bent over M.K. poking the trident between the buttocks. A third picture shows T.V. positioned behind another girl as if engaging in anal sex. In another picture, M.K. poses with money stuck into her lingerie – stripper-style (T.V. ex rel. B.V. v. Smith-Green Community School Corporation, 2011, p. 772).

T.V. had posted most of the photographs on her Myspace and Facebook accounts, which were accessible only to persons with "Friend" status (T.V. ex rel. B.V. v. Smith-Green Community School Corporation, 2011). Some of the photos with the lollipops were posted on Photo Bucket, which was accessible only by password. The photos did not identify the girls as students of the high school. Furthermore, the girls did not bring the photos to school.

After parents complained about the pictures, the students were suspended from the volleyball team for a part of the school year in accordance with the school's code of conduct relating to extra-curricular activities (T.V. ex rel. B.V. v. Smith-Green Community School Corporation, 2011). The code of conduct, which applied to on-campus and off-campus activities, authorized the school to suspend students from extra-curricular activities if they brought discredit to the school.

The students challenged their suspension in federal district court on First Amendment grounds (T.V. ex rel. B.V. v. Smith-Green Community School Corporation, 2011). The defendants moved for summary

Child Pornography

judgment on the ground that the pictures constituted child pornography and were thus unprotected. The court rejected this motion, finding that the pictures were not child pornography under state or federal statutes. Indiana's child pornography legislation referred to images depicting "sexual conduct by a child" (p. 778). Indiana's statutory definition of "sexual conduct" in regards to child exploitation and child pornography stated as follows:

"Sexual conduct" means sexual intercourse, deviate sexual conduct, exhibition of the uncovered genitals intended to satisfy the sexual desires of any person, sadomasochistic abuse, sexual or deviate sexual conduct with an animal, or any fondling or touching of a child by another person or of another person by a child intended to arouse or satisfy the sexual desires of either the child or the other person (T.V. ex rel. B.V. v. Smith-Green Community School Corporation, 2011, p. 778).

The defendants asserted that the photographs constituted "deviate sexual conduct," under state law, which was defined as "an act involving: a sex organ of one person and the mouth and anus of another person; or (2) the penetration of the sex organ or anus of a person by an object" (T.V. ex rel. B.V. v. Smith-Green Community School Corporation, 2011, p. 778). The court rejected this claim because none of the pictures "depicts the sex organ, mouth or anus of two people, and none of the images depicts actual penetration" (p. 778).

The defendants tried to sidestep the state statute by claiming that the students had admitted in a deposition that the photographs portrayed acts of oral and anal sex (T.V. ex rel. B.V. v. Smith-Green Community School Corporation, 2011). The court rejected this attempt, noting that the deposition testimony failed to address the statutory definition of "sexual conduct" and that the law witnesses could not provide such legal conclusions.

The federal child pornography statute defined child pornography as having a "visual depiction involv[ing] the use of a minor engaging in sexually-explicit conduct" (T.V. ex rel. B.V. v. Smith-Green Community School Corporation, 2011, p. 778). The defendants argued that the photographs constituted sexually-explicit conduct according to the federal statute in that they depicted "actual or simulated … sexual intercourse, including genital-genital, oral-genital, anal-genital, whether between persons of the same or opposite sex" (T.V. ex rel. B.V. v. Smith-Green Community School Corporation, 2011, p. 778). The court rejected this contention because the photographs included candy phalluses and toy tridents, and thus failed to create a realistic impression of actual sexual intercourse.

CONCLUSION

Because the United States Supreme Court has held that the First Amendment does not protect child pornography, students cannot challenge school district sanctions for accessing or distributing child pornography online while off-campus on First Amendment grounds. However, T.V. ex rel. B.V. v. Smith-Green Community School Corporation (2011) shows that school districts might not always be able to use the Supreme Court's child pornography cases to justify sanctions of students for posting sexually-ribald pictures onto social media websites while off school grounds. In order to censor student speech as child pornography, school districts must ensure that they strictly comply with the requirements in the Supreme Court's child pornography case law.

REFERENCES

Ashcroft v. Free Speech Coalition (2002). 535 U.S. 234.

Broadrick v. Oklahoma (1973). 413 U.S. 601.

Ginsberg v. United States (1968). 390 U.S. 629.

Miller v. California (1973). 413 U.S. 15.

New York v. Ferber (1982). 458 U.S. 747.

Osborne v. Ohio (1990). 495 U.S. 103.

T.V. ex rel. B.V. v. Smith-Green Community School Corporation (2011). 807 F.Supp.2d 767.

KEY TERMS AND DEFINITIONS

Child Pornography: Visual of a minor in a nude or partially nude state designed to appeal to prurient interests.

Compelling Interest: A strong constitutionally-recognized justification for certain government action.

De Minimus: This refers to state of something being legally inconsequential or insignificant.

Jurisprudence: The body of case law governing a particular area of American life.

***Miller* Test:** The three-part test the United States Supreme Court created in Miller v. California (1973) for determining whether the government can censor speech as obscenity. Under this test, courts inquire into: (a) whether, under contemporary community standards, the average person would deem the speech as a whole as appealing to a prurient interest; (b) whether the speech describes or shows sexual conduct defined by state law in a manifestly offensive way; and (c) whether the speech as a whole has no serious political, scientific, literary or artistic value (Miller v. California, 1973).

Obscene Speech: Speech that satisfies the three-part *Miller* test, consequently qualifying as obscene under the First Amendment. Obscene speech is also sometimes referred to as legally-obscene speech.

Overbroad: This describes when a law or government action censors constitutionally-protected speech while censoring speech that is constitutionally censorable.

Scienter: The intent or knowledge of wrongdoing.

Underinclusive: This describes when a government action or law censors some constitutionally-censorable speech while not censoring similar speech.

Section 3

Student Free Speech and the United States Supreme Court

Chapter 7
Material and Substantial Disruption/Infringement of Rights

ABSTRACT

This chapter focuses on the Tinker v. Des Moines Independent Community School District (1969) case – the first United States Supreme Court decision about student speech under the Free Speech Clause of the First Amendment. It discusses the two tests established in Tinker v. Des Moines Independent Community School District for determining the scope of school authority over student speech. These tests are the "material and substantial disruption" test and the "infringement-of-rights" test. The ultimate goal of the chapter is to analyze the Tinker v. Des Moines Independent Community School District case in order to determine if it authorizes schools to censor off-campus student speech.

INTRODUCTION

This chapter examines the United States Supreme Court's decision in Tinker v. Des Moines Independent Community School District (1969). It is important for scholars, the judiciary and schools to understand Tinker v. Des Moines Independent Community School District because it is the case most often applied in student speech cases (Frederick, 2007). The chapter begins with a background discussion of the Supreme Court's entry into students' First Amendment constitutional rights in West Virginia State Board of Education v. Barnette (1943). It then discusses per the authors the speech incident that inspired the Tinker v. Des Moines Independent Community School District case. This chapter also includes an analysis of the Court's reasoning in the case in order to determine the scope of students' free speech rights recognized in the case. The two tests for determining whether schools can censor students' free speech rights are explored. The objective is to analyze the Supreme Court decision in order to facilitate an understanding of the authority of schools over student speech. Since the United States Supreme Court's precedents are critical to free speech jurisprudence all over the country, it is essential to understand the Supreme Court's first decision about students' right to free speech under the Free Speech Clause. The *Tinker* decision is

DOI: 10.4018/978-1-4666-9519-1.ch007

Material and Substantial Disruption/Infringement of Rights

also important because it encouraged the free exchange of ideas for students rather than the unilateral transmission of ideas from schools to students (Harpaz, 2000). Additionally, it established the material and substantial disruption test as well as the infringement-of-rights test as barriers to school censorship of students' speech; despite the need for schools to have authority to maintain discipline and order in schools. Finally, even though the student-speakers in Tinker v. Des Moines Independent Community School District were young students, the Supreme Court endorsed their right to speak about controversial issues (Harpaz, 2000).

BACKGROUND

The United States Supreme Court first opened the door to the constitutional protection of students' right to free expression in West Virginia State Board of Education v. Barnette (1943). While the case was not decided under the Free Speech Clause, the language the Supreme Court used in the case signaled a willingness to protect students' right to free speech. In that case, a group of Jehovah's Witnesses challenged a West Virginia Board of Education regulation which compelled students and teachers to salute the flag of the United States. The regulation provided that anyone who refused to salute the flag would be punished for insubordination. Based on their belief that the Scripture prohibited the salute of any image such as the flag, the Jehovah's Witnesses sought a religious exception to the salute mandate from the board of education; they were, however, denied. In its review of the constitutional challenge to the regulation, the Supreme Court ruled that the salute constituted symbolic speech designed to communicate a political idea. The regulation, however, was a "compulsion of students to declare a belief" (p. 631) that could force students to "forego any contrary convictions of their own and become unwilling converts to the prescribed ceremony" (p. 632). This is clearly unacceptable and contrary to the conscience of the United States Constitution.

The Supreme Court warned that "censorship or suppression of expression of opinion is tolerated by our Constitution only when the expression presents a clear and present danger of action of a kind the State is empowered to prevent and punish" (West Virginia State Board of Education v. Barnette, 1943, p. 633). This is a very stringent standard since it requires that danger must be clear as well as imminent in order to censor speech. The West Virginia Board of Education failed to allege that a clear and present danger would result from a failure to salute the flag. Consequently, the regulation could not pass constitutional muster. The Court ruled that boards of education must comply with the United States Constitution's Bill of Rights even as they perform their critical and very discretionary responsibilities for students' education. The very fact that boards of education are "educating the young for citizenship is reason for scrupulous protection of Constitutional freedoms of the individual" (p. 637). Further, the Court cautioned schools against compelling students into a unified state-sanctioned viewpoint on issues: "Those who begin coercive elimination of dissent soon find themselves exterminating dissenters. Compulsory unification of opinion achieves only the unanimity of the graveyard" (p. 641). The Constitution does not allow any official to dictate orthodoxy in religion, politics, nationalism or "other matters of opinion" (p. 642). Finally, the Court emphasized that the right to free expression entails respecting the right of others to be eccentric and intellectually different from social norms:

We can have intellectual individualism and the rich cultural diversities that we owe to exceptional minds only at the price of occasional eccentricity and abnormal attitudes. When they are so harmless to others or to the State as those we deal with here, the price is not too great. But freedom to differ is not limited to things that do not matter much. That would be a mere shadow of freedom. The test of its substance is the right to differ as to things that touch the heart of the existing order (West Virginia State Board of Education v. Barnette, 1943, pp. 641-42).

These statements foreshadowed the Supreme Court's official recognition of the rights of students, under the Free Speech Clause, to express views contrary to school-approved views in Tinker v. Des Moines Independent Community School District (1969) – the main focus of this chapter.

MAIN FOCUS OF THE CHAPTER

In Tinker v. Des Moines Independent Community School District (1969), the United States Supreme Court recognized the right of students to express their views as a protected constitutional right under the Free Speech Clause. In this case, the Supreme Court created two different tests for determining whether student speech is protected:

1. The "material and substantial disruption" test; and
2. The "infringement of rights" test.

These tests are known as the *Tinker* tests. The Tinker v. Des Moines Independent Community School District case as well as the two tests are examined next.

The Speech Incident

In 1965, 15-year old John Tinker, a student in the Des Moines Independent Community School District, and his mother traveled from Iowa to Washington, DC to attend an anti-war rally organized for people to voice concerns about the Vietnam War (Borkoski, 2013). At the time, there was limited national opposition to the war (Moss, 2011). There were approximately 72,000 United States troops in Vietnam and 500 Americans had been killed in the war; though these numbers increased significantly to 385,000 troops and more than 6,000 deaths by 1966 when the opposition to the war gained national traction (Moss, 2011). During the bus ride home from the rally, John met 16-year old Christopher Eckhardt who had also attended the rally (Borkoski, 2013). Christopher was "in part a stereotypically quaint Midwestern boy-but he was also part of a disillusioned clique that 'sat in [its] own section of the auditorium [at school events] and refused to cheer . . . or to rise for the National Anthem'" (p. 1416). John and Christopher discussed the rally's impact on them, the voice it gave them for their views on the Vietnam War and the feelings of acceptance they experienced. Years later, John would say that he "was used to the idea that my beliefs were not very widely appreciated" (Moss, p. 1416). As they brainstormed ideas to continue the momentum they experienced at the rally, they decided to wear black armbands to their school. When they arrived in Iowa, they discussed their ideas with other students (Borkoski, 2013).

Material and Substantial Disruption/Infringement of Rights

Officials in the Des Moines Independent Community School District learned, through an announcement for the school newspaper, that some students were planning to wear armbands to school to express their opposition to the Vietnam War and support of a détente (Tinker v. Des Moines Independent Community School District, 1969; Borkoski, 2013). In order to deter the students from wearing the armbands to school, officials promulgated a policy that would mandate high school as well as junior high school students to remove armbands or face suspension from school until the student complied with the policy (Tinker v. Des Moines Independent Community School District, 1969). The policy was also motivated by the fact that the Vietnam War was a "subject of major controversy" and because several draft-card burning incidents were taking place around the country (p. 510; Roberts, 2008). School officials had previously permitted students to wear black armbands to school for another subject – grieving the "loss of school spirit" (Borkoski, 2013, p. 1). Additionally, the school did not censor students who chose to wear symbols on controversial subjects unrelated to the Vietnam War such as the Iron Cross (which typically represents Nazism) (Tinker v. Des Moines Independent Community School District, 1969).

John and Christopher wore black armbands to their high school in violation of the policy against armbands (Tinker v. Des Moines Independent Community School District, 1969). John's 13-year old sister, Mary Beth Tinker, a junior high schooler wore a black armband to school as well even though she was initially hesitant to participate (Moss, 2011). The siblings of John and Mary Beth – 8-year old Paul and 11-year old Hope – also wore armbands to their elementary school; however, since the policy ban did not apply to elementary schools, they were not a part of the case. Each armband was about a two-inch wide band of cloth. One of the students characterized their message as the "witness of the armbands" (Tinker v. Des Moines Independent Community School District, p. 514). The parents of the students were fully supportive of their decision to wear the armband to school (Moss, 2011). In the case, the Supreme Court ruled that the armbands were a form of speech analogous to any other speech under the First Amendment. Unlike verbal speech, however, the armbands were a "silent, passive expression of opinion" (Tinker v. Des Moines Independent Community School District, p. 508).

While at school, the students did not communicate their views on the Vietnam War beyond their wearing of the armbands (Tinker v. Des Moines Independent Community School District, 1969). Nevertheless, a football player tried to tear the armband off of Christopher's sleeve (Borkoski, 2013). Additionally, school officials asked the students to remove the armbands (Tinker v. Des Moines Independent Community School District, 1969). In fact, an administrator told Christopher that he could get a "busted nose" for wearing the armband (Borkoski, 2013). The administrator also tried to get Christopher to remove his armband by telling him that "[n]o college would accept a protestor" (Borkoski, p. 1). Christopher felt intimidated and cried as a result of the administrator's comments but refused to remove his armband. School officials contacted his mother to implore her to urge Christopher to remove his armband (Borkoski, 2013). Instead, she told them that he had a constitutional right to wear the armband. Christopher recalled years later that his girlfriend broke off their relationship because he wore the armband to school and she told him he was no longer welcome at her house (Moss, 2011).

Mary Beth, Christopher and John did not interrupt any class at their schools (Tinker v. Des Moines Independent Community School District, 1969). According to John, "only the students sitting near me in class could see that I had the armband on. The teachers apparently did not notice it. Or, if they did, they did not make an issue of it" initially (p. 1421). John's armband was not discovered until he was changing for gym class as his armband was "camouflaged" (Borkoski, p. 1). One of the football players defended him after some students expressed opposition to his armband (Borkoski, 2013). Upon noticing Mary Beth's armband, her math teacher sent her to the principal's office. While Mary Beth removed her armband at the principal's office, she was still suspended from school (Moss, 2011). After Christopher and John refused to remove their armbands, they were also suspended from school (Tinker v. Des Moines Independent Community School District, 1969). Additionally, John was prohibited from performing with the marching band (Borkoski, 2013). The parents of the three students filed suit against the school district, under the Free Speech Clause, seeking an injunction and nominal damages. When the students returned from their suspensions, they wore black clothing the rest of the school year in order to protest the decision of the school to censor their speech (Moss, 2011). Subsequent to the events at the school, some people threw red paint on the home of the Tinker family and Mary Beth got a death-threat phone call (Borkoski, 2013). Mary Beth recalled that her family received "threats on our lives and on our house. Someone called on Christmas eve and said that the house would be blown up by morning. Some other people threw red paint on our house and threatened to kill me" (Moss, p. 1416).

Analysis

The United States Supreme Court's decision in Tinker v. Des Moines Independent Community School District (1969) was laden with language firmly supportive of students' free speech rights. To this day, *Tinker* remains the only case, under the Free Speech Clause, in which students have been victorious in the United States Supreme Court. The Court began its decision in the case with a declaration that students and teachers have First Amendment rights "applied in light of the special characteristics of the school environment" (Tinker v. Des Moines Independent Community School District, p. 506). The Court, however, did not define what constitutes the special characteristics of the school, making it very difficult to fully delimit the scope of free speech rights at school. Had the Court identified some of the characteristics, scholars and the judiciary would be able to examine them in order to determine if those characteristics exclude off-campus speech from First Amendment; and if off-campus speech were determined to be protected under the First Amendment, the characteristics would have helped define the extent of the protection.

The Supreme Court did, however, make a seminal statement that has appeared in almost every case involving students' free speech rights since the *Tinker* case: "It can hardly be argued that either students or teachers shed their constitutional rights to freedom of speech or expression at the schoolhouse gate" (Tinker v. Des Moines Independent Community School District, 1969, p. 506). This statement implies that teachers and students bring free speech rights to the schoolhouse gate. Surely, in order to shed rights at the schoolhouse gate, students and teachers must have those rights outside the gate. Even though Justice Black disagreed with the Court's decision to give students free speech rights, his dissenting opinion in the case shed some light on what the Supreme Court meant in its use of the "schoolhouse gate" term. Specifically, Justice Black stated that he disagreed with the Court's view that the clear rule of law is that "students and teachers take with them into the schoolhouse gate constitutional rights to freedom of speech or expression" (p. 521). In other words, Justice Black interpreted the Court's intended meaning of the term "schoolhouse gate" as a recognition that students actually bring the constitutional rights to free speech with them to the schoolhouse gate; and that they can also take those rights into the schoolhouse gate. It is also worthy of note that the school district prominently titled the second section of its brief submitted to the Supreme Court as "Disturbances in Schools Are Not Properly Measured by Identical Standards Used to Measure Disturbances on the Streets, in Eating Houses or Bus Depots" (Moss, 2011, p. 1420).

Material and Substantial Disruption/Infringement of Rights

The Supreme Court was, in essence, well aware of the school district's arguments that separate standards should apply to students' free speech rights off-campus as opposed to on-campus. As indicated earlier, the Court did not dispute the fact that students have rights outside the schoolhouse gate. The failure of the Supreme Court to explicitly authorize school officials to censor students' off-campus speech as well as the "overall pro-students' rights tone of the decision" might be indicative of a *Tinker* Court unwilling to expand school powers over student speech beyond the schoolhouse gate (Tuneski, 2003, p. 161).

In the *Tinker* case, the Supreme Court noted that students must retain free speech rights within the schoolhouse gate so that they can begin to appreciate the importance of constitutional rights critical to citizenship (Tinker v. Des Moines Independent Community School District, 1969). A failure to recognize students' rights within the school might lead students to "discount important principles of our government as mere platitudes" (p. 508). The Court also appeared to limit its reasoning in the case to on-campus speech by its focus on the classroom when it stated that "[t]he classroom is peculiarly the marketplace of ideas" (p. 512). This focus on the classroom is not surprising, given that Christopher, John and Mary Beth wore their armbands in the classroom. However, the Court also stated that the principles it discussed in the case were "not confined to the supervised and ordained discussion which takes place in the classroom" (p. 512). Moreover, the rights of students "do not embrace merely the classroom hours" (p. 512). In its discussion of students' rights outside of the classroom, however, the Court only identified the playground, the cafeteria and other locations "on the campus during the authorized hours" (pp. 512-13).

Further complicating the question of whether the Supreme Court's reasoning in the *Tinker* case applies to off-campus speech is an observation by Justice Black in his dissenting opinion in the case. Justice Black reminded the Court that the petition for certiorari in the case raised *only one* question for the Court to address: "Whether the First and Fourteenth Amendments permit officials of state supported public schools to prohibit students from wearing symbols of political views within school premises where the symbols are not disruptive of school discipline or decorum" (Tinker v. Des Moines Independent Community School District, 1969, p. 515). The phrase "within school premises" clearly limits the question presented to the Court in the case to on-campus speech. As a result, it would appear that any reasoning of the Court beyond the scope of this question is mere dicta. In essence, it appears that, the campus-centric nature of the case might make it challenging to reliably extend the Supreme Court's reasoning in the *Tinker* case to off-campus speech. Furthermore, in Hazelwood v. Kuhlmeier (1988), the Supreme Court stated that the *Tinker* case applies to "educators' ability to silence a student's personal expression that happens to occur on the school premises" (p. 271). In other words, the *Hazelwood* Court interpreted *Tinker* as governing on-campus personal expressions of students.

The *Tinker* case revealed the boundaries of school authority over students. In his dissenting opinion in the case, Justice Harlan called for giving schools the "widest authority" to discipline students so as to ensure "discipline and good order" in the school (Tinker v. Des Moines Independent Community School District, 1969, p. 526). However, the majority of the Supreme Court Justices disagreed. The Court declared that "state-operated schools may not be enclaves of totalitarianism" (p. 511). Consequently, schools do not have "absolute authority over their students" (p. 511). Given that schools do not have absolute authority over students, they should not be able to exercise around-the-clock authority over students' speech. Indeed, the "vigilant protection of constitutional freedoms is nowhere more vital than in the community of American schools" (p. 512). The Court notably reaffirmed its ruling in West Virginia State Board of Education v. Barnette (1943) recognizing students as persons under the United States Constitution, entitling them to constitutional protection. The Court stated that "[s]tudents in school as well as out of school are 'persons' under our Constitution. They are possessed of fundamental rights which the State must respect" (Tinker v. Des Moines Independent Community School District, p. 511). In other words, students have constitutional rights on-campus as well as outside the campus. Additionally, it is unconstitutional for schools to force students to only hear or communicate school-approved ideas or sentiments. The notion that schools can attempt to create a "homogenous people" has been repudiated (p. 511).

In delineating the boundaries of school-censorship authority over students, the Supreme Court stated that the right to free speech would not be a genuine right "if the right could be exercised only in an area that a benevolent government has provided as a safe haven for crackpots" (Tinker v. Des Moines Independent Community School District, 1969, p. 513). This means that the government is not empowered to restrict freedom of speech to areas the government chooses as the only avenues for free speech. Schools, therefore, cannot restrict students' right to free speech to a safe haven for crackpots. Expanding on the constitutional limits on the government's power to restrict speech to only specified locales, the Court pointed out that free speech rights are not confined to "a telephone booth or the four corners of a pamphlet, or to supervised and ordained discussion in a school classroom" (p. 513).

Further, as long as a school cannot specifically demonstrate that it has sound constitutional reasons for censoring student speech, students retain the right to express their personal views (Tinker v. Des Moines Independent Community School District, 1969). What is unclear from the case is whether there is any constitutionally-sound reason to censor off-campus student speech, particularly since Tinker v. Des Moines Independent Community School District (1969) arose in the context of on-campus student speech. As the pioneer case on students' free speech rights under the Free Speech Clause, the case could enlighten scholars and schools about the scope of schools' authority over student speech, despite its on-campus origin. As Justice Black noted in his dissent, the case introduced "an entirely new era" with respect to the judicial view of schools' "power to control pupils" (p. 515). In Tinker v. Des Moines Independent Community School District, the Supreme Court effectively repudiated the idea that schools have unlimited power under the United States Constitution to censor student speech (Caplan, 2003).

For the first time, the Supreme Court set forth tests for determining if schools can censor student speech. First, school officials can censor student speech that has or would "materially and substantially interfere with the requirements of appropriate discipline in the operation of the school" (Tinker v. Des Moines Independent Community School District, 1969, p. 509). This is the material and substantial disruption test. Second, student speech can be censored if the speech has or would "impinge upon the rights of other students" (p. 509). This is the infringement-of-rights test. According to Frederick (2007), when courts apply the material and substantial disruption test, they tend to overrule school censorship of students' speech. However, when courts use the infringement-of-rights test, they tend to authorize the censorship of students' speech. Each of these tests is discussed next.

Material and Substantial Disruption Test

The material and substantial disruption test was the only test the Supreme Court truly applied in the *Tinker* case. The Court found that the speech of Christopher, John and Mary Beth – wearing of the armbands – did not constitute "aggressive, disruptive action" (Tinker v. Des Moines Independent Community School District, 1969, p. 508). This is evident in the fact that Christopher, Mary Beth and John expressed their message silently and passively. Further, none of them materially and substantially disturbed the school or caused disorder. While it is acceptable under the United States Constitution for schools to censor speech that is materially and substantially disruptive, they cannot censor speech that merely disrupts the school. The Court concluded that "[t]here is here no evidence whatever of petitioners' [Christopher,

Material and Substantial Disruption/Infringement of Rights

Mary Beth and John] interference, actual or nascent, with the schools' work" (p. 508). If there was no evidence that Mary Beth, John and Christopher disrupted the school or caused disorder in class, there was a fortiori no evidence that they caused material and substantial disruption – the legal standard for the test of censorship. Any commotion that arose at the school could not be attributed to Mary Beth, John and Christopher. The absence of material and substantial disruption was also echoed in the fact that "there were no threats or acts of violence on school premises" (p. 508). This was language that further indicated that the Supreme Court might have limited its ruling in the *Tinker* case to on-campus speech.

As further evidence for its analysis of material and substantial disruption of the speech in the case, the Supreme Court compared the ratio of students who wore armbands to the number of students in the district (Tinker v. Des Moines Independent Community School District, 1969). Only about five (the other two were not involved in the lawsuit) of the 18,000 students in the Des Moines Independent Community School District wore the armbands. In other words, the number of speakers was too "few" (p. 508). The Court also examined whether the reactions of the other students to Christopher, Mary Beth and John caused material and substantial disruption. While some students directed "hostile" comments at Christopher, Mary Beth and John, those comments did not include any threats of violence or actual violence on the school's campus. Besides, the number of hostile remarks was insignificant as only "a few students made hostile remarks" (p. 508). Additionally, those remarks were made "outside the classroom" (p. 508). The characterization of the reaction to the speech as "outside the classroom" could be interpreted as a finding that reactions of others, outside the classroom, to the student-speaker's speech do not constitute material and substantial disruption. The decision to emphasize that the speech was "outside the classroom" also raises questions about how far outside the classroom the Court is willing to embrace here. If "outside the classroom" was intended as merely a reference to outside the physical classroom at a school, yet within the schoolhouse gate, this amplifies the view that the Supreme Court's decision in the *Tinker* case is limited to on-campus student speech. If, on the other hand, "outside the classroom" was intended to encompass any area beyond not just the physical classroom, but also beyond the schoolhouse gate, then there is room to interpret the *Tinker* case as covering off-campus student speech. After all, off-campus student speech is clearly speech outside the classroom. If, indeed, the Supreme Court decision in *Tinker* case applies to off-campus speech, then the off-campus reaction of others to the student-speaker's speech should not constitute material and substantial disruption.

The *Tinker* decision emphasized to schools that "undifferentiated fear or apprehension of disturbance" cannot constitute material and substantial disruption (Tinker v. Des Moines Independent Community School District, 1969, p. 508). The Supreme Court stated that fear can arise at a school when views contrary to those of the majority emerge. Further, a student's "departure from absolute regimentation may cause trouble" (p. 508). "Any word spoken, in class, in the lunchroom, or on the campus, that deviates from the views of another person may start an argument or cause a disturbance. But our Constitution says we must take this risk" (p. 508). The on-campus focus in this statement aligns with the on-campus context of the speech in the *Tinker* case. This further limits the opportunities from the case to successfully contend that, in *Tinker*, the Supreme Court left open the possibility of applying its rules in the case to off-campus speech.

However, the Court also stated that "conduct by the student, in class or out of it, which for any reason—whether it stems from time, place, or type of behavior—materially disrupts classwork or involves substantial disorder ... is, of course, not immunized by the constitutional guarantee of freedom of speech" (Tinker v. Des Moines Independent Community School District, 1969, p. 513). The Court's inclusion of the phrase about conduct outside the class left open the possibility that, through that phrase, the Court intended the material and substantial disruption test to apply off-campus; especially since off-campus speech is clearly out of the class. Tuneski (2003) views that phrase as the "only one phrase in the entire decision that could possibly suggest that the Court would consider applying the substantial disruption test to off-campus expressive activity" (p. 160). The Court's failure to expand on the meaning of the phrase "in class or out of it" equally left open the possibility that outside the classroom only referred to locations outside the class yet within the four walls of the school. In fact, if taken in context, the sentence is part of a paragraph explicating the need to protect student rights as opposed to restricting those rights (Tuneski, 2003). This protective focus, along with the schoolhouse gate statement by the Court discussed earlier, might indicate that the Supreme Court was not inclined to restrict students' off-campus speech in Tinker v. Des Moines Independent Community School District (1969), but rather to protect students' speech in all forums.

The Supreme Court stated that, while the right to dissenting views in a school is a "hazardous freedom" (Tinker v. Des Moines Independent Community School District, 1969, p. 508), it is part of living in America which is a "relatively permissive, often disputatious, society" (p. 509). This was an acknowledgment that schools are a microcosm of society where controversial views are commonplace. The Court stated that dissent actually strengthens our nation by fostering independence and independent thinking of Americans. The fear of difference must not drive censorship of student speech. The unsettling nature of speech is also inadequate justification for censorship. The Court warned schools that censorship of "a particular expression of opinion" must be justified by "something more than a mere desire to avoid the discomfort and unpleasantness that always accompany an unpopular viewpoint" (p. 509). In other words, viewpoint discrimination is unconstitutional unless the school can show that the particular viewpoint that it seeks to censor would materially and substantially disrupt the school. The Court found it disturbing that, in the case of Mary Beth, John and Christopher, school officials in the Des Moines Independent Community School District testified at trial that they passed the policy ban against armbands because they were uneasy with the principle of protesting the Vietnam War through armbands in the halls of the public school. In fact, the "action of the school authorities appears to have been based upon an urgent wish to avoid the controversy which might result from the expression, even by the silent symbol of armbands, of opposition to this Nation's part in the conflagration in Vietnam" (p. 510). It was constitutionally unacceptable that the school officials chose to discriminate against a particular controversial subject while students in the district were not censored for wearing political and other symbols, including the Iron Cross.

In any lawsuit challenging censorship of any student speech, including controversial speech, courts will examine the record to determine if schools have provided evidence that the student's speech actually led to material and substantial disruption at the school (Tinker v. Des Moines Independent Community School District, 1969). School officials do not need to wait till the disruption actually occurs, however, before censoring speech. Courts will also uphold censorship of speech if the record shows that school officials had reasonable grounds to forecast that the speech would cause material and substantial disruption to the school. In the case of Christopher, John and Mary Beth, the Supreme Court found that, not only was there no actual disruption, the school failed to provide evidence that it had reasonable grounds to forecast that their speech would lead to material and substantial disruption. For example, the Court pointed out that the school's official memorandum identifying the reasons for the armband policy failed to indicate any expectation of material and substantial disruption. The only evidence in the court record indicating that school officials feared disruption was in the following statements in the memorandum:

Material and Substantial Disruption/Infringement of Rights

1. "A former student of one of our high schools was killed in Viet Nam. Some of his friends are still in school and it was felt that if any kind of a demonstration existed, it might evolve into something which would be difficult to control" (Tinker v. Des Moines Independent Community School District, 1969, p. 509);
2. "Students at one of the high schools were heard to say they would wear arm bands of other colors if the black bands prevailed" (p. 509).

These statements, however, did not rise to the level of fear of material and substantial disruption.

Additionally, the fact that student speech distracts students from classwork and turns their focus to discussion of an emotionally-charged subject is not grounds for censorship unless there was actual or reasonable forecast of material and substantial disruption (see Justice Black's dissenting opinion, on pages 517-18 of Tinker v. Des Moines Independent Community School District, discussing actions the Court did not find materially and substantially disruptive). Justice Black argued to his Supreme Court colleagues that students would not be able to focus on their classwork if black armbands were "ostentatiously displayed in their presence to call attention to the wounded and dead of the war, some of the wounded and the dead being their friends and neighbors" (p. 524). The majority of the Court was not persuaded, however, that this was enough to constitute reasonable forecast of material and substantial disruption. Further, Justice Black argued that it was critical to censor students' speech because "groups of students all over the land are already running loose, conducting break-ins, sit-ins, lie-ins, and smash-ins" (p. 525). His colleagues were not responsive to this concern and his fears that abrogation of the ban on armbands would unleash more students to engage in similar acts. In essence, hysteria about ongoing events at other schools or general student misbehavior nationally is not an adequate ground for censoring students' speech unless the material and substantial disruption test is satisfied.

While there is no "precise test" for determining what constitutes material and substantial disruption (Erb, 2008, p. 266; Denning & Taylor, 2008), the following are some questions courts consider in analyzing whether school censorship satisfies the material and substantial disruption test:

1. Did a teacher or student have to be absent or take a leave from the school?;
2. What was the magnitude of the reaction of teachers and students to the speech?;
3. Did a teacher lose control of class as a result of the speech?;
4. Did the speech lead to cancellation of classes?; and
5. Did the school officials respond promptly to the speech or did they treat it as an incident that did not merit prompt attention? (Erb, 2008).

While schools do not need to show that total chaos occurred as a result of the speech, in order to justify censorship pursuant to the material and substantial disruption test, there must be "more than some mild distraction or curiosity created by the speech" (p. 266). Additionally, if the school has reasonable grounds to believe that "a particular type of student speech will lead to a decline in students' test scores, an upsurge in truancy, or other symptoms of a sick school—symptoms therefore of substantial disruption—the school can forbid the speech" (Nuxoll ex rel. Nuxoll v. Indian Prairie School District #204, 2008, p. 674). It is unclear, however, if disruption needs to be pervasive in order to constitute material and substantial disruption (Denning & Taylor, 2008). While some courts hold that material and substantial disruption can be "concentrated within a small group", others have found the effect of speech on a single person sufficient to constitute material and substantial disruption (Denning & Taylor, p. 844; see also Saxe v. State College Area School District, 2001, p. 217).

The failure of the United States Supreme Court to articulate a precise test for determining what constitutes material and substantial disruption makes it difficult to predict how a court will ultimately rule in a case; unless the case involves disruption that is so pervasive and clear that its nature is indisputable. The absence of a precise test also exposes the material and substantial disruption test to "potential malleability" at the discretion of a court, exposing speech to risk of increased censorship (Denning & Taylor, 2008, p. 844). As Denning and Taylor observed, "[h]ow much less protective is hard to know"; however, it should be cause for concern that "it is not entirely clear that there is any logical stopping point to this power" to apply the test without clearly-defined boundaries (p. 844). Some courts have, for instance, approved school censorship simply because a teacher decided not to teach after student speech that would be protected if the speaker had not been a student (Papandrea, 2008). Situations like this have led some scholars like Papandrea (2008) to express fear that courts will allow the "unreasonable reaction of teachers and school officials" to satisfy the material and substantial disruption test (p. 1067). Despite this concern, students can take some comfort in the fact that the *Tinker* case excluded more speech from the purview of school discipline than it authorized for inclusion. While schools had unlimited power to censor student speech prior to the *Tinker* case, the Supreme Court's imposition of the material and substantial disruption test, as well as the infringement-of-rights test (discussed next), effectively made all student speech protected under the First Amendment (unless the school can make a case for excluding specific speech based on either of these tests).

Infringement-of-Rights Test

In Tinker v. Des Moines Independent Community School District (1969), the Supreme Court described the infringement-of-rights test as an evaluation of whether student speech resulted in "collision with the rights of other students to be secure and to be let alone" (p. 508). However, the Court provided very limited insight into the test. In fact, the Court's application (if that) of the test in analysis of the speech of Christopher, Mary Beth and John was cursory. For example, the Court stated there was no evidence in the case to support a conclusion that "the school authorities had reason to anticipate that the wearing of the armbands would … impinge upon the rights of other students" (p. 509). Additionally, the Court stated that "[t]here is here no evidence whatever … of collision with the rights of other students to be secure and to be let alone" (p. 508). The Court's failure to develop the test might have been fueled by the school's failure to present vigorous evidence to make a case that the students' armbands infringed upon the rights of the other students at the school. Apparently, the Court was not convinced that the armbands infringed the rights of students, even though the school provided the Court with an official memorandum which explained that current students would be impacted by the speech because their friend – a former student of the school – was killed in Vietnam (Tinker v. Des Moines Independent Community School District, 1969, p. 509). The Court left no doubt that it was not applying the infringement-of-rights test when it stated that "this case does not concern speech or action that intrudes upon the work of the schools or the rights of other students" (p. 509).

The United States Supreme Court established in the *Tinker* case that school officials cannot discriminate against a viewpoint because of their "mere desire to avoid the discomfort and unpleasantness that always accompany an unpopular viewpoint" (Tinker v. Des Moines Independent Community School

Material and Substantial Disruption/Infringement of Rights

District, 1969, p. 509). An exception to this rule is if schools demonstrate that the viewpoint will infringe the rights of other students. The Supreme Court stated that student speech "in class or out of it, which for any reason—whether it stems from time, place, or type of behavior— … involves … invasion of the rights of others is, of course, not immunized by the constitutional guarantee of freedom of speech" (p. 513). As under the material and substantial disruption test, the phrase "in class or out of it" could equally suggest that the infringement-of-rights test applies on-campus as off-campus.

Since *Tinker*, the Supreme Court is yet to apply the infringement-of-rights test. For a long time, the lower courts also failed to apply the test. It is possible that the lower courts either did not recognize that, in the *Tinker* case, the Supreme Court created the infringement-of-rights test as a test for censorship of speech; or they simply did not know how to apply it. The lower courts might also have viewed the test as dicta since the Supreme Court did not entirely apply it to the facts of the *Tinker* case (Frederick, 2007). Indeed, only a few courts have applied the test since 1969 when the *Tinker* case was decided. Since the lower courts have not widely applied this test and the Supreme Court has failed to define the parameters of the test, there is very little insight available about the test. The United States Court of Appeals for the Third Circuit emphasized this point, stating that the "[t]he precise scope of *Tinker's* 'interference with the rights of others' language is unclear" (Saxe v. State College Area School District, 2001, p. 217; J.C. ex rel. R.C. v. Beverly Hills Unified School District, 2010). In this section of the book, we will provide some insight into the current understanding of the test. With the uncertainty and lack of clarity from the Supreme Court about the import of the test, we have to rely on the lower court interpretations of the test.

One of the first cases to acknowledge and use the infringement-of-rights test to decide censorship of student speech, since the test was introduced 36 years earlier, was Nixon v. Northern Local School District Board of Education (2005). In that case, seventh-grader James Nixon wore a t-shirt that he recently bought at a church camp meeting to Sheridan Middle School. Before he wore the t-shirt to school, his father told him that if the school tried to censor his speech, he did not have to comply with the censorship. The following message was printed on the front of the t-shirt:

INTOLERANT
Jesus said … I am the way, the truth and the life.
John 14:6 (p. 967).

The back of the t-shirt stated:

Homosexuality is a sin!
Islam is a lie!
Abortion is murder!
Some issues are just black and white! (p. 967).

Even though James did not disrupt the school with his t-shirt, school officials insisted that he turn the t-shirt inside out or remove it because the speech was not appropriate and offensive (Nixon v. Northern Local School District Board of Education, 2005). James informed the school officials that his parents authorized him to wear the t-shirt and that he did not believe the speech was inappropriate. He also refused to turn the t-shirt inside out or remove it. The school then made various other attempts to censor the speech. The assistant principal called James' father to request his intervention so as to stop James from wearing the t-shirt. After James' father refused to stop James, the assistant principal told him that he needed to pick his son up from school otherwise he would be assigned to an alternative school for the day. When James' father picked him up from school, the principal told him that James would be suspended from school if he wore the t-shirt to school again. The father demanded an explanation of the school's reasoning for characterizing James' message as offensive. When the father insisted on not leaving the school premises until an acceptable explanation was provided, the school called in the county sheriff's office. James and his parents then sued the school, under the First Amendment, seeking an injunction and nominal damages.

Prior to the censorship of James' speech, Sheridan Middle School officials had allowed some t-shirt messages and censored others (Nixon v. Northern Local School District Board of Education, 2005). For example, school officials did not censor a t-shirt message that featured President George W. Bush's picture with the phrases "International Terrorist" and "Which Side are You On?" imprinted on his forehead (p. 968). Other students' t-shirt messages that were not censored read: "For Good Luck Rub My Belly"; "The Dark Carnival Presents Insane Clown Posse" (p. 968). The school also did not censor James when he wore a t-shirt with the message "WWJD" (i.e. What Would Jesus Do?) (p. 968). On the other hand, the school censored t-shirt messages that featured a rebel flag, the Playboy Bunny logo and a message about Malcolm X that read, "You wear your X and I'll wear mine" (p. 968).

In the federal district court, school officials contended that James' t-shirt message violated the infringement-of-rights test (Nixon v. Northern Local School District Board of Education, 2005). The district court acknowledged that the test is a basis for censoring student speech: "It is true that, according to *Tinker*, schools can regulate speech that invades on the rights of others" (p. 974). As noted earlier, this test went mostly unacknowledged before this case. The court observed that school officials at Sheridan Middle School identified "no authority [legal precedent] interpreting what 'invasion on the rights of others' really entails" (p. 974). Besides, the court itself was "not aware of a single decision that has focused on that language in *Tinker* as the sole basis for upholding a school's regulation of student speech" (p. 974). The court's cursory interpretation of the infringement-of-rights test was that the test "entails invading on other students' rights to be secure and to be let alone" (p. 974). James' t-shirt did not violate the test because his speech was silent and it was passive. As passive silent speech, James' speech could not invade the right of other students to be left alone and to be secure. Furthermore, he did not actively try to force his speech on other students. While James rode the school bus, and in his classes, neither students nor teachers directed any negative comment at his t-shirt messages. Consequently, under the infringement-of-rights test, school officials were wrong to censor James' speech.

The United States Court of Appeals for the Ninth Circuit was the first federal court of appeals to apply the infringement-of-rights test (Frederick, 2007; Waldman, 2008; Harper v. Poway Unified School District, 2006). It was also the first court to approve school censorship of speech while using only the infringement-of-rights test for its analysis (Waldman, 2008). While the United States Supreme Court vacated the case as moot because the student (Tyler Harper) had graduated (Harper ex rel. Harper v. Poway Unified School District, 2007), the case is instructive on the infringement-of-rights test. In Harper v. Poway Unified School District (2006), the United States Court of Appeals for the Ninth Circuit had to decide if schools could constitutionally censor student t-shirt messages that disparage other students because of their sexual orientation. Prior to the specific speech incident in the case, there was a history of altercations related to anti-homosexual comments at Poway High School. Consequently, the school

Material and Substantial Disruption/Infringement of Rights

decided to allow the Gay–Straight Alliance student organization to hold a Day of Silence. The day was designed to promote tolerance of sexual-orientation differences (Harper v. Poway Unified School District, 2006). The day was also designed as an acknowledgment of, and response to, the silencing of homosexuals that occurs through bullying (Gay, Lesbian & Straight Education Network, 2013).

Some heterosexual students decided to hold Straight–Pride Day as their response to the Day of Silence (Harper v. Poway Unified School District, 2006). On that day, the students wore t-shirts with disparaging comments about homosexuals. School officials asked the students to remove the t-shirts and suspended those who refused to do so. One day after the following year's Day of Silence, Tyler Harper wore a t-shirt to school that stated in the front of the t-shirt: "BE ASHAMED, OUR SCHOOL EMBRACED WHAT GOD HAS CONDEMNED" (p. 1171). The back of the t-shirt stated: "HOMOSEXUALITY IS SHAMEFUL 'Romans 1:27.'" (p. 1171). Conscious of the school's prior history with altercations about anti-homosexual comments, school officials asked Tyler to remove his t-shirt because they believed it was inflammatory and would contribute to a hostile environment. Tyler refused to remove his t-shirt and declined the alternative proposals from the school officials for conveying his message. The principal consequently held Tyler in the school's front office the rest of the school day. He was not suspended from school, however, and no discipline was recorded in his file. Tyler challenged the school's censorship of his speech as violative of his right to free speech under the First Amendment.

In its review, the federal circuit court of appeals stated that Tyler's t-shirt "embodies the very sort of political speech that would be afforded First Amendment protection outside of the public school setting" (Harper v. Poway Unified School District, 2006, p. 1176). However, within the public school, those rights are more limited. The court acknowledged that the *Tinker* case had created the infringement-of-rights test as one of two tests for determining when schools can limit students' right to free speech. The court, however, disagreed with Tyler's contention that the infringement-of-rights test should be interpreted narrowly so as to only apply when a "student's right to be free from direct physical confrontation is infringed" (Harper v. Poway Unified School District, p. 1177). The test is not limited to situations where a student-speaker physically accosts other students such as when a student-speaker tries to forcefully pin buttons with his message on other students. Instead, speech that is vulgar, indecent, obscene, plainly offensive and lewd may infringe other students' rights without proof that the student-speaker directly accosted other students with the speech. The court ruled that another form of speech that could be censored under the infringement-of-rights test is speech that could lead to psychological harm. Recall that the Supreme Court stated in the *Tinker* case that the infringement-of-rights test entitles students to be secure (security) and left alone (privacy) from interference with their rights. According to the federal circuit court of appeals in Harper v. Poway Unified School District, this freedom to be secure and left alone includes freedom from physical confrontations. It also includes freedom from "psychological attacks that cause young people to question their self-worth and their rightful place in society" (p. 1178).

The federal circuit court of appeals concluded that Tyler's t-shirt infringed upon the rights of other students in the "most fundamental way" (Harper v. Poway Unified School District, 2006, p. 1177). The court reasoned that "students who may be injured by verbal assaults on the basis of a core identifying characteristic such as race, religion, or sexual orientation, have a right to be free from such attacks while on school campuses" (p. 1178). The court refused to address whether gender should be included as one of the core characteristics and it is unclear why gender was not included. In fact, the court excluded Whites and Christians from the infringement-of-rights test, stating that "any verbal assault targeting majorities that might justify some form of action by school officials is more likely to fall under the '[material and] substantial disruption' prong of *Tinker*" (p. 1183). Alternatively, the speech of students who are White or Christian will have to be evaluated under the test created in Bethel School District No. 403 v. Fraser (1986) – discussed in the next chapter of this book. The court explained that this was necessary because Whites and Christians have "always enjoyed a preferred social, economic and political status" (Harper v. Poway Unified School District, p. 1183). It cited no precedent justifying its decision to limit the infringement-of-rights test to students with religious, sexual orientation and racial minority status.

As for race, sexual orientation and religion, the court stated that speech attacking students who belong to historically-oppressed minority groups that have been treated as inferior, and faced physical and verbal abuse, is injurious, intimidating and damaging to the students (Harper v. Poway Unified School District, 2006). Such speech also hampers their education. While the court ruled that the gay and lesbian students at Poway High School did not need to present evidence that they actually suffered any of these verbal, physical or psychological injuries, it took judicial notice that these injuries were the likely consequences of the messages on Tyler's t-shirt. The court ruled that such injuries were "self-evident" (p. 1180). Therefore, it concluded that "the School had a valid and lawful basis for restricting Harper's wearing of his T-shirt on the ground that his conduct was injurious to gay and lesbian students and interfered with their right to learn" (p. 1178). Moreover, people's right to avoid unwanted communication should be most protected, particularly when they have no power to avoid the communication. This is the case in public schools where compulsory attendance laws require students to be in attendance. The court also reasoned that even though "name-calling is ordinarily protected outside the school context", while at school, students cannot use the First Amendment as a shield against punishment when they intimidate and abuse other students (p. 1180). In essence, the court seemed to limit the infringement-of-rights test to on-campus student speech.

Despite Judge Kozinski's criticism, in his dissent, that the court's ruling might empower schools to censor students' off-campus online criticism of the Day of Silence, it appears that the court's interpretation of the infringement-of-rights test as a test for on-campus speech effectively excludes the test from off-campus censorship reviews in the United States Court of Appeals for the Ninth Circuit (Harper v. Poway Unified School District, 2006). This has not stopped courts from applying the infringement-of-rights test in the context of off-campus speech, however (see e.g., J.C. ex rel. R.C. v. Beverly Hills Unified School District (2010) discussed later in this book). Further evidence that the United States Court of Appeals for the Ninth Circuit limited its interpretation of the infringement-of-rights test to on-campus speech is evident in the following language: "To say that homosexuality is shameful is to say, necessarily, that gays and lesbians are shameful. There are numerous locations and opportunities available to those who wish to advance such an argument. It is not necessary to do so by directly condemning, to their faces, young students trying to obtain a fair and full education in our public schools" (Harper v. Poway Unified School District, 2006, p. 1181). The court acknowledged the right of students off-campus, even under the infringement-of-rights test when it stated that it is important to ensure that "students have the opportunity to engage in full and open political expression, both in and out of the school environment" (p. 1182).

According to the United States Court of Appeals for the Ninth Circuit, a student t-shirt or other message that reads "Negroes: Go Back To Africa", or messages that refer to homosexual students as "shameful", black students as "inferior" or Jews as "doomed to Hell" could be censored under the infringement-of-rights test (Harper v. Poway Unified School District, 2006, pp. 1180, 1181). The court also stated that messages that condemn homosexuality are equivalent to condemnation of homosexuals. The infringement-of-rights test is not violated by student t-shirts or speeches with a political message

Material and Substantial Disruption/Infringement of Rights

such as "Young Democrats Suck", "Young Republicans Suck" or messages that "denigrate the President, his administration, or his policies, or otherwise invite political disagreement or debate, including debates over the war in Iraq" (p. 1182).

The federal circuit court of appeals emphasized that its approval of school censorship of student speech, under the infringement-of-rights test, was limited to "instances of derogatory and injurious remarks directed at students' minority status such as race, religion, and sexual orientation" (Harper v. Poway Unified School District, 2006, p. 1182). The court effectively ruled that all anti-homosexual speech, racist speech and speech disparaging a religious minority within a school can be censored (Frederick, 2007). Recall that the Supreme Court had ruled, in the *Tinker* case, that viewpoint discrimination was unconstitutional unless it satisfied either the material and substantial disruption test or the infringement-of-rights test (Tinker v. Des Moines Independent Community School District, 1969, p. 509). In singling out racist speech, anti-homosexual speech and speech disparaging a religious minority, the federal circuit court of appeals in *Harper* effectively endorsed viewpoint discrimination. The court essentially ruled that, as a matter of law, schools can engage in viewpoint discrimination on the subjects of religion, race and sexual orientation because disparaging speech on those subjects inherently infringes the rights of others. On the other hand, verbal bullying of White students, heterosexual students and Christian students could not be censored under the infringement-of-rights test. Such broad censorship would not, however, be allowed at the higher-education level because of the maturity of those students (Harper v. Poway Unified School District, 2006).

Judge Kozinski cautioned the court against a broad interpretation of the infringement-of-rights test (Harper v. Poway Unified School District, 2006). He opined that "[t]he 'rights of others' language in *Tinker* can only refer to traditional rights, such as those against assault, defamation, invasion of privacy, extortion and blackmail, whose interplay with the First Amendment is well established" (p. 1198). Without such a limitation, the infringement-of-rights test could be manipulated to give students the right not to hear speech that offends them. The court, however, dismissed the concern as ungrounded in the *Tinker* case because that case had no language listing any of those traditional rights (the court overlooked the fact that the endorsement of viewpoint discrimination based on race, religion and sexual orientation was not mentioned in the *Tinker* case either). Further, the federal district court of appeals rejected Judge Kozinski's concern because it found no legal basis to believe that the rights to be left alone and to be secure only encompass freedom from torts such as extortion, blackmail, defamation, invasion of privacy and assault. There was also no legal basis for Judge Kozinski to exclude "verbal assaults that cause psychological injury to young people" from the list of rights protected under the infringement-of-rights test (Harper v. Poway Unified School District, p. 1178).

In a very brief review of the infringement-of-rights test, the United States Court of Appeals for the Third Circuit mentioned that "at least one court has opined that it covers only independently tortious speech like libel, slander or intentional infliction of emotional distress" (Saxe v. State College Area School District, 2001, p. 217). That court also stated that schools must not be allowed to censor speech under the test simply because the speech is offensive. The United States Court of Appeals for the Eighth Circuit and a federal district court in Pennsylvania have also ruled that speech must be tortious before it can infringe the rights of other students (Kuhlmeier v. Hazelwood School District, 1986; Slotterback v. Interboro School District, 1991). Indeed, no other court has interpreted the infringement-of-rights test as expansively as the United States Court of Appeals for the Ninth Circuit did in Harper v. Poway Unified School District (2006) (Harvard Law Review Association, 2007). A federal district court in Massachusetts opined that Harper v. Poway Unified School District has no precedential value because the United States Supreme Court vacated the judgment, albeit for mootness rather than the expansive infringement-of-rights reasoning of the federal circuit court of appeals (Bowler v. Town of Hudson, 2007, p. 179). Further, the Harvard Law Review found that "the weight of legal authority counsels against the *Harper* majority's approach" (Harvard Law Review Association, p. 1694).

The United States Court of Appeals for the Seventh Circuit has also applied the infringement-of-rights test. In Nuxoll ex rel. Nuxoll v. Indian Prairie School District #204 (2008), the Gay-Straight Alliance student organization at Neuqua Valley High School held a Day of Silence to give a voice to harassment experienced by homosexuals and to foster tolerance. As support for the Day of Silence, various teachers and students wore t-shirts to school with messages that neither criticized heterosexuality nor advocated homosexuality. The t-shirts included messages such as: "Be Who You Are" (p. 670). A number of students who discommended homosexuality chose to hold a Day of Truth as a response to the Day of Silence. They urged participants in the Day of Truth to wear t-shirts with the following messages: "day of truth" and "The Truth cannot be silenced" (p. 670). One of the student-participants wore a t-shirt to school with the following message imprinted in the front "*My* Day of Silence, Straight Alliance" (p. 670). The back of the t-shirt read: "Be Happy, Not Gay" (p. 670).

When a school official noticed the t-shirt, the official inked out the words "Not Gay" (Nuxoll ex rel. Nuxoll v. Indian Prairie School District #204, 2008, p. 670). The school also banned t-shirts with the message "Be Happy, Not Gay" on the grounds that they violated a school rule prohibiting disparaging remarks about sexual orientation, race, gender, disability and religion. Additionally, the school stated that students of a particular sexual orientation, race, gender, disability or religion could make positive comments about their own group; however, they could not make a disparaging comment about students outside their own group. A student who participated in the Day of Truth sued the school, claiming that the school violated the students' right to free speech under the First Amendment. The student argued that he had a First Amendment right, on-campus and off-campus, to make "any negative comments he wants about the members of a listed group, including homosexuals" as long as his comments were not fighting words (fighting words are categorically excluded from First Amendment protection) (p. 671). The student conceded that he could not wear a t-shirt with the words "homosexuals go to Hell" to school because those would be fighting words (pp. 671, 674). Additionally, while the student could advocate heterosexuality, the school could censor him if he wore a t-shirt that read: "homophobes are closeted homosexuals" (p. 674).

The United States Court of Appeals for the Seventh Circuit ruled that while schools cannot educate students in an "intellectual bubble", they are not precluded from censoring student speech (Nuxoll ex rel. Nuxoll v. Indian Prairie School District #204, 2008, p. 671). They can constitutionally censor disparaging student speech on "unalterable or otherwise deeply rooted personal characteristics about which most people, including—perhaps especially including—adolescent schoolchildren, are highly sensitive" (p. 671). Additionally, remarks about sexual orientation, race, gender, disability and religion tend to impact a person at his very core because these characteristics are integral to the individual's identity. The court observed that "for most people these are major components of their personal identity—none more so than a sexual orientation that deviates from the norm" (p. 671). This is very similar to the view of the United States Court of Appeals for the Ninth Circuit in Harper v. Poway Unified School District (2006), discussed earlier. The one key difference between the approach of the United States Court of Appeals for the Seventh Circuit and that of the United States Court of Appeals for the Ninth Circuit is that the United States Court of Appeals for the Seventh Circuit included gender and disability as protected classes,

Material and Substantial Disruption/Infringement of Rights

The United States Court of Appeals for the Seventh Circuit explained that it was necessary to exclude disparaging speech about characteristics like sexual orientation from constitutional protection because such speech could negatively impact the education of students with those characteristics (Nuxoll ex rel. Nuxoll v. Indian Prairie School District #204, 2008). The speech could also "poison the school atmosphere" (p. 672). Moreover, the school is not a place for students to "practice attacking each other with wounding words" (p. 674). Nonetheless, in accord with the Supreme Court's ruling in the *Tinker* case, the court ruled that the mere offensiveness of speech is not a constitutional basis for censorship. Consequently, the mere fact that speech is offensive cannot satisfy the infringement-of-rights test. The court ruled that there is also no constitutional or other legal right to preclude others from criticizing one's "way of life" (p. 672). The school officials in the case failed to present evidence to the court showing that the "Be Happy, Not Gay" message would poison the school environment (p. 676). They did not show that the speech was not merely offensive. Moreover, since the student who filed the suit was not seeking to target or name specific individuals in his speech, he was not infringing the rights of others. Additionally, he was not seeking to defame a specific individual with his speech. The court indicated that if the student had sought to defame a specific individual, the school could censor the speech under the infringement-of-rights test. On the other hand, if his speech defamed a group, the speech could not be censored under the test.

The United States Court of Appeals for the Fourth Circuit is one of the other courts to acknowledge the existence of an infringement-of-rights test. The court described the test as a standard intended to ensure that student speech does not "collide with other students' rights 'to be secure and to be let alone'" (Kowalski v. Berkeley County Schools, 2011, p. 572). The court, however, did not further develop the test. Recently, the United States Court of Appeals for the Ninth Circuit pointed out that, as of 2013, only a few circuit courts of appeals had applied the infringement-of-rights test (Wynar v. Douglas County School District, 2013). The federal circuit court of appeals also observed that, even Justice Alito of the United States Supreme Court once stated (while he was a federal circuit court of appeals judge) that the infringement-of-rights test was not clear.

While the United States Court of Appeals for the Ninth Circuit agrees with the United States Court of Appeals for the Third Circuit that the infringement-of-rights test must not be used to censor speech simply because it is offensive, the court refused to "elaborate on when offensive speech crosses the line" (Wynar v. Douglas County School District, 2013, p. 1072). However, the court did state that student speech which threatens a school shooting can be censored as an infringement of the rights of other students. Additionally, a federal district court in Oregon has ruled that student harassment of other students just off the school's premises on the routes students take to and from school can be censored under the infringement-of-rights test (C.R. ex rel. Rainville v. Eugene School District 4J, 2013). This court also ruled that, under the test, a school might be able to censor speech that is indecent, vulgar, lewd, obscene or plainly offensive even when a student-speaker has not directly confronted specific students with speech.

Since the United States Supreme Court has not used the infringement-of-rights test since it was introduced in Tinker v. Des Moines Independent Community School District (1969), the Court needs to expressly affirm that the infringement-of-rights test remains a valid test for analyzing the authority of schools to censor student speech. This will help clear up the uncertainty in the lower court about how to interpret the test. In 1986 as well as 1988, the Supreme Court quoted the infringement-of-rights test but only as part of quoting the same sentence that introduced the material and substantial disruption test (Bethel School District No. 403 v. Fraser, 1986; Hazelwood v. Kuhlmeier, 1988). However, in 2007, in identifying the test created in Tinker v. Des Moines Independent Community School District, the

Supreme Court left out the infringement-of-rights language when quoting that same sentence (Morse v. Frederick, 2007, p. 403). In Morse v. Frederick, Justice Alito authored a concurring opinion (joined by Justice Kennedy) that similarly failed to mention the infringement-of-rights test. Likewise, Justice Breyer authored an opinion in which he omitted the infringement-of-rights language when discussing the test created in Tinker v. Des Moines Independent Community School District. Justice Stevens' dissenting opinion (joined by Justice Ginsburg and Justice Souter) referenced, without elaboration, the infringement-of-rights language when identifying the test that emerged from the *Tinker* case but only as part of the sentence that also quotes the material and substantial disruption test. Indeed, the material and substantial disruption test was the only test the *Morse* case consistently identified as the test created in the *Tinker* case.

In 1988, in Hazelwood v. Kuhlmeier, the Supreme Court acknowledged that a lower court had used the infringement-of-rights test but the Court decided not to clarify the test: "We therefore need not decide whether the Court of Appeals correctly construed *Tinker* as precluding school officials from censoring student speech to avoid 'invasion of the rights of others,' except where that speech could result in tort liability to the school" (Hazelwood v. Kuhlmeier, pp. 273). In the same case, Supreme Court Justice Brennan mentioned, in his dissenting opinion that the *Tinker* case created the infringement-of-rights test. He also opined that the rights covered under this test must be restricted to rights that are "protected by law" such as tortious or criminal rights (Hazelwood v. Kuhlmeier, p. 289). He reasoned that "[a]ny yardstick less exacting than [that] could result in school officials curtailing speech at the slightest fear of disturbance" (p. 289). Given the context of the statement about protection of the law, it appears that Justice Brennan was referring to the traditional torts, identified earlier herein, but this is not definitive. The Supreme Court needs to clarify which rights are covered by the infringement-of-rights test. The Court needs to rule on whether only traditional torts such as assault, extortion, defamation, invasion of privacy and blackmail are covered by the test. Otherwise the lower courts and schools will be uncertain about the valid scope of students' free speech rights under the test (Denning & Taylor, 2008).

The language of the infringement-of-rights test as well as that of the material and substantial disruption test focuses on the impact of the speech as opposed to the mode or location of the speech (Wheeler II, 2004). Consequently, an argument could be made that the applicability of both tests is not limited to a location (on-campus or off-campus) or the communication mode (internet or face-to-face). This implies that "[w]hether a student writes 'I am against the Vietnam War,' shouts it as a slogan at a protest, wears a black armband, or posts a Web site, the message remains the same and is either protected or not based on content, not mode of communication" (p. 27). Until the United States Supreme Court clarifies this, however, scholars, attorneys, schools and the judiciary can only speculate about the reach of the tests. The malleability of the infringement-of-rights test coupled with its current vacuousness and the uncertainty of the test could threaten students' free exchange of ideas while they are off-campus.

CONCLUSION

In this chapter, we analyzed the United States Supreme Court's landmark student-speech decision – Tinker v. Des Moines Independent Community School District (1969). We analyzed the Supreme Court's reasoning in the case to determine whether the Court gave any indication that students retain their free speech rights against school censorship while off-campus. Our analysis revealed that there is some language in the case that proponents and opponents of off-campus censorship can rely on to strengthen their divergent positions. We also noted that the *Tinker* Court created two tests for analyzing the constitutionality of school censorship of student speech: the material and substantial disruption test; and the infringement-of-rights test. While the material and substantial disruption test is widely applied in censorship of student speech, it remains a malleable test. Further, the scope of the infringement-of-rights test remains nebulous and often unknown. In order to avoid an erosion of students' speech rights under either test, the United States Supreme Court needs to speak clearly on their applicability or non-applicability to off-campus student speech.

REFERENCES

Bethel School District No. 403 v. Fraser (1986). 478 U.S. 675

Borkoski, K. (2013). Tinker v. Des Moines Independent Community School District: Kelly Shackelford on symbolic speech. *SCOTUSblog*. Retrieved December 22, 2013, from http://www.scotusblog.com/2013/11/tinker-v-des-moines-independent-community-school-district-kelly-shackelford-on-symbolic-speech/

Caplan, A. H. (2003). Public school discipline for creating uncensored anonymous internet forums. *Willamette Law Review*, *39*, 93–194.

C.R. ex rel. Rainville v. Eugene School District 4J (2013). 2013 WL 5102848.

Denning, B. P., & Taylor, M. C. (2008). Morse v. Frederick and the regulation of student cyberspeech. *Hastings Constitutional Law Quarterly*, *35*, 835–896.

Erb, T. D. (2008). A case for strengthening school district jurisdiction to punish off-campus incidents of cyberbullying. *Arizona State Law Journal*, *40*, 257–287.

Frederick, D. D. (2007). Restricting student speech that invades others' rights: A novel interpretation of student speech jurisprudence in Harper v. Poway Unified School District. *University of Hawaii Law Review*, *29*, 479-500.

Gay, Lesbian & Straight Education Network (2013). Info + Resources. *Glsen Day of Silence*. Retrieved December 27, 2013, from http://www.dayofsilence.org/resources/

Harpaz, L. (2000). Internet speech and the First Amendment rights of public school students. *Brigham Young University Education and Law Journal*, *123*, 142–143.

Harper ex rel. Harper v. Poway Unified School District (2007). 549 U.S. 1262.

Harper v. Poway Unified School District (2006). 445 F.3d 1166 (vacated by Harper ex rel. Harper v. Poway Unified School District (2007), 549 U.S. 1262 and dismissed as moot in Harper ex rel. Harper v. Poway Unified School District (2007), 485 F.3d 1052).

Harvard Law Review Association. (2007). Recent Cases: Constitutional Law—Freedom of Speech—Ninth Circuit Upholds Public School's Prohibition of Anti-Gay T-Shirts – Harper v. Poway Unified School District. *Harvard Law Review*, *120*(1691), 1694-95.

Hazelwood v. Kuhlmeier (1988). 484 U.S. 260, 265-66, 271-73, 289.

J.C. ex rel. R.C. v. Beverly Hills Unified School District (2010). 711 F.Supp.2d 1094, 1108.

Kowalski v. Berkeley County Schools (2011). 652 F.3d 565.

Kuhlmeier v. Hazelwood School District (1986). 795 F.2d 1368.

Morse v. Frederick (2007). 551 U.S. 393.

Moss, S. A. (2011). The overhyped path from Tinker to Morse: How the student speech cases show the limits of Supreme Court decisions–for the law and for the litigants. *Florida Law Review*, *63*, 1407–1457.

Nixon v. Northern Local School District Board of Education (2005). 383 F.Supp.2d 965.

Nuxoll ex rel. Nuxoll v. Indian Prairie School District #204 (2008). 523 F.3d 668.

Papandrea, M. (2008). Student speech rights in the digital age. *Florida Law Review*, *60*, 1027–1102.

Roberts, C. E. (2008). Is Myspace their space?: Protecting student cyberspeech in a post-Morse v. Frederick world. *UMKC Law Review*, *76*, 1177–1192.

Saxe v. State College Area School District (2001). 240 F.3d 200, 217.

Slotterback v. Interboro School District (1991). 766 F.Supp. 280, 289.

Tinker v. Des Moines Independent Community School District (1969). 393 U.S. 503.

Tuneski. (2003). Online, not on grounds: Protecting student internet speech. *Virginia Law Review*, *89*, 139-87.

Waldman, E. G. (2008). A Post–Morse Framework for Students' Potentially Hurtful Speech (Religious and Otherwise). *Journal of Law and Education*, *37*, 463–503.

West Virginia State Board of Education v. Barnette (1943). 319 U.S. 624.

Wheeler, T. E. II. (2004). Slamming in cyberspace: The boundaries of student First Amendment rights. *Res Gestae*, *47*, 24–32.

Wynar v. Douglas County School District (2013). 728 F.3d 1062, 1071-72.

KEY TERMS AND DEFINITIONS

Dicta: A statement made within a judicial opinion that was not central to the determination of the legal issue(s) under consideration in the case. Due to its incidental nature, such a statement has only persuasive rather than binding precedential value.

First Amendment: This is the first right listed within the bill of rights added to the United States Constitution in 1791 to guarantee Americans certain rights free from government infringement. It covers the right to free speech, the right to free exercise of religion, right against government establishment of religion, the right to a free press, the right to peaceable assembly and the right to petition for redress of grievances.

Infringement-of-Rights Test: The judicial standard that conditions censorship of student speech on whether the speech impinges the rights of other students.

Material and Substantial Disruption Test: The judicial standard that conditions censorship of student speech on whether the speech is reasonably foreseeable to cause or actually caused material and substantial disruption to the school.

Off-Campus Student Speech: Student speech that occurs in any locale outside the borders or premises of a school and outside school hours. It includes student speech away from the school bus and school-sponsored events such as school trips.

On-Campus Student Speech: Student speech that occurs in any area inside the school or on school premises. It includes speech on the school bus or at school-sponsored events.

Schoolhouse Gate: The terminology that the United States Supreme Court introduced in Tinker v. Des Moines Independent Community School District (1969) as the borderline separating a school and its premises from locales outside the school.

Tinker **Tests:** The two tests – the material and substantial disruption test and the infringement-of-rights test – created in Tinker v. Des Moines Independent Community School District (1969) for reviewing the constitutionality of school censorship of student speech.

Chapter 8
Lewd, Vulgar, Plainly-Offensive, and Obscene Speech

ABSTRACT

This chapter focuses on the Bethel School District No. 403 v. Fraser (1986) case – the United States Supreme Court's second review of students' speech rights under the Free Speech Clause of the First Amendment. It discusses the test created in the case for determining when schools can regulate students' speech. This test, referred to as the Bethel test or the Fraser test authorizes schools to censor students' speech if the speech is vulgar, lewd, plainly offensive or obscene. The chapter also discusses the Supreme Court's decision on the scope of students' free speech rights. The ultimate goal of the chapter is to analyze the Bethel School District No. 403 v. Fraser case in order to determine if it empowers schools to censor off-campus student speech.

INTRODUCTION

This chapter examines the United States Supreme Court's decision in Bethel School District No. 403 v. Fraser (1986). This case is important in student-speech jurisprudence as it retreated from the expansive recognition of students' right to free speech in Tinker v. Des Moines Independent Community School District (1969). The Court removed an entire category of student speech from First Amendment protection. The chapter discusses the new test for student-speech censorship created in the case. This test authorizes schools to censor student speech that is vulgar, lewd, obscene or plainly offensive. As discussed in chapter five, obscenity is unprotected speech. Given that the Supreme Court had already created a test for obscenity many years before Bethel School District No. 403 v. Fraser (1986), this chapter per the authors examines the Court's decision to specifically identify obscenity as unprotected student speech in the *Bethel* case. The chapter discusses what this seemingly redundant decision to exclude obscene student speech from First Amendment protection could mean for students' right to free speech. While the Supreme Court did not define the terms "vulgar, lewd, plainly offensive or obscene" the chapter per the authors analyzes the case to determine keys for assessing whether student speech qualifies as one of those terms. The chapter also analyzes the Court's reasoning in the case in order to determine whether,

DOI: 10.4018/978-1-4666-9519-1.ch008

Lewd, Vulgar, Plainly-Offensive, and Obscene Speech

in Bethel School District No. 403 v. Fraser, the Supreme Court intended to empower schools to censor students' off-campus speech that is vulgar, lewd or plainly offensive; and whether schools are authorized to censor off-campus student speech that is obscene according to the *Bethel* case but not obscene under the traditional-obscenity jurisprudence.

MAIN FOCUS OF THE CHAPTER

After Tinker v. Des Moines Independent Community School District in 1969, the United States Supreme Court was silent on students' First Amendment right to free speech for almost two decades. Finally, in 1986, in Bethel School District No. 403 v. Fraser, the Court revisited the scope of school authority to censor students' speech under the Free Speech Clause. In this case, the Supreme Court created another test for determining whether schools can constitutionally censor student speech: if the speech is vulgar, lewd, plainly offensive or obscene, it can be constitutionally censored. The Court, however, failed to define these terms, appearing to leave them to common understanding. Unlike the expansive approach to student speech in Tinker v. Des Moines Independent Community School District (1969), the Bethel School District No. 403 v. Fraser (1986) case constricted students' free speech rights as it carved out an entire category of speech for school censorship. While the case involved on-campus student speech, it sheds some light on the Court's thinking about off-campus student speech. However, as the Supreme Court stated in 2007, the "mode of analysis employed in *Fraser* [*Bethel* case] is not entirely clear" (Morse v. Frederick, 2007, p. 404). We examine the *Bethel* case as well as the test created in the case in order to determine what guidance we can glean therein about the rights of students to speak off-campus.

The Speech Incident

In 1983, Bethel High School in Washington conducted an assembly to teach students about self-government (Bethel School District No. 403 v. Fraser, 1986). One of the students, Matthew Fraser, spoke at the assembly in support of his friend and schoolmate's candidacy for a student government position. Matthew delivered his speech despite warnings from his teachers not to deliver the speech. The teachers had told him that the speech was not appropriate and that he could face serious repercussions for the speech. The school also had a policy that was based on the material and substantial disruption test created in Tinker v. Des Moines Independent Community School District (1969). This policy stated that "[c]onduct which materially and substantially interferes with the educational process is prohibited, including the use of obscene, profane language or gestures" (Bethel School District No. 403 v. Fraser, p. 678). The case arose during a period of increased sexual programming on television that was opposed by many parents and politicians (Moss, 2011).

In the speech, laden with double entendre, Matthew stated:

'I know a man who is firm—he's firm in his pants, he's firm in his shirt, his character is firm—but most ... of all, his belief in you, the students of Bethel, is firm.

'Jeff Kuhlman is a man who takes his point and pounds it in. If necessary, he'll take an issue and nail it to the wall. He doesn't attack things in spurts—he drives hard, pushing and pushing until finally—he succeeds.

'Jeff is a man who will go to the very end—even the climax, for each and every one of you.

'So vote for Jeff for A.S.B. vice-president—he'll never come between you and the best our high school can be.' (Bethel School District No. 403 v. Fraser, 1986, p. 687).

The mandatory assembly was attended by about 600 students, a good portion of which were 14-year olds (Bethel School District No. 403 v. Fraser, 1986). As Matthew spoke, three students used graphic gestures to simulate the sexual references in his speech, while others "hooted and yelled" (pp. 678, 694). The speech seemed to leave some students feeling embarrassed and perplexed. A teacher subsequently had to devote part of her class to discussions with her students about the speech. The school counselor testified, however, that the general reaction of students at the assembly "was not atypical to a high school auditorium assembly" (p. 694). In a meeting with the assistant principal after the speech, Matthew acknowledged that he intentionally used the sexual references in his speech. Pursuant to the school policy noted earlier, the assistant principal suspended Matthew from school for three days. He was allowed to return to school after two days. As further punishment for the speech, the school withdrew Matthew's name from consideration for graduation speaker. Nonetheless, his peers voted him as the graduation speaker through a write-in campaign. Matthew and his father filed suit against the school for monetary damages and an injunction. They claimed that the school censored Matthew in violation of his First Amendment right to free speech (Bethel School District No. 403 v. Fraser, 1986). In an interview almost two decades after his speech, Matthew insisted that, while he expected his speech to inspire some form of reaction from his schoolmates, he did not expect to be punished for the speech which he wrote just an hour prior to the assembly (Hudson, 2001).

Analysis

In Bethel School District No. 403 v. Fraser (1986), the United States Supreme Court reaffirmed its ruling in Tinker v. Des Moines Independent Community School District (1969) that students do not shed their constitutional rights at the schoolhouse gate. However, the Court took a constrictive view of students' First Amendment right to free speech, in contrast to the expansive view it took in the *Tinker* case (discussed in chapter seven of this book). The Court explained this difference in approach as a distinction based on the nature of the speech: in Tinker v. Des Moines Independent Community School District, the student speech was political speech while in Bethel School District No. 403 v. Fraser, the speech was sexual. It also appeared significant that the speech in the *Tinker* case was personal speech while the speech in the *Bethel* case was at an official school assembly. Further, the Court seemed quite uncomfortable with Matthew's speech to the point that it referred to him as a "confused boy" (Bethel School District No. 403 v. Fraser, p. 683), even though, as Justice Stevens observed in his dissent, Matthew was "an outstanding young man with a fine academic record" who was elected the graduation speaker by his peers (p. 692).

The Supreme Court characterized Matthew's speech as obscene, indecent, plainly offensive, vulgar and lewd without providing a legal foundation for this conclusion (Bethel School District No. 403 v. Fraser, 1986). This might be due to the Court's reliance on the commonly-understood meanings of those words. That would appear to be the case even more so because the Court failed to conduct the

Lewd, Vulgar, Plainly-Offensive, and Obscene Speech

traditional-obscenity test (discussed in chapter five of this book) before characterizing Matthew's speech as obscene. It might also be an indication that a different level of analysis applies to obscenity off-campus than on-campus. Recall that in Miller v. California (1973), the Supreme Court created the *Miller* test – a three-part test. Under this test, courts inquire:

1. "Whether the average person, applying contemporary community standards, would find that the work, taken as a whole, appeals to the prurient interest";
2. "Whether the work depicts or describes, in a patently offensive way, sexual conduct specifically defined by the applicable state law"; and
3. "Whether the work, taken as a whole, lacks serious literary, artistic, political, or scientific value" (p. 24).

In that case, the Court indicated that the *Miller* test applies to visual as well as non-visual descriptions of sexual conduct. We also know that the *Miller* test is the standard for all determinations of obscenity and that the Court has never specifically limited the test to any particular forum. Moreover, since the *Miller* test – created in 1973 – preceded Bethel School District No. 403 v. Fraser (1986), the Supreme Court was clearly aware of the test at the time it characterized Matthew's speech as obscene. The Supreme Court's failure to even acknowledge the *Miller* test in the *Bethel* case might be indicative of an expectation that this test should not apply within the school setting.

Evidence that the Supreme Court's use of the term "obscenity" in the *Bethel* case might not be the same term used in traditional-obscenity jurisprudence can be found in Justice Brennan's concurring opinion in the case. While his concurring opinion does not carry the weight of a majority opinion, Justice Brennan obviously participated in the Supreme Court deliberations in the case; therefore, he was aware of the Justices' thinking about the term "obscenity." In light of this, Justice Brennan indicated that Matthew's speech did not qualify as obscene speech under the traditional-obscenity jurisprudence which applies to all Americans (Bethel School District No. 403 v. Fraser, 1986). He stated that Matthew's speech was "far removed from the very narrow class of 'obscene' speech which the Court has held is not protected by the First Amendment" (p. 688). This was an acknowledgment that a different standard for obscenity applies to off-campus student speech than on-campus student speech.

Justice Brennan also cautioned us against interpreting the Supreme Court's repeated use of the term "obscene" in its characterization of Matthew's speech as equivalent to the traditional legal understanding of the term (Bethel School District No. 403 v. Fraser, 1986). Even though Justice Brennan did not mention the *Miller* test, the traditional legal understanding of obscenity is the *Miller* test which applies regardless of forum, off-campus and on-campus. Since the *Miller* test excludes the off-campus obscene speech of students as well as all obscene speech of adults from First Amendment protection, the Supreme Court would be denying students even more free speech rights if a lower standard than the *Miller* test were allowed for censorship of their off-campus speech. It would also be a duplication of the jurisprudence on obscenity because two standards would be applicable to off-campus speech – the *Miller* test and the *Bethel* test. It is more logical to assume that the Court intended the *Miller* test to remain off-campus but also apply on-campus as it already did. However, the Court wanted to give schools authority to censor speech on school grounds that did not meet the *Miller* test. Accordingly, the obscenity that the *Bethel* test empowered schools to censor would be on-campus speech. The on-campus context of the *Bethel* case might further limit or preclude the applicability of the rules in the case to off-campus student speech.

There was a strong on-campus undertone in the *Bethel* case. Even though Justice Brennan agreed with the Court's limitation of students' rights to obscene, vulgar, lewd, or plainly-offensive speech while they on-campus, he did not exclude such speech from all on-campus locations (Bethel School District No. 403 v. Fraser, 1986). For instance, he opined that Matthew's speech might be entitled to First Amendment protection on one condition upon which he did not elaborate: "where the school's legitimate interests in teaching and maintaining civil public discourse were less weighty" (p. 689). Justice Stevens agreed, noting that in places such as the school hallway as well as the locker room, Matthew's speech was "rather routine comment" (p. 696). He pointed out that the key is for students to keep the pig in the barnyard rather than the parlor. In other words, while vulgar, lewd and plainly-offensive speech might be acceptable in the locker room, it would not be appropriate in a classroom. Similarly, as long as the "pig-speech" remains off-campus rather than on-campus, schools must be required to respect it as constitutionally-protected speech. The exception would be for school-sponsored events that take place off-campus where the pig must remain in the barnyard (Tuneski, 2003).

In the case of sexual speech, traditional-obscenity law could be implicated as discussed earlier. Where traditional-obscenity law is applicable, speech determined obscene is unprotected for both adults and students alike (Roth v. United States, 1957; Jacobellis v. Ohio, 1964; Ginsberg v. New York, 1968; Stanley v. Georgia, 1969; Miller v. California, 1973; Oluwole, Green & Stackpole, 2013). The Supreme Court affirmed this in Bethel School District No. 403 v. Fraser (1986). When children are in the audience, even adults do not have the absolute right to free speech that they are otherwise entitled to. This limitation on adults and students applies in all forums. The Supreme Court has identified sexual speech as an area for judicial sensitivity to ensure that students, particularly in a "captive audience" do not read or see sexually-explicit speech (p. 684). In fact, the authority of schools to censor sexually-explicit speech is so expansive that it allows them to prohibit and purge books with such content from the school library (Board of Education v. Pico, 1982; Bethel School District No. 403 v. Fraser, 1986). In order to censor the off-campus sexual speech of students as vulgar, lewd or plainly-offensive speech, however, courts must rely on the *Miller* test for obscenity. Otherwise, they leave no refuge for students to express political or other views in constitutionally-protected vulgar, plainly offensive or lewd terms as adults can.

As noted earlier, the *Miller* test is designed to ensure that only speech that legally qualifies as obscene is censored, protecting a wide breadth of speech. The potentially corrupting nature of sexually-explicit speech that precludes giving adults absolute constitutional protection for such speech should similarly support denying students the right to sexually-explicit speech before a captive audience of other students. While such speech might fall short of the obscenity standard under the *Miller* test, the vulnerability of students to sexually-explicit content is reason to allow schools to censor such speech on-campus as well as off-campus. It is unclear, however, that Matthew's speech in the *Bethel* case constituted sexually-explicit speech as opposed to double entendre; particularly since the speech could have a valid non-sexual purpose and meaning for a poetry class or an English class on effective use of metaphors, for example. As a double-entendre speech, the speech clearly had two meanings to students in the audience. While some might have seen the sexual metaphors in the speech, others could just as likely viewed the speech as a motivational nomination speech for a friend's election for a student government office.

The speech certainly had the desired impact as Matthew's friend was elected with a strong majority of the votes (Moss, 2011). Only three of the 600 students at the assembly simulated the sexual undertones of the speech (Bethel School District No. 403 v. Fraser, 1986). The speech could be viewed as a passionate description of the attributes that would make his friend successful in the office. Justice Brennan observed that there was "no evidence in the record that any students, male or female, found the speech

Lewd, Vulgar, Plainly-Offensive, and Obscene Speech

'insulting'" (p. 689). In fact, students at the school responded to the school's censorship of Matthew by voting him the graduation speaker as a write-in candidate after the school removed him from the ballot. Further, Matthew's speech was in no way close to the level of vulgarity, lewdness or plainly-offensive speech that society has featured or accepted off-campus on the "bulk of programs currently appearing on prime time television or in the local cinema" such as programs on MTV (p. 689). In 2001, Fraser recalled that, in their efforts to censor him, the "school officials martyred me" among his peers (Hudson, 2001, p. 3). For example, the final student newspaper of the year "was like an ode to Matt Fraser" and football players created signs supporting him that read "Stand firm for Matt" (Hudson, 2001, p. 3). In essence, most of the student body supported the speech.

The Supreme Court chose to categorically exclude speech that is vulgar, lewd, plainly offensive or obscene from the right to free speech that students enjoy under the First Amendment (Bethel School District No. 403 v. Fraser, 1986). Consequently, the Court empowered schools to censor student speech as long as the speech is vulgar, lewd, plainly offensive or obscene. This is known as the *Bethel* test (or *Fraser* test) for school censorship of student speech. There is no need to show material and substantial disruption or infringement of the rights of others as the *Bethel* test is a separate test unrelated to the *Tinker* tests. The justification for the categorical exclusion was that schools are institutions designed to teach students "fundamental values", manners and habits that are critical to self-government and civility in a democratic society (p. 681). While these values include tolerance of opposing views, they also include sensitivity to the feelings of others, particularly other students at the school. These values also include an appreciation of appropriate social behavior. The Court stated that the "undoubted freedom to advocate unpopular and controversial views in schools and classrooms must be balanced against the society's countervailing interest in teaching students the boundaries of socially appropriate behavior (p. 681). Beyond the overall on-campus factual context of the case, the "in schools and classroom" focus of this justification for the categorical denial of First Amendment protection to vulgar, obscene, plainly-offensive or lewd student speech is further reason to believe that the Court limited the scope of its decision in the case to on-campus speech.

Additionally, while the Court acknowledged that students in schools do not have the same free speech rights as adults, it did not state anywhere in the case that students do not have the same free speech rights as adults when students are outside school. What the Court did state is that "simply because the use of an offensive form of expression may not be prohibited to adults making what the speaker considers a political point [does not mean] the same latitude must be permitted to children in a public school" (Bethel School District No. 403 v. Fraser, 1986, p. 682). The focus of this statement on the school setting amplifies the view that the *Bethel* test is limited to on-campus student speech. The Court's framing of the legal issue in the case further supports the view that the *Bethel* test was intended for on-campus speech as the issue focused on the on-campus forum for the speech: "we turn to consider the level of First Amendment protection accorded to Fraser's utterances and actions before an official high school assembly attended by 600 students" (p. 681). A second phrasing of the issue confirms this: "We granted certiorari to decide whether the First Amendment prevents a school district from disciplining a high school student for giving a lewd speech at a school assembly" (p. 677). The Court's holding in the case similarly highlights the on-campus nature of its decision: "high school assembly or classroom is no place for a sexually explicit monologue directed towards an unsuspecting audience of teenage students" (p. 685).

The *Bethel* Court noted that adults have a robust right to engage in speech (Bethel School District No. 403 v. Fraser, 1986). This right of adults includes the right to engage in vulgar speech which does not rise to the level of obscene speech under the *Miller* test, discussed earlier (Miller v. California, 1973).

It also includes the right to engage in speech that is "highly offensive to most citizens" (Bethel School District No. 403 v. Fraser, p. 682). Under the reasoning of the *Bethel* case, it appears that students would retain these same rights of adults while students are outside the schoolhouse gate. After all, the Supreme Court stated that the "constitutional rights of students in public school are not automatically coextensive with the rights of adults in other settings" (p. 683). In other words, while students are in the school, they do not automatically have the constitutional rights of adults. However, when students are not in the school setting and instead in the "other settings" (i.e. non-school settings) referred to in the statement, they should have the same rights as adults in those same settings. There is no language in Bethel School District No. 403 v. Fraser (1986) indicating otherwise.

It is fair to ask why the Supreme Court used the phrase "rights of adults in other settings" (Bethel School District No. 403 v. Fraser, 1986, p. 683) rather than using the phrase "rights of students/children in other settings." If indeed the Court believed students were already entitled to the rights of adults in off-campus settings, the Court would have simply stated that the rights of students on-campus are not automatically coextensive with the rights of students when they are outside the campus. Thus, one could reason from this that the Court implicitly acknowledged that the off-campus speech rights of students are not at the level granted to adults under the United States Constitution. While this might be true, it does not change the fact that the Supreme Court also stated that students do not shed their rights to free speech at the schoolhouse gate. In essence, students bring free speech rights to school but those rights are not wholly shed at the schoolhouse gate. This could mean that students do not shed, at the schoolhouse gate, the "rights of adults in other settings" that they bring with them to the schoolhouse gate. It therefore appears that the Court merely acknowledged the limitations on-campus without restricting in anyway the off-campus speech rights of students.

The on-campus nature of the Court's reasoning is further heightened by the following quote from the Court: "the First Amendment gives a high school student the *classroom* right to wear Tinker's armband, but not Cohen's jacket" (Bethel School District No. 403 v. Fraser, 1986, p. 682). In other words, students have a classroom right to wear the Tinker armband but they do not have a classroom right to wear Cohen's jacket. Cohen's jacket was a reference to the jacket Paul Cohen, an adult, wore through a courthouse in 1968 in protest of the draft and the Vietnam War (Cohen v. California, 1971). On the jacket was a message that read 'Fuck the Draft' (p. 16). Paul was arrested and convicted for offensive conduct. The Supreme Court reversed the conviction, reasoning that the government could not justify the censorship by "acting as guardians of public morality" (p. 22). The Court stated that the government cannot constitutionally "remove this offensive word from the public vocabulary" (p. 23).

In essence, what the Supreme Court was stating in the *Bethel* case through its reference to Cohen's jacket was that students do not have a right to wear the jacket while they are in school (Bethel School District No. 403 v. Fraser, 1986). The Court, however, did not prohibit students from wearing such a jacket in a non-school setting (It would have been absurd for the Court to tell students not to wear such a jacket off-campus). Further, the Court did not authorize schools to censor such student speech in off-campus settings. Thus, a school would not be able to constitutionally discipline a student for wearing Cohen's jacket to a courthouse like Paul Cohen did. The one area where the Court has limited the right of adults and students to wear Cohen's jacket is on the public airwaves. The First Amendment right of adults to engage in speech that, while vulgar, plainly offensive or lewd, does not satisfy the *Miller* test for obscenity excludes the right to such language over broadcast radio and television (Federal Communications Commission v. Pacifica Foundation, 1978). This rule applies to both students and adults in all forums; and the Supreme Court affirmed this in Bethel School District No. 403 v. Fraser (1986). The

Lewd, Vulgar, Plainly-Offensive, and Obscene Speech

Court's rationale for this rule is society's interest in morality and the need to protect children in their developmental stages from speech that could corrupt their morals before the age of maturity when they can make prudent decisions for themselves (Federal Communications Commission v. Pacifica Foundation, 1978; Bethel School District No. 403 v. Fraser, 1986; Chaplinsky v. New Hampshire, 1942). The reasoning is that children are more likely to be an involuntary unsuspecting captive audience on the public airwaves, relative to other off-campus settings.

The Supreme Court appeared to lift the on-campus limitation of its reasoning in the *Bethel* case when it stated without qualification that "it is a highly appropriate function of public school education to prohibit the use of vulgar and offensive terms in public discourse" (Bethel School District No. 403 v. Fraser, 1986, p. 683). Here, the Court seemed to give schools carte blanche power to censor students' use of vulgar and offensive speech in any public discussion regardless of forum. Interpreted accordingly, the statement would also leave only the use of vulgar and offensive speech during private discourse under First Amendment protection. However, it would be absurd to think that the Court would allow schools to discipline students for wearing Cohen's jacket in a mall, courthouse, restaurant, park, or other non-school setting simply because the speech was in public discourse. The context of the statement similarly shows that it was likely intended to be limited to public discourse *within* the school setting. For example, the Court concluded the paragraph with a summative sentence that supports an on-campus focus: "The determination of what manner of speech in the classroom or in school assembly is inappropriate properly rests with the school board" (p. 683).

A part of the Supreme Court decision that could provide support for anyone who seeks to extend the *Bethel* test beyond the on-campus context is the following statement: "The process of educating our youth for citizenship in public schools is not confined to books, the curriculum, and the civics class; … teachers—and indeed the older students—demonstrate the appropriate form of civil discourse and political expression by their conduct and deportment in and out of class" (Bethel School District No. 403 v. Fraser, 1986, p. 683). Whenever the Supreme Court eventually reviews an off-campus student speech case involving vulgar, lewd, plainly-offensive or obscene speech, the Court itself could rely on this language as rationale for extending the *Bethel* test to off-campus speech. The key to the Court's decision in such a review will be the scope of the location covered by the phrase "out of class" used in the above statement. The Court will need to clarify whether the phrase should be interpreted as confined to locations outside the classroom but within the schoolhouse gate; or if the phrase encompasses locations outside the schoolhouse gate.

Recall that in the Supreme Court statement quoted in the prior paragraph, the Court indicated that the education of students is not confined to the class, the curriculum and books (Bethel School District No. 403 v. Fraser, 1986). If that is the case, and if students set examples by their speech in and out of class as noted in the statement, it seems logical that schools should be able to demand those examples from students even when they are off campus and engaged in speech. It would be unreasonable, however, to expect the United States Constitution to allow schools to have unbridled power to reach into students' homes to demand students' compliance with the school's code of acceptable civil speech. If schools have such unbridled power to censor students' speech off-campus, even in their homes, the First Amendment would be of no meaning and use for students. Moreover, the Supreme Court's statement that students do not shed their constitutional rights at the schoolhouse gate would be a mere platitude. To students, this Supreme Court aphorism as well as the United States Constitution would become "but a walking shadow, a poor player that struts and frets his hour upon the stage and then is heard no more: it is a tale told by an idiot, full of sound and fury, signifying nothing" (Crowther, 2005, p. 2). Despite the opportunity for those seeking to apply the *Bethel* test to off-campus speech, there is evidence that the Court's reference to deportment in and out of class might actually only apply within the schoolhouse gate. The concluding part of the discussion of deportment included the following rule: "schools, as instruments of the state, may determine that the essential lessons of civil, mature conduct cannot be conveyed in a school that tolerates lewd, indecent, or offensive speech and conduct such as that indulged in by this confused boy" (Bethel School District No. 403 v. Fraser, p. 683). This rule, indeed, empowers schools to decide not to accept lewd speech in a school. Interestingly, however, the rule does not foreclose schools from determining that the lessons of civil conduct cannot be taught within the school if students use lewd speech off-campus.

While the Supreme Court did not explicitly define what would make student speech vulgar, lewd, plainly offensive or obscene for purposes of censorship, some elements can be gleaned from the case. For example, vulgar, lewd, plainly-offensive or obscene speech is speech that is contrary to manners and habits of civility (Bethel School District No. 403 v. Fraser, 1986). Such speech is also outside the "boundaries of socially appropriate behavior" and offends the "personal sensibilities of the other participants and audiences" involved in the discussion or debate (p. 681). Further, vulgar, lewd, plainly-offensive or obscene speech is speech that involves "the use of terms of debate highly offensive or highly threatening to others" (p. 683). Vulgar, lewd, plainly-offensive or obscene speech is speech that violates the "shared values of a civilized social order" (p. 683). It is also speech that is "plainly offensive to both teachers and students—indeed to any mature person" (p. 683). Courts are also expected to look at whether the speech is "acutely insulting to teenage girl students"; especially, where male sexuality is glorified in the speech (p. 683). Speech such as Matthew's speech that has "pervasive sexual innuendo" is vulgar, lewd, plainly-offensive or obscene speech (p. 683). Additionally, review of student speech under the *Bethel* test includes consideration of whether the speech is "seriously damaging to its less mature audience" (p. 683). In the case of sexual speech, a determination of whether speech is seriously damaging to an audience includes consideration of whether the audience is "on the threshold of awareness of human sexuality", creating heightened concern to protect them under the law from exposure to the speech (p. 683). Given the Supreme Court's failure to provide more specific definitions for the terms vulgar, lewd, plainly offensive or obscene, the common understanding of those terms in the school's community and the school setting would factor into whether students' speech meets the *Bethel* test. This is evident in the Court's reference to the importance of the "shared values of a civilized social order" in determining speech that can be constitutionally censored (p. 683).

The Court concluded that Matthew's speech satisfied the various considerations, discussed above, for determining if speech is vulgar, lewd, plainly-offensive and obscene speech (Bethel School District No. 403 v. Fraser, 1986). Some of the 14-year old students seemed alarmed at the speech and mimicked the sexual innuendo in the speech as Matthew spoke. Since the students were merely on the verge of sexuality, it was critical for the law to step in to protect them from exposure to such speech. The Court ruled that, in its parental role, the school has authority to censor student speech "to protect children—especially in a captive audience—from exposure to sexually explicit, indecent, or lewd speech" (p. 684). This paternalistic approach was further evident through the Court's emphasis of the need to empower schools to teach students proper manners, the lack of maturity of students and consequent need to protect students from speech on human sexuality which the Court viewed as significantly threatening to students'

Lewd, Vulgar, Plainly-Offensive, and Obscene Speech

development and ability to function civilly in society. This paternalism is contrary to the expansive view expressed in Tinker v. Des Moines Independent Community School District (1969) where the Court ruled that "students may not be regarded as closed-circuit recipients of only that which the State chooses to communicate" (p. 511).

By empowering schools to censor speech that does not meet boundaries of socially-acceptable behavior, the Court effectively made students closed-circuit recipients of only those manners and habits that the school finds acceptable or non-offensive. Even if that is sanctioned within the school, that power must not be allowed to reach outside the schoolhouse gate. The Free Speech Clause does not serve its purpose if it only protects non-offensive speech. After all, it is offensive speech, rather than non-offensive speech, that people object to. If students are not allowed to speak outside their school without a school speech filter, schools would become "enclaves of totalitarianism" – something the Court was firmly opposed to about two decades earlier, as noted in the previous chapter (Tinker v. Des Moines Independent Community School District, p. 511). In 2001, Matthew was asked to reflect on his speech and the Supreme Court decision in his case. He stated that his case merely empowered schools to exert more power over students rather than deter school overreaching as he had intended (Hudson, 2001). He concluded that "*Tinker* may still be good law de jure, but it has been de facto obliterated" by the Supreme Court decision in Bethel School District No. 403 v. Fraser (p. 4). The *Bethel* Court's grant of expansive power to schools over student speech was also evident in its authorization of schools to justify their censorship of vulgar or lewd student speech with their educational mission. The Court ruled there is no First Amendment limitation on the authority of schools to censor students' speech using the rationale that lewd or vulgar speech "undermines the school's basic educational mission" (Bethel School District No. 403 v. Fraser, p. 685). This authority includes the power to censor student speech in order to "make [a] point" to students – the point that vulgar, lewd speech is inconsistent with values underlying education (p. 685). Such values include tolerance of others and appreciation of proper etiquette (Papandrea, 2008). Moreover, the Court implied that the denial of censorship authority to schools over vulgar, lewd, obscene or plainly-offensive speech would be surrendering the control of schools to students.

Even if schools are constitutionally authorized to censor Matthew's speech on-campus, they should not be permitted to censor the same speech off-campus. As Justice Brennan wrote in his concurring opinion, if Matthew had "given the same speech outside of the school environment, he could not have been penalized" (Bethel School District No. 403 v. Fraser, 1986, p. 688). Even though Justice Brennan voted with the Court to authorize schools to censor Matthew's speech on-campus, he wrote a separate concurrence to "express my understanding of the breadth of the Court's holding" (p.688). In his view, as one of the Justices influential in the decision, the Court's decision in *Bethel* should not be read as an endorsement of authority for schools to censor Matthew's speech if delivered off-campus. Specifically, he stated that "the Court's opinion does not suggest otherwise" (p. 688). Not only should schools not be constitutionally permitted to censor Matthew's speech off-campus, they should not be permitted to prohibit students from wearing Cohen's jacket off-campus. We believe the First Amendment protects the right to use vulgar, lewd or plainly-offensive speech off-campus.

As Justice Brennan emphasized, courts must solemnly approach their responsibility as guardians of the First Amendment to ensure that students' free speech rights are not violated because of "prudish failures to distinguish the vigorous from the vulgar" (Bethel School District No. 403 v. Fraser, 1986, p. 690, citing Thomas v. Board of Education, Granville Central School District, 1979). In his dissenting opinion, Justice Stevens echoed the importance of distinguishing the vulgar from the vigorous. He observed that when he was in high school, Clark Gable's use of the word "damn" in the line "Frankly, my dear, I don't give a damn" (during the film *Gone with the Wind*) was viewed as culturally shocking. However, by 1986, it was no longer shocking. Today it is even less shocking that it is unlikely to qualify as plainly offensive. As the United States Court of Appeals for the Seventh Circuit stated in 2011, Matthew's speech "involved student speech that, from the perspective enabled by 25 years of erosion of refinement in the use of language, seems distinctly lacking in shock value" (Zamecnik v. Indian Prairie School District No. 204, 2011, p. 877). Moreover, students are more up-to-date on what their peers find offensive than are schools and judges. Justice Stevens echoed this sentiment when he stated that a student is more apt at judging whether "his contemporaries would be offended by the use of a four-letter word—or a sexual metaphor—than is a group of judges who are at least two generations and 3,000 miles away" (Bethel School District No. 403 v. Fraser, p. 692). Even if schools are empowered to censor vulgar, lewd or plainly-offensive speech on-campus, judges and schools are often metaphorically 3,000 miles from the teenage culture. Consequently, if schools are given authority to censor off-campus student speech in addition to their authority over on-campus speech, more constitutionally-protected speech is exposed to risk of censorship on a mistaken classification of speech as vulgar, lewd or plainly offensive. School administrators, teachers and the judiciary need to be culturally-relevant to ensure that they are not being prudish in censoring students' speech on-campus and off-campus.

Justice Brennan provided keen insight on what the Supreme Court might have intended with respect to the reach of its decision in the *Bethel* case to off-campus speech:

In the course of its opinion, the Court makes certain remarks concerning the authority of school officials to regulate student language in public schools. For example, the Court notes that '[n]othing in the Constitution prohibits the states from insisting that certain modes of expression are inappropriate and subject to sanctions.' These statements obviously do not, and indeed given our prior precedents could not, refer to the government's authority generally to regulate the language used in public debate outside of the school environment (Bethel School District No. 403 v. Fraser, 1986, p. 688).

Justice Marshall, who dissented from the Supreme Court's decision, endorsed Justice Brennan's opinion (Bethel School District No. 403 v. Fraser, 1986). Justice Stevens, in his dissent, similarly emphasized the on-campus nature of the scope of the Bethel decision. For example, he appeared to interpret the Supreme Court's decision as merely giving authority to schools to censor students' vulgar, lewd, plainly-offensive and obscene speech in classrooms, at other locations on the school's campus and at school-sponsored extracurricular activities – which activities could obviously be off-campus or on-campus. Assuming that Justices Stevens and Brennan's interpretations represent an accurate perspective of the Supreme Court majority's views in Bethel, it would appear settled that while schools can punish students for obscene off-campus speech without violating the First Amendment, students have leeway under the Free Speech Clause to use vulgar, lewd or plainly-offensive speech off-campus (at non-school-sponsored events) without fear of school punishment. However, it is not settled because the majority opinion in the case did not explicitly rule on off-campus speech. Moreover, the Supreme Court has acknowledged that its analysis in the Bethel case is not very clear (Morse v. Frederick, 2007).

CONCLUSION

In this chapter, we reviewed the United States Supreme Court's decision in Bethel School District No. 403 v. Fraser (1986). Relative to the Court's broad grant of free speech rights to students in Tinker v. Des Moines Independent Community School District (1969), the *Bethel* case diminished students' speech rights by removing vulgar, lewd, plainly-offensive and obscene speech from First Amendment protection. The factual context of the case suggests that its reach is limited to the school's campus. Furthermore, various concurring and dissenting Justices in the case similarly underscored the on-campus scope of the decision. Thus we are inclined to conclude that the *Bethel* test only applies on-campus. Nonetheless, as we noted, there is language in the case that can be used to permit school censorship of vulgar, lewd and plainly-offensive off-campus speech. This is unlikely to be the Supreme Court's stance, however, as this would eviscerate students' ability to express themselves using colorful vulgar language free from the school's prying eyes even in the privacy of their homes. Moreover, the *Bethel* Court's reasoning overwhelmingly suggests that the *Bethel* test is moored to the on-campus setting. Even then, schools retain censorship authority over obscene off-campus speech. As we noted, obscene speech is already recognized as unprotected speech for adults and students alike off-campus; thus schools can censor such speech pursuant to the *Miller* test. Off-campus student speech such as vulgar speech that falls short of meeting the *Miller* test is likely beyond the censorship reach of schools.

REFERENCES

Bethel School District No. 403 v. Fraser (1986). 478 U.S. 675.

Board of Education v. Pico (1982). 457 U.S. 853.

Chaplinsky v. New Hampshire (1942). 315 U.S. 568, 572.

Cohen v. California (1971). 403 U.S. 15.

Crowther, J. (Ed.). (2005). No Fear Macbeth. *SparkNotes*. Retrieved January 5, 2014, from http://nfs.sparknotes.com/macbeth/page_202.html

Cukor, G., & Fleming, V. (Directors). (1939). *Gone with the wind*. [Motion Picture]. United States: Warner Bros.

Federal Communications Commission v. Pacifica Foundation (1978). 438 U.S. 726.

Ginsberg v. New York (1968). 390 U.S. 629.

Hudson, D. (2001). Matthew Fraser speaks out on 15-year-old Supreme Court free-speech decision. *First Amendment Center*. Retrieved January 5, 2014, from http://www.firstamendmentcenter.org/matthew-fraser-speaks-out-on-15-year-old-supreme-court-free-speech-decision

Jacobellis v. Ohio (1964). 378 U.S. 184.

Miller v. California (1973). 413 U.S. 15.

Morse v. Frederick (2007). 551 U.S. 393.

Moss, S. A. (2011). The overhyped path from Tinker to Morse: How the student speech cases show the limits of Supreme Court decisions–for the law and for the litigants. *Florida Law Review, 63,* 1407–1457.

Oluwole, J., Green, P., & Stackpole, M. (2013). *SextEd: Obscenity versus free speech in our schools.* Santa Barbara, CA: Praeger Publishers.

Papandrea, M. (2008). Student speech rights in the digital age. *Florida Law Review, 60,* 1027–1102.

Roth v. United States (1957). 354 U.S. 476.

Stanley v. Georgia (1969). 394 U.S. 557.

Thomas v. Board of Education, Granville Central School District (1979). 607 F.2d 1043, 1057.

Tinker v. Des Moines Independent Community School District (1969). 393 U.S. 503.

Tuneski (2003). Online, not on grounds: Protecting student internet speech. *Virginia Law Review, 89,* 139-87.

Zamecnik v. Indian Prairie School District No. 204 (2011). 636 F.3d 874, 877.

KEY TERMS AND DEFINITIONS

Bethel **Test:** This is the test the United States Supreme Court created in Bethel School District No. 403 v. Fraser (1986) that authorizes school officials to censor student speech that is vulgar, lewd, plainly offensive or obscene. The test is also sometimes referred to as the *Fraser* test.

Free Speech Clause: The clause in the First Amendment to the United States Constitution which prohibits the government from denying citizens the right to free speech.

Miller **Test:** The three-part test the United States Supreme Court created in Miller v. California (1973) for determining whether the government can censor speech as obscenity. Under this test, courts inquire into: (a) whether, under contemporary community standards, the average person would deem the speech as a whole as appealing to a prurient interest; (b) whether the speech describes or shows sexual conduct defined by state law in a manifestly offensive way; and (c) whether the speech as a whole has no serious political, scientific, literary or artistic value (Miller v. California, 1973).

Off-Campus Student Speech: Student speech that occurs in any locale outside the borders or premises of a school and outside school hours. It includes student speech away from the school bus and school-sponsored events such as school trips.

On-Campus Student Speech: Student speech that occurs in any area inside the school or on school premises. It includes speech on the school bus or at school-sponsored events.

Student-Speech Jurisprudence: The composite of cases governing students' right to free speech under the United States Constitution.

Traditional-Obscenity Jurisprudence: The body of United States Supreme Court case law that governs the censorship of obscene speech of Americans in the community at large (as opposed to the case law governing students on school grounds).

Chapter 9
School-Sponsored Speech

ABSTRACT

This chapter examines the Hazelwood v. Kuhlmeier (1988) case – the United States Supreme Court's third review of students' speech rights under the Free Speech Clause of the First Amendment. It discusses the test created in the case for analyzing when schools can regulate students' speech. This test, referred to as the Hazelwood test (also known as the Kuhlmeier test) authorizes schools to censor school-sponsored student speech. The chapter discusses the Supreme Court's approach to student speech in the Hazelwood v. Kuhlmeier (1988) case. The ultimate goal of the chapter is to analyze the case in order to determine if it authorizes schools to censor students' speech while they are outside the schoolhouse gate.

INTRODUCTION

This chapter reviews the United States Supreme Court's decision in Hazelwood v. Kuhlmeier (1988). This was the first case to address the concept of school-sponsored student speech and its constitutional status under the Free Speech Clause of the First Amendment. The chapter discusses and analyzes the speech incident that ignited the case. The analysis discusses the Supreme Court's cursory interpretation of its schoolhouse gate ruling in Tinker v. Des Moines Independent Community School District (1969). Furthermore, the chapter discusses the Court's definition of school-sponsored student speech and how this relates to off-campus student speech. The chapter per the authors sets forth the new test for speech censorship created in Hazelwood v. Kuhlmeier (1988). It examines the reasoning in the case in order to determine the censorship authority it provided schools over students' speech rights. Additionally, the chapter covers the public forum doctrine which was an essential element of the reasoning for authorizing school censorship of school-sponsored speech. It discusses traditional public forum, limited public forum and closed public forum. It also highlights how the reasoning in *Hazelwood* could impact off-campus student speech. The objective of the chapter is to analyze the rules and reasoning in the case in order to clarify the authority of schools over student speech under Hazelwood v. Kuhlmeier – one of only four Supreme Court cases to rule on students' speech rights under the Free Speech Clause.

DOI: 10.4018/978-1-4666-9519-1.ch009

MAIN FOCUS OF THE CHAPTER

The United States Supreme Court first reviewed the authority of schools to censor student speech in school-sponsored media in Hazelwood v. Kuhlmeier (1988). In this case, the Supreme Court created a new test that allows schools to constitutionally censor student speech: schools can censor all school-sponsored student speech if the school has a legitimate pedagogical reason for the censorship. While the facts of the case involved student speech in a school-sponsored publication, the Court expanded the reach of its decision to all school-sponsored activities. Continuing the trend that started with Bethel School District No. 403 v. Fraser (1986), in Hazelwood v. Kuhlmeier, the Court reined in students' free speech rights recognized in Tinker v. Des Moines Independent Community School District (1969). Specifically, the Court created an entirely new category of student speech for schools to censor. Even though, factually, the case involved on-campus student speech, it could provide some insight on the Court's inclination about off-campus student speech. We examine this case as well as the test next.

The Speech Incident

During the 1982-83 school year, the curriculum at Hazelwood East High School in Missouri included various journalism classes designed to teach students about the art and responsibilities of journalism (Hazelwood v. Kuhlmeier, 1988). In Journalism II, students gained practical journalism experiences by writing and editing Spectrum – the school newspaper. The curriculum guide described Journalism II as a "laboratory situation in which the students publish the school newspaper applying skills they have learned in Journalism I" (p. 268). The practical experiences in the course were designed to teach students about the moral, ethical and legal obligations of journalists and to help them cultivate skills for working under journalistic deadlines. Spectrum was a triweekly publication primarily funded by the school board and supplementally funded by the sale of Spectrum which was widely distributed to school employees, students and the community. The school board policy stated that Spectrum as well as other school-sponsored publications were a part of the curriculum (p. 268). Prior to publication, pursuant to school custom, the journalism teacher submitted page proofs of each issue of Spectrum to the principal for approval.

During the spring semester, Journalism II students wrote articles for Spectrum that explored the effect of divorce on students as well as the pregnancy experiences of students (Hazelwood v. Kuhlmeier, 1988). The article on student pregnancies used pseudonyms in order to protect the identities of the students discussed in the story. Nonetheless, the principal objected to its publication because he believed that the students could still be identified from the article. Additionally, he felt that it was wrong to expose the school's younger students to the article's discussions of birth control and sex. The divorce article quoted a student who stated that, prior to her parents' divorce, her father "wasn't spending enough time with my mom, my sister and I" (p. 263). The student also stated that her father constantly argued with her mother and "was always out of town on business or out late playing cards with the guys" (p. 263). The article used the student's actual name in the story, prompting the principal to preclude its publication. The principal further objected to the speech because he believed that it was inappropriate to publish the comments without consultation with or consent from the student's father and mother.

Moreover, the principal believed that Spectrum's publication deadline would not be met if he allowed the journalism class to further edit the divorce and pregnancy articles (Hazelwood v. Kuhlmeier, 1988).

School-Sponsored Speech

Consequently, he ordered the journalism teacher to delete the two pages featuring the pregnancy and divorce articles from Spectrum. Deletion of the two pages effectively precluded publication of other articles sharing the same pages as the censored articles even though the principal did not find their content objectionable. Those other articles were articles about juvenile delinquents, runaways and teenage marriage as well as a pregnancy article that did not specifically discuss a student at the school. One of the editors, Cathy Kuhlmeier, subsequently revealed that she was left to wonder if the articles could have saved the life of a classmate who committed suicide (Moss, 2011). Cathy and two other students who worked on Spectrum that semester sued the school district claiming that the school's censorship of the divorce and pregnancy articles violated their free speech rights under the First Amendment. They sought monetary damages and an injunction (Hazelwood v. Kuhlmeier, 1988).

Analysis

In Hazelwood v. Kuhlmeier (1988), the United States Supreme Court reaffirmed its ruling in Tinker v. Des Moines Independent Community School District (1969) that public school students' First Amendment free speech rights are not shed at the schoolhouse gate. The Court explained this rule as a warning to schools that students "cannot be punished merely for expressing their personal views on the school premises—whether in the cafeteria, or on the playing field, or on the campus during the authorized hours" unless one of the *Tinker* tests is satisfied (Hazelwood v. Kuhlmeier, p. 266). In other words, students bring free speech rights to their personal views to the schoolhouse gate and those rights are more expansive than the rights they possess within the schoolhouse gate. Even within the schoolhouse gate, however, the authority of schools over student speech is not limitless. While within the schoolhouse gate, the free speech rights of students are not "automatically coextensive" with rights that adults possess (p. 266). The Court ruled that students' speech rights are instead limited "in light of the special characteristics of the school environment" (p. 266). Given that the Court did not state that students' speech rights must be limited in light of special characteristics of the *non*-school environment, it is evident that the *Hazelwood* Court did not limit the off-campus speech rights of students. Instead, the Court's intent was to increase censorship of student speech within the school setting.

Even as the Supreme Court granted expansive authority to schools over students' on-campus speech in Hazelwood v. Kuhlmeier (1988), the Court explicitly indicated that it did not restrict students' off-campus speech rights through the case. For example, the Court ruled that schools can censor student speech that is "inconsistent with its basic educational mission, even though the government could not censor similar speech outside the school" (p. 266). Therefore, a school could, for instance, censor speech that is "sexually explicit but not legally obscene" when the student is on-campus (p. 266). However, in order for the government, including schools, to censor such speech off-campus, the speech must be deemed legally-obscene under the *Miller* test discussed earlier in this book. Additionally, within the schoolhouse gate, unlike off-campus, a school could censor vulgar speech in order to "disassociate itself from the speech in a manner that would demonstrate to others that such vulgarity is wholly inconsistent with the fundamental values of public school education" (Hazelwood v. Kuhlmeier, pp. 266-67). The *Hazelwood* Court pointed to Bethel School District No. 403 v. Fraser (1986) as personification of this rule about censorship of vulgar speech within the schoolhouse gate. The rule that schools can censor student speech that is "inconsistent with its basic educational mission, even though the government could not censor similar speech outside the school" provides further insight on the power of schools over students' off-campus speech (Hazelwood v. Kuhlmeier, p. 266). Specifically, the use of the word "could" suggests that there might be situations in which schools can censor off-campus student speech. The Court did not identify those situations, however.

The Supreme Court stated that the "determination of what manner of speech in the classroom or in school assembly is inappropriate properly rests with the school board rather than with the federal courts" (Hazelwood v. Kuhlmeier, 1988, p. 267). It is notable that the Supreme Court did not state that the determination of what manner of speech that is inappropriate outside the schoolhouse gate properly rests with the school board. This further highlights the fact that Hazelwood v. Kuhlmeier merely restricted students' on-campus speech rights rather than their off-campus speech rights. The *Hazelwood* case involved school-sponsored student speech – speech that "students, parents, and members of the public might reasonably perceive to bear the imprimatur of the school" (p. 271). Additionally, school-sponsored student speech is speech that "may fairly be characterized as part of the school curriculum, whether or not they occur in a traditional classroom setting, so long as they are supervised by faculty members and designed to impart particular knowledge or skills to student participants and audiences" (p. 271). This definition implies that school-sponsored speech relates to on-campus student speech as opposed to off-campus student speech; and that if it relates to off-campus speech, it only relates to school-sponsored off-campus student speech.

The Supreme Court ruled that the *Tinker* tests are inapplicable to school-sponsored student speech because the *Tinker* tests only apply to personal student speech that is not sponsored by the school (Hazelwood v. Kuhlmeier, 1988). The *Tinker* tests govern "educators' ability to silence a student's personal expression that happens to occur on the school premises" (p. 271). This Supreme Court statement in *Hazelwood* implies that *Tinker* merely governs on-campus personal expressions of students. Another distinction between *Tinker* and *Hazelwood* is that *Tinker* examined a school's obligation to "tolerate particular student speech" whereas *Hazelwood* examined whether a school has an obligation to "affirmatively ... promote particular student speech" (p. 271). The Court analogized the substantive distinction between *Hazelwood* and *Tinker* to a distinction between school-sponsored student speech and personal student expression in an "off-campus underground newspaper that school officials merely had allowed to be sold on a state university campus" (p. 271). Unlike the other language above from Hazelwood v. Kuhlmeier which suggested that *Tinker* merely governs on-campus speech, this analogy implied that *Tinker* could apply to off-campus speech under one condition: if students bring the off-campus speech on school grounds. When student speech is part of a "school-sponsored publications, theatrical productions, and other expressive activities", however, censorship of the speech must be governed by the *Hazelwood* test (Hazelwood v. Kuhlmeier, p. 271). The *Hazelwood* test states that schools have "editorial control over the style and content of student speech in school-sponsored expressive activities so long as their actions are reasonably related to legitimate pedagogical concerns" (p. 273).

The Supreme Court also applied the public forum doctrine to the school's censorship of the school-sponsored student speech in the Spectrum newspaper at Hazelwood East High School (Hazelwood v. Kuhlmeier, 1988). This doctrine recognizes three types of public forum:

1. Traditional public forum;
2. Limited public forum; and
3. Closed public forum (also known as reserved forum or non public forum)

Traditional public forums are places that "have immemorially been held in trust for the use of the public, and, time out of mind, have been used for purposes of assembly, communicating thoughts between citizens, and discussing public questions" (Perry Education Association v. Perry Local Educators' Association, 1983, p. 45). A public forum could become a traditional public forum either through:

1. Historical tradition; or
2. Government designation.

In traditional public forums, content-based censorship of speech is constitutional only if the censorship satisfies the strict scrutiny standard of review which requires that the censorship must:

1. Be narrowly tailored; and
2. Serve a compelling government interest.

In traditional forums, regulations of the time, place and manner of speech are constitutional as long as they are:

1. Content-neutral;
2. Narrowly tailored to a significant government interest; and
3. "Leave open ample alternative channels of communication" (Perry Education Association v. Perry Local Educators' Association, 1983, p. 45).

Limited public forums are forums that the school has opened up for speech even though they are not traditional public forums (Perry Education Association v. Perry Local Educators' Association, 1983). While the school "is not required to indefinitely retain the open character of the facility, as long as it does so it is bound by the same standards as apply in a traditional public forum" (p. 45). Once the government opens up the forum to one kind of speech, it cannot discriminate against another kind of speech because of the content of such speech unless it satisfies strict scrutiny (Lamb's Chapel v. Center Moriches Union Free School District, 1993). Additionally, reasonable time, place and manner regulations of speech are permissible in a limited public forum (Perry Education Association v. Perry Local Educators' Association, 1983). However, any content-based censorship "must be narrowly drawn to effectuate a compelling state interest" (p. 45). A public school is not a limited public forum unless, through practice or policy, it has allowed the general public or a part of the public use of the school. For example, if the school permits a student club to indiscriminately use its facility, the facility would become a limited forum. If, however, the school reserves the facility for its intended purposes, the facility constitutes a closed forum.

Closed public forums are places which "have [not] immemorially been held in trust for the use of the public, and, time out of mind, have [not] been used for purposes of assembly, communicating thoughts between citizens, and discussing public questions" (Perry Education Association, p. 46). In other words, a closed public forum is government property which has not been made a traditional public forum either by:

1. Historical traditional; or
2. Government designation.

"In addition to time, place, and manner regulations, the state may reserve the forum for its intended purposes, communicative or otherwise, as long as the regulation on speech is reasonable and not an effort to suppress expression merely because public officials oppose the speaker's view" (p. 46). In essence, the school can regulate content of speech in closed public forum as long as the regulation is:

1. Not designed to suppress a particular viewpoint; and
2. Reasonable.

The rationale for allowing greater censorship of speech within closed public forums is that the "First Amendment does not guarantee access to property simply because it is owned or controlled by the government" (Hazelwood v. Kuhlmeier, 1988, p. 46). The school cannot accidentally convert a closed forum into a limited forum. Instead, in order for a closed public forum to become a limited public forum, the school must intentionally open up the forum to indiscriminate use for public discourse (Cornelius v. NAACP Legal Defense and Educational Fund, Inc., 1985). The school computers, computer lab, web server, library, school mailbox and classroom are some general examples of closed forums. If students are allowed to use these forums for their personal expressions, however, they would become limited public forums (Harpaz, 2000). Schools could retain the closed-forum nature of school computers, computer labs and servers that students could use to access off-campus speech by clearly restricting their use to school projects (Harpaz, 2000; Hudson, Jr., 2000). Such restrictions should be set forth in the school's acceptable use policy. Where such a restriction exists, student speech on the school server, computer or lab would be governed by the *Hazelwood* test. This is because "if a school is somehow subsidizing the student speech, then school officials can control the content of the speech" (Pisciotta, 2000, p. 662). However, the school is not authorized to censor personal student speech "in the cafeteria, or on the playing field, or on the campus during the authorized hours even though those arenas are clearly financed and supported by the school" (West, 2008, p. 37). The nature of speech as school-sponsored speech, rather than the arena of the speech, dictates whether student speech attracts the *Hazelwood* test. If a forum is exclusively devoted to school-sponsored speech, the forum is a closed forum. On the other hand, since schools traditionally allow students to engage in personal discourse on the playing field or the cafeteria, those forums are limited public forums.

If a student prints a hard copy of her personal (non-school-sponsored) speech in the computer lab (or using the school computer or web server) of a school with an acceptable use policy that restricts use to school-sponsored speech, the test applicable to the hard copy should depend on where the speech is distributed. If the hard copy is distributed at the school, the *Tinker* tests should govern the hard copy because *Tinker* is the standard applicable to personal speech (Hudson, Jr., 2000). If the hard copy is distributed off-campus, however, it is not clear that the *Tinker* or *Hazelwood* tests would apply to the hard copy since, as noted in this book, the Supreme Court has not explicitly extended either test to off-campus speech. On the other hand, if journalism or world language students, for example, are required to email pen pals as part of a class assignment, the emails would likely fall under the *Hazelwood* test (Swartz, 2000). Consequently, school officials could require pre-approval of the emails or exercise other censorship of the emails through editorial oversight and filtering software (Swartz, 2000).

The Supreme Court concluded that the Spectrum newspaper was a closed public forum (Hazelwood v. Kuhlmeier, 1988). The Court reasoned that, unlike locations outside the schoolhouse gate such as streets and public parks, public schools are not traditional public forums. Additionally, Spectrum was not a limited public forum because it was never opened to indiscriminate use for public discourse "by its student reporters and editors, or by the student body generally" (p. 270). Instead, it was restricted to students enrolled in the Journalism II course. The school board policy as well as the curriculum guide defined Spectrum as a part of the curriculum. The school never deviated through policy or practice from the reserved curricular use of Spectrum. Students who worked on the newspaper were graded for their work as part of Journalism II. The newspaper was also created with school resources during school hours. Moreover, school officials customarily wielded great editing authority over articles in the Spectrum. The journalism teacher had an established practice of making several decisions about Spectrum without student input. These decisions generally included publication dates, review of quotes, page totals for each issue, assignment of publication ideas to students and selection of student editors. The teacher, not the students, had the "final authority with respect to almost every aspect of the production and publication of Spectrum, including its content" (p. 268). The school's control over the forum – Spectrum – was also ensured through the additional requirement of principal approval before articles could be published in Spectrum. These facts converged to demonstrate that Spectrum was a closed forum. Consequently, school officials were constitutionally authorized to censor the student speech in Spectrum if the censorship was reasonable. Legitimate pedagogical justifications would make such censorship reasonable.

School officials must have authority to regulate school-sponsored student speech in order to ensure that goals of the curriculum or extra-curricular activity are met (Hazelwood v. Kuhlmeier, 1988). This is a legitimate pedagogical justification for empowering schools to censor school-sponsored student speech. The Supreme Court stated that school authority over school-sponsored speech must be broad so that schools can minimize the erroneous attribution of personal student expression to the school. It was important that the Court only applied this rationale to school-sponsored speech; otherwise, schools would have unbridled authority to regulate students' personal expression, making the protections of *Tinker* null. After all, substantial personal student speech off-campus or on-campus could be erroneously attributed to the school. Another rationale for expansive censorship authority over school-sponsored is the need for schools to police content exposed to their less mature audience when speech bears the imprimatur of the school (Hazelwood v. Kuhlmeier, 1988). This is another rationale that must be limited to school-sponsored student speech in order to avoid undermining the free speech rights recognized in Tinker v. Des Moines Independent Community School District (1969). As the Supreme Court noted in the *Tinker* case, "something more than a mere desire to avoid the discomfort and unpleasantness that always accompany an unpopular viewpoint" is needed in order to censor student speech (p. 509).

The broad authority to regulate school-sponsored speech allows the school to censor student speech that it could not otherwise regulate if the speech were merely *personal* student speech that failed to satisfy either the *Tinker* or *Bethel* tests (Hazelwood v. Kuhlmeier, 1988; Tinker v. Des Moines Independent Community School District, 1969; Bethel School District No. 403 v. Fraser, 1986). This authority also allows schools to censor student online speech that is school-sponsored. For example, if students are asked to create a website during a computer class, the school could censor the website's content for pedagogical reasons pursuant to the *Hazelwood* test (Harpaz, 2000). The Supreme Court only imposed one limitation on the broad authority to censor school-sponsored student speech – the *Hazelwood* test's requirement of a legitimate pedagogical reason for censorship: "It is only when the decision to censor a school-sponsored publication, theatrical production, or other vehicle of student expression has no valid educational purpose that the First Amendment is so 'directly and sharply implicate[d],' as to require judicial intervention to protect students' constitutional rights" (Hazelwood v. Kuhlmeier, 1988, p. 273, citing Epperson v. Arkansas, 1968, p. 104). Under this broad authority, the school can censor student "speech that is, for example, ungrammatical, poorly written, inadequately researched, biased or prejudiced, vulgar or profane, or unsuitable for immature audiences" (Hazelwood v. Kuhlmeier, p. 271). This authority also enables the school to distance itself from speech "that might reasonably be perceived to advocate drug or alcohol use, irresponsible sex, or conduct otherwise inconsistent with the shared values of a civilized social order" (p. 272). It empowers schools to censor school-sponsored speech in order to distance itself from "any position other than neutrality on matters of political controversy" (p. 272). The *Tinker* case makes it clear, however, that schools cannot censor personal student speech on matters of political controversy unless one of the *Tinker* tests is satisfied (Tinker v. Des Moines Independent Community School District, 1969). Therefore, the *Hazelwood* test must be confined to school-sponsored speech in order to avoid compromising students' free speech rights on-campus or off-campus.

The Supreme Court found that the school officials at Hazelwood East High School had legitimate pedagogical reasons for censoring the divorce and pregnancy articles as well as the other articles that would have appeared on the same pages of Spectrum (Hazelwood v. Kuhlmeier, 1988). These pedagogical reasons included:

1. The students' failure to sufficiently protect the identities of the subjects in the pregnancy article;
2. This failure might have violated anonymity pledges made to the subjects;
3. Inadequate sensitivity to the privacy interests of parents and boyfriends who were covered in the pregnancy story but not consulted;
4. The failure to seek the publication consent of parents and boyfriends for the pregnancy story;
5. The belief that sex-related "frank talk was inappropriate in a school-sponsored publication distributed to 14–year–old freshmen and presumably taken home to be read by students' even younger brothers and sisters" (pp. 274-75);
6. The journalistic fairness of publishing the divorce article without giving the father criticized in the article the opportunity to offer a rebuttal;
7. The editorial challenges presented by publication deadlines;
8. Concern that the journalism students had not learned the curriculum content dealing with the legal, ethical and moral obligations of journalists that cover and provide news to adolescents;
9. Concern that the students had not learned the curriculum content about the proper ways to handle personal attacks in articles;
10. Concern that the students had not learned the curriculum content about the journalistic standards for addressing controversial issues in articles; and
11. Concern that the students had failed to learn the journalistic standards governing the privacy of subjects (Hazelwood v. Kuhlmeier, 1988).

What is evident from these pedagogical reasons is that schools get significant judicial deference over school-sponsored student speech that they do not enjoy over other student speech. They also highlight the campus-centric nature of *Hazelwood*, limiting any arguments for applying the reasoning beyond the schoolhouse gate. Additionally, the Court distinguished between on-campus and off-campus speech in ruling that schools must have authority to set higher standards over school-sponsored publications than standards "in the 'real' world" (Hazelwood v. Kuhlmeier, 1988, p. 272). This Supreme Court recognition of diametrical standards for on-campus versus off-campus speech needs to resonate with those who contend for symmetry in tests for off-campus and on-campus speech. Hazelwood v. Kuhlmeier (1988) essentially provided schools more authority over on-campus student speech without restricting the free speech rights of students while off-campus. Therefore, the *Hazelwood* test would not apply to underground newspapers that students create off-campus because they are not school-sponsored; instead, underground newspapers exist "in the real world." As noted earlier, the one area where the *Hazelwood* case opened the door to school censorship of off-campus student speech is off-campus speech that students bring on-campus. Beyond that, what emerges from the *Hazelwood* case is that students' off-campus speech rights remain status quo as defined in the *Tinker* and *Bethel* cases discussed earlier in this book.

CONCLUSION

In this chapter, we reviewed the United States Supreme Court's decision in Hazelwood v. Kuhlmeier (1988). This case authorized school officials to censor school-sponsored student speech if they have legitimate pedagogical concerns; this standard is known as the *Hazelwood* test. The Court's reasoning in the case strongly indicates that the *Hazelwood* test is limited to school-sponsored on-campus speech; or school-sponsored off-campus. It would be dangerous to extend the *Hazelwood* test to non-school-sponsored off-campus speech because schools would then be able to censor student speech as long as they can articulate a pedagogical reason. Such a move would empower schools to censor speech simply because it conflicted with the curriculum objectives that the school finds acceptable. It could also inspire schools to tailor their curriculum against ideas they are hostile towards so that they can create a conflict between student speech and the curriculum. As Justice Brennan warned in his dissent, the *Hazelwood* test would, for example, allow a school to censor a student who states that "socialism is good" based on the pedagogical concern that the speech "subverts the school's inculcation of the message that capitalism is better" (Hazelwood v. Kuhlmeier, 1988, p. 279).

If applied to off-campus student speech, the *Hazelwood* test would undermine *Tinker* as it would allow a school to censor student speech opposing war if the student speech contradicts the school's pedagogical message that war is appropriate in certain situations. It would also undermine the Supreme Court's declaration in *Tinker* that "students may not be regarded as closed-circuit recipients of only that which the State chooses to communicate. They may not be confined to the expression of those sentiments that are officially approved" (Tinker v. Des Moines Independent Community School District, 1969, p. 511). We believe that schools must not be allowed to "assume an Orwellian 'guardianship of the public mind'" (Hazelwood v. Kuhlmeier, p. 578, citing Thomas v. Collins, 1945, p. 545), casting a "pall of orthodoxy" over the school environment (Keyishian v. Board of Regents, 1967, p. 603).

REFERENCES

Bethel School District No. 403 v. Fraser (1986). 478 U.S. 675.

Cornelius v. NAACP Legal Defense and Educational Fund, Inc. (1985). 473 U.S. 788, 802.

Epperson v. Arkansas (1968). 393 U.S. 97, 104.

Harpaz, L. (2000). Internet speech and the First Amendment rights of public school students. *Brigham Young University Education and Law Journal, 123*(125), 154–157.

Hazelwood v. Kuhlmeier (1988). 484 U.S. 260.

Hudson, D. L. Jr. (2000). Censorship of student internet speech: The effect of diminishing student rights, fear of the internet and columbine. *Law Review of Michigan State University Detroit College of Law, 199*, 204.

Keyishian v. Board of Regents (1967). 385 U.S. 589, 603.

Lamb's Chapel v. Center Moriches Union Free School District (1993). 508 U.S. 384.

Moss, S. A. (2011). The overhyped path from Tinker to Morse: How the student speech cases show the limits of Supreme Court decisions–for the law and for the litigants. *Florida Law Review, 63*, 1407–1457.

Perry Education Association v. Perry Local Educators' Association (1983). 460 U.S. 37.

Pisciotta, L.M. (2000). Beyond sticks & stones: A First Amendment framework for educators who seek to punish student threats. *Seton Hall Law Review, 30*, 635, 662.

Swartz, J. K. (2000). Beyond the schoolhouse gates: Do students shed their constitutional rights when communicating to a cyber-audience? *Drake Law Review, 48*, 587–604.

Thomas v. Collins (1945). 323 U.S. 516, 545.

Tinker v. Des Moines Independent Community School District (1969). 393 U.S. 503.

West, S. R. (2008). Sanctionable conduct: How the Supreme Court stealthily opened the schoolhouse gate. *Lewis and Clark Law Review, 12*, 27–44.

KEY TERMS AND DEFINITIONS

Closed Public Forum: This is a government-owned forum that has not been made a traditional public forum either by historical traditional or government designation. This forum is also referred to as a reserved forum or a non-public forum (Note: Under the United States Constitution, public schools are viewed as an arm of the government).

***Hazelwood* Test:** This is the test the United States Supreme Court created in Hazelwood v. Kuhlmeier (1988) that authorizes school officials to censor student speech that is sponsored by the school as long as the censorship has a legitimate pedagogical purpose. The test is also sometimes referred to as the *Kuhlmeier* test.

Injunction: An equitable judicial remedy that enjoins a party to a case from engaging in specified conduct.

Limited Public Forum: This refers to a government-owned forum that the government has opened up for people to use for speech even though the forum is not a traditional public forum.

Monetary Damages: A pecuniary judicial remedy that is designed to compensate a party for the injury suffered because of the actions or inactions of another party.

Off-Campus Speech: Student speech that occurs in any locale outside the borders or premises of a school and outside school hours. It includes student speech away from the school bus and school-sponsored events such as school trips.

On-Campus Speech: Student speech that occurs in any area inside the school or on school premises. It includes speech on the school bus or at school-sponsored events.

School-Sponsored Student Speech: Student speech that is part of a school-sponsored publication, a school-sponsored activity or any other activity that would be viewed as bearing the school's imprimatur.

Tinker **Tests:** The two tests – the material and substantial disruption test and the infringement-of-rights test – created in Tinker v. Des Moines Independent Community School District (1969) for reviewing the constitutionality of school censorship of student speech.

Traditional Public Forum: This is a government-owned forum that is historically or by government designation used by the citizenry to engage in communication or assembly. Such forums include public streets and public parks.

Chapter 10
Advocacy of Illegal Drug Use

ABSTRACT

This chapter examines the Morse v. Frederick (2007) case – the most recent United States Supreme Court decision about students' right to free speech under the Free Speech Clause of the First Amendment. It discusses the test created in the case for determining the extent of school-censorship authority over student speech. This test, known as the Morse test, allows schools to censor student speech if the speech advocates illegal drug use. The ultimate goal of the chapter is to analyze the Morse v. Frederick case in order to determine if it gives schools any authority to censor students' off-campus speech.

INTRODUCTION

This chapter reviews the United States Supreme Court's decision in Morse v. Frederick (2007). As the most recent case in the Supreme Court's student-speech jurisprudence, it is critical for scholars, the judiciary and schools to understand its view on students' free speech rights. The chapter per the authors discusses the speech incident that led to the United States Supreme Court's review of the case. In addition, the chapter includes an analysis of the Supreme Court Justices' reasoning in the case in order to determine the scope of students' free speech rights that emerged from the case. The chapter's analysis begins with a discussion of the Supreme Court's decision to move the schoolhouse gate beyond the physical premises of the school. The chapter discusses how this decision effectively enabled schools to classify speech that occurs outside the physical schoolhouse gate within their censorship authority. It identifies factors from the case that schools can use in their determinations of whether speech should be legally classified as occurring off the school's campus or on-campus. The Court introduced a new concept – "school-sanctioned speech" – into its student-speech jurisprudence. This concept is discussed in light of the expanded censorship power it affords schools over student speech. The chapter reviews the case's interpretations of pertinent language in Tinker v. Des Moines Independent Community School District (1969), Bethel School District No. 403 v. Fraser (1986) and Hazelwood v. Kuhlmeier (1988) in relation to off-campus student speech. The chapter also highlights the Supreme Court's decision to create a new test for determining whether schools can censor students' free speech rights. This test pro-

DOI: 10.4018/978-1-4666-9519-1.ch010

Advocacy of Illegal Drug Use

vides that schools can regulate student speech that promotes the illegal use of drugs. The objective of the chapter to analyze the various judicial opinions in the case in order to decipher what this precedent states regarding the authority of schools over students' off-campus speech.

MAIN FOCUS OF THE CHAPTER

In Morse v. Frederick (2007), the United States Supreme Court expanded the authority of schools to censor student speech while coterminously restricting students' speech rights under the Free Speech Clause. This was done through the creation of a new category of unprotected speech for students. The Court's decision to withdraw another category of student speech from First Amendment protection continued the trend toward lesser student-speech protection that began in Bethel School District No. 403 v. Fraser (1986) and Hazelwood v. Kuhlmeier (1988). Under the test created in the case, school officials can censor student speech that advocates illegal drug use. This is known as the *Morse* test. The Morse v. Frederick case is the closest the Supreme Court has come to examining any student-speech facts remotely similar to off-campus student speech. The case and the test are examined next.

The Speech Incident

In 2002, in preparation for the Winter Olympics, the Olympic Torch Relay and torchbearers marched on a street in front of Juneau–Douglas High School (JDHS) as the torch traveled through Juneau, Alaska (Morse v. Frederick, 2007). Several spectators gathered in front of the school to watch the procession. JDHS' cheerleaders and band performed during the relay. The principal of JDHS approved the relay as a class trip. Consequently, teachers were permitted to dismiss their classes so that students and teachers could watch the relay. School officials supervised students as they watched the procession on both sides of the street (Morse v. Frederick, 2007). However, school officials did not stop students from leaving the event nor were students required to attend (Frederick v. Morse, 2006). Neither parents nor students were informed that the principal had approved the relay as a school event (West, 2006). Unlike the school's "routine for field trips and other supervised events off of the school premises", students were not required to submit parental permission forms in order to attend the relay (Frederick v. Morse, p. 1116).

Joseph Frederick (a JDHS student) arrived late to school that morning and immediately went across the street from the school to join his classmates and another friend who was not a JDHS student (Morse v. Frederick, 2007). As the cameras and torchbearers proceeded by them, Frederick and his friends unrolled a 14-foot banner. The banner stated prominently "BONG HiTS 4 JESUS" in sight of students on both sides of the street (p. 397). Frederick averred that the idea for the "BONG HiTS 4 JESUS" expression came after he took an American Justice class and while reading "Albert Camus' existential novel The Stranger" about the meaninglessness of life (Moss, 2011, p. 1428). According to Frederick, he "decided to devise a plan that would clearly be constitutionally protected speech and speech that would be funny and at the same time embarrass . . . school administration" (p. 1429). As he brainstormed with friends about ideas for the plan, his girlfriend showed him a snowboard sticker with the words "Bong Hits For Jesus" that he could use for his "free speech experiment" (p. 1429).

The principal of JDHS crossed the street and ordered the students to furl the banner (Morse v. Frederick, 2007). He believed that the banner advocated illegal drug use (smoking of marijuana) in violation of school policy. The school policy, which governed curricular activities as well as approved class trips, prohibited "public expression that ... advocates the use of substances that are illegal to minors" (p. 398). While the other students complied with the order, Frederick did not, prompting the principal to confiscate the banner. Frederick was subsequently suspended for five days. However, according to Frederick, after he quoted Thomas Jefferson's view on free speech to the principal, his suspension was changed to ten days (Moss, 2011). The principal countered that the suspension was doubled because Frederick "wouldn't cooperate and name the other students who held the banner" (p. 1429). The superintendent later reduced the suspension to eight days (Morse v. Frederick, 2007). The superintendent concluded that Frederick's speech seemed to constitute advocacy of illegal drug use "in the midst of his fellow students, during school hours, at a school-sanctioned activity" (p. 398). The superintendent reasoned that the censorship of Frederick was justified because Bethel School District No. 403 v. Fraser (1986) authorized schools to censor speech contradicting the school's educational mission (Morse v. Frederick, 2007). He stated that Frederick was not communicating a political message such as legalization of marijuana or a religious message, either of which would be constitutionally protected.

Frederick asked the American Civil Liberties Union (ACLU) to intervene and sued the school district seeking monetary damages as well as declaratory and injunctive relief (Morse v. Frederick, 2007; Moss, 2011). He claimed that school officials' actions violated his right to free speech under the First Amendment (Morse v. Frederick, 2007). In his deposition, he contended that he deliberately chose to speak off school grounds and across from the school, on a public sidewalk, because he believed he had free speech rights outside the schoolhouse gate (West, 2008). Conservative and liberal advocacy groups filed amicus briefs in support of Frederick due to fears that the Supreme Court might give expansive censorship power to schools (Waldman, 2008b).

Analysis

Since the focus of our book is students' off-campus speech, it is noteworthy that Morse v. Frederick (2007) was the first case in which the United States Supreme Court provided any semblance of an off-campus student-speech analysis, albeit cursory. The Court's opinion (written by Chief Justice Roberts and joined by Justices Alito, Thomas, Scalia and Kennedy) started with an off-campus versus on-campus analysis as a response to Frederick. Frederick argued that, since his speech was outside the schoolhouse gate, his speech was beyond the censorship purview of school officials. Consequently, Frederick contended that his speech was "not a school speech case" (Morse v. Frederick, p. 400). The Supreme Court disagreed and characterized his speech as school speech. While the Court acknowledged that there is "some uncertainty at the outer boundaries as to when courts should apply school speech precedents", it nevertheless summarily concluded that such uncertainty was absent with Frederick's speech (p. 401). Even though the Court failed to describe the uncertainty referenced here, the context of use suggests that the Court was referring to uncertainty about the applicability of current student-speech jurisprudence to off-campus speech. The statement was made as part of the paragraph devoted to explicating the Court's reasoning for characterizing Frederick's speech as on-campus speech rather than off-campus speech (Morse v. Frederick, 2007). Additionally, the Court cited, without any discussion, Porter v. Ascension Parish School Board (2004) to support its statement about uncertainty in the student-speech jurisprudence. Porter v. Ascension Parish School Board, discussed later in this book, was a federal circuit court of appeals case involving student speech created off campus.

Advocacy of Illegal Drug Use

Despite the fact that Frederick's speech occurred outside the schoolhouse gate (and the fact that Frederick never brought the speech inside the schoolhouse gate), the Court used an aggregate of factors in characterizing the speech as on-campus speech (Morse v. Frederick, 2007). The Court effectively turned a "public sidewalk—the epitome of a quintessential public forum" into an on-campus forum (West, 2008, pp. 27-28). Our review revealed the following as the factors the Court relied upon in determining whether to characterize the speech in Morse v. Frederick (2007) as on-campus speech:

1. Whether the speech was uttered during an event that occurred during regular school hours. The event at which Frederick unfurled the banner took place during the school's regular hours.
2. Whether other students from the district were present at the event. This was the case at the Olympic Torch Relay.
3. Whether the school sanctioned the event as a school-approved class trip or social event. In the case of Frederick, his principal did sanction the event as a class trip or social event.
4. Whether the school policy expressly subjects approved class trips or social events to the same rules governing student conduct. JDHS' policy expressly included approved social events and class trips within its student conduct rules.
5. Whether school officials are interspersed among the students at the event. Administrators and faculty were present among the students during the Olympic Torch Relay.
6. Whether the school district charged school officials with supervising students during the event. The Court answered this in the affirmative in Frederick's case.
7. Whether a school curricular group, school club or other extracurricular group performed during the event. During the Olympic Torch Relay, the cheerleaders and the high school band performed.
8. Whether the speech was "directed … toward the school, making it plainly visible to most students" (p. 401). Frederick directed his banner toward the school and he did it in such a way that it was clearly visible to the students at the relay.

These factors collectively led the Court to conclude that Frederick's speech was on-campus speech rather than off-campus speech (Morse v. Frederick, 2007). The Court ruled that "[u]nder these circumstances, we agree with the superintendent that Frederick cannot stand in the midst of his fellow students, during school hours, at a school-sanctioned activity and claim he is not at school" (p. 401). Given that Frederick's speech occurred physically off school grounds, it is disconcerting that the Court characterized the speech as on-campus speech, expanding the bounds of school authority over student speech (Roberts, 2008). It is also distressing because Frederick spoke at a time when students were not required to be on the school's campus; and he never physically entered the school at any time before his speech (Frederick v. Morse, 2006). As West (2008) fittingly noted, Frederick was a member of the public on that day:

On the day of the incident, Frederick had not stepped foot on school property; rather, he was standing among the public on a public sidewalk. He was present at a commercially sponsored, non-school event—the running of the Olympic Torch Relay through his town. The planning, creation and display of Frederick's speech occurred completely off school grounds and without school resources. Thus it was the school principal, not Frederick, who may have crossed the line (both physically and legally) between the school and non-school environment when she left school property, marched across the street, and grabbed Frederick's banner (West, 2008, p. 29).

Moreover, students were not mandated to attend the event. So like every other member of the public who was present that day, the school and the Supreme Court should have accorded Frederick citizen status rather than student status.

Besides, Frederick's speech originated entirely off-campus and no school resource was used in its creation:

The planning, creation and display of Frederick's speech occurred completely off school grounds and without school resources. Thus it was the school principal, not Frederick, who may have crossed the line (both physically and legally) between the school and non-school environment when she left school property, marched across the street, and grabbed Frederick's banner (West, 2008, p. 29).

Despite these facts, the Supreme Court characterized Frederick's speech as on-campus speech, extending the schoolhouse gate beyond the physical walls of the school. This blurring of off-campus and on-campus locales could be a harbinger of the Supreme Court's willingness to continue to extend the schoolhouse gate. Roberts (2008) observed that "[w]ith students increasingly speaking off school grounds through mediums such as the Internet, *Morse* may lay a framework for school officials to restrict more student speech than ever before" (p. 1180). That remains to be seen as *Morse* is not entirely clear about the direction of the off-campus speech jurisprudence. Until there is definitive clarification from the United States Supreme Court, however, school officials would be wise to pay attention to the factors set forth above as guides to determining when they can classify speech as on-campus speech as opposed to off-campus speech. According to Sonja West, who filed an amicus brief in Morse v. Frederick (2007), the decision to introduce the term "school-sanctioned" into the school-speech lexicon where only the term "school-sponsored" existed prior (see Hazelwood v. Kuhlmeier, 1988) indicates that the Court is willing to create new judicial terminology as needed in order to expand school power over student speech (West, 2008). This new terminology allowed the Court to characterize what was actually an event sponsored by Coca-Cola and other private entities as a school event (Frederick v. Morse, 2006). However, "the Court introduced this new concept without defining it, citing any legal support for it, or explaining its limits" (West, p. 40). In fact, the "failure of the Court to define or limit this sanctioning power raises disturbing questions and potentially could chill a large amount of protected student expression" (p. 29). For instance, the "Court's ruling could encourage school authorities in the future to sanction all sorts of off-campus community events, thereby aggrandizing government power at the expense of expressive liberty" (p. 29). All the school would have to do is tag the event a "school-sanctioned event" and any activity that is educational or otherwise could fall under school-censorship authority:

Under its broadest interpretation, this wide-sweeping view of school power over independent, [physically] off-campus student speech has the potential to chill all types of student expression. The school could sanction attendance at a planned rally on a matter of public debate, such as illegal immigration or gay rights, as an educational activity. It would certainly be reasonable for a school to decide that there are learning opportunities in having students write letters to the editors of local newspapers, produce off-campus publications or create and maintain weblogs thus leading them to sanction these activities. Trips to museums, zoos, aquariums and historical landmarks could certainly qualify as sanctionable educational outings. And a Fourth of July parade or other expression of community pride would seem

Advocacy of Illegal Drug Use

to be as educational, and therefore sanctionable, as the Olympic Torch Relay. The school might wish to encourage students to engage in artistic or literary endeavors during their off-hours as a school-sanctioned activity (West, 2008, p. 42).

Free speech advocates should be concerned that schools and courts could expand the reach of the "sanctioning" power of schools to the point that it cripples students' right to free speech off-campus. The "sanctioning" power could allow schools to classify vast amounts of off-campus speech as on-campus speech providing the gateway for schools to expand censorship over off-campus speech.

Nothing in the Supreme Court's Morse decision, moreover, indicates that the school's sanctioning power must be limited to events and activities with an educational element. Indeed, the torch relay itself was not particularly educational in nature; it was instead an occasion of community celebration and pride. Does the Court mean to suggest that there is no boundary to what a school can sanction, including with regard to social, religious, or work-related events? Might a student be open to punishment for what he says at the grocery store or local shopping mall? (West, 2008, p. 42).

Nevertheless, since the Supreme Court found that Frederick's speech was actually on-campus speech, even though it was uttered outside the schoolhouse gate, the Court's subsequent analysis in the case could be deemed to be peculiarly designed for on-campus speech. The on-campus nature of the case is evident in the Court's phrasing of the issue that limited its scope to a school event: "whether a principal may, consistent with the First Amendment, restrict student speech at a school event, when that speech is reasonably viewed as promoting illegal drug use" (Morse v. Frederick, 2007, p. 403). Nonetheless, we can gain some insight about the Court's approach to student speech that could encompass off-campus speech should the Court choose to extend the *Morse* reasoning to off-campus speech at some point in the future. For instance, the case is instructive on the Supreme Court's approach to interpretation of student messages that have multiple or ambiguous meanings. The Court conceded that the meaning of Frederick's speech was ambiguous and that the speech could be interpreted in multiple ways. However, if the school's interpretation of the speech is reasonable, the Court will defer to the school's interpretation.

In Frederick's case, the Court found that the speech could be interpreted as mere gibberish for the attention of the television cameras – the interpretation Frederick proffered to the Court (Morse v. Frederick, 2007, p. 403). The speech could also be viewed as offensive speech or amusing speech. Alternatively, the speech could be interpreted as communication about drug use: either as an imperative to smoke marijuana or as a celebration of drug use. The speech could also be interpreted as a political message or a religious one; however, neither Frederick nor the school proffered either as the interpretation. The Court accepted as reasonable the principal's interpretation of the speech as advocacy of marijuana use. By allowing schools to censor the words "BONG HiTS 4 JESUS" as advocacy of illegal drug use, while recognizing First Amendment protection for the same words if intended as political or religious speech, the Court effectively empowered schools to practice viewpoint discrimination. The Court did similarly in Bethel School District No. 403 v. Fraser (1986) as discussed in chapter eight of this book. Justice Stevens characterized it as an invitation to "stark viewpoint discrimination" (Morse v. Frederick, p. 437; Waldman, 2008a). This sanction of viewpoint discrimination contradicts a longstanding position of the Court that if censorship is directed at "particular views taken by speakers on a subject, the violation of the First Amendment is all the more blatant" (Rosenberger v. Rector and Visitors of University of Virginia, 1995, p. 829).

Despite its on-campus locus, Morse v. Frederick (2007) is instructive about the reach of the *Bethel* test to off-campus speech. Recall that in Bethel School District No. 403 v. Fraser (1986), the Supreme Court ruled that "the constitutional rights of students in public school are not automatically coextensive with the rights of adults in other settings" (p. 682). In the *Morse* case, the Court interpreted this rule to mean that, if Matthew Fraser's vulgar, lewd or plainly-offensive speech had been delivered "in a public forum outside the school context, it would have been protected" (Morse v. Frederick, p. 405). This statement suggests that the *Bethel* test was intended to govern on-campus speech rather than off-campus speech. It also affirms Justice Brennan's declaration in his Bethel School District No. 403 v. Fraser (1986) concurrence that, if Matthew Fraser had "given the same speech outside of the school environment, he could not have been penalized" (p. 688).

We believe that Morse v. Frederick (2007) reveals that the Supreme Court has thus far only limited school-censorship authority to on-campus student speech. This conclusion is supported by the *Morse* Court's interpretation of a rule created in Tinker v. Des Moines Independent Community School District (1969): students and teachers have First Amendment rights "applied in light of the special characteristics of the school environment" (p. 506). The *Morse* Court interpreted this rule to mean that, while students are "[i]n school", their First Amendment rights are "circumscribed in light of the special characteristics of the school environment" (Morse v. Frederick, p. 405). In essence, students' First Amendment rights outside of school are not circumscribed because of the special characteristics of the school environment. As in Tinker v. Des Moines Independent Community School District, the Supreme Court failed to identify the special characteristics relied upon for this conclusion (Morse v. Frederick, 2007). The Court, however, indicated that one of its prior precedents – Hazelwood v. Kuhlmeier (1988) – had provided some direction regarding off-campus student speech. Specifically, the Court stated that "*Kuhlmeier* acknowledged that schools may regulate some speech even though the government could not censor similar speech outside the school" (Morse v. Frederick, pp. 405-06, citing Hazelwood v. Kuhlmeier, p. 266). This is an implicit acknowledgment that Hazelwood v. Kuhlmeier recognized the limits of school-censorship authority as the confines of the schoolhouse gate.

The Supreme Court stated that, even though "children assuredly do not 'shed their constitutional rights ... at the schoolhouse gate,' ... the nature of those rights is what is appropriate for children in school" (Morse v. Frederick, 2007 p. 406, citing Vernonia School Dist. 47J v. Acton, 1995, pp. 655-56). In other words, the nature of rights not shed at the schoolhouse gate – rights within the schoolhouse gate – is dictated by appropriateness of the speech inside the school. The Court did not state, however, that the nature of students' rights to speech outside the schoolhouse gate is dependent on the appropriateness of the speech inside the school.

The Court's brief comparison of its student-speech jurisprudence to its student-search jurisprudence likewise reveals that students retain their full constitutional rights outside the schoolhouse gate. For instance, the Court stated that "Fourth Amendment rights, no less than First and Fourteenth Amendment rights, are different in public schools than elsewhere" (Morse v. Frederick, p. 406, citing Vernonia School Dist. 47J v. Acton, 1995, p. 656). Additionally, "the school setting requires some easing of the restrictions to which searches by public authorities are ordinarily subject" (Morse v. Frederick, p. 406, citing New Jersey v. T.L.O., 1985, p. 340). These statements imply that students have greater First and Fourth Amendment rights outside the school setting than they do on-campus. Therefore, we can surmise that the Court did not intend to limit students' off-campus speech rights in Morse v. Frederick, even though the speech occurred on a street across from the school.

Advocacy of Illegal Drug Use

The Supreme Court interpreted its creation of the *Bethel* test in Bethel School District No. 403 v. Fraser (1986) as a statement from the Court that courts are not limited to *Tinker* as the governing source of tests when analyzing student speech (Morse v. Frederick, 2007). Consequently, new facts could call for creation of a new test for analyzing student speech as happened in Hazelwood v. Kuhlmeier (1988) with the creation of the *Hazelwood* test (Morse v. Frederick, 2007). As another example, the Court found that neither the *Bethel* test nor the *Tinker* test were applicable to Joseph Frederick's speech. *Tinker* was not applicable because Frederick's speech was not political speech. The *Bethel* test was not applicable because Frederick's speech was not sexual speech and it was not delivered in a classroom or at a school assembly. Additionally, the speech did not involve vulgar or lewd or plainly-offensive speech. In fact, the Court reasoned that it "stretches *Fraser* too far" to view Frederick's speech as plainly offensive because a higher standard than mere offense is required to find speech to be plainly offensive (Morse v. Frederick, p. 409). Unbridled power over offensive speech was the one area, in the *Morse* case, where the Court did not expand the power of schools to censor student speech. While the school district argued that schools should be empowered to censor any offensive speech, the Supreme Court countered that such a rule would put a wide scope of protected speech at risk of censorship (Denning & Taylor, 2008). The *Hazelwood* test was inapplicable to Frederick's speech because the speech was not school-sponsored speech (Morse v. Frederick, 2007).

Since the *Tinker*, *Bethel* and *Hazelwood* tests were inapplicable, the Court decided to create a new test to resolve the question of whether school officials could censor Frederick's speech without violating the Free Speech Clause (Morse v. Frederick, 2007). This test, known as the *Morse* test, authorizes schools to censor student speech that advocates illegal drug use. The justification for this test was the need to protect students from drug abuse and the permanent, serious and potentially grave harm associated with drugs (Morse v. Frederick, 2007). Another justification was the growing drug epidemic in schools which had resulted in illegal drugs being sold, offered to or received by 25% of high school students on school premises (Morse v. Frederick, citing Centers for Disease Control and Prevention, 2006). The Court declared that "[s]tudent speech celebrating illegal drug use at a school event, in the presence of school administrators and teachers, thus poses a particular challenge for school officials working to protect those entrusted to their care from the dangers of drug abuse" (Morse v. Frederick, p. 408). Despite the urgency in the Court's reasoning for empowering schools to take on a paternalistic role with respect to drugs, this rationale was not extended to provide an off-campus reach for schools. In fact, as indicated earlier in this chapter, the Court emphasized that its cases merely eased, within the school, the constitutional restrictions on government power that would otherwise apply outside of school.

The Supreme Court concluded that its holding in the *Morse* case was consistent with three principles from its precedents:

1. Students' free speech rights are not shed at the schoolhouse gate (Morse v. Frederick, 2007);
2. Students' First Amendment rights must be "applied in light of the special characteristics of the school environment" (p. 397, quoting Tinker v. Des Moines Independent Community School District, p. 506);
3. Students' constitutional rights in public schools are not "automatically coextensive" with adults' rights in other settings (Morse v. Frederick, pp. 396-97).

As discussed earlier in this book, none of these principles extends school authority over students while they are off-campus; or limits the off-campus free speech rights of students. Even Justice Thomas, who wrote a concurring opinion to express his belief that students should not have any First Amendment right within the schoolhouse gate, did not suggest that students should not have First Amendment rights outside the schoolhouse gate.

Justice Thomas would completely reverse the Supreme Court's Tinker v. Des Moines Independent Community School District (1969) decision and invalidate the case's recognition of free speech rights for students. In fact, he stated that:

I join the Court's opinion because it erodes Tinker's hold in the realm of student speech, even though it does so by adding to the patchwork of exceptions to the Tinker standard. I think the better approach is to dispense with Tinker altogether, and given the opportunity, I would do so (Morse v. Frederick, 2007, p. 422).

This confirms that there is at least one Supreme Court Justice willing to completely preclude free speech rights for students while they are on-campus.

Justice Thomas focused his opinion on students' on-campus speech because he was trying to counter the Supreme Court's restriction of schools' censorship authority over students' on-campus speech. He stated that public schools should be able to run their classrooms with "an iron hand" as exists in many private schools, in order to "generate a spirit of subordination to lawful authority, a power of self-control, and a habit of postponing present indulgence to a greater future good" (Morse v. Frederick, pp. 410-11, citing Emerson & Potter, 1843, p. 125). He suggested that the Supreme Court's decision to create new tests (the *Bethel*, *Hazelwood* and *Morse* tests) since Tinker v. Des Moines Independent Community School District (1969) was a recognition that the Court's decision in *Tinker* was a mistake. Consequently, those tests have "scaled back *Tinker's* standard, or rather set the standard aside on an ad hoc basis" (Morse v. Frederick, p. 417). There is some merit to this, since as discussed earlier in this book, the *Bethel*, *Hazelwood* and *Morse* tests carved out new categories of speech for schools to censor, eroding the protection introduced in the *Tinker* case.

As disquieting as it is today, Justice Thomas envisioned schools as places where students do not speak until spoken to as teachers command and teach students (Morse v. Frederick, 2007). This sounds almost like military barracks. He argued that schools should fully control students and compel absolute obedience and submission from students when they are in school. The only limitation he saw in the power of schools over students within the school was the legal constraint on "excessive physical punishment" (p. 416). Indeed, he wanted "despotism in the government of schools which has been discarded everywhere else" (p. 414, citing Cooper v. McJunkin, 1853, p. 291). Withal, he did not argue similarly about students outside the schoolhouse gate. He opined that parents who are displeased with an iron-hand public school "can send their children to private schools or homeschool them; or they can simply move" (Morse v. Frederick, p. 419). This notion that students seeking greater free speech rights can get them at a homeschool or private school or by moving away from the district is an implicit acknowledgment that students retain free speech rights outside the schoolhouse gate. He stated that, "[i]n the name of the First Amendment, *Tinker* has undermined the traditional authority of teachers to maintain order in public schools" (p. 421). In this statement, he emphasized a traditional authority of teachers but that authority was on-campus rather than off-campus authority. Justice Thomas concluded that school officials could censor Joseph Frederick simply because "the Constitution does not afford students a right to free speech in public schools (pp. 418-19). He added that "it cannot seriously be suggested that the First Amendment 'freedom of speech' encompasses a student's right to speak in public schools" (p. 419). It

Advocacy of Illegal Drug Use

is notable that Justice Thomas did not state that "the Constitution does not afford students a right to free speech outside public schools." Neither did he state that "it cannot seriously be suggested that the First Amendment 'freedom of speech' encompasses a student's right to speak outside public schools." These statements support the conclusion that Justice Thomas understood the Supreme Court decision in the *Morse* case as merely a restriction of students' on-campus speech rights; further, Justice Thomas called for school censorship only within, rather than without, the schoolhouse gate.

Justice Alito wrote a concurring opinion (joined by Justice Kennedy) which could shed further light on the off-campus approach of the Supreme Court. Given that only five Justices voted for the majority opinion, Justice Alito's concurrence – supported by two of those five Justices – is typically viewed by federal courts as the controlling opinion (Moss, 2011; Waldman, 2008b). Justice Alito wrote the opinion in order to preclude any expansive interpretations of the Supreme Court's decision in the *Morse* case (Morse v. Frederick, 2007). His aversion to broad student-speech censorship is clear in his emphatic statement that "[t]he opinion of the Court does not endorse the broad argument advanced by petitioners and the United States that the First Amendment permits public school officials to censor any student speech that interferes with a school's 'educational mission'" (p. 423). He was so adamant about restricting the interpretation of *Morse* that he stated that the broad argument "can easily be manipulated in dangerous ways, and I would reject it before such abuse occurs" (p. 423). He cast his vote in support of the Court opinion based on his understanding that the Court therein intended to only authorize censorship of advocacy of illegal drug use; and his understanding that the Court decision "provides no support for any restriction of speech that can plausibly be interpreted as commenting on any political or social issue" (p. 422). The limited-interpretation disposition of Justice Alito is further supported in his statement that "I join the opinion of the Court on the understanding that the opinion does not hold that the special characteristics of the public schools necessarily justify any other speech restrictions" besides those in *Morse*, *Tinker*, *Bethel* and *Hazelwood* (Morse v. Frederick, p. 423). His limited-interpretation disposition also suggests that he might be loath to using the *Morse*, *Tinker*, *Bethel* and *Hazelwood* tests to expand school authority into censorship of student off-campus speech.

Justice Alito opined that the Court was correct to reaffirm the rule in Tinker v. Des Moines Independent Community School District (1969) that students' free speech rights are not shed at the schoolhouse gate (Morse v. Frederick, 2007). He characterized this as a "fundamental principle" (p. 422). As discussed earlier in this book, this principle implies that students bring free speech rights with them to the schoolhouse gate; in order words, they already have free speech rights outside the schoolhouse gate. If this is a fundamental principle to Justice Alito, it seems fair to surmise that, with his limited-interpretation disposition in the *Morse* case, he is unlikely to authorize an expansive use of the *Morse* test to censor off-campus speech. Justice Alito was clearly cognizant of the free speech rights of students outside the schoolhouse gate. He stated that the *Tinker* case "does not set out the only ground on which in-school student speech may be regulated by state actors in a way that would not be constitutional in other settings" (Morse v. Frederick, p. 422). This statement simultaneously limits *Tinker* to on-campus speech and acknowledges that a different standard governs students' in-school speech as opposed to their off-campus speech.

Justice Alito is against using the educational mission of a school as a basis for extending censorship of student speech (Morse v. Frederick, 2007). He warned that such an approach could lead schools to amend their educational missions in a bid to discriminate against controversial social or political views. Consequently, an educational-mission approach would authorize schools to censor the armbands in Tinker v. Des Moines Independent Community School District (1969) as contravening the educational mission of world peace or solidarity with the military (Morse v. Frederick, p. 423). Justice Alito's opposition to an educational-mission rationale for student-speech censorship effectively signals that he would firmly reject any attempt to use the rationale to extend school censorship to off-campus speech. He is likewise against using the idea of in loco parentis as a basis for censorship of students' speech. He stated that when schools censor students' speech, they are actually acting in a government role and not in loco parentis. He cautioned that "[i]t is a dangerous fiction to pretend that parents simply delegate their authority—including their authority to determine what their children may say and hear—to public school authorities" (p. 424). Additionally, "[i]t is even more dangerous to assume that such a delegation of authority somehow strips public school authorities of their status as agents of the State" (p. 424).

For First Amendment purposes, within the schoolhouse gate, schools merely have governmental authority rather than parental authority over students unless a parent specifically delegates that authority (Morse v. Frederick, 2007). If schools do not have the parental authority to decide what students hear, read or say within the school, a fortiori, they cannot have parental authority in the student's home or other off-campus locale. Justice Alito stated that "[o]utside of school, parents can attempt to protect their children in many ways and may take steps to monitor and exercise control over the persons with whom their children associate" (p. 425). Since parents retain their parental authority outside the schoolhouse gate, "any argument for altering the usual free speech rules in the public schools cannot rest on a theory of delegation but must instead be based on some special characteristic of the school setting" (p. 425). The usual rules referenced here are the *Tinker*, *Bethel* and *Hazelwood* tests; as well as post-*Morse*, the *Morse* test.

Justice Alito argued that creation of the *Morse* test was justifiable because, within the school setting, parents' ability to protect their children from physical danger was significantly constricted (Morse v. Frederick, 2007). The special characteristic of the school setting that prompted his support for amending the usual rules governing student speech was the threat to students' physical safety from drugs within the confines of a school. While students are exposed to this threat outside the school, parents are responsible for protecting them in off-campus settings. Students also have greater freedom to avoid the threat off-campus than they do within the confines of the school's gates. Hence, Justice Alito reasoned that, within the schoolhouse gate, schools should have authority over student speech, beyond that afforded through the *Tinker*, *Bethel* and *Hazelwood* tests, to encompass speech advocating illegal drug use. He added a caveat, however: "I regard such regulation as standing at the far reaches of what the First Amendment permits. I join the opinion of the Court with the understanding that the opinion does not endorse any further extension" (Morse v. Frederick, p. 425). This disposition toward minimizing the extension of school-censorship authority within the school further supports the conclusion that Justice Alito would not vote for an expansion of censorship into student off-campus speech. However, his statement that the usual free speech tests could be altered to protect the physical safety of students could be interpreted as applicable to off-campus speech if a lower court views the off-campus speech as a threat to the physical safety of students within the schoolhouse gate. This will effectively make the *Morse* test borderless.

Even Justice Breyer, who partly concurred and partly dissented from the Court's decision, emphasized the school setting as a critical factor in empowering school officials to censor Joseph Frederick's "BONG HiTS 4 JESUS" speech (Morse v. Frederick, 2007). The school setting of speech – here a school-related event – could trigger censorship if a school official's view that the speech is inappropriate is reasonable. Justice Breyer stated:

Advocacy of Illegal Drug Use

What is a principal to do when a student unfurls a 14–foot banner (carrying an irrelevant or inappropriate message) during a school-related event in an effort to capture the attention of television cameras? Nothing? In my view, a principal or a teacher might reasonably view Frederick's conduct, in this setting, as simply beyond the pale (Morse v. Frederick, 2007, p. 427).

Justice Breyer's dissent from the Court decision was solely based on his view that the case should not have been decided on First Amendment grounds (Morse v. Frederick, 2007). He reasoned that constitutional determinations must be avoided unless necessary because they can be intricate and fractious and provide little guidance that is practical for school officials. Despite his aversion to a constitutional determination, he provided a First Amendment analysis in the case. There is no indication in his in-school-centric opinion, however, that out-of-school speech could trigger valid censorship. He argued instead for judges to defer to schools' decisions to discipline students for speech and conduct within the school setting in order to avoid converting the "judge's chambers into the principal's office" (Morse v. Frederick, p. 428). His unwillingness to apply the *Tinker*, *Hazelwood* and *Bethel* tests to Joseph Frederick's speech due to its differing facts foreshadows an unwillingness to extend current student-speech tests to dissimilar circumstances. This would seem to be the case with off-campus speech which is different from on-campus speech. Justice Breyer concluded that there is ongoing judicial uncertainty about the precise situations in which the current Supreme Court student-speech precedents would be applicable. This uncertainty extends to whether and how those precedents apply to off-campus speech.

Justice Stevens, who is no longer on the Supreme Court, authored a dissenting opinion that Justice Ginsburg and now-retired Justice Souter joined (Morse v. Frederick, 2007). These Justices agreed with Joseph Frederick that his speech was mere gibberish rather than advocacy of illegal drug use; hence, their dissent from the Court decision. They stated that, even if the speech had advocated illegal drug use, it would have been "unquestionably" protected under the First Amendment "had the banner been unfurled elsewhere" (p. 434). This means that the speech would be protected if it was off-campus speech. In another statement addressing the validity of the JDHS's rule against drug advocacy, the Justices stated: "It is also relevant that the display did not take place 'on school premises,' as the rule contemplates" (p. 440). This statement confirms that the dissenters did not view Frederick's speech as on-campus speech.

The dissenting Justices interpreted the Court's ruling in the *Morse* case as limited to on-campus speech (Morse v. Frederick, 2007). The Justices stated that the ruling relied on "the unusual importance of protecting children from the scourge of drugs [which] supports a ban on all speech in the school environment that promotes drug use" (p. 438). It would have been constitutionally absurd for the Court to rule that protection from the dangers of drugs justified a ban on all speech outside the school environment that promotes drug use as that would emasculate the First Amendment. According to the dissenting Justices, "while conventional speech [i.e. off-campus speech] may be restricted only when likely to 'incit[e] ... imminent lawless action,' it is possible that our rigid imminence requirement ought to be relaxed at schools" (p. 439, citing Brandenburg v. Ohio, 1969, p. 449). This lends some, albeit not definitive, credence to the view that Supreme Court Justices expect on-campus student speech to be treated differently than off-campus speech under the First Amendment.

CONCLUSION

In this chapter, we analyzed the United States Supreme Court's decision in Morse v. Frederick (2007). It is evident from the Supreme Court opinion, as well as the concurring and dissenting opinions, that the *Morse* case did not resolve the question of whether students have First Amendment rights off-campus. The Court's decision to characterize Frederick's speech as on-campus speech helped it avoid resolution of the question. Our analysis above shows that the *Morse* case indicates that students might retain greater rights off school grounds than on-campus. The transitory nature of the schoolhouse gate in the Court's decision, however, puts this conclusion in doubt. Given the physical location of Frederick's speech – on a public road outside the actual premises of the school – Morse v. Frederick (2007) would have been a great case for the Court to clarify the off-campus speech jurisprudence. Its failure to do so in the *Morse, Bethel, Hazelwood* and *Tinker* cases has fed greater uncertainty in the lower courts in their review of students' off-campus speech, as discussed in the next chapter.

REFERENCES

Bethel School District No. 403 v. Fraser (1986). 478 U.S. 675.

Brandenburg v. Ohio (1969). 395 U.S. 444.

Centers for Disease Control and Prevention. (2006). Youth risk behavior surveillance—United States, 2005: Surveillance summaries (No. SS-5). *Morbidity and Mortality Weekly Report, 55*, 19. Retrieved from http://www.cdc.gov/mmwr/PDF/SS/ss5505.pdf

Cooper v. McJunkin (1853) 4 Ind. 290, 291.

Denning, B. P., & Taylor, M. C. (2008). Morse v. Frederick and the regulation of student cyberspeech. *Hastings Constitutional Law Quarterly, 35*, 835–896.

Emerson, G. B., & Potter, A. (1843). *The School and the Schoolmaster: A Manual.* New York: Harper & Brothers Publishers.

Frederick v. Morse (2006). 439 F.3d 1114.

Hazelwood v. Kuhlmeier (1988). 484 U.S. 260.

Morse v. Frederick (2007). 551 U.S. 393.

Moss, S. A. (2011). The overhyped path from Tinker to Morse: How the student speech cases show the limits of Supreme Court decisions–for the law and for the litigants. *Florida Law Review, 63*, 1407–1457.

New Jersey v. T.L.O. (1985). 469 U.S. 325.

Porter v. Ascension Parish School Board (2004). 393 F.3d 608.

Roberts, C. E. (2008). Is Myspace their space? Protecting student cyberspeech in a post-Morse v. Frederick world. *UMKC Law Review, 76*, 1177–1192.

Rosenberger v. Rector and Visitors of University of Virginia (1995). 515 U.S. 819.

Tinker v. Des Moines Independent Community School District (1969). 393 U.S. 503.

Vernonia School Dist. 47J v. Acton (1995). 515 U.S. 646.

Waldman, E. G. (2008a). Returning to Hazelwood's core: A new approach to restrictions on school-sponsored speech. *Florida Law Review*, *60*, 63–123.

Waldman, E. G. (2008b). A Post–Morse Framework for Students' Potentially Hurtful Speech (Religious and Otherwise). *Journal of Law and Education*, *37*, 463–503.

West, S. R. (2008). Sanctionable conduct: How the Supreme Court stealthily opened the schoolhouse gate. *Lewis and Clark Law Review*, *12*, 27–44.

KEY TERMS AND DEFINITIONS

Bethel **Test:** This is the test the United States Supreme Court created in Bethel School District No. 403 v. Fraser (1986) that authorizes school officials to censor student speech that is vulgar, lewd, plainly offensive or obscene. The test is also sometimes referred to as the *Fraser* test.

First Amendment: This is the first right listed within the bill of rights added to the United States Constitution in 1791 to guarantee Americans certain rights free from government infringement. It covers the right to free speech, the right to free exercise of religion, right against government establishment of religion, the right to a free press, the right to peaceable assembly and the right to petition for redress of grievances.

Fourth Amendment: This is the fourth right listed within the bill of rights added to the United States Constitution in 1791 to guarantee Americans the right against unreasonable government searches and seizures. It includes the requirement of a warrant and probable cause for government searches.

Fourteenth Amendment: This is the amendment added to the United States Constitution in 1868 to guarantee Americans citizenship, the privileges and immunities of citizenship, right to due process and the right to equal protection of the laws. It was adopted after the American Civil War to recognize rights for the emancipated minorities who had been held in slavery and consequently deprived constitutional rights.

Hazelwood **Test:** This is the test the United States Supreme Court created in Hazelwood v. Kuhlmeier (1988) that authorizes school officials to censor student speech that is sponsored by the school as long as the censorship has a legitimate pedagogical purpose. This test is also sometimes referred to as the *Kuhlmeier* test.

Morse **Test:** This is the test the United States Supreme Court created in Morse v. Frederick (2007) that authorizes school officials to censor student speech that advocates illegal drug use.

Schoolhouse Gate: The terminology that the United States Supreme Court introduced in Tinker v. Des Moines Independent Community School District (1969) as the borderline separating a school and its premises from locales outside the school.

School-Sanctioned Speech: This is student speech that occurs at an event that, while not sponsored by the school, is approved by the school for student participation.

Student-Speech Jurisprudence: The composite of cases governing students' right to free speech under the United States Constitution.

Viewpoint Discrimination: Discrimination against speech based on the view expressed in the speech.

Section 4
Lower Courts and Off-Campus Speech

Chapter 11
Their Stories:
Offline Off-Campus Speech

ABSTRACT

This chapter examines the stories of students who have been censored by their schools for exercising their right to free speech off-campus in an offline forum. It discusses offline off-campus student speech in three categories: (a) speech directed at or against school officials or the school; (b) speech directed at or against students; and (c) speech directed at or against persons who are unaffiliated with the school. The chapter per the authors examines the court decisions regarding students' First Amendment rights to free speech under each of these categories. The goal of the chapter is to analyze the various lower court decisions governing the right of students to speak off-campus when they are not using online media. This chapter will highlight the unsettled nature of students' right to free speech in an off-campus offline setting.

INTRODUCTION

This chapter discusses the various cases in which the lower courts have examined whether students have a First Amendment right to free speech while off-campus. It tells the stories of those students who have been censored for speech in an offline setting. In addition, the chapter examines the reasoning of the courts for upholding or invalidating school censorship of off-campus student speech. In some cases, the rationale was grounded in the material and substantial disruption test that the United States Supreme Court created in Tinker v. Des Moines Independent Community School District (1969). In a few cases, the courts applied the *Bethel* test created in Bethel School District No. 403 v. Fraser (1986) or a version of it. In others, the courts applied the fighting-words doctrine or the true-threat doctrine. It is important for scholars, the judiciary and schools to understand the lower court decisions about off-campus offline speech if we are to bring certainty and clarity to the jurisprudence. As each case is examined, the chapter per the authors presents the censorship story of the student first. All spelling errors within the student speeches included in this book were in the original speech as cited in court documents. They were retained in their original forms in this book for authenticity. After presenting the censorship story, the chapter per the authors analyzes the court's rationale for its ruling about the scope of students' free speech

DOI: 10.4018/978-1-4666-9519-1.ch011

rights in an off-campus offline setting. The objective is to analyze the lower court decisions in order to highlight grounds for school censorship of student off-campus speech which would then form the basis for the discussion in the "Assessing the Current Jurisprudence" chapter. The discussions will also reveal that there is no uniformity in the judicial approach to censorship of off-campus offline student speech.

MAIN FOCUS OF THE CHAPTER

Over the years, various lower courts have tried to apply the four United States Supreme Court precedents – Tinker v. Des Moines Independent Community School District (1969), Bethel School District No. 403 v. Fraser (1986), Hazelwood v. Kuhlmeier (1988) and Morse v. Frederick (2007) – to off-campus student speech cases. Since these Supreme Court cases were decided in the context of on-campus student speech, the lower courts have struggled to determine if and how these precedents govern students' offline off-campus speech. Some courts have also chosen to apply the true-threat doctrine to off-campus offline speech, even though the Supreme Court has never applied the doctrine to student speech. The burgeoning uncertainty in the off-campus offline student-speech jurisprudence thus makes it difficult for students to know the scope of their free speech rights.

In this chapter, we set forth the various court decisions regarding the scope of students' speech rights. We tell the story of students who schools censored for speaking offline in off-campus settings. The chapter includes student-speech cases that occurred before the first Supreme Court student-speech decision – Tinker v. Des Moines Independent Community School District (1969). Additionally, we examine cases since 1969 that have applied the Supreme Court precedents. Our discussion is divided into three categories of students' offline off-campus speech:

1. Speech directed at or against school officials or the school;
2. Speech directed at or against students; and
3. Speech directed at or against persons who are unaffiliated with the school.

SPEECH DIRECTED AT OR AGAINST SCHOOL OFFICIALS OR THE SCHOOL

In this section, we discuss various instances of school censorship of student offline speech. The schools chose to censor the students' speech even though the students spoke in off-campus settings. In this section, we specifically focus on instances of student speech that targeted a teacher, an administrator or the student's school. We examine how courts have approached the offline off-campus student speech and the authority of schools to censor such speech.

1. The Story of Peter Lander, Jr.

The Speech Incident: Old Jack Seaver

The Supreme Court of Vermont was a trailblazer in the judicial review of the right of students to free speech while off-campus. This happened in **Lander v. Seaver** (1859). In that case, 11-year old Peter Lander, Jr., a student in the Burlington school district, directed his speech against his teacher while off-

Their Stories: Offline Off-Campus Speech

campus an hour and a half after the school day had ended. After Peter arrived home from school, he left on a walk with his father's cow. As he drove the cow past his teacher's house, he called the teacher "Old Jack Seaver" in the presence of some of his schoolmates and the teacher (p. 1). The upset teacher reprimanded Peter for the "insulting language" which the court also referred to as "saucy and disrespectful language" (p. 1). The following day, when Peter got to school, the teacher beat him with rawhide as punishment for his speech. Peter claimed the beating was severe but the teacher disputed this. Peter and his father sued claiming that the teacher had no authority to censor the student for his off-campus speech.

Analysis

The Supreme Court of Vermont ruled that school officials have supervisory authority and control over a student not only during school hours but also "from the time he leaves home to go to school till he returns home from school" (Lander v. Seaver, 1859, p. 4). Such a broad scope of authority allows schools to censor off-campus student speech as long as the speech is expressed on the student's trip to and from school. If the student is in the custody of his or her parents on the way to and from school, however, the school has no censorship authority over the student during that time. The court warned the judiciary against equating the school's role to the parental role in student discipline, because, unlike parents, schools do not discipline from the "instinct of parental affection" that comes from a familial attachment to children (p. 6). The court ruled that "[w]hen the child has returned home or to his parent's control, then the parental authority is resumed and the control of the teacher ceases, and then for all ordinary acts of misbehavior the parent alone has the power to punish" (p. 4). The exception to this rule is when the speech has a "direct and immediate tendency to injure the school" and undermine the school official's authority (p. 5). This test was a forerunner for the material and substantial disruption test (see Tinker v. Des Moines Independent Community School District, 1969).

When off-campus student speech is directed against a teacher in front other students, the off-campus nature of the speech does not negate the school's censorship authority because the school needs to be able maintain order within the schoolhouse gate (Lander v. Seaver, 1859). For instance, even though Peter called his teacher "Old Jack Seaver" after he arrived home – at which time parental authority had resumed – the fact that he did so in front of his schoolmates threatened to imminently undermine the teacher's authority over students at the school. Such subversion has a direct and immediate tendency to injure the school by disrupting the ability of the school to maintain order and discipline. Consequently, the court ruled that the teacher could discipline Peter within the schoolhouse gate for his speech outside the schoolhouse gate.

Several rules emerged from Lander v. Seaver (1859). According to the Supreme Court of Vermont, if off-campus student speech is directed at a teacher outside the presence of other students, the parents, rather than the school, have the authority to censor the student. Similarly, if the off-campus speech does not impact the school and is not connected to the school in any way, the parents, not the school, can censor the student. Additionally, if the speech is directed at someone unaffiliated with the school, the school has no censorship authority over the student. This case recognized the right of students to speak off-campus as long as the speech is not related to the school. If the speech is related to the school, the school must show that the speech has more than a remote and indirect impact on the school; the impact must be shown to be immediate and direct. Off-campus student speech that only has a "remote and indirect tendency to injure the school" is speech that does not immediately undermine the ability of school officials to maintain law and order in the school (Lander v. Seaver, p. 5).

In the Lander v. Seaver (1859) case, the presence of teachers and students at the off-campus locale heightened the urgency the court felt to censor the student's speech. The court conceded that it is difficult to distinguish the remote from the immediate when analyzing the impact of speech on the school. According to the Supreme Court of Vermont, however, this distinction is a struggle courts have to grapple with on a case-by-case basis. The only guidance in the case for making this distinction was the list of examples of off-campus speech that could create a direct and immediate impact on the school:

1. Language shared with other students to incite insubordination or disorder at the school;
2. Language designed to "heap odium and disgrace" on the teacher (p. 5); or
3. "Writings and pictures placed so as to suggest evil and corrupt language, images and thoughts to the youth who must frequent the school" (p. 5).

Since Lander v. Seaver, as schools continue to censor students, various other courts have tried to determine the status of students' rights to free speech outside the schoolhouse gate, as evident in the cases discussed next.

2. The Story of Jeffrey Fenton

The Speech Incident: A Teacher Called a Prick

In Fenton v. Stear (1976), Jeffrey Fenton – a senior at Marion Center High School – sued his school district after he was disciplined for speaking outside the schoolhouse gate. Jeffrey spent a Sunday evening in May 1976 with friends at North Plaza in Indiana, Pennsylvania. This shopping center was a considerable distance from Marion Center High School so there was absolutely no doubt that Jeffrey was off-campus. While Jeffrey and his friends were seated in a car at North Plaza, they noticed a teacher from the school. One of the occupants shouted "There's [Donald] Stear" (p. 769). At that point, Jeffrey shouted, "He's a prick" (p. 769). The teacher heard the comment as he drove past Jeffrey and his friends.

The following day, the teacher reported Jeffrey to the school principal (Fenton v. Stear, 1976). When Jeffrey arrived at school, the vice principal questioned him about the speech. After admitting that he called his teacher a prick, Jeffrey was immediately suspended for three days. This was an in-school suspension which barred Jeffrey from curricular and extracurricular activities as well as any form of instruction; though he was allowed to attend school. He was required to report to a small classroom referred to as "the jail" during each of the three days he was suspended (p. 769). He spent the time alone in the classroom while assigned teachers "guarded" him (p. 769). As further punishment for his off-campus speech, Jeffrey was banned from the senior class trip to historic sites during a bicentennial celebration. School officials called Jeffrey's parents to inform them of his off-campus speech and the discipline. Jeffrey's mother then called the district superintendent to express concern about the censorship of her son. The superintendent, however, supported the school officials' decision to discipline Jeffrey. Jeffrey's parents insisted that the school board president bring up the issue for discussion at the school board meeting later that evening. At the end of the school board discussion, the board concluded that, since Jeffrey admitted to calling his teacher a prick, the school had the authority to discipline him.

Subsequent to the board hearing, the vice principal informed Jeffrey's parents of a hearing to address the scope of the discipline (Fenton v. Stear, 1976). The notice stated that the school could add seven more days to the suspension after the hearing. At the informal hearing, however, the principal expressed a

Their Stories: Offline Off-Campus Speech

desire to impose a more significant punishment on Jeffrey. The principal stated that if Jeffrey had called him a prick, unlike the teacher, he would have "wrung" Jeffrey's neck (p. 770). He imposed a complete school restriction on Jeffrey for the rest of the school year – a total of eleven days (in addition to the three-day suspension he served earlier). Under the complete school restriction, Jeffrey was required to seek school permission to go anyway inside or outside of the school during the school day. The restriction also prohibited him from speaking to anyone while walking from one class to another. Additionally, he was barred from all extracurricular activities. Finally, in the cafeteria, he was only allowed to sit at the restriction table alongside other students under restriction. These multiple disciplinary actions were taken against Jeffrey simply because of his off-campus speech. In his First Amendment suit against the district, Jeffrey sought an injunction, monetary damages and expungement of his discipline record.

Analysis

Jeffrey argued that school officials had no authority to censor his speech since it was delivered "on Sunday evening at a public parking lot" (Fenton v. Stear, 1976, p. 772). The federal district court for the western district of Pennsylvania rejected this argument, stating that the "validity of this argument is subject to some doubt" (p. 772). The court reasoned that, in a public place, Jeffrey's teacher had a right to be free from loud insulting words that are lascivious, lewd or indecent. Further, in a public place, the teacher had a right to be free from fighting words or insulting remarks that "by their very utterance inflict injury or tend to incite an immediate breach of the peace" (p. 771). Jeffrey violated these rights by calling the teacher a prick. Additionally, speech that includes "fighting words, the lewd and obscene, the profane and libelous, is not safeguarded by the Constitution" (p. 771). Therefore, the school could censor Jeffrey's speech without violating the First Amendment. The court's simultaneous references to fighting words, obscene speech and defamatory speech – unprotected speech categories that govern adults – suggest that the court would analyze off-campus student speech in the same way it would analyze the speech of adults.

The federal district court ruled that "when a high school student refers to a high school teacher in a public place on a Sunday by a lewd and obscene name in such a loud voice that the teacher and others hear the insult it may be deemed a matter for discipline in the discretion of the school authorities" (Fenton v. Stear, 1976, p. 772). Failure to empower schools to discipline students for off-campus speech directed against a teacher in a public place, could have "devastating consequences" on the ability of school officials to maintain order within the school (p. 772). The court's blind decision to automatically correlate loud insulting off-campus speech directed against a teacher to a disastrous disruption of order in the school is disturbing. Particularly because it was Jeffrey's teacher, rather than Jeffrey, who took the speech to the school when the teacher reported him to the principal. No evidence was presented that Jeffrey or his friends took the speech to school. Nonetheless, the court was willing to expand school-censorship authority beyond the schoolhouse gate.

The federal district court rejected Jeffrey's argument that, since his remark was off-campus speech, the only remedy available to the teacher should be in criminal or civil court (Fenton v. Stear, 1976). The court reasoned that a criminal or civil court might view the remark as a de minimus insult, foreclosing the teacher's opportunity for a remedy. Consequently, it was important to authorize schools to discipline students for their off-campus speech in order to assure the targeted teacher some form of remedy. The court effectively elevated the interests of the teacher for justice or vengeance above the student's constitutional right to free speech. This is deeply disturbing.

The federal district court emphasized the need for courts to defer to school decisions about discipline, even when the speech occurs outside the schoolhouse gate (Fenton v. Stear, 1976). Under the court's approach, as long as off-campus student speech is deemed lewd, lascivious, obscene, profane, libelous or fighting words, schools have unbridled authority to censor the speech. The focus on lewd, lascivious, obscene or profane speech is similar to that which arose ten years later in Bethel School District No. 403 v. Fraser (1986); though unlike the *Bethel* case, the federal district court in Fenton v. Stear explicitly extended the focus beyond the schoolhouse gate.

An overarching theme in the court's analysis was the need for judicial restraint in second-guessing school-discipline decisions (Fenton v. Stear, 1976). This deference applies even when school officials make mistakes, if the mistake is insignificant. Besides, the court ruled that the discipline imposed on Jeffrey for his off-campus speech was negligible because it was merely an in-school suspension rather than an out-of-school suspension or expulsion. As a result, there was no need to second-guess the school decision. The problem with deference to school mistakes or classification of censorship as negligible, in order to further deference, is that deprivation of First Amendment rights, even for a brief period of time, causes irreparable harm (Beussink v. Woodland R-IV School District, 1998). Thus, such deprivation cannot be deemed an insignificant mistake or negligible censorship.

A court, like the federal district court in Fenton v. Stear (1976), threatens the First Amendment free speech rights of students who speak off-campus because of its willingness to give significant deference to schools. Schools, on the other hand, would welcome this approach as it expands their censorship authority beyond the four walls of the school.

3. The Story of Shasta Hatter

The Speech Incident: Boycotting the Chocolate Drive

Shasta Hatter, a student at Venice High School in California, decided to protest her school's dress code through a boycott of the school's annual chocolate drive – a fundraiser to support student activities (Hatter v. Los Angeles City High School District, 1971). She chose to rally other students in support of her protest by handing out flyers before school hours outside the schoolhouse gate. Shasta distributed the flyers, which called for a boycott of the drive, at a street corner located across from the school. She used no school resource or time for the speech. Upon learning of the speech, school officials suspended her from the school until the drive was over. The court noted that this suspension threatened to prejudice Shasta's employment and college opportunities. Shasta sued her school district, claiming that school officials violated her First Amendment free speech rights. She sought an injunction and declaratory judgment that she had a constitutional right to distribute the flyers off-campus.

Analysis

The United States Court of Appeals for the Ninth Circuit emphasized that, even though students are not adults, they are persons under the United States Constitution within the schoolhouse gate as well as outside the schoolhouse gate (Hatter v. Los Angeles City High School District, 1971). Here the court was simply echoing a similar ruling of the United States Supreme Court in Tinker v. Des Moines Independent Community School District (1969) (discussed in chapter seven of this book). The court declared that

Their Stories: Offline Off-Campus Speech

students could enjoy constitutional protection even for matters that are of no import to adults (Hatter v. Los Angeles City High School District, 1971). Indeed, "[t]hey are entitled in the absence of compelling countervailing considerations to exercise their First Amendment right to freely express themselves upon those issues which concern them" (p. 675). The court rejected the contention that schools should have unbridled authority to censor student speech unless the speech relates to a matter of significant national concern. It warned judges to avoid the treacherous path of using and assigning relative social importance to speech when making determinations of constitutional protection; otherwise, judicial bias might become a factor in First Amendment analysis as judges pick and choose issues to accord protection.

The federal circuit court of appeals relied on the material and substantial disruption test created in Tinker v. Des Moines Independent Community School District (1969) for its analysis (Hatter v. Los Angeles City High School District, 1971). The school district argued that Shasta's off-campus speech disrupted the school because teachers found it difficult to convince students to focus on their class subjects rather than discussing the boycott. Shasta countered that she did not encourage students to disrupt their classes; accordingly, the school could not attribute the disruption to her. The court found insufficient evidence of material and substantial disruption to justify the school's censorship of Shasta. In its remand of the case, the court directed the lower court to further assess the record in order to determine if the school had evidence that could show material and substantial disruption or reasonable forecast of such disruption.

What is remarkable about this case, which was decided two years after the *Tinker* case, is that the federal circuit court of appeals chose to apply the material and substantial disruption test without discrimination. While the *Tinker* material and substantial disruption test involved on-campus speech, the federal circuit court of appeals in Hatter v. Los Angeles City High School District (1971) applied the test to off-campus speech. The court seemed to assume that the test was universally applicable to student speech. Had the school shown material and substantial disruption consequent to Shasta's speech, such a showing would have created a nexus between her off-campus speech and events within the school. That could have provided some justification for applying the material and substantial disruption test to Shasta's off-campus speech. However, since the federal circuit court of appeals failed to provide any justification for its decision to use the test for off-campus speech, we may never know the true rationale.

4. The Story of Jason Klein

The Speech Incident: Jason's Middle Finger

On Monday April 14, 1986, a teacher at Oxford Hills High School in Maine drove his son to a restaurant in South Paris, Maine (Klein v. Smith, 1986). The teacher waited in the car while his son went into the restaurant to apply for a job. While the teacher waited, Jason Klein – a student at the school – arrived at the restaurant in a vehicle that his companion parked perpendicular to the teacher's car. Before leaving the car for the restaurant, Jason "extended the middle finger of one hand" at the teacher – a gesture "commonly understood to mean 'fuck you'" (p. 1441). The teacher viewed it as a sign of disrespect and was quite offended. Jason did not use any school time or school resource for his speech.

The next day when Jason returned to school he was suspended from school for ten days for his speech (Klein v. Smith, 1986). School officials relied on a school rule prohibiting student use of vulgar language against school employees. Jason filed suit against the school district, seeking an injunction. He alleged that the school district violated his First Amendment right to free speech.

Analysis

Jason's speech took place outside school hours and outside the schoolhouse gate. As the United States District Court for the District of Maine observed, the speech "occurred in a restaurant parking lot, far removed from any school premises or facilities at a time when teacher Clark was not associated in any way with his duties as a teacher" (Klein v. Smith, 1986, p. 1441). It was also at a time when Jason "was not engaged in any school activity or associated in any way with school premises or his role as a student" (p. 1441). In other words, both the teacher and Jason were in their roles as private citizens in a public place. The dissociated status of Jason and the teacher in relation to the school, at the time of the speech, led the court to conclude that the speech had no nexus to the school that could justify censorship. The dissociation also meant that the mere fact that a teacher was the target was an insufficient basis for linking the speech to orderly functioning of the school. The court stated that, at the restaurant, the teacher was a person, a private citizen, who simply happened to be Jason's teacher. In order to show a nexus between the school and the speech, school officials must show much more than the "far too attenuated" evidence presented in Jason's case (p. 1441). They cannot simply rely on the identities of the speaker and the target.

The school officials argued that Jason's speech had weakened their resolve to discipline him and other students within the schoolhouse gate (Klein v. Smith, 1986). Indeed, sixty-two teachers (including the teacher that Jason targeted) signed a letter claiming that they feared a recurrence of Jason's speech and that their ability to discipline had been undermined as had the teacher-student relationship of respect. They argued, therefore, that under the material and substantial disruption test, school officials should be allowed to censor Jason. The federal district court scathingly rightly rejected this argument:

The Court cannot accept, however, this body of evidence as accurately predicting, however heartfelt it may presently be, the future course of the administration of discipline at Oxford Hills High. The Court cannot do these sixty-two mature and responsible professionals the disservice of believing that collectively their professional integrity, personal mental resolve, and individual character are going to dissolve, willy-nilly, in the face of the digital posturing of this splenetic, bad-mannered little boy. I know that the prophecy implied in their testimony will not be fulfilled. I think that they know that, too (Klein v. Smith, 1986, p. 1441).

It is interesting that, in its response to the school's argument that Jason's off-campus speech caused disruption inside the school, the court applied the material and substantial disruption test – created in an on-campus context – to an off-campus speech context. The court seemed completely oblivious to the distinction in contexts. In other words, a court that was very aware of the off-campus status of Jason's speech and protective of the speech, was oblivious to the on-campus context of the material and substantial disruption test which it extended to Jason's off-campus speech.

The federal district court indicated that schools could censor off-campus speech that constitutes fighting words because such speech enjoys no First Amendment protection (Klein v. Smith, 1986). However, it concluded that Jason's speech did not constitute fighting words. The court reasoned that, even though the teacher was quite offended by the speech and felt like taking violent action against Jason, he actually showed restraint. Additionally, the court found that teachers and administrators at Oxford Hills High School had commonly encountered the middle finger gesture from students; yet those teachers and administrators did not respond violently to the students. Consequently, the teacher's encounter at the restaurant was not so unique as to trigger a just violent response from the teacher. The federal district

Their Stories: Offline Off-Campus Speech

court stated that "[t]he Court can only conclude, contrary to what might be its reflexive, uninformed judgment, that 'the finger,' at least when used against a universe of teachers, is not likely to provoke a violent response" (p. 1441).

The federal district court ruled that, even when schools find students' off-campus to be crude and vulgar, they must not overstep constitutional bounds (Klein v. Smith, 1986). The price of sophisticated and refined student language cannot be the sacrifice of First Amendment free speech rights, regardless of the locale of the speech. According to the court, parents, rather than teachers, are responsible for students' speech outside the schoolhouse gate. The willingness to recognize the supremacy of parents over students outside the schoolhouse gate secured the right of free speech for students when off-campus against school interference in this court. Consequently, once school ends, school-censorship authority ends as well. The two exceptions to this rule arise when off-campus student speech qualifies as unprotected speech such as fighting words; or when the speech is reasonably forecast to cause or actually causes material and substantial disruption to the school.

5. The Story of Alan Burch

The Speech Incident: The Bad Astra

In 1983, five students at Lindbergh High School in Washington decided to create an outlet for the students to express their views beyond the official school-approved outlets (Burch v. Barker, 1988). This led to their creation of a four-page newspaper which they called "Bad Astra" (p. 1150). The newspaper was created off-campus and outside school hours. The students funded their newspaper with their own resources. School officials were not aware of the publication and it was an unofficial newspaper, making it an underground newspaper. The school district, however, had a policy that required students to seek school review and approval before distributing any student-authored publication on the school campus or at school functions. The policy authorized the district to censor articles that included obscenity, drug, liquor or cigarette advertisements, epithets, defamatory language or an incitement to commit illegal acts. Bad Astra did not include any advertisement, profanity, obscenity, religious epithet, or defamatory language.

Some of the articles in Bad Astra criticized the school's student attendance policy, the student service card policy and the school activities policy (Burch v. Barker, 1988). A mock poll evaluating Lindbergh High School's teachers was also included. The students also included poems from various well-known poets such as Edgar Lee Masters. On May 20, 1983, the students distributed several copies of the newspaper at a school-sponsored senior class barbeque. The mother of one of the students who was also the school's parent-teacher association president distributed copies through the faculty and staff mailboxes. The principal claimed that the students violated the school's pre-distribution policy which required review and approval of student-written publications. Consequently, he censured the students and put reprimand letters in their files. The students sued the school district under the Free Speech Clause of the United States Constitution. They asked the court to order expungement of the letters from their files and to enjoin the school from enforcing the pre-distribution policy.

Analysis

The school district and the students stipulated that Bad Astra's contents were not objectionable under the school's policy (Burch v. Barker, 1988). Nonetheless, the district insisted that the students should have complied with the policy by seeking school pre-approval of the newspaper. In other words, the school used the failure to seek pre-approval as a basis to censor the student speech in Bad Astra. The United States Court of Appeals for the Ninth Circuit decided to apply the material and substantial disruption test to the case. It reasoned that the school's actual reason for censoring the speech was "undifferentiated fear of disruption" (p. 1154). According to the court, the "policy appears to be based upon far less justification than the action of the school principals in *Tinker*, which was directed at specific expression in an atmosphere of political turmoil. The school's action in this case is contrary to the principles laid down in *Tinker*" (p. 1154).

The court of appeals found no evidence of material and substantial disruption from the underground newspaper (Burch v. Barker, 1988). As the court observed, even though the newspaper was distributed while the rock band was playing at the barbeque, the distribution did not disrupt the band or the ongoing socialization. The court compared the district to the largest school district in the state – Seattle School District. It reasoned that, if such a large district had no history of material and substantial disruption from an underground newspaper, Lindbergh High School was even less likely to face material and substantial disruption from Bad Astra. Besides, Lindbergh High School had no history of material and substantial disruption from the distribution of underground newspapers. Additionally, the court found no material and substantial disruption because the school presented no statistical evidence that, without a pre-distribution policy, underground newspapers are more likely to cause material and substantial disruption in schools. These various indicia led the court to conclude that the censorship of Bad Astra could not be justified under the material and substantial disruption test. Accordingly, the school could not censor Bad Astra. Further for similar reasons, the pre-distribution policy was deemed unconstitutional; and, as a consequence, the school district could not keep reprimand letters in the students' files.

The court of appeals further objected to the pre-distribution policy because it was censorship based on prior restraint (Burch v. Barker, 1988). The court stated that if students are to be punished for speech, they should be punished after speaking rather than before. Except in extraordinary cases such as imminent national security concerns, prior restraints are an unconstitutional means of censoring speech of Americans. The court extended this rule to school censorship of students' off-campus speech. Specifically, the court stated that a school "policy subjecting all written communications to prior review for possible censorship would be invalid outside the school context" (Burch v. Barker, 1988, p. 1155). The rationale for heightened protection of speech against prior restraint censorship is grounded in its stifling effect on thought:

A system of prior restraint is in many ways more inhibiting than a system of subsequent punishment: It is likely to bring under government scrutiny a far wider range of expression; it shuts off communication before it takes place; ... the system allows less opportunity for public appraisal and criticism; the dynamics of the system drive toward excesses, as the history of all censorship shows (Burch v. Barker, 1988, p. 1155, citing Emerson, 1970, p. 506).

In order to be constitutional, the focus of any pre-distribution policy must be to prevent off-campus speech from causing material and substantial disruption at the school (Burch v. Barker, 1988). For on-campus speech, pre-distribution policies can be constitutional if they satisfy the material and substantial disruption test or if the speech is school-sponsored speech. As the court rightly observed, the United States Supreme Court upheld a prior restraint policy for on-campus speech in Hazelwood v. Kuhlmeier (1988). That case involved a school district's pre-publication policy which required students to seek

Their Stories: Offline Off-Campus Speech

review and approval of articles for the school newspaper. However, unlike the *Hazelwood* test, Burch v. Barker did not involve school-sponsored speech. In fact, Bad Astra was an unauthorized underground newspaper. Therefore, even if Bad Astra were viewed as on-campus speech by virtue of its on-campus distribution, the *Hazelwood* test would be inapplicable to the speech.

This case essentially concluded that school districts cannot use the material and substantial disruption test or the *Hazelwood* test to justify censoring off-campus speech simply because the speech is critical of school policies. Moreover, pre-distribution policies are unconstitutional unless they satisfy the material and substantial disruption test. Effectively, this means that, for off-campus speech, pre-distribution policies are effectively immaterial. This is so because the material and substantial disruption test is the governing standard for prior restraint of off-campus speech. And since a pre-distribution policy cannot be constitutional unless the material and substantial disruption test is part of the policy, the policy itself has no real legal significance independent of the test.

6. The Story of Adam Porter

The Speech Incident: The Sketch of a Violent Siege

In 1999, fourteen-year old Adam Porter, a student at East Ascension High School in Louisiana, drew a sketch of his school in his personal sketchpad (Porter v. Ascension Parish School Board, 2004). The sketch was a crude drawing created at home after school hours without any use of school resources. It showed the school under siege by several armed people, a missile launcher, a helicopter and a tanker truck. It included a drawing of Adam's principal being attacked with a brick as someone yelled the words "shut the fuck up faggot" at the principal (Porter ex rel. LeBlanc v. Ascension Parish School Board, 2004, p. 580). Various racial epithets and obscene language were used in the sketch against the persons featured therein (Porter v. Ascension Parish School Board, 2004). Adam showed the sketch to his mother, his brother and a friend who lived with the family. He never took the sketch to school. Instead, he stored it away in his home closet.

In 2001, Adam's brother, a 12-year old student at Galvez Middle School, found the sketchpad in the closet as he searched for paper to use to draw a llama (Porter v. Ascension Parish School Board, 2004). After drawing the llama in the sketchpad, he took it to his middle school so that his teacher could give him feedback on the llama. Apparently, the teacher did not see Adam's sketch while reviewing his brother's llama nor did anyone during the school day. On the bus ride back home, however, Adam's brother allowed another student to see his llama. As this student looked through the sketchpad, he noticed Adam's sketch and promptly reported it to the bus driver shouting, "Miss Diane, look, they're going to blow up EAHS [East Ascension High School]" (p. 611). The driver seized the sketchpad from Adam's brother and reported him to school officials who questioned him about the siege drawing. Despite his revelation that Adam drew the school siege, school officials suspended Adam's brother from school for possessing the drawing on campus.

The middle school officials forwarded the sketchpad to the school resource officer and administrators at Adam's school (Porter v. Ascension Parish School Board, 2004). When confronted, Adam admitted to drawing the siege but explained that it was drawn two years prior, he had no malicious intent and presented no danger to the school. Nonetheless, due to safety concerns about the drawing, the school officials searched him. During the search, they discovered a box cutter with a one-half inch exposed blade in his wallet. Adam claimed that the cutter was a tool for his job at a grocery store. The school officials' search of his bag revealed various notebooks that referenced death, gang symbols, drugs and sex. Adam explained that the death reference was part of a homework assignment. He also claimed that the gang symbols were merely references to friends whom the principal conceded were not threatening. Nevertheless, school officials decided to immediately suspend Adam and recommend his expulsion. They informed his mother of the sketchpad and the expulsion recommendation. After she learned that expulsion recommendations were typically upheld, she waived the expulsion hearing so that Adam could immediately enroll in an alternative education program. The school resource officer arrested Adam on charges of possession of an illegal weapon and terrorizing of the school. He spent four nights in the local jail. Even though the school permitted Adam to return to school in the fall semester, he dropped out of school during the 2002 spring semester. Adam's mother sued the school district under the Free Speech Clause because the school disciplined him for speech created off-campus that Adam did not bring to school.

Analysis

In its review of Adam's speech, the United States Court of Appeals for the Fifth Circuit classified censorship of student speech into five groups:

1. Censorship of a student's specific viewpoint;
2. Censorship that is unrelated to a student's specific viewpoint;
3. Censorship of lewd, vulgar, obscene or plainly-offensive speech;
4. Censorship of school-sponsored student speech; and
5. Censorship of true threats (Porter v. Ascension Parish School Board, 2004).

The *Morse* test was not included in the list because it was created after this case. As the court noted, the *Hazelwood* test, which governs censorship of school-sponsored student speech, was inapplicable to Adam's speech because his speech was personal student speech. The court found the *Bethel* test inapplicable because the school district did not state that it disciplined Adam for lewd, vulgar, obscene or plainly-offensive speech. This suggests that the court would have applied the *Bethel* test to off-campus speech if the school had disciplined Adam for vulgarity or obscenity of the off-campus speech.

The court ruled that the *Tinker* material and substantial disruption test governs when a school censors a student's specific viewpoint (Porter v. Ascension Parish School Board, 2004). When censorship is unrelated to a viewpoint, however, schools must satisfy three factors in order to validly censor student speech:

1. The censorship must promote a substantial government interest;
2. The government interest must have no relation to suppressing the student's speech; and
3. The incidental speech restrictions due to the censorship must not go beyond what is necessary to promote the government interest.

Even though Adam's speech was unrelated to a viewpoint, the court did not apply the three factors and failed to explain its rationale for not doing so.

Their Stories: Offline Off-Campus Speech

The court ruled that Adam's speech was off-campus speech rather than on-campus speech. Specifically, the court stated that because of "the unique facts of the present case, we decline to find that Adam's drawing constitutes student speech on the school premises" (Porter v. Ascension Parish School Board, 2004, p. 615). The unique facts the court relied upon for this conclusion include the fact that Adam:

1. Created the sketch in his home;
2. Stored the sketch in his closet and it stayed there for two years;
3. Had no intention of ever bringing the sketch to the school (the sketch got to the school unintentionally because of Adam's brother);
4. "Took no action that would increase the chances that his drawing would find its way to school" (p. 615).

The second and fourth factors suggest that if a student takes action to prevent speech from getting to the school campus or avoids action that would bring the speech to school, his off-campus speech would have a better chance of remaining classified as off-campus speech. The court stated, without elaboration, that it is challenging to decide cases where speech created off-campus is brought on-campus by either the student-speaker or another party. According to the court, "[t]he line dividing fully protected 'off-campus' speech from less protected 'on-campus' speech is unclear, however, in cases such as this involving off-campus speech brought on-campus without the knowledge or permission of the speaker" (p. 619). Despite this lack of clarity, the court ruled that, if speech is intentionally brought within the schoolhouse gate, the speech would be converted to "on-campus speech subject to special limitations" (pp. 618-19). The special limitations referenced here are a mystery since the court did not explicate the rule.

The federal circuit court of appeals identified off-campus speech that is "directed at the campus" as a form of off-campus speech that can be censored on-campus (Porter v. Ascension Parish School Board, 2004, p. 615). However, the court did not reveal what would turn off-campus speech into "speech directed at the campus" and thus subject such speech to the United States Supreme Court's student-speech precedents. The lack of clarity is amplified by the court's conclusion that Adam's speech was not speech directed at the campus. This is surprising, given that the sketch ostensibly targeted his principal and showed the school under siege. If that did not constitute speech directed at the school, it is difficult to determine what would unless the court speaks clearly on this.

The federal circuit court of appeals observed that several courts apply the *Tinker* test to off-campus speech without even considering the distinction between off-campus speech and on-campus speech: "Refusing to differentiate between student speech taking place on-campus and speech taking place off-campus, a number of courts have applied the test in *Tinker* when analyzing off-campus speech brought onto the school campus" (Porter v. Ascension Parish School Board, 2004, p. 615). As evident in some of the cases discussed in this book, these courts have applied the *Tinker* test even when someone other than the student-speaker brought the speech to the school. The federal circuit court ruled, however, that the *Tinker* test does not apply to off-campus speech that has unique facts as existed with Adam's speech. These unique facts kept Adam's speech as purely off-campus speech, despite the fact that his brother took the speech to school. As purely off-campus speech, Adam's speech was therefore not governed by the material and substantial disruption test.

The court's focus on unique facts, purity of off-campus speech like Adam's and on-campus targeting by off-campus speech implies that the court did not foreclose school censorship of students' off-campus speech (Porter v. Ascension Parish School Board, 2004). In fact, the court indicated that schools have censorship authority over off-campus student speech though that authority is more circumscribed than that over on-campus speech. The court did not identify or explain the extent of the circumscribed authority, however. This makes it difficult for students to know when they are truly engaged in off-campus speech and when they transition into on-campus speech. It also makes it challenging for schools to know the extent of their censorship authority. Additionally, not every student speech will have a unique fact like the two-year storage in a home closet that played a key factor in the court's conclusion that Adam's speech was purely off-campus speech.

Given the off-campus nature of Adam's speech, the court chose the true-threat doctrine as the governing standard (Porter v. Ascension Parish School Board, 2004). According to the court, "[s]peech is a 'true threat' and therefore unprotected if an objectively reasonable person would interpret the speech as a 'serious expression of an intent to cause a present or future harm'" (p. 616, citing Doe v. Pulaski County Special School District, 2002, p. 622). True-threat analysis is not triggered unless the speaker intended to communicate the alleged threat to the target or a third party; or if the speaker "publicized [the speech] in a way certain to result in its appearance" within the schoolhouse gate (Porter v. Ascension Parish School Board, 2004, p. 620). The speech does not constitute a true threat if the speech does not satisfy this threshold determination. The speaker's subjective intent to execute the alleged threat is irrelevant to a true-threat analysis; as is the speaker's capability to execute the alleged threat. The court chose not to apply the reasonable-speaker or reasonable-recipient view of true threats because it found that the case could be decided strictly based on the intent-to-communicate threshold requirement.

The federal circuit court of appeals ruled that, even though Adam intentionally communicated the speech to his mother, his brother and his friend, that communication was not enough to make the speech unprotected (Porter v. Ascension Parish School Board, 2004). This was because, as the court explained, a speaker must intentionally communicate the alleged threat beyond the confines of his home in order for the speech to even merit a true-threat analysis. Adam's speech could not constitute a true threat because he only communicated the speech to people inside his home and because the speech stayed in the home for two years. The fact that the speech got to the campus accidentally rather than because of Adam's intent buffered the decision not to deem his speech a true threat.

Additionally, Adam did not publicize his sketch in a way that would have made it a certainty that the speech would get to the school campus (Porter v. Ascension Parish School Board, 2004). The court observed that the on-campus presence of the speech was not connected to the in-home communication of the speech to his mother, brother and friend. The two-year interval between this communication and the on-campus arrival of the speech supported this conclusion. The court ruled that "[p]rivate writings made and kept in one's home enjoy the protection of the First Amendment ... For such writings to lose their First Amendment protection, something more than their accidental and unintentional exposure to public scrutiny must take place" (pp. 617-18). Consequently, the court ruled that the school had no constitutional authority to censor Adam's off-campus speech.

The court highlighted the uncertainty in the off-campus student-speech jurisprudence:

[S]ome [courts] have found that off-campus speech is entitled to full First Amendment protection even when it makes its way onto school grounds without the assistance of the speaker. Still others have adopted a combination approach, analyzing off-campus speech under a flurry of standards in an effort to comprehensively address all possible legal approaches. Frustrated by these inconsistencies, commentators

Their Stories: Offline Off-Campus Speech

have begun calling for courts to more clearly delineate the boundary line between off-campus speech entitled to greater First Amendment protection, and on-campus speech subject to greater regulation (Porter v. Ascension Parish School Board, 2004, pp. 619-20).

This book is designed to call attention to this lack of clarity. As the court noted, the lack of clarity makes it difficult for school officials to perform their discipline responsibilities while respecting students' rights to free speech. The court observed:

[A] reasonable school official facing this question [the First Amendment right of students to off-campus speech] for the first time would find no 'pre-existing' body of law from which he could draw clear guidance and certain conclusions. Rather, a reasonable school official would encounter a body of case law sending inconsistent signals as to how far school authority to regulate student speech reaches beyond the confines of the campus (Porter v. Ascension Parish School Board, 2004, p. 620).

Until the United States Supreme Court provides a clear and definitive ruling on the off-campus speech rights of students, the uncertainty will linger.

7. The Story of Jeffrey Schwartz

The Speech Incident: "King Louis" in the High School Free Press

On Monday April 2, 1968, school officials at Jamaica High School in New York, found Jeffrey Schwartz, a senior, distributing materials at the school during school hours (Schwartz v. Schuker, 1969). The materials, which were created off-campus, asked students to join a student-strike effort. While Jeffrey was not disciplined, the dean informed him that students could not distribute outside publications at the school without prior approval. Almost a year later, the principal approached Jeffrey about another off-campus publication called the High School Free Press. The principal, who had read the fourth issue of the publication, told Jeffrey that he would not be allowed to distribute the fifth issue of the publication on the school's campus. The principal was concerned because the fourth issue used "four-letter words, filthy references, abusive and disgusting language and nihilistic propaganda" (p. 240).

Four days later, Jeffrey distributed thirty-two copies of the fifth issue off-campus but near the school's campus (Schwartz v. Schuker, 1969). Other students distributed copies on school grounds. This fifth issue sharply criticized the principal. The publication referred to the principal as "'King Louis', 'a big liar', and a person having 'racist views and attitudes'" (p. 240). While Jeffrey did not distribute the publication on-campus, he did ask a student not to comply with the dean's order to stop distribution on-campus. The school informed Jeffrey's parents that he was suspended from school for "contumelious behavior" (p. 240). Despite the suspension, Jeffrey returned to school in compliance with his mother's instruction who opposed the suspension. The superintendent then recommended the school either force Jeffrey to graduate within a week or that he be transferred to another school in the district. Jeffrey and his parents did not accept the recommendation. They filed suit against the district claiming that the school district violated Jeffrey's free speech rights by suspending him for distributing the publication "off school grounds near the property of the high school" (p. 239). They sought declaratory judgment and an injunction against further deprivation of Jeffrey's rights.

Analysis

The United States District Court for the Eastern District of New York chose to focus more on Jeffrey's disobedience and defiant behavior rather than his free speech rights (Schwartz v. Schuker, 1969). The court stated that, rather than defiance, "[t]here surely was another way if he and his parents so desired, to squarely present the issue of his right to disseminate off but next to school property, copies of the subterranean paper, High School Free Press" (p. 241). The court chided Jeffrey for not respecting the various directives of school officials and for bringing the newspaper on-campus. The court even chided him for his disobedience after he was punished – returning to school during his suspension. Even though Jeffrey brought the case as a First Amendment challenge to the censorship of his off-campus speech, the court's decision to frame the issue as a defiance issue conveniently allowed the court to skirt the free speech issue. The court opined that Jeffrey should have exercised his free speech rights obediently. Requiring students to exercise free speech rights obediently stifles the freedom that free speech seeks to inspire. While a jurisprudence focused on student obedience would allow courts to avoid deciding the complicated issue of students' off-campus speech rights, it empowers schools to censor student speech.

Even when schools censor student speech because of a dislike of the speech, they could make a pretextual claim that they merely disciplined the students for defiance or disobedience. It is interesting that the court took this approach despite its acknowledgment that Tinker v. Des Moines Independent Community School District (1969) established the right of students to free speech. The court also conceded that schools have no authority to censor student speech that offends school officials (Schwartz v. Schuker, 1969). Nonetheless, the court declared that "[g]ross disrespect and contempt for the officials of an educational institution may be justification not only for suspension but also for expulsion of a student" (Schwartz v. Schuker, p. 242). When a court, such as in this case, fails to rule on a First Amendment off-campus speech issue, it allows the perpetuation of uncertainty in the off-campus speech jurisprudence. Jeffrey likely emerged from the case not knowing whether he had a First Amendment right to distribute his off-campus speech outside, but near, the schoolhouse gate. He probably also emerged from the case wondering if he had to subordinate his First Amendment speech rights to school directives against the speech, in order not to be disciplined for insubordination. Finally, the school likely emerged from the case with a renewed sense that it could censor student off-campus speech with impunity if the censorship is characterized as discipline for insubordination. Indeed, the court indicated that because high school students are not as mature as college students, schools have greater censorship authority over them in order to help them separate propaganda from facts.

8. The Story of Justin Boucher

The Speech Incident: The Diary and the Pseudo-Nazi Group

In April 1997, students at Greenfield High School in Wisconsin launched an underground newspaper called "The Last" (Boucher v. School Board of School District of Greenfield, 1998). The newspaper was an underground newspaper in the sense that it was not a school-sponsored or school-authorized newspaper. The newspaper and its articles were created outside the schoolhouse gate without use of school resources. The students sought to encourage free speech and foster debate so they included a free speech pledge in the newspaper. The pledge, included at the beginning of the newspaper, read as follows: "*No* censorship is impossible to achieve and wouldn't make for a very good paper, so we'll settle for a *minimum* of

Their Stories: Offline Off-Campus Speech

censorship. We will accept anything so long as it has some point or at least some interesting quality" (p. 822). The articles in the newspaper were published without the real names of the student authors in order to maintain their anonymity and protect them from school officials. The first issue stated that "The Last" was designed to "ruffle a few feathers and jump-start some to action" (p. 822). The language used in the newspaper led Judge Cudahy to remark that "The Last is not your father's newspaper" (p. 822).

The June issue of "The Last" featured an anonymous article titled "So You Want To Be A Hacker" with the byline Sacco and Vanzetti (Boucher v. School Board of School District of Greenfield, 1998, p. 822). The introductory section of the article explained the reason for the article as follows:

We would like first to say that Sacco and Vanzetti do not publish 'The Last.' We are merely hackers with anarchistic views who have a little section in 'The Last.' Recently at our school Mrs. Authority (we can't use her real name but you should know who she is) has been harassing the hackers. We have been blamed for virii in the computers, for the printers fucking up, for changing peoples passwords, for windows going too slow and pretty much every other thing caused by Mrs. Authority's own fucking stupidity. There never was a virus in the computers. She just fucked something up and needed a scapegoat so she blamed the hackers. So we have now decided to tell everyone how to hack the schools gay ass computers. We hope you enjoy and remember that your parents tax dollars paid for those fucking computers so you have a right to know what's on them (Boucher v. School Board of School District of Greenfield, 1998, p. 829).

The article described ways for students to determine the identity of anyone using the school's network at any given time (Boucher v. School Board of School District of Greenfield, 1998). This information was designed to help students avoid getting caught. The article also educated students on how to quickly exit the computer in order to avoid being caught while hacking. It cautioned that "[i]f a teacher is on or YoungM or sysop or ghs or admin are on then I would suggest not doing any hacking because you might get caught" (p. 822). The authors included various disclaimers, including one which warned that "if you are a fucking idiot and get caught Sacco and Vanzetti and any publishers or distributors of 'The Last' will not be held responsible. Just say god made me do it and they might let you off" (p. 830). To further stress the importance of not getting caught, the article stated that:

Recently at a school which will remain nameless three hackers, we can't use their real names so we'll just call them Adam D., Brian R., and Justin B, were all accused of doing evil shit on the computers. What was that they were doing that was so evil. Well this is pretty horrible so prepare yourself. They were trying to program computers. I know that's pretty awful they were trying to do something that can get you hired by companies but rather than help them the school saw them as a perfect scapegoat to blame their computer 'experts' stupidity on. We can't use her name so we'll call her Mrs. Old Bitch. Now whenever this dumb bitch fucks something up these three students get blamed. We write this as a warning of what can happen if you get caught. So be careful and remember that when you're in the computer lab they can trace you and everyone is watching you (Boucher v. School Board of School District of Greenfield, 1998, p. 830).

In the technical part of the article, the authors described how students could access the setup utility for the school's computer system (Boucher v. School Board of School District of Greenfield, 1998). It read in pertinent part:

To restart the computer hit 'control-alt-delete' all at the same time. Hit these three buttons twice to exit whatever you were doing very quickly. To enter the computers setup utility restart the computer and start holding the F2 button. It may ask for a password to get in so keep guessing. ... To enter DOS off the network unplug the little black cable in the back that looks like a phone cable. Then restart the computer. Then you're in DOS but you can't enter any of the networked programs.

To see a list of every file on the computer go into professional write, if you don't have it log on as ST20 and go to generic then go to professional write. Now hit control-g. it should say H: but if you change it to say H:\>>> then hit enter you will be given a list of a bunch of cool shit. Go under students then under menus to see all the students login names. Go to classes to see all of the teachers log in names. Surely some of these names won't have passwords on them. Find a name, logout and give it a try. ... To enter DOS on the network you must get to the screen where it says "hit control-a to run a floppy." Hit control-a and then hit control-c it should now say terminate batch job. Hit y then hit f. Now type in H:\ then hit enter. Now hit cd\ then hit enter. Now you can access of the .com or .exe files (Boucher v. School Board of School District of Greenfield, 1998, p. 830).

The article featured various comments about accessing passwords for the school computers, beginning with the statement that "the school isn't all that smart so the password should be real easy to guess or crack" (Boucher v. School Board of School District of Greenfield, 1998, p. 822). It suggested potential passwords to students:

Some commonly used passwords at very stupid schools are: first names, last names, ghs, ghsteacher, williefred, hacker, teacher, and password. Remember that these won't always work and they probably won't but they're a good starting point when your guessing (Boucher v. School Board of School District of Greenfield, 1998, p. 822).

Additionally, the article instructed students on how to access the list of each computer's files. The authors told students to practice their hacking skills and then "when you have mastered all this shit I'll be happy to teach you more" (p. 822). The conclusion section of the article stated:

E-mail SaccoandVanzetti@juno.com. Don't even try to trace my account to find out who I am because it's all under fake ass names and I use a modem jammer when I dial so don't even try to fuck with me. If I catch any of you saying that you made this shit up or that you're Sacco or Vanzetti I will fucking kill you and you will be the biggest lamer in the world. Until next time (Boucher v. School Board of School District of Greenfield, 1998, p. 830).

On June 4, 1997, the newspaper issue that contained this hacking article was distributed on the school's campus in places such as the cafeteria and bathrooms (Boucher v. School Board of School District of Greenfield, 1998). After learning of this distribution and the article, school officials hired computer experts who spent four hours conducting diagnostic testing on the computer system. School officials also changed all the passwords referenced in the article. The school's investigation revealed that Justin Boucher, a junior at Greenfield High School, was the only author of the article (as opposed to the multiple authorship suggested in the article). Justin was suspended for the remaining fifteen days of the school year and recommended for expulsion. Shortly thereafter, the school board expelled him for one school year, reasoning that while Justin created the article off-campus, he had knowledge that the article would be distributed on-campus by other students. The school board argued that the article endangered school property. Justin filed a First Amendment suit against the school district seeking an injunction and other equitable relief.

Analysis

Justin argued that his speech could not be censored because it was protected pursuant to the United States Supreme Court's ruling that "[s]tudents in the public schools do not 'shed their constitutional rights to freedom of speech or expression at the schoolhouse gate'" (Boucher v. School Board of School District of Greenfield, 1998, p. 825, citing Tinker v. Des Moines Independent Community School District, 1969, p. 506). He contended that the censorship authority of schools over students' "off-campus expression is much more limited than it is over expression on school grounds" (Boucher v. School Board of School District of Greenfield, p. 828). In other words, Justin conceded that school-censorship authority extends beyond the schoolhouse gate; it is simply not as far reaching as censorship authority over on-campus speech. The United States Court of Appeals for the Seventh Circuit, however, stated that Justin failed to present any precedent to support the proposition that schools do not have as broad a censorship authority over off-campus speech as they do over on-campus speech.

The court of appeals chose to treat Justin's speech as on-campus speech rather than off-campus speech (Boucher v. School Board of School District of Greenfield, 1998). The court reasoned that, even though Justin did not distribute the article on-campus, the article "appeared with his knowledge ... for distribution at school" (p. 824). In essence, Justin could reasonable foresee that the speech would make it to the school campus. Additionally, even though the article was published off-campus, it advocated for students to take action – hacking – within the schoolhouse gate. In other words, an off-campus speaker's knowledge of on-campus distribution of his speech, as well as the speaker's advocacy of on-campus activity in the speech, would convert off-campus speech into on-campus speech. Given that Justin's speech was classified as on-campus speech, the United States Supreme Court's student-speech precedents were readily applicable since those precedents likewise arose in on-campus contexts.

The court of appeals decided to use the material and substantial disruption test for its review of Justin's speech (Boucher v. School Board of School District of Greenfield, 1998). Justin argued that the school could not punish him for the distribution of the newspaper in the cafeteria and other on-campus locations because the Supreme Court had ruled that students "cannot be punished merely for expressing their personal views on the school premises—'whether in the cafeteria, or on the playing field, or on the campus during the authorized hours'" (Boucher v. School Board of School District of Greenfield, 1998, p. 825, citing Hazelwood School District v. Kuhlmeier, 1988, p. 266). The court of appeals disagreed because school officials had reasonable grounds to forecast material and substantial disruption from Justin's speech. The court concluded that Justin's article had a "palpably transgressive" agenda (Boucher v. School Board of School District of Greenfield, p. 825). In fact, the court seemed so concerned about the speech that it expressed fear that inclusion of the technical part of Justin's article (see above) within the court's opinion could "risk ... jeopardizing the nation's computer security" (p. 828). The court, however, presented no evidence to support the possibility of such risk. As for material and substantial disruption at the school, the court rightly noted that Justin's encouragement of other students to hack the school's computers could destroy the computer system. The need to change passwords and to conduct four hours of diagnostic testing on the computer system buttressed a finding of material and substantial disruption. The court also observed that Justin's promise to teach students more hacking tricks provided a reasonable basis to forecast even more material and substantial disruption at the school.

In this case, the court decided to view Justin's off-campus creation of the speech as part of a single continuous transaction that included the on-campus distribution of the speech; despite the fact that Justin himself never distributed the article at the school (Boucher v. School Board of School District of Greenfield, 1998). This court effectively ruled that off-campus speech can be punished as on-campus speech if the off-campus speech advocates on-campus action; and if the speech is distributed on-campus by a third party on the school's campus with the knowledge of the speaker. Students would thus be wise to take active steps to prevent their peers or anyone else from distributing controversial off-campus speech on the school's campus; particularly, if the speech advocates action on the school campus. Off-campus speech might also be more likely to be protected if the student-speaker does not advocate on-campus action. Even if the speech does not advocate action on the school campus, however, the speaker could still be censored if the speech gets to the school's campus with the knowledge of the speaker. The court's decision to classify Justin's speech as on-campus speech was an easy way to avoid deciding the complicated question of how to extend the United States Supreme Court's free speech precedents from their on-campus contexts to an off-campus context. This escapism, however, failed to bring us any closer to resolution of the scope of schools' censorship authority over off-campus speech. The court seemed to indicate that schools have coextensive censorship authority over off-campus student speech and on-campus student speech. This is surprising, however, given that in Bethel School District No. 403 v. Fraser (1986), the United States Supreme Court indicated that speech outside the school might enjoy greater protection than on the school's campus. This conflicting position of this court with the Supreme Court's merely adds to the confusing state of the off-campus student-speech jurisprudence.

9. The Story of Donna Thomas, John Tiedeman, David Jones, and Richard Williams

The Speech Incident: *Hard Times* Pasquinades the School

In November 1978, Donna Thomas, John Tiedeman, David Jones and Richard Williams – senior students at Granville Junior-Senior High School in New York – decided to create a satirical underground newspaper directed at their school (Thomas v. Board of Education, Granville Central School District, 1979). Over the next several months, as they finalized plans for the publication, they decided to pattern it after the National Lampoon which satirizes sexual issues. They did some of their preparations for the publication in the classroom of George Mager, a teacher who they consulted "on isolated grammar and content" questions (p. 1045). The on-campus preparations, however, were relatively minor compared to the significant work done wholly off-campus at the students' homes. The most work the students did on-campus was the occasional writing or typing of an article inside the school building. The on-campus preparations for the publication took place after school hours.

Donna, John, David and Richard asked students at Granville Junior-Senior High School to suggest topics for coverage in the newspaper which they called "Hard Times" (Thomas v. Board of Education, Granville Central School District, 1979). Based on the suggestions, Donna, John, David and Richard composed articles that pasquinaded various facets of the school, including teachers, students and school lunches. They also wrote about castration, prostitution, masturbation and sodomy. Additionally, the

Their Stories: Offline Off-Campus Speech

newspaper featured a cartoon and various puzzles. The cover page stated that the newspaper's contents were "uncensored, vulgar, immoral" (p. 1045). In January 1979, after George Mager saw a draft of one of the articles, he reported the students to the assistant principal. The assistant principal confronted John and informed him of the repercussions of offensive publications, including suspension from school. He also warned him against using students' names in the newspaper and against bringing the newspaper on school grounds. Subsequently, John, Donna, David and Richard made wholesale changes to the newspaper, including removal of student names and elimination of various articles. They took great pains to dissociate the newspaper from the school, including incorporation of a disclaimer legend on the publication's cover. In the disclaimer, they disavowed responsibility for any on-campus presence of the publication.

John, Donna, David and Richard printed 100 copies of the newspaper at a local business (Thomas v. Board of Education, Granville Central School District, 1979). They stored the copies in George's classroom closet, with his permission, until they were able to retrieve them for sale to students at an off-campus store. John, Donna, David and Richard only retrieved and sold the newspapers after school hours. Besides, they only sold them to high school students to ensure that only mature students got the newspaper. Despite John, Donna, David and Richard's efforts to exclude the newspaper from the school campus, a teacher found a student with a copy on school grounds and notified the principal (Thomas v. Board of Education, Granville Central School District, 1979). In spite of this on-campus presence, the newspaper caused no disruption to the school. Accordingly, the principal and superintendent decided to delay disciplinary action until they could fully determine the on-campus impact of the newspaper. In the interim, the school board president and mother of a student who learned of the newspaper demanded that the school officials take disciplinary action. She also threatened to convene a board meeting to address the situation. The principal promptly commenced an investigation during which George revealed that he only had a role, albeit a small role, in the newspaper's storage and editing for publication. The investigation also identified John, Donna, David and Richard as the newspaper's publishers.

After the students' parents were notified of the investigation's findings, the school district decided to take several disciplinary actions against the students (Thomas v. Board of Education, Granville Central School District, 1979). In the letter to the parents, the school officials characterized the newspaper as "morally offensive, indecent, and obscene" (p. 1046). Each student was given a five-day suspension with a possibility of reduction to three days if the student wrote an essay discussing the dangers of obscene and irresponsible publications. Additionally, during the suspension, the students were stripped of all their school privileges. For the entire month of February, students who failed to submit a satisfactory essay were segregated from their peers during study hall. The suspension letters were also placed in the students' files. Their parents filed a First Amendment suit against the school district seeking injunctive as well as declaratory relief.

Analysis

The United States Court of Appeals for the Second Circuit acknowledged that school officials need substantial authority to discipline students (Thomas v. Board of Education, Granville Central School District, 1979). However, that authority must comport with the United States Constitution which has a "deeply held preference for free discourse over enforced silence" (p. 1047). The court stated that its "willingness to defer to the schoolmaster's expertise in administering school discipline rests, in large measure, upon the supposition that the arm of authority does not reach beyond the schoolhouse gate" (pp. 1044-45). This is one of the rare cases on record where a court explicitly limited the censorship authority of schools to the confines of the schoolhouse gate. The court added that, "[w]hen an educator seeks to extend his dominion beyond these bounds, therefore, he must answer to the same constitutional commands that bind all other institutions of government" (p. 1045). This ruling indicates that outside the schoolhouse gate, students have the same constitutional protections as non-students. Additionally, in order to censor students' speech outside the schoolhouse gate, schools must comply with traditional constitutional standards that govern adults. In such cases, schools cannot rely on the in-school free speech precedents of the United States Supreme Court. The court reasoned that outside the schoolhouse gate, the right to speak freely about controversial subjects is foundational to the effective functioning of our democratic system. Therefore, the strict standards that traditionally govern speech of non-students outside the schoolhouse gate must similarly apply to students' speech in the same realm. Otherwise, students would not understand the import of liberal preservation of speech rights for sustenance of our democracy.

The court observed that residents of prisons and military barracks retain free speech rights, albeit limited rights (Thomas v. Board of Education, Granville Central School District, 1979). However, free speech restrictions that govern in a prison or barracks do not follow the soldier or prisoner into the larger community. Similarly free speech rules within school should not follow students outside the schoolhouse gate. The court favored a marketplace of ideas where speech and counter-speech rule rather than censorship. This approach prevails outside the schoolhouse gate and favors exposure to all viewpoints and ideas which then compete for acceptance in public discourse. This approach is important because "[e]mbodied in our democracy is the firm conviction that wisdom and justice are most likely to prevail in public decisionmaking if *all* ideas, discoveries, and points of view are before the citizenry for its consideration" (p. 1047). The only exception to this broad rule favoring free speech occurs where the speech has exceedingly small value and poses great harm. The limited speech categories that fit under this exception are obscenity, defamation, true threats, fighting words and child pornography. For such speech, there is no First Amendment protection. Rather than expanding these categories, courts must practice intentional judicial frugality in authorizing censorship. Otherwise there would be a "chilling effect that inexorably produces a silence born of fear" of discipline for speech (p. 1048).

Thomas v. Board of Education, Granville Central School District (1979) was a unique case in that the court explicitly rejected application of *Tinker* and its progeny to off-campus speech. The court reasoned that the Supreme Court's precedents occurred in an on-campus context which is factually distinct from an off-campus context. It also reasoned that in *Tinker* and its progeny, the Supreme Court Justices merely envisioned on-campus settings for speech. The court characterized the entirety of the work that John, Donna, David and Richard did within the school for the publication as "scant and insignificant school contacts" that were constitutionally immaterial (p. 1045). This made the off-campus and on-campus nexus "[d]e minimis" (p. 1050). In fact, the students took deliberate steps to ensure that "all but an insignificant amount of relevant activity in this case was deliberately designed to take place beyond the schoolhouse gate" (p. 1050). Therefore, their speech, which was conceived, printed and sold off-campus, could not be viewed as on-campus speech. The school was therefore reaching beyond the schoolhouse gate to censor these speech activities. "Here, because school officials have ventured out of the school yard and into the general community where the freedom accorded expression is at its zenith, their actions must be evaluated by the principles that bind government officials in the public arena" (p. 1050).

Earlier, we pointed out that, in the letter notifying the students' parents of the disciplinary actions, the principal characterized the newspaper as "morally offensive, indecent, and obscene" (Thomas v. Board of Education, Granville Central School District, 1979, p. 1046). The court indicated that, as off-campus speech, the *Miller* test (Miller v. California, 1973) for obscenity rather than an in-school standard

Their Stories: Offline Off-Campus Speech

for obscenity should govern the students' speech. The court's insistence that the *Miller* test apply to determinations of obscenity in off-campus student speech aligns with its insistence that *Tinker* and its progeny apply only within the schoolhouse gate; and that the same traditional free speech jurisprudence governing in the adult community apply off-campus to students. The school district's characterization of the newspaper was found wanting because the school district failed to provide documentation that it applied the *Miller* test before concluding that the speech was obscene. The court also noted, without elaboration, that morally-offensive speech is not necessarily synonymous with obscene speech; the school failed to make such a distinction in its letter to the parents. School officials' lack of understanding or even knowledge of foundational constitutional principles such as the *Miller* test brings into question their ability to properly safeguard students' rights even if off-campus censorship were authorized.

Even though the court of appeals indicated that traditional speech jurisprudence must govern school censorship of off-campus student speech, in another rule, the court apparently nullified the off-campus censorship power of schools. Specifically, the court ruled that outside the schoolhouse gate, punishment for speech must originate from an impartial adjudicator that is independent of the school (Thomas v. Board of Education, Granville Central School District, 1979). Ostensibly, a school is not an impartial and independent adjudicator when it punishes students for the content of the off-campus speech. The court explained that, when punishing a student for off-campus speech, "a school official acts as both prosecutor and judge when he moves against student expression. His intimate association with the school itself and his understandable desire to preserve institutional decorum give him a vested interest in suppressing controversy" (p. 1051). Adults in the off-campus community could also influence the school to muzzle controversial views further making the school impartial. The adult community's endorsement of censorship for off-campus student speech, however, must not override the First Amendment prohibition of censorship. Consequently, the First Amendment precluded the school from censoring John, Donna, David and Richard in response to a community leader (on the school board) and mother's call for censorship. The problem with the impartial-adjudicator rationale for precluding off-campus censorship is that, besides the judiciary, there is no truly independent adjudicator of censorship. Law enforcement has an interest in punishing people for speech they consider harmful. At the point of punishment, law enforcement acts as prosecutor and judge; yet, courts allow law enforcement to punish speech that presents imminent and present danger.

On the other hand, if we view the impartial-adjudicator rationale merely as a requirement that the judge be a separate entity from the prosecutor, this separation consistently occurs even when schools censor off-campus speech. For instance, in Thomas v. Board of Education, Granville Central School District (1979), the school was the prosecutor. The students' parents appealed the case to the federal court, giving the court the opportunity to fulfil its role as judge in the case. A parallel system exists with law enforcement outside the schoolhouse gate as the accused or charged gets a hearing in court where an independent and impartial adjudicator determines the outcome. Therefore, authorization of off-campus censorship of students' rights would not necessarily unite prosecutorial and judicial roles in one entity. Accordingly, the impartial-adjudicator rationale is not as strong a basis for denying off-campus speech. The stronger rationale is the importance of free speech, discussed earlier, in which the court emphasized the importance of free speech to our constitutional democracy.

However, if the impartial-adjudicator rationale is viewed through the lenses of the comparative length of student discipline and time for judges to hear appeals of cases, the rationale takes on greater validity. As the court noted, student suspensions, for instance, are typically of such short duration that by the time a court hears the case, the student has already completed the discipline (Thomas v. Board of Education, Granville Central School District, 1979). In such a situation, the school would become the *de facto* prosecutor and judge by the mere fact that the judicial review has little to no opportunity to prevent the student from serving the sentence imposed by the prosecutor (the school). "Where, as here, the punishment is virtually terminated before judicial review can be obtained, many students will be content to suffer in silence, a silence that may stifle future expression as well" (p. 1052).

The impartial-adjudicator rationale also takes on added validity if viewed through the lenses of relative costs of censorship to students and school districts. As the court aptly observed, the execution of censorship is costless for the school district; whereas students have to incur significant expenses to initiate a judicial challenge to the censorship (Thomas v. Board of Education, Granville Central School District, 1979). The significant cost to students could create a disincentive to challenging the censorship. In cases where students fail to challenge the censorship, the school essentially becomes the *de facto* prosecutor and judge. Even when students initiate court challenges to censorship, they might have limited resources to pursue a protracted litigation. They might even have less patience for the process. Conversely, the district might have insurance and other resources to support a vigorous defense to the court challenge. Besides, the district's experience with litigation might give it the patience for a protracted litigation. This patience might in turn wear out the student and preclude the district's willingness to negotiate settlement that would be meaningful and favorable to the student. In such a case, the district has the better opportunity to sustain and win the case, making it the *de facto* prosecutor and judge. In the various situations discussed in this and the prior paragraphs about the validity of the impartial-adjudicator rationale, "the promise of judicial review is virtually an empty one" (p. 1052).

School censorship of off-campus student speech could lead to a slippery slope that effectively whittles away parental authority and leaves students with no privacy of speech away from the off-campus prying eyes and iron hand of the school. Schools would then be able to do what traditional police officers and other government entities are not constitutionally permitted to do: take twenty-four hour residence in students' homes. As the court rightly observed:

It is not difficult to imagine the lengths to which school authorities could take the power they have exercised in the case before us. If they possessed this power, it would be within their discretion to suspend a student who purchases an issue of National Lampoon, the inspiration for Hard Times, at a neighborhood newsstand and lends it to a school friend. And, it is conceivable that school officials could consign a student to a segregated study hall because he and a classmate watched an X-rated film on his living room cable television. While these activities are certainly the proper subjects of parental discipline, the First Amendment forbids public school administrators and teachers from regulating the material to which a child is exposed after he leaves school each afternoon. Parents still have their role to play in bringing up their children, and school officials, in such instances, are not empowered to assume the character of Parens patriae. The risk is simply too great that school officials will punish protected speech and thereby inhibit future expression (Thomas v. Board of Education, Granville Central School District, 1979, pp. 1050-51).

Unlike the impartial-adjudicator rationale, the slippery slope rationale is a more valid concern as it could effectively eradicate the schoolhouse gate, making the school borderless. It could also make students' home and bedroom doors mere physical doors of no constitutional consequence. With such broad school power accompanying school officials' lack of training in the constitutional intricacies, unlike judges

Their Stories: Offline Off-Campus Speech

and police officers, school officials could use the power "arbitrarily, erratically, or unfairly" (Thomas v. Board of Education, Granville Central School District, 1979, p. 1051). This would undoubtedly jeopardize sacred free speech rights.

This case gave students the right to speak off-campus free from school censorship. It also recognized that, once the school day ends, students can speak free of school censorship even if they are on the school's campus. Presumably, because at that point, the censorship authority of schools ceases. This case also stated that punishment, if any, for off-campus speech must be initiated from an entity or person that is independent of the school. This effectively stripped the school of any power to initiate censorship of students' off-campus speech. Although the court ruled that the traditional free speech jurisprudence applicable to adults must govern school censorship of students' off-campus speech, this ruling was essentially emptied of significance with the court's ruling that the school cannot initiate or mete out off-campus punishment. Accordingly, this case strictly confined school-censorship authority to on-campus student speech.

10. The Story of Dan Sullivan and Mike Fischer

The Speech Incident: The Pflashlyte Criticizes School Policies and Administrators

Dan Sullivan and Mike Fischer transferred to Sharpstown High School in Texas for their senior year (Sullivan v. Houston Independent School District, 1969). As they began the 1968-69 school year, they realized that their new school did not have any clear regulations about student conduct. Specifically, they were concerned that Sharpstown High School did not have any written rules to provide guidance and notice to students about potential violations of regulations. Consequently, unwritten and maybe ad hoc rules governed the school. Dan and Mike noticed various inconsistencies in the application of the rules. For instance, school officials sometimes banned students from using the park across the school before the start of the school day; while at other times they allowed students to use the park. It was not clear, however, how the school made these decisions since students had nothing in writing to review in determining whether or not they could use the park.

In another situation, Dan was told to remove a neckerchief because it violated unwritten regulations of which he had no prior knowledge (Sullivan v. Houston Independent School District, 1969). On another occasion, Dan, Mike and another student asked the principal if they could conduct a fundraiser for the American Red Cross during school hours in order to support starving citizens of Biafra. The Red Cross fully supported the students' proposal. The principal, however, told the students that the district office prohibited fundraisers during school hours. Additionally, the principal denied the students permission to place small cans for donations on lunch tables, stating that it violated regulations. When Dan sought permission from the district office, he was informed that the principal, not the district office, made decisions about approval of fundraisers. Later that semester, the principal organized a fundraiser during school hours to buy some tropical plants. Dan refused to contribute to the fundraiser after a teacher asked him to during class time. Dan believed that it was hypocritical for the principal to organize a fundraiser during school hours after he and his classmates were denied this opportunity. The teacher then accused Dan of being under Communist influence.

Given that several other students shared the concerns about inconsistencies and lack of clarity about the rules, Dan and Mike decided to organize a rally after school hours at a park close to the school (Sullivan v. Houston Independent School District, 1969). During this rally, students, teachers and coaches heard the students express their criticism of the school. As the students spoke, some of the coaches called them Communists and Fascists. The coaches also tore student notebooks and flung books through the park. Apparently, some students who attended the rally had their grades cut. Several incidents happened beyond the rally that got Dan and Mike even more frustrated with the school administration. A coach verbally abused Dan while another told him that he would have Dan's "block knocked off" (p. 1332). Additionally, after Dan and other students came to school with American flags on their shirt lapels in honor of patriotism, a coach threatened them with suspension unless they removed the flags. The coach claimed that the flags were disruptive.

The culmination of these events prompted Dan and Mike to create an underground newspaper called Pflashlyte to express their views, concerns and criticism of the school, its policies and officials (Sullivan v. Houston Independent School District, 1969). A section of the newspaper known as "Edmund's Thoughts" used sarcasm to ridicule school administrators. It used the voice of a hypothetical administrator, Edmund P. Senile, to present sarcastic criticism of the school, drawing the ire of school officials. The "Edmund's Thoughts" section provided (see Appendix for the entire first issue of the newspaper):

EDMUND'S THOUGHTS

Some students are confused by the regulations here. To make these rules clearer, I will explain—

1/ No boy shall be allowed to wear his hair longer than two inches. There have been numerous reports of students stranggling themselves while sharpening their pencils. But there are more important reasons. It is feared that another outbreak of Bubonic Plague is on its way very soon. Any day now, they may to start cleaning the floors of the school. Still another reason exists. The members of the coaching department obviously have a definite sight problem. The don't seem to be able to distinguish male and female students unless the males have hair cut in the style of a Tibetian monk. Several accounts of forcible rape have been filed by boys in all gym classes.

2/ No one shall wear a neckercheif or scarf about their neck. It has been reported that one of the faculty members is actually a missing link between man and the Orangutan. Necties are permissable since Orangutangs do not know there are such things and therefore will not strangle you.

3/ There is strong evidence that there are some students at this school who actually beleive in Democracy. NASTY, NASTY... All of this garbage about rights and dignity of man went out the same tiem justice, peace, love and sanity did (when you registered at Sharpstown). So get all of that out of your system. We want the school to be just as sterile and smooth-running as we can make it. Just act like a vegetable waiting to be eaten, close your eyes and you won't feel a thing.

4/ Due to an excessive number of students losing their eyeballs, no one will be permitted to give the peace sign. Medical authorities agree that the best way to cope with the problem is to break the students fingers so they will swell up and not fit into the eye sockets. Science wins again.......

Their Stories: Offline Off-Campus Speech

5/ Students are not allowed to remain across the street from school before classes. Geologists report that there is a very large crack in the earth in the park. Years ago it was sealed with 17 tons of bubble gum, but since we are now closer to the sun than we were at that time, there is a great danger that it will all melt and result in students falling to China.

6/ All fire alarms have been disconnected so that no one will miss all the excitement. If anyone discovers some-one reporting a fire, take him to the office where he will be promptly be stoned to death with wet erasers.

7/ No one shall bear the American flag in the presence of the Administration. Although very quaint, it is also very dangerous as there are people in the school who do not believe in Life, Liberty and the Pursuit of Happiness.

8/ Beware of what type literature you posess. Excerpts from the PTA bulletins and the Handbook for Principals and Teachers— Secondary Schools are thought to be coded messages to communist agents seeking the overthrow of the schools. It is a well known fact the the Bible preaches communal living and in fact perpetrates a fanatic cult of weirdos called Christians. Beware of these people. They are occassionally seen nailed to the office walls.

9/ Do not, under any curcumstances, collect money for the starving children of Biafra. Some of the money goes to Nigeria and as soon as the babies are born there, they are inducted into the Communist Party.

10/ Last of all, do not think. This practice has recently been found to cause irreparable damage to brainwashed minds. This type of activity causes the brain to overheat and warp your values until instilling such beliefs as dressing as one wants and thinking and saying as one feels. You may even degenerate to the point of belief in love. remember the Sharpstown slogan:

ALL FOR NOTHING AND NOTHING FOR ALL.............

yours sincerely, Edmund P. Senile (this was translated by

Mr. Senile's secretary due to the disaster of his last article) (Sullivan v. Houston Independent School District, 1969, pp. 1351-52).

Dan and Mike took various steps to ensure that the newspaper did not get to the school campus (Sullivan v. Houston Independent School District, 1969). Additionally, they paid for the newspaper's printing at the University of Houston using their personal finances. They also used their own stencil for the production. The research and preparation for the newspaper, which had no connection to school curriculum, were done after school hours. Moreover, Dan and Mike did not distribute the newspaper on school grounds or during school hours. The first distribution occurred at the park across from the school as students walked to school. Subsequent distributions took place at the local shopping center and other stores where a critical mass of students could be found.

Dan and Mike told students who helped with the distribution not to do so during school hours or on school grounds (Sullivan v. Houston Independent School District, 1969). They urged students not to even take the newspaper to the school. They also told students that, if they ended up with the newspaper at school, they should store it away in a notebook. A few of the students failed to comply with Dan and Mike's instructions. Therefore, copies of the newspaper were discovered in school during school hours. Some were found hidden in sewing machines and in a paper towel dispenser. Others were found in the boys' restroom below a sign that encouraged students to take copies. Teachers seized copies of the newspaper from at least four students who read the newspaper during their classes. Another teacher seized a copy from five students found reading the newspaper before her class. While some teachers claimed that the newspaper disrupted their classes, others reported no disruption. Two teachers reported that the newspaper's presence on school grounds led to relatively more than typical traffic in the hallways. The assistant principal also claimed that, although he could not identify a specific disruptive incident, he felt "a difference in the attitude" of the student body during the week when the copies were found at the school (p. 1334). In fact, the assistant principal was incredibly vague in his assessment of the attitude and disruption from the newspaper:

There seemed to be, the attitude seemed to be, I don't know if its [sic] going to say what I, more concerned with something else. I wanted to say that you often see a group in the hall standing together and talking in between classes, passing time. You might see a group, a large group gathering at a lunch table. This in itself may or may not be attributed to something like this. It's difficult to say. There seemed to be, if I might describe it this way, there seemed to be something of concern that was generally among the student body ... I would say that they had been, let me think a minute. They had something on their minds that was causing them to be of great concern. That's my own choice of words (Sullivan v. Houston Independent School District, 1969, pp. 1334-35).

The principal learned of the newspaper's presence on school grounds from both teachers and students (Sullivan v. Houston Independent School District, 1969). He also received a copy of the introductory issue in the mail from an unidentified source. As teachers and students increasingly brought copies to show to the principal, he got "quite anxious about the situation and resolved that the students responsible would be expelled immediately" (p. 1335). His investigation revealed that Dan and Mike were the publishers of the newspaper. He also learned that they distributed the newspaper before the start of the school day at the park across from the school. After Dan and Mike admitted their involvement with the newspaper, they were both expelled for the rest of their senior year. The principal rejected their offers to stop publication in exchange for reduced discipline. Over the nine-day period between the school's initial discovery of the newspaper on-campus and the expulsions of Dan and Mike, the school only issued one student a discipline card in relation to the newspaper. However, that student's discipline was merely one of several violations unrelated to the newspaper that the student was disciplined for.

Dan and Mike's parents tried unsuccessfully to enroll them in other schools (Sullivan v. Houston Independent School District, 1969). However, the superintendent chose not to overrule the principal despite informing them that Dan and Mike only had a slim likelihood of getting into another school. The students' parents filed suit for injunctive and declaratory relief against the school district claiming a violation of their children's First Amendment free speech rights. Mike's gymnasium teacher told him that, if he could get away with it, he would give Dan a failing grade in the class because he filed a lawsuit against the school district.

Their Stories: Offline Off-Campus Speech

Analysis

The United States District Court for the Southern District of Texas refused to give schools broad censorship authority over students' off-campus speech (Sullivan v. Houston Independent School District, 1969). According to the court, the only conceivable justification for such authority arises when speech creates a nexus with the school through material and substantial disruption of the school (pursuant to the eponymous test created in Tinker v. Des Moines Independent Community School District (1969)). Nonetheless, the court was very hesitant to use the test to extend school authority to reach Dan and Mike's off-campus speech: "In this court's judgment, it makes little sense to extend the influence of school administration to off-campus activity under the theory that such activity might interfere with the function of education" (Sullivan v. Houston Independent School District, 1969, p. 1340). The court even stated that it is "questionable" to grant schools censorship authority over off-campus student speech which has enduring disruptive impact on other students (p. 1340). Despite its hesitancy, the court chose to extend the material and substantial disruption test beyond the schoolhouse gate. However, the court emphasized that this test must be the only basis for censorship of students' off-campus speech. The court's reason for extending the material and substantial disruption to off-campus speech, in spite of its hesitancy to do so, is unclear. Besides, since the court acknowledged that the off-campus student-speech jurisprudence was unclear, it did not have to muddy the jurisprudence by extending a test created in an on-campus context (Tinker v. Des Moines Independent Community School District) to an off-campus context. The fact that the court extended the material and substantial disruption test off-campus without explanation makes it difficult to determine when the other on-campus student-speech tests (*Morse*, *Fraser* and *Hazelwood*) might conceivably be embraced as applicable to off-campus speech in future cases.

The district court's decision to extend the material and substantial disruption test to off-campus speech is even more surprising because the court decidedly stated that the school and off-campus locales are constitutionally distinct (Sullivan v. Houston Independent School District, 1969). The court was right to emphasize a constitutional distinction between the school's campus and places outside the schoolhouse gate. This distinction is vital because, as the court explained, when students are off-campus, they have the same status as other citizens subject to criminal and civil laws that hold them accountable for their actions. The mere fact that a child is also student should not make the student a twenty-four hour ward of the school. Therefore, the school should not be able to censor the student's speech when he is off-campus; this role should be left to the same government entities that have authority to censor the speech of adults outside the schoolhouse gate. Rather than follow this sound conclusion and the court's own declaration that on-campus sites are constitutionally distinct from off-campus sites, the court chose to import the material and substantial disruption test into off-campus jurisprudence (Sullivan v. Houston Independent School District, 1969). Under this approach, the school can censor the student's off-campus speech, whether the student speaks in the privacy of his home or on a public street off-campus, if the speech causes material and substantial disruption inside the school.

The United States Supreme Court's decision in Morse v. Frederick (2007), however, has slightly modified this approach. As discussed in chapter ten of this book, the Supreme Court ruled that student speech that occurs outside the schoolhouse gate on a public street can be reclassified as on-campus speech if two key conditions are satisfied:

1. The event at which the student spoke was school-sanctioned; and
2. Students and faculty were present at the school-sanctioned event.

In the case of Mike and Dan, the Pflashlyte newspaper was not school-sanctioned. While the newspaper was the focal speech in Sullivan v. Houston Independent School District (1969), the students' speech at the rally inside the park across from the school is worthy of examination under the Morse v. Frederick approach to off-campus speech. Even though teachers and students were present at the rally, the rally was not school-sanctioned. Therefore, Morse v. Frederick did not require reclassification of the rally as an on-campus speech. When a court reclassifies off-campus speech as on-campus speech, there is less room for controversy if the Supreme Court's student-speech precedents are applied to the speech because those precedents similarly arose in on-campus speech contexts.

School officials argued that, even though Dan and Mike only published and distributed the newspaper off-campus, their involvement with the newspaper caused material and substantial disruption on-campus (Sullivan v. Houston Independent School District, 1969). The district court, however, ruled that school officials could not censor Dan and Mike's speech because their speech did not cause material and substantial disruption to the school. The court also ruled that schools can implement reasonable time, place and manner regulations in order to ensure that on-campus student speech does not cause material and substantial disruption at the school. The only thing Dan and Mike did in relation to the school was enter the schoolhouse gate for classes; they did not distribute or publish the newspaper on school grounds. As the court observed, students do not abandon their First Amendment rights simply because they cross into the schoolhouse gate. In order to censor off-campus student speech, school officials must prove that student speech created a nexus to the school beyond the student's mere entrance into the school.

Additionally, in order to censor the speaker, the material and substantial disruption at the school must be attributable to the speaker (Sullivan v. Houston Independent School District, 1969). Otherwise, any discipline for the on-campus impact of the speech must be imposed on the students who caused the material and substantial disruption on the school grounds rather than the speaker. School officials could not attribute any material and substantial disruption at the school to Dan and Mike. Both students took great pains to avoid distributing the newspaper on-campus. They even adjured their schoolmates not to bring the newspaper on-campus.

The assistant principal's vague descriptions of disruption consequent to the newspaper were clearly insufficient to constitute material and substantial disruption (Sullivan v. Houston Independent School District, 1969). In fact, they appeared to be fueled by administrative discomfort with the newspaper's criticism of school policy and the administration. As the court noted, students' First Amendment right to free speech allows them to engage in vigorous debate of controversial subjects. Schools must provide a strong justification to override that right:

A function of free speech under our system of government is to invite dispute. It may indeed best serve its high purpose when it induces a condition of unrest, creates dissatisfaction with conditions as they are, or even stirs people to anger. Speech is often provocative and challenging. It may strike at prejudices and preconceptions and have profound unsettling effects as it presses for acceptance of an idea. That is why freedom of speech, though not absolute, is nevertheless protected against censorship or punishment, unless shown likely to produce a clear and present danger of a serious substantive evil that rises far above public inconvenience, annoyance, or unrest (Sullivan v. Houston Independent School District, 1969, p. 1340, citing Terminiello v. City of Chicago, 1948, p. 4).

Additionally, the fact that the school only disciplined one student in relation to the newspaper before expelling Dan and Mike suggested that there was no material and substantial disruption at the school

Their Stories: Offline Off-Campus Speech

(Sullivan v. Houston Independent School District, 1969). Besides, the school failed to discipline the students who hid the newspapers in the sewing machines and paper towel dispensers; indicating that the hiding of the newspapers was not of sufficient disruptive concern for school officials.

The district court also used the material and substantial disruption test to protect on-campus distribution and publication of underground newspapers (Sullivan v. Houston Independent School District, 1969). Specifically, the court ruled that schools cannot totally prohibit the on-campus publication or distribution of underground newspapers unless they can show that the distribution violates the material and substantial disruption test. This rule provides an on-campus distribution outlet for students' off-campus speech as long as the speech does not cause material and substantial disruption. Under this rule, students do not have to distribute their newspapers or other off-campus speech outside the schoolhouse gate or surreptitiously on-campus. Rather than censoring the speech, however, school officials can regulate the time, place and manner of the speech if the regulation is not designed to suppress a disfavored viewpoint. Thus, the court gave license to Dan and Mike to publish and distribute the newspaper on-campus as long as they complied with reasonable time, place and manner regulations; and if the school was unable to show a reasonable forecast of or actual material and substantial disruption. Dan and Mike indeed published and distributed the newspapers outside school hours in order to avoid any potential time and place regulations. As the court observed, "if a student complies with reasonable rules as to times and places for distribution within the school, and does so in an orderly, nondisruptive manner, then he should not suffer if other students, who are lacking in self-control, tend to over-react thereby becoming a disruptive influence" (p. 1340).

The school district's strongest objection to Dan and Mike's speech was the Edmund's Thoughts section of the newspaper because it ridiculed the school (Sullivan v. Houston Independent School District, 1969). The district asked the court to classify the Edmund's Thoughts section as fighting words. As unprotected speech, the school officials would have been able to censor the speech with immunity from a First Amendment challenge. The court, however, ruled that the Edmund's Thoughts section did not constitute fighting words because it did not inflict injury by its very utterance. The same reasons that led the court to find no material and substantial disruption supported this conclusion. Additionally, the court indicated that the Edmund's Thoughts section did not constitute obscene or defamatory speech; thus school officials could not censor it. However, as the court noted, they could seek civil remedy against students for obscene or defamatory off-campus speech through the judicial system. Indeed, it appears that the district court would rather have school officials pursue remedies through the criminal or civil process against students for their off-campus speech rather than exercise school-censorship authority outside the schoolhouse gate. This would ensure that students' off-campus rights are protected by the relatively more rigorous judicial process outside the schoolhouse gate than the discipline process that rules inside schools.

11. The Story of Paul Kitchen

The Speech Incident: Profanity in "Space City!"

After Sharpstown High School censored Dan Sullivan and Mike Fischer's publication and distribution of Pflashlyte (Sullivan v. Houston Independent School District, 1969), the United States District Court for the Southern District of Texas ordered the Houston Independent School District to revamp its policy to specify times and places where student speech could be regulated (Sullivan v. Houston Independent

Their Stories: Offline Off-Campus Speech

School District, 1973, p. 1073). The policy also had to specify that school officials would not censor student speech unless the speech caused material and substantial disruption at the school. The district court also authorized school officials to censor actionable obscene or defamatory speech.

Within the first three months of 1970, the Houston Independent School District promulgated a new policy which required students to submit all underground publications to their principal for prior approval (Sullivan v. Houston Independent School District, 1973). The policy covered publications that students planned to distribute on school grounds as well as those distributed off-campus that were reasonably calculated to get to the school campus. As the federal district court had authorized, the policy provided that school officials could censor publications because of obscene or defamatory speech. It, however, prohibited censorship of publications simply because of its controversial content. The policy further provided that publications that advocated illegal action or non-compliance with student-conduct rules of the district could be censored. It authorized students to distribute publications on school grounds as long as the distribution was done before or after school hours. The policy, however, banned sale of publications within the schoolhouse gate. Additionally, it required student publishers and contributors to use their actual names in publications.

Like Dan Sullivan and Mike Fischer in the same district, Paul Kitchen, a junior student at Waltrip Senior High School, decided to publish an underground newspaper called "Space City!" (Sullivan v. Houston Independent School District, 1973, p. 1074). The newspaper used vulgar language to express Paul's opinions on various issues. It included a letter titled "High Skool is Fucked" (p. 1074). Before school hours on October 20, 1970, Paul sold the newspaper to students close to but outside the schoolhouse gate. Paul's principal bought a copy from him. As the principal skimmed through the newspaper, he discovered that it included vulgar language. He confronted Paul and told him that he violated school policy because he failed to submit "Space City!" for prior approval. He ordered Paul to immediately cease sale of the publication but Paul refused to do so. The principal, consequently, decided to suspend Paul for his refusal to cease the sale and for the violation of the prior approval policy. After notifying Paul's parents, the principal suspended Paul until a meeting with his parents six days later. The suspension upset Paul so much that, as he left the principal's office, he slammed the door and yelled out within hearing of other students and the secretary: "I don't want to go to this goddamn school anyway" (p. 1074).

Despite his suspension, Paul returned to the school several times over the six-day suspension (Sullivan v. Houston Independent School District, 1973). Each time, however, school officials asked him to leave. Before school hours on October 26, 1970 (the principal's meeting date with Paul's parents), Paul returned to the same off-campus location where he had sold "Space City!" six days earlier. There he again sold copies to students as they arrived for school. The principal showed the prior approval policy to Paul and threatened to call the police if he did not cease the sale. Instead of ceasing the sale, Paul yelled "the common Anglo-Saxon vulgarism for sexual intercourse" at the principal who called the police (p. 1074). Although Paul was taken into police custody, no charges were filed. Due to the incidents that day, the scheduled meeting with Paul's parents was cancelled. The principal, however, informed Paul's parents that he would be suspended for the rest of the semester for violating the prior approval policy and using profanity in the presence of the secretary. The assistant superintendent as well as the superintendent affirmed the suspension. Paul's "academic career suffered severely from continued suspension" (p. 1076). Paul and his father filed a First Amendment suit against the school district. They asked the court to hold the district in contempt for failing to follow the order issued in Dan and Mike's case in Sullivan v. Houston Independent School District (1969), discussed earlier. They also sought injunctive relief and monetary damages.

Analysis

Paul and his father argued that the school could not censor sale of the newspaper because, as protected speech under the First Amendment, the newspaper did not cause material and substantial disruption within the school (Sullivan v. Houston Independent School District, 1973). Since Paul and his father made their arguments based on the material and substantial disruption test, the United States Court of Appeals for the Fifth Circuit applied it without taking the time to distinguish the on-campus context of Tinker v. Des Moines Independent Community School District (1969) from the off-campus context of Paul's case. Even though the court found that Paul's speech did not materially and substantially disrupt the school, it nevertheless ruled that school officials could censor the newspaper.

The court of appeals posited the issue in the case as a balance between the First Amendment right to free speech and the competing authority of schools to ensure order within the schoolhouse gate (Sullivan v. Houston Independent School District, 1973). This balance weighed in favor of school censorship of Paul because he did not protest his disagreement with the prior approval policy appropriately. The court was troubled by Paul's defiance of the principal's orders to cease sale and comply with the prior approval policy. Besides, Paul continued to defy the principal during his six-day suspension. He also audaciously sold the newspapers the morning of a meeting with his parents, flaunting the school policy. Indeed, this defiance continued until the police intervened. On two different occasions, Paul yelled profanities at the principal. These various acts of defiance led the court to minimize the First Amendment right of Paul to his off-campus speech.

Interestingly, the court did not review Paul's profanities under a test like *Bethel* which authorizes schools to censor on-campus vulgar speech (Sullivan v. Houston Independent School District, 1973). Instead, the court viewed the vulgarities as merely part of Paul's acts of defiance. Under the *Bethel* test, the school officials would have been able to regulate Paul's on-campus profanity when he slammed the door as he left the principal's office. However, if the court reviewed Paul's case as a First Amendment case (as opposed to a school-defiance case), it is unclear if the court would have recognized school-censorship authority over his profanity outside the schoolhouse gate. This lack of clarity stems from the fact that, as noted earlier, the court disregarded the on-campus context of the material and substantial disruption test in applying it to Paul's speech. If the court did that for one student-speech test, it could do similarly with the *Bethel* test. On the other hand, as Justice Brennan wrote in his concurring opinion in Bethel School District No. 403 v. Fraser (1986), and the Supreme Court affirmed in Hazelwood School District v. Kuhlmeier (1988), if vulgar speech is given off-campus, school officials cannot censor it.

According to the court of appeals, the appropriate response for Paul would have been to submit the newspaper for review in compliance with the school policy (Sullivan v. Houston Independent School District, 1973). He could then have brought a First Amendment challenge if the school censored him. Paul instead chose to engage in too many acts of defiance that could undermine the ability of school officials to maintain order within the schoolhouse gate. These acts distracted from his First Amendment claim. As the court observed, Paul's defiance was unlike the "pristine, passive acts of protest 'akin to pure speech' involved in *Tinker*" (p. 1075). Consequently, the discipline Paul incurred as well as its impact on his academic career were self-inflicted.

The court ruled that a student's acts of defiance could change the tenor of his First Amendment case into a student-defiance case (Sullivan v. Houston Independent School District, 1973). In such a case, the school can censor the student's off-campus speech even in the absence of material and substantial disruption. The court stated that "[i]n the years since *Tinker* was decided courts have refused to accord

Their Stories: Offline Off-Campus Speech

constitutional protection to the actions of students who blatantly and deliberately flout school regulations and defy school authorities" (p. 1076). Besides, "the open disregard of school regulations is a sufficient and independent ground for imposing discipline" (p. 1076). In order to successfully change the tenor of a case, the school must frame the censorship as a response to the student's defiance of policy rather than as censorship based on content. This ruling empowers schools to censor off-campus student speech as long as they craft policies that are not patently unconstitutional or pretexts for viewpoint or content discrimination. The student, on the other hand, needs to work within the school policy in order to preserve his First Amendment challenge. If the student is censored after complying with school policy, he should then file a First Amendment challenge against the censorship consequent to enforcement of the school policy. As the court stated, in order to have a successful First Amendment case, students must "come into court with clean hands" (p. 1076).

12. The Story of Mark Shanley, Clyde Coe, Jr., William Jolly, John Alford, and John Graham

The Speech Incident: Marijuana, Birth Control, and the Newspaper

Five MacArthur High School, Texas, seniors – Mark Shanley, Clyde Coe, Jr., William Jolly, John Alford and John Graham – decided to publish an underground newspaper which they called the Awakening (Shanley v. Northeast Independent School District, 1972). These academically-successful students created the newspaper to provide a non-school-sponsored forum to share their views with other students. In the newspaper, they provided information on birth control. They also advocated that politicians reexamine their approach to regulation of marijuana. The other subjects in the newspaper were noncontroversial. In fact, the United States Court of Appeals for the Fifth Circuit described the newspaper as "probably one of the most vanilla-flavored ever to reach a federal court" (p. 964).

The newspaper was published off-campus after school hours (Shanley v. Northeast Independent School District, 1972). Mark, Clyde, William, John and Graham neither distributed the newspaper on school grounds nor encouraged their schoolmates to distribute it on school grounds. Instead, they distributed it on the sidewalk of a street adjoining the school. A parking lot separated the school from the sidewalk. Additionally, Mark, Clyde, William, John and Graham only distributed the newspaper on two occasions: one morning before school hours; and another day after school hours. They used no school resource in the newspaper's publication or distribution.

MacArthur High School had a policy which required prior approval for all on-campus and off-campus student publications. It read in pertinent part:

Be it further resolved that any attempt to avoid the school's established procedure for administrative approval of activities such as the production for distribution and/or distribution of petitions or printed documents of any kind, sort, or type without the specific approval of the principal shall be cause for suspension and, if in the judgment of the principal, there is justification, for referral to the office of the Superintendent with a recommendation for expulsion (Shanley v. Northeast Independent School District, 1972, pp. 964-65).

School officials discovered copies of the newspaper at the school and decided to discipline Mark, Clyde, William, John and Graham (Shanley v. Northeast Independent School District, 1972). The school

Their Stories: Offline Off-Campus Speech

claimed that the students violated the school policy because they failed to seek prior approval for the publication and distribution of Awakening. Each student was suspended from school for three days. The suspension had a significant impact on their grades as they lost all grades during the three days. This happened at a time when they were applying to colleges and for college scholarships. The school conceded that the students distributed the newspaper civilly and in a non-disruptive manner. Moreover, the publication and distribution did not disrupt any school function. In their appeal to the school board, the students argued that they could not be punished for speech that occurred wholly off-campus and outside school hours. The school board, however, upheld the suspensions. The students' parents sued the school district under the First Amendment based on this same argument used before the school board. They asked the court to enjoin school officials from enforcing the censorship and the zero grade each student received during the suspension.

Analysis

The United States Court of Appeals for the Fifth Circuit ruled that while schools must have authority to maintain order in the school, that authority must be exercised within the dictates of the First Amendment (Shanley v. Northeast Independent School District, 1972). The court acknowledged, however, that the question and scope of school-censorship authority over off-campus speech was unresolved in precedents. Accordingly, the First Amendment dictates governing off-campus student speech were unclear. Despite the lack of clarity, schools do not have unbridled authority over students and their speech. Students are not mere wards of the state subject to the whims and caprices of school officials. Even with the unsettled jurisprudence, the question and scope of school-censorship authority over off-campus speech is relatively less complicated than questions about on-campus censorship because school authority to censor off-campus student "cannot exceed" the authority over on-campus speech (p. 968). The conditions that call for increased censorship authority over on-campus speech simply are not applicable to off-campus. For instance, there is no classroom setting on a sidewalk or street corner that risks disruption from off-campus speech. Additionally, within a school setting, the educational function would be hampered by "the milling, mooing, and haranguing, along with the aggressiveness that often accompanies a constitutionally-protected exchange of ideas on the street corner" (p. 968). As the court observed, inside the schoolhouse gate, students and teachers are in such close quarters that they cannot easily escape on-campus speech targeting them. Schools also have a limited time during the day to cover various subjects. Unbridled on-campus speech could further constrict that time; particularly if the speech hampers the ability of teachers to teach and maintain their classrooms. In this rationale, the court overlooked the fact that off-campus speech could make its way to the school campus and have the same impact as speech originating on school grounds.

Without distinguishing the on-campus context of Tinker v. Des Moines Independent Community School District (1969) from the off-campus context of Shanley v. Northeast Independent School District (1972), the United States Court of Appeals for the Fifth Circuit chose the *Tinker* tests as governing. Although the court acknowledged the infringement-of-rights test, it did not apply it. Therefore, it is difficult to know how the court would have ruled using this test; given that the test remains clouded in the courts, as we discussed in chapter ten. The court, however, applied the material and substantial disruption test. Specifically, the court found that the school had no reasonable basis to forecast material and substantial disruption from the Awakening (Shanley v. Northeast Independent School District, 1972). Additionally, no actual disruption occurred at the school because of the publication and distribution of the Awakening. Besides, in its defense of the censorship, the school did not make any claim of potential or actual disruption. The court ruled that if a school can reasonably forecast that persons with opposing views will cause material and substantial disruption because of student speech, the school can impose reasonable time, place and manner regulations on the speech through such avenues as a prior approval policy. It is evident from this ruling that the student-speaker need not originate the material and substantial disruption. The court cautioned, however, that a small but vocal minority should not be allowed to censor speech under the guise of material and substantial disruption.

The court of appeals read the material and substantial disruption test to cover disruptions that occur off-campus when it stated that "there were no disturbances of any sort, on or off campus, related to the distribution of the Awakening" (Shanley v. Northeast Independent School District, 1972, p. 970). In other words, off-campus material and substantial disruption from the publication or distribution of the Awakening could have validated the school's censorship of the newspaper. However, Mark, Clyde, William, John and Graham were very peaceful in their off-campus distribution of the newspaper. With respect to actual or potential material and substantial disruption, the court observed that:

All parties to this case agree that distribution of the 'Awakening' was polite, orderly, and non-disruptive. None of the students tried to force papers on anyone; no one attempted to block ingress or egress to a building; students were, in fact, discouraged from taking the papers onto the school grounds. The distributors of the 'Awakening' merely handed newspapers to those who wished to read them, nothing more. We find nothing whatsoever in the means of distribution followed by these students that is offensive to the rights of others or potentially disruptive in a material and substantial way to the conduct of school activities (Shanley v. Northeast Independent School District, 1972, p. 971).

As a general rule, school officials cannot censor speech simply because of disagreement with its content (Shanley v. Northeast Independent School District, 1972). However, the court identified three categories of student speech that can be censored, based on content, irrespective of location: obscene speech; defamatory speech; and inflammatory speech. Even though the Bethel School District No. 403 v. Fraser (1986) case had not been decided at the time, the court recognized that school-censorship authority extended to obscene speech. It is unclear how the court would have ruled if the *Bethel* test had existed at the time. If the court failed to give significance to the on-campus context of the *Bethel* case as it did with the *Tinker* tests, then it would have extended the *Bethel* test to off-campus. This would have extended the reach of schools over the content of off-campus student speech because the *Bethel* test is a less stringent standard than the *Miller* test for obscenity (Miller v. California, 1973) (see our discussion of the *Miller* test in chapter five). Had the court applied the *Miller* test and found the speech obscene, the speech would be constitutionally unprotected; consequently, the school would have had license to censor the off-campus speech. Given that the court did not find the speech in Awakening to be obscene under its *Bethel*-test approach, it would not have found the speech obscene under the more stringent *Miller* test.

The court of appeals did not describe the parameters of inflammatory speech (Shanley v. Northeast Independent School District, 1972). Consequently, it is unclear if the court limited or equated inflammatory speech to fighting words; or if the court extended it to the kind of speech that the *Bethel* test would deem vulgar. However, as Justice Brennan noted in Bethel School District No. 403 v. Fraser (1986), if speech that is vulgar under the *Bethel* test is delivered off-campus, the school cannot censor the speech. Since controversial protected speech typically tends to inflame passions on both sides of an issue, more

Their Stories: Offline Off-Campus Speech

than inflammation is required to validate censorship of off-campus speech. As the court stated, "[i]deas in their pure and pristine form, touching only the minds and hearts of school children, must be freed from despotic dispensation by all men, be they robed as academicians or judges or citizen members of a board of education" (p. 972). The court found that the two subjects – marijuana and birth control – that the school district identified as controversial were not fighting words because they did not "inherently prompt only divisiveness and disruption" (p. 972). Additionally, the school had books on birth control in its library that were indistinguishable from the information provided in the Awakening. The court warned schools against stifling student speech on controversial subjects, such as marijuana and birth control, on which the citizenry is engaged in debate.

The court of appeals rebuked the school district for unconstitutionally usurping the power of parents and turning into super-parent (Shanley v. Northeast Independent School District, 1972). According to the court, parents should be shocked that "their elected school board had assumed suzerainty over their children before and after school, off school grounds, and with regard to their children's rights of expressing their thoughts" (p. 964). Despite the strong admonishment, the court refused to completely rule out extending school-censorship authority to cover off-campus speech. It conceded, however, that geography could define the jurisdiction of a school, confining the school's authority to inside the schoolhouse gate. This is reasonable because a speaker's geographical location sometimes determines whether the speaker is entitled to constitutional protection (see our discussion of public forums in chapter nine). The court stated that even the "width of a street" between a school and the student-speaker could make a difference in the reach of a school's jurisdiction (p. 974).

The court observed "it is not at all unusual in our system that different authorities have responsibility only for their own bailiwicks" (Shanley v. Northeast Independent School District, 1972, p. 974). Under this approach, schools would only be responsible for speech within the schoolhouse gate. Civil and criminal laws applicable to citizens would then govern students outside the schoolhouse gate. Since these laws are already applicable to students while they are off-campus, it would be doubly punishing students to allow a school to impose further punishment on students for off-campus speech that can be censored under civil and criminal laws. Notwithstanding this risk of double punishment, the court left open the door for school censorship of off-campus student speech. The court ruled that, at minimum, a school must show reasonable forecast of material and substantial disruption before censoring student speech that occurs wholly outside school hours and outside the schoolhouse gate. Accordingly, MacArthur High School's policy was unconstitutional as it did not include language limiting the reach of the school to speech reasonable forecast to cause material and substantial disruption at the school.

13. The Story of James LaVine

The Speech Incident: The "Last Words" Poem

During an evening in the summer of 1998, James LaVine, an eleventh grade student at Blaine High School in Washington, decided to compose a poem to capture his imaginative thoughts (Lavine v. Blaine School District, 2001). The poem, which he called "Last Words" was written after school hours while he was at home. His mother warned him not to take the poem to school out of concern that teachers might overreact to it; particularly in light of the various school-shooting incidents that had occurred nationally around that time. The poem read as follows:

As each day passed, I watched, love sprout, from the most, unlikely places, wich reminds, me that, beauty is in the eye's, of the beholder.
As I remember, I start to cry, for I, had leared, this to late, and now, I must spend, each day, alone, alone for supper, alone at night, alone at death.
Death I feel, crawlling down, my neck at, every turn, and so, now I know, what I must do.
I pulled my gun, from its case, and began to load it.
I remember, thinking at least I won't, go alone, as I, jumpped in, the car, all I could think about, was I would not, go alone.
As I walked, through the, now empty halls, I could feel, my hart pounding.
As I approched, the classroom door, I drew my gun and, threw open the door, Bang, Bang, Bang–Bang. When it all was over, 28 were, dead, and all I remember, was not felling, any remorce, for I felt, I was, clensing my soul,
I quickly, turned and ran, as the bell rang, all I could here, were screams, screams of friends, screams of co workers, and just plain, screams of shear horor, as the students, found their, slayen classmates,
2 years have passed, and now I lay, 29 roses, down upon, these stairs, as now, I feel, I may, strike again. No tears, shall be shead, in sarrow, for I am, alone, and now, I hope, I can feel, remorce, for what I did, without a shed, of tears, for no tear, shall fall, from your face, but from mine, as I try, to rest in peace, Bang! (Lavine v. Blaine School District, 2001, pp. 983-84).

After writing the poem, James completely forgot about it for approximately three months (Lavine v. Blaine School District, 2001). However, on September 30, 1998, he found the poem in his living room and took it to school two days later. While at school, he showed the poem to many of his friends. Additionally, as he submitted various assignments to his English teacher, he turned in the poem as well. Even though it was not a class assignment, he asked the teacher to give him feedback on the poem (He had a practice of seeking feedback on some of his poems from his English teachers). When the English teacher read "Last Words" she was alarmed. She interpreted the poem as a quiet student's silent cry for help. Therefore, she reported the poem's contents to the school counselor the following day – a Saturday. Alarmed, the counselor scheduled a Saturday meeting with the English teacher and the vice principal to discuss the poem. During this meeting, the counselor disclosed various incidents that James had shared with her to the teacher and the vice principal. These incidents included a fight with his father in September 1998 which led to James moving out of his family's house temporarily; his suicidal ideations and a no-contact order against his father. James also recently broke up with his girlfriend and her mother accused him of allegedly stalking her daughter. Further, James' school discipline record included a fight and insubordination. Moreover, the vice principal, who described James as "somewhat of a loner", had recently disciplined him for coming to school in a shirt that read "ear shit and die" (p. 985).

Due to the vice principal's concerns about the poem, and all he had learned about James during the Saturday meeting, he alerted security at the evening's scheduled homecoming dance to keep an eye on James if he showed up at the dance (Lavine v. Blaine School District, 2001). He also called the police for advice on how to address the situation. The police recommended contacting the state's child protective services, which in turn suggested calling the Community Mental Health Crisis Line. The crisis line connected the school officials to a psychiatrist who recommended that the police pick up James for a psychological evaluation. When the police arrived at James' house, he and his mother assured them that he was not a danger, that he had no plan to commit the acts in the poem and that he had no weapons.

Their Stories: Offline Off-Campus Speech

He also told the police that, prior to "Last Words", he had never written such a poem; and that he had no reason for writing the poem. He told them that he was not crying out for help when he submitted the poem to his teacher; instead he was merely following his longstanding practice of seeking feedback from his teachers about his poems. With no probable cause for involuntary commitment of James, and with his refusal to voluntarily submit to a psychological evaluation, the police left without James. After the psychiatrist consulted the police about their visit, she decided against involuntarily committing James. She concluded that there was no adequate basis to classify James as an imminent danger to himself or others. The next day, the vice principal deliberated with the principal who decided to emergency-expel James. The state law allowed school officials to emergency-expel any student reasonably believed to present an imminent danger to himself or others. In his letter notifying James' parents of the expulsion, the principal cited James' poem as justification. The letter stated that the poem "implied extreme violence to our student body" (p. 986).

James' parents appealed the expulsion to the school board (Lavine v. Blaine School District, 2001). The school district's attorney informed them that James could return to school if he underwent a psychological evaluation of his danger to himself and others at the district's expense. After three evaluation sessions, the psychiatrist recommended James' return to the school. Therefore, after seventeen days away from school, James was permitted to return for the rest of the school year and the expulsion was overturned. His parents continued their appeal to the school board because they wanted the school district to remove the principal's letter from James' file. They were concerned that the letter would negatively impact James' opportunity to get into the military. The board revised the letter but did not remove it from his file. It also affirmed the emergency expulsion. James and his father brought a First Amendment claim against the school district for an injunction and monetary damages. They asked the court to order the school to remove the letter from James' file.

Analysis

The United States Court of Appeals for the Ninth Circuit conceded that, amidst the rise in school shootings around the country, schools need to react decisively, quickly and seriously to threats of violence (Lavine v. Blaine School District, 2001). The second-guessing of school officials after school shootings adds to the urgent need to take a proactive and serious approach toward every threat of violence. As the court observed, if school officials fail to take action, people will confront them with questions about "how teachers or administrators could have missed telltale 'warning signs,' why something was not done earlier and what should be done to prevent such tragedies from happening again" (p. 987). The court emphasized that, although schools enjoy significant deference in defining the bounds of acceptable speech inside the school, students retain free speech rights within the schoolhouse gate. Despite the gravity of school safety, schools must operate within the confines of the United States Constitution by balancing safety with First Amendment rights. James claimed that the school incorrectly weighed school safety above his First Amendment right to free speech when it disciplined him for his poem which was merely an exercise of his right to free speech. Even when according deference to schools in this balancing, courts must not abdicate their responsibility to safeguard student speech rights when schools overstep constitutional bounds. As the court observed, "[j]ust as the Constitution does not allow the police to imprison all suspicious characters, schools cannot expel students just because they are 'loners,' wear black and play video games" in the name of safety (p. 987).

Despite the fact that the United States Supreme Court's student-speech precedents only involved on-campus speech, the federal court of appeals in Lavine v. Blaine School District (2001) stated that judicial review of all student speech must be conducted within the framework of those precedents. According to the court, the material and substantial disruption test from Tinker v. Des Moines Independent Community School District (1969) governs any case not falling under any of the other free speech tests. At the time, Morse v. Frederick (2007) had not been decided so the court only considered the *Hazelwood* test and the *Bethel* test. The *Hazelwood* test was inapplicable to James' poem because it was not school-sponsored speech; nor was it part of a school assignment (Lavine v. Blaine School District, 2001). The poem was not vulgar, lewd or obscene speech because it was not "an elaborate, graphic, and explicit sexual metaphor as was the student's speech in [Bethel School District No. 403 v. Fraser]" (Lavine v. Blaine School District, p. 989). Therefore, the *Bethel* test was not applicable to the poem.

As the catch-all test when both the *Hazelwood* and *Bethel* tests are not applicable, the material and substantial disruption test governed the court's review of James' speech (Lavine v. Blaine School District, 2001). Under this test, schools are authorized to censor student speech if they have reasonable grounds to forecast material and substantial disruption at the school. The court determined that the totality of the circumstances revealed reasonable grounds for such a forecast in James' case: The suicidal ideations James disclosed to the school counselor, James' fight with his father, his temporary removal from his family home, the breakup with his girlfriend, the accusation of alleged stalking, the content of the poem, the references to death, suicide and violence in the poem, the recent school shooting in a neighboring state as well as incidents in James' school disciplinary record. The court ruled that a police or psychiatric decision not to commit a student is not a dispositive factor when assessing material and substantial disruption. This is so because, while the police and psychiatrist might be required to show mental illness in order to involuntarily commit a person, the material and substantial disruption test does not have such a requirement. Even if there are other competing reasonable grounds *not* to find material and substantial disruption (like the assurances from James and his mother during the police visit to their house or the psychiatrist's conclusion that James was not an imminent danger), as long as the school's basis for forecasting material and substantial disruption is also reasonable, the court would uphold the school's grounds.

The court ruled in favor of the school district based on its underlying theme of deference to the difficult decisions schools have to make regarding student safety (Lavine v. Blaine School District, 2001). It observed that:

In retrospect, it may appear that, as James' mother predicted, the school overreacted. James very well may have been using his poetry to explore the disturbing topic of school violence and chose to do so through the perspective of a suicidal mass murderer. In fact, James strongly contends this was all he was doing and that he had no intention of hurting himself or others. We have no reason now to disbelieve James, as he did return to Blaine High School without further incident. We review, however, with deference, schools' decisions in connection with the safety of their students even when freedom of expression is involved (Lavine v. Blaine School District, 2001, pp. 991-92).

Despite ruling in the school district's favor, the court gave James a small victory. It ruled that once James was no longer deemed a threat, the district should not have kept the principal's letter or the revised school board letter in James' disciplinary record.

Their Stories: Offline Off-Campus Speech

In its analysis of James' speech, the United States Court of Appeals for the Ninth Circuit never distinguished between on-campus speech and off-campus speech. This could be because James brought the speech to school. The ninth circuit court seemed to confirm this in 2013 in Wynar v. Douglas County School District when it stated that Lavine v. Blaine School District (2001) "dealt with speech created off campus but brought to the school by the speaker. This is not a minor distinction" (p. 1068). In other words, the court distinguished off-campus speech brought on school grounds from off-campus speech. In essence, off-campus speech brought on school grounds is actually on-campus speech. Consequently, even though James created the poem off-campus, he converted it to on-campus speech when he brought it within the schoolhouse gate.

The court of appeals refused to use the true-threat analysis to review James' case (Lavine v. Blaine School District, 2001). If it had, it could have avoided distinguishing off-campus speech from on-campus without misgivings. This is because, under a true-threat analysis, the distinction between off-campus speech and on-campus speech is redundant. True threats are unprotected speech off-campus as well as on-campus. When a court fails to distinguish between off-campus and on-campus speech, however, it simply leaves the off-campus speech case law muddled as it leaves scholars and other courts to speculate about the role of the off-campus status of speech in First Amendment analysis.

14. The Story of Zachariah Paul

The Speech Incident: The Top Ten List

Zachariah Paul, a student and member of the track team at Franklin Regional High School in Pennsylvania, was upset after the school implemented several track team rules (Killion v. Franklin Regional School District, 2001). He was also upset because school officials denied him a permit to park at the school. Consequently, in March 1999, Zachariah decided to express his anger by creating a Top Ten list ridiculing several things about the athletic director, including his appearance and his genitals. The list stated:

10) The School Store doesn't sell twink[i]es.
9) He is constantly tripping over his own chins.
8) The girls at the 900 #'s keep hanging up on him.
7) For him, becoming Franklin's "Athletic Director" was considered "moving up in the world".
6) He has to use a pencil to type and make phone calls because his fingers are unable to hit only one key at a time.
5) As stated in previous list, he's just not getting any.
4) He is no longer allowed in any "All You Can Eat" restaurants.
3) He has constant flashbacks of when he was in high school and the athletes used to pick on him, instead of him picking on the athletes.
2) Because of his extensive gut factor, the "man" hasn't seen his own penis in over a decade.
1) Even it is wasn't for his gut, it would still take a magnifying glass and extensive searching to find it (Killion v. Franklin Regional School District, 2001, p. 448).

Zachariah compiled the list after school hours in the privacy of his home (Killion v. Franklin Regional School District, 2001). Several days later, he used his personal computer and email to send the list to his friends. He made no use of school resources in creating or sending the list. Prior to this, school officials

163

had threatened him with punishment when he brought lists to school. As a result, he made a conscious decision not to take the Top Ten list to school. Nonetheless, copies of the list ended up at the school through an undisclosed student who changed the format of Zachariah's original list before distributing it at school. Copies of the list were also found in the teachers' lounge at the high school as well as at the middle school. The list was distributed at the school for several days before school officials learned of it. After learning of it, school officials failed to address it for at least a week. When the principal, assistant principal and athletic director eventually confronted Zachariah, he admitted creating the list but denied bringing the list to school. He informed them that he created the list off-campus and that he emailed the list from his home computer to the personal emails of his friends. The following day, the school officials suspended Zachariah from school for ten days. The suspension covered curricular as well as extracurricular activities, including the track team. The school proffered three reasons for the suspension: the use of offensive speech to target a school official; Zachariah's admission that he created the list; and the fact that the list was discovered within the schoolhouse gate. Essentially, the school chose to disregard the absence of evidence showing that Zachariah brought the list to school. In fact, the only time Zachariah touched the list while on-campus was when he showed a copy, which he discovered in the hallway, to his track-team coaches. About a week after the suspension, Zachariah and his mother filed suit against the school district seeking monetary damages and an injunction. They claimed that, by punishing Zachariah for his off-campus speech, the school district infringed his First Amendment right to free speech.

Analysis

Even though the United States District Court for the Western District of Pennsylvania rightly observed that "there is limited case law" on the off-campus speech rights of students, it nonetheless ruled that schools have some censorship authority over students' off-campus speech (Killion v. Franklin Regional School District, 2001, p. 454). The court did not circumscribe the off-campus authority of schools so it is unclear how far reaching that authority is. The court, however, stated that the censorship authority of school officials over off-campus student speech is "much more limited than" that over on-campus speech (p. 454). While this comparative view of on-campus and off-campus authority is reasonable (given the academic needs within the school setting), it does not define the scope of schools' off-campus censorship authority. It also does not provide parameters for determining how much more limited the off-campus authority is relative to the on-campus authority. Acknowledging the off-campus censorship authority without defining its precise scope leaves the door open for schools to push the limits of censorship which could in turn considerably muzzle student speech off-campus.

The school district argued that it could censor Zachariah's speech because it was disruptive under the material and substantial disruption test; and because it was lewd and obscene under the *Bethel* test (Killion v. Franklin Regional School District, 2001). Zachariah and his mother argued, however, that since his speech was created off-campus, the school had no constitutional authority to censor him. They also argued that since someone other than Zachariah brought the speech to the school, Zachariah could not be disciplined for the presence of the speech on the school's campus unless the school district proved extraordinary circumstances. Although the federal district court conceded that the United States Supreme Court's student-speech precedents were decided in on-campus contexts, it ruled that those precedents must serve as the framework for reviewing off-campus student speech. According to the district court, the *Tinker* tests govern any student speech that does not fall under any of the other free speech tests (Killion v. Franklin Regional School District, 2001, citing Saxe v. State College Area School District, 2001).

Their Stories: Offline Off-Campus Speech

The court ruled that the *Tinker* tests also govern off-campus speech brought on-campus by someone other than the student-speaker, even if the person is unknown. The court rejected Zachariah's request for a more stringent standard than *Tinker* for off-campus speech, reasoning that several courts already use the *Tinker* test in off-campus speech contexts.

The federal district court found that the school district could not censor Zachariah's off-campus speech because the district failed to satisfy the material and substantial disruption test (Killion v. Franklin Regional School District, 2001). There was no evidence that the Top Ten list handicapped the ability of teachers to teach or manage their classrooms. Even though the list offended the athletic director, it did not so offend him that he had to take a leave of absence. Additionally, the list was at the school for several days before school officials learned of it – an indication that it could not have caused material and substantial disruption. Besides, even after learning about it, school officials waited at least a week before addressing it, taking away the urgency to any concern about the list. Moreover, the speech did not include a threat which would have otherwise provided a basis for a reasonable forecast of material and substantial disruption. Based on these factors, the court concluded that Zachariah's speech did not cause material and substantial disruption at the school.

The district court concluded that "[w]e cannot accept, without more, that the childish and boorish antics of a minor could impair the administrators' abilities to discipline students and maintain control" (Killion v. Franklin Regional School District, 2001, p. 456). The fact that the speech was related to the high school was insufficient in itself to find or forecast material and substantial disruption. Likewise, the offense of school officials at Zachariah's speech does not constitute material and substantial disruption. Neither does the demeaning, rude or abusive nature of speech. "However, if a school can point to a well–founded expectation of disruption—especially one based on past incidents arising out of similar speech—the restriction may pass constitutional muster" (p. 455, citing Saxe v. State College Area School District, 2001, p. 212). Indeed, Zachariah had brought prior lists to school; however, none of those lists caused disruption. The school also did not discipline him for bringing the prior lists to school. Therefore, the school could not use those past incidents as grounds for a reasonable forecast of material and substantial disruption from the Top Ten list.

The court also applied the *Bethel* test to Zachariah's off-campus speech (Killion v. Franklin Regional School District, 2001). Zachariah and his mother argued that, if the list was viewed as lewd and obscene pursuant to the *Bethel* test, the person who brought the list to school, rather than Zachariah, should be punished. They argued that the use of the *Bethel* test "to punish the author for work created outside of school is certainly beyond the First Amendment pale" (p. 456). The court agreed, relying on Justice Brennan's concurrence in Bethel School District No. 403 v. Fraser (1986) in which he stated that a school could not censor lewd and obscene on-campus speech if the speech were delivered off-campus. Although the *Bethel* test empowered schools to teach students fundamental values and civility, the authority does not extend to off-campus speech decorum. The court ruled that schools do not have constitutional authority to censor students' off-campus lewd and obscene speech "absent exceptional circumstances" (Killion v. Franklin Regional School District, p. 457). The court, however, failed to define what would constitute an "exceptional circumstance", leaving both schools and students in the dark about their censorship authority and free speech rights respectively.

One reason the court might have imposed the exceptional-circumstances requirement could be that, unlike with the material and substantial disruption test which inherently includes a school nexus via its school-disruption requirement, there is no nexus element within the *Bethel* test. The exceptional-circumstances requirement might thus serve as the nexus should the court chose to apply the *Bethel* test to off-campus speech. The court found several items in the Top Ten list lewd, obscene and vulgar, including the following: "he's just not getting any .... Because of his extensive gut factor, the 'man' hasn't seen his own penis in over a decade .... Even if it wasn't for his gut, it would still take a magnifying glass and extensive searching to find it" (Killion v. Franklin Regional School District, p. 457). Nonetheless, the school could not censor the speech because the speech was created in Zachariah's home, far away from the school campus, at a time when he was not involved in any school function or his role as a student. Effectively, this lack of a nexus limited the ability of the school to rely on the *Bethel* test in censoring Zachariah. It does appear that if Zachariah had brought the list to school, the court would have found the *Bethel* test applicable as that would have provided a nexus to the school. In that case, the school might actually be censoring on-campus speech (the list brought on-campus by Zachariah) rather than his off-campus speech (the list not brought on-campus by Zachariah). The court stated that, because of "the out of school creation of the list, absent evidence that Paul [Zachariah] was responsible for bringing the list on school grounds, and absent disruption, ... defendants could not, without violating the First Amendment, suspend Paul for the mere creation of the Bozzuto Top Ten list" (p. 458).

It is interesting that the court ruled that schools have no censorship authority over students' off-campus obscene speech. After all, as noted in chapter five of this book, if student speech qualifies as obscenity under the *Miller* test (Miller v. California, 1973), the speech is not protected under the First Amendment. In order to determine if speech is obscene under the *Miller* test, courts inquire

1. "Whether the average person, applying contemporary community standards, would find that the work, taken as a whole, appeals to the prurient interest";
2. "Whether the work depicts or describes, in a patently offensive way, sexual conduct specifically defined by the applicable state law"; and
3. "Whether the work, taken as a whole, lacks serious literary, artistic, political, or scientific value" (Miller v. California, p. 24).

As unprotected speech, obscenity is exposed to censorship. The court's failure to recognize this is an oversight.

While the district court's exceptional-circumstances requirement might apply to lewd off-campus student speech, it should not apply to off-campus student speech that qualifies as obscenity under the *Miller* test. If the district court intended to merely apply the exceptional-circumstances requirement to off-campus student speech that is only obscene under the *Bethel* test (as opposed to the *Miller* test) then the exceptional-circumstances requirement would validly apply to obscene off-campus student speech. As we explained earlier in this book, the *Bethel* test expects a higher level of civil discourse within the schoolhouse gate than obtains in society outside the schoolhouse gate. As a result, relatively more speech can be censored in school pursuant to the *Bethel* test than outside of school under the *Miller* test. The *Miller* test seeks to protect speech from being censored as obscene while the *Bethel* test seeks to empower censorship of speech as obscene. Schools cannot constitutionally require the sanitation of off-campus student speech that is only obscene pursuant to the *Bethel* test. However, they can constitutionally require such sanitation if the speech is obscene pursuant to the *Miller* test.

Their Stories: Offline Off-Campus Speech

15. The Story of Janet Bystrom, Adam Collins, and David Drangeid

The Speech Incident: Tour de Farce: Sophomoric Humor and "Trash & Slash '86"

During the 1984-85 school year, a group of students at Fridley High School in Minnesota created an underground newspaper which they called Tour de Farce (Bystrom By and Through Bystrom v. Fridley High School, 1987). After some students distributed the newspaper on school property during school hours, school officials ordered them to cease the distribution. The school officials informed the students that the distribution violated the school district's policy requiring prior approval of all unofficial publications distributed on-campus. As a result, some students decided to distribute the newspaper on the sidewalk adjacent to the school's campus. This off-campus distribution, and a lawsuit challenging the prior approval policy, prompted the district to amend the policy in order to expressly limit its jurisdiction to speech distributed on school grounds. The district court found the district's policy unconstitutional as a prior restraint on speech.

Following the court's ruling, during the 1985-86 school year, Janet Bystrom, Adam Collins and David Drangeid created a newspaper which they called Tour de Farce (Bystrom By and Through Bystrom v. Fridley High School, 1987). The eight-page newspaper which was littered with sophomoric humor and vulgarities featured the students' own articles as well as material reproduced from other publications. It also criticized the school's policy which barred students from going off-campus during lunch. The newspaper called for the school to promulgate a strict policy against restroom smoking. Another article titled "Trash & Slash '86" discussed the recent vandalism at a teacher's house (p. 1390). In that article the author stated that "many students attending Fridley [Fridley High School] would like to claim responsibility for this act [vandalism], and I can't say that I blame them" (p. 1390). This article also stated: "I would like to say that we at Tour de Farce find this act pretty damn funny" (p. 1390).

On a Monday morning in 1986, between 7:45 to 7:55 a.m. just before school started, Janet, Adam and David distributed the newspaper in the school's cafeteria as students socialized (Bystrom By and Through Bystrom v. Fridley High School, 1987). This distribution did not disrupt the school. However, after the school day started, as other students circulated, read and reacted to the newspaper, classes were disrupted and teachers were forced to suspend teaching at various points. The teacher who was the focus of the "Trash & Slash '86" article left the school early as she did not want to subject herself to student reactions to the story. Janet, Adam and David did not participate in any of the disruptions at the school. Nevertheless, school officials suspended them from school for the remaining three days of the school year. The assistant principal told the students that they were suspended for advocating violence against a teacher's house. In other words, the school was not disciplining the students for the on-campus distribution but rather for the speech in the newspaper. Janet, Adam and David's parents sued the district under the First Amendment seeking injunctive relief.

Analysis

The United States District Court for the District of Minnesota applied the material and substantial disruption test to Janet, Adam and David's speech (Bystrom By and Through Bystrom v. Fridley High School, 1987). While the court recognized the existence and applicability of the infringement-of-rights test, it followed the same course as a majority of courts that have recognized the test: the court merely referenced the test without describing it or circumscribing its scope. The court also found the *Bethel* test applicable to Janet, Adam and David's off-campus speech. It appears that the court found the *Tinker* and *Bethel* tests applicable to the newspaper because, even though the students created the newspaper off-campus, they distributed it on school grounds. Ostensibly, the on-campus distribution provided a nexus to the school that sufficiently converted the off-campus speech into on-campus speech for purposes of school censorship. The fact that school officials punished the students for the content of their off-campus speech rather than for the on-campus distribution of the newspaper was immaterial to the on-campus versus off-campus status of the speech. This is surprising because the newspaper content that the school used to punish the students was created entirely off-campus. Therefore, since the punishment was for content rather than distribution, the newspaper should have retained its off-campus status. Moreover, Janet, Adam and David distributed the newspaper before school started, albeit on school grounds; thus, the on-campus distribution was de minimis at best.

Since the newspaper materially and substantially disrupted classes, school officials could censor the newspaper (Bystrom By and Through Bystrom v. Fridley High School, 1987). The court ruled that, even if the student-speaker(s) was not the direct cause of the material and substantial disruption, school officials could censor the speech. Additionally, even if the student-speaker(s) did not encourage or advocate disruption, school officials can censor the speech if material and substantial disruption ensues. Accordingly, while Janet, Adam and David did not participate in the disruptions at the school, the other students' disruptions could be attributed to them because their newspaper played a role in the disruptions. Moreover, the court ruled that even though, under traditional free speech standards, the vandalism discussion in the newspaper could not be censored as advocacy of violence, it was still censorable. The court ruled that school-censorship authority is not governed by the same traditional free speech standards applicable to adults. In so concluding, the court went rogue, in light of its acknowledgment that "[t]he Supreme Court has not yet addressed the question when school officials can punish students for advocating violence or other unlawful conduct" (p. 1393). This court statement is puzzling, particularly since it implies that the true-threat doctrine is also not applicable to school censorship of student speech. While the Supreme Court has never applied the true-threat doctrine to student speech, other courts have. Thus, the court could have safely applied the true-threat doctrine here without much controversy since the doctrine originated in the context of off-campus speech (see chapter two for discussion of the true-threat doctrine). Had the court applied the doctrine, it would have concluded that the newspaper's references to vandalism were not threats at all. The students did not threaten any future act; they simply mused at a past act of vandalism and claimed responsibility for it.

Given that the newspaper used vulgarities, it was not surprising that application of the *Bethel* test led the district court to conclude that the newspaper was censorable (Bystrom By and Through Bystrom v. Fridley High School, 1987). It was surprising, however, that the court extended the *Bethel* test beyond the schoolhouse gate to censorship of off-campus speech. Particularly because the only nexus to the school was the one-day ten-minute before-school distribution which the school admitted was not the reason for its censorship of the students. Instead of explaining its decision to extend the *Bethel* test outside the schoolhouse gate, the court summarily concluded that the newspaper was censorable because it was more vulgar and lewd than Matthew Fraser's boorish speech in Bethel School District No. 403 v. Fraser (1986) (see Matthew's speech in chapter eight). The district court, however, missed the mark because, as the United States Supreme Court stated in Morse v. Frederick (2007), if Matthew Fraser had delivered his vulgar speech "in a public forum outside the school context, it would have been protected" (p. 405).

The district court's conclusions in this case are perplexing because they contradict the court's own strong advocacy of a vibrant marketplace of ideas:

Their Stories: Offline Off-Campus Speech

The constitutional right of free expression is powerful medicine in a society as diverse and populous as ours. It is designed and intended to remove governmental restraints from the arena of public discussion, putting the decision as to what views shall be voiced largely into the hands of each us, in the hope that the use of such freedom will ultimately produce a capable citizenry and more perfect polity and in the belief that no other approach would comport with the premise of individual dignity and choice upon which our political system rests. To many, the immediate consequence of this freedom may often appear to be only verbal tumult, discord and even offensive utterance (Bystrom By and Through Bystrom v. Fridley High School, 1987, pp. 1324-25, citing Cohen v. California, 1971, pp. 24–25).

Given the plain language of this quote, one would have expected the court to endorse First Amendment protection for students' off-campus speech, even if the speech had vulgarities. At minimum, one would have expected the court to insist that students' off-campus speech should only be censorable under the same free speech standards applicable to the community at large such as the *Miller* test for obscenity. The language above clearly values expression and supports private-citizen, rather than government, regulation of speech. Its broad regard for speech contravenes the court's decision to use the one-day ten-minute on-campus distribution between 7:45 to 7:55 a.m. before school started as the basis to convert the off-campus speech into on-campus speech. The language also does not align with the court's willingness to allow censorship of off-campus student-speakers for material and substantial disruption attributable to others. In essence, in broadly authorizing censorship of off-campus student speech, the court hypocritically failed to be the guardian of free speech it endorsed in the above language.

16. The Story of Chris Pangle

The Speech Incident: *OUTSIDE!*, Snake Bite Antidote And Visine

During the 1996-97 school year, Chris Pangle, a junior at Mountain View High School in Oregon, contributed various articles to an underground newspaper called "OUTSIDE!" which he helped create (Pangle v. Bend-Lapine School District, 2000, p. 277). The newspaper featured quotations as well as articles from several student-authors who identified themselves using pseudonyms. Chris, for example, wrote as "Stryfe" and "Chuck M. Hall" (p. 281). Chris contributed an article called "We Want Your Letters!!" to each issue of the newspaper (p. 283). In this article, he informed readers that he would read and respond to all correspondence unless the reader specifically requested a response from a different author. This responsibility highlighted the prominence of Chris' role in the newspaper's publication and operation. In that same article, Chris discussed the authors' commitment to a free newspaper while appealing to readers for support. He suggested a nefarious way for readers to support the newspaper's publication:

We are strong believers in the belief that knowledge should be free to anyone who wants it! Going with that theory, if you e-mail us and request any of the information that we have within our magazine, it will be yours as fast as I can reply to it ... Now, to contradict myself, we do need a certain amount of money to operate this newsletter. We aren't even considering charging for this wonderful pamphlet of papers, but we will lease out our services. Would you like a home made virus to distribute to other people's computers? We can do it! Just tell us what you want it to do, or say, and we will get it to you (With a small fee ...). This is the only way we could think of to generate funds. If you can think of any others, please let us know. We are now a lil' hesitant to do this ... An absolutely gorgeous friend of Stryfe and Krimson recieved a virus in an e-mail the other day and messed up her comp. If we do decide to distribute virii, please be responsible in the targets you choose ... (Pangle v. Bend-Lapine School District, 2000, p. 283).

The front cover of the newspaper included the following disclaimer:

Well, now we need to get some legal crap out of the way. None of us are lawyers none of us know lawyers, but this should cover our asses pretty well:

OUTSIDE! is not responsible for the actions of other people. The articles within this newsletter are meant to distribute information, and anyone applying the methods or using the information within this document, we are not responsible for (Pangle v. Bend-Lapine School District, 2000, p. 281).

Chris' articles mostly criticized school officials, school policies, school culture as well as administrators' management of a student activity (Pangle v. Bend-Lapine School District, 2000). One of his articles titled "TOP TEN THINGS ..." described top ten things that Chris wanted done at the school (p. 281). Before listing the ten things, he provided readers the following rationale for the list:

These are the top ten things I would like to see happen at school ... to the people who 'run' it, or just some things to cause them Stryfe.

What is wrong with school you may ask ... ? I can't imagine too many people don't have their own individual responses to this question, but perhaps you would like to hear mine? Schools are a breeding ground for hatred and segregation. Students are persecuted by their peers, judged by their appearances and treated differently because of them. Cliques dominate their surroundings, and torment those who don't fit in ... The teachers preach nothing more than conforming to the 'norm' and obeying authority when we reach the 'REAL WORLD', slowly destroying each young mind which enters the public school system. Most within know they are in classes which will never benefit them and they will be lost when they leave this institution of imbeciles.

That is just my two cents on this subject, and justification for this article. These ten items are not meant to be used on the student population, and make the environment they must suffer through everyday worse. It is intended to be used against the 'forces that be' in our society (Pangle v. Bend-Lapine School District, 2000, p. 281).

Chris' top ten list read as follows:

10) Create an underground newsletter that shows how ignorant and overpowering the administration is. (Oops.. that has now been done!)

Their Stories: Offline Off-Campus Speech

9) A citizens arrest of the administrators which are unjust ... Some good proof would be needed, of course. Apparently destroying the minds of America's youth isn't a good enough reason, but one can wish.

8) Feed snake bite antidote or Visine to someone. The former will make a person vomit. (Make sure it is a harmless type ... most are.) The Visine will send them to the bathroom almost instantly. It is one of the world's greatest laxatives ...

7) Deposit some very disgusting smelling liquid in the school commons. Some possible sources?

Dog training liquid: smells like concentrated piss

Cadaver scent: used for Search and Rescue, it is the smell of a dead human body. Call a chemical company (Need some company names? Just write us! We will get you some!) and tell them you are training a dog for search and rescue ... it is a great smell ...

Hydrogen Sulfide: what most stink bombs are composed of. The chemistry room has an abundance of this I am told ...

6) A collection of teacher's signatures. They are not hard to obtain ... teachers are usually pretty free with them. Progress reports, hall passes, anywhere. If a substantial list of them were established, it would be great to post around school!

5) Epoxy glue any lock you can come to, aside from lockers. It will cause a lot of Kaos [chaos] among the teachers.

4) Blowing things up is always a great form of release ... as long as people aren't endangered, life is good! How about toilets? Put calcium Carbide (sold as 'Gopher–Go' in some places) in a gelatin capsule (available at any drug store ... dir cheap) and flush it. It causes a violent explosion when it hits water and some damage if it is flushed. Some other forms of exciting flushables? Firecrackers, balloons partly filled with air ... be creative! Express yourself!

3) Bomb threats are great, aren't they? We get to leave early, and if it is after 2:00 we don't have to make the day up at the end of the year. Anyway, if you attempt to call in a bomb threat, be careful. I am told it is a federal offense ... not to scare anyone off. It would be great to have some more! However, don't be an IDIOT and tell everyone what it is you have done. Don't do it for the recognition, do it because you believe in the cause.

2) How do you like the schools use of theh intercom system? Would you like to adapt it to your own private intercom show? That would be nice! And definitely possible! Splicing communication wires isn't hard at all! All you need is alligator clips, wire, a stereo with a pre-recorded tape and a remote location to splice in at. Above the panels of the ceiling, you can find the wire to the PA system.

1) PORN ADDS! We have all the phone numbers and addresses of the teachers in the Bend/LaPine school district at our disposal! Using them, it would be nice to place them in a wonderful homosexual personal add! ... or even replying to one wit their name and number! If you would like any teachers number or address, please write us and we will get it to you!

(Special thanks to the Youth International Pary (The Yippies) for giving me the inspiration for this top ten list ...)

Well, there you have it. Enjoy, and I hope to see some of these employed in the nea future (Pangle v. Bend-Lapine School District, 2000, pp. 281-82).

In another article, Chris criticized the fact that school officials had easy access to students' addresses, telephone numbers and school records. He stated:

Now, do you really think it is fair that the teachers and staff have access to our phone numbers, our home addresses and our records? I don't. I think that is a load of shit. Here we have a list of every teacher, disciplinary bastard, cook and janitor at Mountain View High School. The idiots actually have a book with EVERY number to everyone who works for the district. No, not just our district, but Crook County as well. Did they really think that if it was only distributed to teachers that it would ensure privacy?

*Well, I hope you have fun with these. If you need any 'inspiration', just flip through this newsletter and I'm sure you will find some. However, be careful. Although teachers aren't noted for raking in a great income, they could still have Caller I.D. To avoid this? Just type in *67 before you call, and it will not be able to display your number .... (Pangle v. Bend-Lapine School District, 2000, pp. 282-83).*

He then revealed the telephone numbers and addresses of Mountain View High School's teachers. Right after listing the teachers' information, he wrote:

*I do believe that all the numbers are here. In my haste of typing them up, I may have missed a few, so please let me know if there are any numbers which I have left out. The only number I know that I don't have is that hall monitor bastard who looks like a large penis. You know who I am talking about ... I think the bastards name is ' * * * '? Commonly known as dumb fuck. Well, if you do get his Name, Number and Address, I would REALLY appreciate it if you would sent it to us! ... actually, I think his son attends MVHS [Mountain View High School], so it may not be too hard to obtain after all ..." (Pangle v. Bend-Lapine School District, 2000, p. 282).*

Even though Chris composed the articles off-campus, he distributed the newspaper on school grounds without seeking the prior approval of school officials, in contravention of school policy (Pangle v. Bend-Lapine School District, 2000). After the assistant principal learned of Chris' articles, his on-campus distribution of the newspaper and his role in its creation, he suspended Chris from school. Upon the assistant principal's recommendation, the assistant superintendent changed the suspension to an expulsion through the first semester of the 1997-98 school year. The assistant superintendent, however, also offered Chris probationary enrollment for the first semester of the 1997-98 school year if Chris' parents and school officials could agree on a probation plan. Chris' parents filed a First Amendment lawsuit against the school district asking for injunctive and declaratory relief.

Analysis

The Court of Appeals of Oregon failed to acknowledge the off-campus nature of Chris' speech or distinguish his off-campus speech from the on-campus distribution of the newspaper (Pangle v. Bend-Lapine School District, 2000). Instead, the court treated Chris' speech as on-campus speech because of his distribution of the newspaper on school grounds. Even though Chris' speech originated outside the schoolhouse gate, the court ruled that the United States Supreme Court's student-speech precedents governed his speech because students' "First Amendment rights of expression must comport with the ability of schools to carry out their educational mission" (pp. 283, 285). The court effectively tempered students' free speech rights while elevating as priority the educational mission of the school. Using this educational-mission rationale, for example, the court ruled that Chris' speech could be censored as vulgar under the *Bethel* test. As we noted in chapter ten, however, Justice Alito's controlling opinion in Morse v. Frederick (2007) opposed use of a school's educational mission to justify any censorship of student speech. While the *Morse* case had not been decided when the Court of Appeals of Oregon considered Chris' case, it is now evident that the court's rationale would no longer be valid in the United States Supreme Court. As Justice Alito warned, an educational-mission rationale would enable schools to manipulate their educational missions in order to discriminate against controversial views (Morse v. Frederick, 2007).

Recall that the United States Supreme Court ruled in Hazelwood v. Kuhlmeier (1988) that schools can censor student speech that is "inconsistent with its basic educational mission, even though the government could not censor similar speech outside the school" (p. 266). The Court of Appeals of Oregon acknowledged this rule but failed to explicate or apply the rule to Chris' speech. Indeed, the court refused to consider any persuasive or binding precedent involving off-campus speech. The court explained: "Because First Amendment rights are applied based on the special characteristics of a high school environment, cases that do not involve First Amendment rights in a high school setting do not aid our analysis" (Pangle v. Bend-Lapine School District, 2000, p. 284). This was clearly a mistake as it furthered the conflation of on-campus and off-campus speech in the nebulous student-speech jurisprudence evident in this book. The court chose to ignore off-campus precedents despite the court's recognition that the Supreme Court had emphasized that the "the unique facts of each case" could dictate creation and application of a new student-speech test (p. 284). The decision to ignore off-campus precedents is also puzzling because the Court Appeals of Oregon conceded that "[s]o far as we can discern, the United States Supreme Court has not ruled on any case involving facts that are analogous to this case" (p. 284).

While the Court of Appeals of Oregon acknowledged the infringement-of-rights test and summarily concluded that Chris' speech violated the rights of other students, it did not distinguish the infringement-of-rights test from the material and substantial disruption test (Pangle v. Bend-Lapine School District, 2000). As a result, the court's interpretation of the infringement-of-rights test is not entirely clear. Nevertheless, a thorough review of the court's opinion provides information that could help provide some minor, albeit cramped, clarity. In fact, the court framed the issue in the case around the material and substantial disruption test and the educational-mission rationale, omitting the infringement-of-rights test:

"the task confronting us in this case is to focus on the issue of any disruption, actual or potential, that the dissemination of OUTSIDE! caused to school's educational mission" (p. 285). Yet, the court used the same facts to conclude in consonance that Chris' speech violated the infringement-of-rights test as well as the material and substantial disruption test. Consequently, it is possible that the court sees no material difference between the two tests. If the court does view the tests as materially different, it is unclear what the court would look for in an infringement-of-rights review if the facts do not also support a finding of material and substantial disruption.

It was indisputable that school officials could have reasonably forecast material and substantial disruption from Chris' speech (Pangle v. Bend-Lapine School District, 2000). In his "We Want Your Letters!!" article, he spoke of infecting computers with a virus. As the court noted, his top ten list provided ample support for such a forecast. For example, in the list, Chris described how students could tamper with the school's intercom system. Moreover, he called for citizen's arrests of school officials. He also spoke of placing the names, phone numbers and addresses of school officials in a pornographic advertisement. Additionally, he called for the placement of stink bombs in the school commons and provided directions for students to get stink bombs. He encouraged students to "[f]eed snake bite antidote or Visine to someone", knowing that it would lead to health issues for the targets (p. 281). He urged students to "[e]poxy glue any lock you can come to, aside from lockers. It will cause a lot of Kaos [chaos] among the teachers" (p. 282). In essence, Chris knew that the epoxy-glue prank would cause material and substantial disruption at the school.

Chris encouraged students to blow up toilets using firecrackers or calcium carbide which he indicated "causes a violent explosion when it hits water and some damage if it is flushed" (Pangle v. Bend-Lapine School District, 2000, p. 282). He also discussed how students can procure calcium carbide. Further, despite acknowledging that bomb threats are a federal offense, Chris urged students to make bomb threats at the school. He concluded his top ten list with the following exhortation: "Enjoy, and I hope to see some of these employed in the nea[r] future", showing intent and willingness to execute the items on the list (pp. 282, 286). The specificity of the items in Chris' list amplified their gravity; and thus created appropriate concern for school officials. As the court stated, school officials were right to take the items on the list seriously, given the increased violence in schools today. Further, the court concluded that the items on the list undermined the school's educational mission, heightening the concerns about the speech. While it is true that the speech undermined the educational mission, the United States Supreme Court has never restricted censorship under the material and substantial disruption test to disruption that undermines a mission. Under the Supreme Court's student-speech jurisprudence, even if speech does not undermine the educational mission, it can be censored as long as there is actual or reasonable forecast of material and substantial disruption.

17. The Story of Casey Riggan

The Speech Incident: The Suburban Photographs of Alleged Sexual Improprieties

During the spring of 1999, a local newspaper in Midland, Texas revealed that it purportedly had an intimate videotape of Midland Senior High School's principal (Riggan v. Midland Independent School District, 2000). The newspaper identified the source of the video as "Cody Owens" (p. 650). While this

Their Stories: Offline Off-Campus Speech

video was never released, the revelation prompted the Midland Independent School District to investigate the principal for alleged sexual improprieties amid rumors of other videos and photographs. The school district found no student called Cody Owens in its database. In the course of the investigation, school officials interviewed 18-year old student Casey Riggan after learning from various sources that he might have pertinent pictures and information. He denied being Cody Owens. He also told school officials that he was not the source of any rumors about the principal and that he was not the newspaper's source.

Casey revealed that he and two friends heard rumors that the principal was allegedly engaged in sexual improprieties (Riggan v. Midland Independent School District, 2000). Therefore, as part of a prank, the three friends trailed the principal in their vehicle after they saw him off-campus at a local restaurant. Casey had his camera with him during the drive. When they saw the principal park in front of a teacher's home, Casey asked one of his friends to take pictures of the principal's car on the public street where the teacher's house was located. After the three students left the scene, Casey stored the two pictures that his friend took off-campus; he never brought them on-campus. No school resource or school time was used in taking the pictures. When the principal learned of the pictures' existence through the local paper and the rumor mill, he ordered the student who took the pictures for Casey to meet with him to answer questions about the pictures. During their meeting in the principal's car, the friend admitted taking the pictures and apologized. The principal told this student that he would not be disciplined. The principal also confronted Casey's second friend who admitted his role and apologized. This friend was likewise not disciplined. Both friends failed to provide a written statement promised to the principal averring that Casey was the pictures' mastermind.

The principal convened a meeting in his office with Casey and his father to discuss the pictures (Riggan v. Midland Independent School District, 2000). At the meeting, the principal accused Casey of planning to distribute one of the pictures on T-shirts over the caption "I never had sex with that woman" (p. 651). He claimed that Casey planned to distribute the T-shirts during graduation ceremonies. He also accused Casey of spreading the sexual impropriety rumors about him. Casey, however, denied these accusations. The meeting became so intensely acrimonious that the principal had Casey's father escorted out of his office. Subsequently, the principal decided to punish Casey for taking the picture of his car on a public street. Initially, he wanted to send Casey to an alternative education program – a program that separated students from their peers and teachers – for the rest of the school year. However, he opted to suspend Casey for three days until another meeting with Casey's father to discuss further discipline for the rest of the school year. During this follow-up meeting, the principal decided to send Casey to the alternative education program for five days. Additionally, he told Casey that he would not be permitted to take part in graduation ceremonies unless he wrote two letters of apology. Casey appealed to the assistant superintendent. The principal argued that Casey planned the picture-taking incident as retaliation for prior disciplinary action he had taken against Casey. While the assistant superintendent disagreed with this retaliation argument, he nonetheless ruled that Casey disrespected an adult. Therefore, he affirmed the three-day suspension, the five-day assignment to the alternative education program and the requirement of two letters of apology. Casey was also placed on probation for the rest of the semester. The school board affirmed the decision. Casey filed suit against the school district claiming that the punishment for taking pictures of the principal on an off-campus public street violated his First Amendment right to free speech. The school board then passed a motion stating that Casey would be banned from graduation ceremonies if he did not dismiss his lawsuit or write the apology letters.

Analysis

Casey argued that the school district had no authority to discipline him for his speech (the taking and possession of the pictures) because it was off-campus speech; and because it involved no use of school resource or time (Riggan v. Midland Independent School District, 2000). The school district countered that it could discipline Casey because students do not have the same First Amendment right as adults outside the schoolhouse gate. The school also argued that it could censor student speech as long as the speech materially and substantially interfered with the school. Casey argued, however, that the United States Supreme Court's free speech precedents only applied to on-campus speech. The United States District Court for the Western District of Texas ruled that school officials can censor student speech that does not pass muster under the Supreme Court's student-speech precedents. The district court chose to make the rumored T-shirt distribution the focus of its review despite acknowledging that students have a First Amendment right to silly opinions and to sharing those opinions. Apparently, the planned on-campus distribution of the T-shirt provided the nexus between the off-campus picture-taking and the school campus, triggering the Supreme Court's student-speech precedents (Riggan v. Midland Independent School District, 2000).

By anchoring its analysis in the planned on-campus distribution, the court either sought to avoid deciding an off-campus speech case (due to the lingering uncertainty in the jurisprudence) or the court genuinely viewed the case as an on-campus speech case because of the nexus referenced earlier. Viewing the case as an on-campus case allowed the court to apply the Supreme Court's student-speech precedents then existing –Tinker v. Des Moines Independent Community School District (1969), Hazelwood v. Kuhlmeier (1988) and Bethel School District No. 403 v. Fraser (1986). Thus, it is not surprising that the court chose to make central to its analysis Casey's "plan [of] a public humiliation of his principal at graduation ceremonies" (Riggan v. Midland Independent School District, p. 661). What is surprising is that the court did not give greater credence to Casey's denial of the rumored on-campus T-shirt distribution. The court gave greater credence to the principal's assertion that Casey planned to distribute the T-shirts at graduation ceremonies on the school's campus. It is perplexing that the court accepted the word of the school because later on in the case the court chose not to simply accept the assertion of school officials that the speech would materially and substantially disrupt the school. Indeed, the court stated that "intuition or the simple pronouncement of the superintendent or principal that disruption is likely to occur" is not sufficient (p. 661). The court failed to explain its reasons for giving credence to one assertion of school officials while giving no credence to another assertion of the same school officials. In its review under the material and substantial disruption test, the court found insufficient evidence in the record showing that material and substantial disruption occurred or would occur at the school as a result of Casey's off-campus speech. The court, however, did not rule out the possibility of such a finding: "Defendants may be able to show a reasonable belief that Riggan's other conduct in taking and possessing the picture was substantially disruptive to the educational process" (p. 661).

The court found the *Hazelwood* test inapplicable because the taking and possession of the pictures did not constitute school-sponsored speech (Riggan v. Midland Independent School District, 2000). As for the *Bethel* test, the court ruled that this test empowers schools to broadly censor student speech in order to teach and maintain civility as well as sensitivity to others. However, the court interpreted Bethel School District No. 403 v. Fraser (1986) and thus the *Bethel* test narrowly. According to the court, the *Bethel* case merely governs speech at a mandatory assembly. The court stated that it might apply the *Bethel* test to the T-shirt distribution if the school district could make a convincing case that distribution of T-shirts at a graduation ceremony is similar to speech at a mandatory assembly (Riggan v. Midland Independent School District, 2000). Despite this apparent willingness to embrace an expansive interpretation of the *Bethel* test, the court ruled that the test was not applicable to Casey's speech because his speech was not at a mandatory school assembly.

In essence, this case extended the Supreme Court's student-speech tests, with the exception of the *Hazelwood* test and possibly the *Bethel* test, to students' off-campus speech even though those tests were created in the context of on-campus student speech.

18. The Story of K.G.S.

The Speech Incident: The Golf Ball With Vulgar Words

K.G.S., a ninth-grade student at Martin High School in Texas, spent May 4, 2009 with friends playing golf at a public golf course (K.G.S. v. Kemp, 2011). Even though K.G.S. was a member of his school's golf team, the golf get-together was not related to any school function. It was a purely personal social gathering of friends. While on the golf course, K.G.S. used a golf bag imprinted with the name "Martin High School" (p. 1). This was the only school resource that K.G.S. used during the outing. Coincidentally, a school district employee and her friend were playing golf on the course at the same time as K.G.S. and his friends. The district employee wore a shirt with the school district logo so she was identifiable. As the ladies played the sixth hole, one of them unexpectedly drove a ball into the area occupied by K.G.S. and his friends but failed to apologize. Additionally, while playing the tenth hole, the ladies decided to "play through" K.G.S. and his friends instead of first seeking permission from them (p. 1). These actions upset K.G.S. and his friends. Therefore, they decided to retaliate. When the ladies got to the twelfth hole, K.G.S. wrote on one of his personal golf balls the phrase "fucking nigger bitch" and strategically placed it in the twelfth-hole cup (p. 1). When the school employee saw the speech on the golf ball, she confronted K.G.S. and his friends in an effort to determine the source of the speech. She got K.G.S. to admit that he was the speaker and that he was a Martin High School student.

The following day, the employee reported K.G.S. to a district administrator who directed the golf coach as well as the assistant principal of Martin High School to discipline K.G.S. for his off-campus speech (K.G.S. v. Kemp, 2011). K.G.S. never took his speech to school. Nonetheless, the golf coach decided to dismiss him from the golf team. The assistant principal sent K.G.S. to the district's disciplinary alternative education program for the rest of the semester. K.G.S.'s parents sued the district claiming a violation of his First Amendment right to free speech.

Analysis

The United States District Court for the Northern District of Texas found no controlling precedent on off-campus student speech (K.G.S. v. Kemp, 2011). As the court observed, for instance, the United States Court of Appeals for the Third Circuit had issued conflicting opinions on the First Amendment status of off-campus student speech: one opinion upholding the right to off-campus free speech and the other giving censorship authority to schools over off-campus student speech. The United States Court of Appeals for the Second Circuit, on the other hand, had concluded that its earlier off-campus speech precedent "did not clearly establish[ ] that off-campus speech-related conduct may never be the basis for discipline by school officials" (p. 3, citing Doninger v. Niehoff, 2011). As the United States District

Court for the Northern District of Texas observed, at the time that K.G.S. spoke, "judges did not agree on the parameters of a school official's ability to discipline students for off-campus speech; much less could school officials such as the defendants be expected to clearly understand their limitations in that regard" (K.G.S. v. Kemp, 2011, p. 4).

Additionally, the district court found no binding precedent that would have provided "fair warning that disciplining a student for writing a vulgar, racist statement on a golf ball would infringe on that student's First Amendment rights" (K.G.S. v. Kemp, 2011, p. 3). In other words, there was no fair warning to school officials that they could be violating students' speech rights by censorship of vulgar off-campus speech under the *Bethel* test or any other test. The uncertainty in the law prompted the district court to rule for the school district as the school officials could not have anticipated that the censorship would violate the First Amendment. Therefore, the court dismissed the case with prejudice. While it is laudable that the court acknowledged the judicial uncertainty about the First Amendment status of off-campus student speech, its decision to dismiss the case on that basis merely left the uncertainty in place. This in turn leaves students unsure of their rights and schools empowered to censor off-campus speech as they operate in the gray areas of the law. The court missed a great opportunity to add to the understanding of students' rights to off-campus speech. Arguably, the court could rightly contend that, rather than missing an opportunity, it simply chose not to add to the existing misunderstanding or uncertainty about the law – misunderstanding and uncertainty that will exist until the United States Supreme Court specifically addresses the issue of students' off-campus speech.

SPEECH DIRECTED AT OR AGAINST STUDENTS

In this section, we present the stories of students whose offline speech has been censored by their schools, despite the fact that the speech occurred off-campus. We focus specifically on student speech directed at or against other students. We examine how various courts have addressed this offline student speech as well as the authority of schools to censor such speech.

1. The Story of Spencer Sherrell

The Speech Incident: His Dad's Gun and the Seventh Grade

Spencer Sherrell, a 16-year old student at Tri–Central Junior–Senior High School in Indiana, spent the evening of March 6, 2001 at a get-together in a schoolmate's home (Sherrell ex rel. Sherrell v. Northern Community School Corporation of Tipton County, 2004). During his interaction with two friends that evening, Spencer told them that he planned to "get his dad's gun in Indianapolis, bring it to school, start with the seventh grade, and work his way up" (p. 698). Spencer made this statement because he was upset at the school's handling of an issue he had with a friend. An unidentified person relayed the statement to the school. Spencer's father owned several guns so there was presumably increased gravity to his statement.

The following day when Spencer arrived at school, both the principal and assistant principal confronted him about his statement (Sherrell ex rel. Sherrell v. Northern Community School Corporation of Tipton County, 2004). Spencer acknowledged making the threat. He also conceded that it violated the school rule prohibiting threats that could interfere with the school. School officials searched his locker for a gun but found none. They then asked the sheriff's office to intervene. After a probation officer and a sheriff's deputy interviewed Spencer, the probation officer opted not to pursue criminal charges against him because she could not find an appropriate law for charging him. Nevertheless, school officials decided to punish Spencer for his speech. Two days after the speech, he was suspended for ten days. The principal also asked the superintendent to initiate the district's expulsion process against Spencer. At the conclusion of the process, the school board found it appropriate to expel Spencer in light of the threatening nature of his speech as well as the increasing violence in schools. The school board concluded that the off-campus nature of Spencer's speech did not preclude the expulsion. Spencer then sought judicial review of the school board's decision.

Analysis

The Court of Appeals of Indiana took a very deferential approach toward school censorship of student speech (Sherrell ex rel. Sherrell v. Northern Community School Corporation of Tipton County, 2004). Under this approach, irrespective of the location of the speech, schools have broad censorship authority over student speech. In fact, the court stated that, if the school decision is not arbitrary or capricious, the judiciary should abstain from overruling the school. It found that school officials at Tri–Central Junior–Senior High School did not act arbitrarily or capriciously because Spencer's speech threatened violence against the school. The willingness of the court to defer to the school in a case where speech occurred in a private home (and a case where the student-speaker did not himself take the speech to school), creates a borderless school with far reaches into students' homes. The imposition of an arbitrary or capricious standard as one of only two checks on school authority effectively makes it more likely that school censorship will pass First Amendment muster (see the next paragraph for our discussion of the second check). However, it is arguably arbitrary and capricious in itself to give schools authority over students' off-campus speech; particularly when such speech is in a home and after school hours. This is even more so because the court's decision deprives students of all spheres of private communication. Even though Spencer directed his speech against his schoolmates, and although his speech was in the presence of his school friends, the statement was made off-campus at a friend's home where the schoolhouse gate should not extend.

The other restraint the court placed on school-censorship authority was the requirement that off-campus speech must be reasonably likely to interfere with the school before it can be censored (Sherrell ex rel. Sherrell v. Northern Community School Corporation of Tipton County, 2004). This reasonable-likelihood approach is similar to the material and substantial disruption test even though the court did not apply any of the student-speech precedents of the United States Supreme Court (Tinker v. Des Moines Independent Community School District, 1969). The similarity lies in the fact that the requirement helps establish a nexus between off-campus speech and events within the school campus. The court concluded that, as a threat, Spencer's speech was reasonably likely to interfere with the school (Sherrell ex rel. Sherrell v. Northern Community School Corporation of Tipton County, 2004). The fact that Spencer's father owned several guns gave added credence to the conclusion that the speech was a credible threat to the school. The court rejected the idea that the government's failure to prosecute a student who utters a threat could be dispositive of the credence of speech as a threat. The decision not to prosecute Spencer, consequently, was not probative of the authority of the school to suspend and expel him for his speech. Instead, schools are authorized to make their own disciplinary decisions independent of the criminal law. Accordingly, the court ruled that the school was justified in disciplining Spencer.

2. The Story of Christopher Donovan

The Speech Incident: The List with the Scatological Title

On Sunday September 18, 1994, Christopher Donovan, a senior at Winchester High School in Massachusetts, visited a friend's house with thirteen other students (Donovan v. Ritchie, 1995). During their time at the home, one of the students created a nine-page document titled the "THE SHIT LIST" (p. 15). The document included churlish comments attacking the behavior and character of each of the 140 students identified therein. The document, which was not created with school resources or time, insulted about twelve freshmen students, for their appearances and social behaviors. It also vilified over thirty sophomores, more than thirty juniors and over sixty seniors with various epithets. The epithets went beyond the insults about appearance directed at the freshmen students. They included explicit comments about the students' sexual proclivities, their sexual promiscuities and their capacities to engage in sexual relations. They also included general crude comments.

On Thursday September 22, 1994, while away from school, Christopher and two other students made copies of the document (Donovan v. Ritchie, 1995). Even though they put the copies in a trash barrel at an off-campus location, a few days later, a teacher found the copies at the school. The document troubled the principal who told the student body and staff that he believed the list was disparaging and damaging. He also asked students to help identify those behind the list. He met with various students who revealed the names of fifteen students alleged to have been at the home when the list was created. On Monday September 26, Christopher and the two other students who hid the copies in the trash barrel met with the principal and denied involvement with the list. The following day, however, they changed their story. While they now admitted copying the list, they claimed that they had no knowledge of its contents. They also insisted that, since the copies were made off-campus using no school resource, the principal had no authority to punish them. Nonetheless, the principal suspended Christopher indefinitely after meeting with him and his mother. The principal claimed that Christopher and the other students violated the school's rules against name calling, put downs and obscene language. The principal also met with the other fourteen students and their parents about their discipline. As further punishment for Christopher, the principal asked him to write an apology letter. On Monday October 3, Christopher turned in his letter, apologizing for making a "bad mistake" (p. 16). The letter also admitted Christopher's role in the delivery of the list to the school campus:

My involvement in the list is such; I had the list copied with 2 other boys and we then proceeded to take the list put it in a trash bag and put it in the barrel at Gin [Ginn Field] where it was to be picked up (Donovan v. Ritchie, 1995, p. 16).

Following this apology and admission, the principal changed Christopher's suspension to ten days (Donovan v. Ritchie, 1995). He was also barred from all interscholastic athletics, including lacrosse in which Christopher participated. Additionally, he was prohibited from attending any school social event. These disciplinary actions were also placed in his file. As a condition precedent to his reinstatement to interscholastic athletics, and to the removal of the discipline from his file, Christopher was required

Their Stories: Offline Off-Campus Speech

to make efforts to fix any harm done to the school and the students. He complained to the principal that his punishments were excessive. The superintendent and the school board, however, supported the principal's decision. Consequently, Christopher sued the school district, asking the court to enjoin the school district and award him monetary damages.

Analysis

Despite the fact that Christopher was never shown to have created the list, the United States Court of Appeals for the First Circuit attributed preparation of the list to him (Donovan v. Ritchie, 1995). The court apparently presumed that since he was at the scene of the speech creation, he was jointly responsible for the speech. Further, the court gave no credence to Christopher's claim that he was ignorant of the list's contents. It concluded:

Moreover, as we reflect on the giant-sized capital letters spelling out the title ["The Shit List"] of the list on the cover, and the following listing names with, generally, a salacious one-line commentary, we can be skeptical of the likelihood of one remaining oblivious to content after feeding into and retrieving from the copying machine multiple copies of this nine-page document (Donovan v. Ritchie, 1995, p. 18).

The court stated that, even if Christopher was unaware of the list's contents, he was involved in the list's off-campus preparation (Donovan v. Ritchie, 1995). The court also indicated that his photocopying of the list, albeit off-campus, played a role in the list's distribution on the school's campus. This apparently created a satisfactory nexus between the off-campus speech and the school's campus. Consequently, the court ruled that the school could punish him for the list as well as the preparation and distribution of the list. The court suggested that if Christopher had submitted strong evidence disavowing his involvement in the speech's preparation and distribution, school officials might not have the purview to discipline him. Christopher had the opportunity to do so if he had such evidence yet he failed to. The evidence for Christopher was so scant that the principal could have reasonably concluded that his argument about the off-campus nature of his actions was not credible. Nonetheless, the court found a sufficient nexus between the off-campus speech and the school campus. The court was "entirely satisfied" to conclude that Christopher's "admitted off-premises conduct led to the distribution of the list on school premises" (p. 19).

A lesson here is that students in this court might not be able to use an ignorance-of-content defense to avoid discipline for off-campus speech if they played a role in the list ultimately getting to the school. Such a role would include making copies of the speech that end up at the school. If a student cannot establish a clear chain of custody for copies of the speech, showing that he was not involved in the list's presence within the schoolhouse gate, the court might allow the school to punish the student. Additionally, a student's role in the off-campus preparation of a speech might not exculpate the student of an on-campus rule violation. Particularly if the court views the preparation as part of a single transaction that resulted in the speech's presence on-campus. In Christopher's case, the court appeared to actually view his speech outside the schoolhouse gate as on-campus speech. When a court views off-campus speech as on-campus speech, it removes the constitutional concerns about school censorship of off-campus speech; and empowers schools to exercise their censorship authority over off-campus under the guise of censoring on-campus speech.

It appears that the court was actively looking for a nexus between Christopher's speech and the school campus. Christopher's actions (the preparation and photocopying of the list) provided that nexus. Unlike what happened with Christopher, students seeking to escape censorship of their off-campus speech need to present the court with strong evidence detailing how they clearly had no role whatsoever in the speech getting within the schoolhouse gate. Strong evidence might be to show that the student actually took deliberate steps to prevent the speech from getting to campus. If Christopher had actually torn the speech rather than merely placing it in the trash barrels, he would have been able to show an active effort to keep the speech away from the schoolhouse gate.

3. The Story of C.R.

The Speech Incident: The B.J. Double Entendre Speech

During the 2011-12 school year, C.R., a seventh-grade student in the Eugene School District in Oregon, walked home after school with several seventh-graders and two sixth-graders (C.R. ex rel. Rainville v. Eugene School District 4J, 2013). The two sixth-graders in the walking group had special needs: the male had autism while the female was hearing impaired. On the first day that the group walked together, C.R. introduced himself to them using a fictitious name. The following day, during the walk home, two male students in the group made several sexual comments that made the sixth-graders uncomfortable. For instance, they "talked about blowjobs and BJ's" (p. 1). They also asked the group, "do you watch porn and stuff like that?" (p. 1). The male students in the group laughed at the two students with special needs when they indicated that they had not watched pornography. C.R. claimed that his response after the pornography question was simply, "I like BJ's restaurant pizza" (p. 1). He claimed to have made this comment merely because the two male students who made the sexual comments also referred to the restaurant. He conceded, however, that he "heard them say porn when they said BJs, but I just kind of really wasn't thinking" (p. 1). During the walk, one of the students stated that a "'BJ is something that you'—'It's a sandwich that you can enjoy by yourself, but it's really better to enjoy it with another person'" (p. 2). The students also made comments about the two students with special needs going to BJ's as a couple. One of the students said to the male student with special needs, "Why don't you take her to BJ's or she can take you to BJ's?" (p. 2). They tried to pressure the two students to repeat various cuss words, some of which had sexual connotations.

On the third day, during the walk home, an instructional aide for students with disabilities sensed that the group was not friendly to the two students with special needs (C.R. ex rel. Rainville v. Eugene School District 4J, 2013). Consequently, she asked the two students if they felt safe walking with the group. The girl confirmed that she was not comfortable. The aide then asked the boys in the group to walk on without the two students with special needs. The aide walked with both students to ensure that the boys did not come back to tease them. During their walk, the girl revealed that the boys had been discussing BJ's. She told the aide that, while the students claimed that they were discussing the restaurant, she felt they might have been using BJ's as a double entendre. The girl, however, refused to elaborate further or discuss any other aspect of the incident.

The aide, a friend of C.R.'s mother, reported C.R. and the walking group's conversation to the vice principal (C.R. ex rel. Rainville v. Eugene School District 4J, 2013). She told the vice principal that the male students made the girl with special needs uncomfortable. The girl confirmed this to the vice principal; and told him that she felt unsafe because of the conversation. The girl informed the vice principal that, during the walk, she heard swearing among the students. She also revealed that the male students discussed Ben and Jerry's as well as BJ's Ice Cream during the walk. School officials confronted C.R. who denied knowledge of any conversation that could have made the girl uncomfortable. Interviews of the other male students in the walking group confirmed C.R.'s involvement, however. These students also told school officials that C.R. had more involvement in the conversation than simple profession of love for BJ's restaurant and BJ's pizza. The students claimed that C.R. as well as the girl knew that the entire conversation was about blow jobs. Subsequent to these interviews, C.R. admitted that he made inappropriate comments during the walk. After meeting with C.R.'s parents to discuss the incident, school officials suspended C.R. from school for two days citing sexual harassment. The vice principal described the reason for the suspension in a disciplinary form:

[Plaintiff] along with some other boys verbally harassed two students with disabilities. One victim was a female hearing impaired, 6th grader, and one student was a 6th grade autistic male. The comments contained sexual connotations referring to blowjobs in connection to B.J.'s restaurant. [Plaintiff] admitted that the comments were inappropriate. It should be noted that the female student stated that she understood what the B.J. comment was referring to and did not feel safe (C.R. ex rel. Rainville v. Eugene School District 4J, 2013, p. 1).

After the suspension was imposed, C.R.'s parents asked him to send a letter of apology to the parents of the students with special needs. In that letter, C.R. stated:

... very sorry I didn't stand up for your kids. I was walking home with some people and they started to harass them and I stood there and accidently intimidated them. It was wrong not to stand up to them and tell the people to stop.

I'm also sorry for lying about my name for about a minute. It's a joke I have used since first grade. I didn't mean to harass your kids and I'm very sorry about it.

I've learned lots about harassment and have paid the price for my actions. I'm sorry that I scared your kids and I will never do it again (C.R. ex rel. Rainville v. Eugene School District 4J, 2013, p. 4).

C.R. wrote a similar letter to the principal in which he continued to disavow any leadership role in the walking group's conversations (C.R. ex rel. Rainville v. Eugene School District 4J, 2013). He never delivered the letter to the principal, however. C.R. instead sued the school district for injunctive relief claiming a violation of his right to free speech under the First Amendment.

Analysis

C.R. argued that the school unconstitutionally censored his speech even though it occurred after school hours outside the schoolhouse gate (C.R. ex rel. Rainville v. Eugene School District 4J, 2013). The United States District Court for the District of Oregon, however, dismissed this argument. According to the court, C.R.'s characterization of his case as a free speech case was designed to distract from his real motive – second-guessing the school district. This conclusion is flaccid, however, because every student-speech case is brought to second-guess a school's disciplinary decision. In essence, the second-guessing of school decisions and a First Amendment claim are not mutually exclusive nor are they diametrically opposed. The court's framing of C.R.'s motive merely foreboded the pro-school direction of its decision.

The federal district court did not make an in-depth constitutional distinction between on-campus and off-campus speech because C.R. and the school district agreed that Tinker v. Des Moines Independent Community School District (1969) governed the case (C.R. ex rel. Rainville v. Eugene School District 4J, 2013). Instead the court chose to rely on language from the *Tinker* case in which the United States Supreme Court stated that "conduct by the student, in class or out of it, which for any reason—whether it stems from time, place, or type of behavior—materially disrupts classwork or involves substantial disorder ... is, of course, not immunized by the constitutional guarantee of freedom of speech" (C.R. ex rel. Rainville v. Eugene School District 4J, p. 5, citing Tinker v. Des Moines Independent Community School District, p. 513). The key language from this case was "in class or out of it" which the district court apparently interpreted as extending school censorship to off-campus student speech. Even though the court stated that the location of speech could make a difference in a case, it ruled that "off-campus speech is within the reach of school officials" (C.R. ex rel. Rainville v. Eugene School District 4J, p. 5, citing Wynar v. Douglas County School District, 2013, p. 1068). Clearly, this bright line rule gives schools authority over student speech. Therefore, it is puzzling that the court stated that location can make a difference. The court failed to explain how location can make a difference after granting schools censorship authority over off-campus student speech.

Since the federal district court chose to authorize school censorship of off-campus student speech, the court extended the United States Supreme Court's student-speech precedents to off-campus speech (C.R. ex rel. Rainville v. Eugene School District 4J, 2013). The court ruled that schools can censor off-campus student speech that presents a threat of violence as long as the school satisfies the material and substantial disruption test. The court was either not aware that the true-threat doctrine could be applied to student off-campus speech or it chose not to apply the doctrine to student speech, reserving it strictly for censorships that non-school entities initiate. As we discussed in chapter two, speech deemed a true threat is constitutionally unprotected, exposing it to broad school censorship. Under the true-threat doctrine, schools do not need to show material and substantial disruption. Nonetheless, the court imposed the material and substantial disruption test as the governing censorship standard for off-campus student speech constituting a violent threat.

The federal district court also ruled that schools can censor off-campus student speech that is degrading and sexually explicit (C.R. ex rel. Rainville v. Eugene School District 4J, 2013). The court apparently ignored or was ignorant of Justice Brennan's statement in Bethel School District No. 403 v. Fraser (1986) that "[i]f respondent had given the same [vulgar, lewd, plainly-offensive] speech outside of the school environment, he could not have been penalized simply because government officials considered his language to be inappropriate" (p. 688). As we noted earlier, the Supreme Court affirmed this in Hazelwood v. Kuhlmeier (1988). The district court appeared to have extended the *Bethel* test to off-campus speech rather than imposing the *Miller* test (Miller v. California, 1973) (discussed in chapter five) as the governing standard for censorship of degrading or sexually-explicit off-campus speech. The court's mere limitation on school-censorship authority over degrading or sexually-explicit off-campus speech was that the speech must fail the material and substantial disruption test or the infringement-of-rights test created in Tinker v. Des Moines Independent Community School District (1969) in order to qualify for censorship. The court effectively blended the *Bethel* test with the *Tinker* tests in order to expand the authority of schools to censor student speech that is sexually explicit or degrading.

Their Stories: Offline Off-Campus Speech

The federal district court ruled that school officials had reasonable grounds to forecast substantial and material disruption from C.R.'s speech (C.R. ex rel. Rainville v. Eugene School District 4J, 2013). It stated that any incident of bullying and harassment is so important that failure to censor the speech could multiply such incidents at the school. This could then breed a school culture that embraces harassment and bullying. Consequently, schools are authorized to censor off-campus speech in order to preclude such deterioration of school culture. This ruling arguably constitutes "undifferentiated fear or apprehension of disturbance" which the United States Supreme Court has ruled cannot constitute material and substantial disruption (Tinker v. Des Moines Independent Community School District, 1969, p. 508). The ruling is based on piling inference upon inference to reach a conclusion that an off-campus conversation could have such significant and widespread impact on a school as material and substantial disruption.

The court also relied on the infringement-of-rights test in its expansion of school-censorship authority beyond the schoolhouse gate (C.R. ex rel. Rainville v. Eugene School District 4J, 2013). It ruled that, under the infringement-of-rights test, any harassing speech that occurs outside the school's premises but on the route that students regularly travel on their way to and from school can be censored as an impingement of the rights of other students. Actual or forecast of material and substantial disruption is not required in this case because the infringement-of-rights test is independent of the material and substantial disruption test. C.R. could be disciplined under the infringement-of-rights test because he participated in the walking group's conversation about pornography; and understood that the entire group conversation about BJ's was actually a conversation about blow jobs. The censored student is not required to have directly accosted a specific student with his comments; the mere participation in the conversation suffices. The court also ruled that when off-campus speech is vulgar, lewd, obscene or plainly offensive, the school can censor it under the infringement-of-rights test. The on-campus context of the *Bethel* test suggests that the Supreme Court limited the test to speech that occurs within the schoolhouse gate. In order to get around that limitation, the district court essentially subsumed the *Bethel* test into the infringement-of-rights test, so as to give schools expansive censorship authority over off-campus student speech. As noted, earlier, this contradicts Justice Brennan's statement in Bethel School District No. 403 v. Fraser (1986) that schools cannot censor vulgar, lewd, obscene or plainly-offensive off-campus student speech. However, without a clear ruling from the United States Supreme Court on the scope of school authority over off-campus student speech, courts are likely to continue such creative expansions of the current off-campus student-speech jurisprudence if they desire to expand school-censorship reins.

4. The Story of E.P.

The Speech Incident: The Diary and the Pseudo-Nazi Group

In 2005, E.P., a sophomore at Montwood High School in Texas, created a diary in which he described the formation and activities of a pseudo-Nazi group (Ponce v. Socorro Independent School District, 2007). The extensive diary entries presented a first-person narrative of how E.P. formed the group at his school as well as other schools in the district. The diary also described how E.P. burned another student's house and killed the student's dog as punishment for something the student did. The diary described how E.P. directed the pseudo-Nazi group "to brutally injure two homosexuals and seven colored" individuals (p. 766). Additionally, it described the group's plans for a Columbine-style shooting at E.P.'s school or a simultaneous shooting at all schools within the district. The day for the shooting was listed as the graduation day for E.P.'s close friends. The diary was replete with entries in which E.P. described his state of mind. For instance, he stated that "[my] anger has the best of me"; and "it will get to the point where I will no longer have control" (p. 766).

The diary was created off-campus without use of resources or time (Ponce v. Socorro Independent School District, 2007). However, during school, E.P. showed the diary to another student who promptly reported E.P. to a teacher. The teacher reported E.P. to the assistant principal about 24 hours later. After the assistant principal questioned the informant, he confronted E.P. about the diary and proceeded to search E.P.'s backpack where he found the diary. E.P. defended the diary's entries as mere fiction. After reviewing the diary, the assistant principal contacted E.P.'s mother who similarly defended the entries as fictional writing. The mother also told the assistant principal that her son was simply practicing creative writing like his mother. The assistant principal promised to call her back after thoroughly reviewing the diary in light of student safety. E.P. was allowed to return to his classes for the rest of the school day.

Later that day, after the assistant principal read the diary, he concluded that the diary entries constituted a "terroristic threat" (Ponce v. Socorro Independent School District, 2007, p. 767). Consequently, he had the police arrest E.P. The county attorney chose not to prosecute him, however. Nevertheless, the assistant principal suspended E.P. for three days. He also decided to send E.P. to an alternative education program for the rest of his sophomore year. The principal, assistant superintendent and the school board supported the assistant principal's discipline of E.P. E.P.'s parents did not want him enrolled at the alternative education program because his school record in that program as well as in all the district's schools would reflect the terroristic-threat determination. They were concerned that such a record would negatively impact his opportunities for admission to a desired college. As a result, they enrolled him in private school for the rest of his sophomore year. The parents filed suit against the school district claiming a violation of E.P.'s First Amendment right to free speech. They asked the court to enjoin the school district from discussing the terroristic-threat determination and from documenting it in E.P.'s file. They also sought an injunction against the placement of E.P. in the alternative education program.

Analysis

In its review of whether school officials could constitutionally censor E.P.'s diary, even though it was created off-campus, the United States Court of Appeals for the Fifth Circuit applied the United States Supreme Court's decision in Morse v. Frederick (2007) (Ponce v. Socorro Independent School District, 2007). As we noted in chapter ten, in *Morse*, the Supreme Court ruled that student speech which advocates illegal drug use is unprotected speech because of the compelling school interest in preventing drug use in schools. Under this rationale, schools can censor student speech even if the speech causes no actual material and substantial disruption and is not reasonably forecast to cause such disruption (Morse v. Frederick, 2007). The court of appeals interpreted this rationale to mean that, if the prevention of "a harmful activity may be classified as an important-indeed, perhaps compelling interest, speech advocating that activity may be prohibited by school administrators with little further inquiry" (Ponce v. Socorro Independent School District, p. 769). In essence, the court of appeals ruled that the *Morse* test authorized schools to censor any student speech that advocates a dangerous activity because of the school's compelling interest in preventing such an activity. Even though the Supreme Court, in the *Morse* case, failed to explain "how the particular harms of a given activity add up to an interest sufficiently compelling to forego *Tinker* [material and substantial disruption] analysis", the court of appeals chose to extend the *Morse* test to terroristic threats in a diary (p. 769). The court conceded that this extension,

Their Stories: Offline Off-Campus Speech

without a clear voice from the Supreme Court, could empower schools to censor student "speech advocating an activity entailing arguably marginal harms" (p. 769). "Political speech in the school setting, the important constitutional value *Tinker* sought to protect, could thereby be compromised by overly-anxious administrators" (p. 769).

In his concurrence in the *Morse* case Justice Alito explicitly stated that the Court's holding was limited to advocacy of illegal drug use (Morse v. Frederick, 2007). Yet perplexingly the court of appeals in Ponce v. Socorro Independent School District (2007) relied on Justice Alito's concurrence to justify extending the *Morse* test beyond its illegal drug use moorings. Specifically, the court of appeals seized on the following language in Justice Alito's concurrence:

[A]ny argument for altering the usual free speech rules in the public schools cannot rest on a theory of delegation but must instead be based on some special characteristic of the school setting. The special characteristic that is relevant in this case is the threat to the physical safety of students. ... Experience shows that schools can be places of special danger (Ponce v. Socorro Independent School District, 2007, p. 770, citing Morse v. Frederick, p. 424).

The court of appeals interpreted this language as making "explicit that which remains latent in the [*Morse*] majority opinion: speech advocating a harm that is demonstrably grave and that derives that gravity from the 'special danger' to the physical safety of students arising from the school environment is unprotected" (Ponce v. Socorro Independent School District, 2007, p. 770). The court considered the references to the physical safety of students and the potential for special danger as applicable to E.P.'s diary because his diary's contents presented a danger to the physical safety of students at the school. Accordingly the court altered one of the Supreme Court tests for analyzing student speech – the *Morse* test – to cover off-campus speech such as E.P.'s. In essence, the court chose between two apparently contradictory statements in Justice Alito's concurrence in order to support its extension of the *Morse* test to E.P.'s diary. Specifically, the court chose language that suggested that schools could censor speech presenting danger over language that explicitly limited the *Morse* ruling to advocacy of illegal drug use. The court could have easily reconciled the conflicting statements in Justice Alito's concurrence by interpreting them conjunctively as follows: the *Morse* test is only applicable to school censorship of advocacy of illegal drug use because drug use presents a peculiar danger to students. In that way, the court of appeals would have maintained the integrity of the *Morse* test.

In chapter ten, we noted that, when taken in context, Justice Alito's statement about danger to students was designed to focus on physical dangers within the school setting (Morse v. Frederick, 2007). In-school physical dangers are dangers that parents are unable to protect students from as students are outside parental custody while at school. Besides, as Justice Alito indicated, when students are outside the schoolhouse gate, parents are able to take responsibility for the safety of their children. In other words, Justice Alito argued that schools should have censorship authority over on-campus speech that advocates illegal drug use because parents cannot exercise their protective power over their children within the schoolhouse gate. Justice Alito did not at any point extend school-censorship authority beyond the schoolhouse gate, however. The court of appeals glossed over this clear posture in Justice Alito's concurrence. Instead, the court read Justice Alito's statement as extending school-censorship authority to even off-campus speech that advocates dangerous activity that threatens the in-school physical safety of students. The court declared that:

187

The constitutional concerns of this case ... fall precisely within the student speech area demarcated by Justice Alito in Morse. That area consists of speech pertaining to grave harms arising from the particular character of the school setting. The speech in question here is not about violence aimed at specific persons, but of violence bearing the stamp of a well-known pattern of recent historic activity: mass, systematic school-shootings in the style that has become painfully familiar in the United States ... Such shootings exhibit the character that the concurring opinion identifies as particular to schools. As the concurring opinion points out, school attendance results in the creation of an essentially captive group of persons protected only by the limited personnel of the school itself (Ponce v. Socorro Independent School District, 2007, pp. 770-71).

The court of appeals, therefore, made the *Morse* test a new test for determining the authority of schools to censor students' off-campus test as long as the speech presents a threat of violence to the school. The court was a trailblazer in this respect. The court explained that:

Lack of forewarning and the frequent setting within schools give mass shootings the unique indicia that the [Alito] concurring opinion found compelling with respect to drug use. If school administrators are permitted to prohibit student speech that advocates illegal drug use because 'illegal drug use presents a grave and in many ways unique threat to the physical safety of students,' then it defies logical extrapolation to hold school administrators to a stricter standard with respect to speech that gravely and uniquely threatens violence, including massive deaths, to the school population as a whole (Ponce v. Socorro Independent School District, 2007, pp. 771-72, citing Morse v. Frederick, 2007, p. 425).

As we observed in chapter ten, in Morse v. Frederick (2007), the United States Supreme Court dismissed Joseph Frederick's argument that he intended the words "BONG HiTS 4 JESUS" as mere gibberish (Morse v. Frederick, 2007, pp. 398, 402). The court of appeals in Ponce v. Socorro Independent School District (2007) followed this same path in dismissing as irrelevant E.P.'s explanation of the diary as mere fiction. Instead, as in *Morse*, the court focused on how a reasonable observer would view the speech. In this case, the reasonable observer was the assistant principal who interpreted the diary entries as terroristic threats to students.

The court of appeals indicated that the traditional student-speech tests should only be altered when speech threatens the physical safety of students within the schools (Ponce v. Socorro Independent School District, 2007). Since the material and substantial disruption test readily applies to speech threatening students' physical safety, that test needed no alteration in order to make it conform to the censorship of speech presenting physical danger. Despite its extension of the *Morse* test to off-campus speech, the court suggested that the material and substantial disruption test should continue to be the touchstone test for analyzing off-campus student speech; particularly because that test provides a nexus between off-campus speech and the school campus as it requires actual or reasonably forecast material and substantial disruption at the school campus before there is censorship.

The court of appeals decided not to use the material and substantial disruption test, however, because, unlike the *Morse* test, it is not a *per se* rule (Ponce v. Socorro Independent School District, 2007). In other words, whereas schools are required to make a determination of material and substantial disruption before censoring speech under the *Tinker* test, speech that advocates illegal drug use or other danger to students' physical safety is *per se* unprotected, irrespective of material and substantial disruption. A *per se* rule thus makes it easier for schools to take proactive prophylactic action against school dangers. The court indicated that if the threats in E.P.'s diary had been directed against teachers rather than students, it would have applied the material and substantial disruption test. It reasoned that, in such a situation, the speech would not trigger Justice Alito's language about the physical safety of students and the inability of parents to protect students within the school (Ponce v. Socorro Independent School District, p. 771). Therefore, there would be no basis for altering the usual free speech rules.

The court also noted, without analysis, that E.P.'s speech constituted a true threat (Ponce v. Socorro Independent School District, 2007). Therefore, it was unprotected speech. It is curious that the court chose to focus on extending the *Morse* test rather than applying the true-threat doctrine. Had the court simply applied the true-threat doctrine using the reasonable-observer perspective that it used in its *Morse* analysis, it would have come to the same conclusion it did under its extension of the *Morse* test: the censorship of E.P. did not violate the First Amendment. Clearly, the diary entries threatened the students at E.P.'s school as well as those at all the district's schools. Its reference to plans for a Columbine-style shooting would be very troubling for a reasonable observer in light of the multitude of shootings around the country. Additionally, the identification of a specific day for the shooting added urgency and gravity to the entries. As did the statements that "anger has the best of me" and "it will get to the point where I will no longer have control" (Ponce v. Socorro Independent School District, p. 766).

This case gives courts and schools the option of using either the *Morse* test or the true-threat doctrine when faced with off-campus speech that presents a physical danger to student safety. It is unclear, however, if the court was implicitly viewing the speech as on-campus speech since E.P. brought the diary to school (the principal found it in his backpack and E.P. shared it with a student while he was at school). If the court implicitly viewed it as on-campus speech, then there would be no controversy about the court's use of the Supreme Court's student-speech precedents since those precedents involved on-campus contexts. Since the court did not address the on-campus presence of the diary or E.P.'s on-campus disclosure of the diary to another student, it is unclear if either or both provided nexus sufficient to convert off-campus speech to on-campus speech. The court's failure to address this leaves one with the impression that the court's analysis was focused on speech created off-campus rather than on-campus speech.

5. The Story of Anthony Latour

The Speech Incident: The Four Rap Songs

Over a two-year period, Anthony Latour, a student at Riverside Beaver Middle School in Pennsylvania, wrote and recorded various rap songs while he was at home after school hours (Latour v. Riverside Beaver School District, 2005). He never took any of the rap songs to school though he sold them in the local community and made them available to the public on the internet. He used no school resource in the writing and recording of the songs. The four songs in question are described below:

1. A song written in 2003 that mentions another middle school student (Jane Smith);
2. The first track on a CD recorded in November 2004, titled "Murder, He Wrote";
3. A battle rap song with John Doe titled "Massacre"; and
4. Another battle rap song he wrote and uploaded onto his personal internet website titled "Actin Fast ft. Grimey." (Latour v. Riverside Beaver School District, 2005).

The school first learned of the songs around March, 2005 but they took no action until May of that year when school officials claimed that they could censor the rap songs because they threatened student safety (Latour v. Riverside Beaver School District, 2005). Yet, after learning of the songs, they did not investigate Anthony for weapons possession at the school. Furthermore, they did not speak to Jane Smith – a student who was the subject of one of the songs. School officials also failed to take steps to keep John Doe – the subject of the song "Massacre" – away from Anthony. Additionally, they did not confront Anthony or speak to his parents about the songs for the two-month period. Nonetheless, on May 5, 2005, school officials suspended Anthony from school because of his writing and recording of four of the rap songs. About two weeks later, he was expelled from school for two years for the same reason. He was also prohibited from attending any school-sponsored activity and from visiting the school campus after school hours. Anthony was arrested after school officials notified the police of the songs. After the suspension, several students wore T-shirts to school with the slogan "Free Accident" in support of Anthony (p. 2). Anthony and his parents filed suit against the school district seeking injunctive relief. They claimed that the district violated his First Amendment right to free speech.

Analysis

The school district argued that it had constitutional authority to censor Anthony's speech as a true threat (Latour v. Riverside Beaver School District, 2005). The United States District Court for the Western District of Pennsylvania disagreed, however. The court stated that true threats must be "statements where the speaker means to communicate a serious expression of an intent to commit an act of unlawful violence to a particular individual or group of individuals" (p. 1). This is similar to the various true-threat definitions that we presented in chapter two of this book. The true-threat doctrine is not tied to locale. Therefore, it applies on-campus and off-campus alike.

The district court used the reasonable-speaker view of true threats (Latour v. Riverside Beaver School District, 2005). In its review under the reasonable-speaker view, the court examined the following factors:

1. The intent of the speaker;
2. Whether the target had reasonable grounds to believe that the speaker has a propensity to be violent;
3. Whether the speaker directly communicated the alleged threat to the target;
4. Whether the threat was conditional; and
5. The targeted victim's reaction to the threat.

The court concluded that Anthony did not intend to communicate a threat through his rap songs (Latour v. Riverside Beaver School District, 2005). It reasoned that rap is a music genre that sometimes involves use of violent metaphors and imagery; yet, there is typically no intent to threaten in the songs. The school district failed to establish that Anthony intended to communicate an actual threat of violence through the rap songs. Besides, the school district did not present any evidence showing that the targets (John Doe and Jane Smith) of the songs had reasonable grounds to believe that Anthony had a propensity to be violent. Moreover, even though Anthony sold the songs in the local community and distributed them on the internet, he did not communicate them directly to the targets. Furthermore, Jane Smith's reaction to the song about her was a broken heart and humiliation rather than a feeling of endangerment. John Doe's reaction was also muted as well. John Doe indicated that he viewed the song "Massacre" as a bluff rather than as a threat. The school district's failure to immediately investigate Anthony for access to weapons as well as the district's failure to remove John Doe from an area where he would encounter Anthony at the school undercut any argument from the district that the songs were true threats. The fact that the school waited for a while before informing Anthony or his parents that they viewed his songs as true threats further undermined the district's argument.

The school district also argued that it could censor Anthony's speech under the material and substantial disruption test (Latour v. Riverside Beaver School District, 2005). The court rejected this argument, however, because there was no reasonable basis for forecasting material and substantial disruption; and such disruption did not actually occur. There was no evidence that the song disrupted any class or school function. Indeed, the district did not show that Anthony's songs were ever distributed at the school. While several students attended school wearing t-shirts with the slogan "Free Accident", the school's punishment of Anthony, rather than his songs, inspired the t-shirt campaign (p. 2). Even then, the campaign did not materially and substantially disrupt the school. Although the school argued that Jane Smith and John Doe left the school district because of the songs, the court found no merit to this argument. Jane Smith withdrew from the school district for different reasons. John Doe was held out of school by his mother because she feared repercussions from Anthony's arrest; not because of the song about John Doe.

Despite recognizing Anthony's rap songs as off-campus speech, the district court chose to review it under the material and substantial disruption test (Latour v. Riverside Beaver School District, 2005). In so doing, the court effectively extended the material and substantial disruption test to off-campus speech. The court did not even demand a nexus between the off-campus speech and the school campus before deciding to apply the test beyond the schoolhouse gate. The court's failure to acknowledge the on-campus origin of the material and substantial disruption test in Tinker v. Des Moines Independent Community School District (1969) leaves one to wonder if the court even saw the test as an on-campus test. If it did see the test as such, its failure to provide an explanation for extending an on-campus speech test to off-campus speech shrouds the court's reasoning in mystery. Without an understanding of the court's reasoning, it is impossible to circumscribe the court's view of the full reach of the material and substantial disruption test when analyzing the right of students to speak off-campus.

6. The Story of J.M.

The Speech Incident: The Breakup Letter

While in seventh grade at Northwood Junior High School in Arkansas, J.M. started dating one of his classmates K.G. (Doe v. Pulaski County Special School District, 2002). They spent time together both on-campus and off-campus. Over the course of the school year, they ended and rekindled their dating relationship several times. At some point during the relationship, J.M. told K.G., K.G.'s best friend and D.M. (a friend of J.M. and K.G.) that he was a member of the Bloods gang. Despite this information, J.M. and K.G. dated through the seventh grade. K.G. terminated the relationship with J.M. after deciding to date another student. The breakup greatly upset J.M., prompting him to express his anger in "two violent, misogynic, and obscenity-laden rants expressing a desire to molest, rape, and murder K.G." (p. 619). J.M. wrote the two rants as songs, while at home, without any school resource. He claimed that he wrote the songs to imitate the violent and vulgar lyrics in the songs of rappers such as Eminem, Kid Rock and Juvenile. However, after finding that the song rants had no rhythm or beat, he decided to turn them into letters which he signed and stored away inside his house.

The letter that formed the basis of the case was titled "Fuck that bitch [K.G.]" (Doe v. Pulaski County Special School District, 2002, p. 625). The letter, written as if it was a direct communication to K.G., showed J.M.'s "pronounced, contemptuous and depraved hate for K.G." (p. 625). More than 80 times in a four-page span, J.M.'s letter characterized K.G. as "a 'bitch,' 'slut,' 'ass,' and a 'whore'" (p. 625). It expressed the desire to rape, sodomize and kill K.G. The letter included at least ninety uses of the f-word. "The most disturbing aspect of the letter, however, is J.M.'s warning in two passages, expressed in unconditional terms, that K.G. should not go to sleep because he would be lying under her bed waiting to kill her with a knife" (p. 625).

About a month before the following school year, while D.M was visiting J.M.'s home, he found the letter atop the dresser in J.M.'s bedroom (Doe v. Pulaski County Special School District, 2002). When J.M. saw D.M. with the letter, he immediately took it away from him in an effort to prevent him from reading it. D.M. insisted on reading the letter and getting a copy. J.M. eventually relented, allowing D.M. to read the letter though he refused to give him a copy. K.G. ultimately heard about the letter and its content. There was conflicting testimony about how she learned of the letter. J.M. claimed that D.M. disclosed the letter's existence and its contents to K.G. K.G., however, claimed that J.M. first revealed the letter's existence to her in a phone call during which J.M told her that another student had penned a letter threatening to kill K.G. During a subsequent phone call with K.G., J.M. told her that he authored the threatening letter.

K.G. was deeply troubled by the letter so she asked D.M. to help her get a copy from J.M. (Doe v. Pulaski County Special School District, 2002). A week before the school year started, D.M. spent the night at J.M.'s house so that he could surreptitiously retrieve the letter. During his stay at the house, D.M. took the letter from J.M.'s bedroom without his permission or knowledge. He gave the letter to K.G. when they returned to school. K.G. read the letter in her gymnasium class and was shaken to the point of being fearful to leave the classroom. Indeed, she was reduced to tears. For the first few nights afterwards, she left her bedroom lights on while sleeping. One of the students who heard K.G. read the letter told the school resource officer that someone had threatened K.G. K.G. acknowledged to the resource officer that she had been threatened. Following his investigation, the resource officer told the principal about J.M.'s letter. The school investigation revealed that D.M. took the letter from J.M. without J.M.'s permission and knowledge; and that D.M., not J.M., brought the letter to school. Nonetheless, the principal decided to expel J.M. from the school for the rest of the school year. The principal informed J.M. that his speech violated the school's rule against terroristic threats. J.M.'s parents appealed to the director of student services and athletics who recommended a one-semester suspension and that the district permit J.M. to attend the district's alternative school. While attending the alternative school, J.M's parents appealed the one-semester suspension to the school board. The school board, however, decided to expel J.M. from both the alternative school as well as Northwood Junior High School – his regular resident school. J.M.'s mother sued the school district claiming a violation of his right to free speech under the First Amendment. She asked for a restraining order against the school district, the reinstatement of J.M. and the removal of any expulsion references from his school record.

Analysis

J.M.'s mother argued that he had a First Amendment right against school censorship because his speech was created in his house and he had no intent to convey the content of the letter to K.G. (Doe v. Pulaski County Special School District, 2002). The United States Court of Appeals for the Eighth Circuit dis-

Their Stories: Offline Off-Campus Speech

missed this argument because it considered J.M.'s speech a true threat. The court conceded that the school district has "no business telling an individual what he may read or view in the privacy of his own home" (p. 624). The school district "similarly has no valid interest in the contents of a writing that a person, such as J.M., might prepare in the confines of his own bedroom" (p. 624). The court, however, indicated that when violence is threatened and communicated, the censorship power can reach into the privacy of a person's bedroom because of the government's need to prevent the violence expressed in a true threat.

As discussed in chapter two – the "True Threat" chapter, regardless of locale, true threats are unprotected under the First Amendment. Therefore, true threats "fall within the realm of speech that the government can proscribe without offending the First Amendment" (Doe v. Pulaski County Special School District, 2002, p. 622, citing Watts v. United States, 1969). The court reasoned that school districts have a censorship interest that overrides free speech when speech that includes violence constitutes a true threat (Doe v. Pulaski County Special School District, 2002). The challenge lies in distinguishing true threats from protected speech so that protected speech is not falsely classified as a true threat, violating sacred constitutional rights. Since the court found no guidance for this distinction in the United States Supreme Court's precedents, the court examined the approaches used by the other federal circuit courts of appeals. These courts use an objective standard that falls into one of two categories: reasonable-recipient view; and reasonable-speaker view. Under the reasonable-speaker view, courts inquire "whether a reasonable person standing in the shoes of the speaker would foresee that the recipient would perceive the statement as a threat" (Doe v. Pulaski County Special School District, 2002, p. 623). The United States Court of Appeals for the Eighth Circuit adopted the reasonable-recipient view which inquires into "how a reasonable person standing in the recipient's shoes would view the alleged threat" (p. 623) (see chapter two for further discussion of the reasonable-recipient and reasonable-speaker views).

Under the reasonable-recipient view, a true threat is defined as "a statement that a reasonable recipient would have interpreted as a serious expression of an intent to harm or cause injury to another" (Doe v. Pulaski County Special School District, 2002, p. 624). Since this view dismisses the speaker's perspective in true-threat analysis, the federal circuit court of appeals' decision to adopt that view effectively dismissed J.M.'s perspective regarding whether his letter constituted a threat. K.G.'s views only mattered in the form of the letter he already wrote. His subsequent explanation of his intent behind the letter was immaterial. His views, embodied in the letter, took center stage in the determination of whether the letter expressed an intent to harm now or in the future. The court examined the following factors in its analysis of the letter under the reasonable-speaker view:

1. The reaction of listeners;
2. Whether the speaker directly and intentionally communicated the threat to the target or some other person (this is referred to herein as the intentional-communication factor);
3. Whether the speaker had a history of threatening the target;
4. Whether the target had reasonable grounds to believe that the speaker had an inclination to be violent; and
5. "Whether the threat was conditional" (p. 623). The speaker need not have the capability or intent to execute the threat.

As the federal circuit court observed, J.M. directly and intentionally communicated his threat to D.M. when he chose to allow D.M. to read the letter (Doe v. Pulaski County Special School District, 2002). Besides, J.M. knew that D.M., a friend of K.G., was likely to communicate the speech to K.G.

While the communication to D.M. satisfied the intentional-communication factor, J.M. also directly and intentionally communicated the threat to K.G. (the target) during the phone call in which he admitted writing the letter threatening to kill her. According to the court, the intentional-communication factor is a reasonable-recipient factor so as to make it difficult for the government to censor people's speech within their homes. The court stated that "[r]equiring less than an intent to communicate the purported threat would run afoul of the notion that an individual's most protected right is to be free from governmental interference in the sanctity of his home" (p. 624). The fact that J.M. intentionally communicated the threat to at least one other person meant that he did not intend to "keep the letter, and the message it contained, within his own lockbox of personal privacy" (p. 625). In essence, once J.M. intentionally and directly communicated the threat to the target or a third party, his bedroom was no longer a sphere of privacy for his speech. Accordingly, students can lose their in-home free speech rights to threatening speech if they intentionally communicate the threat to the target or a third party.

Even though J.M. had no history of threats, the court found that other reasonable-recipient factors supported the determination that J.M.'s speech constituted a true threat (Doe v. Pulaski County Special School District, 2002). For instance, the speech was clearly an unconditional threat because J.M. explicitly warned K.G. in two passages of the letter that he would wait for her under her bed and kill her with a knife. He repeated this threat to K.G.'s best friend, knowing and fully expecting that this friend would convey the threat to K.G. He also expressly stated several times that he would sodomize and rape her. Additionally, the fact that J.M. referred to K.G. as a "bitch", "slut", "ass" and a "whore" more than eighty times within a four-page span suggested a level of disdain and "depraved hate" (p. 625). When these excessive vulgarities are coupled with the threats to kill, sodomize and rape K.G., it indubitably leads to the conclusion that the threat was not conditional. Besides, after J.M. realized that K.G. felt threatened by his speech, he took no action to allay her fears; evidencing the unconditional nature of the threats in the letter. His failure to allay her fears supports the conclusion that, by the time K.G. received the letter from D.M., K.G. already had a reasonable basis to believe that J.M. had an inclination to be violent. K.G. also had reason to believe that K.G. had a propensity to be violent because he had told her that he belonged to the Bloods gang. Further, K.G. had prior knowledge of J.M.'s inclination for violence against animals, knowledge that could have served as reasonable basis for her inference that he was inclined to be violent toward her.

As the court observed, the reaction of the listeners also supported the conclusion that J.M.'s speech constituted a true threat (Doe v. Pulaski County Special School District, 2002). For instance, a student reported the speech to the school resource officer because that student viewed J.M.'s speech as a threat. Moreover, as the court pointed out, the typical 13-year old recipient of J.M.'s speech would feel threatened by its content and tone. The noted that K.G. herself cried in her classroom after reading the letter and was afraid to leave the class. She slept with her bedroom lights on for a few nights after this. D.M. was another listener who reacted to the letter with concern about its intent and gravity. Indeed, he "purloined it from his friend's home because he felt that something should be done about it" (p. 626). School officials also reacted to the letter with earnest concern, prompting an investigation that culminated in an affirmation of their immediate reaction to the speech as terroristic threat.

Based on its application of the reasonable-recipient factors above, the court ruled that J.M.'s speech constituted a true threat under the reasonable-recipient view (Doe v. Pulaski County Special School District, 2002). Consequently, J.M. had no First Amendment defense to the school's censorship of his

Their Stories: Offline Off-Campus Speech

speech. Similarly, any student who makes a true threat off-campus would not enjoy First Amendment protection if the speech satisfies the reasonable-recipient factors. For such, speech even in the bedroom is not venerable. It is interesting that the court did not even focus on the fact that the off-campus speech was brought to the school; or the fact that a person other than the speaker brought the speech to school. The mere fact that the speech constituted a true threat apparently made every other issue irrelevant because the true-threat determination removed the shield of the First Amendment from the speech, leaving it utterly exposed to censorship. The court, in essence, ruled that the off-campus nature of true-threat speech does not provide refuge from school censorship.

HYBRID SPEECH: SPEECH DIRECTED AT OR AGAINST SCHOOL OFFICIALS AS WELL AS NON-SCHOOL ENTITIES

This category focuses on the judicial response to off-campus student speech that is not strictly directed at the school. An example would be speech that simultaneously criticizes the school principal and the president of the United States. Our research only revealed one case in this category. Unlike in previous sections of this chapter, we did not assign a number to this case because it was the only one in this category. This case is examined next.

1. The Story of David Baker and William Schaffner

The Speech Incident: Vulgarity and the Oink Newspaper

In November 1968, two senior students – David Baker and William Schaffner – at Earl Warren High School in California created an underground newspaper which they called "Oink" (Baker v. Downey City Board of Education, 1969, p. 519). David was the senior class president while William was the student body president. The students wanted to use the newspaper as an outlet, beyond the school-sponsored publications, to express their opinions on various issues. They published the newspaper off-campus without using school resources. Both students distributed copies of the newspaper to their fellow students "just outside the main gate to the campus" as students reported to the school (p. 519). The distribution lasted for about 30 minutes: from 7:30 a.m. to approximately 8 a.m. right before classes started.

On November 5, 1969, William distributed copies of a new issue of the newspaper to students outside the school's main gate while David stood nearby inside the gate (Baker v. Downey City Board of Education, 1969). David, however, did not distribute any newspaper that morning while he was within the schoolhouse gate. That morning, about 450 copies of the issue were distributed to students as they entered the school. In the issue, David and William used vulgar language to express their views. They heavily criticized school administrators even though the principal had previously warned them to be more constructive in their criticisms. The issue also featured "vulgar retouching of what appears to be a photograph of President Nixon … by the adding and positioning of a finger" (p. 520). When school officials learned of the profanities in the issue, they decided to punish David and William. Both of them were deposed from their student positions. School officials claimed that both students violated the oath of their offices which provided:

I solemnly promise that I will do my best to fulfill the requirements of the office to which I have been elected by the students of Warren Senior High School, that I will uphold and support the rules and regulations of the student body and the school, and I will set an example in scholarship and leadership which will be a pattern for conduct among the students and do everything within my power to uphold the highest standards of the school (Baker v. Downey City Board of Education, 1969, p. 519).

School officials also suspended David and William from school for ten days. Their parents sued the school district claiming a First Amendment violation. They asked for injunctive relief as well as declaratory judgment.

Analysis

David and William argued that the school district had no authority to censor their speech since they did not create or distribute the speech within the school (Baker v. Downey City Board of Education, 1969). The United States District Court for the Central District of California dismissed this argument: the "insistence that Oink was not distributed on campus is of little aid to their case" (p. 526). Additionally, the court stated that "the fact the acts which resulted in the distribution on campus were not actually performed on campus is of no consequence" (p. 526). According to the court, the distribution near the school gate was sufficient to attribute knowledge and intent of the newspaper's on-campus presence to William and David. Clearly, even though David and William technically did not distribute the newspaper issue within the schoolhouse gate, they knew that the students would take the newspaper into the school. In other words, it was reasonably foreseeable to them that the students to whom they gave copies of the newspaper would take them inside the schoolhouse gate, creating an on-campus presence for the off-campus speech. In fact, the court stated that David and William distributed the newspaper near the gate because they intended for students to take the issue on school grounds. Thus, the distribution outside the school gate was merely designed to skirt the school policy while still achieving the ultimate goal of an on-campus distribution.

The federal district court took a deferential posture toward school authority to censor students' off-campus speech (Baker v. Downey City Board of Education, 1969). For instance, the court declared that "school authorities are responsible for the morals of the students while going to and from school, as well as during the time they are on campus" (p. 526). Therefore, since William and David were in the process of going to school between 7:30 a.m. and 8 a.m. when the distribution occurred, the school had authority over their speech. This ruling also means that school officials retain censorship authority over off-campus student speech until students reach their homes or another location where parental custody takes effect. Parental custody might be inconsequential, however, because the court also ruled that "when the bounds of decency are violated in publications distributed to high school students, whether on campus or off campus, the offenders become subject to discipline" (p. 526). Furthermore, the court stated that students do not have a First Amendment right to speak anywhere they wish. This gives carte blanche authority to censor off-campus speech (as long as the speech is distributed to students) simply because the speech violates bounds of decency. This particular ruling might no longer be valid, however, because in Hazelwood v. Kuhlmeier (1988), the United States Supreme Court endorsed Justice Brennan's declaration in Bethel School District No. 403 v. Fraser (1986) that "[i]f respondent had given the same [vulgar, lewd, plainly offensive] speech outside of the school environment, he could not have been penalized simply because government officials considered his language to be inappropriate" (p. 688).

Their Stories: Offline Off-Campus Speech

The federal district court chose to apply the material and substantial disruption test to analyze the case without providing a rationale for this choice (Baker v. Downey City Board of Education, 1969). It could be that, since David and William conceded that the material and substantial disruption test was the applicable test, the court simply accepted that premise; especially since the school district did not object. The court might also have applied the material and substantial disruption test because, at the time, it was the only extant student-speech test in the United States Supreme Court. Pursuant to this test, David and William contended that the newspaper issue did not materially and substantially disrupt the school. While the court acknowledged that students have free speech rights, it stated that schools must have broad authority to censor student speech in order to maintain discipline in schools. The court relied on Schwartz v. Schuker (1969) (discussed earlier in this chapter) in stating that schools should have greater authority over off-campus speech distributed near the school because high school students are not sufficiently mature to properly discriminate content they are exposed to (Baker v. Downey City Board of Education, 1969). As we pointed out earlier, Schwartz v. Schuker similarly gave deferential authority to school officials. Like in Schwartz v. Schuker, the federal district court in Baker v. Downey City Board of Education emphasized that students must learn to obey and submit to school officials. The court also stated that students must speak within school rules because those rules are designed to foster the "educational program in a good moral environment" (p. 527). It is, however, shortsighted for the court to presume that school rules are motivated by purely pedagogical concerns as opposed to ulterior motives designed to suppress constitutional rights.

The federal district court cautioned the judiciary against second-guessing the decisions of school administrators even when the censored speech is not necessarily directed at the school (Baker v. Downey City Board of Education, 1969). It appears that, if school officials argue, as pretext, that speech would impact the school, deference would be accorded to the school. Indeed, the district court deferred to the school district's averment that the profane and vulgar speech in the newspaper issue threatened to undermine education and the ability to control students. The court also credited the superintendent's "apprehension that unless action was taken promptly to discipline the plaintiffs there would be further disruption of and interference with the educational program" (p. 522). This is surprising because in Tinker v. Des Moines Independent Community School District (1969), when the United States Supreme Court created the material and substantial disruption test, it specifically stated that apprehension could not be the premise for censoring student on-campus speech. While the district court did not rely solely on the superintendent's apprehension, it gave apprehension credence and significant weight in censorship of off-campus speech (Baker v. Downey City Board of Education, 1969).

The federal district court also ruled that school officials could censor the newspaper issue because students in 25 to 30 classes were distracted because they were discussing the article (Baker v. Downey City Board of Education, 1969). The Supreme Court, however, rejected a similar argument in Tinker v. Des Moines Independent Community School District (1969) as sufficient ground for finding material and substantial disruption. The district court itself conceded that some teachers testified that there was no disruption in their classes; thus, the decision to allow censorship based on distractions seems to be more about judicial deference to exercise of school-censorship authority. The court stated that condemnation of students' free speech rights is justified when the end is compelling. According to the court, the need for law and order within the school constitutes such an end.

The court further extended school officials' censorship tentacles beyond the schoolhouse gate by imposing a duty on student leaders to be role models on-campus and off-campus (Baker v. Downey City Board of Education, 1969). The court also warned student leaders to avoid fighting their administrators' decisions. In line with this, the court urged David and William to make efforts to avoid being "remembered as leaders who finished high school contesting the rights of the administration to encourage and enforce good moral standards for the members of the student body, both on and off campus" (p. 528). The court's willingness to empower schools to enforce role-model expectations or morals when students are off-campus leaves students (especially student leaders), no room to experiment, grow and choose their own values. Contrary to the commands of Tinker v. Des Moines Independent Community School District, it gives schools "absolute authority over their students" (p. 511). The case also makes students, even in the privacy of their own homes, "closed-circuit recipients" of only those values that the school district approves (p. 511). Further, this case made it clear that school-censorship authority over students' off-campus speech is not limited to speech that targets the school, teachers, administrators or students. Schools can also censor off-campus student speech that targets non-school entities as well.

CONCLUSION

In this chapter, we reviewed lower courts cases that have considered whether students have a First Amendment right to speak off-campus free from school censorship. We presented stories of students censored by their schools for speaking offline off-campus. We also analyzed the judicial reasoning in each case for affirming, abrogating or curtailing school censorship of off-campus student speech. Our analysis revealed that most cases relied on the material and substantial disruption test as the driving force for their ruling. A minority of cases ruled based on the *Bethel* test (or a version of it) while others used the true-threat doctrine or the fighting-words doctrine. Our analysis also revealed that the off-campus offline speech jurisprudence remains unsettled and courts are inconsistent in their rulings even when interpreting the United States Supreme Court's student-speech precedents and applying them to off-campus offline student speech. The precarious jurisprudence in the lower courts exists because the Supreme Court has yet to decide an off-campus offline speech case. Consequently, the lower courts themselves appear uncertain as to how to proceed. It is therefore vital and time for the Supreme Court to bring clarity to the jurisprudence to ensure that students' First Amendment rights are not unconstitutionally denied.

REFERENCES

Baker v. Downey City Board of Education (1969). 307 F.Supp. 517.

Bethel School District No. 403 v. Fraser (1986). 478 U.S. 675.

Boucher v. School Board of School District of Greenfield (1998). 134 F.3d 821.

Burch v. Barker (1988). 861 F.2d 1149.

Bystrom By and Through Bystrom v. Fridley High School (1987). 686 F.Supp. 1387.

Cohen v. California (1971). 403 U.S. 15.

C.R. ex rel. Rainville v. Eugene School District 4J (2013). 2013 WL 5102848.

Their Stories: Offline Off-Campus Speech

Doe v. Pulaski County Special School District (2002). 306 F.3d 616.

Doninger v. Niehoff (2011). 642 F.3d 334, 347.

Donovan v. Ritchie (1995). 68 F.3d 14.

Emerson, T. I. (1970). *The System of Freedom of Expression.* New York: Random House.

Fenton v. Stear (1976). 423 F. Supp. 767.

Hatter v. Los Angeles City High School District (1971). 452 F.2d 673.

Hazelwood v. Kuhlmeier (1988). 484 U.S. 260.

K.G.S. v. Kemp (2011). 2011 WL 4635002.

Killion v. Franklin Regional School District (2001). 136 F.Supp.2d 446.

Klein v. Smith (1986). 635 F. Supp. 1440.

Lander v. Seaver (1859). 32 Vt. 114.

Latour v. Riverside Beaver School District (2005). 2005 WL 2106562.

Lavine v. Blaine School District (2001). 257 F.3d 981.

Miller v. California (1973). 413 U.S. 15.

Morse v. Frederick (2007). 551 U.S. 393.

Pangle v. Bend-Lapine School District (2000). 10 P.3d 275.

Ponce v. Socorro Independent School District (2007). 508 F.3d 765.

Porter ex rel. LeBlanc v. Ascension Parish School Board (2004). 301 F.Supp.2d 576.

Porter v. Ascension Parish School Board (2004). 393 F.3d 608.

Riggan v. Midland Independent School District (2000). 86 F.Supp.2d 647.

Saxe v. State College Area School District (2001). 240 F.3d 200.

Schwartz v. Schuker (1969). 298 F.Supp. 238.

Shanley v. Northeast Independent School District (1972). 462 F.2d 960.

Sherrell ex rel. Sherrell v. Northern Community School Corporation of Tipton County (2004). 801 N.E.2d 693.

Sullivan v. Houston Independent School District (1969). 307 F.Supp. 1328.

Sullivan v. Houston Independent School District (1973). 475 F.2d 1071.

Terminiello v. City of Chicago (1948). 337 U.S. 1.

Thomas v. Board of Education, Granville Central School District (1979). 607 F.2d 1043.

Tinker v. Des Moines Independent Community School District (1969). 393 U.S. 503.

Watts v. United States (1969). 394 U.S. 705.

Wynar v. Douglas County School District (2013). 728 F.3d 1062, 1068.

KEY TERMS AND DEFINITIONS

Bethel **Test:** This is the test the United States Supreme Court created in Bethel School District No. 403 v. Fraser (1986) that authorizes school officials to censor student speech that is vulgar, lewd, plainly offensive or obscene.

Fighting Words: Speech which inflicts injury simply from being uttered or speech with the tendency to incite a disturbance.

Hybrid Speech: Speech that is directed at or against school officials as well as at an entity unaffiliated with the school.

Lower Court: Any court in America other than the United States Supreme Court which is the highest court in the United States.

Material and Substantial Disruption Test: The judicial standard that conditions censorship of student speech on whether the speech is reasonably foreseeable to cause or actually caused material and substantial disruption to the school.

Miller **Test:** The three-part test the United States Supreme Court created in Miller v. California (1973) for determining whether the government can censor speech as obscenity. Under this test, courts inquire into: (a) whether, under contemporary community standards, the average person would deem the speech as a whole as appealing to a prurient interest; (b) whether the speech describes or shows sexual conduct defined by state law in a manifestly offensive way; and (c) whether the speech as a whole has no serious political, scientific, literary or artistic value (Miller v. California, 1973).

Off-Campus Speech: Speech that occurs in any locale outside the borders or premises of a school and outside school hours. It includes student speech away from the school bus and school-sponsored events such as school trips.

Off-Campus Offline Student-Speech Jurisprudence: The composite of cases governing students' right to free speech under the United States Constitution in off-campus offline settings.

On-Campus Speech: Speech that occurs in any area inside the school or on school premises. It includes speech on the school bus or at school-sponsored events.

True Threat: Speech that expresses a genuine intent to cause harm.

Their Stories: Offline Off-Campus Speech

APPENDIX: PFLASHLYTE NEWSPAPER ISSUE NO. 1

The Christmas holidays have just passed us by and, for most people, the expression can be taken literally. As in one of the current tunes, it was the time of the season for loving. During Christmas most people put on their masks of peace and good will toward men, and after struggling find they can almost be tolerant of one another. The problem is that too many restrict their efforts to a minimum. They find that they can appease their puny minds by talking about equality, justice, tolerance, and love of fellow men. If they would make a sincere effort to practice the ideology of the democracy that they supposedly hold so dear they might find that refreshing and productive relationships are possible.

People are able to meet on common ground and establish a productive rapport providing that all parties make a sincere effort. They can overcome their differences and search for solutions to common problems and means to reach common ends.

It is well known that the relationships between school administrators, faculty members, and students have been more than slightly hostile in the past, and that in the wake of incidents such as the intolerable locker checks one would discover that the basic underlying problem was one of misunderstanding and lack of communications. The communications could be more closely described as ultimatums, threatening the use of destructive forces at the disposal of both parties. It is evident that this type of situation renders more harm than good. A reversal of these ills can be accomplished only through sincere co-operation of all factions.

The first phase of this rehabilitation is renewal of faith in the intentions of the opposing parties. This factor was obviously lacking in the past. As we enter the closing months of this school year, it is still possible to establish a worthwhile relationship between the power of the schools and students.

We cannot neglect the fact that both the schools and the students, if antagonized, are capable of using force sufficient to disrupt the well being of each other. It is also obvious that a confrontation of this nature would result in regression rather than progression.

The common goal of both students and school administrators is development of the students minds in order that the well being of our constantly changing society will be enhanced by the intelligence that may be gained from a formal education. The role of the school is to present necessary technical and historical information; and the students responsibility is to assimilate this information, along with his own moral code, into a working philosophy of existence. A dispute arises in regard to what constitutes necessary and valid ideas.

As in the past, those in authority resent being told that their ideas are outmoded and those governed equally resent attempts to stifle their individuality and mold them into puppets of old guard authoritarians. This resentment prohibits objective discourse on the validity of old ideas and the necessity of new concepts. But this type of evaluation is a prerequisite for reform. In order for this to be accomplished the issues and their proposed solutions must be articulated and rational arguments presented and examined in an objective manner. This cannot be done if either party decides to be the infallible authority.

WE ARE PRESENTING A SERIES OF ARTICLES IN AN ATTEMPT TO MAKE CLEAR OUR PROTESTS AND TO OFFER THE FACULTY AND ADMINISTRATION AN OPPORTUNITY TO INTELLIGENTLY DISCUSS THE ISSUES WHICH DIVIDE US AND DIVERT US FROM THE COMMON GOAL OF PROGRESS

— the editors
'PFLASHLYTE

The Pflashlyte is made possible only by donations. All labor, time, writing, distribution, and use of printing equipment is supplied to us free of charge. The only money spent on this paper is for the purchase of paper, ink, and staples. We rely only on contributions made by students. If you are solicited for funds please contribute anything you can afford. Your donations will be greatly appreciated.

SCHOOL SPIRIT VS. CONSCIENCE

The Pflashlyte has found it imperative to speak out on an issue which is presently somewhat obscure. Far too few students are aware of the absurdity of the fund drive for the Senior Project. The student body is only told that the drive is short by $350 and that its goal is $500 for the planting of shrubbery in the planter box. Announcements are made (by order of the Administration) to the effect that all students are expected to 'co-operate' in the raising of money for this noteworthy project. Yet how many know that Mr. Stewart refused to let a group of students, in association with the International Red Cross, collect money for starving children in Biafra. The students were told that there is a school policy banning solicitations from students except when approved by the downtown Administration; later it was acceptable to begin a drive to solicit $500 from students in order to buy a bunch of bushes.

Mr. Cobb, of the downtown office of HISD, told Pflashlyte investigators that the decision of which fund drives are to be allowed at schools lies in the individual principal's interpretation of school rules. In view of this, it is reasonable to assume that noble Mr. Stewart feels that planting bushes is far more important than feeding starving children. Pflashlyte sincerely hopes that Mr. Stewart will get his bushes and that his conscience doesn't bother him too much.

Anyone wishing to donate money for the needy in Biafra should contact the Red Cross headquarters, 2006 Smith— 227-1151.

EDMUND'S THOUGHTS

Pflashlyte brings you an inspirational dissertation from a model administrator.

Ah wosh tew thank yew all for yore generosity en givin me this oppertunity tew express mahself. Furst of all, ah wosh to say that ah'm proud as punch to be here an ah'm shure yew all are proud as punch to be en mah school. For mah fine capacity to suppress ideas, ah have been awarded this school and all yore minds. If yew all should fall from the path we'll have them athletic boys put you raht back on the track real quick like. And there ain't no need to thank me, its mah sacred mission to save yew from them bastard hippies and sech like. Remember ah'm here for yor-benefit and ah will employ evry means available under the divine raht of kings. In closin, ah wont to inform yew of the next Senior Project. 'Under mah direction, the senior class is formin one of them extortion rackets to collect $500 for a 17-foot facsimile of mah posterior to be erected at the front gate so that all students might kiss the baloney stone each day before classes.'

sincerely yours— Edmund P. Senile

'The school program should be sufficiently flexible to meet all the needs of the student, whether physical, mental, moral, or social; and the teaching staff should give adequate consideration to the mental health, the emotional stability, and the physical well-being of every individual student.

Their Stories: Offline Off-Campus Speech

Every phase of the school program should be explored for opportunities to promote democratic behavior through developing individual initiative, co-operation, and self-discipline. True democracy is attained only when every member of a group participates actively in planning and carrying out those activities which concern the group as a whole.

Every student should be taught to understand and appreciate the rights, duties, and privileges of citizenship in a democracy; he should be taught to realize fully his own obligations as a member of his home, his school, his community, his state, and his nation.'

The above is the way many of us feel that the school should be run. The points about democracy, and the schools striving for the welfare of the individual students are things I am sure none of us can deny as desireable. These points do seem fantastic, however, in that to have a school system as the above implies necessitates having school system personnel who accept these ideas. What is more fantastic, though, is that these three paragraphs are excerpts from the 'Philosophy of the Secondary Schools' by Dr. Woodrow Watts, Deputy Superintendent Secondary Schools, Houston Independent School District.

We can now clearly see the humor and hypocrisy in the way the philosophy of the schools reads and its in fact application. Let us review the first paragraph and pick the major fallacies and discuss the reasons why they are false.

One, the school program is inflexible, and practically none of the physical, mental, moral, or social needs of the students (save for a small gr-up) are provided for. Many teachers, especially those in the Athletic Department, could give a damn about the mental health, emotional stability, or physical well-being of any student.

The second paragraph states that democratic behavior should be encouraged. This is probably the biggest farce which exists in the school system. How can a school be democratic when locker searches are made, people are suspended for bearing flags, people are suspended for carrying literature that the administration doesn't agree with, suspending people for exercising free speech rights, and suspending students for repulsing teacher aggression? And if a student speaks out on these issues he is punished for questioning authority.

The third paragraph says that every student should be taught citizenship, its rights, privileges, and duties. Since we have just noted that we are certainly not being shown citizenship's duties either. We learn from example, and this is the example that is shown to us. The school tells us to be good American children and do what we are told, not because we have to, but because we want to. On page 2 of the Handbook for Secondary School Principals and Teachers, though, it states that, under 'Jury Duty,' teachers are not required to serve on a jury, and so if they elect to do so they will be penalized by having the days they miss deducted from their salary. Jury duty is a duty of all Americans, who should want to do it, but teachers can not serve even if they want to, because they cannot afford the deduction from their salary.

The school system has, for the preceding reasons, shown themselves to be weak because they have violated their own code of conduct and when an organization violates its own rules, there is an indication of corruption and incompetence.

Students for a Democratic Society

'PFLASHLYTE'
THIS PAPER PROTECTS THE RIGHT OF STUDENTS TO KNOW WHAT IS GOING ON AND TO EXPRESS THEIR OPINIONS ON IMPORTANT ISSUES.
— the editors

JUSTICE vs. SCHOOL POWER

If their is any fixed star in our constitutional constellation, it is that no official, high or petty, can prescribe what shall be orthodox in politics, nationalism, religion, or matters of opinion or force citizens to confess by word or act their faith therein.

— Justice Robert H. Jackson

Are high-school students citizens? The fourteenth amendment to the Constitution of the United States answers this question; 'all persons born or naturalized in the United States, and subject to the jurisdiction thereof, are citizens of the United States and to the state wherein they reside.' (notice the word 'all') The 14th Amendment further states 'no state shall make or enforce any law which shall abridge the privileges or immunities of citizens * * * nor deny to any person within its jurisdiction the equal protection of the laws.' An even more emphatic answer to the question is found in the recent Supreme Court ruling in favor of three Des Moines, Iowa high-school students who were expelled for peacefully protesting the Viet-Nam War. By its decision, the Supreme Court underscored the fact that high-school students are citizens under jurisdiction of the law and therefore entitled to equal protection under the law.

It is the duty of all governmental agencies, including school boards, to operate within the limits of the Constitution and protect the people's rights. Unfortunately there are a few die-hard school administrators who, over in the light of Constitutional amendments and precedent setting Supreme Court decisions, continue to openly and ruthlessly violate the basic civil rights guaranteed to all citizens. Students are suspended or expelled for exercising their legal rights of freedom of speech, press, and assembly. In an effort to justify their actions, administrators claim that forms of expression such as newspapers printed without their approval and the display of American flags are in violation of civil law. Those who use this reasoning only make themselves look ridiculous because they are using laws as a basis for suppressing laws. For some reason, administrators never answer student proposals in a calm and intelligent manner; nor do they attempt to rationalize their stand on any particular issue. They merely hand down ultimatums. (Could it be that they are afraid to meet students as equals?) The days of 'blind obedience' are over; intelligent people want reasons before they act.

In the long run, we must be prepared to work for the reforms we want. We cannot sit back and relax just because of a few Amendments and court rulings. Establishments are reluctant to change and are apt to ignore the escence of the justice that they themselves teach. To protect our rights we must understand them fully and we must be willing to work to preserve them. If we give up and knuckle under to injustices dealt us by a 'dime store dictator' what will happen later in life when we have to face abominations considerably more unbearable than the ones we face here in school? Get on your knees and bow to autocratic administrators or hold our for something that fits a little better in a supposedly democratic society. ITS OUR CHOICE.

YOUR RIGHTS

This paper will present a series of articles discussing the rights insured by the Bill of Rights and how they specifically apply to students

— the editors

If you read the final edition of the Chronicle of Monday, February 24, 1969, you would have undoubtedly read the article on the Supreme Court's ruling on student protests. 'The Supreme Court, insured today, the right of school children to hold protest demonstrations but emphasized officials may impose restraints in there are intrusions upon the work of the school or the rights of other students. The Chronicle quoted Justice Abe Fortas as saying 'It can hardly be argued that either students or teachers shed their Constitutional rights to freedom of speech or expression at the schoolhouse gate.' Further, 'they (students) are possessed of fundamental rights which the state must respect * * *.' This position was affirmed by the clear majority of support from the other justices. The decision was verified by 7-2 vote.

The primary principles in question involved the dispute over to what degree freedom of speech and expression should be extended. We do not see how anyone can decy students the right to express themselves as they desire when not endangering the lives or rights of others. The principle of equal treatment was one of the most fundamental rights guaranteed by the Bill of Rights.

A good discussion of freedom of expression may be found in A Living Bill of Rights, written by Justice William O. Douglas, published by Doubleday & Co., Inc. In his book, Douglas states, 'man has responded to this power of expression in one of two ways. Some have said that since ideas may be dangerous, their expression must be carefully controlled by those in power. This has been the approach of * * * all totalitarians.' The other approach is that taken by the United States Constitution; 'Congress shall make no law * * * abridging the freedom of speech or of the press.' Which approach has the Administration of Sharpstown taken? If you are cunning enough to glimpse at a Handbook for Principals and Teachers— Secondary Schools, be sure to read the paragraph entitled 'Principals.' You will find that school principals '* * * may enforce obedience to all rules and regulations which are lawful and reasonable.' In other words, principals, or schools, may enact rules only if they are lawful and reasonable, not lawful or reasonable, but lawful and reasonable. The Supreme Court and even the Constitution of the United States have asserted that it is unsawful to restrict human beings the right of expression. Therefore, schools may not enact a rule contrary to this principal. Yet schools have tried to place themselves in a higher position them the Supreme Court by in effect overruling the rights insured by the Constitution. Is the school so sovereign? We don't think so and neither does the Supreme Court.

EDMUND'S THOUGHTS

Some students are confused by the regulations here. To make these rules clearer, I will explain—

1/ No boy shall be allowed to wear his hair longer than two inches. There have been numerous reports of students straggling themselves while sharpening their pencils. But there are more important reasons. It is feared that another outbreak of Bubonic Plague is on its way very soon. Any day now, they may to start cleaning the floors of the school. Still another reason exists. The members of the coaching department obviously have a definite sight problem. The don't seem to be able to distinguish male and female students unless the males have hair cut in the style of a Tibetian monk. Several accounts of forcible rape have been filed by boys in all gym classes.

2/ No one shall wear a neckercheif or scarf about their neck. It has been reported that one of the faculty members is actually a missing link between man and the Orangutan. Necties are permissable since Orangutangs do not know there are such things and therefore will not strangle you.

3/ There is strong evidence that there are some students at this school who actually beleive in Democracy. NASTY, NASTY... All of this garbage about rights and dignity of man went out the same tiem justice, peace, love and sanity did (when you registered at Sharpstown). So get all of that out of your system. We want the school to be just as sterile and smooth-running as we can make it. Just act like a vegetable waiting to be eaten, close your eyes and you won't feel a thing.

4/ Due to an excessive number of students losing their eyeballs, no one will be permitted to give the peace sign. Medical authorities agree that the best way to cope with the problem is to break the students fingers so they will swell up and not fit into the eye sockets. Science wins again.......

5/ Students are not allowed to remain across the street from school before classes. Geologists report that there is a very large crack in the earth in the park. Years ago it was sealed with 17 tons of bubble gum, but since we are now closer to the sun than we were at that time, there is a great danger that it will all melt and result in students falling to China.

6/ All fire alarms have been disconnected so that no one will miss all the excitement. If anyone discovers some-one reporting a fire, take him to the office where he will be promptly be stoned to death with wet erasers.

7/ No one shall bear the American flag in the presence of the Administration. Although very quaint, it is also very dangerous as there are people in the school who do not believe in Life, Liberty and the Pursuit of Happiness.

8/ Beware of what type literature you posess. Excerpts from the PTA bulletins and the Handbook for Principals and Teachers— Secondary Schools are thought to be coded messages to communist agents seeking the overthrow of the schools. It is a well known fact the the Bible preaches communal living and in fact perpetrates a fanatic cult of weirdos called Christians. Beware of these people. They are occassionally seen nailed to the office walls.

9/ Do not, under any curcumstances, collect money for the starving children of Biafra. Some of the money goes to Nigeria and as soon as the babies are born there, they are inducted into the Communist Party.

10/ Last of all, do not think. This practice has recently been found to cause irreparable damage to brain-washed minds. This type of activity causes the brain to overheat and warp your values until instilling such beliefs as dressing as one wants and thinking and saying as one feels. You may even degenerate to the point of belief in love. remember the Sharpstown slogan:

ALL FOR NOTHING AND NOTHING FOR ALL..............
yours sincerely, Edmund P. Senile (this was translated by
Mr. Senile's secretary due to the disaster of his last article)

ATTEMPT TO COMMUNICATE

Many students have legitimate gripes about their school (and it is their school, supported by their parents' tax money) which they would like to express openly to the Administration. Some are able to do so indirectly through a faculty member who really cares about the student, but more often than not he is unable to do so and will not go to the Administration because of a deep fear of the office. We would like to encourage students to go to the office and find someone to talk to there and express their gripes, because, believe it or not, there are some people in the office who want to help. Unfortunately, this attempt often fails because of several reasons. One, the student fails to make an appointment and finds the administrator at a very busy part of his day and is subsequently brushes off and leaves scared, dissapointed, and angry. Two, the student fails to clearly state his idea to the administrator; or, the administrator jumps to the conclusion. Third, the student seems beligerent and the administrator gets angry and yells at the student without listening to what is to be said. Worse, however, is the mutual misunderstanding between the student and administrator. All to often, something of importance to the student seems quite unimportant to the administrator to ignores the student. This attitude eventually results in a great wall of hostility between the student body and the office.

There are many faults with our school system which will be presented, but this is one which can be corrected easily, and should be corrected. But to correct it will take work and giving from both sides. Several times this year the Administration has offered us talk sessions and then retracted the offer. It is this paper's opinion that much unrest in the school could be eased if this plan were brought into effect, and certain rules under the jurisdiction of the principal (and we know what these are) were changed somewhat according to popular student vote and ideas. We hope that the Administration will consider all that has been said in an open light and do something about it because, then, we of this paper will have done something to help our school.

ARGUMENT FOR PREE SPEECH AND PRESS

As anticipated, the second issue of Pfsashlyte brought about unconstitutional and suppressive reprisals from the Administration. The School has obviously taken upon itself the sovereignty to overrrule the Constitution of the United States, thereby castrating the ideals of democracy and suppressing the production of creative ideas.

They should pull the wax out of their ears and listen to the works of our forefathers; 'Congress shall make no law * * * abridging the freedom of speech or of the press; or the right of the people peacefully to assemble and to petition the government for a redress of greviences' (Amendment I).
and
'the Fourteenth Amendment, as now applied to the states, protects the citizens against the state itself ad- all of its creatures'— boards of education not excluded. These have, of course, delicate and highly discretionary functions, but none that they cannot perform within the limits of the Bill of Rights. That they are educating the young for citizenship is reason for scrupulous protection of Constitutional freedom of the individual if we are not to strangle the free mind at its source and teach youths to discount important principles of government as mere platitudes.

Such boards are numerous and their territorial jurisdiction often small. But small and local authority may feel less sense of responsibility to the Constitution and agencies of publicity may be less vigilant in calling it to account. '* * * there are village tyrants as well as village Hampdens, but none who acts under the color of law is beyond reach of the Constitution.'

Chapter 12
Their Stories:
Online Off-Campus Speech

ABSTRACT

This chapter presents the stories of students censored by their schools for speaking in an off-campus online forum. It discusses online off-campus student speech in two categories: (a) speech directed at or against school officials or the school; and (b) speech directed at or against students. The chapter examines and analyzes the various legal precedents governing students' First Amendment speech rights under each of these categories. The analysis highlights the lack of clarity and the unsettled nature of the jurisprudence governing students' free speech rights in an off-campus online setting.

INTRODUCTION

This chapter examines the various lower court decisions on the First Amendment right of students to speak off-campus. It discusses these cases in the context of the stories of students censored for their off-campus speech in an online setting. In addition, the chapter analyzes the judicial reasoning for affirming or restricting school-censorship authority beyond the schoolhouse gate. The chapter reveals that, in most cases, the judicial rationale was founded on the material and substantial disruption test that the United States Supreme Court created in Tinker v. Des Moines Independent Community School District (1969). Some courts employed the true-threat doctrine – a gateway to censorship of speech that constitutes a true threat. A few courts chose to employ the *Bethel* test created in Bethel School District No. 403 v. Fraser (1986). Scholars, students, school officials and the judiciary need to understand the current state of the off-campus online student-speech jurisprudence if needed certainty and clarity are to emerge in the jurisprudence. In the examination of the cases, the censorship story of the student is presented first. The chapter per the authors then analyzes the court's rationale for its ruling about the scope of students' free speech rights in an off-campus online setting. The objective is to analyze the lower court decisions in order to highlight grounds for school censorship of student off-campus speech which would then form the basis for chapter thirteen's analysis. The discourse will reveal that there is no uniformity in the judicial approach to censorship of off-campus online student speech.

DOI: 10.4018/978-1-4666-9519-1.ch012

Their Stories: Online Off-Campus Speech

MAIN FOCUS OF THE CHAPTER

Since the emergence of the digital age, lower courts have tried to apply the United States Supreme Court's student-speech precedents – Tinker v. Des Moines Independent Community School District (1969), Bethel School District No. 403 v. Fraser (1986), Hazelwood v. Kuhlmeier (1988) and Morse v. Frederick (2007) – to off-campus student speech cases. Given that these Supreme Court cases involved speech within the schoolhouse gate, lower courts have struggled to provide clarity about how these precedents govern students' online speech outside the schoolhouse gate. Some courts have also applied the true-threat doctrine to students' off-campus digital speech, even though the Supreme Court has never extended the doctrine to such speech. As courts reach for ways to address school censorship of digital off-campus speech without clarity from the Supreme Court, the jurisprudence becomes a nebulous collection of inharmonious cases. This uncertainty clouds the scope of students' speech rights. In this chapter, we tell the story of students that schools have censored for speaking electronically off-campus. Our discussion is divided into two categories based on the target of the online off-campus speech:

1. Speech directed at or against school officials or the school; and
2. Speech directed at or against students.

SPEECH DIRECTED AT OR AGAINST SCHOOL OFFICIALS OR THE SCHOOL

In this section, we present the stories of students censored for their online speech created or distributed outside the school's campus. We specifically focus on student speech that targeted teachers, administrators or the student's school. We examine how courts have approached the student speech and the authority of schools to censor such speech.

1. The Story of Brandon Beussink

The Speech Incident: Retaliation and Criticism

In February 1998, during his junior year at Woodland High School in Missouri, Brandon Beussink created a homepage on the internet in order to provide a forum for his personal views (Beussink v. Woodland R-IV School District, 1998). He made the entire page publically viewable so that anyone with internet access could find it. According to Brandon, he never intended for anyone at his school to view or access the page. Indeed, he did not reveal the homepage's existence to other students. The entire creation and posting of the homepage took place in the privacy of his home. He also created the homepage outside school hours without using any school resource. Instead he created it on his personal computer with a program he found on the internet.

On his homepage, Brandon criticized teachers as well as the principal using vulgar and coarse language (Beussink v. Woodland R-IV School District, 1998). Vulgar language was also used in criticism of his school and the school's homepage. Brandon's homepage included a hyperlink to the school's official homepage. He asked visitors to his page to contact his school principal to voice concerns about the school. During a classmate's visit to Brandon's home, about two weeks after the homepage's creation, the classmate discovered the homepage on Brandon's personal computer. Shortly after this discovery, she had a squabble with Brandon that was unrelated to the homepage. She was so upset by the squabble that she decided to retaliate against him. Accordingly, she intentionally accessed his homepage at the school, showing it to the computer teacher. Brandon had no prior knowledge of her plan to access the homepage at school and never gave her its address. She was able to access the homepage simply based on recall from her earlier accidental discovery of the page while in Brandon's home. The contents of the page offended and angered the teacher who reported it to the principal. Immediately after the principal saw the homepage, he decided to discipline Brandon because he was angry about its contents and display on school grounds. Before making the decision to discipline Brandon, the principal did not investigate whether other students knew of or saw the homepage. During the entire time that the principal and teacher viewed the homepage, Brandon was unaware that the homepage had been accessed at the school.

Around the fourth period, the computer teacher authorized her students to access the homepage on the school computers during her class (Beussink v. Woodland R-IV School District, 1998). She also had a conversation with the class about the homepage's contents. Brandon did not authorize this classroom access of his homepage. In fact, he was oblivious to it. The teacher claimed that she only granted her entire class authorization to view the homepage after she learned that three students had discovered the homepage. After the class discussion, however, the teacher stopped students viewing the homepage. The librarian claimed that Brandon accessed the page at school; the court, however, gave no credence to this claim as Brandon denied it and the librarian could not prove he did. The student whom the librarian claimed witnessed Brandon's on-campus access of the homepage denied seeing Brandon access the homepage. Additionally, there was no evidence that the homepage caused any disruption at the school.

During the fourth period, the principal informed Brandon that he would be suspended from school for five days (Beussink v. Woodland R-IV School District, 1998). When the suspension notice was delivered to Brandon at his class, he offered to give the homepage address to his teacher to show he did nothing wrong; the teacher, however, was not interested. Had the teacher accessed the homepage on-campus with Brandon's authorization, the school might have been able to claim that Brandon encouraged an on-campus access that could be the basis for punishing him for on-campus speech. Despite the fact that Brandon had not accessed the homepage on-campus, around the seventh period, the principal decided to increase Brandon's suspension to ten days. When the second suspension notice was delivered to his class, Brandon showed a hard copy of the homepage's first page to his seventh-period teacher. He asked the teacher to review the copy in order to advise him as to whether the school had valid legal grounds for the suspension. Brandon claimed that he did not personally access the hard copy of the speech on-campus; he merely showed the teacher the hard copy attached to his suspension notice. The school secretary claimed, however, that she did not attach a copy to the notice. Brandon and the school district agreed that no student saw the hard copy's contents. The principal denied Brandon's request to amend his suspension. Instead, he instructed Brandon to either delete his homepage or clean it up. When Brandon returned home, he deleted the homepage from the internet. The ten-day absence from school significantly impacted Brandon's grades for the semester. As a result of the absence, he failed all his classes. Brandon and his mother sued the school district, asserting a violation of his First Amendment right to free speech. Brandon asked the court to enjoin the school's censorship of his speech as well as the record of his failing grades.

Analysis

Beussink v. Woodland R-IV School District (1998) was the first case in the United States to rule on the right of students to speak off-campus in an online forum. Consequently, this case is often cited in other off-campus online speech cases. The United States District Court for the Eastern District of Missouri applied the material and substantial disruption test to Brandon's off-campus speech without acknowledging the on-campus origin of the test. The court's decision to extend the material and substantial disruption test to off-campus speech on the internet implied that the test was borderless. However, since the court did not provide any rationale for such an extension, it is impossible to decipher the court's reasoning for disregarding the on-campus origin of the test. Despite this inaugural decision to extend the test to digital off-campus speech, the court stated that school officials should not have unbridled authority over students. It appears that the material and substantial disruption test was the court's way of ensuring that school officials do not have unfettered reach over off-campus speech. Therefore, the court emphasized that, without evidence of a reasonable forecast of or actual material and substantial disruption, school officials cannot deprive students of their First Amendment right to digital off-campus speech.

The district court concluded that the school's censorship of Brandon did not satisfy the material and substantial disruption test (Beussink v. Woodland R-IV School District, 1998). This conclusion was supported by the principal's concession that the decision to suspend Brandon was made immediately after viewing the homepage without any evidence of disruption. The principal made the suspension decision solely because he was upset at the content and its display inside the school. As the court explained, the *Tinker* test does not authorize school censorship of student speech merely because a school official dislikes the speech or finds it upsetting. Besides, the significant activities at the school related to the homepage occurred because of the actions of school officials and other students (rather than because of Brandon). As evident in the record, only the school officials and other students actually viewed the homepage on the school's campus; Brandon never did.

The district court ruled that school officials cannot censor off-campus speech simply because it is controversial or critical of school officials; the material and substantial disruption test also governs censorship of such speech (Beussink v. Woodland R-IV School District, 1998). As the court pointed out, the First Amendment exists to protect controversial and offensive speech such as Brandon's:

Indeed, it is provocative and challenging speech, like Beussink's, which is most in need of the protections of the First Amendment. Popular speech is not likely to provoke censure. It is unpopular speech that invites censure. It is unpopular speech which needs the protection of the First Amendment. The First Amendment was designed for this very purpose (Beussink v. Woodland R-IV School District, 1998).

The district court also ruled that, irrespective of its brevity, deprivation of First Amendment rights causes irreparable harm (Beussink v. Woodland R-IV School District, 1998). This rule was particularly applicable to the principal's ultimatum to Brandon to close his homepage or clean it up. The rule was also especially important in protecting students' digital speech because it afforded Brandon a remedy after he felt he had to delete his entire homepage in order to avoid further repercussions from his school. The rule also applied to the failing grades that Brandon received in all his courses because the suspension was a means of censoring Brandon's speech.

Like Tinker v. Des Moines Independent Community School District (1969), Beussink v. Woodland R-IV School District (1998) was a trailblazer in students' rights. While the *Tinker* case heralded the right of students to free speech, the *Beussink* case heralded the right of students to off-campus online speech. In both cases, students were victorious as their rights were recognized while school-censorship authority was constricted. If there were no progenies of these cases, students would continue to enjoy the broad protections announced in those cases. Unfortunately, as evident from Bethel School District No. 403 v. Fraser (1986), Hazelwood v. Kuhlmeier (1988) and Morse v. Frederick (2007), progenies of cases sometimes constrict the rights of students. Additionally, despite Tinker v. Des Moines Independent Community School District and Beussink v. Woodland R-IV School District, censorship of students' speech remains vibrant in schools as evident in the other censorship stories discussed below.

2. The Story of Gregory Requa

The Speech Incident: The YouTube Video of the Pelvic Thrust and Rabbit Ears

During the 2005-06 school year, Gregory Requa, a junior student at Kentridge High School in Washington, and some classmates ostensibly created a video recording of their teacher (Requa v. Kent School District No. 415, 2007). The video, in the form of a motion picture with musical soundtrack, was taken furtively during class time on two different days. S.W. – a student involved in the filming – claimed that Gregory was responsible for posting it on YouTube. The video was edited and posted from a personal computer outside school hours away from the school's campus. Over the summer, while school was not in session, Gregory put a link to the YouTube video on his Myspace.com page. The school computers were configured to block all access to YouTube and Myspace.com; accordingly no student accessed the video on school grounds through either of these sites.

The YouTube video featured a student standing behind the teacher while making rabbit ears – two fingers vertically-placed or inclined above the back of the teacher's head (Requa v. Kent School District No. 415, 2007). In the video, the student with the rabbit ears thrust his pelvic in the teacher's direction while making various facial gestures. The video also included a section titled "Caution Booty Ahead" (p. 1274). This section featured numerous pictures of the teacher's buttocks in diverse situations, including when she was bent over. The recording of the teacher's buttocks was a close-up and extensive. The "Caution Booty Ahead" section had its own special rap music called "Ms. New Booty" (p. 1274). The video also featured comments critical of the teacher's hygiene and disorganization. It showed the teacher's cluttered desk and shelves as well as the chalk litter on her classroom floor. The video caused no disruption at the school.

In February 2007, while preparing a report on students' YouTube criticisms of teachers, a local television station found Gregory's video on YouTube (Requa v. Kent School District No. 415, 2007). The reporter called Kentridge High School administrators to solicit their comments. The station then aired the video (along with others) as part of a news segment. Prior to this airing, the only students aware of the video appeared to be those involved in its creation. Once Gregory heard of the news segment, amid concerns that the video might constitute harassment, he deleted it from his Myspace.com page.

The principal learned of Gregory's involvement with the video from S.W. (Requa v. Kent School District No. 415, 2007). Four other students confirmed that Gregory was involved in the filming though two of them could not definitively state that Gregory was the videographer for any film segment. S.W. revealed that "[a]bout the last 5 days of school Greg Requa and I filmed [Ms. M.] without her consent and

Their Stories: Online Off-Campus Speech

posted it online. Greg did editing and posted it online. All I did was some filming" (p. 1274). Gregory claimed that his only role was linking the YouTube site for the video to his Myspace.com page. He denied any role with the filming, editing and posting of the video.

Despite Gregory's denial, the principal decided to suspend him from school for 40 days (Requa v. Kent School District No. 415, 2007). He informed Gregory and his parents that the later 20 days of the suspension would be deferred if Gregory wrote a research paper during the first 20 days of the suspension. The principal also assigned Gregory to contract school – an alternative education process that allows a student to complete his school assignments at home while working with a tutor after school hours. The other students involved with the video got similar suspension terms. The school board did not find Gregory's denial of involvement credible. Instead, the board gave credence to S.W.'s statement that Gregory was involved. The board concluded that all students involved with the video were equally censorable. Additionally, the board ruled that any off-campus activity (such as editing and posting on YouTube) were merely incidental to the on-campus filming. Therefore, Gregory's discipline did not violate the First Amendment because his speech was actually on-campus speech. Accordingly, the board affirmed Gregory's discipline. Gregory sought judicial review of his First Amendment claim and an injunction against the district.

Analysis

The school district argued to the court, as it contended during its review of Gregory's discipline, that Gregory was punished for his on-campus filming of the teacher rather than for off-campus speech (Requa v. Kent School District No. 415, 2007). The district argued that the off-campus editing and posting of the YouTube video were merely incidental to the primary on-campus filming. In fact, the school district conceded that it could not punish Gregory for his off-campus speech. Gregory, on the other hand, argued that the district punished him for his off-campus speech; specifically his posting of the YouTube link on his Myspace.com page. The United States District Court for the Western District of Washington rejected Gregory's argument, however. The court reasoned that, since the school district imposed the same punishment on all students involved with the video, the students were punished for the same speech. Given that all the students punished were involved with the on-campus filming, and only Gregory was involved with the off-campus editing and posting, Gregory's punishment must have been for the filming. Accordingly, the court determined that Gregory's punishment was for his on-campus speech rather than the editing and posting of the YouTube video. While this might be the case, it is incredulous to believe that the posting of the video did not play a magnified role in the discipline. Clearly, the media report on the video's presence on YouTube, rather than their actual filming of the video, instigated the investigation of Gregory and his friends. Additionally, unlike the school district, the court itself conceded that the off-campus editing and posting constituted "considerable off-campus activity" rather than mere incidentals (p. 1278). In essence, the court ignored two considerable parts of the trio of filming, editing and posting to focus on one – filming – as the basis for the discipline. The filming happened to be the on-campus part of the trio, allowing the district court to conveniently bring the entire speech within the on-campus school-censorship authority recognized by the United States Supreme Court.

The federal district court rightly observed that school officials did not censor Gregory's Myspace. com link to the YouTube video (Requa v. Kent School District No. 415, 2007). Gregory made a personal voluntary decision to delete the link from his Myspace.com page even before school officials confronted him. Moreover, the district did not bar him from reposting the link. Besides, after the news segment aired, several other students at Gregory's school posted links to the YouTube video on their webpages. Yet, school officials did not punish them. These facts supported the court's conclusion that Gregory was not punished for linking the YouTube video to his webpage. Additionally, the video remained on YouTube even after Gregory's deletion of his webpage link and imposition of his punishment. As the court observed, the school never asked YouTube's web administrators to delete the video. If the school had wanted to censor the speech, it would have taken steps to remove the video from the YouTube link and barred Gregory from reposting it on YouTube, his Myspace.com page or any other site.

Despite conceding that Bethel School District No. 403 v. Fraser (1986) differed from Gregory's case, the federal district court ruled that the *Bethel* test governed Gregory's speech (Requa v. Kent School District No. 415, 2007). As the court readily acknowledged, Gregory's speech, unlike the speech in the *Bethel* case, was not wholly on school grounds. However, the on-campus component of Gregory's speech exposed him to censorship under the *Bethel* test:

The facts of this case are not on all fours with Fraser [Bethel School District No. 403 v. Fraser (1986)] in the sense that the 'speech' at issue here was ultimately published in an off-campus location (i.e., the internet). But an inseparable part of the speech which Plaintiff seeks to protect is the filming of the footage in the classroom. That is an inextricable part of the activity which comprises the 'speech' of the completed video and, in singling out that discreet portion of the 'speech' for punishment, Defendants have localized the sanctionable behavior to the area in which their authority has been upheld by the Supreme Court (Requa v. Kent School District No. 415, 2007, p. 1280).

Under the *Bethel* test, the court ruled that the pelvic thrust and the rabbit ears constituted plainly-offensive and lewd speech (Requa v. Kent School District No. 415, 2007). Additionally, the recording of the teacher's buttocks, the "Caution Booty Ahead" section as well as the rap music "Ms. New Booty" were lewd and plainly offensive. The court rejected Gregory's argument that the recording of the teacher's buttocks was merely a commentary on her hygiene rather than sexual speech. Moreover, the court ruled that students cannot avail themselves of an unlimited audience for sexual speech. If sexual speech has a political purpose, however, the court would find it constitutionally protected under the *Bethel* test. Gregory failed to qualify for this exception because he did not articulate a political purpose.

Since the district court viewed Gregory's speech as on-campus speech, it found the *Tinker* tests – material and substantial disruption test and the infringement-of-rights test – applicable to the speech; despite the fact that the editing and online posting occurred off-campus (Requa v. Kent School District No. 415, 2007). The *Tinker* tests were also applicable because of the court's rule that, when speech does not fit precisely under any of the other Supreme Court student-speech precedents, the *Tinker* tests govern. Even though the court acknowledged the infringement-of-rights test and its applicability, it neither applied the test nor explained it. Therefore, we do not know the court's interpretation of this test which, as discussed in chapter seven, remains clouded in various courts.

The court's application of the material and substantial disruption test led to a ruling in favor of the school district's censorship (Requa v. Kent School District No. 415, 2007). Despite the fact that Gregory's speech did not result in any actual disruption of the school, the court found that it caused material and substantial disruption. The court ruled that there is *per se* material and substantial disruption when a student makes rabbit ears behind a teacher and directs pelvic thrusts at the teacher. Additionally, filming a teacher's buttocks while she bends over constitutes material and substantial disruption. Any "demeaning, derogatory, sexually suggestive behavior toward an unsuspecting teacher in a classroom" also constitutes material and substantial disruption (p. 1280).

The district court apparently extended the material and substantial disruption test beyond its moorings (Requa v. Kent School District No. 415, 2007). Tinker v. Des Moines Independent Community School District (1969) required actual evidence of material and substantial to the school's work or maintenance of discipline; or at minimum, evidence of reasonable forecast of material and substantial disruption to the school's work or discipline at the school. A *per se* finding ignores this need for evidence of material and substantial disruption. To justify its extension of the test, the court surprisingly stated, in contravention of the Supreme Court's ruling in the *Tinker* case, that material and substantial disruption is not limited to disruption of the school's work or maintenance of discipline (Requa v. Kent School District No. 415, 2007). Instead, the test encompasses disruption of a "civil and respectful atmosphere toward teachers and students alike" (p. 1280). This is a very fluid concept that would allow school officials to censor virtually any student speech based on a subjective interpretation that the speech impacted civility and respect at the school. The court concluded that, even though students have a right to criticize their teachers, the right must be exercised in compliance with the *Bethel* test as well as the material and substantial disruption test.

Students need to be aware that some courts, as in Requa v. Kent School District No. 415 (2007), might choose to extricate any on-campus component of their speech from the off-campus component in order to empower school censorship. Consequently, filming, editing and posting of speech need to occur wholly off-campus. If any component of the off-campus student speech occurs on the school's campus, a student would be wise to avoid sexual speech about her teachers or colleagues as well as derogatory or demeaning speech directed at the teacher or student. Such speech, as noted above, could be deemed as *per se* material and substantial disruption. It could also violate the *Bethel* test.

3. The Story of Christopher Barnett, Kevin Black, and Gary Moses

The Speech Incident: The Fake Myspace.com Profiles

In October 2006, Christopher Barnett, a student at Brighton High School in Tennessee posted a fake profile of his assistant principal on Myspace.com (Barnett ex rel. Barnett v. Tipton County Board of Education, 2009). Christopher created the profile using the assistant principal's biography and photograph taken directly from the school district's website. He also included crude sexually-suggestive remarks about various female students at his school. Kevin Black, who was also a Brighton High School student, created a fake Myspace.com profile of one of the school's coaches similar to Christopher's. Gary Moses, a student with special needs and classmate of Christopher and Kevin, participated in the websites' creation. Christopher accessed his website in the school's computer lab during one of his classes.

School officials first learned of the websites from a parent and a reporter (Barnett ex rel. Barnett v. Tipton County Board of Education, 2009). The local reporter who discovered both websites thought that the assistant principal created them. The reporter also believed that the assistant principal was using the websites for sexual communications with students. As a result, the reporter called the school district to alert school officials to the websites. Similarly, the parent called the school district out of concern that the assistant principal might be involved with the websites. During the school district's investigation, school officials discovered that Gary Moses was involved. When confronted, Gary revealed that

Christopher and Kevin created the websites. He claimed that he merely contributed to the websites. A search of the school's computers showed that Christopher accessed his website on school grounds. School officials then suspended Christopher from school for two days. He also received eight days of in-school suspension. Kevin received eleven days of in-school suspension while Gary received two days of in-school suspension. While away from school on suspension, Christopher created another website targeting a student who he wrongly believed disclosed his website to the school officials. This website featured the student's picture in a "Wanted Person" poster. Shortly thereafter, the school board decided to assign Christopher to an alternative school for the remainder of the school year as punishment for his speech on the websites. The board affirmed Kevin's suspension and informed him that he would be subjected to the district's zero-tolerance policy for the rest of the school year. Gary's suspension was affirmed after a special needs meeting. The parents of all three students filed a First Amendment lawsuit against the school district claiming a violation of the students' free speech rights.

Analysis

In one of the most breviloquent court decisions that we found, instead of analyzing the off-campus nature of the speech, the United States District Court for the Western District of Tennessee chose to frame its decision around the students' argument that their speech constituted parodies (Barnett ex rel. Barnett v. Tipton County Board of Education, 2009). The court ruled that a parody would enjoy First Amendment as long as a reasonable observer does not view it as a description of actual facts about the parody's subject matter. According to the court, parodies are clear exaggerations designed to inspire humor. They are also "not reasonably believable" (p. 984, citing Hustler Magazine, Inc. v. Falwell, 1988, p. 57). The court characterized the websites in this case, however, as fraudulent sites designed to lead viewers to believe that the coach and the assistant principal were engaged in inappropriate communication with students. Moreover, Christopher, Kevin and Gary failed to present evidence showing that viewers of their websites would interpret their comments thereon as parodies. Indeed, both the parent and the local reporter reasonably and actually believed that school officials created the websites. They also considered the websites as a serious discussion of actual facts, prompting them to report the websites to the school district. Consequently, the websites were not protected as parodies under the First Amendment.

It appears that the court viewed Christopher's speech as on-campus speech because he accessed his website on the school's campus (Barnett ex rel. Barnett v. Tipton County Board of Education, 2009). Besides, Christopher used the school's resources in creation of his website – the assistant principal's biography and photograph were taken directly from the school district's website. The court failed to give any rationale for ignoring the off-campus nature of Kevin and Gary's speech, however. Presumably, since Kevin's website used the coach's biographical information and photograph from the district's website, his speech was converted to on-campus speech. While Gary was not one of the website's creators, his role as a contributor to websites created using school resources might have led the court to view his speech as on-campus speech.

Since the court did not reveal any rationale for its disregard of the off-campus versus on-campus components of the students' speeches, it is impossible to know how the court views the two components. It is unclear if the court simply believes that there is no constitutionally-significant distinction between off-campus and on-campus speech. In other words, it is unclear if the court views school-censorship

Their Stories: Online Off-Campus Speech

authority as borderless. If the court believed that the students transformed their off-campus speech into on-campus speech by accessing it on school grounds or using school resources, school-censorship authority would remain confined within the schoolhouse gate. If, however, the court viewed school-censorship authority as borderless, then clearly schools would have the power to censor students' speech even in the privacy of their homes.

4. The Story of Karl Beidler

The Speech Incident: The Lehnis Web

In January 1999, Karl Beidler, a student at Timberline High School in Washington, created a website that ridiculed his assistant principal (Beidler v. North Thurston School District, 2000). He called the website the Lehnis Web based on the assistant principal's last name. The website featured an image of the assistant principal drinking alcohol. Moreover, the site showed the assistant principal painting a wall with graffiti. It also portrayed the assistant principal in a Viagra advertisement. Additionally, the website represented the assistant principal as a Nazi involved in a Nazi book burning. Various screens on the website read as follows: "Lehnis as a Nazi"; "Lehnis hitting on a student"; "Lehnis with drugs and guns"; "The homo-loving photo"; "Lehnis flirting with male teacher"; "Lehnis 'baked' on drugs"; and "Lehnis defecating in class" (p. 6). The website included comments regarding a "girl about to be raped; and the pig taken for sodomizing" (p. 6). In a contradiction, the website portrayed the assistant principal as a police officer. The site also included comments which referred to a female student as "fat" and "whore" (p. 6). The website was not entirely distasteful. Karl included some innocuous comments taken from a prior Lehnis website that three other students had created on-campus using school resources.

Karl created the website in the privacy of his home (Beidler v. North Thurston School District, 2000). He never viewed his website on the school's campus. While on-campus, however, he told classmates about the website and discussed ideas for the site with some of them. The only school resource he used were some photographs taken from a school annual. When the principal learned about the website, he imposed an emergency expulsion on Karl. The principal explained that Karl deserved the punishment because the website was offensive and because teachers did not want him in their classrooms. The emergency expulsion was later changed to a long-term suspension. Karl was also assigned to an alternative school for his junior year. He sued the school district, alleging a violation of his right to free speech under the First Amendment. He asked the court to award him monetary damages and injunctive relief.

Analysis

The Thurston County Superior Court in Washington ruled that, while school officials must have censorship authority over student speech, the authority must not be extended beyond the schoolhouse gate (Beidler v. North Thurston School District, 2000, citing Thomas v. Board of Education, Granville Central School District, 1979). When schools extend their power beyond the schoolhouse gate, they are bound by the same speech-censorship rules (such as the fighting-words doctrine, defamatory speech rules, obscenity standards and the public forum doctrine discussed in earlier chapters) governing non-school government entities. The court rejected the school district's argument that it could censor Karl's off-campus speech as defamatory speech, without complying with the rules governing non-school government entities:

[W]here lawful government proscription of defamation has occurred, it has been by statute or ordinance, and such laws are subject to constitutional scrutiny under the traditional tests of overbreadth and public interest. In the instant case, there is no statute, ordinance or school regulation proscribing defamation relied upon by the school district in imposing [Karl] Beidler's suspension. Rather, defendants merely assert the defense that the school district's disciplinary action is exempt from the First Amendment scrutiny because Beidler's speech defames another. In summary, I conclude that the defamation defense is not available as a matter of law, and accordingly the factual issue of whether defamation occurred is not material (Beidler v. North Thurston School District, 2000, pp. 7-8).

The court stated that, even if it wanted to consider Karl's statements on the website as defaming the assistant principal, "that action is not this action ... and [t]he First Amendment does not permit such a result" (Beidler v. North Thurston School District, 2000, p. 7). In other words, the assistant principal should have filed a separate legal action alleging defamation against Karl rather than using the extrajudicial measure of school censorship. The court also rejected the school district's argument that it could censor Karl's speech under the fighting-words doctrine. The court, however, did not preclude schools from using this doctrine to censor off-campus student speech. It simply ruled that, "as a matter of law", this doctrine was inapplicable to the school's censorship of Karl's off-campus speech because the school failed to provide evidence in the record that satisfied the doctrine's requirements (p. 7).

The superior court stated that, even though the internet has changed the landscape of student communications, the boundaries of school-censorship authority remain unchanged (Beidler v. North Thurston School District, 2000). In other words, First Amendment protection is not a fluid concept that changes with innovations in technology. The court emphasized that, student speech over the internet is protected under the First Amendment (Beidler v. North Thurston School District, citing Reno v. American Civil Liberties Union 1997). Additionally, "[s]chools can and will adjust to the new challenges created by such students [as Karl] and the internet, but not at the expense of the First Amendment" (Beidler v. North Thurston School District, p. 3). Although the court viewed Karl as "immature and foolishly defiant" for posting the comments on the website, it ruled that he was still entitled to First Amendment protection beyond the school's purview (p. 3). It also ruled that Karl's on-campus discussion of the website's existence (and ideas for the website) with classmates was so de minimis that it did not convert his off-campus speech into on-campus speech. His use of photographs from the school annual was also deemed de minimis and insufficient to convert the speech to on-campus speech. Furthermore, even though Karl took some innocuous comments from a website that his friends created on-campus, he was the source of his own website's objectionable comments. Since the school punished him for the publication of his own website, rather than the republication of his friends' website comments, the pertinent censored comments were Karl's. Besides, Karl's censored comments occurred off-campus. Consequently, the court ruled that the school had no legal basis to treat Karl's speech as on-campus speech.

The superior court rejected the school district's contention that the United States Supreme Court's student-speech precedents authorized the school to censor Karl's off-campus speech (Beidler v. North Thurston School District, 2000). According to the court, because of the on-campus context of Tinker v. Des Moines Independent Community School District (1969), the material and substantial disruption test only applies to on-campus student speech. Despite this conclusion, the court applied the test to Karl's speech simply to reinforce its ruling that school officials had no authority to censor his off-campus speech

Their Stories: Online Off-Campus Speech

(Beidler v. North Thurston School District, 2000). Specifically, it found that the school failed to prove that the speech caused material and substantial disruption at the school. Therefore, "[r]egardless of where the geographical limits of school district authority may lie, *Tinker* does not support defendants" (p. 4).

The *Hazelwood* test was inapplicable because Karl's speech was not school-sponsored speech. Besides, unlike in Hazelwood v. Kuhlmeier (1988), it did not occur as part of a course (Beidler v. North Thurston School District, 2000). Instead, Karl's speech contained content, such as "whore", rape and the portrayal of his assistant principal as a Nazi that could be deemed plainly offensive, obscene or vulgar under the *Bethel* test. However, the court ruled that the *Bethel* test could not provide the basis for the school's censorship of Karl's off-campus speech; particularly because the context of Bethel School District No. 403 v. Fraser (1986) was speech at a mandatory school assembly with a captive audience of students (Beidler v. North Thurston School District, 2000). This on-campus context limited the *Bethel* test to on-campus speech in contrast to the off-campus context of Karl's speech. The court concluded that "*Fraser* [Bethel School District No. 403 v. Fraser] might provide support for disciplining [Karl] Beidler if the defendants could show that the circumstances of his speech were in any way analogous to the circumstances in *Fraser*" (Beidler v. North Thurston School District, p. 5).

This case was clearly very protective of students' off-campus speech. The court's requirement that schools adjust to the First Amendment rather than the First Amendment adjusting to schools is evidence of this. However, the court's declaration that the First Amendment does not evolve with changing technological landscape might be naïve. Particularly because as evident in this book, courts have struggled to determine the boundaries of school-censorship authority over off-campus speech. The absence of a clear voice from the United States Supreme Court about off-campus speech is the obvious reason for this struggle. The superior court's decision to minimize the impact of technology on the First Amendment shows a lack of understanding of the internet's ubiquity and the challenges of circumscribing the schoolhouse gate's borders.

In toto, the superior court chose a bright line rule that off-campus student speech is wholly excluded from school-censorship authority. This rule ensures that only non-school government entities can censor students' off-campus speech under rules applicable to the larger community. However, it does not clarify for students, teachers, scholars or lawyers when speech is off-campus versus on-campus. For instance, this case does not answer the question of whether on-campus access of speech that originated off-campus converts the off-campus speech into on-campus speech. The case simply does not explain where the schoolhouse gate is anchored for students' off-campus digital speech.

5. The Story of J.S.

The Speech Incident: The "Teacher Sux" Website

During the 1998 spring semester, J.S., an eighth-grade student at Nitschmann Middle School in Pennsylvania, created a website which he called "Teacher Sux." (J.S. v. Bethlehem Area School District, 2002, p. 850). The website was created on his personal computer inside his home after school hours without use of any school resource. J.S. created the website to provide an outlet for his views about school officials at Nitschmann Middle School. The first page of the website included a disclaimer which stated that any visitor to the website who clicked on the webpages consented to conceal the website's existence from the school district's employees and administrators. The disclaimer also asked visitors to warrant that they were not administrators or district employees. Additionally, the disclaimer asked visitors to keep confidential J.S.'s identity as the website's designer. The disclaimer also asked visitors to represent that they would not get J.S. into trouble because of the website. The disclaimer did not preclude people who disagreed with its terms from accessing the website, however. J.S. had no way of verifying that the visitors would actually abide by the disclaimer's terms as visitors could enter the website without a password.

The publically-accessible website, included several webpages featuring threatening, vulgar and disparaging pictures, words, sound clips and animation directed against his principal and teachers (J.S. v. Bethlehem Area School District, 2002). One of the webpages, for instance, greeted readers with the words, "Welcome to Kartsotis [the principal] Sux" (p. 851). On another webpage, J.S. used vulgar terms to accuse the principal of a sexual relationship with another principal in the district. The website also included pages targeting J.S.'s algebra teacher. For example, on the page called "Why Fulmer [teacher] Should be Fired", J.S. sniped at the teacher's physique and disposition and argued that the teacher should be fired for her disposition and physique (p. 851). On another page, J.S. included the teacher's picture alongside cartoon images from the television show "South Park" (p. 851). Next to these pictures, J.S. stated: "That's right Kyle [a South Park character]. She's a bigger bitch than your mom" (p. 851). He devoted a webpage to a hand-drawn image of the teacher dressed up as a witch. Another page used a sound clip and vulgarity in stating that "Mrs. Fulmer Is a Bitch, In D Minor" (p. 851).

One of the webpages portrayed the teacher's face morphing into Adolph Hitler, along with the following statement: "The new Fulmer Hitler movie. The similarities astound me" (J.S. v. Bethlehem Area School District, 2002, p. 851). Another page about the teacher was titled "Why Should She Die?" (p. 851). Below this title, J.S. asked visitors to "[t]ake a look at the diagram and the reasons I gave, then give me $20 to help pay for the hitman" (p. 851). The diagram accentuated and critiqued various physical attributes of the teacher. He drew lines to various parts of her face, listing some of the reasons why she should die: "Puke Green Eyes"; "Zit!"; and "Hideous smile" (p. 851). For her hair, he stated, "Is it a rug, or God's Mistake?" (pp. 851, 858). On this same webpage, J.S. included a section titled "Some Words from the writer" (p. 851). In this section, he used the phrase "Fuck You Mrs. Fulmer. You Are A Bitch. You Are A Stupid Bitch" one hundred and thirty six times (p. 851). On another page, J.S. included a pint-sized headless picture of the teacher as blood dribbled down her neck. He also included a webpage that shared answers to mathematics questions with classmates while criticizing the teacher. Several visitors to the website indicated in posted comments that they found its contents humorous.

While J.S. was at school, he told some of his schoolmates about the website (J.S. v. Bethlehem Area School District, 2002). Additionally, during the school day, he showed the website to a classmate. A teacher heard about the website and reported it to the principal – a website subject. The principal believed that the threats on the website were serious so he called a faculty meeting to notify teachers of the website. He also notified the police department as well as the Federal Bureau of Investigation (FBI) who conducted an investigation. Subsequently, the law enforcement agencies informed the school that J.S. was the website's creator. However, the agencies refused to charge J.S. School officials never spoke to J.S. about the website that school year and did not refer him to counseling either.

The website had a great impact on the algebra teacher as she believed that the website conveyed a serious plan to kill her (J.S. v. Bethlehem Area School District, 2002). She experienced appetite loss, sleeplessness, weight loss, headaches, short-term memory loss, anxiety and stress. Additionally, she was unable to leave her house. She also became terrified to be in crowded places. As a result of these various health issues, she was placed on antidepressants. The teacher also took medical leave from the school because she unable to continue teaching that school year. Consequently, the school had to hire three substitute teachers to fulfil the algebra teacher's responsibilities. The website impacted students as well. Some students, for instance, expressed anxieties about their safeties. Others requested counseling sessions to deal with the fallout from the website. The website became a major topic of discussion at the school. Parents expressed concern about student safety and outrage that the school had to hire substitutes to teach their children. According to the principal, the school became demoralized beyond anything he had seen in forty years. The morale of the school was described as "comparable to the death of a student or staff member" (p. 852). Nonetheless, the school allowed J.S. to continue attending classes and extracurricular activities. He also participated in a field trip with students and faculty.

The school did not punish J.S. during that school year (J.S. v. Bethlehem Area School District, 2002). Even though the school district did not ask J.S. to delete the website, he did so on his own volition about a week after the principal learned of it. After the school year ended, school officials notified J.S. and his parents for the first time that the school was aware of the website and that J.S. would be suspended from school for three days. School officials subsequently extended the suspension to ten days to be served at the beginning of the next school year. A month after this increased suspension, the school district expelled J.S. The district explained that J.S.'s statements constituted harassment of two school officials and a threat against the teacher. The district also cited the impact on the teacher's health as justification. At the time of the expulsion, J.S.'s parents had already enrolled him in another state for the following school year. His parents filed a First Amendment suit against the school district seeking injunctive relief.

Analysis

The Supreme Court of Pennsylvania conceded that it is "difficult" to determine the scope of school-censorship authority over students' off-campus speech (J.S. v. Bethlehem Area School District, 2002, p. 850). The court's framing of the issue in the case also highlighted this difficulty. Specifically, the court framed the issue as a determination of the scope of school-censorship authority over off-campus student speech that is vulgar or threatening. Both of these forms of off-campus speech have no pertinent precedents from the United States Supreme Court, making the issue an even more difficult one. While the United States Supreme Court ruled on vulgar on-campus student speech in Bethel School District No. 403 v. Fraser (1986), it has never decided a case involving such off-campus speech. The closest we have to a United States Supreme Court view on such speech was Justice Brennan's concurrence in the *Bethel* case which stated that on-campus speech which is vulgar would not be censorable off-campus. The Supreme Court affirmed this statement in Hazelwood v. Kuhlmeier (1988) and Morse v. Frederick (2007); however, both cases were on-campus student-speech cases.

As for threatening speech, the only proximate test, in the student-speech context, from the United States Supreme Court is the material and substantial disruption test created in Tinker v. Des Moines Independent Community School District (1969). The Supreme Court, however, specifically described the speech in the *Tinker* case as a "silent, passive expression of opinion" (Tinker v. Des Moines Independent Community School District, p. 508). This is a far cry from threatening speech. The only reason the material and substantial disruption test could be proximate is that threats can cause material and substantial disruption to a school. As a result, threats could conceivably be fitted into the material and substantial disruption test. Nonetheless, it is indubitable that the material and substantial disruption test arose in the context of wholly on-campus speech, unlike J.S.'s speech which originated off-campus.

It is also irrefragable that each student-speech case that the United States Supreme Court has considered had different facts. Each case also led to the creation of a new student-speech test (the *Tinker* tests, the *Bethel* test, the *Hazelwood* test and the *Morse* test). Consequently, it is fair to expect that the United States Supreme Court might seek to create a new test if new facts – off-campus speech – are presented to it. The Supreme Court of Pennsylvania observed that "the breadth and contour of these cases [the United States Supreme Court's student-speech precedents] and their application to differing circumstances continues to evolve. Moreover, the advent of the Internet has complicated analysis of restrictions on speech" (J.S. v. Bethlehem Area School District, p. 863). As the court poignantly noted, "[o]nly a few courts have considered whether the off-campus posting of email or a web site, and the accessing of the mail or site at school, constitutes on-campus or off-campus speech. These cases have differed in their conclusions" (p. 864). Until the United States Supreme Court clearly rules on off-campus speech, the issue of school-censorship authority will continue to be a difficult one for the lower courts.

Despite the announced difficulty of the issue of off-campus student speech, the Supreme Court of Pennsylvania chose to apply the material and substantial disruption test to the school's censorship of J.S.'s speech (J.S. v. Bethlehem Area School District, 2002). It reasoned that this test was applicable because some courts had already applied this it to off-campus speech. The court chose the material and substantial disruption test despite acknowledging that J.S.'s speech was factually distinct from the speech in the *Tinker* case: "*Tinker's* simple armband, worn silently and brought into a Des Moines, Iowa classroom, has been replaced by J.S.'s complex multi-media web site, accessible to fellow students, teachers, and the world" (J.S. v. Bethlehem Area School District, p. 863). The court also chose the material and substantial disruption test despite emphasizing that the analysis of student-speech censorship cases must begin with a threshold determination of the location of the speech. This was one of the few cases that explicitly required schools to distinguish between the on-campus and off-campus locations of student speech. The court explained that in both Bethel School District No. 403 v. Fraser (1986) and Hazelwood v. Kuhlmeier (1988) Justice Brennan and the Supreme Court respectively had indicated that schools could not censor vulgar off-campus student speech (J.S. v. Bethlehem Area School District, 2002). Accordingly, courts and school districts must acknowledge the distinction between locales of speech. The location of the speech must be examined in order to determine if the speech implicates concerns that are unique to a school setting such as the need for school officials to maintain order and ensure effective education for students. If this analysis reveals that, despite its off-campus nature, the speech would cause material and substantial disruption at the school, the speech would implicate those concerns.

The threshold determination of the speech's location could lead a court to find that the off-campus speech was not purely off-campus speech (J.S. v. Bethlehem Area School District, 2002). For instance, the Supreme Court of Pennsylvania agreed with the school district that J.S.'s access of the website on school grounds converted the off-campus speech into on-campus speech. If off-campus speech is converted to on-campus speech, the United States Supreme Court's student-speech precedents would readily apply to the speech since those precedents themselves involved on-campus speech. According to the Supreme Court of Pennsylvania, a student-speaker can convert speech wholly created off-campus into on-campus speech if the student accesses the speech on school grounds. Additionally, such conversion can occur if the student-speaker shows the speech to at least one student while within the schoolhouse gate. How much of the speech the student accesses on-campus or shows to another student is immaterial. If the student-speaker informs other students of the speech while at school, the student also creates a nexus to the school that converts the speech into on-campus speech. Moreover, even if neither the student-speaker nor any other student accesses the off-campus speech on school grounds, the speech could still be converted into on-campus speech if school officials access the speech on school grounds.

Additionally, as long as the student-speaker somehow facilitates the on-campus access of the speech, the speech would become on-campus speech. Off-campus speech can also be converted into on-campus speech if the speech is aimed at an audience connected to the school.

The Supreme Court of Pennsylvania ruled that "where speech that is aimed at a specific school and/ or its personnel is brought onto the school campus or accessed at school by its originator, the speech will be considered on-campus speech" (J.S. v. Bethlehem Area School District, 2002, p. 866). As we noted earlier, the court did not limit this ruling to the originator (i.e. the student-speaker). Indeed, the court declared:

[W]e do not discount that one who posts school-targeted material in a manner known to be freely accessible from school grounds may run the risk of being deemed to have engaged in on-campus speech, where actual accessing by others in fact occurs, depending upon the totality of the circumstances involved (J.S. v. Bethlehem Area School District, 2002, p. 866).

This should be troubling for students because they have no control over the conversion of their speech rights from an off-campus status to an on-campus status. As the court stated, it only takes one student or school official to access the site on the school's campus in order for off-campus speech to be converted to on-campus speech.

According to the Supreme Court of Pennsylvania, if off-campus speech is reasonably foreseeable to reach the school, the speech would be converted into on-campus speech (J.S. v. Bethlehem Area School District, 2002). While the standard of reasonable foreseeability might seem to protect the off-campus status of students' speech, the standard is hollow; especially because students can always reasonably foresee that their online speech will reach the school. Even when they use privacy settings on their online websites and only share the information with their friends, there is no guarantee that the speech will not reach the school. Besides, reasonable foreseeability is merely one of the myriad of ways that a conversion can occur. We agree with Chief Justice Zappala of the Supreme Court of Pennsylvania that we should be concerned about the "overly broad" reach of the court's decision (p. 870). In fact, the Chief Justice was so concerned about this overreaching that he wrote an entirely separate opinion to raise alarm about it.

In its *Tinker* test analysis, the Supreme Court of Pennsylvania found that J.S.'s speech caused material and substantial disruption within the school (J.S. v. Bethlehem Area School District, 2002). The impact on the algebra teacher's health was foremost in establishing such disruption. Additionally, the teacher had to take a medical leave from the school. Material and substantial disruption was also found in the fact that the school had to hire three substitute teachers just to ensure that students in the algebra class would continue to receive quality education. Furthermore, material and substantial disruption was evident in the fact that some students requested counseling and the website was a major focus of discussions at the school. The court found that material and substantial disruption also occurred because the website heightened some students' concerns about their safeties. The parental outrage over the website's threats to student safety and the educational quality of substitute teachers also constituted material and substantial disruption. Moreover, according to the court, the grave impact of the website on school morale also sufficed as material and substantial disruption of the school. While the court ruled that the infringement-of-rights test was applicable to J.S.'s speech, like several other courts, the court neither applied the test nor expounded upon it (see chapter seven for more on this test).

Despite acknowledging that the circumstances of J.S.'s speech were factually distinct from those in Bethel School District No. 403 v. Fraser (1986), the court ruled that the *Bethel* test was applicable to his speech (J.S. v. Bethlehem Area School District, 2002). Unlike the speech in Bethel School District No. 403 v. Fraser, J.S.'s speech was not before a captive audience of students gathered at an official school function. J.S.'s speech, on the other hand, required viewers to specifically and voluntarily click on the website to access its pages. Even though the Supreme Court of Pennsylvania required that student speech have factual proximity to the speeches in the United States Supreme Court's student-speech precedents before it would apply the pertinent precedent, it ignored its own requirement. Indeed, the court declared that "questions exist as to the applicability of *Fraser* to the instant factual scenario" (p. 868). Despite the lack of factual proximity, the court decided not to explain its rationale for using the *Bethel* test because it was convinced that under either the material and substantial disruption test or the *Bethel* test, the school would be victorious. In other words, since the court already found that school officials had a constitutional right to censor J.S.'s speech under the material and substantial disruption test, it chose not to devote time explaining its *Bethel* test reasoning. Instead, the court cursorily and correctly concluded that the language on J.S.'s website was vulgar and plainly offensive. The court stated that the language J.S. used on the website was at least as vulgar as that used in the *Bethel* case. This is undoubtedly true. While J.S. used words such as "Fuck" and "Bitch" (J.S. v. Bethlehem Area School District, p. 851), the student's speech in the *Bethel* case was much tamer. Recall that the student in the *Bethel* case simply stated that "I know a man who is firm—he's firm in his pants, he's firm in his shirt, his character is firm—but most ... of all, his belief in you, the students of Bethel, is firm. ... 'Jeff is a man who will go to the very end—even the climax, for each and every one of you" (Bethel School District No. 403 v. Fraser, 1986, p. 687).

Under the true-threat doctrine, the Supreme Court of Pennsylvania ruled that, since true threats are unprotected speech irrespective of location, school officials should have the authority to censor off-campus student speech that qualifies as a true threat (J.S. v. Bethlehem Area School District, 2002). Although the United States Supreme Court has never applied the true-threat doctrine to student-speech, the court was persuaded to use the doctrine because some other lower courts had so applied the doctrine (see chapter two for more on the doctrine). Nevertheless, the court indicated that student speech can only be viewed as a true threat if the speech is of a "criminal nature" (p. 859). The court also emphasized that the true-threat doctrine is a very narrow exception to the First Amendment right to free speech. This is even more important in the context of a school because the school is a "laboratory-like setting" for teaching students about the values of free speech (p. 649). The doctrine guards against censorship by allowing people to make threats as long as the threat is not a true threat. The court chose the reasonable-speaker view of true threats for off-campus student speech (see chapter two for further discussion of the reasonable-speaker view).

Under the reasonable-speaker view, courts examine whether the reasonable speaker would reasonably foresee that a listener would reasonably view the speech as a serious expression of intent to inflict harm as opposed to a joke or hyperbole (J.S. v. Bethlehem Area School District, 2002). The court subsumed the reasonable-recipient view into its reasonable-speaker analysis by making the reaction of the listeners a critical factor. The court considered the following factors in its analysis: the nature of J.S.'s comments; the reaction of the listeners; and the context in which he made the comments. The court also considered whether the threats were equivocal or conditional (conditional or equivocal statements cannot be true threats). Other factors used in the court's reasonable-speaker analysis included: whether the threat was communicated directly to the target; whether the student-speaker had expressed similar threats to

Their Stories: Online Off-Campus Speech

the target in the past; and whether the listener had reasonable grounds to believe that the student had a propensity for violence. The court emphasized that the totality of the circumstances must be considered in the reasonable-speaker analysis. This approach effectively allowed the court to use the reasonable-recipient view as a factor within the reasonable-speaker analysis.

The nature and context of J.S.'s comments showed that a reasonable speaker would reasonably foresee that a reasonable viewer would interpret the website as a serious expression of intent to inflict harm. For instance, J.S. asked for donations for a hitman. He also showed the teacher in blood and a headless body. Besides the vitriol directed at the teacher in his various remarks on the website added earnestness to the website's comments directed at the teacher. His decision to write the words "Fuck You Mrs. Fulmer. You Are A Bitch. You Are A Stupid Bitch" one hundred and thirty six times amplified the seriousness (J.S. v. Bethlehem Area School District, 2002, p. 851). Additionally, the algebra teacher had various health issues and took medical leave after viewing the website. J.S.'s threats were also not conditional or equivocal. Nevertheless, the court ruled that J.S.'s speech did not constitute a true threat.

According to the court, the context of the speech supported the conclusion that J.S.'s speech did not constitute a true threat (J.S. v. Bethlehem Area School District, 2002). This context included the fact that visitors to the website indicated that they found the website humorous. Besides, after an investigation, the FBI and local police department decided not to pursue criminal charges against J.S., suggesting that they did not view the website as a true threat. Additionally, school officials never discussed the website with J.S. after its discovery and even after reporting it to law enforcement agencies. Instead, they allowed him to mingle with other students in classrooms, extracurricular activities and a field trip. These facts showed that the school itself did not view the speech serious enough to warrant separating J.S. from other students out of fear of an expectation of harm. School officials also did not require J.S. to undergo counseling. Moreover, the fact that J.S. did not communicate his threats directly to the principal or the algebra teacher – the targets of the website – minimized the threatening nature of the speech.

Further, the court explained that the disclaimer on the website's first page expressed J.S.'s clear intent to prevent disclosure of the website to its targets (J.S. v. Bethlehem Area School District, 2002). There was also no evidence in the record that J.S. had previously expressed similar threats to the website's targets. School officials also failed to articulate reasonable grounds to believe that J.S. had a propensity for violence. Additionally, the court found that J.S.'s use of cartoons and a hand-drawing of the teacher undermined the seriousness of any threats on the webpages. While the use of the cartoon could support a finding that the speech was a joke, the court's reliance on the hand-drawn nature of the picture is curious. The two other curious grounds the court cited for finding the speech to be a joke was the student's decision to attack the teacher's physique and the comparison of the teacher to Adolph Hitler. According to the court, these showed the lightheartedness of the website; therefore, J.S. could not have reasonably foreseen that a reasonable viewer would consider the website as a genuine expression of intent to harm. The court's decision to dismiss the Adolph Hitler comparison as a joke is baffling and unsubstantiated.

Even though the teacher suffered health consequences from the website's contents targeting her, the court perplexingly concluded that:

We believe that the web site, taken as a whole, was a sophomoric, crude, highly offensive and perhaps misguided attempt at humor or parody. However, it did not reflect a serious expression of intent to inflict harm. This conclusion is supported by the fact that the web site focused primarily on Mrs. Fulmer's physique and disposition and utilized cartoon characters, hand drawings, song, and a comparison to Adolph Hitler. While Mrs. Fulmer was offended, certain others did not view it as a serious expression of intent to inflict harm (J.S. v. Bethlehem Area School District, 2002, p. 859).

It appears that the linchpin to the court's decision was its overarching view that true threats have a criminal nature, even in the case of student speech. The law enforcement agencies' decision not to pursue criminal charges against J.S. seemed critical. It undermined any argument that J.S.'s speech had a criminal nature. When this linchpin is considered with all the other circumstances the court examined, the court's conclusion that J.S.'s off-campus speech was not a true threat becomes less perplexing.

6. The Story of O.Z.

The Speech Incident: The Slideshow – The Killing of the English Teacher

In March 2008, O.Z., a seventh-grade student at Hughes Middle School in California, created a slideshow with a classmate while they were on their spring break vacation (O.Z. v. Board of Trustees of Long Beach Unified School District, 2008). The slideshow presented in dramatic fashion the murder of their English teacher. The students used no school resource in the creation of the slide show which they uploaded on to YouTube under the title "[O.Z.] Kills Mrs. Rosenlof" (p. 1). The photographs of the teacher featured in the slideshow were actually photographs of O.Z. made to look like the teacher. The students used red text on each of their slide photographs presumably to represent blood. In their first slide photograph, they included the words "Mrs. Rosenlof dies" (p. 1). In another slide photograph, they included the words "Jelly Donut's knife: haha fat bastard. here i come!" (p. 1). This same slide photograph showed a butcher knife targeting the teacher as if she was about to be stabbed. They also included a photograph that showed the teacher dead with the butcher knife on top of her. In this slide photograph, they included the words "hehehe. i'm a shank yoooooooooo!" (p. 1). They concluded the slideshow with the words "your [sic] dead, BITCH!:D" (p. 1).

About two months after the slideshow was created, the targeted teacher discovered the YouTube video while she was "Googling" her name at home (O.Z. v. Board of Trustees of Long Beach Unified School District, 2008). The following description next to the slide show caught her attention:

[O.Z.], a student of Ms. Rosenlof, kills her over YouTube somehow. This video shows the video of Ms. Rosenlof dying. This was made by [O.Z.] and [Student 2] in her first and second period classes (O.Z. v. Board of Trustees of Long Beach Unified School District, 2008, p. 1).

The teacher was so troubled by the video that she reported the video to the principal the next day, even though it was a Saturday (O.Z. v. Board of Trustees of Long Beach Unified School District, 2008). She also became physically ill and sleepless for many nights because of the video's contents. After the principal concluded his investigation, he suspended O.Z. from school and transferred him to another school for eighth grade. O.Z.'s mother sued the school district seeking injunctive relief. She claimed that the school district violated O.Z.'s First Amendment right to free speech.

Analysis

The United States District Court for the Central District of California ruled that the material and substantial disruption test governs off-campus student speech that can be reasonably interpreted as a threat of violence (O.Z. v. Board of Trustees of Long Beach Unified School District, 2008). While this rule might read like a merger of the material and substantial disruption test and the true-threat doctrine, that would be a misreading. This is because, in actuality, the court chose not to apply the true-threat doctrine: "the Court need not ask whether this slide show was a 'true threat,' because the Court concludes that even if the slide show was protected speech, the school's actions were justified" (p. 2). Even though the court was aware that the true-threat doctrine traditionally governs the censorship of threats by citizens, it instead opted for a test that is a staple of student-speech jurisprudence – the material and substantial disruption test. As we noted in chapter two, unlike the material and substantial disruption test, the United States Supreme Court has never applied the true-threat doctrine to student speech. The district court also chose not to apply the true-threat doctrine because it concluded that the school would be victorious under either the true-threat doctrine or the material and substantial disruption test. There was no reason to bring a doctrine that is outside the United States Supreme Court's student-speech precedents into the student-speech jurisprudence. The court's decision to use the rationale of school victory is not completely remarkable; particularly because the court expressed a preference for judicial deference to schools unless the First Amendment violation is indubitable. The court stated that "[a] court's interference with the school's disciplinary decisions in this case would undermine the administration of the school and encourage parents to simply file suit if they are unhappy with a school's disciplinary action" (p. 6).

The court's decision to apply the material and substantial disruption test to O.Z.'s off-campus speech, despite its off-campus nature, suggests that the court does not see geographic limitations to the test (O.Z. v. Board of Trustees of Long Beach Unified School District, 2008). This is buttressed by the fact that the court failed to acknowledge that the material and substantial disruption test arose in an on-campus context which would distinguish it from O.Z.'s speech which was entirely off-campus. Not only did O.Z. create the speech outside school, he did so during spring break when he had no obligation to the school. Moreover, the teacher discovered the video while she was at home. There was no evidence that any student or teacher accessed the video on-campus or that O.Z. encouraged such access. The court ruled that, even though O.Z. did not intend for any student other than his collaborator to see the video, it was reasonably foreseeable that such speech would impact the school. Accordingly, "the fact that Plaintiff's creation and transmission of the slide show occurred away from school property does not necessarily insulate her from school discipline" (p. 4).

The district court emphasized that school officials only needed reasonable forecast of material and substantial disruption from O.Z.'s off-campus speech in order to censor it (O.Z. v. Board of Trustees of Long Beach Unified School District, 2008). Consequently, it was immaterial that the speech caused no actual disruption at the school. Even though O.Z. expressed regret for the speech and claimed that the entire video was a joke, the court concluded that the violent language and photographs in the slideshow provided reasonable grounds for a forecast of material and substantial disruption. Based on the language and the photographs, school officials were justified to take action against O.Z. in order to protect the teacher. The language and photographs also provided grounds for school officials to reasonably forecast that the teacher could face physical attack from O.Z. The school could also have reasonably forecast that other students would ridicule the teacher once they learned of the video. According to the court, any such ridicule of the teacher would have caused material and substantial disruption at the school. While the court's ruling that ridicule of the teacher could lead to material and substantial disruption is surprising, it is understandable; especially, if viewed in the context of the physical illness the teacher suffered as a result of the video. In other words, if the physically-ill teacher were ridiculed at the school, things could escalate to the point where material and substantial disruption ensues. It must be noted that the court did not rule that ridicule itself would constitute material and substantial disruption; only that ridicule could lead to such disruption. The court's decision to apply the material and substantial disruption test without amending it for off-campus speech supports our conclusion that the court views the test as borderless.

7. The Story of Avery Doninger

The Speech Incident: The "Douchebag" Blog Posting

Avery Doninger, a junior at Lewis S. Mills High School in Connecticut, was her school's junior class secretary and served on the student council (Doninger v. Niehoff, 2007). In her role on the student council, she worked with other members of the council to organize Jamfest – an annual musical festival in which different bands performed. This festival traditionally occurred in the school auditoriums. However, during the 2005-06 school year, it was held in the cafeteria because the auditorium was unavailable due to construction. The cafeteria was not ample for the festival, however, because it was only designed for acoustic performances (as opposed to the electrical performances that the bands preferred). The auditorium's construction delayed the 2006-07 school year's Jamfest twice. When the new auditorium opened during the spring semester, Avery and her colleagues received administrative approval to move the festival back to the auditorium for an April 28, 2007 Jamfest.

About three weeks prior to Jamfest, however, Avery was informed that the festival could not be held in the auditorium because the teacher-coordinator for the auditorium's sound and light systems would be unavailable (Doninger v. Niehoff, 2007). This late notice made it challenging to properly plan for alternatives as it came just before students left for school on spring break which started on April 6. Avery and her student-council colleagues proposed hiring an external technician or recruiting a parent to supervise the sound and light system. The principal declined their proposals, however, just four days before Jamfest, He explained that the school board policy allowed only the teacher-coordinator to operate the sound and light system. The venue change greatly frustrated Avery and her colleagues. They were concerned that the change would require a complete overhaul of their band sets within a four-day window, something they worried could not be done. It also meant that they would have to perform acoustics again. They were further concerned that, since the school year was ending, they might not be able to reschedule Jamfest for that academic year. Besides, there was no guarantee that all the invited bands would be able to attend on a rescheduled date. Avery and her colleagues were also worried that some of the bands would choose not to participate because they had previously been rescheduled twice.

On the same morning that Avery and her student-council colleagues learned of the venue change, they sent out a mass email to taxpayers (Doninger v. Niehoff, 2007). In the email, they explained the situation surrounding the venue change. They also asked taxpayers to contact the superintendent to demand the auditorium for April 28, 2007 for Jamfest. In addition, they asked the taxpayers to forward the email to other taxpayers. Avery and her colleagues sent the email from the school's computer lab using the personal email account of one of their parents. The list of addresses used for the email came from this parent's email as well as Avery. Avery and her colleagues signed the email in their real names. Avery claimed that the student council's faculty advisor suggested the mass emails as a way to rally taxpayer

Their Stories: Online Off-Campus Speech

support after she and her colleagues failed to secure a meeting with the principal. According to Avery, the advisor told them that this was the proper course because the auditorium was taxpayer funded. The advisor denied this assertion. She claimed that she merely told the students to speak to their parents, not taxpayers, about it. She insisted that her only other recommendation was that the students draft a list of rationales for presentation to the principal and the superintendent highlighting the paramountcy of the auditorium. More student-council members supported the teacher's account more closely than they did Avery's; thus, the court accorded greater credence to the teacher's account.

The superintendent as well as the principal received several phone calls and emails about the auditorium from taxpayers, including Avery's mother (Doninger v. Niehoff, 2007). The superintendent unsuccessfully tried to explain the school's rationale for the venue change to Avery's mother. The mass emails from Avery and her student-council colleagues as well as the resulting torrent of calls from taxpayers upset the superintendent and the principal. Accordingly, the principal asked Avery and her colleagues to write a letter of apology to the superintendent. She also told the students that their use of the school computer lab to send personal emails violated the school's internet policy. She informed them that the school had always been willing, and remained willing, to reschedule Jamfest for the auditorium. She then required them to email taxpayers to correct any information in the mass emails that might have suggested otherwise. Additionally, she instructed them to avoid mass emails. She told them that such emails were not an acceptable or proper means of addressing student disagreements or grievances against school officials. She informed them that the school expected its student officers to speak directly with school administrators about their disagreements or concerns about administrative decisions.

When Avery returned home that day, she was still upset about the events that transpired at the school (Doninger v. Niehoff, 2007). As a result, she decided to post an entry on her personal blog at livejournal.com expressing her views about the venue change. Avery used no school resource in the blog posting. She used a privacy setting on her blog that allowed any member of the public to see her posting. Further, Avery intended for her schoolmates to see the blog posting and for them to respond to it. In her blog posting, Avery stated:

… jamfest is cancelled due to douchebags in central office. … basically, because we sent [the original Jamfest email] out, Paula Schwartz [the superintendent] is getting a TON of phone calls and emails and such. … however, she got pissed off and decided to just cancel the whole thing all together, anddd [sic] so basically we aren't going to have it at all, but in the slightest chance we do[,] it is going to be after the talent show on may 18th (Doninger v. Niehoff, 2007, p. 206).

She also included in her posting the mass email that she and her colleagues previously sent to taxpayers as well as the email her mother sent to the superintendent complaining about the venue change (Doninger v. Niehoff, 2007). She urged her readers, including her schoolmates, to refer to these two emails in order to "get an idea of what to write if you want to write something or call [the superintendent] to piss her off more" (p. 206). One of the several students who responded to Avery's posting blogged that the superintendent was a "dirty whore" (p. 207).

Students believed Avery's blog assertion that Jamfest had been cancelled (Doninger v. Niehoff, 2008). Therefore, the following day, April 25th, they were "all riled up" and planned a sit-in (p. 51). That same day, school officials who were unaware of the blog posting offered to hold Jamfest on April 28th in the cafeteria or June 8th in the auditorium (Doninger v. Niehoff, 2007). Given that the students really wanted the auditorium, for the various reasons noted earlier, they chose the latter date. The superintendent as well as the principal reiterated to Avery and her student-council colleagues that student officers should not use mass emails to express disagreement with school officials' decisions. After this meeting, school officials continued to receive phone calls and emails from taxpayers about the auditorium. The superintendent and principal's schedules were disrupted because they had to address issues surrounding the phone calls and emails.

The superintendent learned of the blog on May 7th and sent the link to the principal (Doninger v. Niehoff, 2008). The principal, however, waited until May 17th, after Avery's advanced placement examinations, to confront her. She required Avery to write an apology letter to the superintendent for the blog posting. She also required Avery to show the posting to her mother. In addition, the principal asked Avery to withdraw her candidacy for the senior class secretary. After she refused, the principal withheld her administrative endorsement of Avery's candidacy, effectively barring her from running for the position. This also meant that Avery would be ineligible to speak at graduation. Avery was, however, allowed to remain junior class secretary and to serve out her term on the student council. Despite the decision to eliminate Avery from the ballot for senior class secretary, she won a plurality of the votes through a write-in campaign that several of her classmates organized. Nevertheless, the school gave the position to the second-place candidate (Doninger v. Niehoff, 2007).

The principal explained that the discipline was justified because the posting used vulgar language (Doninger v. Niehoff, 2007). It was also misleading because it suggested that Jamfest had been cancelled. The principal also stated that Avery failed to comply with the principal's earlier admonishment about the appropriate means for school officers to communicate disagreements with administrative decisions. Avery's mother conceded that the blog posting was offensive but asked the principal to reconsider the discipline because it was overly harsh. The principal rejected Avery's mother's request for an alternate punishment – barring Avery from involvement with Jamfest for the rest of her time at the school. Avery's mother then filed a First Amendment claim against the school district that sought monetary damages and injunctive relief. She asked the court to order school officials to run a new senior class secretary election in which Avery would be eligible. As an alternative, she asked the court to require Avery's appointment, alongside the second-place candidate, as senior class secretary.

Analysis

The United States Court of Appeals for the Second Circuit acknowledged that, because the United States Supreme Court has never ruled on off-campus student speech, the jurisprudence is unclear (Doninger v. Niehoff, 2008). Nevertheless, the court ruled that school officials can censor students' off-campus speech under the material and substantial disruption test even without the speech actually getting to campus. All they need to show is that the materially and substantially disruptive speech was reasonably foreseeable to reach the school (this is a modification of the material and substantial disruption test). Off-campus speech can certainly pose a foreseeable risk of on-campus material and substantial disruption without the speech itself getting on school grounds. Thus the modified test is sensible if a court, as in this case, is willing to extend school-censorship authority. The court emphasized that under the modified material and substantial disruption test, schools do not need to wait for actual disruption either. If the school can show that the off-campus speech is reasonably likely to cause material and substantial disruption inside the school house gate, the school's censorship authority will be triggered under the modified test. In essence, reasonable foreseeability underscores the modified approach: reasonable foreseeability to reach campus and reasonable foreseeability of material and substantial disruption.

Their Stories: Online Off-Campus Speech

According to the federal circuit court of appeals, school-censorship authority must extend beyond the schoolhouse gate because digital communication modes have made geographical boundaries insignificant in the student-speech jurisprudence (Doninger v. Niehoff, 2008). In this borderless digital terrain, the modified material and substantial disruption test provides a nexus between the school and the off-campus. This nexus helps ensure that schools do not exercise authority over speech that is unrelated to the school's campus. Another rationale for the modification in the material and substantial disruption test – reasonably foreseeability that the speech would get onto the school grounds – might be to ensure that the speaker can reasonable foresee that the speech would come to the attention of school officials. In other words, it preserves fair warning of administrative discipline for the student. Furthermore, the modification adds another layer to the stringency of the material and substantial disruption test. Specifically, it requires the school to not only show actual or reasonable forecast material and substantial disruption but also requires that the speech's presence on-campus be reasonably foreseeable. In other words, even if speech is reasonably forecast to cause material and substantial disruption, it cannot be censored by a school unless school officials prove that the speech is reasonably foreseeable to get on-campus. It is immaterial that the speech actually does not make it to the campus; all that is required is reasonable foreseeability that it could. An indicium of reasonable foreseeability of an on-campus presence is the intent of the student-speaker. Off-campus speech would be deemed reasonably likely to get to the school's campus if the student-speaker intended the speech to be read by her schoolmates or other members of the school's community. Another indicium is the subject matter of the speech: if the speech addresses issues directly related to activities at the school, the court is likely to find it reasonably foreseeable that the speech would reach school grounds.

Pursuant to the modified material and substantial disruption test, the United States Court of Appeals for the Second Circuit ruled that the school had authority to censor Avery's off-campus speech (Doninger v. Niehoff, 2008). Since Avery intended for her schoolmates to read her blog posting, it was reasonably foreseeable that student readers would take the speech to campus. Indeed, several students responded to the blog posting. Avery also encouraged readers of the blog posting to contact the superintendent using information in her posting. Moreover, her subject matter directly related to activities at the school, supporting the conclusion that the speech was reasonably likely to reach the school. Besides, the blog actually reached the school when it was brought to the attention of the superintendent as well as the principal.

Avery's speech also satisfied the other component of the modified material and substantial disruption test – reasonable foreseeability of material and substantial disruption at the school (Doninger v. Niehoff, 2008). The plainly-offensive language Avery used in urging readers to contact the superintendent supported a finding that the speech was reasonably likely to cause material and substantial disruption at the school (Doninger v. Niehoff, 2008). For instance, Avery urged readers to write the superintendent "to piss her off more" (Doninger v. Niehoff, 2007, p. 206). This language likely inspired one of the student-readers to call the superintendent a "dirty whore" (p. 207). As the court observed, Avery also referred to the superintendent and other school officials as "douchebags in central office" (Doninger v. Niehoff, 2008, p. 51). These salty words in Avery's posting "were hardly conducive to cooperative conflict resolution" (p. 51). They could simply inflame passions that could materially and substantially disrupt the school.

The court also found that Avery included inaccurate information in the posting in order to inflame students' anger (Doninger v. Niehoff, 2008). Specifically, Avery indicated that Jamfest had been cancelled, even though the principal previously informed her that she was flexible about rescheduling in order to accommodate the use of the auditorium. Since students believed the blog's assertion that the festival had been cancelled, they were exasperated and planned a sit-in that threatened material and substantial disruption. The court rightly concluded that it was reasonably foreseeable that school officials would have to take time away from other functions in order to address the misinformation spread through the blog. Indeed, the superintendent and the principal had their schedules disrupted as they responded to the torrent of calls, emails and other issues surrounding Avery's speech. The court ruled that, even if the actual disruption on the school's campus resulted from the mass emails rather than the blog posting, this did not change the fact that school officials could reasonably foresee material and substantial disruption from the blog. In other words, *actual* material and substantial disruption from the *mass emails* is not mutually exclusive of or diametrically opposed to a finding of reasonable foreseeability of material and substantial disruption from the *blog*. Recall, the material and substantial disruption test is satisfied with *reasonable foreseeability* of material and substantial disruption, even in the absence of actual material and substantial disruption.

The court ruled that Avery's positions as a student-council member and as junior class secretary were material to analysis of student speech under the material and substantial disruption test (Doninger v. Niehoff, 2008). According to the court, since Avery was a school officer, her speech risked material and substantial disruption through "frustration of the proper operation of LMHS's [Lewis S. Mills High School] student government and undermining of the values that student government, as an extracurricular activity, is designed to promote" (p. 52). Further, student officers, as representatives of the school and other students, must uphold the responsibility of their privileged positions, both on and off campus, as they are role models for other students. The court explained that Avery abused the privilege to hold her position when she included misleading information in her posting as well as when she tried to undermine school officials through the tenor of her speech. Moreover, she defied the admonishment of her principal earlier in the day about inappropriate ways to communicate disagreement with school officials by posting the blog the very same evening. Consequently, the school could censor Avery's off-campus speech, in her role as a school officer, because she materially and substantially disrupted the school's student-government expectations; especially, the expectations of good citizenship inside the schoolhouse gate as well as outside it. The court stated that "we have no occasion to consider whether a different, more serious consequence than disqualification from student office would raise constitutional concerns" (p. 53). This implied that student officers' off-campus speech are subject to gradations of censorship. In other words, disqualification from office might not raise the same constitutional censorship concerns as some other forms of censorship. However, since the court failed to define the contours of those gradations and no other court has defined them either or even implied such gradations, the court's outlook here is a mystery.

The court did not foreclose application of the *Bethel* test to student off-campus speech (Doninger v. Niehoff, 2008). In fact, the court stated that "[v]ulgar or offensive speech—speech that an adult making a political point might have a constitutional right to employ—may legitimately give rise to disciplinary action by a school" (p. 48). Despite this broad statement, the court conceded that "[i]t is not clear, however, that *Fraser* [Bethel School District No. 403 v. Fraser (1986)] applies to off-campus speech" (Doninger v. Niehoff, p. 49). While Avery's speech included vulgar and plainly-offensive speech (douchebag and "piss her off more") that are censorable inside the schoolhouse gate, it is unclear that a school could regulate such speech off-campus (Doninger v. Niehoff, 2007, p. 206). Both Bethel School District No. 403 v. Fraser (1986) and Hazelwood v. Kuhlmeier (1988) (discussed in chapters eight and nine) indicated that schools are not constitutionally authorized to censor vulgar off-campus student speech. Justice Brennan stated, and the Supreme Court endorsed the view, that school officials would not have been constitutionally authorized to censor the on-campus speech in the *Bethel* case if it had been delivered off-campus. Avery's speech was not necessarily more vulgar than the speech in the *Bethel* case. The circuit court of appeals needs to tread carefully and pay close attention to those two Supreme Court precedents – Bethel School District No. 403 v. Fraser and Hazelwood v. Kuhlmeier, even though they involved on-campus speech. These precedents' ostensible reluctance to extend the *Bethel* test to off-campus vulgar speech should give the circuit court of appeals pause in determining whether to extend the test to off-campus speech. As we noted earlier, the court failed to rule out extension of the *Bethel* test to off-campus speech. While the court successfully and conveniently avoided making the tough decision about the *Bethel* test's applicability to off-campus speech in this case, another opportunity will be presented to the court in the future. In such a case, the court might not be able to avoid making the tough decision. We have to wait for such a case, however, to get any clarity on the court's thinking. In the interim, the court's view of the *Bethel* test's scope will remain a puzzler.

8. The Story of Aaron Wisniewski

The Speech Incident: The Instant Message, Pistol, and Splattered Blood

In the course of the 2001 spring semester, school officials at Weedsport Middle School in New York told students that they would no longer condone students' use of threatening language (Wisniewski v. Board of Education of the Weedsport Central School District, 2007). They warned students that any threat would be considered a violent act and punished accordingly. A few weeks after this warning, Aaron Wisniewski (an eighth-grade student at the school) used his personal computer, while inside his home, to create an icon featuring a pistol and splattered blood. The icon presumably showed the demise of Aaron's English teacher. The icon portrayed a human head above the words "Kill Mr. VanderMolen [Aaron's teacher]" (p. 36). It also included a pistol shooting directly at the teacher's head with dots signifying blood squirts above the head. Aaron used the icon as the identifier for his America Online (AOL) Instant Messaging (IM) account. Aaron never showed the icon to the English teacher or any other school official.

Since AOL allowed IM participants (known as "buddies") to see each other's icon during their communications, Aaron was able to share the gory icon with his buddies (Wisniewski v. Board of Education of the Weedsport Central School District, 2007). Indeed, for three weeks, Aaron used the icon during IM exchanges with about fifteen buddies, some of whom were his classmates. Ultimately, a student outside of Aaron's buddy list learned of the icon. This student brought the icon to school and showed it to the English teacher who, fearing for his safety, reported it to school administrators. The administrators granted the teacher's request to no longer teach Aaron's class. Consequently, the school had to find a replacement teacher. School officials notified the local police department about the icon. The police, however, decided not to press charges because that they found that the icon was a joke and that Aaron was not a threat to anyone, including the English teacher. A psychologist found similarly. Aaron apologized to school officials for creating the icon and for communicating it to his buddies. Nonetheless, they suspended him from school for five days. The suspension was subsequently increased to a full-semester suspension to be served in the 2001 fall semester. The ensuing community outrage directed at Aaron's icon prompted his family to move to another city. His parents sued the school district for monetary damages claiming a First Amendment violation of his right to free speech.

Analysis

The United States Court of Appeals for the Second Circuit ruled that off-campus student speech is within the censorship purview of schools (Wisniewski v. Board of Education of the Weedsport Central School District, 2007). The court ruled that off-campus student speech is censorable under the material and substantial disruption test as long as it is reasonably foreseeable that the speech would be brought to the attention of school officials. In other words, the court ruled that schools can censor off-campus student speech under a modified material and substantial disruption test. Recall that in some cases, such as J.S. v. Bethlehem Area School District (2002) discussed earlier in this chapter, courts converted off-campus speech to on-campus speech based on the reasonably foreseeability of the speech getting to the school. Unlike these courts, the federal circuit court did not sanction such a conversion.

The circuit court of appeals was divided, however, on whether speech *actually* had to reach the school's campus or whether reasonable foreseeability that the speech would reach the school's campus should suffice to trigger the material and substantial disruption test (Wisniewski v. Board of Education of the Weedsport Central School District, 2007). Apparently, the panel of judges came to a compromise by merely requiring reasonable foreseeability that the speech would be brought to the attention of school officials. This modification to the material and substantial disruption test means that, even if a student-speaker cannot reasonably foresee that her speech would get to the school, the school can censor the speech under the test; as long as it was reasonably foreseeable that the speech would be brought to the attention of school officials. It also means that, even if a student's speech does not actually reach the school's campus, the school can censor the speech as long as it was reasonably foreseeable that the speech would be brought to the attention of school officials. It is immaterial that the student-speaker had no intention of bringing the speech to the attention of school officials.

The court found that Aaron's speech satisfied the modified material and substantial disruption test (Wisniewski v. Board of Education of the Weedsport Central School District, 2007). It was reasonably foreseeable that the icon would be brought to the attention of school officials because Aaron shared the icon with fifteen IM participants which included his classmates. He also made it viewable for three weeks, increasing the likelihood that someone would bring it to the attention of school officials, including the English teacher. Furthermore, the court found that it was reasonably foreseeable that Aaron's speech would lead to material and substantial disruption at the school. It was reasonably foreseeable that the speech would impact the threatened English teacher; and cause him not to want to teach a class in which Aaron was a student. It was also reasonably foreseeable that the school would be forced to find a replacement for the English teacher because of the speech's impact on him. However, these appear too de minimis to constitute material and substantial disruption. The English teacher merely transferred from one class to another. He did not take medical leave or suffer health consequences to our knowledge. It is was also not out of the ordinary that the school looked for a replacement teacher. Schools routinely have to find replacement teachers for myriad reasons. Therefore, Aaron's speech did not cause anything out of the norm. Besides, the court ignored the police department's conclusion that Aaron was merely joking. Since the police determined that Aaron was not a threat and that he simply tried to be humorous, presumably, a reasonable person communicating facetiously through an icon like Aaron's would not have foreseen that the icon would cause material and substantial disruption at the school.

The federal court of appeals ruled that the true-threat doctrine was inapplicable to Aaron's speech (Wisniewski v. Board of Education of the Weedsport Central School District, 2007). According to the court, the true-threat doctrine is limited to cases where speech is criminalized as a true threat rather than merely school-censored. The court explained that the context of Watts v. United States (1969) – the first United States Supreme Court decision on true threats – justified its ruling. As the court rightly observed, that case involved criminalized speech outside the schoolhouse gate (Wisniewski v. Board of Education of the Weedsport Central School District, 2007). Even though, as highlighted in chapter two of this book, some lower courts have applied the true-threat doctrine to school censorship of student speech, the second circuit court of appeals was unpersuaded. The key concern for the court was that the United States Supreme Court itself had not extended the doctrine to censorship of student speech. This is sound reasoning because it is yet unclear that the Supreme Court would want the doctrine extended to student speech. However, since students are citizens like other adults outside the schoolhouse gate, they are governed by the true-threat doctrine. Therefore, law enforcement officials can arrest and prosecute students for true threats. Consequently, while the court's reasoning is sound, it is unpersuasive. The doctrine already applies to students outside the schoolhouse gate; therefore, the court's failure to acknowledge its applicability is immaterial. Since the doctrine governs students outside the schoolhouse gate, when they make true threats, the speech is unprotected and subject to the full censorship authority of the government, including schools.

Another reason that the federal court of appeals decided not to apply the true-threat doctrine was because school officials have greater censorship authority under the material and substantial disruption test than they would have under the true-threat doctrine (Wisniewski v. Board of Education of the Weedsport Central School District, 2007). According to the court, this broader authority would enable school officials to maintain order in the school at a level that they would be unable to under the true-threat doctrine. The true-threat doctrine only allows censorship of speech that is considered a genuine threat. The material and substantial disruption test, however, allows censorship of any speech that is reasonably forecast to or actually causes material and substantial disruption in the school. The presumption is that the true-threat doctrine would not allow censorship of speech that constitutes a threat (but not a true threat) which causes material and substantial disruption. While this is accurate, it is only partially so. It is also true that speech that creates material and substantial disruption does not necessarily constitute a true threat. The problem with this reasoning is that the true-threat doctrine and the material and substantial disruption are not mutually exclusive or diametrically opposed. They can coexist. In other words, a school can censor speech under both the true-threat doctrine and the material and substantial disruption. If the true-threat doctrine does not allow the censorship, the school could simply use the material and substantial disruption test. Thus, the court's decision to rely on the rationale of greater censorship authority under the material and substantial disruption test is weak.

The court's rationale that the material and substantial disruption test provides "significantly broader authority" than the true-threat doctrine faces another problem which further weakens the rationale (Wisniewski v. Board of Education of the Weedsport Central School District, 2007, p. 38). The true-threat doctrine might actually give school officials relatively more censorship authority over student speech than the material and substantial disruption test. This is because speech that is deemed a true threat is unprotected on-campus as well as off-campus. Whereas Tinker v. Des Moines Independent Community School District (1969) which provides the context for the material and substantial disruption test suggests that the test might be limited to on-campus speech. Since the combination of on-campus and off-campus speech is broader than merely on-campus speech, the true-threat doctrine might actually give schools more censorship authority over student speech.

Even though the court chose not to apply the true-threat doctrine, its decision to authorize censorship of off-campus speech under the material and substantial disruption test expands the scope of school authority. This is because school officials can now censor off-campus speech even when the speech could not reasonably be foreseen to reach the school's campus. It particularly puts off-campus online speech at risk because, with the ubiquitous nature of the internet, any online student speech could be reasonably foreseen to get to the school's attention; even if the speech itself never gets inside the schoolhouse gate. The court also significantly increased school authority over off-campus speech through its decision to find the replacement hiring for the English teacher along with the teacher's distress at the speech materially and substantially disruptive. This dilutes the material and substantial disruption test in contravention of the United States Supreme Court's ruling in Tinker v. Des Moines Independent Community School District (1969) that undifferentiated fear or discomfort of speech should not justify censorship of controversial student speech. The First Amendment future of student speech is bleak if schools are allowed to censor speech merely because of discomfort with the speech since discomfort is a malleable concept.

9. The Story of Joshua Mahaffey

The Speech Incident: Satan's Webpage

Joshua Mahaffey and another student at Waterford Kettering High School in Michigan collaborated to create a website which they called "Satan's web page" (Mahaffey ex rel. Mahaffey v. Aldrich, 2002, p. 781). Joshua claimed that the website was created out of boredom "for laughs" (p. 781). The main architect of the website was the other student though Joshua contributed to the website. A parent of one of Joshua's schoolmates discovered the website and reported it to the police who in turn informed the school. Joshua revealed to the police that the school's computers "may have been used to create the website" (p. 782). There was no evidence, however, that Joshua told other students about the website or that he intended for them to see it. Indeed, he insisted that he did not want "anyone else to see it" (p. 786). The introductory section of the website read in pertinent part:

This site has no purpose. It is here to say what is cool, and what sucks. For example, Music is cool. School sucks. If you are reading this you probably know me and Think Im [sic] evil, sick and twisted. Well, Some [sic] might call it evil. I like to call it__ well evil I guess. so [sic] what? If you don't know me you will see. I hope you enjoy the page (Mahaffey ex rel. Mahaffey v. Aldrich, 2002, pp. 781-82).

The website covered several topics including "movies that rock"; "music I hate"; and "music that is cool" (Mahaffey ex rel. Mahaffey v. Aldrich, 2002, p. 782). It also provided a list of the "people I wish would die" and the "people that are cool" (p. 782). The end of the website included the following language about stabbing someone along with the disclaimer:

SATAN'S MISSION FOR YOU THIS

WEEK: Stab someone for no reason then set them on fire throw them off of a cliff, watch them suffer and with their last breath, just before everything goes black, spit on their face. Killing people is wrong don't do It [sic]. unless [sic] Im [sic] there to watch. __ Or just go to Detroit. Hell is right in the middle. Drop by and say hi.

Their Stories: Online Off-Campus Speech

PS: NOW THAT YOU'VE READ MY WEB PAGE PLEASE DON'T GO KILLING PEOPLE AND STUFF THEN BLAMING IT ON ME. OK? (Mahaffey ex rel. Mahaffey v. Aldrich, 2002, p. 782).

After school officials learned about the website, they placed Joshua on a short-term suspension from school (Mahaffey ex rel. Mahaffey v. Aldrich, 2002). They also informed Joshua and his parents that the district planned to expel him. The expulsion hearing was cancelled, however, after Joshua's parents enrolled him in another district because the district viewed this enrollment as a withdrawal from the district. Joshua's parents, however, claimed that the enrollment was necessary to ensuring that Joshua's education did not suffer. After school officials held a hearing to consider Joshua's parents request to re-enroll him in the district, they decided not to expel Joshua. As a result of Joshua's enrollment in the other district, the delay in the hearings and the time of the hearings, his short-term suspension effectively only lasted till the beginning of the spring semester. Joshua, however, remained enrolled in the other district till he graduated. His parents filed a First Amendment suit against the school district seeking equitable relief.

Analysis

Even though the United States District Court for the Eastern District of Michigan clearly recognized that the material and substantial disruption test was created in an on-campus context, the court reluctantly chose to apply the test to Joshua's speech (Mahaffey ex rel. Mahaffey v. Aldrich, 2002). The reluctance arose from concern that extending the material and substantial disruption test beyond its on-campus origins to off-campus speech would be overreaching. In spite of this concern, the court decided to extend the material and substantial disruption test off-campus because other courts, such as J.S. v. Bethlehem Area School District (2002) (discussed earlier in this chapter), had applied the test to off-campus speech. This case was not like some other cases in which off-campus speech was converted into on-campus speech in order to apply the material and substantial disruption test. In fact, the court emphasized that Joshua's speech was off-campus speech. His statement to the police about their use of school computers for the website's creation did not change the website into on-campus speech. The court explained that Joshua's use of the word "may" in the police statement made the statement at best "equivocal" (Mahaffey ex rel. Mahaffey v. Aldrich, p. 784). Besides, the school's failure to investigate the veracity of Joshua's statement or search the school computers to verify on-campus access undermined the credibility of the statement. Presumably, if the investigation had shown that the speech was accessed on school grounds, the court would have found that sufficient to convert Joshua's off-campus speech to on-campus speech. Thus, even though the court did not convert Joshua's off-campus speech to on-campus speech, it did not necessarily foreclose such a possibility.

The federal district court found no evidence in the record that Joshua's speech caused material and substantial disruption at the school (Mahaffey ex rel. Mahaffey v. Aldrich, 2002). The glaring disclaimer on the website also counseled against finding reasonable foreseeability of material and substantial disruption. Further, as the court pointed out, Joshua had no history of material and substantial disruption that would have provided reasonable grounds to forecast material and substantial disruption. Additionally, the court observed that Joshua's speech was unlike J.S. v. Bethlehem Area School District (2002) where material and substantial disruption was found. Specifically, unlike in J.S. v. Bethlehem Area School District, no one had health issues or took medical leave as a result of Joshua's speech (Mahaffey ex rel.

Mahaffey v. Aldrich, 2002). The court also found that Joshua's speech did not encourage anyone to take specific steps to materially and substantially disrupt the school. The prominence of the disclaimer apparently inspired this conclusion. Recall, the disclaimer stated in large caps: "PS: NOW THAT YOU'VE READ MY WEB PAGE PLEASE DON'T GO KILLING PEOPLE AND STUFF THEN BLAMING IT ON ME. OK?" (p. 782). We can conclude from this that glaring student disclaimers on websites could impact judicial interpretation of the speech for purposes of the material and substantial disruption test. A disclaimer, however, is unlikely to help speech retain its off-campus status if the speech is accessed on school grounds. It is also likely that if the speech is accessed outside the schoolhouse gate using the school's computer, the court would view the speech as on-campus speech. The court ruled that the school district's censorship of Joshua's "speech on the website without any proof of disruption to the school or on campus activity in the creation of the website was a violation of Plaintiff's First Amendment rights" (p. 786). This ruling encapsulated the court's view about how schools could constitutionally censor off-campus speech under the United States Supreme Court's student-speech precedents. Of course, if off-campus speech is converted to on-campus speech, there would be no controversy in applying those Supreme Court on-campus speech precedents to their proper contexts – on-campus speech.

The district court applied the reasonable recipient view of the true-threat doctrine to Joshua's off-campus speech (Mahaffey ex rel. Mahaffey v. Aldrich, 2002). This view examines whether "a reasonable person would foresee that the statement would be interpreted by those to whom the maker communicates the statement as a serious expression of an intention to inflict bodily harm upon or take the life of [the target]" (p. 785, citing United States v. Lineberry, 2001, p. 524; United States v. Lincoln, 1972, p. 1369). Given that Joshua had no intention of threatening the school, it was not reasonably foreseeable that the website would be interpreted as a threat (Mahaffey ex rel. Mahaffey v. Aldrich, 2002). Besides, Joshua included a clear disclaimer of violence on the website. The court noted that Joshua did not reveal the website to any student and no student was threatened on the website. It concluded that "plaintiff's listing of names under the heading 'people I wish would die,' did not constitute a threat to the people listed therein any more than plaintiff's listing of names under the heading 'people that are cool,' make those listed therein 'cool'" (p. 786).

The district court was right to apply the true-threat doctrine to off-campus speech. As we discussed in chapter two, this doctrine should govern speech both on-campus and off-campus. Even though the United States Supreme Court has never applied the doctrine to student speech, the district court's application of the doctrine to off-campus speech is a recognition that students are not just wards of the state but American citizens as the rest of us. In other words, they are entitled to the same constitutional rights, protections and standards outside the schoolhouse gate as are traditionally recognized for citizens. Ironically, while the court's decision to apply the true-threat doctrine to students expands school-censorship authority, it actually expanded the free speech rights of students outside the schoolhouse gate because it treats them in a similar way as adults while they are off-campus. Moreover, the court's reluctance to extend the material and substantial disruption test – a student test – to off-campus speech makes us think even more that the court actually believed that students are like other citizens once they leave the school. Unfortunately, the court succumbed to peer pressure from other courts by following the crowd of courts that had applied the material and substantial disruption test to off-campus speech. This is sad because the district court ignored its genuine conviction against applying a student test to children once they exit the schoolhouse gate.

Their Stories: Online Off-Campus Speech

10. The Story of A.B.

The Speech Incident: The Rant about Greencastle and Mr. Gobert

During the 2005-06 school year, R.B., a student at Greencastle Middle School in Indiana, was expelled from school after she created a private Myspace profile off-campus using the name of her principal Mr. Gobert (A.B. v. State, 2008). R.B. designed the profile to convey the impression that the principal was its actual author. She made the profile viewable by only twenty-six people (including R.B.'s classmate – A.B.) granted "friend" status. Readers with "friend" status were able to post comments about the profile. A.B. took advantage of this opportunity, posting very critical and vulgar comments about the principal's enforcement of the school policy regarding student appearance. She stated:

… hey you piece of greencastle shit. what the fuck do you think of me know [sic] that you cant [sic] control me? huh? ha ha ha guess what ill [sic] wear my fucking piercings all day long and to school and you cant [sic] do shit about it.! ha ha fucking ha! stupid bastard! (A.B. v. State, 2008, p. 1225).

A.B.'s other postings on R.B.'s profile included: "FUCK MR. GOBERT AND GC SCHOOLS!"; and "die ... gobert ... die" (p. 1225). She also included the symbolic representations of the vulgarities.

A.B. subsequently created her own MySpace page which she titled with vulgarity attacking her principal and the district schools for R.B.'s expulsion (A.B. v. State, 2008). She made this profile publically viewable and posted the following:

[R.B.] made a harmless joke profile for Mr. Gobert. and [sic] some retarded bitch printed it out and took it to the office. [R.B.] is expelled, has to go to court, might have to go to girl [sic] school, and has to take the 8th grade over again! that's [sic] just from the school, her paretns [sic] have grounded her, and took [sic] her computer, she cant [sic] be online untill [sic] 2007! GMS is full of over reacting idiots! (A.B. v. State, 2008, p. 1227).

Certain students who learned of the postings notified the principal who confronted A.B. and R.B. and asked to see both profiles (A.B. v. State, 2008). Afterwards, school officials pursued delinquency proceedings against A.B. for her off-campus speech. They claimed that she was delinquent for electronically transmitting harassing statements against the school and the principal. A.B. countered that the school had no authority to censor her speech.

Analysis

In its overly brief decision, the Supreme Court of Indiana ruled that, in order for speech to constitute harassment, the speaker must have had an intent to harass (A.B. v. State, 2008). This means that foundationally the speaker must have had a subjective expectation that the target of the speech would become aware of the speech. It must also be evident that the alleged harassing speech was not intended as communication of a legitimate issue. The court observed that A.B. postings on R.B.'s Myspace page were on a private profile restricted to twenty-six "friends." Therefore, A.B. neither intended nor anticipated that the principal – the target – would see the speech or that the speech on a private profile with "friends" would come to the attention of the principal. Besides, the principal did not actually see the postings until he required A.B. and R.B. to make the private profile accessible to him.

As for A.B.'s speech on her own Myspace page, there is ample evidence in the record indicating that she had a subjective expectation that the speech would reach the school (A.B. v. State, 2008). For instance, instead of restricting her page to "friends" as R.B. did, A.B. made her page publically viewable. As a result, any student or school official could find the page and report it to the target of the postings. Despite this subjective expectation, A.B.'s speech did not meet the standard for harassment because, as the court observed, her speech was intended as legitimate communication. Specifically, she created her own page to legitimately criticize the school's expulsion of her friend A.B. for the creation of the private profile. Thus, A.B. could not be adjudicated a delinquent and her off-campus speech could not be censored. The court effectively held that online off-campus student-speech would receive greater protection if the student-speaker restricts access to a limited group using the privacy settings of the website. If the student-speaker makes the speech publically viewable, however, she must be careful to only post communications about a legitimate concern. The student must also ensure that her postings make it clear that she does not intend for the target of her speech to ever see the speech. A prominently-placed disclaimer expressing a desire not to communicate the speech to the target could serve this purpose. The disclaimer could also be used to make it clear to readers that the speech constitutes legitimate criticism rather than harassment.

11. The Story of J.S. Snyder

The Speech Incident: The Fake Myspace Profile Called M-Hoe

During the 2006-07 school year, school officials at Blue Mountain Middle School in Pennsylvania disciplined J.S., an eighth-grade student, for twice violating the school's dress code (J.S. ex rel. Snyder v. Blue Mountain School District, 2011). Subsequently, on Sunday March 18, 2007, while at home, J.S. used her parents' computer to create a fake Myspace profile of her principal who she called "M-Hoe" (p. 920). J.S.'s friend and classmate, K.L., assisted with the profile's creation at the URL www.myspace.com/kidsrockmybed. They intended the profile as a joke; and their friends understood it as such. Visitors to the site did not view it a genuine profile of the principal because of the outlandish nature of most of the comments. In fact, several students told J.S. that they found the profile humorous. After J.S. learned that several students had seen the page, she changed the publically-viewable profile to a private profile. This change limited access to those granted "friend" status on Myspace, which included twenty-two students. Students had no access to the speech at school because the district's computers did not allow access to Myspace.

The profile featured the principal describing himself as a bisexual middle school principal in Alabama (J.S. ex rel. Snyder v. Blue Mountain School District, 2011). While J.S. and K.L. did not include the principal's actual name or school in the profile, the principal could be easily identified from his official photograph which K.L. copied from the district website. J.S. used vulgar and churlish language, including juvenile jokes and profanities in the profile. The profile also included ribald personal comments targeting the principal and his family. In the "About me" section of the profile, J.S. wrote:

Their Stories: Online Off-Campus Speech

HELLO CHILDREN[.] yes. It's your oh so wonderful, hairy, expressionless, sex addict, fagass, put on this world with a small dick PRINCIPAL[.] I have come to myspace so i can pervert the minds of other principal's [sic] to be just like me. I know, I know, you're all thrilled[.] Another reason I came to myspace is because—I am keeping an eye on you students who[m] I care for so much[.] For those who want to be my friend, and aren't in my school[,] I love children, sex (any kind), dogs, long walks on the beach, tv, being a dick head, and last but not least my darling wife who looks like a man (who satisfies my needs) MY FRAINTRAIN [Frain is the principal's wife and school's counselor] (J.S. ex rel. Snyder v. Blue Mountain School District, 2011, p. 921).

In the general interests part of the site, J.S. listed the following as the principal's interests: "detention, being a tight ass, riding the fraintrain, spending time with my child (who looks like a gorilla), baseball, my golden pen, fucking in my office, hitting on students and their parents" (J.S. ex rel. Snyder v. Blue Mountain School District, p. 920). The profile stated that the fraintrain was "a slow ride but you'll get there eventually" (p. 941).

A student told the principal about the profile two days after its creation (J.S. ex rel. Snyder v. Blue Mountain School District, 2011). The principal asked this student, who also identified J.S. as the profile's author, to bring a hard copy to school the following day. This was the only hard copy of the profile that was brought on school grounds. The principal also searched Myspace.com for a copy of the profile to no avail. During the ensuing school investigation, the social networking site denied the principal's request for information about the identity of the computer used for the profile's creation. Myspace, however, removed the profile at the principal's request.

The school district claimed that the profile caused disruption at the school because some students discussed the profile during their classes (J.S. ex rel. Snyder v. Blue Mountain School District, 2011). The mathematics teacher was forced to yell at approximately seven students after they defied his prior two requests to stop their discussions of the profile during class. The teacher conceded, however, that the students' discussions of the profile were not extraordinary; and that he encountered similar situations weekly. The school district also claimed that the profile disrupted the school counselor's (the principal's wife) schedule for about thirty minutes. Specifically, she was forced to cancel a few counseling sessions in order to serve as a substitute test supervisor for another counselor who participated in the school's investigation of the profile. Cancellation of the counseling sessions did not disrupt any class.

The principal confronted J.S. and K.L. and told them that he was furious that they created the website. He also threatened to sue them and their parents (J.S. ex rel. Snyder v. Blue Mountain School District, 2011). After meeting with their parents, the principal suspended both students from school for ten days. He also barred them from school dances that occurred during the suspension. The principal disciplined both students for violating the school's policy prohibiting false statements about a school official despite conceding that the profile was a pretentious rather than accusatory representation of him. This disciplinary action was also taken in spite of the school district's lack of evidence that any viewer of the profile, besides the school officials, took the profile seriously. The principal also claimed that the students could be punished for their speech because they used his district photograph in violation of the school policy against copyright infringement. He also claimed that the disruption to the school justified the suspension. After learning of his suspension, J.S. wrote a letter of apology to the principal. The principal, however, refused to reconsider the suspension which was also affirmed by the superintendent. Additionally, the principal asked the police to press criminal charges against J.S. and K.L. but was told that the charges would be unsuccessful. As a result, he withdrew his pursuit of charges. Instead, he asked the state police to call the students and their parents to convey to them the gravity of the students' actions. The police complied and ordered the students and their parents to the police station where they discussed the profile with the families. The suspension as well as the police experience greatly upset J.S. and her parents. Consequently, her family filed a First Amendment suit against the school district. They asked the court to grant injunctive relief against the suspension.

Analysis

Even though the United States Court of Appeals for the Third Circuit acknowledged that the off-campus online nature of the case was an issue of first impression for the court, it chose to apply the material and substantial disruption test to the students' speech (J.S. ex rel. Snyder v. Blue Mountain School District, 2011). The court reasoned that, since its precedents as well as the United States Supreme Court's precedents had applied the material and substantial disruption test to many student-speech cases, albeit on-campus speech, it was logical to extend the test to off-campus student speech. In essence, the court implied that the on-campus context of the precedents was immaterial in those precedents. As a result, there is no constitutionally-significant difference between off-campus student speech and on-campus student speech. This ruling appears to be an oversight. Particularly because, although the court quoted the Supreme Court rule in Tinker v. Des Moines Independent Community School District (1969) that students do not shed their constitutional rights at the schoolhouse gate, it failed to analyze the rule or the schoolhouse gate as a legal boundary-marker for students' rights (J.S. ex rel. Snyder v. Blue Mountain School District, 2011). Indeed, the court stated:

The appellants argue that the First Amendment 'limits school official[s'] ability to sanction student speech to the schoolhouse itself.' While this argument has some appeal, we need not address it [emphasis added] to hold that the School District violated J.S.'s First Amendment free speech rights (J.S. ex rel. Snyder v. Blue Mountain School District, 2011, p. 926).

Moreover, the court referenced the Supreme Court's ruling in the *Tinker* case that students' rights inside the school are not coextensive with those of adults outside the school; yet, the court failed to consider the possibility that this ruling could be an acknowledgment that students' rights outside the school are different from those inside the school.

Although the *Tinker* case involved political speech (and the Supreme Court reaffirmed this context in Bethel School District No. 403 v. Fraser (1986)), the third circuit court of appeals disregarded that context (J.S. ex rel. Snyder v. Blue Mountain School District, 2011). Instead, the court of appeals declared that the material and substantial disruption test "has never been confined to such speech" (p. 926). The court was persuaded by Justice Alito's view of the material and substantial disruption test during his time on the third circuit court of appeals. Specifically, Justice Alito stated that the material and substantial disruption test is the default test when other Supreme Court student-speech tests are not contextually applicable to a case. The third circuit court of appeals, however, failed to give proper import to Justice Alito's opinion about school-censorship authority after he joined the Supreme Court. As a member of the Supreme Court, Justice Alito has argued against expanding school-censorship authority (Morse v. Frederick, 2007). He has similarly argued for limiting school authority to speech inside the schoolhouse gate (see discussion in chapter ten). As evident in the following statement, the third circuit court of appeals was clearly aware of Justice Alito's position in the *Morse* case:

Justice Alito only joined the Court's opinion [in Morse] 'on the understanding that the opinion does not hold that the special characteristics of the public schools necessarily justify any other speech restrictions' than those recognized by the Court in Tinker, Fraser, Kuhlmeier, and Morse. ... Moreover, Justice Alito engaged in a detailed discussion distinguishing the role of school authorities from the role of parents, and the school context from the '[o]utside of school' context (J.S. ex rel. Snyder v. Blue Mountain School District, 2011, p. 927, citing Morse v. Frederick, 2007, pp. 424-25).

Undeterred by this, the court concluded that it would simply "assume, without deciding" that the material and substantial disruption test governed J.S.'s off-campus online speech (J.S. ex rel. Snyder v. Blue Mountain School District, 2007, p. 926). This failure to clearly explain its decision to extend the material and substantial disruption test from its on-campus origins to off-campus speech could only further the confusion in the off-campus student-speech jurisprudence. Particularly because the third circuit court of appeals essentially requires lower courts to simply apply the material and substantial disruption test without knowing or understanding whether the test is anchored in sound jurisprudence. The court of appeals instead chose to anchor application of the material and substantial disruption test in assumption – a blind assumption that the test also covers off-campus speech.

The court of appeals concluded that J.S.'s off-campus online speech did not cause material and substantial disruption at the school (J.S. ex rel. Snyder v. Blue Mountain School District, 2011). The school district's lawyer actually agreed with the court that the disruptions at the school did not constitute material and substantial disruption. Instead, the district argued that it had reasonable grounds to forecast material and substantial disruption from the off-campus speech. The court rejected this argument based on its relative assessment of reasonability foreseeability of disruption from J.S.'s speech and that from the armband in Tinker v. Des Moines Independent Community School District (1969):

If Tinker's black armbands—an ostentatious reminder of the highly emotional and controversial subject of the Vietnam war—could not 'reasonably have led school authorities to forecast substantial disruption of or material interference with school activities,' neither can J.S.'s profile, despite the unfortunate humiliation it caused for McGonigle [the principal] (J.S. ex rel. Snyder v. Blue Mountain School District, 2011, pp. 929-30).

The court has a valid point. As we noted in chapter seven, the Supreme Court ruled in Tinker v. Des Moines Independent Community School District (1969) that students' on-campus discussion of a controversial subject matter does not constitute material and substantial disruption or provide reasonable grounds for such forecast. Additionally, in that case, the Supreme Court found the record devoid of reasonable basis for forecast of material and substantial disruption, despite the fact that a mathematics teacher's class was "practically 'wrecked' chiefly by disputes with Mary Beth Tinker, who wore her armband for her 'demonstration'" (Tinker v. Des Moines Independent Community School District, pp.

514, 517). Therefore, the federal circuit court of appeals correctly ruled that the disruption to classes at J.S.'s school that resulted from student discussions of the speech and the cancellation of the counseling sessions did not provide grounds for a reasonable forecast (J.S. ex rel. Snyder v. Blue Mountain School District, 2011).

The court of appeals also concluded that J.S.'s speech did not provide any reasonable ground to forecast material and substantial disruption because J.S. intended the profile as a joke; and no one, except school officials, took its contents seriously (J.S. ex rel. Snyder v. Blue Mountain School District, 2011). Additionally, even though the profile included the principal's picture, his name and school were not identified in the profile. J.S. also did not take the profile to school. Besides, after J.S. learned that some students at her school had found the profile, she restricted access to the profile to only twenty-two students. Further, since the school blocked students' on-campus access to Myspace, no student ever saw the profile inside the schoolhouse gate. The court ruled that the hard copy of the profile also caused no actual disruption and provided no reasonable basis for forecast of material and substantial disruption. According to the court, even if this copy had caused significant disruption, it could not have provided a reasonable basis for forecast of material and substantial disruption. After all, the hard copy only got to campus because the principal directed a student to bring it on school grounds.

This case made clear that disruptions from off-campus speech brought on school grounds pursuant to a school's investigation are impertinent to a material and substantial disruption analysis (J.S. ex rel. Snyder v. Blue Mountain School District, 2011). As are disruptions which arise at the school because a student filed a First Amendment censorship claim against the school. This case also revealed that off-campus student speech cannot be censored simply because it reaches the school's campus unless the school also satisfies the material and substantial disruption test. The court refused to allow censorship founded on reasonable foreseeability that the off-campus speech will make it to the school's campus. Instead, schools must show that the student-speaker subjectively intended the speech to reach the school. The mere fact that a student shared her speech with her classmates in an off-campus setting does not mean that the speech was designed to reach the school. The court reasoned that students' friendship networks outside the schoolhouse gate includes their schoolmates. Therefore, it would be improper to broadly sweep all their off-campus communications with schoolmates as speech designed to reach the school.

In J.S.'s case, the record revealed that she did not intend for the speech to reach the school (J.S. ex rel. Snyder v. Blue Mountain School District, 2011). In fact, she took proactive steps to ensure that the speech did not reach the school. These steps included her change of the profile to a private profile as well as her decision not to list the principal's name or location. Nevertheless, school officials can still censor speech such as J.S.'s despite the subjective intent to keep the speech off-campus if they can satisfy the material and substantial disruption test. This case also established that off-campus online speech will not fall within the school's purview simply because the student used an official school photograph; instead, school officials must show that the speech or use of the photograph caused material and substantial disruption. Besides, the use of an official district photograph in an off-campus online speech constitutes a de minimis use of school resource that cannot convert off-campus speech to on-campus speech.

This case was also one of the few to apply the infringement-of-rights test, albeit cursory (J.S. ex rel. Snyder v. Blue Mountain School District, 2011). The school district argued to the court that it could censor J.S.'s off-campus speech because the speech infringed the right of the principal to be free from defamatory speech. As the court rightly observed, the language which formed the basis for this test in Tinker v. Des Moines Independent Community School District (1969) included, "the rights of other students to be let alone" as well as "invasion of the rights of others" (J.S. ex rel. Snyder v. Blue Mountain

School District, p. 931, citing Tinker v. Des Moines Independent Community School District, pp. 508, 513). While the second phrase's use of the word "others" could conceivably encompass adults, as the court of appeals noted, no court has interpreted the infringement-of-rights test to protect the rights of adults from student infringement (J.S. ex rel. Snyder v. Blue Mountain School District, 2011).

The Supreme Court needs to bring clarity to the infringement-of-rights test. Otherwise, student speech rights could be jeopardized if courts expand the scope of this test to off-campus speech because the test is amorphous (see chapter seven for more on this test). Indeed, the court of appeals cautioned against expanding the infringement-of-rights test because it could endanger students' free speech rights: "if that portion of *Tinker* [i.e. the infringement-of-rights test] is broadly construed, an assertion of virtually any 'rights' could transcend and eviscerate the protections of the First Amendment" (J.S. ex rel. Snyder v. Blue Mountain School District, 2011, p. 931). Nevertheless, the court used the test and concluded that J.S.'s speech did not constitute defamatory speech. This was because his speech was clearly understood as a joke and no one, except school officials, took it seriously. In essence, even if the infringement-of-rights test protects adults, if no reasonable observer views the speech as a factual narrative, school officials have no actionable claim for defamation.

The court of appeals decided not to extend the *Bethel* test to off-campus speech (J.S. ex rel. Snyder v. Blue Mountain School District, 2011). The court ruled that this test should be limited to on-campus speech because of language the United States Supreme Court used in Morse v. Frederick (2007). Specifically, in that case, the Supreme Court affirmed Justice Brennan's statement in Bethel School District No. 403 v. Fraser (1986) that if the student in the *Bethel* case had given "the same speech in a public forum outside the school context, it would have been protected" (Morse v. Frederick, p. 932). The court of appeals interpreted this to mean that, outside the schoolhouse gate, students are governed by the same speech rules applicable to adults (J.S. ex rel. Snyder v. Blue Mountain School District, 2011). Accordingly, students' obscene off-campus speech is governed by the traditional standard for obscenity – the *Miller* test (discussed in chapter five).

As with the material and substantial disruption test, the court of appeals ruled that school officials cannot convert off-campus student speech into on-campus speech for purposes of the *Bethel* test if a school official is responsible for the speech's on-campus presence:

[T]he fact that McGonigle [principal] caused a copy of the profile to be brought to school does not transform J.S.'s off-campus speech into school speech. The flaws of a contrary rule can be illustrated by extrapolating from the facts of Fraser itself. As discussed above, the Supreme Court emphasized that Fraser's speech would have been protected had he delivered it outside the school. Presumably, this protection would not be lifted if a school official or Fraser's fellow classmate overheard the off-campus speech, recorded it, and played it to the school principal. Similarly here, the fact that another student printed J.S.'s profile and brought it to school at the express request of McGonigle does not turn J.S.'s off-campus speech into on-campus speech (J.S. ex rel. Snyder v. Blue Mountain School District, 2011, pp. 932-33).

For purposes of the *Bethel* test, the court also warned against extending school-censorship authority to off-campus speech simply because the speech was directed at a school official or the school or because the speech was brought to the attention of the school (J.S. ex rel. Snyder v. Blue Mountain School District, 2011). This ruling is great news for students. However, it would have been even much better had the court applied the same rule to speech that the court subjects to the material and substantial disruption test. As Judge Smith stated in his concurrence, the material and substantial disruption test should not apply to off-campus student speech. Instead, courts need to recognize that "the First Amendment protects students engaging in off-campus speech to the same extent it protects speech by citizens in the community at large" (p. 936).

Essentially, this case recognized off-campus student speech as constitutionally distinct from on-campus student speech. This is evident in the court's statement that "a student's free speech rights outside the school context are coextensive with the rights of an adult" (J.S. ex rel. Snyder v. Blue Mountain School District, 2011, p. 932). This broad statement, however, conflicts with the court's refusal to distinguish off-campus speech from on-campus speech in its application of the material and substantial disruption test to J.S.'s speech. These conflicting positions are reconcilable, however, by interpreting the broad statement as only applicable to obscene, vulgar, plainly-offensive or lewd off-campus speech. Otherwise, the statement would be nonsensical; particularly since the court did not find students' off-campus speech rights coextensive with those of adults under the material and substantial disruption test. If the material and substantial disruption test is applied to off-campus student speech, it necessarily means that the pertinent court does not consider the rights of adults and students to be coextensive. After all, adult speech cannot be censored merely because it causes material and substantial disruption. Instead, the government must show that the adult speech is "directed to inciting or producing imminent lawless action and is likely to incite or produce such action" (Brandenburg v. Ohio, 1969, p. 447) – a higher standard than the material and substantial disruption test.

12. The Story of Justin Layshock

The Speech Incident: The "Big" Myspace Profile

In December 2005, Justin Layshock, a 17-year old senior at Hickory High School in Pennsylvania, created a fake Myspace profile of his principal designed to highlight the principal's size as a "big" man (Layshock ex rel. Layshock v. Hermitage School District, 2011, p. 208). The profile, created with his grandmother's computer in her house, included the principal's photograph copied from the district website – the only school resource used for the profile. He listed the principal's interests as "Transgender, Appreciators of Alcoholic Beverages" and identified his club membership as "Steroids International" (p. 208). He filled the Myspace profile template with spurious responses designed to portray his principal as a big man. He also used the word "big" repeatedly as evident in his following responses to the template question "tell me about yourself":

Birthday: too drunk to remember
Are you a health freak: big steroid freak
In the past month have you smoked: big blunt [marijuana cigarette]
In the past month have you been on pills: big pills
In the past month have you gone Skinny Dipping: big lake, not big dick
In the past month have you Stolen Anything: big keg
Ever been drunk: big number of times
Ever been called a Tease: big whore

Their Stories: Online Off-Campus Speech

Ever been Beaten up: big fag
Ever Shoplifted: big bag of kmart
Number of Drugs I have taken: big (Layshock ex rel. Layshock v. Hermitage School District, 2011, p. 208).

Justin granted "friend" status to several students at his school, enabling them to view the profile (Layshock ex rel. Layshock v. Hermitage School District, 2011, p. 208). Shortly after its creation, virtually all students at his school learned about the profile though they did not know the author. Students were also able to access the profile on school grounds. The principal discovered the profile online. Justin accessed the profile, in class, on a school computer and showed it to several classmates without disclosing that he authored the profile. On another occasion, a group of students viewed the profile on a school computer while giggling during class, forcing their teacher to interrupt class to disperse them. Around the same time that Justin created his profile, three other students created fake profiles of the principal using more profane language than Justin used in his profile. The principal learned of this profile from his daughter.

After school officials learned of the various profiles, they sought to block student access to Myspace (Layshock ex rel. Layshock v. Hermitage School District, 2011). They were unsuccessful, however, because the technology coordinator was on vacation. Therefore, they instead chose to limit use of school computers to the library and the computer lab so that they could monitor students' online access. Ultimately, the school disabled access to Myspace. School officials took this step in spite of the principal's admission that he never felt threatened by the profiles. The principal claimed the censorship was justified because he feared that the "degrading," "demeaning," "demoralizing," and "shocking" profiles would damage his reputation (p. 209). He also asked the local police department to press criminal charges against the profiles' authors but the department declined.

School officials confronted Justin who apologized to the principal in person as well as in writing (Layshock ex rel. Layshock v. Hermitage School District, 2011). The principal indicated that he felt the apology was genuine. Nevertheless, the school district decided to suspend Justin from school for ten days. Additionally, Justin, a gifted student, was transferred to the alternative education program for the rest of the school year. This program was designed to provide education, in a segregated setting, to students with behavioral issues for three hours per day. The school district prohibited him from his graduation ceremony as well as all extracurricular activities. He was also precluded from continuing to serve as a French tutor to middle school students under the school's foreign-language tutoring program. School officials notified Justin's parents that they planned to increase the suspension to an expulsion. Justin's parents were very disappointed in him for creating the profile. As a result, they took away his computer and other privileges. However, the parents felt that the school had no right to censor their son. Therefore, they filed a First Amendment claim against the school district seeking monetary damages as well as injunctive and declaratory relief.

Analysis

The United States Court of Appeals for the Third Circuit declared that "[i]t would be an unseemly and dangerous precedent" to authorize school censorship over off-campus student, particularly speech within a student's home, to the same extent as on-campus speech (Layshock ex rel. Layshock v. Hermitage School District, 2011, p. 216). Despite this strong statement in support of student speech, the court ruled that schools have censorship authority over off-campus online student speech because the schoolhouse gate has been extended beyond mortars and bricks. The censorship authority is, however, constrained through the material and substantial disruption test. The court's framing of the issue under consideration signaled right away that the court was intent on extending the material and substantial disruption test to off-campus speech: "if a school district can punish a student for expressive conduct that originated outside of the schoolhouse, did not disturb the school environment" (p. 206). This focus on disturbance is a reference to the material and substantial disruption test. This test provides and ensures a nexus between the school and the speech before censorship can be sanctioned.

The school district argued that Justin's use of the principal's official photograph created a sufficient nexus with the school such that the profile could be censored as on-campus speech (Layshock ex rel. Layshock v. Hermitage School District, 2011). As it did in J.S. ex rel. Snyder v. Blue Mountain School District (2011), the United States Court of Appeals for the Third Circuit ruled that the use of the photograph was de minimis for First Amendment purposes (Layshock ex rel. Layshock v. Hermitage School District, 2011). The court similarly ruled that Justin's on-campus access of the profile was constitutionally de minimis. In this regard, the court found the ruling in Thomas v. Board of Education, Granville Central School District (1979) persuasive. In that case, the United States Court of Appeals for the Second Circuit held that the students' on-campus activities were constitutionally de minimis and did not change the off-campus nature of the speech. The students in that case were punished for their off-campus publication because they did some preparatory work for the publication, including writing articles, on school property. The students also consulted their teacher about the publication's content and grammar. In addition, they stored copies of the publication in a classroom with the teacher's permission. Most of the work for the publication was done at the students' homes, however. Despite all their on-campus activities, the court concluded that:

[A]ll but an insignificant amount of relevant activity in this case was deliberately designed to take place beyond the schoolhouse gate. Indeed, the [students] diligently labored to ensure that [the publication] was printed outside the school, and that no copies were sold on school grounds. That a few articles were transcribed on school typewriters, and that the finished product was secretly and unobtrusively stored in a teacher's closet do not alter the fact that [the publication] was conceived, executed, and distributed outside the school. At best, therefore, any activity within the school itself was [d]e minimis (Thomas v. Board of Education, Granville Central School District, 1979, p. 1050).

The United States Court of Appeals for the Third Circuit reasoned from the above language that, if the students' on-campus activities in the *Thomas* case were deemed de minimis so must Justin's (Layshock ex rel. Layshock v. Hermitage School District, 2011). This is valid reasoning, particularly because Justin's on-campus activities were limited to his on-campus access of the profile and his use of a district photograph (unlike the publication in Thomas v. Board of Education, Granville Central School District (1979) which was partly created on-campus). The de minimis nature of these on-campus activities supported the conclusion that Justin's off-campus speech did not cause material and substantial disruption at the school. Besides, the school district agreed that the speech did not cause such disruption at the school. As a result, the court found that the school could not censor Justin's off-campus speech under the material and substantial disruption test:

Their Stories: Online Off-Campus Speech

> [B]ecause the School District concedes that Justin's profile did not cause disruption in the school, we do not think that the First Amendment can tolerate the School District stretching its authority into Justin's grandmother's home and reaching Justin while he is sitting at her computer after school in order to punish him for the expressive conduct that he engaged in there (Layshock ex rel. Layshock v. Hermitage School District, 2011, p. 216).

The court also ruled that off-campus speech is not censorable simply because it is reasonably foreseeable that the speech would be brought to school attention (Layshock ex rel. Layshock v. Hermitage School District, 2011). Neither is off-campus speech censorable merely because it is directed at or against the school. In either case, school officials must still satisfy the material and substantial disruption test. Requiring the material and substantial disruption test in either of these two situations actually renders each situation redundant. This is because, under the court's holding, school officials can censor any off-campus speech that materially and substantially disrupts the school, irrespective of whether the speech was reasonably foreseeable to get to school attention or whether the speech targeted the school.

Finally, the school district argued that it could censor Justin's speech as on-campus speech under the *Bethel* test because he accessed the vulgar, plainly-offensive and lewd speech on school grounds (Layshock ex rel. Layshock v. Hermitage School District, 2011). The court rejected this argument, however, based on its ruling that Justin's on-campus access of the profile was constitutionally de minimis. As constitutionally de minimis on-campus access, the off-campus speech was not converted into on-campus speech. Furthermore, as the court ruled, the *Bethel* test is not applicable to off-campus speech. The court stated emphatically, "we reject out of hand any suggestion that schools can police students' out-of-school speech by patrolling 'the public discourse'" (p. 217). If, however, the vulgar, plainly-offensive or lewd speech creates material and substantial disruption at the school or a reasonably foreseeable risk of such disruption, it can be censored as on-campus speech under the *Bethel* test. Clearly, if the speech was reasonably foreseeable to cause or actually causes material and substantial disruption, the *Tinker* test can provide the basis for censorship of off-campus speech – speech that would otherwise fall under the *Bethel* test if shed of its off-campus nature. In such a situation, application of the *Bethel* test is effectively redundant. Consequently, the material and substantial disruption is all that a school needs in order to censor off-campus student speech.

13. The Story of Katherine Evans

The Speech Incident: The "Worst" Teacher Facebook Post

On November 9, 2007, Katherine Evans, a senior at Pembroke Pines Charter High School in Florida, created a Facebook group page to provide students a forum for criticism of one of their teachers (Evans v. Bayer, 2010). She included the teacher's photograph on the Facebook page which she titled "Ms. Sarah Phelps is the worst teacher I've ever met" (p. 1367). She encouraged students to express animus toward the teacher:

> *Ms. Sarah Phelps is the worst teacher I've ever met! To those select students who have had the displeasure of having Ms. Sarah Phelps, or simply knowing her and her insane antics: Here is the place to express your feelings of hatred (Evans v. Bayer, 2010, p. 1367).*

Two days after creation of the page, Katherine deleted the above posting after some students posted critical comments about Katherine for creating the page. Those students also voiced support for the teacher. Despite the animus-themed nature of Katherine's page, she did not post any threat on the page. Besides, the page did not cause any disruption at the school even though several students were aware of the page. Moreover, she did not access or talk about the page at school. The page was created after school hours on Katherine's personal computer inside her home. The targeted teacher and other school officials only learned of the posting after Katherine had already deleted it from Facebook. Nonetheless, the principal suspended her from school for three days. He also transferred her from advanced placement (AP) courses to lesser-weighted honors courses. Katherine sued the principal for injunctive relief and nominal damages, alleging a violation of her First Amendment right to free speech.

Analysis

The United States District Court for the Southern District of Florida ruled that student-speech censorship decisions must begin with a threshold determination of whether the speech constitutes on-campus speech or off-campus speech (Evans v. Bayer, 2010). According to the court, Morse v. Frederick (2007) mandated this threshold determination in ruling that the physical schoolhouse gate is not dispositive on the boundaries of school-censorship authority. Earlier we observed that, in that case, the Supreme Court authorized a principal to censor speech across the street from the school even though the student never physically brought the speech to school (see chapter ten). The *Morse* Court ruled that, since the speech occurred at a school-sanctioned event, the school had censorship authority over the speech; in spite of the fact that the speech occurred across the street from the school. Even though the *Morse* Court did not explicitly require a threshold determination of speech location, it was appropriate for the federal district court to require it. This is because, as we noted in chapter ten, the Supreme Court made such a threshold determination at the outset of its review of its first student-speech case that occurred outside the four walls of a school.

The federal district court ruled that the location of every student speech must be "determined at the outset in order to decide whether the 'unique concerns' of the school environment are implicated" (Evans v. Bayer, 2010, p. 1370). The court failed to identify these unique concerns. Therefore, it is impossible to predict how those concerns might vary based on the peculiar facts of each off-campus case presented to a court or school district. However, the court stated that when a student-speaker brings off-campus speech on to school grounds, the unique concerns of the school environment are implicated. Since Katherine did not bring her speech on school grounds, her speech retained its off-campus nature.

The federal district court ruled that off-campus speech is not converted into on-campus speech simply because the off-campus speech targeted the student-speaker's school (Evans v. Bayer, 2010). Additionally, the student-speaker's on-campus access of online off-campus speech does not necessarily convert the speech to on-campus speech. The court did not foreclose such conversion, however, stating that "[t]his is not to suggest that speech made off-campus and accessed on-campus cannot be handled as on-campus speech" (pp. 1371-72). Since Katherine did not access the speech on school grounds, the court found it unnecessary to make a definitive ruling on whether on-campus access can conclusively change off-campus speech into on-campus speech. This is a curious decision, given that the court made a definitive ruling about the impact of bringing speech on-campus; despite the fact that Katherine did not bring her speech on-campus.

Their Stories: Online Off-Campus Speech

The mere fact that speech is determined to be off-campus speech does not make it uncensorable (Evans v. Bayer, 2010). Even though the federal district court ruled that off-campus speech is "generally protected" under the First Amendment, it recognized an exception to the rule for speech that satisfies the material and substantial disruption test (p. 1370). The court chose to apply this test to off-campus speech in spite of its explicit recognition that Tinker v. Des Moines Independent Community School District (1969) – the origin of the test – only involved on-campus speech. The court relied upon the following language from the *Tinker* case:

[C]onduct by the student, in class or out of it, which for any reason—whether it stems from time, place, or type of behavior—materially disrupts classwork or involves substantial disorder or invasion of the rights of others is, of course, not immunized by the constitutional guarantee of freedom of speech (Tinker v. Des Moines Independent Community School District, 1969, p. 513).

The court appears to have plausibly but inaccurately interpreted the phrase "in class or out of it." When considered in context, this *Tinker* quote is more accurately interpreted as encompassing speech in and out of the classroom but within the schoolhouse gate (rather than speech in and out of the four walls of the school). Nevertheless, the district court interpreted the quote to authorize use of the material and substantial disruption test for censorship of off-campus student speech.

The federal district court modified the material and substantial disruption test for purposes of off-campus speech censorship (Evans v. Bayer, 2010). The modified test provides that schools can censor off-campus student speech under the material and substantial disruption test as long as "the speech raises on-campus concerns" (p. 1370). The court, however, failed to specify the parameters for determining whether speech raises on-campus concerns. It is surprising that the court extended the material and substantial disruption test to off-campus speech, given its acknowledgment that the "Supreme Court [has] recognized that there is some uncertainty at the outer boundaries as to when courts should apply school-speech precedents" (p. 1370, citing Morse v. Frederick, 2007, p. 401).

The federal district court concluded that Katherine's off-campus speech did not cause material and substantial disruption at the school; and that there was no reasonable basis for forecast of such disruption (Evans v. Bayer, 2010). In fact, Katherine removed the posting from Facebook before school officials ever learned of it. Moreover, the targeted teacher never actually saw the posting. The court rejected the principal's argument that he could censor Katherine's speech as materially and substantially disruptive because it was defamatory to the teacher. The court stated that if the potential for defamation sufficed as material and substantial disruption, "students everywhere would be prohibited from the slightest criticism of their teachers, whether inside or outside of the classroom" (p. 1373). Besides, as the court ruled, calling her teacher the worst teacher ever is purely an opinion and thus not defamation.

The federal district court also ruled that the *Bethel* test was not applicable to off-campus speech (Evans v. Bayer, 2010). The court relied on the following statement by the Supreme Court in Morse v. Frederick (2007): "[h]ad Fraser delivered the same speech in a public forum outside the school context, it would have been protected" (p. 1374, citing Morse v. Frederick, p. 405). Furthermore, the *Bethel* test was created in a case involving speech at a school assembly distinct from Katherine's off-campus speech which occurred on the internet. According to the court, "equat[ing] a school assembly to the entire internet would set a precedent too far reaching" (Evans v. Bayer, p. 1374). Besides, Katherine's speech was not even vulgar, lewd, plainly-offensive or obscene speech. The court's decision to use context as a reason not to extend the *Bethel* test to off-campus speech contradicts its decision to extend the material and substantial disruption beyond its on-campus context. Students, however, can take comfort in the court's decision not to extend the *Bethel* test to off-campus speech. Had the court done so, school officials would be able to broadly censor vulgar, plainly-offensive or obscene speech even if the speech caused no material and substantial disruption to the school.

14. The Story of Landon Wynar

The Speech Incident: Bragging About Weapons and the Plan to "Take Out" People

On Monday April 14, 1986, Landon Wynar, a sophomore at Douglas High School in Nevada, used Myspace's instant messaging (IM) function several times to communicate from his home with classmates (Wynar v. Douglas County School District, 2013). The IM conversations took place after school hours on his personal computer. Landon, an avid weapons collector and owner of several riffles and ammunitions, often centered the conversations on weapons. He frequently discussed his practice shooting sessions. He also engaged in many conversations about World War I and Hitler. During one of those conversations, he called Hitler "our hero" (p. 1065). Some of Landon's messages revealed his struggle with insecurity. For instance, in one conversation, he stated that "[my parents] also dont like me just like everyone at school" (p. 1065). He also stated that "its ignore landon day everyday" (p. 1065).

Landon's classmates thought his violence-laden messages were merely wisecracks (Wynar v. Douglas County School District, 2013). However, as the school year proceeded, they grew increasingly distressed as violence became a prominent theme of his messages. For example, he talked about a school shooting scheduled for April 20th – a date chosen because it was Hitler's birthday and the anniversary of the Columbine High School massacre that occurred in 1999. It was also a few days from the anniversary of the massacre at Virginia Tech University which occurred on April 16, 2007. During an IM conversation, Landon posted the following messages:

its pretty simple / i have a sweet gun / my neighbor is giving me 500 rounds / dhs [Douglas High School] is gay / ive watched these kinds of movies so i know how NOT to go wrong / i just cant decide who will be on my hit list / and thats totally deminted and it scares even my self

i havent decided which 4/20 i will be doing it on / by next year, i might have a better gun to use such as an MI cabine w/ a 30 rd clip.... or 5 clips.... 10?

and ill probly only kill the people i hate?who hate me / then a few random to get the record

[in response to a statement that he would "kill everyone"] no, just the blacks / and mexicans / halfbreeds / athiests / french / gays / liberals / david

[referring to a classmate] no im shooting her boobs off / then paul (hell take a 50rd clip) / then i reload and take out everybody else on the list / hmm paul should be last that way i can get more people before they run away ...

she only reads my mesages and sometimes doesnt even do that. / shes # 1 on 4/20 ya i thought about ripping someones throat out with one. / wow these r weird thoughts... / then raping some chicks dead bodies to? no. maybe. idk.

that stupid kid from vetch [Virginia Tech]. he didnt do shit and got a record. i bet i could get 50+ people / and not one bullet would be wasted.

i wish then i could kill more people / but i have to make due with what i got. / 1 sks & 150 rds / 1 semi-auto shot gun w/sawed off barrle / 1 pistle (Wynar v. Douglas County School District, 2013, pp. 1065-66).

Some of Landon's classmates involved in the IM conversations with him discussed amongst themselves how to respond to these threatening postings (Wynar v. Douglas County School District, 2013). One of them sent the messages to another student who wrote back: "thats [f ...] crazy / landon and i have and messages like that too / he told me he was going to rape [redacted] / then kill her / then go on a school shotting / maybe we should be worried" (p. 1066). These two students chose to consult their football coach on how to address the situation so as "not to make him [Landon] tick and go on a rampage" (p. 1066). Another student who joined the conversation between the two students expressed dread: "Jesus Christ dude!!! / this is some really serious shit!!! / wat do we do? / i mean that is really really sico shit and this is not something to be taking lightly seriously" (p. 1066). The two students and the football coach decided to report Landon to the principal who contacted the police. The school resource officer reported that the two students "were vis[i]bly shaken and believe[d] the suspect is mentally disturbed" (p. 1071). One of the students targeted in Landon's speech told school officials that she was afraid of Landon and would not return to school if he remained at the school. While Landon was in police custody, he told school officials that he intended his Myspace postings to be merely facetious. Nevertheless, school officials suspended him from school for ten days. The school board subsequently expelled him for ninety days. Landon and his father filed a First Amendment claim against the school district seeking injunctive relief.

Analysis

The United States Court of Appeals for the Fifth Circuit ruled that "the location of the speech can make a difference, but that does not mean that all off-campus speech is beyond the reach of school officials" (Wynar v. Douglas County School District, 2013, p. 1068). Even though the court recognized that the United States Supreme Court has never ruled on the rights of students to off-campus speech, it chose to apply both *Tinker* tests – the infringement-of-rights test and the material and substantial disruption test – to off-campus speech. The court reasoned that schools should be able to censor students' off-campus speech if the speech threatens student and school safety. According to the court, "when faced with an identifiable threat of school violence, schools may take disciplinary action in response to off-campus speech that meets the requirements of *Tinker*" (p. 1069). Besides, "[i]t is an understatement that the specter of a school shooting qualifies under either prong [infringement-of-rights prong or material and substantial disruption prong] of *Tinker*" (p. 1070).

The court's decision to extend the *Tinker* tests to off-campus speech is surprising. Particularly because the court also acknowledged that each of the Supreme Court's student-speech precedents "governs a different area of student speech" (Wynar v. Douglas County School District, 2013, p. 1067). Given this fact, one would expect the Supreme Court to create another test when it eventually considers an off-campus student speech case. The Supreme Court is yet to use the same test twice in a student-speech case. It seems logical, therefore, that a new area – off-campus speech – would require its own test. In fact, the court of appeals itself stated that different areas could require different tests. The court should have heeded its own assessment of the jurisprudence as well as its caution about using one test for a broad category of speech: "One of the difficulties with the student speech cases is an effort to divine and impose a global standard for a myriad of circumstances involving off-campus speech" (p. 1069).

It is also surprising that the federal court of appeals chose to extend the *Tinker* tests to off-campus speech because the court knew of and acknowledged the Supreme Court's clear declaration that "[t]here is some uncertainty at the outer boundaries as to when courts should apply school speech precedents" (Wynar v. Douglas County School District, 2013, citing Morse v. Frederick, 2007, p. 401). Moreover, the court of appeals conceded that "[a] number of our sister circuits have wrestled with the question of *Tinker's* reach beyond the schoolyard" (Wynar v. Douglas County School District, p. 1068). These statements which emphasized the unstable nature of the jurisprudence should have given the court pause before extending the *Tinker* tests to off-campus speech. Instead, the court ruled that when the *Morse* test, the *Bethel* test or the *Hazelwood* test are not applicable to a student's speech, the *Tinker* tests govern. In essence, as the default tests, the *Tinker* tests automatically encompass off-campus speech since such speech does not fit any of the other tests. The problem with this reasoning is that the *Morse*, *Bethel* and *Hazelwood* tests are not applicable to off-campus speech because the contexts of those cases involved school-sponsored or school-sanctioned activities or speech. The court's decision to use the on-campus context as reason for precluding the applicability of the *Morse*, *Bethel* and *Hazelwood* tests is disingenuous as it willfully ignores the fact that the *Tinker* tests also originated in an on-campus context. Furthermore, the court applied the *Tinker* tests to Landon's off-campus speech despite stating that "[w]e do not need to consider at this time whether *Tinker* applies to all off-campus speech [because different factual contexts could call for different approaches]" (p. 1068). Besides, by applying the *Tinker* tests to Landon's off-campus speech, the court failed to adhere to its own caution against trying to fit off-campus speech into one test: "we are reluctant to try and craft a one-size fits all approach" (Wynar v. Douglas County School District, p. 1068).

The court of appeals stated that it was not prepared to decide whether censorship of off-campus speech should include a nexus requirement (Wynar v. Douglas County School District, 2013). This decision clearly ignored the fact that the material and substantial disruption test *is* a nexus requirement since it focuses on the impact of speech at the school. Additionally, the court left open the possibility of requiring schools in future cases to establish before censoring off-campus speech that there was reasonable foreseeability of the speech reaching campus. The court found it unnecessary to decide these two issues in this case because the student's threats were so serious that the court felt a need to bypass a nexus or reasonable-foreseeability requirement. In effect, the court ruled that where there is a genuine student threat, the location of the student's speech is immaterial to the school's censorship authority. The court effectively subsumed the true-threat doctrine into the *Tinker* tests. Given the fallacy in the court's reasoning, highlighted above, for extending the *Tinker* tests to off-campus, it might have been more prudent for the court to simply apply the true-threat doctrine.

Even though the Supreme Court has never applied the true-threat doctrine to off-campus speech, that analysis governs the speech of all American citizens, irrespective of location. Accordingly, under the true-threat doctrine, the court of appeals would not have been confronted with justifying extension of a test arising in on-campus contexts to off-campus contexts. Instead, the court would simply have applied an off-campus doctrine – the true-threat doctrine – to off-campus speech. Earlier, we noted that, under the true-threat doctrine, speech that constitutes a true threat is unprotected speech and therefore subject to censorship. Consequently, the school would have been able to censor Landon's speech if it passed the reasonable-speaker view of true threats used in the federal circuit court of appeals for the ninth circuit (see chapter two for more on true threats). The court, however, chose not to definitively apply the true-threat doctrine because the *Tinker* tests authorized the school's censorship (Wynar v. Douglas County School District, 2013). The court instead chose to merely speculate about the potential outcome of Landon's case under a true-threat doctrine. It stated that "[i]n the criminal arena, for speech to be deemed a 'true threat,' the speaker must have 'subjectively intended the speech as a threat'" (p. 1070). As a result, the court suggested that Landon's speech might not be true threat because he subjectively intended it as a joke.

The court overlooked the traditional definition of the reasonable-speaker view of true threats (Wynar v. Douglas County School District, 2013). As we noted in chapter two, this traditional view focuses on the reasonable person rather than on subjective intent. The reasonable-speaker view examines whether "a reasonable person would foresee that the statement would be interpreted by those to whom the maker communicates the statement as a serious expression of intent to harm or assault" (United States v. Orozco–Santillan, 1990, p. 1265). In fact, this is the same definition that the ninth circuit court of appeals itself uses in true-threat cases involving society at large. Given the strong violent language in the student's Myspace messages, as well as his public revelation to classmates that he had access to weapons, a reasonable speaker would have foreseen that listeners would view his speech as a serious expression of intent to harm. The court implied without elaboration that different standards might govern true threats in criminal and civil cases. However, the court only applied subjective intent which it considered a criminal standard. In so doing, the court incorrectly interpreted the reasonable-speaker standard with respect to Landon's speech; unless the court plans to use the reasonable-person standard for civil cases while reserving subjective intent strictly for criminal cases. If the court had elaborated on the civil and criminal standards beyond its cursory note in the case, we would have better clarity on its views about schools' use of the true-threat doctrine to censor students' off-campus speech. Unfortunately, the court merely left school officials with great uncertainty by implying the possibility of different standards and yet providing no explanation of the standards.

The court concluded that school officials were authorized to censor Landon's speech under the material and substantial disruption test (Wynar v. Douglas County School District, 2013). This conclusion is supported by the fact that Landon openly acknowledged that he had access to weapons and 500 rounds of ammunition. Additionally, the rhetoric in his Myspace messages was laden with violent images. He also identified specific individuals and groups that he planned to target in a rampage. The court determined that the shooting rampage he referenced was apparently already scheduled – evidence of planning. Besides, the chosen date for the rampage was the anniversary of other school massacres and Hitler's birthday. The seriousness of Landon's threats was also evident in the fact that his conversation classmates, who viewed his initial comments as jokes, changed their perspectives once he amplified his violent rhetoric which they considered to be serious expressions of intent to harm. Additionally, the court noted that the two students who reported the posting were visibly shaken. Furthermore, the court pointed out that another student targeted in the speech told school officials that she was afraid of Landon. Besides, as the court observed, if the school took no preventive action, a deadly rampage could have occurred at the school. These facts persuaded the court that the school had reasonable grounds to forecast material and substantial disruption. These same facts should have persuaded the court to classify the student's messages as a true threat.

With respect to the infringement-of-rights test, as evident in this book, courts rarely apply this test (see chapter seven for more on this test). In fact, the federal court of appeals acknowledged as much:

"Few circuit cases address the 'invasion of the rights of others' prong of *Tinker*" (Wynar v. Douglas County School District, 2013, p. 1071). The court also acknowledged that Justice Alito had once declared the scope of this test unclear. Nonetheless, the court applied the test to Landon's off-campus speech. Although the court stated that offensiveness of speech does not satisfy the infringement-of-rights test, it "decline[d] to elaborate on when offensive speech crosses the line" (p. 1072). Instead, it summarily concluded (apparently as a matter of law) that speech that threatens a school shooting undoubtedly infringes on the rights of other students. Given the court's conclusion that Landon's Myspace messages threatened the entire student body and identified students, his off-campus speech could be censored under the infringement-of-rights test. According to the court, his speech was the "quintessential harm" that the infringement-of-rights test was designed for. The court's decision to apply the test without explaining the test or defining its scope adds to the uncertainty that Justice Alito articulated about the test. The court was able to avoid explaining the test by ruling as a matter of law. This makes it difficult to fully understand the constitutional import of the ruling because matter-of-law rulings conveniently allow a court to abdicate its responsibility to develop its reasoning. Therefore, even after this case, the infringement-of-rights test remains shrouded in mystery.

15. The Story of Juliano Roasio

The Speech Incident: Cussing on Twitter

In 2012, coaches at Desert Oasis High School in Nevada dismissed Juliano Roasio, a senior student and basketball player, from the school's team (Roasio v. Clark County School District, 2013). His father complained about this decision to school officials. Later in the year, Juliano was conditionally reinstated to the basketball team after a tryout. In February 2013, after the team played its final game of the season, Juliano and his family visited a local restaurant. While at this off-campus location, Juliano posted comments on Twitter criticizing his coaches and athletic director. His tweets stated:

1. "Mr. Isaacs [athletic director and assistant principal] is a bitch too"
2. "I hope Coach brown [boys varsity basketball coach] gets fucked in tha ass by 10 black dicks"
3. "Now I can tweet whatever I want and I hope one of y'all mother fuckers snitch on me"
4. "Fuck coach browns bitch ass"
5. "Finally this bitch ass season is over"
6. "Aiight I'm done y'all can go snitch now like before"
7. "Oh yeah and Mr. Dinkel's [athletic director] square ass"
8. "AND Ms. Evans [a coach at the school] bitch ass boyfriend [another coach at the school] too He a pussy ass nigga tryna talk shit while walking away" (Roasio v. Clark County School District, 2013, p. 3).

When the school officials mentioned in the tweets learned about them, they filed disciplinary complaints against Juliano at the school (Roasio v. Clark County School District, 2013). The record is not entirely clear but it appeared that school administrators initially suspended or expelled Juliano for the tweets. He was, however, subsequently transferred to another high school within the district. Juliano and his father then sued the school district under the First Amendment seeking injunctive relief.

Their Stories: Online Off-Campus Speech

Analysis

The United States District Court for the District of Nevada was clearly not opposed to giving schools censorship authority over student speech outside the schoolhouse gate (Roasio v. Clark County School District, 2013). Indeed, the court declared it "well-established that schools may discipline students for off-campus speech in certain situations" (p. 4). According to the court, one of those situations is obscene student speech. Remarkably, the court that was ostensibly eager to give schools censorship authority over off-campus speech chose to apply a more stringent test than the *Bethel* test to school censorship of students' obscene off-campus speech. Specifically, the court applied the *Miller* test for obscenity to Juliano's tweets. Recall that, under the *Miller* test, schools examine the speech in question in order to determine:

1. "Whether the average person, applying contemporary community standards, would find that the work, taken as a whole, appeals to the prurient interest";
2. "Whether the work depicts or describes, in a patently offensive way, sexual conduct specifically defined by the applicable state law"; and
3. "Whether the work, taken as a whole, lacks serious literary, artistic, political, or scientific value" (Miller v. California, 1973, p. 24).

It is possible that the court chose to apply the *Miller* test, as opposed to the *Bethel* test, to off-campus speech because of the off-campus nature of the speech. Since the court did not identify this or any other reason as its rationale for using the *Miller* test, we can only try to deduce the rationale from the court's opinion. We believe that it is more likely that the court chose the *Miller* test because the school district presented its case to the court using that test rather than the *Bethel* test; and Juliano did not object to its application. The school district argued that Juliano's tweets were obscene and therefore unprotected speech open to school censorship despite its off-campus locale. Regardless of the court's rationale for using the *Miller* test, as evident in this book, it is rare for a court to apply the *Miller* test in analyzing the obscenity of off-campus student speech; even though that is the appropriate test to use.

The federal district court concluded that Juliano's second tweet was obscene as a matter of law under the *Miller* test (Roasio v. Clark County School District, 2013). That tweet, stated, "I hope Coach brown [boys varsity basketball coach] gets fucked in tha ass by 10 black dicks" (p. 3). The court found the tweet obscene because it satisfied each prong of the *Miller* test. Under contemporary community standards, it clearly appealed to prurient interests. It also lacked serious literary, artistic, scientific or political scientific value. Finally, it described, in an indubitably offensive way, sexual conduct that Nevada law had specifically defined. While the school district argued that the other tweets were obscene because they were racist, violent or hateful speech, the court ruled otherwise. The other tweets did not constitute obscene speech because they did not appeal to prurient interests and they did not describe sexual conduct at all. Since the school district did not present other legal grounds for censoring the speech as hateful, violent or racist, the court was unable to rule on whether another ground would suffice for censorship.

The federal district court – a court within the jurisdiction of the United States Court of Appeals for the Ninth Circuit – conceded that the ninth circuit court has never ruled on off-campus student speech that occurs on social media (Roasio v. Clark County School District, 2013). Nonetheless, the district court chose to extend the material and substantial disruption test to off-campus student speech on social media. Specifically, the court chose to adopt from other courts a modified material and substantial disruption test for online off-campus student speech. Under this test, schools can censor student speech that satisfies two conditions:

1. There is reasonable foreseeability that the speech will reach campus; and
2. There is reasonable grounds to forecast material and substantial disruption at the school from the speech.

Because more facts needed to be developed in the case, the court chose to delay its review, under this modified test, of the school's censorship of Juliano's speech. There was no basis in the record at the time of the decision to adequately determine if the tweets were reasonably foreseeable to reach campus. There was also insufficient evidence in the record to determine if the tweets caused material or substantial disruption at the school; or that there was reasonable ground to forecast such disruption. Given the inconclusive nature of this case, there are only two key points we can deduce from this case: school censorship of obscene off-campus speech must be evaluated under the *Miller* test; and non-obscene speech must be analyzed under the modified material and substantial disruption test.

16. The Story of R.S.

The Speech Incident: Dislike, Salty Curiosity, and Naughty Conversations on Facebook

In the course of the 2011 spring semester, R.S., a sixth-grade student at Minnewaska Area Middle School in Minnesota, used her Facebook page to express dislike of her school's hall monitor (R.S. ex rel. S.S. v. Minnewaska Area School District No. 2149, 2012). Specifically, R.S. stated, "[I hate] a Kathy person at school because [Kathy] was mean to me" (p. 1133). R.S. posted the message in her house, after school hours, without any school resource. Further, R.S. restricted access to her postings through Facebook's privacy setting. As a result, only those persons whom she granted Facebook "friend" status could view her postings. Students could not view her postings from school because school officials blocked access to Facebook on school grounds. One of the students whom R.S. granted "friend" status shared R.S.'s posting about the hall monitor with the principal. The principal then confronted R.S., telling her that the posting constituted bullying and disrespectful behavior in contravention of school policy. He imposed detention on her and ordered her to apologize to the hall monitor. Out of curiosity and frustration at the "friend" who tattled, R.S. posted a salty message on her Facebook page: "I want to know who the fuck told on me" (R.S. ex rel. S.S. v. Minnewaska Area School District No. 2149, pp. 1133-34). Like her earlier postings, this message was posted after school hours while R.S. was at home. As punishment for this new posting, the principal barred R.S. from a class ski trip. She also received in-school suspension for one day.

Later that semester, a male student's guardian informed school officials that R.S. and the male student had been engaging in sexual conversations on the internet (R.S. ex rel. S.S. v. Minnewaska Area School District No. 2149, 2012). The male student, who started the conversations, admitted his role to school officials. R.S. admitted to the school counselor that she had discussed "naughty things" with the male

Their Stories: Online Off-Campus Speech

student (p. 1134). However, she insisted that the conversations took place off-campus after school hours without use of school resources. Nonetheless, that same day, the school resource officer (a deputy sheriff in police uniform with a taser) along with counselor and another staff member questioned R.S. about the online sexual conversations. R.S. again admitted that she engaged in naughty conversations with the male student. According to R.S., during the interrogation, the three school officials ordered her to disclose her Facebook and email passwords and usernames. She also claimed that she was threatened with detention and called a liar after she told them that she could not recall the passwords. Ultimately, she disclosed the usernames and passwords to the school officials who then searched her public and private Facebook postings for the naughty conversations. The officials were dismayed when they found that R.S. had taken a Facebook sex quiz and that she had used profane language in several of her Facebook postings. R.S. claimed she felt scared and demeaned as the school officials accessed her Facebook page and criticized her postings. She also claimed that the encounter caused her to cry and suffer depression. Additionally, she was unable to attend school for two days after the interrogation and access of her Facebook page. R.S. contended that she had "lost her sense of security" and safety by the time she returned to school (p. 1135). R.S.'s mother filed a First Amendment claim against the school district asking for injunctive relief.

Analysis

The United States District Court for the District of Minnesota declared that it is settled that "students do not check their First Amendment rights at the schoolhouse door" (R.S. ex rel. S.S. v. Minnewaska Area School District No. 2149, 2012, p. 1138). Further, the court ruled that "[o]ut-of-school speech by a student is subject to even less stringent school regulation than in-school speech" (p. 1138). These two rules are noteworthy for what they did not state as much as what they stated. They did not state that school officials have no censorship authority whatsoever over off-campus student speech. This means that, even though students have First Amendment rights to off-campus speech – rights which they bring to the schoolhouse door – school officials can reach beyond the schoolhouse door to censor the speech. What these rules actually state is that school officials can exercise less censorship authority over off-campus student speech than they can over on-campus speech. In essence, the question of school-censorship authority over off-campus speech is a matter of degree or scope rather than one of validity. Moreover, off-campus speech and on-campus speech are not coterminous. The court, however, ruled that, as with on-campus speech, school officials cannot censor student speech merely because of its offensive nature.

According to the district court, the advent of the internet has not changed the rules governing school censorship of off-campus student speech; rules which the court indicated were established in the United States Supreme Court's first student-speech decision – Tinker v. Des Moines Independent Community School District (1969) (R.S. ex rel. S.S. v. Minnewaska Area School District No. 2149, 2012). The district court recognized that the "movement of student speech to the internet poses some new challenges, but that transition has not abrogated the clearly established general principles which have governed schools for decades" (p. 1139). The problem with this statement is that, as evident in this book, the off-campus student-speech jurisprudence is hardly clear, established or certain. Additionally, all the Supreme Court's student-speech cases have involved on-campus student speech. Yet, the district court stated that "[s]everal high-profile Supreme Court cases have distinguished between regulation of in-school speech and out-of-school speech" (p. 1141). This statement is not completely accurate. First, the Supreme Court has only decided four, not several, student-speech cases. Second, the Supreme Court has only acknowledged a distinction between on-campus and off-campus speech in two cases – Hazelwood v. Kuhlmeier

(1988) and Morse v. Frederick (2007); and those acknowledgments were desultory. As we noted earlier, the only other clear statement about this distinction, in a Supreme Court case, was in Justice Brennan's concurring opinion in Bethel School District No. 403 v. Fraser (1986).

The federal district court ruled that school officials can censor students' off-campus speech pursuant to the material and substantial disruption test if the speech is reasonably foreseeable to reach the school (R.S. ex rel. S.S. v. Minnewaska Area School District No. 2149, 2012). In spite of their authority under this modified material and substantial disruption test, school officials cannot actively monitor or search for students' off-campus speech in order to censor the speech unless the speech involves violent and serious threats that could materially and substantially disrupt the school. The court also ruled that schools can alternatively censor student speech under the true-threat doctrine without having to use the modified material and substantial disruption test. Under this doctrine, school officials can censor the speech pursuant to the reasonable-recipient view as long as the speaker intended to communicate the threat to someone. According to the court, the true-threat doctrine as well as the modified material and substantial disruption test are rare exceptions to the general rule that "school officials may not simply 'reach out to discover, monitor, or punish any type of out of school speech'" (p. 1140, citing D.J.M. ex rel. D.M. v. Hannibal Public School District No. 60, 2011, p. 765). The court's jurisprudence on off-campus student speech under both the true-threat doctrine and the modified material and substantial disruption test was aptly described in the case:

The law on out-of-school statements by students can thus be summarized as follows: Such statements are protected under the First Amendment and not punishable by school authorities unless they are true threats or are reasonably calculated to reach the school environment and are so egregious as to pose a serious safety risk or other substantial disruption in that environment (R.S. ex rel. S.S. v. Minnewaska Area School District No. 2149, 2012, p. 1140).

In other words, schools cannot censor non-violent, non-disruptive off-campus speech albeit offensive.

The federal district court determined that R.S.'s online postings and conversations did not constitute true threats because they did not contain any violence or threat (R.S. ex rel. S.S. v. Minnewaska Area School District No. 2149, 2012). Besides, her postings and conversations did not satisfy the modified material and substantial disruption test. As the court noted, even though the postings and conversations were reasonably calculated to reach the school's campus, they did not cause material and substantial disruption at the school. Her statement about hating the hall monitor was just that – a statement. There was nothing in the statement that could serve as a basis to reasonably forecast material and substantial disruption. Although she used vulgar language in her posted inquiry about the "friend" who told the principal about her prior posting, there was nothing in the posting that school officials could have used to reasonably forecast material and substantial disruption. Furthermore, neither of these statements/postings was so egregious as to threaten serious danger or other significant disruption to the school. As a result, the court concluded that R.S.'s speech passed the modified material and substantial disruption test.

This case effectively recognized broad protections for students' non-disruptive non-violent, non-threatening off-campus speech. The broad protections afforded off-campus speech can only be overcome in the limited circumstance where there is a true threat; or if speech that is reasonably likely to reach the school campus is so egregious that it portends material and substantial disruption at the school.

Their Stories: Online Off-Campus Speech

17. The Story of Taylor Bell

The Speech Incident: The Rap Song: Drool, Pistol, Middle Finger, and the N-Word

In August 2001, Taylor Bell, a senior at Itawamba Agricultural High School in Mississippi, composed a rap song which used vulgar language to criticize two of his school's coaches identified in the song (Bell v. Itawamba County School Board, 2012). The coaches were also teachers at the school. After recording himself singing the song, Taylor uploaded the song on YouTube for public access. Additionally, he posted the song on his Facebook page for more than 1,300 Facebook "friends", many of whom were his schoolmates. Taylor composed, sang, recorded and posted the song online while he was off-campus after school hours. He did not use any school resource to compose, record or post the song. The song accused the coaches of inappropriate acts toward female students. The last two verses described some of the acts and Taylor's feelings about them:

1. "Looking down girls' shirts/drool running down your mouth/messing with wrong one/going to get a pistol down your mouth"; and
2. "Middle fingers up if you can't stand that nigga/middle fingers up if you want to cap that nigga" (p. 836).

Additionally, Taylor described one of the coaches as "a "dirty ass nigger [who] is fucking with the whites and now fucking with the blacks" (Bell v. Itawamba County School Board, 2012, p. 839). He described this coach as a "pussy nigger [who] is fucking with the students he just had a baby … [and is] … fucking around cause his wife ain't got no titties" (p. 839). He accused the coach of telling female students that they "are sexy" (p. 839). In addition, he mentioned that he left the basketball team because the coach "is a pervert" (p. 839). Taylor described the second coach as a 30-year old "pervert" who is "fucking with juveniles" and "fucking with students at the school" (p. 839). Taylor then stated that he would "hit ya [the second coach] with my ruler" (p. 839). He compared this coach to a former coach at the school who was arrested for sexting a minor. Specifically, Taylor referred to the second coach as "another Bobby Hill [the former coach]" (p. 839). Taylor also accused this coach of coming "high" to football practice (p. 839).

An undisclosed person reported Taylor's song to school officials who accused him of threatening the coaches and making false accusations (Bell v. Itawamba County School Board, 2012). The wife of one of the coaches texted the coach while he was at school to inform him of Taylor's song. The coach, who was understandably upset, reported his concern to the principal. Both coaches claimed that their teaching was negatively impacted after the song became common knowledge at the school as students viewed them suspiciously. Taylor insisted that the song did not constitute a threat and refused to recant his accusations of inappropriate sexual acts toward female students. He averred to school officials that the coaches committed the acts referenced in his song. In order to prevent Taylor from returning to his classes for the rest of the day, the principal drove Taylor off school grounds to his friend's house. This was not a formal suspension so Taylor returned to school the next school day. After classes ended that day, school officials suspended Taylor indefinitely until a disciplinary hearing. At the conclusion of the hearing, they changed the suspension to seven days. Taylor was also transferred to an alternative school for the rest of the nine-week marking period. The school board affirmed the discipline, claiming that Taylor harassed and threatened school employees in his song. Taylor's mother sued the school district for injunctive relief under the First Amendment.

Analysis

The United States District Court for the Northern District of Mississippi ruled that schools can censor student speech pursuant to the material and substantial disruption test (Bell v. Itawamba County School Board, 2012). The court relied on Tinker v. Des Moines Independent Community School District (1969) – the origin of the material and substantial disruption test – where the United States Supreme Court stated:

[C]onduct by a student, in class or out of it which for any reason ... materially disrupts classwork or involves substantial disorder or invasion of the rights of others is, of course, not immunized by the constitutional guarantee of freedom of speech" (Bell v. Itawamba County School Board, 2012, p. 837, citing Tinker v. Des Moines Independent Community School District, p. 506).

The court highlighted the phrase "in class or out of it" to suggest that the material and substantial disruption test (also highlighted in the quote) applied to off-campus speech. The court apparently interpreted the phrase to not only encompass on-campus speech outside the classroom but also off-campus speech since off-campus speech *is* speech outside the classroom. The court emphatically stated that "the U.S. Supreme Court in *Tinker* specifically ruled that off-campus conduct causing material or substantial disruption at school can be regulated by the school" (Bell v. Itawamba County School Board, 2012, pp. 837-38). However, as we explained in chapter seven, when taken in context, the Supreme Court's use of the phrase "in class or out of it" appeared to have been restricted to speech outside the classroom yet within the schoolhouse gate. Therefore, the district court used the quote out of context. The court's interpretation was however, clever, as it provided a rationale grounded in Supreme Court precedent for extending the material and substantial disruption test beyond the schoolhouse gate. The court also decided to apply the material and substantial disruption test to off-campus student speech because other courts had applied the test to off-campus speech.

The court modified the material and substantial disruption test with the additional requirement that, before the off-campus speech can be censored under the test, the student-speaker must have intended the speech to reach the school (Bell v. Itawamba County School Board, 2012). The speech is not required to actually reach the school. Additionally, if the speech includes *threatening* content and the content reaches the school's campus, these would be sufficient to constitute material and substantial disruption. The threatening nature of speech also suffices to establish reasonable foreseeability that the speech would cause material and substantial disruption at the school, even if the speech does not reach the school. The court found the references to "pistol down your mouth" and "middle fingers up if you can't stand that nigga/middle fingers up if you want to cap that nigga" to be threatening speech (p. 836). The court also implied that the vulgar nature of the speech was sufficient to make the speech threatening.

After speech is determined to be threatening, the next question for consideration is whether the student-speaker intended the speech to reach the school (Bell v. Itawamba County School Board, 2012). As the court noted, since Taylor made the rap song accessible to 1,300 Facebook "friends" who were mostly his schoolmates, it was evident that he intended the speech to reach the school. Besides, he uploaded the

Their Stories: Online Off-Campus Speech

song on YouTube where the general public had unrestricted access to it, supporting the inference that he intended the speech to ultimately get to the school. Additionally, the content of the song reached the school's campus when the undisclosed person reported the song to school officials as well as when the coach's wife texted him at the school about the song. Finally, the song apparently impacted both coaches' teaching negatively. Accordingly, the court ruled that the school district had the constitutional authority to censor his off-campus speech. This case essentially and unfortunately used an erroneous interpretation of language in Tinker v. Des Moines Independent Community School District (1969) to expand school-censorship authority to off-campus student speech while restricting students' First Amendment right to off-campus speech.

18. The Story of Justin Neal and Ryan Kuhl

The Speech Incident: The Neal and Kuhl Websites

In 2004, while Greenwood High School in Arkansas was still on its summer break, two of its students – Justin Neal and Ryan Kuhl – created two different websites on their personal computers inside their homes without use of school resources (Neal et al. v. Efurd, 2005). Justin included a hyperlink on his website to Ryan's website as did Ryan to Justin's website. During the fall semester, which started on August 19, 2004, they continued to run and use the website though they did so entirely off-campus. They neither accessed the websites at school nor encouraged any student to access the website at the school. Justin and Ryan used the websites to express their views about their school and their town. Their sites also featured images of school officials doing violent things to students but they did not make any threat on the website. Additionally, they used boorish language to refer to athletes and band members.

Justin's website featured an online comic called "Greentree" who satirized "people who live in Greenwood, Arkansas" and conveyed his thoughts about "life in the small town" (Neal et al. v. Efurd, 2005, p. 11). Justin included cartoon frames that described the principal as "'E-Firdcom,' an intercom wheeled about on a cart" (p. 11). The first frame portrayed E-Firdcom, the principal, saying to students at the first school assembly of the school year, "Hello students. Welcome back to school. Who's excited to be back?" The second frame showed a student's raised hand in response to the question. The third frame featured the assistant principal with a smoking gun and a bullet hole in the head of the student with the raised hand as well as that of another student. This third frame then showed E-Firdcom asking, "Anyone else?" (p. 11). A number of other cartoon frames portrayed the assistant principal as "Abominable Vice Principal", "monster" or "Sasquatch" (p. 11). Justin's website also included several message boards with the following titles:

1. "Discuss the quality of education at GHS [Greenwood High School]";
2. "Discuss GHS's budget";
3. "Discuss the academic aspects of GHS versus the athletic aspects";
4. "Talk about Greenwood, Arkansas in general";
5. "Speak your mind about the comic";
6. "Discuss national politics";
7. "Discuss local politics";
8. "How can the boards be improved?"

9. "Talk about anything not covered by other categories including music, movies, or anything else that comes to mind"; and
10. "wild card topic" which provided an opportunity for visitors to discuss miscellaneous topics (Neal et al. v. Efurd, 2005, pp. 11-12).

Justin's website also featured a message board named "Talk about Greenwood High School in general" (Neal et al. v. Efurd, 2005, p. 12). One of the visitors to this board described it as a forum for "the creation of mayhem within the school" (p. 12). The student, however, merely used the word "mayhem" figuratively to call for criticism of school officials and change at the school. In addition to the above topics, visitors to Justin's website engaged in vigorous debates about the First Amendment, teachers' salaries, students' standardized test scores, the district's report card, the need for increased diversity, smaller class sizes and new textbooks. They discussed the water quality in Greenwood, Arkansas and businesses that should move to Greenwood. They also discussed effecting change at their school through creation of a new student club and election of a student representative. Furthermore, they debated whether the website's content would inspire violence. No one, however, posted any threat on the website. The most extreme posting was from a visitor who talked about damaging the football field.

While Ryan's website covered similar topics to Justin's website, it appeared that his views were expressed with anger and hostility that had been repressed for quite some time (Neal et al. v. Efurd, 2005, p. 13). His website also used significantly more vulgarity than Justin's. The website portrayed Ryan's dislike of his school and persons at the school. It also featured a cartoon which he called the "Bulldog Death of the Week" which was "a takeoff on a song entitled 'Kill Your Idols'" (p. 13). The bulldog was the school's mascot; hence the reference in the cartoon title. In the cartoon, he only included the cartoon title and a mace over the head of the bulldog. Ryan encouraged visitors to suggest the Bulldog Death of the Week but there was no significant discussions under this posting. Like Justin, Ryan also included message boards on his website.

Before the start of the fall semester, a parent complained to the principal about the websites because she was agitated at the messages targeting athletes and band members (Neal et al. v. Efurd, 2005). She also expressed concern about vulgar and hateful language on the websites. Shortly after the school year began, Justin and Ryan were removed from their classes for the day as school officials interrogated them about the websites. The following day, school officials suspended both students from school for three days. Several teachers told the assistant principal that they felt the websites might impact their teaching. Additionally, about twenty students told the assistant principal that they found the vulgarities and violent images on the websites troubling. As a result of the suspension, both students, who until then had stellar academic records, received zero grades on all missed assignments. The district informed Justin that his suspension was for creation of his website and for including a hyperlink to "an inappropriate website that [sic] encouraged mayhem and dissension among GHS [Greenwood High School] students" (p. 6). The district told Ryan his suspension was for "posting inappropriate website. Inappropriate material on the website" (p. 6). The principal sent the entire faculty an email notifying them that unidentified students had been suspended for making "threatening statements" directed at a few staff members (p. 5). When the principal sent the email, he was fully aware that neither Justin nor Ryan had any threats on their websites. Even though the principal did not mention Justin and Ryan in the email, the teachers were able to determine their identities. Teachers became very leery of both students because of the content of the principal's email. The principal subsequently conceded that he never once thought that either student posed a danger to the faculty or students.

Justin and Ryan sued the school district for violating their First Amendment right to free speech (Neal et al. v. Efurd, 2005). They asked the court for an injunction and monetary damages. The principal defended the suspensions of Justin and Ryan, claiming that he suspended them because he thought the websites could disrupt the school, cause divisiveness and offend some members of the school community. He also felt that the websites harassed and intimidated people at the school. Disruption, harassment and intimidation were never identified as grounds for the suspension until after the lawsuit was filed. The principal claimed that the websites disrupted the school because there was "buzz" at the school after students learned of the investigation (p. 7). He, however, acknowledged that buzz was routine at the school during student investigations. The assistant principal also stated that the start of the year was typically a little chaotic as students returned to school. Thus, the impact of the website on the school was not atypical. Several teachers stated that the websites did not cause any disruption at the school. In a few classes, students unsuccessfully asked their teachers to discuss the First Amendment implications of Justin and Ryan's suspensions. No disruption resulted from these requests or the denials of these requests, however. The teachers conceded that their concerns about the websites stemmed from the principal's characterization of the websites' contents and from subsequent rumors about the contents. The teachers never actually saw the websites' contents.

Analysis

The United States District Court for the Western District of Arkansas ruled that schools have a "limited degree of control" over students' off-campus speech (Neal et al. v. Efurd, 2005, p. 6). The words "limited" and "degree" opened the door to school censorship of off-campus student speech because they imply that censorship of off-campus speech is not precluded but merely circumscribed in scope. The court chose the *Tinker* tests – the material and substantial disruption test as well as the infringement-of-rights test – as the means of circumscribing the scope of school-censorship authority over off-campus student speech. This is surprising because the court acknowledged that "*Tinker* did not reach the issue of whether a school may constitutionally regulate the speech of a student on his own time, while away from campus and not at any school-related activity" (p. 18). Nevertheless, the court reasoned that, since other courts had applied the material and substantial disruption test (and a few times the infringement-of-rights test) to off-campus speech, the test must be applicable to off-campus speech. In essence, the court succumbed to a herd mentality. It is dangerous constitutional practice and a threat to student-speech jurisprudence for courts to blindly follow other courts without showing any curiosity about the soundness of those other courts' decisions. While the court recognized both the material and substantial disruption test and the infringement-of-rights test, it did not apply the infringement-of-rights test. Therefore, the court's interpretation of the infringement-of-rights test and the test's nuances are a mystery.

The federal district court ruled that when off-campus student speech satisfies the following conditions, it will be analyzed under the material and substantial disruption test:

1. The speech is on the internet;
2. The speech was created in the student's home or other off-campus locale;
3. No part of the speech was created on school property;
4. The student created the speech outside school hours on the student's time; and
5. The speech is not school sponsored (Neal et al. v. Efurd, 2005).

Given that Justin and Ryan's websites satisfied these conditions, the material and substantial disruption test was applicable. As noted above, however, the websites did not cause any disruption at the school. The disruptions at the school were caused by other factors such as the typical start-of-the-school-year frenzy. The buzz surrounding the school's investigations of Justin and Ryan was also routine for student investigations. The court minimized the fact that approximately twenty students complained to the assistant principal that they found the websites' vulgarities and violent images disturbing. The court reasoned that those students constituted less than three percent of the entire student body which was comprised of 750 students. This is sound reasoning, given that no disruption occurred at the school from the twenty students' complaints about the website. The court indicated that student attempts to discuss, during class, the First Amendment issues surrounding the website and the suspension did not constitute material and substantial disruption. Instead such discussions should be viewed as opportunities for learning rather than for censorship. The court ruled that "student expression may not be suppressed simply because it gives rise to some slight, easily overlooked disruption, including but not limited to a showing of mild curiosity by other students, discussion and comment among students, or even some hostile remarks or discussion outside of the classrooms by other students" (Neal et al. v. Efurd, 2005, p. 23, quoting Holloman ex rel. Holloman v. Harland, 2004, pp. 1271-72).

The teacher concerns about the websites' impact on their teaching did not constitute material and substantial disruption as it was speculative (Neal et al. v. Efurd, 2005). As the court noted, the teachers' concerns about the websites were founded on rumors and the principal's inaccurate characterization of the websites' contents as threats against staff members. The court concluded that:

Absent the understandable apprehensions generated by the memo and general rumors, the Court believes these capable teachers would have properly ignored the rather crude and ineffectual attempts to annoy and harass via the internet in the same way they ignore the usual nonsense that a few high school students offer them on a day-to-day basis (Neal et al. v. Efurd, 2005, p. 22).

In essence, the court viewed Ryan's use of the words "Bulldog Death of the Week", and his solicitation of suggestions for the Bulldog Death of the Week, as so trifling that teachers would generally ignore them in the course of the day (Neal et al. v. Efurd, 2005, p. 13). This seems shortsighted, however. Despite the fact that Ryan did not fully develop the "Bulldog Death of the Week" feature of his website, the shootings at Columbine High School and various other school shootings remind us of the importance of not ignoring potential signals of violence, even at the incipient stages. Therefore, it was reasonable to forecast that Ryan's reference to Bulldog Death of the Week could lead to material and substantial disruption at the school. Moreover, Justin's cartoon, which featured the assistant principal shooting two students, provided reasonable grounds to forecast material and substantial disruption from the school. It was important to forecast material and substantial disruption and act accordingly because an actual shooting at the school would not only cause material and substantial disruption at the school but also potential carnage.

The district court applied the reasonable-recipient view of the true-threat doctrine (Neal et al. v. Efurd, 2005). Under this view, a true threat is "a statement that a reasonable recipient would have interpreted as a serious expression of an intent to harm or cause injury to another" (p. 16, quoting Doe v. Pulaski County Special School District, 2002, p. 624). The court found that Justin did not post any content on his website that a reasonable recipient would have viewed as a true threat. Even though Justin's cartoon showed the assistant principal shooting two students, the court explained that it was merely a figurative expression. Justin intended the cartoon to convey that his "school is deathly dull, and that the administration does not want it any other way" (p. 16). This is a remarkable conclusion, given that the reasonable-recipient focuses on the recipient's interpretation rather than the speaker's. It might be reasonable to conclude that a reasonable recipient would not have interpreted the cartoon as a threat that Justin himself would shoot students at the school. However, it is unreasonable to conclude, as the court did, that no reasonable recipient would have interpreted the cartoon as a threat. The website clearly portrayed the assistant principal shooting students. The website represented the cartoon as the assistant principal's creation. A justifiable reason for the finding of no true threat lies in the fact that it might be unreasonable and even absurd to think an assistant principal would use a cartoon to convey threats to kill students. The court, however, did not articulate this rationale for its finding. Another rationale is that the use of a cartoon betrayed the unserious nature of the shooting (Neal et al. v. Efurd, 2005).

The district court also found that Ryan did not post any true threat on his website (Neal et al. v. Efurd, 2005). Even though Ryan encouraged visitors to suggest the "Bulldog Death of the Week", this website feature was so undeveloped that reasonable visitors to the website could not have been viewed it as a serious expression of intent to harm (p. 16). The court ignored the hostility toward the school that pervaded the tone of his postings; and the fact that Ryan actually encouraged visitors to suggest a death of the week. The court apparently considered the inchoateness of the threatening thoughts as vitiating the finding of a true threat. According to the court, since the school mascot, rather than the students, was the bulldog, "Bulldog Death of the Week" could not be interpreted as a plan to harm students (p. 17). The court seemed to discount a potential grave threat to the mascot. According to the court, "it would be no less facetious to suggest that the actual death of either a bulldog or a student was being threatened by the use of the words [Bulldog Death of the Week] and/or [bulldog] images" on Ryan's website (p. 17).

The district court ruled that third-party postings of threats could not be attributed to Justin and Ryan merely because they created, operated or used the website (Neal et al. v. Efurd, 2005). Thus, the school district incorrectly relied on third-party postings as a basis for disciplining Justin. The court ruled that the "Bulldog Death of the Week" and "Kill Your Idols" mentions on Ryan's website were simply reflections of teenage communication in today's culture (pp. 25-26). Moreover, such language is pervasive in movies, music and video games. This perspective minimized the threatening nature of the speech; as did the principal's acknowledgment that he never viewed Justin or Ryan as dangers to students or faculty.

Even though the district court extended the material and substantial disruption test to off-campus student speech, it warned schools against overreaching censorship, noting that:

The real issue of how far a school can go in regulating off-campus speech is determined by the Constitution and existing case law, and a school district cannot by the creation or implementation of its own rules, override that precedent (Neal et al. v. Efurd, 2005, p. 27).

The court used both the material and substantial disruption test and the true-threat doctrine to *deny* school officials censorship authority over Justin's speech (Neal et al. v. Efurd, 2005). Therefore, application of the test and the doctrine to off-campus speech did not necessarily expand school-censorship authority. The court's stringency in application of the doctrine and the test makes it difficult for schools to censor off-campus student speech. While one could have deemed Justin's shooting cartoon and Ryan's Bulldog Death of the Week solicitation as censorable under the true-threat doctrine and the material and substantial disruption test (based on reasonable forecast of such disruption), the court's decision otherwise reflects an expectation that schools must present a very strong and unequivocal case that speech is threatening in order to extend censorship authority beyond the schoolhouse gate.

The court summarily concluded that Justin and Ryan's websites did not constitute fighting words, defamation or obscenity; as such we do not know the court's rationale for these conclusions (Neal et al. v. Efurd, 2005). Given that the court ruled that school officials had no reasonable ground to forecast material and substantial disruption from the speech, and since the websites did not include true threats, it is not surprising that the court similarly ruled that the websites did not constitute fighting words. The same evidence used for analyzing speech under the true-threat doctrine and the material and substantial disruption test is applicable to analysis of fighting words. We agree with the court that there was absolutely nothing in the speech that was obscene. The speech was not even sexual speech. The one area that is a mystery is the court's defamation conclusion in light of the website's violent graphic representation of the assistant principal in the act of killing students. Finally, based on the fact that the court mentioned fighting words, defamation or obscenity together as unprotected speech categories (and since these speech categories traditionally apply to speech outside the schoolhouse gate), it appears to us that the court would apply off-campus standards to students' off-campus obscene speech. In other words, the court would rely on the *Miller* test instead of the *Bethel* test in reviewing off-campus student speech for obscenity. This approach would protect relatively more student-speech rights, since as we discussed earlier in this book, the *Miller* test is more exacting than the *Bethel* test.

SPEECH DIRECTED AT OR AGAINST STUDENTS

In this section, we present the stories of students who have been censored by their schools for their online speech, in spite of the fact that the speech occurred outside the four walls of the school. We focus in particular on student speech that is directed at or against other students. We highlight how various courts have ruled on the right of students to speak off-campus and the authority of schools to censor such speech.

1. The Story of Jack Flaherty, Jr.

The Speech Incident: Taunting a Volleyball Player and His Mom

Keystone Oaks High School in Pennsylvania scheduled a volleyball game against Baldwin High School (also located in Pennsylvania) for the 2000-01 school year (Flaherty v. Keystone Oaks School District, 2003). In the days leading up to the game, Jack Flaherty, Jr., a senior student and volleyball player at Keystone Oaks High School, posted four messages on the message board of a website unaffiliated with his school district. Three of the messages were posted at home using his own personal computer after school hours. The fourth message was posted while he was at school using a school computer.

In his first posting from home, Jack expressed his opinion about his school's fledgling basketball program as well as the upcoming game and season (Flaherty v. Keystone Oaks School District, 2003). He also criticized a volleyball player at Baldwin High School and the student's mother. The posting stated:

Their Stories: Online Off-Campus Speech

I think that V.P. richard [sic] has made some very great points (especially about Baldwin) no one said that ko [Keystone Oaks High School] was winning states this year. I don't know where you got this outlandish idea. this [sic] is only the fourth year of mens volletball [sic] in our school and we don't have middle-school teams like some other teams in our section do. we [sic] are also a triple a team going against some teams with twice the enrollment as us. you [sic] also have to admit that our section is arguably the toughest in the state. Also our secret weapon [redacted] will show the 'Icon' what's up. Im [sic] not out to make excuses I think we are gonna hold our own this year just ask North Hills.

PS Bemis [Bemis is Pat Bemis, a student at Baldwin High School and on their volleyball team] from Baldwin: you're no good and your mom [Pat Bemis' mother is an art teacher at KOSD (Keystone Oaks School District)] is a bad art teacher (Flaherty v. Keystone Oaks School District, 2003, p. 700).

In the second posting from home, Jack continued his criticism of the Baldwin High School volleyball player and his mother. He also predicted a decisive win of the volleyball game that would embarrass players and fans of Baldwin High School (Flaherty v. Keystone Oaks School District, 2003). He stated:

I couldn't agree with you more. Someone better call the Guiness [sic] book of world records, for the biggest lashing in mens volleyball history. These purple panzies [sic] are in for the suprise [sic] of their lives. I predict players and fans will want to transfer to Ko [Keystone Oaks High School] after this game is through. I also predict that Bemis is going to shed tears on the court. So people from baldwin [sic] I will tell you this, you better save the ridiculous price of 2 dollars to go watch your school get embarrassed at for Bemis to make a spectacle of himself [sic]

P.S. My dog can teach art better than Bemis' mom (Flaherty v. Keystone Oaks School District, 2003, p. 700).

Jack's third posting from home was a response to an individual with the username "Kauffmoney. bitch please" (Flaherty v. Keystone Oaks School District, 2003, p. 700). In that posting, he touted volleyball players at his school as prospects for the all-Western Pennsylvania Interscholastic Athletic League (W.P.I.A.L.) team. The posting read as follows:

bitch please

Keystone Oaks has a few prospects for the all W.P.I.A.L [sic] team for example Middle hitter [redacted]. He stands 6 foot 7 inches and is ready to show those plum foreigners how to spike in America. Also another player is # 5 Jack Flaherty (The True Icon) he is 72 inches of mullet madness who is ready to let loose. Last but not least is [redacted]. He is young but is a strong canidate [sic] for W.P.I.A.L. MVP this year. watch [sic] out he is only a freshman! P.S. Kaufmoney eat my wad ho (Flaherty v. Keystone Oaks School District, 2003, p. 700).

Jack posted his fourth message during his journalism class (Flaherty v. Keystone Oaks School District, 2003). The message continued the same themes of his prior postings. The fourth message simply stated, "how [sic] bad is ko [Keystone Oaks High School] going to beat Baldwin [sic] I predict a lashing and for Bemis to shed tears" (p. 700). This was the only message he posted while he was at school. When the school officials learned about the posting, he was expelled from the volleyball team (Simonich, 2002). He was also barred from the school's premises after 3PM and from using the schools' computers. Jack and his parents filed a First Amendment suit against the school district claiming that the censorship violated his free speech rights (Flaherty v. Keystone Oaks School District, 2003). After the court ruled for Jack, reinstating him to the team, some players and coaches left the team in protest. This led Keystone Oaks High School to disband its volleyball team (Simonich, 2002).

Analysis

Jack and his parents claimed that school officials had no constitutional authority to censor his off-campus speech (Flaherty v. Keystone Oaks School District, 2003). They argued that the school's censorship authority was limited to speech on school grounds or at school-related events. They also contended that the school discipline policy needed to contain a geographical limitation on the reach of school authority in order for it to pass First Amendment muster; otherwise school officials would have unbridled power over student speech. The United States District Court for the Western District of Pennsylvania agreed. The court ruled that a school discipline policy must include a geographical limitation in order to avoid violating the First Amendment. Such a limitation must confine the jurisdiction of the school to the school's campus or school-related functions. The policy could also define school-censorship authority to include the times when students are in transit to and from school as long as the students are in the custody of the school.

The principal of Keystone Oaks High School contended that he had the constitutional authority to punish students for internet postings created in the privacy of the student's home on the student's personal computer (Flaherty v. Keystone Oaks School District, 2003). The principal also argued that he had the authority to punish students for off-campus speech (even if the speech was not at the school or a school-related function) that brought negative publicity or disrespect to the school or the volleyball team. Similarly, the coach claimed that he could punish a student for speech posted online in the student's home if the speech embarrassed the volleyball team or other players on the team:

Q. Coach Sieg, explain to me what you think are the limits of your authority to punish your volleyball players for speech that takes place outside of school.

A. If it is going to bring shame to the school or my program, I basically do what I did. I could suspend; I could expel (Flaherty v. Keystone Oaks School District, 2003, p. 706).

The court rejected these arguments as an ultra vires exercise of power. To rule otherwise would be to "permit a school official to discipline a student for an abusive, offensive, harassing or inappropriate expression that occurs outside of school premises and not tied to a school related activity" (Flaherty v. Keystone Oaks School District, 2003, p. 706). The court warned schools to respect the First Amendment rights of students to speak off-campus and to confine exercise of their powers within the schoolhouse gate. If school-censorship authority is to be exercised over speech that occurs off-campus, that speech must have occurred at a school-related function. If the student's off-campus speech is wholly personal speech that is not uttered at a school-related function, the school has no censorship authority over the speech. In Jack's case, even though his home postings were about a school-related function, they were not made at a school-related function. Therefore, the school's jurisdiction was limited to Jack's fourth

Their Stories: Online Off-Campus Speech

posting which occurred during his journalism class. Despite the ostensibly offensive nature of Jack's speech, and the taunts of an opposing player and his mother in his home postings, the school could not constitutionally exercise censorship jurisdiction over those postings. The court ruled that school policy should at least satisfy the material and substantial disruption test in order to be upheld.

2. The Story of J.C.

The Speech Incident: The YouTube Video of R.S.

After Beverly Vista High School, California, closed on Tuesday May 27, 2008, J.C. and a group of her thirteen-year old classmates visited a local restaurant (J.C. ex rel. R.C. v. Beverly Hills Unified School District, 2010). During the early dinner, J.C. used her personal video recorder to document the conversations among her friends about C.C – their classmate. The video, which lasted four minutes and thirty-six seconds, featured one of the students calling C.C. a "slut" and a "spoiled" child (p. 1098). The student's comments included various profanities. For instance, she referred to C.C. as "the ugliest piece of shit I've ever seen in my whole life" (p. 1098). She also discussed "boners" (p. 1098). As the student spoke, J.C. could be heard in the background cheering on the student's comments about C.C. with phrases such as "continue with the Carina rant" (p. 1098). One of the students was troubled by the group's attacks against C.C., prompting her to ask her classmates if she was "the only one that doesn't hate Carina?" (p. 1108).

Later that evening, after J.C. returned home, she used her personal computer to upload the video of the group's attacks on C.C. to YouTube for public viewing (J.C. ex rel. R.C. v. Beverly Hills Unified School District, 2010). Shortly after the video was uploaded, J.C. asked ten students to view it. She also told C.C. about the video. All of these contacts originated from J.C.'s home. After watching the video, C.C. told J.C. that she felt the comments in the video were mean. J.C. then offered to delete the video from YouTube. However, since C.C.'s mother planned to report the video to school officials the following morning, J.C. declined the offer. At least fifteen people viewed the video that evening, resulting in 90 "hits" (p. 1098). By the beginning of school the following morning, the video had 100 "hits" (p. 1119). J.C. never accessed the video at school. Additionally, while at school, she never encouraged anyone to view the video. About a month before this YouTube recording, J.C. had been disciplined in another case for surreptitiously recording her teachers.

On the morning of May 28, 2008, C.C. and her mother reported the video to school officials (J.C. ex rel. R.C. v. Beverly Hills Unified School District, 2010). C.C. was visibly agitated about the video and cried at school. During a twenty-five minute counseling session with the school counselor, C.C. revealed that she felt humiliated and hurt. She also expressed reluctance to return to class though the counselor successfully persuaded her to return. That morning, J.C. heard approximately ten students talking about the video. However, students were not able to view the video from the school's computers because the computers were configured to block student access to YouTube. While students could view the video on their cellphones, there was no proof that students used their cellphone for this purpose. Moreover, the school had a cellphone policy that banned on-campus cellphone use. Even though school officials required J.C. and the other students involved with the video to provide written statements about their roles in the video, only J.C. was disciplined. After school officials watched the video, they ordered J.C. to remove it from YouTube as well as her personal computer. They also suspended her from school for two days. J.C.'s mother sued the school district claiming that the school's censorship violated J.C.'s First Amendment right to free speech. They asked the court for injunctive relief and monetary damages.

Analysis

J.C.'s mother argued that the school had no censorship authority over J.C.'s speech because the entire speech occurred outside the schoolhouse gate (J.C. ex rel. R.C. v. Beverly Hills Unified School District, 2010). The United States District Court for the Western District of Pennsylvania, however, chose to focus more on the impact of the speech within the schoolhouse gate rather than the geographical origin of the speech. Accordingly, the court framed the issue in the case as whether school officials can constitutionally censor off-campus student speech that has an effect inside the school's campus. The court framed the issue this way because of its belief that Tinker v. Des Moines Independent Community School District (1969) governs the regulation of off-campus student speech (J.C. ex rel. R.C. v. Beverly Hills Unified School District, 2010). The court was firm in this belief despite recognizing that the United States Supreme Court has never decided a case involving off-campus student speech. The court reasoned that since cases such as Shanley v. Northeast Independent School District (1972), Boucher v. School Board of School District of Greenfield (1998), Beussink v. Woodland R-IV School District (1998), Lavine v. Blaine School District (2001), Killion v. Franklin Regional School District (2001) had applied the material and substantial disruption test to off-campus speech, the test must necessarily apply to J.C.'s speech (J.C. ex rel. R.C. v. Beverly Hills Unified School District, 2010). As evident in our earlier discussions in this book, these cases extended the material and substantial disruption test to off-campus speech without giving any significance to the difference between on-campus speech and off-campus speech. In fact, the United States District Court for the Western District of Pennsylvania was well aware of this. The district court observed that, "[i]n these cases, the courts have directly applied the *Tinker* substantial disruption test to determine if a First Amendment violation occurred, without first considering the geographic origin of the speech" (p. 1104). Additionally, "the substantial weight of authority indicates that geographic boundaries generally carry little weight in the student-speech analysis" (p. 1104). Consequently, the court viewed the material and substantial disruption test as a borderless test not tied to its origins in the on-campus factual context of Tinker v. Des Moines Independent Community School District. In other words, the court disregarded the existence of the very schoolhouse gate that the United States Supreme Court recognized in Tinker v. Des Moines Independent Community School District as the border between the school campus and off-campus settings. The court stated that, even more so in the current age where student communications are increasingly digital, school-censorship authority must not be limited by geography (J.C. ex rel. R.C. v. Beverly Hills Unified School District, 2010).

The district court ruled that, with the exception of Bethel School District No. 403 v. Fraser (1986), the Supreme Court's student-speech precedents govern in both on-campus and off-campus settings (J.C. ex rel. R.C. v. Beverly Hills Unified School District, 2010). The court excepted the *Bethel* test because the Supreme Court limited the test to on-campus student speech in Hazelwood v. Kuhlmeier (1988). The district court explained its other rationales for excepting the *Bethel* test:

The Court is not aware of any authority from the circuit courts applying Fraser [Bethel School District No. 403 v. Fraser] to speech that takes place off campus. Moreover, the reasoning of Fraser, which is anchored in the school's duty to teach norms of civility to its students, does not support extending Fraser to lewd or offensive speech occurring off campus (J.C. ex rel. R.C. v. Beverly Hills Unified School District, 2010, p. 1110).

While the court was correct that no circuit court of appeals had applied the *Bethel* test to off-campus student speech, as revealed in our earlier discussions of Killion v. Franklin Regional School District (2001) and Requa v. Kent School District No. 415 (2007), some district courts had. Thus, this rationale for excluding the *Bethel* test from off-campus student speech is weak. The stronger rationale is that the Supreme Court has indicated that different rules govern on-campus and off-campus vulgar, lewd, plainly-offensive and obscene speech.

The district court also refused to extend the *Bethel* test to off-campus speech because of its concern that such extension would give schools too much power over students (J.C. ex rel. R.C. v. Beverly Hills Unified School District, 2010). The court stated that it "does not wish to see school administrators become censors of students' speech at all times, in all places, and under all circumstances" (p. 1110). The court chose this approach to the *Bethel* test as its limitation on the broad authority it granted schools, in the same case, to censor all student speech in all situations. Limiting school authority by refusing to extend the *Bethel* test to off-campus speech is curious. Particularly because schools retain extensive authority over students' off-campus speech under the court's broad rule which made schools borderless entities for purposes of censorship. Apparently, the court wanted schools to have extensive authority as long as it was not too extensive. The court might have been concerned that it would be overruled by a higher court if it granted overly-extensive censorship authority to schools. Certainly, the material and substantial disruption test also imposes a limitation on school-censorship authority. However, with the court wholly disregarding the geographical origins of speech, the material and substantial disruption test does not preclude schools from censoring off-campus speech to the same extent that they would censor on-campus speech. The sweeping reach of the material and substantial disruption test also suggests that the test could undermine a wide range of student speech. This is because the court ruled that the material and substantial disruption test is the governing test whenever a student's off-campus speech does not fall under the *Morse*, *Hazelwood* and *Bethel* tests.

The district court tried to limit the scope of school-censorship authority under the material and substantial disruption test by making it difficult for schools to satisfy the test (J.C. ex rel. R.C. v. Beverly Hills Unified School District, 2010). Specifically, the court ruled that schools can censor students' off-campus speech only if there is a foreseeable risk that the speech will lead to material and substantial disruption within the school or at school activities; or if the speech actually causes material and substantial disruption on the school's campus or at school activities. This attempt to make it difficult for schools to use the test was tepid and disingenuous, however. While the court's requirement of reasonability foreseeability of material and substantial disruption limits the censorship reach of schools, this was not an original creation of the court. The United States Supreme Court wrote that requirement into the material and substantial disruption test when it created it in Tinker v. Des Moines Independent Community School District (1969).

The district court expanded school-censorship authority over off-campus speech by ruling that the use of school resource or time for off-campus is immaterial (J.C. ex rel. R.C. v. Beverly Hills Unified School District, 2010). In essence, in order to censor off-campus speech, school officials do not need to show that the student-speaker used school resource or time. Thus, school officials can, for instance, censor off-campus student speech created on the student's personal computer over the weekend; as long as the school satisfies the material and substantial disruption test. Additionally, how speech reaches the school campus is generally immaterial to whether schools can censor off-campus student speech. Accordingly, the student-speaker can be censored for off-campus speech that is brought to campus by either the speaker or a third party, even if the speaker did not encourage or facilitate the on-campus presence of the speech. There is one caveat to this general rule: reasonable foreseeability.

As long as it was reasonably foreseeable to the student-speaker that the off-campus speech would reach the school's campus, the school can censor the speech (J.C. ex rel. R.C. v. Beverly Hills Unified School District, 2010). This reasonable-foreseeability standard provides a nexus requirement between the school campus and the speech. If the student-speaker takes active steps to prevent the speech from reaching the school's campus, the speech cannot be censored even if the speech reaches the school. Additionally, if the evidence clearly establishes that the student never intended for the speech to get to the school, the speech cannot be censored. In the latter two situations, the school cannot use the material and substantial disruption test to censor the speech. Instead, the school must meet the same standards for censoring speech applicable to non-school entities such as the public forum analysis, fighting-words doctrine and defamatory speech discussed earlier in this book.

The district court ruled that, even if there was a schoolhouse gate confining the censorship authority of school officials over J.C.'s off-campus speech, the speech was still censorable because it had a nexus to the campus (J.C. ex rel. R.C. v. Beverly Hills Unified School District, 2010). Interestingly, the court found this nexus in the fact that C.C. and her mother brought the speech to school when they reported J.C. to school officials. In essence, a nexus between off-campus speech and the school is created when parents or students targeted in a student's speech bring the speech to school to call administrators' attention to it. As indicated earlier, the court ruled that the source of the speech's on-campus presence is constitutionally insignificant. Therefore, it was immaterial that no student besides C.C. viewed the speech at school. The court also ruled that J.C. could reasonably foresee that her speech would get to the school campus. The mere fact that the speech was posted on an internet site – YouTube – created this foreseeability because the internet is borderless. Moreover, it was reasonably foreseeable that one of J.C.'s classmates would bring the speech to campus because J.C. asked approximately ten students to view the YouTube clip on the weeknight that he posted the video. Besides, J.C. made no effort to prevent the speech from getting to the school.

The district court considered the fact that J.C.'s YouTube posting occurred on a weeknight material to finding reasonable foreseeability (J.C. ex rel. R.C. v. Beverly Hills Unified School District, 2010). This was because the weeknight provided proximate opportunity for the video to get on school grounds during the remaining days of the school week; making it reasonably foreseeable that the speech would get to the school's campus. Besides, J.C. informed C.C. of the video, creating reasonable foreseeability that an upset C.C. would bring the speech to campus. Furthermore, the court observed that the content of the speech was of such a nature that it was reasonably foreseeable that it would reach the school. According to the court, the speech's sexual, derogatory and defamatory nature made it inevitable that the speech would get to the school; particularly because it targeted a thirteen-year old. The court summarily deemed the speech defamatory without any legal analysis. Apparently the court equated the derogatory and sexual nature of the speech targeting the thirteen-year old to defamation. In essence, the court's determination was driven by the clearly disgusting nature of the speech.

The court concluded that the school's strict policy against student cellphone use did not vitiate the reasonable foreseeability of the speech getting to the school (J.C. ex rel. R.C. v. Beverly Hills Unified School District, 2010). The court reasoned that when speech is as offensive as J.C.'s, it is inevitable that school officials would view it on-campus when the speech is brought to their attention. In other words, the reasonable-foreseeability standard is not dependent on the foreseeability of students accessing the off-campus speech on-campus. Recall that reasonable foreseeability is satisfied even if only school officials access the speech on school grounds. Clearly this rule makes a policy banning student cellphone use immaterial to reasonable foreseeability. Accordingly, students need to take into account all persons that could reasonably access the speech at their school when determining if their off-campus speech is reasonably likely to reach the school.

The district court ruled that the mere on-campus discussion of J.C.'s video among ten students did not constitute material and substantial disruption (J.C. ex rel. R.C. v. Beverly Hills Unified School District, 2010). Just like with the armband speech in Tinker v. Des Moines Independent Community School District (1969), students could reasonably be expected to discuss J.C.'s video on school grounds once they learned about it. The school must show more than mere on-campus student discussion of off-campus speech before material and substantial disruption can be found (J.C. ex rel. R.C. v. Beverly Hills Unified School District, 2010). However, if the off-campus speech leads to a "widespread whispering campaign", that might suffice to constitute material and substantial disruption (p. 1118). Alternatively, schools must prove that the classroom was disrupted or that some kind of violence resulted from the speech. Furthermore, if the school's investigation of the off-campus speech has "ripple effects on class activities or the work of the school", that might suffice to constitute material and substantial disruption (p. 1117).

If the student-speaker and the target of the speech have a history of physical or verbal altercations between them, that would also provide the basis for reasonable forecast of material and substantial disruption (J.C. ex rel. R.C. v. Beverly Hills Unified School District, 2010). The school's history of material and substantial disruption from similar off-campus speech could also be a reasonable ground for forecasting that the current student's speech would cause material and substantial disruption. Additionally, schools would be right to forecast material and substantial disruption if the off-campus speech is by a student with a history of causing material and substantial disruption at the school. J.C. had a history of surreptitiously videotaping her teachers and she was actually previously punished for it. However, the court viewed that prior discipline as punishment for violation of school policy rather than punishment for speech. This conclusion effectively took that prior discipline history outside the scope of the First Amendment for purposes of judicial review of the current censorship of J.C.'s speech.

The district court ruled that the material and substantial disruption test can also be satisfied if off-campus speech causes school officials to be "pulled away from their ordinary tasks to respond to or mitigate the effects of a student's speech"; or if there is a reasonable basis to forecast this occurrence (J.C. ex rel. R.C. v. Beverly Hills Unified School District, 2010, p. 1114). The nature of the disruption to an administrator's time and routine must, however, be "highly out of the ordinary, not a response to the everyday emotional conflicts that students often get into" (p. 1118). In J.C.'s case, the disruption to school officials' time and routine during the investigation of speech was typical of school disciplinary investigations:

[T]he record demonstrates that Hart and Lue–Sang [the school counselor and the administrative principal respectively] took steps to investigate the nature of the conflict between J.C. and C.C., to counsel C.C. when she was upset, and to decide, along with Warren's input, whether to impose discipline. That is what school administrators do. As long as students have attended school, some get sent to the principal's office for possible discipline, some seek counseling from the school counselors, and upset parents *on occasion voice concerns to the school, whether it be about a child's poor grades, a student-teacher personality conflict, or otherwise. There is nothing in the record to demonstrate that J.C.'s conduct presented an unusual or extraordinary situation (J.C. ex rel. R.C. v. Beverly Hills Unified School District, 2010, pp. 1118-19).*

The district court also ruled that school officials' "emotional reaction" or disapproval of the content of speech will not suffice for censorship under the material and substantial disruption test (J.C. ex rel. R.C. v. Beverly Hills Unified School District, 2010, p. 1115, citing Beussink v. Woodland R-IV School District, 1998; Killion v. Franklin Regional School District, 2001; Saxe v. State College Area School District, 2001). This aligns with the Supreme Court's ruling in Tinker v. Des Moines Independent Community School District (1969) that offensiveness of speech is not an adequate ground for censorship. The district court also concluded that C.C.'s emotional reaction to the speech did not provide a constitutional basis for censorship under the material and substantial disruption test (J.C. ex rel. R.C. v. Beverly Hills Unified School District, 2010).

C.C.'s temporary refusal to return to class and her twenty-five minute counseling session with the school counselor also did not constitute material and substantial disruption of the school (J.C. ex rel. R.C. v. Beverly Hills Unified School District, 2010). According to the court, a twenty-five minute session is too short to constitute material and substantial disruption, particularly where, as here, the counselor is successful in calming the student down. Furthermore, the court ruled that material and substantial disruption "must be anchored in something greater than one individual student's difficult day (or hour) on campus" (p. 1119). Accordingly, C.C.'s hurt feelings and humiliation did not suffice for school censorship under the material and substantial disruption test. The court might have found material and substantial disruption from the speech, however, if C.C. physically or verbally confronted any of the students involved with the video. Moreover, had the off-campus speech impacted the student body's morale in a similar manner to the death of a student, the court would have found material and substantial disruption.

The district court ruled that the fact that C.C. was thirteen-years old, and emotionally immature at that age to be the target of mean taunts, was insufficient to constitute material and substantial disruption: "The Court cannot uphold school discipline of student speech simply because young persons are unpredictable or immature, or because, in general, teenagers are emotionally fragile and may often fight over hurtful comments" (J.C. ex rel. R.C. v. Beverly Hills Unified School District, 2010, p. 1122). This decision, however, did not foreclose students' tortious claims against those students who target them with derogatory, defamatory or threatening speech. The resolution for such students lies in the judicial system rather than through school censorship of off-campus speech under the material and substantial disruption test.

While the court acknowledged the existence of the infringement-of-rights test, it only found one case which had applied the test; and that case – Harper ex rel. Harper v. Poway Unified School District (2007) (discussed in chapter seven) – limited the test to student speech attacking a student's religion, race or sexual orientation (J.C. ex rel. R.C. v. Beverly Hills Unified School District, 2010). Courts rarely acknowledge the infringement-of rights test; therefore this test has scarcely been applied to any student speech. Even when courts acknowledge the test, they are ostensibly unsure of its meaning. The court in J.C.'s case conceded this lack of clarity:

Their Stories: Online Off-Campus Speech

[T]he precise scope of Tinker's 'interference with the rights of others' language is unclear, as the Court's analysis in Tinker focused primarily on whether a substantial disruption was reasonably foreseeable. Moreover, lower courts have not often applied the 'rights of others' prong from Tinker (J.C. ex rel. R.C. v. Beverly Hills Unified School District, 2010, p. 1123).

Notwithstanding this lack of clarity, the district court declared that, undoubtedly, mere emotional harm to a student cannot satisfy that test (J.C. ex rel. R.C. v. Beverly Hills Unified School District, 2010). The court ruled this way because no other court had found such harm sufficient under the infringement-of-rights test. Consequently, of the two *Tinker* tests, only the material and substantial disruption test actually governed J.C.'s off-campus speech. According to the court, the most substantial impact that J.C.'s speech had on the school's campus was the school's suspension of J.C. The school, however, cannot discipline a student and then claim that the very discipline of the student was material and substantial disruption. In essence, even though the court ruled that school officials had censorship authority over J.C.'s off-campus speech, the authority was not meaningful. This is because, as evident in the discussions above, the court set forth too many requirements that made it a little more challenging for school officials to actually satisfy the test. This case illustrates the hollowness of the judicial extension of school-censorship authority to off-campus speech under the material and substantial disruption test when schools cannot satisfy the test.

3. The Story of Jonathan Coy

The Speech Incident: Lewd Language in the "Losers" Website Section

At the start of the 2000-01 school year, parents of students in the North Canton City Schools in Ohio were asked to sign the school district's acceptable use policy governing student use of the district's computers and internet (Coy ex rel. Coy v. Board of Education of North Canton City Schools, 2002). This policy warned students against abusing the privilege of on-campus computer and internet access. It also prohibited students from using or accessing the school' computers or any website or other databases without school authorization. Additionally, it banned the display of offensive pictures and comments on the computers.

During the 2001 spring semester, Jonathan Coy, an eighth-grade student at North Canton Middle School, created a website on his personal computer to express his opinions about skateboarding and three of his schoolmates (Coy ex rel. Coy v. Board of Education of North Canton City Schools, 2002). His parents signed the acceptable use policy earlier in the school year. The website, which used profane language, was created outside school hours inside his home without use of any school resource. It described the adventures of NBP – a team of skateboarders that Jonathan belonged to. It also included the biographies, photographs and quotes of the skateboarders. A section of the website included photographs of students giving the middle-finger gesture. Jonathan targeted three of his schoolmates in another section of the website called "losers" (p. 795). He included disparaging comments below the photographs of each of these three students. Under one of the boys' photographs, Jonathan wrote that the boy's mother had sexually aroused her own son.

When the school district's technology specialist found out about the website, he asked the company hosting Jonathan's website to shut it down because it was offensive speech (Coy ex rel. Coy v. Board of Education of North Canton City Schools, 2002). At the time of this request, Jonathan had neither accessed the website at school nor done anything to bring it to the attention of school officials. After some students at Jonathan's school learned about his website from an unknown source, they reported him to their teacher. Troubled by the website's content, the teacher reported Jonathan to the principal. The following day, Jonathan appeared to access the website at the school. A teacher saw Jonathan switching between screens on a school computer during class while he was supposed to be working on an assignment. Suspecting that Jonathan was viewing his website, this teacher reported Jonathan to the principal who initiated an investigation. The principal asked the district's technology specialist to examine the school computer that Jonathan used during class in order to determine which websites he accessed. The technology specialist confirmed that Jonathan accessed his website on the school's computer without authorization in contravention of the acceptable use policy.

The principal suspended Jonathan from school for four days and notified Jonathan that he could face expulsion (Coy ex rel. Coy v. Board of Education of North Canton City Schools, 2002). The superintendent subsequently added an eighty-day expulsion to Jonathan's punishment. During the expulsion, Jonathan was allowed to attend school on probation with the stipulation that any further violation of school rules would reactivate the expulsion. Jonathan was barred from attending and participating in extracurricular activities for the rest of the school year. According to school officials, Jonathan was punished for creating his website. The expulsion letter sent to Jonathan's family stated that "[t]he inappropriate website is a major concern in this disciplinary matter" (p. 796). School officials also claimed that Jonathan violated the school district's acceptable use policy through his on-campus unauthorized access of an unauthorized website. They also claimed that the website accessed on school grounds was lewd and obscene in violation of school policy. In pertinent part, this policy provided that "[a] student shall not use obscenity, profanity ... or other patently offensive language or gesture, nor shall a student be in possession of patently offensive material on school property" (p. 796). School officials reported Jonathan's website to the local police department which launched an investigation that included a visit to Jonathan's home. Jonathan's parents filed a First Amendment claim against the school district asking the court for injunctive relief.

Analysis

The United States District Court for the Western District of Pennsylvania chose not to apply the *Bethel* test to Jonathan's speech (Coy ex rel. Coy v. Board of Education of North Canton City Schools, 2002). The court instead applied the state's statutory definition of obscenity. The statutory definition traditionally governs off-campus censorship initiated by non-school government entities. This is not unlike the *Miller* test which, as we noted in chapter five, governs government censorship of obscenity in the community at large (Miller v. California, 1973). The applicable Ohio statute defined obscenity as content that satisfied any of the following requirements:

1. *Its dominant appeal is to prurient interest;*
2. *Its dominant tendency is to arouse lust by displaying or depicting sexual activity, masturbation, sexual excitement, or nudity in a way that tends to represent human beings as mere objects of sexual appetite;*

3. *Its dominant tendency is to arouse lust by displaying or depicting bestiality or extreme or bizarre violence, cruelty, or brutality;*
4. *Its dominant tendency is to appeal to scatological interest by displaying or depicting human bodily functions of elimination in a way that inspires disgust or revulsion in persons with ordinary sensibilities, without serving any genuine scientific, educational, sociological, moral, or artistic purpose;*
5. *It contains a series of displays or descriptions of sexual activity, masturbation, sexual excitement, nudity, bestiality, extreme or bizarre violence, cruelty, or brutality, or human bodily functions of elimination, the cumulative effect of which is a dominant tendency to appeal to prurient or scatological interest, when the appeal to such an interest is primarily for its own sake or for commercial exploitation, rather than primarily for a genuine scientific, educational, sociological, moral, or artistic purpose (Coy ex rel. Coy v. Board of Education of North Canton City Schools, 2002, p. 795, citing Ohio Revised Code Annotated § 2907.01, 2002).*

The court's decision to rely on the traditional statutory definition of obscenity when discussing the obscenity of off-campus student speech suggests that the court expects schools to satisfy a higher standard than the *Bethel* test before censoring off-campus student speech. Indeed, it means that, when it comes to off-campus speech, schools must satisfy the same standards as non-school government entities in the state before they can constitutionally censor off-campus student speech. Jonathan's speech did not fit any of the definitions above: "the website contains no material that could remotely be considered obscene" (Coy ex rel. Coy v. Board of Education of North Canton City Schools, 2002, p. 795). As the court observed, Jonathan's speech was at most juvenile and boorish. The court actually ignored the language of the school policy governing obscenity in favor of the traditional statutory definition of obscenity. This again indicates that school policy governing censorship of obscene off-campus student speech must adhere to the same standards governing non-student citizens of the state.

The district court ruled that the applicability of the Supreme Court's student-speech precedents to specific student-speech cases is determined by the factual proximity of the case to the precedent in question (Coy ex rel. Coy v. Board of Education of North Canton City Schools, 2002). In other words, the Supreme Court precedent that most factually approximates the particular student-speech case will govern the case. This rule was another reason for the district court's refusal to apply the *Bethel* test to Jonathan's speech. Specifically, the court viewed the factual proximity of Jonathan's speech to that in Bethel School District No. 403 v. Fraser (1986) as weak. The court considered Jonathan's speech to be closer to the personal armband speech in Tinker v. Des Moines Independent Community School District (1969) than the vulgar speech before 600 captive-audience students at the mandatory school assembly in the *Bethel* case. The district court explained this rule quite aptly in its decision about the applicability of the *Bethel* test to Jonathan's case:

While Jon Coy accessed the website on a school computer in the school's computer lab, the Court finds the circumstances of this case nearer those of Tinker than Fraser [Bethel School District No. 403 v. Fraser (1986)]. Most important, Coy simply accessed his own website, a website he created on his own time and with his own equipment. At the time the defendants expelled Coy, they had no evidence that he had displayed the information contained in the website to any other student. Unlike Fraser, there was no evidence that he compelled 600 other students to view his website. And unlike Fraser, Coy's website, while crude, was not the 'elaborate, graphic, and explicit sexual metaphor' at issue in that case (Coy ex rel. Coy v. Board of Education of North Canton City Schools, 2002, p. 799, citing Bethel School District No. 403 v. Fraser, p. 678).

Apparently, an important factor in determining the *Bethel* test's applicability to student speech is whether other students saw the off-campus speech accessed on school grounds (Coy ex rel. Coy v. Board of Education of North Canton City Schools, 2002). Another is whether students were compelled to view the website as happened with the speech at the mandatory assembly in the *Bethel* case. The court also observed that the *Bethel* case involved an offline speech at an assembly whereas Jonathan's speech was speech on a website. This last factor is unpersuasive, however, given that the court found the *Tinker* case closer to Jonathan's speech despite the fact that the speech in the *Tinker* case, like that in the *Bethel* case, was offline speech. The *Tinker* case and the *Bethel* case were also factually similar in that they were wholly on-campus speech. Granted, an argument could be made that the students in the *Tinker* case created their armbands off-campus before accessing it on-campus; as likely did the student in the *Bethel* case. Under this perspective, both the *Bethel* case and the *Tinker* case would approximate Jonathan's speech because his speech was created off-campus but accessed on school property. The key distinction would be that, in *Bethel* and *Tinker*, the issue before the Supreme Court involved school-censorship authority over the on-campus components of the speeches in those cases. The Supreme Court never addressed the off-campus components and the school districts did not present the off-campus components as the basis for censorship.

As it did with the *Bethel* test, the federal district court insisted on factual proximity to Supreme Court precedent in its determination of whether the *Hazelwood* and *Morse* tests were applicable to Jonathan's speech. The court ruled that the *Hazelwood* test was not applicable to Jonathan's speech because, even though he was on school grounds when he accessed the speech, he was not engaged in school-sponsored speech. According to the federal district court, "[t]he extent of Jon Coy's expressive activity was the private viewing of his own website" (Coy ex rel. Coy v. Board of Education of North Canton City Schools, 2002, p. 799). Additionally, "[h]is expressive activity was not sanctioned by the school nor did the school knowingly provide any materials to support the expression" (Coy ex rel. Coy v. Board of Education of North Canton City Schools, p. 800). The *Morse* test was inapplicable to Jonathan's speech because, unlike the student in Morse v. Frederick (2007), Jonathan did not engage in speech at a school-sanctioned event. Besides, his speech did not advocate illegal drug use.

The federal district court considered Jonathan's on-campus access of his website as too de minimis to be constitutionally significant (Coy ex rel. Coy v. Board of Education of North Canton City Schools, 2002). The court reasoned that he only accessed the speech during one class as opposed to a pervasive all-day access. Even though he viewed the website multiple times during the class, he only did so periodically. He also did it surreptitiously "in a manner designed to draw as little attention as possible to what he was viewing" (p. 800). This made Jonathan's speech akin to the silent passive armbands in Tinker v. Des Moines Independent Community School District (1969) designed to draw as little attention as possible during class (Coy ex rel. Coy v. Board of Education of North Canton City Schools, 2002). These similarities led the district court to conclude that the same test that the Supreme Court applied to the armbands in the *Tinker* case must govern Jonathan's speech. The court also ruled that when student speech does not fit on all fours with the other Supreme Court precedents, the *Tinker* case will govern.

Even though the court found the on-campus component of Jonathan's speech de minimis, it ruled that the material and substantial disruption test – created in an on-campus context – governed his speech

Their Stories: Online Off-Campus Speech

(Coy ex rel. Coy v. Board of Education of North Canton City Schools, 2002). Given that the court found the on-campus component of Jonathan's speech de minimis, it effectively extended the material and substantial disruption test to off-campus speech. The court, however, failed to provide a rationale for extending the test to off-campus speech. As noted earlier, the court merely presumed and ruled that the material and substantial disruption test is the default test for student speech, irrespective of locale. The court's failure to provide a rationale is surprising, given the court's insistence on factual proximity of cases to Supreme Court precedents. Recall that the district court ruled that applicability of the Supreme Court student-speech precedents must be based on how closely the case sub judice approximates the facts of those precedents (Coy ex rel. Coy v. Board of Education of North Canton City Schools, 2002). While the on-campus component of Jonathan's speech was similar to the silent passive expression in the *Tinker* case, his speech was nonetheless off-campus speech. The fact that the court dismissed the on-campus component of Jonathan's speech as de minimis confirms this. Since none of the Supreme Court's student-speech precedents involved off-campus speech, as off-campus speech, Jonathan's speech was not factually proximate to those precedents. The court should have been consistent with its factual-proximity requirement or at least explained its rationale for departing from this requirement. All we know for certain is that the court enforced this requirement for the *Bethel*, *Morse* and *Hazelwood* tests but not for the material and substantial disruption test.

The district court found insufficient evidence in the record to determine whether the school district punished Jonathan only for his on-campus access or for his off-campus creation of the site (Coy ex rel. Coy v. Board of Education of North Canton City Schools, 2002). Initially, the district claimed that it punished him for creation of the speech, including content of the speech. Indeed, as noted earlier, the expulsion letter stated that "[t]he inappropriate website is a major concern in this disciplinary matter" (p. 796). Subsequently, however, the school district contended that the punishment was merely for the on-campus access of the site, presumably to limit the court's review to discipline for on-campus speech. As the court observed, however, even before school officials had any evidence that Jonathan had accessed the website on the school's campus, the district's technology specialist sought to censor Jonathan's speech. The specialist called the site-hosting company to request that Jonathan's website be shut down because it contained offensive language before there was evidence that Jonathan accessed the speech on school grounds. In spite of the insufficient evidence, the court stated that it was "implausible" that Jonathan was punished for his on-campus access as opposed to the creation and content of the website.

As the court rightly noted, if school officials only censored Jonathan for accessing an unauthorized website on school grounds in violation of school policy, they did not violate his First Amendment rights (Coy ex rel. Coy v. Board of Education of North Canton City Schools, 2002). Such censorship would be valid regulation of the time, place and manner of speech as long as the censorship was not motivated by the content of the speech. In Jonathan's case, school officials censored his speech because of its content. They made clear that they found the content offensive and unacceptable. Accordingly, the censorship was not a valid regulation of the time, place or manner of his speech. Finally, irrespective of locale, school officials could not censor Jonathan's speech under the material and substantial disruption test. There was no evidence in the record that Jonathan's off-campus creation of the website, or his on-campus access of the website, materially and substantially disrupted the school. Further, as noted earlier, the on-campus access was de minimis. As a result, school officials could not censor his speech through an on-campus lens of the speech (i.e. the on-campus access of the website) or an off-campus lens (i.e. the creation of the website).

4. The Story of Nick Emmett

The Speech Incident: The Mock Obituary Website

During the 1999-2000 school year, students in a creative writing class at Kentlake High School in Washington were asked to compose their own obituaries (Emmett v. Kent School District No. 415, 2000, p. 1089). The assignment galvanized Nick Emmett, an 18-year old senior and basketball team co-captain at the school who decided to simulate the assignment on a website. While at home on Sunday February 13, 2000, Nick created a website which he called the "Unofficial Kentlake High Home Page" (p. 1089). In spite of this reference to the school in the title, no school resource was used in the creation of the website. Nick included a disclaimer on the website notifying visitors that it was not a school-sponsored website. The disclaimer also emphasized that the site was merely designed for entertainment. The site featured facetious mock obituaries of two friends. It also featured a poll for visitors to vote on the next person to "die"– the next person to be featured in a facetious mock obituary (p. 1089). Nick also wrote various critical remarks about his school administrators and teachers on the site.

Over the next few days at the school, students as well as school officials discussed the mock obituaries on Nick's website but no disciplinary action was taken against Nick (Emmett v. Kent School District No. 415, 2000). On the evening of February 16, 2000, a local television station aired a news segment about the website. Even though Nick included the disclaimer on the site, the station characterized the obituaries as a hit list of persons that the student-speaker planned to kill. It is unclear how the station came to characterize the obituaries as a hit list, especially since Nick did not use the term "hit list" on the site. That same evening, after Nick learned of the news segment, he deleted the website from the internet. The following day, the principal placed Nick on emergency expulsion, even though there was no evidence that the website intimidated students or disrupted the school. The expulsion was later changed to a five-day suspension. The principal also banned Nick from his basketball team and all other sports. Nick filed suit against the school district for injunctive relief claiming a violation of his First Amendment right to free speech.

Analysis

The United States District Court for the Western District of Washington ruled that Nick's website was off-campus speech even though the site had a target audience related to the school (Emmett v. Kent School District No. 415, 2000). Specifically, the court declared that, while "the intended audience was undoubtedly connected to Kentlake High School, the speech was entirely outside of the school's supervision or control" (p. 1090). In other words, the court felt that school officials should not have unfettered power over off-campus speech. The court came to this conclusion because of Justice Brennan's concurrence in Bethel School District No. 403 v. Fraser (1986) which stated that "[i]f respondent had given the same speech outside of the school environment, he could not have been penalized simply because government officials considered his language to be inappropriate" (p. 688). This is sound reasoning as we explicated in chapter eight. Moreover, the United States Supreme Court endorsed Justice Brennan's statement in both Hazelwood v. Kuhlmeier (1988) and Morse v. Frederick (2007).

While Nick's speech was not vulgar/lewd speech like the speech in the *Bethel* case, it was arguably plainly-offensive speech despite its facetious nature. Asking for people to vote for someone to die next is clearly offensive, particularly to those named in the obituary who might not view it as a joke. The district court ruled, however, that the *Bethel* test was not applicable to Nick's speech (Emmett v. Kent School District No. 415, 2000). Therefore, the plainly-offensive nature of the obituaries was immaterial. The court chose not to extend the *Bethel* test to Nick's speech because Nick's speech was not presented at a school assembly as occurred in *Bethel* case. The court also concluded that the *Hazelwood* test was not applicable to Nick's speech because his speech was neither in a school-sponsored forum nor part of a class assignment as was the case in Hazelwood v. Kuhlmeier (1988). In other words, the court looked for factual proximities between Nick's speech and the United States Supreme Court's student-speech precedents in determining their applicability to Nick's speech.

Even though the district court insisted on factual proximities between Supreme Court precedent and the speech in the case sub judice, it chose to apply the material and substantial disruption test to Nick's off-campus speech (Emmett v. Kent School District No. 415, 2000). This is puzzling because Nick's speech is factually distinct from the speech in Tinker v. Des Moines Independent Community School District (1969) which created the material and substantial disruption test. In fact, the district court characterized Nick's speech as "entirely outside of the school's supervision or control" (Emmett v. Kent School District No. 415, p. 1090). A literal interpretation of this statement suggests that the school had absolutely no authority to censor the speech. That would mean that, irrespective of actual or reasonable forecast of material and substantial disruption from the speech, school officials could not censor it. The decision to apply the material and substantial disruption test, however, indicated that Nick's speech was not wholly outside the school's control. It indicated that the speech was not beyond the school's censorship authority as long as the school could show actual or reasonable forecast of material and substantial disruption of the speech. Although the court extended the material and substantial disruption test to Nick's off-campus speech, it indicated that the off-campus nature of Nick's speech might make it more difficult to satisfy the test than would obtain with on-campus speech. Since the court did not expound on this statement, however, it is impossible to know what additional hurdles the court would impose for off-campus versus on-campus speech.

The court found no evidence of material and substantial disruption from Nick's speech (Emmett v. Kent School District No. 415, 2000). As the court observed, the website was facetious. While the court did not use the true-threat doctrine, it still considered whether the speech had a threatening nature and violent tendency. The court incorporated the true-threat analysis into its material and substantial disruption analysis of Nick's speech. Based on the satirical nature of the speech, the court found that Nick's mock obituaries as well as the polling of who should die next presented no violent tendencies. Nick also did not intend the speech to be threatening. Further, he did not intend to facilitate violence through his speech. In fact, he included a disclaimer, which proved important to the court as it expressly warned visitors that the site was only for entertainment. Besides, there was no evidence that the speech threatened any student or that any student actually felt threatened by the speech. Requiring the analysis of off-campus speech under the material and substantial disruption test to include determination of whether the speech is threatening or violent might be an added hurdle that could ensure greater protection for off-campus speech relative to on-campus speech under the material and substantial disruption test. We are simply speculating here, however. Given that the court did not reveal the hurdles that it alluded to we are unable to make a firm declaration about them. Finally, the court emphasized that, while schools must be empowered to address increasing violence within the schoolhouse gate, they must work within the parameters of the First Amendment. That simply means school officials must comply with the material and substantial disruption test.

5. The Story of T.V. and M.K.

The Speech Incident: The Lollipop Pictures

In the summer of 2009, T.V. and M.K., ninth-grade volleyball players at Churubusco High School in Indiana, had sleepovers with friends at M.K's house (T.V. ex rel. B.V. v. Smith-Green Community School Corporation, 2011). M.K. was also a school cheerleader and a show choir member. The sleepovers took place a few weeks before the July tryout for the following season's volleyball team. During the first sleepover, T.V. and M.K. took some risqué photographs of themselves sucking on rainbow-colored lollipops in the shape of a phallus. One photograph showed M.K. sucking on a lollipop as T.V. acted like she was sucking on another lollipop between M.K.'s legs. Both students were fully clothed in this photograph. Another photograph featured three girls with the following caption from M.K.: "Wanna suck on my cock" (p. 772).

At one of the sleepovers, T.V. snapped a photograph of M.K. simulating a kiss with another girl (T.V. ex rel. B.V. v. Smith-Green Community School Corporation, 2011). Several other photographs were taken at their final sleepover, including one which featured all the girls in pajamas with the exception of M.K. who was in lingerie. In another photograph, T.V. simulated anal sex as she was photographed behind another girl who was on her knees. Another photograph showed M.K. standing as a girl held up one of her legs. While the leg was held up, T.V. could be seen holding a toy trident between M.K.'s legs to simulate a phallus. The students also took a photograph of T.V. bending over as M.K hit a trident placed between T.V.'s derrière. One other photograph showed M.K. posing as a stripper with money in her lingerie. T.V. and M.K. claimed that they were "just joking around" when they took the photographs (p. 772).

After T.V. returned home from the sleepovers, she uploaded several of the photographs on her Facebook and Myspace pages but restricted access to those that she granted "friend" status (T.V. ex rel. B.V. v. Smith-Green Community School Corporation, 2011). She also uploaded some lollipop photographs to Photo Bucket which is password-restricted. The girls chose to upload the photographs to these sites because they wanted to share the humor in the photographs with friends. No school resource or time was used in creating or uploading the photographs.

A parent who learned of the photographs through her daughter took printouts to the school superintendent at the beginning of the school year (T.V. ex rel. B.V. v. Smith-Green Community School Corporation, 2011). She informed the superintendent that the students had posted the photographs on Photo Bucket, Facebook and Myspace. She also told the superintendent that the photographs had divided the volleyball team into two camps: girls who favored the photographs against those who opposed them. Based on this claim that the photographs had fueled dissension within the team, the superintendent ordered the principal to take action against the students involved. Another parent and employee of the district complained similarly about the photographs to the principal. Before taking action against T.V. and M.K., the principal did not even attempt to verify with the volleyball coaches or players the veracity of the divisiveness complaint.

The principal suspended T.V. and M.K. from extracurricular and co-curricular activities for an entire calendar year (T.V. ex rel. B.V. v. Smith-Green Community School Corporation, 2011). Unlike with extracurricular activities, students earned academic credit for co-curricular activities; thus suspension from co-curricular activities impacted the students' grades. The principal claimed that the suspensions were

Their Stories: Online Off-Campus Speech

justified because T.V. and M.K. violated school policy which required members of the extracurricular teams to be good citizens on campus as well as outside the campus. The policy required good citizenship for the entire calendar year, including the summer when school was not in session. The principal also claimed that posing for the photographs, and posting them on the internet, discredited the school. He claimed that it was reasonable to forecast material and substantial disruption from the posing and posting of the photographs.

The principal made a non sequitur reasonable-forecast argument: he claimed that he could reasonably forecast that the photographs would lead to material and substantial disruption because the school recently lost two students in a fatal automobile accident (T.V. ex rel. B.V. v. Smith-Green Community School Corporation, 2011). He also claimed that he could reasonably forecast material and substantial disruption from the photographs because, during the prior spring semester, the school encountered increased student discussions in the gymnasium and hallways after some students appeared drunk in online photographs. The principal believed that the drunken photographs presented similar concerns to the photographs taken by T.V. and M.K. He told T.V. and M.K. that their suspensions would be reduced if they attended three counseling sessions and apologized to the athletic board. After they fulfilled these requirements, their suspensions were indeed reduced to twenty-five percent of their fall semester's extracurricular and co-curricular activities. T.V. and M.K. filed a First Amendment claim against the school district seeking injunctive relief and monetary damages.

Analysis

The United States District Court for the Northern District of Indiana framed the issue in the case as an inquiry into "the limits school officials can place on out of school speech by students in the information age where Twitter, Facebook, MySpace, texts, and the like rule the day" (T.V. ex rel. B.V. v. Smith-Green Community School Corporation, 2011, p. 771). This framing of the issue made it unequivocal that the court's rules and holding were specifically directed at online speech created outside the schoolhouse gate. Further, the court ruled that off-campus speech does not become on-campus speech simply because it gets to the school's campus unless the speech was brought to the campus by the student-speaker (as opposed to another person). Since M.K. and T.V. did not take their photographs or online postings to school, the speech retained its off-campus status. The speech's off-campus status was also amplified by the fact that the speech was created entirely within the students' homes. As evident in the various censorship stories in this book, it is extraordinary to see a court preclude conversion of off-campus speech into on-campus speech merely on the premise that the speech was brought to school by someone other than the student-speaker. Typically, courts that choose to convert off-campus speech into on-campus speech do so once the speech is determined to have been brought on-campus; irrespective of who brought the speech to the school.

The federal district court seemed particularly displeased with the students' lewd speech; and with the fact that the federal judiciary had to decide a case with such speech:

Let's be honest about it: the speech in this case doesn't exactly call to mind high-minded civic discourse about current events. And one could reasonably question the wisdom of making a federal case out of a 6–game suspension from a high school volleyball schedule (T.V. ex rel. B.V. v. Smith-Green Community School Corporation, 2011, p. 771).

Notwithstanding the court's displeasure, it chose not to apply the test that would have easily allowed censorship of lewd speech – the *Bethel* test. The refusal to apply the *Bethel* test was founded on the importance of precedential context to the court. Specifically, the court emphasized that the context of a United States Supreme Court student-speech precedent must be considered in determining whether to apply the precedent to a case sub judice. The context of T.V. and M.K.'s online speech was clearly different from that of Bethel School District No. 403 v. Fraser (1986). Unlike T.V. and M.K.'s speech which was accessed volitionally in an online context, the context of the speech in the *Bethel* case was a mandatory assembly of a captive student audience. T.V. also restricted public access to the photographs through a password-protected website – Photo Bucket. In addition, she restricted Facebook and Myspace access to persons she invited as friends. The student-speaker in the *Bethel* case had no such restrictive ability. The court also reasoned that the *Bethel* test was inapplicable to T.V. and M.K.'s speech because of Justice Brennan's statement in the *Bethel* case that was affirmed in subsequent Supreme Court cases. Recall that Justice Brennan stated that the school would not have been authorized to censor Matthew Fraser's plainly-offensive, vulgar and lewd student speech if it had been off-campus speech (Bethel School District No. 403 v. Fraser, 1986).

As the federal district court observed, in Hazelwood v. Kuhlmeier (1988), the United States Supreme Court accepted Justice Brennan's premise when it stated that "[a] school need not tolerate student speech that is inconsistent with its 'basic educational mission,' even though the government could not censor similar speech outside the school" (T.V. ex rel. B.V. v. Smith-Green Community School Corporation, 2011, p. 779, citing Hazelwood v. Kuhlmeier, p. 266). Later on, in Morse v. Frederick (2007), the Supreme Court declared that "[h]ad Fraser delivered the same speech in a public forum outside the school context, it would have been protected" (T.V. ex rel. B.V. v. Smith-Green Community School Corporation, p. 779, citing Morse v. Frederick, p. 405). Based on these Supreme Court statements, the district court concluded that the *Bethel* test cannot be used to censor off-campus speech that is plainly offensive, vulgar, obscene or lewd (T.V. ex rel. B.V. v. Smith-Green Community School Corporation, 2011). Therefore, the court ruled that the school district could not "prevail on a characterization of the photographs as lewd and vulgar in reliance on *Fraser* because, simply put, [t]he School District's argument fails at the outset because *Fraser* does not apply to off-campus speech" (p. 779, citing, J.S. ex rel. Snyder v. Blue Mountain School District, 2011, pp. 930–32). The problem with this conclusion lies in the court's insistence on parallel contexts before applying the Supreme Court's student-speech precedents to a case. While the statements referenced certainly apply to off-campus speech, they arose in the context of cases involving on-campus speech as opposed to the off-campus context of T.V. and M.K.'s speech. Therefore, the on-campus contexts of the Supreme Court precedents suggest that the Court's off-campus statements referenced above are at best dicta.

In spite of the court's insistence that context matters, it chose to apply the material and substantial disruption test to T.V. and M.K.'s off-campus speech (T.V. ex rel. B.V. v. Smith-Green Community School Corporation, 2011). As we noted in chapter ten, the material and substantial disruption test arose in the context of on-campus speech. It also arose in the context of offline speech on armbands which is different from the online context of T.V. and M.K.'s speech. The following concession by the court makes it is even more surprising that the court chose to apply the material and substantial disruption to off-campus speech:

The Supreme Court has not considered whether Tinker applies to expressive conduct taking place off of school grounds and not during a school activity and has in fact noted that '[t]here is some uncertainty

Their Stories: Online Off-Campus Speech

at the outer boundaries as to when courts should apply school speech precedents' (T.V. ex rel. B.V. v. Smith-Green Community School Corporation, 2011, p. 781, citing Morse v. Frederick, 2007, p. 401 and Porter v. Ascension Parish School Board, 2004, p. 615).

Undeterred by the uncertainty in the jurisprudence, the court extended the material and substantial disruption test to off-campus student speech because other federal courts as discussed in this book had already extended the test beyond its on-campus context (T.V. ex rel. B.V. v. Smith-Green Community School Corporation, 2011). In essence, the court was hypocritical by turning a blind eye to its own context-matters principle when the principle was not convenient to its decision. This inconsistency merely adds to the uncertainty in the jurisprudence as it says context matters but then it does not matter. The court concluded that, despite the contextual restraints of the *Tinker* case, it would "assume without deciding that *Tinker* applies" to T.V. and M.K.'s off-campus speech (p. 781). Assumption without decision was a convenient escape hatch that the district court used to avoid engage in thoughtful intellectual reasoning to clarify the off-campus speech rights of students.

The federal district court ruled that schools must prove that disruption is "specific and significant" in order for censorship to pass muster under the material and substantial disruption test (T.V. ex rel. B.V. v. Smith-Green Community School Corporation, 2011, p. 782, citing Saxe v. State College Area School District, 2001, p. 211). As the court stated, the volleyball team disagreements about the photographs did not constitute specific and significant disruption. The disagreements were nothing more than "unremarkable dissension" or "[p]etty disagreements among players on a team ... [which] is utterly routine" (p. 783). Further, the court opined that the parent who complained about divisiveness on the volleyball team was likely a "busybody" who chose to magnify trivial disagreements (T.V. ex rel. B.V. v. Smith-Green Community School Corporation, p. 782). Besides, only two parents on the entire volleyball team and school complained about T.V. and M.K.'s speech. The principal also failed to investigate the parents' complaints in order to determine whether any team disruption was material and substantial. As the court poignantly observed, the Supreme Court requires more than the innuendos and rumors that school officials relied upon in censoring T.V. and M.K.'s:

[A]t most, this case involved two complaints from parents and some petty sniping among a group of 15 and 16 year olds. This can't be what the Supreme Court had in mind when it enunciated the 'substantial disruption' standard in Tinker. To find otherwise would be to read the word 'substantial' out of 'substantial disruption' (T.V. ex rel. B.V. v. Smith-Green Community School Corporation, 2011, p. 784).

If the school officials had shown that the students' speech caused debilitated school morale or a decline in test scores/student attendance, it would have proved material and substantial disruption.

Not only did school officials fail to show actual material and substantial disruption, they also had no reasonable grounds to forecast material and substantial disruption (T.V. ex rel. B.V. v. Smith-Green Community School Corporation, 2011). As we noted earlier, the school argued that it had reasonable grounds to forecast material and substantial disruption from T.V. and M.K.'s photographs because of an accident at the school two weeks before school officials learned of the photographs. This accident was non sequitur, however, as it was unrelated to T.V. and M.K.'s photographs. School officials also claimed that they had reasonable grounds to forecast material and substantial because drunken photographs of some others students caused increased hallway chatters and gymnasium discussions during the prior semester. The hallway chatters and gymnasium discussions did not substantially disrupt the school, however. Consequently, school officials could not use this prior incident, which did not even involve T.V. and M.K. as a reasonable basis for forecasting material and substantial disruption from T.V. and M.K.'s photographs.

The district court is willing to scrutinize school evidence of reasonable forecast of or actual material and substantial disruption in order to monitor school officials' exercise of their censorship authority over off-campus speech (T.V. ex rel. B.V. v. Smith-Green Community School Corporation, 2011). This is important because, as the court indicated, school officials must not be authorized to censor off-campus speech as easily as they do speech inside the schoolhouse gate. We agree with the court that this monitoring of school evidence is critical to the judiciary's role as guardian of the First Amendment; particularly in the light of the reality that several courts have eroded students' speech rights by granting schools censorship authority over off-campus speech. It is even more critical because of the judicial trend toward an "unseemly and dangerous precedent to allow the state, in the guise of school authorities, to reach into a child's home and control his/her actions there to the same extent that it can control that child when he/she participates in school sponsored activities" (T.V. ex rel. B.V. v. Smith-Green Community School Corporation, 2011, pp. 784-85, citing Layshock ex rel. Layshock v. Hermitage School District, 2011, p. 216). In all, schools could expect this court to require incontrovertible evidence of material and substantial disruption before censorship of off-campus speech is sanctioned. This is good news for students as it makes censorship more difficult for schools.

6. The Story of D.J.M.

The Speech Incident: The 357 Magnum Conversation

Almost daily during the 2006 fall semester, D.J.M., an eleventh-grade student at Hannibal High School in Missouri, communicated through Instant Messaging (IM) with various friends, including classmate C.M. (D.J.M. ex rel. D.M. v. Hannibal Public School District No. 60, 2011). These IM conversations occurred on his home computer after school hours. During one of those IM sessions, D.J.M. engaged in a conversation with C.M. that spanned nine pages. C.M. used her home computer for the conversation. D.J.M. started the IM session with C.M. and other friends by discussing classes, music, televisions shows, masturbation and body piercings. D.J.M. then revealed that he was frustrated that L., a female classmate whom he wanted to date, rejected him. C.M. then asked D.J.M.: "what kidna gun did your friend have again?" (p. 758). D.J.M. responded that the friend had a "357 magnum" (p. 758). C.M. then stated: "haha would you shoot [L.] or let her live?" to which D.J.M. responded: "i still like her so i would say let her live" (p. 758). C.M. then asked D.J.M., "well who would you shoot then lol?" (p. 758). D.J.M.'s response was "everyone else" (p. 758). He then listed some students that he would "have to get rid of" (p. 758). This list included students who belonged to groups that he disliked such as "midget[s]," "fags," and "negro bitches" (p. 758). He stated that some of these students "would go" or "would be going" but that he would spare a named girl during the shooting (p. 758). Even though D.J.M. had a gothic appearance, he had never engaged in violence or threatened anyone at the school prior to the IM conversation with C.M.

C.M. as well as D.J.M. used "lol [laughing out loud]", "haha" and "YAYAYYAY" consistently during the conversation to signal their amusement at the idea of shooting their classmates (D.J.M. ex rel.

Their Stories: Online Off-Campus Speech

D.M. v. Hannibal Public School District No. 60, 2011, p. 758). As the conversation progressed, however, C.M.'s view of D.J.M.'s comments changed. C.M. increasingly considered D.J.M.'s comments about killing classmates to be a genuine and serious threat. As a result, she reached out to an adult friend on IM to express her concerns. C.M. shared some of D.J.M.'s comments with the adult friend and told the friend that the comments frightened her. She also told the friend that D.J.M. had access to a gun and that he planned to take it to school to kill "fags" and "shoot everyone he hates then shoot himself" (p. 758). She revealed that D.J.M. "want [ed] hannibal [Hannibal High School] to be known for something" (p. 758). Additionally, C.M told the friend that D.J.M. was on various medications and had previously been hospitalized. The friend asked C.M. to continue the IM conversation with D.J.M. in order to determine if he was merely venting out of depression that day or if he genuinely intended to threaten the school. Nevertheless, the adult friend informed D.J.M.'s principal of the comments because she thought that the comments were sufficiently serious to warrant school attention.

When C.M. resumed the IM session, she asked D.J.M if his tirade about shooting classmates was due to frustration over the unrequited romantic interest (D.J.M. ex rel. D.M. v. Hannibal Public School District No. 60, 2011). The question agitated D.J.M. who responded: "wtf how did me shooting people at school come up into that [conversation about L.]? ... i still like [L.] and i don't want to do anything hurting or wrong to her" (p. 758). D.J.M. then identified a classmate who "would be the first to die" if he got access to a gun (p. 758). He added, "anyways I'm not going to do that[.] not anytime soon I feel better than I did earlier today" (pp. 758-59). C.M. and D.J.M. then proceeded to discuss several other unrelated topics while C.M. continued her conversation about D.J.M.'s comments with the adult friend. The friend told C.M. that she believed D.J.M.'s threats were genuine and serious. She implored C.M. to tread cautiously in her conversations with D.J.M. That same day, C.M. emailed parts of her conversation with D.J.M. to the principal. The email also stated in pertinent part:

[D.J.M.] had told me earlier before I started saving the messages that he had a friend who had a gun that he could get. A revolver I think he said. He told me he wanted Hannibal [Hannibal High School] to be known for something and that after he shot the people he didnt like he would shoot himself .... I asked him if he had a way to buy a gun and I asked if he had anyone old enough to get one for him and he said someone who was 21 could get one but he doesnt think he would buy it for him (D.J.M. ex rel. D.M. v. Hannibal Public School District No. 60, 2011, p. 759).

School officials received several calls from parents who expressed concern about D.J.M.'s comments (D.J.M. ex rel. D.M. v. Hannibal Public School District No. 60, 2011). Parents also called to inquire if their children were on a hit list. School officials implemented security measures at the school to ensure student safety and to allay parent concerns. The police arrested D.J.M. after the principal (in consultation with the superintendent) reported his comments. He was sent to juvenile detention and required to undergo a psychiatric examination. During the examination, D.J.M. revealed that he had experienced suicidal ideations. School officials suspended him for ten days while he was in juvenile detention. The superintendent, however, extended the suspension for the remainder of the school year because she felt that his speech caused disruption at the school and because he had been sentenced to juvenile detention. His parents filed a First Amendment claim against the district seeking rescission of the suspension as well as monetary damages.

Analysis

The United States Court of Appeals for the Eighth Circuit acknowledged that there is uncertainty in the student-speech jurisprudence because the United States Supreme Court has never considered a case involving off-campus student speech (D.J.M. ex rel. D.M. v. Hannibal Public School District No. 60, 2011). The court also noted that the Supreme Court's student-speech precedents were strictly limited to speech in on-campus settings. In addition, the court of appeals observed that the Supreme Court's failure to rule on off-campus speech has resulted in conflicting rulings in the lower courts about school-censorship authority over off-campus speech. In spite of the uncertainty in the jurisprudence, the court of appeals chose to extend the material and substantial disruption test to off-campus student speech because the Supreme Court's student-speech precedents were "instructive" for off-campus student speech (p. 760). In particular, the court relied on the following language from Tinker v. Des Moines Independent Community School District (1969):

[C]onduct by the student, in class or out of it, which for any reason—whether it stems from time, place, or type of behavior—materially disrupts classwork or involves substantial disorder or invasion of the rights of others is, of course, not immunized by the constitutional guarantee of freedom of speech (p. 513).

The court of appeals interpreted the phrase "in class or out of it" as authorization of school censorship of off-campus speech if the speech causes material and substantial disruption (D.J.M. ex rel. D.M. v. Hannibal Public School District No. 60, 2011). While the phrase "in class or out of it" could be interpreted to encompass censorship of off-campus speech under the material and substantial disruption test, it must be viewed in context. In light of the on-campus context of the *Tinker* case, the phrase likely refers to speech that occurs outside of the classroom but within the schoolhouse gate (see chapter seven). In the two sentences preceding the *Tinker* quote above, the United States Supreme Court stated:

A student's rights, therefore, do not embrace merely the classroom hours. When he is in the cafeteria, or on the playing field, or on the campus during the authorized hours, he may express his opinions, even on controversial subjects like the conflict in Vietnam, if he does so without 'materially and substantially interfere[ing] with the requirements of appropriate discipline in the operation of the school' and without colliding with the rights of others (Tinker v. Des Moines Independent Community School District, 1969, pp. 512-13).

These two sentences appear to confirm our interpretation of the phrase "in class or out of it" as limited to speech inside the schoolhouse gate. It is significant that the Supreme Court did not use the phrase "in school or out of it." Had the court used "school" instead of "class", there would be less reason to doubt the off-campus reach of the quote above, despite the on-campus context of the case. Besides, the court could have easily use the word "school" in the quote given that it was addressing a school-related case; yet it chose the word "class" for that quote. Thus, the court of appeals appears to have misinterpreted the Supreme Court precedent.

The court of appeals ruled that school officials are not authorized to go on a fishing expedition or neighborhood patrol of students' off-campus speech (D.J.M. ex rel. D.M. v. Hannibal Public School

Their Stories: Online Off-Campus Speech

District No. 60, 2011). In particular, the court stated that "[s]chool officials cannot constitutionally reach out to discover, monitor, or punish any type of out of school speech" (p. 765). Instead, they must wait for the speech to be brought to their attention. Accordingly, the court modified the material and substantial disruption test. Under the modified test, school officials can censor off-campus student speech if:

1. It is reasonably foreseeable that the speech would be brought to the attention of school officials; and
2. There is reasonable forecast of material and substantial disruption or actual material and substantial disruption from the speech.

The court observed that threatening speech like D.J.M.'s IM comments would satisfy this test. The court, however, conceded that judges would find it challenging to apply this test to off-campus speech because the lack of Supreme Court clarity makes it difficult to "decide what degree of foreseeability or disruption to the school environment must be shown to limit speech by students" (D.J.M. ex rel. D.M. v. Hannibal Public School District No. 60, p. 767).

The court of appeals also applied the true-threat doctrine to D.J.M.'s speech despite acknowledging that the Supreme Court has never considered a case involving student threat of violence (D.J.M. ex rel. D.M. v. Hannibal Public School District No. 60, 2011). Apparently, the court believed that schools can censor students' off-campus speech using the same rules that govern censorship of other citizens outside the schoolhouse gate. One of those rules is the true-threat doctrine which readily applies to D.J.M.'s conversation since it included threats. The court used the reasonable-recipient view of true threat which regards a true threat as a "statement that a reasonable recipient would have interpreted as a serious expression of an intent to harm or cause injury to another" (p. 762, citing Doe v. Pulaski County Special School District, 2002, p. 624). In order for a threat to constitute a true threat, school officials must also show that the student-speaker intended to communicate the speech to either the target of the threat or a third party. Clearly, D.J.M. intentionally communicated his IM comments to C.M. – a third party. It was also reasonably foreseeable that the targets of the speech would become aware of it because C.M. was their classmate. Besides, as the court noted, D.J.M. took no proactive steps to prevent the target or a third party from learning about the threats expressed on IM.

The court also concluded that D.J.M.'s speech constituted a true threat because a reasonable recipient would view his comments about access to guns and killing classmates as serious threats (D.J.M. ex rel. D.M. v. Hannibal Public School District No. 60, 2011). Additionally, a reasonable recipient would have interpreted D.J.M.'s comments as true threats because of the specificity of the threats. For instance, D.J.M. specifically identified the 357 magnum as his weapon of choice. He also listed specific students that he wanted to kill. He mentioned a particular student as the "first to die" if he got a gun (p. 758). Furthermore, he stated ominously that he wanted his school "to be known for something" (pp. 758, 763). D.J.M.'s admission of depression and plan to commit suicide after killing classmates also made it likely that a reasonable recipient would regard his threats as genuine. D.J.M. countered that C.M. used "lol" during the speech because she found his comments amusing and innocuous rather than threatening. This was a weak argument, however, because C.M. actually interpreted D.J.M.'s comments as a genuine threat; as evident in the content and tone of her communications with the adult friend and the principal. The fact that C.M. did not inform D.J.M. that she viewed his comments as a genuine threat did not vitiate their nature as a true threat. The reaction of other recipients of the comments, such as the principal, superintendent, police and the juvenile court, also revealed that they likewise viewed D.J.M.'s comments as a serious expression of intent to harm his classmates. As the court observed, no one who saw the comments considered them a joke. Given these facts, and the reality that the First Amendment does not protect true threats, the court concluded that school officials validly censored D.J.M.'s off-campus online speech.

This case assured that the true-threat doctrine and a modified material and substantial disruption test govern school censorship of off-campus student speech.

7. The Story of S.J.W and S.W.W.

The Speech Incident: The Twin Brothers' North Press Blog

In December 2011, twin brothers S.J.W and S.W.W., juniors at Lee's Summit North High School in Missouri, created a website to express their opinions about various issues related to their school (S.J.W. v. Lee's Summit R–7 School District, 2012). One of the brothers used the school computer to upload files utilized in creating their website – North Press. The school district's records showed that an unknown person(s) accessed the website through the district's computers on at least three different school days. On one of those days, six school district computers were used. On the second day, two different district computers were used. On the third day, several more computers were used to either access or attempt to access the website.

The website included a blog designed for discussions, satire and venting about school events (S.J.W. v. Lee's Summit R–7 School District, 2012). The brothers posted several racist comments, including ridicule of black students, on the blog. They also posted sexually-explicit comments which disparaged named female classmates. Other blog postings discussed various fights at the school. The blog postings used derogatory and other offensive language. While the website was not password-protected, it was hosted on a domain site that precluded American users from finding it through a Google search. An American user could only find the website if the user knew its address. The brothers shared the address with some of their school friends, one of whom posted a racist comment on the blog.

While the brothers only intended for their friends to know about the website, the entire student body learned about it during the same week that the website was created as the site became a topic of discussion at the school (S.J.W. v. Lee's Summit R–7 School District, 2012). Certain teachers claimed that the website created classroom-management challenges for them amidst student discussions of the site. Two teachers described the last day of that week as the most disruptive of their careers. On that same day, the local media descended on the school and school officials received several calls from parents concerned about their children's safety as well as bullying and discrimination at the school. The disruptions at the school primarily resulted from the brothers' postings and their schoolmate's racist posting.

Immediately after school administrators learned about the website from both teachers and students, they suspended S.J.W and S.W.W. from school for ten days (S.J.W. v. Lee's Summit R–7 School District, 2012). The suspension was later changed to a 180-day suspension. The brothers were permitted to enroll at another district school during the suspension. School officials also blocked access to the website on school computers. The school district argued that their actions were justified because the speech disrupted the school. S.J.W and S.W.W.'s parents filed a First Amendment claim against the school district seeking injunctive relief. They contended that the other district school did not offer some classes that S.J.W and S.W.W. needed. They also argued that the suspension would harm their opportunities to pursue college scholarships and career opportunities.

Their Stories: Online Off-Campus Speech

Analysis

The United States Court of Appeals for the Eighth Circuit ruled that schools can censor off-campus student speech under the material and substantial disruption test if it is reasonably foreseeable that the speech will be brought to the attention of school officials or reach the school (S.J.W. v. Lee's Summit R–7 School District, 2012). The court found this modified material and substantial disruption test applicable because other courts had already extended the test to off-campus speech. According to the court, in the constitutional analysis of off-campus speech, the origin of the speech might not be as important as the reasonable foreseeability of the speech getting to the school or school officials.

Earlier we mentioned that S.J.W and S.W.W. created North Press to address school-related issues (S.J.W. v. Lee's Summit R–7 School District, 2012). Since North Press was "targeted at" the school, it was reasonably foreseeable to come to the attention of school officials or reach the school (p. 778). Even though S.J.W and S.W.W. hosted North Press on a foreign domain site so as to ensure that no one in America could access the website without the address, they shared the website address with some classmates. This made it reasonably foreseeable that the speech would be brought to the attention of school officials or reach the school.

Moreover, the various incidents at the school after the speech got to the campus constituted material and substantial disruption (S.J.W. v. Lee's Summit R–7 School District, 2012). These incidents included the media presence at the school as well as the high volume of parent calls about student safety, bullying and discrimination. The court noted that students targeted on the site could experience distress if S.J.W and S.W.W. returned to the school.

The key lesson from this very brief case is that schools have broad censorship authority over all online off-campus student speech that targets the school; as long as school officials can satisfy the modified material and substantial disruption test. This is unfortunate for students because a grant of broad censorship authority is concomitant with restriction of students' free speech rights.

8. The Story of Kara Kowalski

The Speech Incident: The S.A.S.H. Website

On Thursday April 1, 2005, after Kara Kowalski, a senior student at Musselman High School in West Virginia, returned home from school, she used her personal computer to create a Myspace webpage for group discussions (Kowalski v. Berkeley County Schools, 2011). Kara claimed that she created this group webpage titled "S.A.S.H." in order to create student awareness of STDs (sexually-transmitted diseases) which had become a major topic of discussion at the school (p. 567). In reality, however, the webpage primarily targeted a female classmate – Shay N.

Kara wrote "No No Herpes, We don't want no herpes" below the webpage title (Kowalski v. Berkeley County Schools, 2011, p. 567). She invited about 100 people, including schoolmates, from her Myspace "friends" list to the webpage (p. 567). Only about twenty-four students accepted the invitation, however. One of those students was Ray Parsons, who used a school computer to join the webpage during a class which took place after regular school hours. Ray posted a photograph of himself and a friend holding their noses as they displayed a sign that read, "Shay Has Herpes" (p. 567). Kara responded to Ray's posting with the following comments: "Ray you are soo funny!-)"; and "the best picture [I]'ve seen on myspace so far!!!!" (p. 567). Many students indicated that they found the photograph funny.

Ray subsequently added two photographs of Shay to the webpage after editing them (Kowalski v. Berkeley County Schools, 2011). One of the photographs portrayed Shay's face with red dots representing herpes. It also showed Shay's pelvic region with an accompanying sign which stated, "Warning: Enter at your own risk" (p. 568). The second photograph showed Shay's face with a sign that read, "portrait of a whore" (p. 568). Some students on the webpage thought Kara, rather than Ray, posted the photographs. One of those students stated to Kara: "your so awesome kara ... i never thought u would mastermind a group that hates [someone] tho, lol [laugh out loud]" (p. 568). Another student lauded Kara as a hero for posting the photographs.

During depositions, Kara claimed that her website title "S.A.S.H." stood for "Students Against Sluts Herpes" (Kowalski v. Berkeley County Schools, 2011, p. 567). Ray, however, disagreed, claiming that the title actually referred to Shay. According to Ray, S.A.S.H. stood for "Students Against Shay's Herpes" (p. 567). In fact, many student comments on the webpage focused on Shay. For instance, one student stated that "shay knows about the sign, wait til she sees the page lol" (p. 568). Another student responded with the comment "Haha.. screw her" (p. 568). This student then stated several times, "This is great" (p. 568). In a nod to Ray and his sign "Shay Has Herpes", this same student stated, "Kara sent me a few interesting pics ... Would you be interested in seeing them Ray?" (p. 568).

Immediately after Shay's father learned of the webpage, he called Ray to tell him that he was very upset about the photographs (Kowalski v. Berkeley County Schools, 2011). This happened on the same day that the webpage was created. When Kara learned of the call, she unsuccessfully tried to delete the photographs and the webpage. Consequently, she simply changed the title from "S.A.S.H." to "Students Against Angry People" (p. 568). The following day, Shay's parents took a hard copy of the webpage to school officials. They also filed a harassment complaint about the webpage. Shay did not attend school that day because she felt that the students' comments had created a hostile environment for her.

In the course of the subsequent investigation, school officials learned that, even though Kara created the website, Ray posted the photographs and herpes comments directed at Shay (Kowalski v. Berkeley County Schools, 2011). Nevertheless, they decided to discipline Kara for creating a "hate website" in violation of school policy against harassment, bullying and intimidation during school-related activities (p. 568). The school policy also required students to promote an atmosphere of respect, care and compassion which Kara's website failed to do. Kara was suspended from school for ten days. The assistant superintendent, however, changed the ten-day suspension to a five-day suspension. Kara also received a 90-day "social suspension" barring her from attending all school events unless she was a direct participant in the event (p. 568). Kara was also banned from the cheerleading squad for the rest of the school year. Additionally, she was prohibited from crowning her successor as the new "Queen of Charm" at the Charm Review (p. 568). Kara contended that school officials and students ostracized her because of her punishments. This left her depressed and on depression medication. Kara sued the school district under the First Amendment seeking injunctive and declaratory relief as well as monetary damages.

Analysis

Kara argued that school officials should not have censorship authority over her off-campus speech because the United States Supreme Court has never authorized school censorship of off-campus speech (Kowalski v. Berkeley County Schools, 2011). She argued that the Supreme Court's student-speech precedents were inapplicable because they were decided in the context of on-campus speech. The school

Their Stories: Online Off-Campus Speech

district countered that school officials could censor off-campus speech if the speech was reasonably foreseeable to reach the school's campus and cause material and substantial disruption. The United States Court of Appeals for the Fourth Circuit agreed with the school even though the court acknowledged that the Supreme Court has never ruled on off-campus speech or student speech involving the verbal abuse of a student. The court believed it was sufficient that the Supreme Court had authorized schools to censor student speech that "interfered with the school's work and discipline" (p. 571, citing Tinker v. Des Moines Independent Community School District, 1969, p. 513). Indeed, this quote was one of the Supreme Court's descriptions of the material and substantial disruption in the *Tinker* case. However, as Kara rightly noted, the *Tinker* case involved on-campus speech. The court's decision to apply the broad language in the quote from an on-campus case – the *Tinker* case – to an off-campus speech context is faulty. Particularly, because each time the Supreme Court has confronted a wholly different factual context of student speech, it has created a new test. In other words, since the Supreme Court has not extended the same test to two wholly different contexts, it is unlikely that the Court would borrow one of its on-campus tests in its first off-campus student speech case. Indeed, in Morse v. Frederick (2007), the Supreme Court stated that its student-speech jurisprudence is not limited to a specific test; and that the Court will consider creating a new test in wholly new factual contexts.

Even though the United States Court of Appeals for the Fourth Circuit relied on Morse v. Frederick (2007), the court apparently did not notice the part of the *Morse* case which indicated that wholly new factual circumstances could require a different test. Instead, the court of appeals ruled that schools can censor harassing off-campus student speech under the material and substantial disruption test if the speech presents a safety concern similar to that in Morse v. Frederick (2007) (Kowalski v. Berkeley County Schools, 2011). The court explained that schools can censor harassing speech because such speech is analogous to speech advocating illegal drug use – speech the Supreme Court deemed censorable in the *Morse* case. Recall from our discussions in chapter ten that the Supreme Court justified the censorship of illegal-drug advocacy on the basis of harm from drugs, drug epidemic in schools and student safety (Morse v. Frederick, 2007). The court of appeals concluded that harassing speech can be censored using these same justifications; especially because harassing student speech has become epidemic in schools (Kowalski v. Berkeley County Schools, 2011). Harassing speech has also caused student depression, suicidal ideations and suicides, thus creating student-safety concerns. The court of appeals relied on these *Morse*-like safety rationales in ruling that school officials could censor Kara's speech. The court declared that "[j]ust as schools have a responsibility to provide a safe environment for students free from messages advocating illegal drug use, schools have a duty to protect their students from harassment and bullying in the school environment" (Kowalski v. Berkeley County Schools, p. 572).

While student safety was an overarching concern in Morse v. Frederick (2007), Justice Alito (author of the controlling opinion in the case) explicitly emphasized that the *Morse* case should not be interpreted to authorize censorship of speech other than the advocacy of illegal drugs. Justice Alito's opinion was controlling because, Justice Kennedy who was one of the five Justices in the majority in the 5-4 decision joined Justice Alito's concurring opinion (Morse v. Frederick, 2007). Given that these two Justices were pivotal to getting five votes for the majority opinion, the Alito opinion became controlling. Thus, the Alito opinion should be accorded significant weight. Yet, in its review of Kara's case, the United States Court of Appeals for the Fourth Circuit, apparently ignored the limited drug-advocacy interpretation of the *Morse* case that Justices Kennedy and Alito emphasized as the basis for the Supreme Court majority's decision (Kowalski v. Berkeley County Schools, 2011).

The court of appeal's curious decision to apply the *Morse* case as rationale for censorship of off-campus student speech presents another problem: In the *Morse* case, the Supreme Court did not discuss student safety in order to facilitate using the material and substantial disruption test to censor the advocacy of illegal drugs. The Supreme Court instead created a new test independent of the material and substantial disruption test that allows censorship of advocacy of illegal drug use. The court of appeals on the other hand, used its *Morse*-like safety rationales as an avenue to facilitate its application of the material and substantial disruption test to Kara's speech (Kowalski v. Berkeley County Schools, 2011). This was evident in the court's ruling that schools can censor harassing off-campus student speech under the material and substantial disruption test if the speech presents a safety concern similar to that in Morse v. Frederick.

The court of appeals rightly noted that the determination of whether online speech is off-campus speech or on-campus speech is a "metaphysical question" (Kowalski v. Berkeley County Schools, 2011, p. 573). This is because online speech can be ubiquitous. Accordingly, students should reasonably expect their online speech to get to their schools. Kara's case illustrates the reality that location might be immaterial for online speech. As the court observed, even though Kara "pushed her computer's keys in her home, ... she knew that the electronic response would be, as it in fact was, published beyond her home and could reasonably be expected to reach the school or impact the school environment" (p. 573). Additionally, Kara invited her classmates to the webpage making it reasonably foreseeable that the discussions on the webpage would reach the school's campus. With student access to smartphones and other devices for surreptitious as well as covert online access at schools, it might be unreasonable for students to expect their online speech to be confined outside the schoolhouse gate. Even when students use privacy settings on their websites, those granted "friend" status might access it on school grounds, creating an on-campus presence for the speech.

According to the court of appeals, the first letter of the webpage's title, "S.A.S.H." also made it reasonably foreseeable that the speech would reach the school (Kowalski v. Berkeley County Schools, 2011, p. 568). While Ray and Kara disagreed about the full meaning of the acronym S.A.S.H., they both agreed that the first letter of the title stood for "Students" (p. 567). The fact that the speech targeted students was evidence that Kara expected her schoolmates to become aware of the webpage, making it likely that one of them would take the webpage or its contents to school. In fact, as noted earlier, a student comment on the webpage indicated that the target of the webpage – Shay – would find out about its contents: "shay knows about the sign, wait til she sees the page lol" (p. 568). As the court noted, this posting made it reasonably foreseeability that the speech would reach the school campus because the commenting student indicated a willingness to disclose the webpage. The comment also created the possibility that Shay would become aware of the webpage contents, get upset and then report the webpage to school officials as actually happened in this case. Besides, Ray accessed the webpage on-campus using a school computer. Therefore, even though Kara herself did not access the speech on-campus, the speech actually reached campus. Based on these facts, the court ruled that Kara's speech was "made in the school context" (p. 573).

The United States Court of Appeals for the Fourth Circuit effectively ruled that school officials can censor off-campus student speech as speech "in the school context" if the school can show two factors (Kowalski v. Berkeley County Schools, 2011, p. 577). These two factors, which would give the online off-campus speech "a sufficient nexus with the school" follow: (a) the speech was reasonably foreseeable to reach the school's campus; and (b) there was reasonable forecast of material and substantial disruption or actual material and substantial disruption from the speech (p. 577). The court adopted this modified material and substantial disruption test because other courts had already applied the test to censorship of student speech originating outside the schoolhouse gate. Apparently, the court regarded speech "made in the school context" as distinct from on-campus speech (p. 577).

While the material and substantial disruption test applies to on-campus speech, the modified material and substantial disruption test governs speech "made in the school context" (Kowalski v. Berkeley County Schools, 2011, p. 577). It appears that the "made in the school context" language was simply used to distinguish censorable off-campus speech from uncensorable off-campus speech. Censorable off-campus speech is speech "made in the school context" and this is defined by the modified material and substantial disruption test. Despite ruling that off-campus speech could be censored as speech "made in the school context", the court declared that "[w]e need not resolve, however, whether this [Kara's] speech] was in-school speech" (p. 573). The statement could be interpreted in one of two ways: The court declined to determine if Kara's speech was on-campus speech; or the court declined to determine if Kara's speech constituted off-campus speech "made in the school context". Since the court actually applied the modified material and substantial disruption test to Kara's speech, the former interpretation is more likely. Besides, the court applied its "made in the school context" rule to hold that the school policy prohibiting harassment, bullying and intimidation during school-related activities encompassed Kara's speech; supporting our conclusion that the former interpretation is more faithful to the court of appeal's thinking.

The federal court of appeals determined that school officials had reasonable grounds to forecast material and substantial disruption from Kara's speech (Kowalski v. Berkeley County Schools, 2011). This was because Kara created the online forum that enabled other students to harass one of their classmates. Kara was not absolved of responsibility even though Ray, rather than Kara, posted the comments and photographs about Shay and herpes. The court effectively attributed Ray's comments on Kara's webpage to Kara. In addition, the court concluded, as a matter of law, that the comments on the webpage constituted harassing and defamatory speech and therefore materially and substantially disruptive speech. This nature of the comments also provided reasonable basis to forecast material and substantial disruption from the webpage. As the court explained, "[g]iven the targeted, defamatory nature of Kowalski's [Kara's] speech, aimed at a fellow classmate, it created 'actual or nascent' substantial disorder and disruption in the school" (p. 574). The speech also caused material and substantial disruption because Shay missed school, became depressed and had to use depression medication. The court suggested that, without censorship, Kara's speech might have had a "snowballing effect" at the school as other students imitated Kara by creating webpages similar to Kara's in order to harass other students (p. 574). Finally, the court was convinced that Ray's access of the webpage during a class justified censorship because the access had the potential to materially and substantially disrupt the class. This appears to be very speculative, however; especially because the United States Supreme Court found no reasonable basis for forecast of material and substantial disruption in Tinker v. Des Moines Independent Community School District (1969) despite the fact that a mathematics teacher's class was "practically 'wrecked'" by a student's in-class access of speech (pp. 514, 517). If the practical wrecking of class did not suffice in the *Tinker* case, neither should Ray's mere in-class access.

While the United States Court of Appeals for the Fourth Circuit mentioned the infringement-of-rights test, it did not explicitly apply this test independently of the material and substantial disruption test (Kowalski v. Berkeley County Schools, 2011). We use the term "explicitly" because the infringement-of-rights test is certainly different from the material and substantial disruption test; but it was not clear that the court saw this distinction. If the court saw the distinction, it failed to articulate a distinction. The court instead appeared to view the infringement-of-rights test as just another iteration of the material and substantial disruption test. For instance, this was evident in the court's interpretation of the United States Supreme Court's decision in Tinker v. Des Moines Independent Community School District (1969). According to the court of appeals, the *Tinker* case "recognized the need for regulation of speech that interfered with the school's work and discipline, *describing that interference as* [emphasis added] speech that 'disrupts classwork,' creates 'substantial disorder,' or 'collid[es] with' or 'inva[des]' 'the rights of others'" (Kowalski v. Berkeley County Schools, pp. 571-72, quoting Tinker v. Des Moines Independent Community School District, p. 513). Accordingly, it appears that, the court of appeals would have come to the same conclusion that it did under the material and substantial disruption test if it had conducted a separate analysis using the infringement-of-rights test (independent of the material and substantial disruption test).

We believe the federal court of appeals applied the *Bethel* test to Kara's speech though this is not entirely clear (Kowalski v. Berkeley County Schools, 2011). If the court indeed applied the test, it did so without distinguishing the on-campus context of Bethel School District No. 403 v. Fraser (1986) from the off-campus context of Kara's speech. We believe that the court applied the *Bethel* test because it based approval of censorship of Kara's speech on quotes from the *Bethel* case. These quotes (such as set forth later in this paragraph) were integral to the *Bethel* test which authorizes censorship of speech in order to teach students civility and fundamental values. Yet, the court stated that "[w]e need not resolve ... whether *Fraser* [*Bethel* test] could apply because the School District was authorized by *Tinker* to discipline Kowalski, regardless of where her speech originated" (p. 573). The court appeared to apply the *Bethel* test when it declared that the speech on Kara's webpage was "not the conduct and speech that our educational system is required to tolerate, as schools attempt to educate students about 'habits and manners of civility'" (Kowalski v. Berkeley County Schools, p. 573, quoting Bethel School District No. 403 v. Fraser, p. 681). The speech on the webpage was also not the kind of speech or conduct that schools need to accept as they teach students about "fundamental values necessary to the maintenance of a democratic political system" (Kowalski v. Berkeley County Schools, quoting Bethel School District No. 403 v. Fraser, p. 681). While the court of appeals quoted these statements from the *Bethel* case correctly, the court failed to account for the fact that Kara's speech occurred inside her home while the student speech in the *Bethel* case occurred at an official school assembly. The contradictions in the court's apparent application of the *Bethel* test and its declaration of not applying the test are potentially reconcilable through the court's ruling under the modified material and substantial disruption test: It is possible that the court's ruling, under the modified material and substantial disruption test, that Kara's speech was "made in the school context" carried over to its review under the *Bethel* test (p. 573). In other words, the court might have viewed Kara's speech as speech "made in the school context", for purposes of the *Bethel* test, based on the fact that the speech was reasonably foreseeable to reach the school's campus. If so, this would be the rare court to extend the *Bethel* test to off-campus speech using the mere fact that the speech is reasonably foreseeable to reach the school campus.

The court's decision to apply the material and substantial disruption test to speech originating off-campus, and to seemingly apply the *Bethel* test while pretending not to, creates confusion for school officials, legal scholars, lawyers and other courts. In spite of the confusion the court already created in its analysis, it muddled the jurisprudence even further by failing to provide clarity:

Their Stories: Online Off-Campus Speech

There is surely a limit to the scope of a high school's interest in the order, safety, and well-being of its students when the speech at issue originates outside the schoolhouse gate. But we need not fully define that limit here (Kowalski v. Berkeley County Schools, 2011).

This abdication of responsibility to clarify an obfuscated jurisprudence is very unfortunate. As evident in this book, it is because of such abdication of responsibility by the Supreme Court and the lower courts that the off-campus student-speech jurisprudence is in such quandary. The abdication might encourage schools to abuse the jurisprudence's lack of clarity by testing how far they can censor student speech. The truth is that schools have no reason to do otherwise until the courts provide unequivocal clarity.

CONCLUSION

In this chapter, we presented the stories of students censored by their schools after speaking off-campus in online settings. We reviewed and analyzed lower court decisions that grappled with the issue of whether the First Amendment accords protection to students against school censorship of off-campus online speech. We parsed the judicial reasoning in the cases to determine whether they included language that could be interpreted to give students even a modicum of constitutional right to off-campus online speech. Our discussions show that most cases relied on the material and substantial disruption test from Tinker v. Des Moines Independent Community School District (1969) in determining the right to off-campus online speech. Some courts chose to modify the material and substantial disruption test in order to make it a little more difficile for schools to censor off-campus online speech. A few courts opted to rely on the rarely-used, mysterious and malleable infringement-of-rights test (see chapter seven for more on this test).

Various courts also relied on the true-threat doctrine which allows broad censorship of off-campus online speech that is deemed a true threat. In a very small minority of cases, courts extended the *Bethel* test to off-campus online speech. This was so despite language from Justice Brennan of the United States Supreme Court in Bethel School District No. 403 v. Fraser (1986) that apparently restricts the reach of the *Bethel* test to on-campus speech: "[i]f respondent had given the same speech outside of the school environment, he could not have been penalized simply because government officials considered his language to be inappropriate" (p. 688). This language which ostensibly denies schools censorship authority, pursuant to the *Bethel* test, over off-campus vulgar, lewd and plainly-offensive speech was endorsed by the Supreme Court in Hazelwood v. Kuhlmeier (1988) and Morse v. Frederick (2007). Nevertheless, a handful of cases opted to extend the *Bethel* test off-campus, expanding school-censorship authority.

Decisions that choose to extend on-campus tests (the material and substantial disruption test and the *Bethel* test) to off-campus online speech sadly and veritably expand school-censorship authority beyond the schoolhouse gate while concomitantly restricting student speech. Even when those tests are modified, their mere application off-campus is a recognition and endorsement of the existence of school-censorship authority beyond the schoolhouse gate. Until the Supreme Court decidedly rules on the rights of students to off-campus online speech, students will remain vulnerable to erosion of their First Amendment rights in light of the lack of uniformity in the extant lower court and school approaches to censorship of off-campus online student speech.

REFERENCES

Barnett ex rel. Barnett v. Tipton County Board of Education (2009). 601 F.Supp.2d 980.

Beidler v. North Thurston School District (2000). No. 99-2-00236-6.

Bell v. Itawamba County School Board (2012). 859 F.Supp.2d 834.

Bethel School District No. 403 v. Fraser (1986). 478 U.S. 675.

Beussink v. Woodland R-IV School District (1998). 30 F.Supp. 2d 1175.

Boucher v. School Board of School District of Greenfield (1998). 134 F.3d 821.

Brandenburg v. Ohio (1969). 395 U.S. 444.

Coy ex rel. Coy v. Board of Education of North Canton City Schools (2002). 205 F.Supp.2d 791.

D.J.M. ex rel. D.M. v. Hannibal Public School District No. 60 (2011). 647 F.3d 754.

Doe v. Pulaski County Special School District (2002). 306 F.3d 616.

Doninger v. Niehoff (2007). 514 F.Supp.2d 199.

Doninger v. Niehoff (2008). 527 F.3d 41.

Emmett v. Kent School District No. 415 (2000). 92 F.Supp.2d 1088.

Evans v. Bayer (2010). 684 F. Supp. 2d 1365.

Flaherty v. Keystone Oaks School District (2003). 247 F.Supp.2d 698.

Harper ex rel. Harper v. Poway Unified School District (2007). 549 U.S. 1262.

Hazelwood v. Kuhlmeier (1988). 484 U.S. 260.

Holloman ex rel. Holloman v. Harland (2004). 370 F.3d 1252.

Hustler Magazine, Inc. v. Falwell (1988). 485 U.S. 46.

J.C. ex rel. R.C. v. Beverly Hills Unified School District (2010). 711 F.Supp.2d 1094.

J.S. ex rel. Snyder v. Blue Mountain School District (2011). 650 F.3d 915.

J.S. v. Bethlehem Area School District (2002). 807 A.2d 847.

Killion v. Franklin Regional School District (2001). 136 F.Supp.2d 446.

Kowalski v. Berkeley County Schools (2011). 652 F.3d 565.

Lavine v. Blaine School District (2001). 257 F.3d 981.

Layshock ex rel. Layshock v. Hermitage School District (2011). 650 F.3d 205.

Mahaffey ex rel. Mahaffey v. Aldrich (2002). 236 F.Supp.2d 779.

Miller v. California (1973). 413 U.S. 15.

Their Stories: Online Off-Campus Speech

Morse v. Frederick (2007). 551 U.S. 393.

Neal et al. v. Efurd (2005). No. 04-2195.

Ohio Revised Code Annotated § 2907.01 (West 2002).

O.Z. v. Board of Trustees of Long Beach Unified School District (2008). 2008 WL 4396895.

Porter v. Ascension Parish School Board (2004). 393 F.3d 608.

Reno v. American Civil Liberties Union (1997). 521 U.S. 844.

Requa v. Kent School District No. 415 (2007). 492 F.Supp.2d 1272.

Roasio v. Clark County School District (2013). 2013 WL 3679375.

R.S. ex rel. S.S. v. Minnewaska Area School District No. 2149 (2012). 894 F.Supp.2d 1128.

Saxe v. State College Area School District (2001). 240 F.3d 200.

Shanley v. Northeast Independent School District (1972). 462 F.2d 960.

Simonich, M. (2002, December 2). Newsmaker: Jack Flaherty Jr. / Teen fought school district in court, won. *Pittsburgh Post-Gazette*. Retrieved March 11, 2014, from http://old.post-gazette.com/localnews/20021202newsmakerreg5p5.asp

S.J.W. v. Lee's Summit R–7 School District (2012). 696 F.3d 771.

State, A.B. v. (2008). 885 N.*E. 2d* 1223.

Thomas v. Board of Education, Granville Central School District (1979). 607 F.2d 1043.

Tinker v. Des Moines Independent Community School District (1969). 393 U.S. 503.

T.V. ex rel. B.V. v. Smith-Green Community School Corporation (2011). 807 F.Supp.2d 767.

United States v. Lincoln (1972). 462 F.2d 1368.

United States v. Lineberry (2001). 7 Fed.Appx. 520.

United States v. Orozco-Santillan (1990). 903 F.2d 1262.

Watts v. United States (1969). 394 U.S. 705.

Wisniewski v. Board of Education of the Weedsport Central School District (2007). 494 F.3d 34.

Wynar v. Douglas County School District (2013). 728 F.3d 1062.

KEY TERMS AND DEFINITIONS

Bethel **Test:** This is the test the United States Supreme Court created in Bethel School District No. 403 v. Fraser (1986) that authorizes school officials to censor student speech that is vulgar, lewd, plainly offensive or obscene.

Infringement-of-Rights Test: The judicial standard that conditions censorship of student speech on whether the speech impinges the rights of other students.

Lower Court: Any court in America other than the United States Supreme Court which is the highest court in the United States.

Material and Substantial Disruption Test: The judicial standard that conditions censorship of student speech on whether the speech is reasonably foreseeable to cause or actually caused material and substantial disruption to the school.

***Miller* Test:** The three-part test the United States Supreme Court created in Miller v. California (1973) for determining whether the government can censor speech as obscenity. Under this test, courts inquire into: (a) whether, under contemporary community standards, the average person would deem the speech as a whole as appealing to a prurient interest; (b) whether the speech describes or shows sexual conduct defined by state law in a manifestly offensive way; and (c) whether the speech as a whole has no serious political, scientific, literary or artistic value (Miller v. California, 1973).

***Morse* Test:** This is the test the United States Supreme Court created in Morse v. Frederick (2007) that authorizes school officials to censor student speech that advocates illegal drug use.

Off-Campus Speech: Speech that occurs in any locale outside the borders or premises of a school and outside school hours. It includes student speech away from the school bus and school-sponsored events such as school trips.

Online Speech: Speech in online communication forums, including Twitter, Facebook, Myspace, Friendster, IM (Instant Messaging), YouTube and Instagram.

True Threat: Speech that expresses a genuine intent to cause harm.

Section 5
Reflections

Chapter 13
Assessing the Current Jurisprudence

ABSTRACT

This chapter assesses the current state of the off-campus student-speech jurisprudence. It discusses the lower courts' application of the United States Supreme Court's student-speech tests to off-campus student speech. The discussion reveals that there is no uniformity in this application. It further reveals that the lower courts do not uniformly embrace school-censorship authority over off-campus speech. While a majority of courts have been willing to extend school-censorship authority beyond the school campus, a few courts remain resistant to this extension. The chapter also presents data on the judicial trends in the off-campus student-speech jurisprudence. This data reveals that most courts use the material and substantial disruption test when reviewing the constitutionality of school censorship of off-campus student speech. On the other hand, no court has applied the Hazelwood test to off-campus speech. The data also shows that most off-campus speech cases involve speech directed at or against school officials rather than students. The ultimate goal of the chapter is to provide insight into the current unsettled off-campus student-speech jurisprudence.

INTRODUCTION

This chapter reviews the state of the off-campus student-speech jurisprudence. It discusses examples of lower courts that recognize school-censorship authority in off-campus settings, including the nineteenth century decision of the Supreme Court of Vermont which recognized such authority during student transit to and from school (Lander v. Seaver, 1859). It also discusses examples of lower courts that confine school-censorship authority to the school campus, giving students broad liberty to express themselves off-campus. The chapter highlights the fact that, some courts find the identity of the speaker as a student and that of the target as a teacher, administrator or student sufficient to trigger schools' off-campus censorship authority. Other courts, however, require school officials to establish a more substantive nexus between the school and the off-campus student speech before censoring the speech. This nexus is customarily satisfied through the material and substantial disruption test – one of the United States Supreme Court's student-speech tests.

DOI: 10.4018/978-1-4666-9519-1.ch013

Assessing the Current Jurisprudence

Even though several lower courts use the material and substantial disruption test in reviewing off-campus student speech, unfortunately, there is inconsistency among the courts on whether and how this test and others apply to off-campus speech. Many of the courts that apply the Supreme Court's student-speech tests to off-campus speech struggle with whether the tests should be extended from their on-campus contexts to off-campus speech. In order to avoid dealing with this difference in contexts, various courts opt not to distinguish off-campus speech from on-campus speech. This lack of distinction effectively allows the courts to apply the student-speech tests without regard for geography. It also empowers school officials to censor off-campus speech as they would on-campus speech. The discussion in the chapter further shows that some courts empower censorship by authorizing school officials to convert off-campus speech into on-campus speech. Courts using this approach essentially avoid dealing with the difficult question of whether the Supreme Court's student-speech tests should apply to off-campus speech. Beyond the discussion of the student-speech tests, the chapter highlights the fact that some courts use the true-threat doctrine (rather than the material and substantial disruption test) to analyze off-campus speech that evinces intent to cause harm at a school.

This chapter presents tabulated information on the lower courts' application of the Supreme Court's student-speech tests to off-campus speech. Additionally, it reports on the proportion of off-campus speech cases that have been reviewed under the true-threat doctrine, the fighting-words doctrine, defamation law and the *Miller*-test approach to obscenity. It also reports on the number of courts that have distinguished (and those that have failed to distinguish) on-campus speech from off-campus speech. Recall, the discussions of student-censorship incidents in chapters eleven and twelve revealed that student use of school resource or time plays a role in the judicial analysis of off-campus speech. The discussions also showed that courts give consideration to the student-speaker's (as opposed to a third party) role in bringing the speech to the school's attention. Similarly, when the speaker accesses the speech on-campus, some courts tend to view the speech as on-campus speech. This chapter presents data on the courts that embrace these conclusions in order to determine the prevalence of these conclusions. Moreover, as earlier discussions revealed, some courts impose a reasonable-foreseeability standard that schools must satisfy in order to censor off-campus speech. This chapter provides data on the courts using this requirement. It also underscores the winning party in cases where speech targeted school officials and those where speech targeted students. Finally, it presents data on the number of cases adjudicated in federal courts and state courts.

MAIN FOCUS OF THE CHAPTER

While the United States Supreme Court has ruled on school censorship of on-campus speech, the Supreme Court has been silent on students' First Amendment right to speak off-campus. As evident in our earlier discussions in this book, this silence has led to great confusion in the lower courts regarding the scope of school-censorship authority over off-campus student speech. Courts have also struggled to determine the applicable standard for such speech. As the United States District Court for the Northern District of Texas observed in 2011, "judges [do] not agree on the parameters of a school official's ability to discipline students for off-campus speech; much less could school officials such as the defendants be expected to clearly understand their limitations in that regard" (K.G.S. v. Kemp, 2011, p. 4). In this chapter, we review the current state of the off-campus student-speech jurisprudence in order to provide some systematic insight for the judiciary, scholars, lawyers, legal advocates, policymakers, students and school officials. We also detail data from our research on the judicial trends in the jurisprudence.

The State of the Off-Campus Student-Speech Jurisprudence

Thus far in this book, we have reviewed the stories of students censored for speaking off-campus in an online or offline setting. We have also discussed the judicial responses to school censorship of off-campus student speech. Our research showed that, regardless of setting, there is a lack of consistency in the judicial approach to off-campus student speech. While some courts recognize the authority of schools to censor off-campus speech, others deem such speech beyond the purview of schools.

As far back as 1859, for example, the Supreme Court of Vermont ruled that school officials have authority over students beyond the regular school hours (Lander v. Seaver, 1859). According to the court, this authority extends over a student "from the time he leaves home to go to school till he returns home from school" (p. 4). Since this decision, courts have expanded the reach of off-campus school censorship. For example, in 1976, the United States District Court for the Western District of Pennsylvania ruled that school officials can censor students' obscene off-campus speech if directed at a teacher in a loud voice at an off-campus setting, even when the student is not in transit between home and school (Fenton v. Stear, 1976). The court ruled that "when a high school student refers to a high school teacher in a public place on a Sunday by a lewd and obscene name in such a loud voice that the teacher and others hear the insult it may be deemed a matter for discipline in the discretion of the school authorities" (p. 772).

Some courts are unwilling to embrace school-censorship authority over off-campus speech. The United States Court of Appeals for the Second Circuit, for instance, has ruled that school officials must confine their censorship authority within the schoolhouse gate (Thomas v. Board of Education, Granville Central School District, 1979). The court explained that its "willingness to defer to the schoolmaster's expertise in administering school discipline rests, in large measure, upon the supposition that the arm of authority does not reach beyond the schoolhouse gate" (pp. 1044-45). Under this approach, censorship of off-campus student speech must originate from an impartial adjudicator independent of the school. Furthermore, outside the schoolhouse gate, school officials must comply with the same speech-censorship rules applicable to adults. As the United States Court of Appeals for the Fifth Circuit elucidated, "it is not at all unusual in our system that different authorities have responsibility only for their own bailiwicks" (Shanley v. Northeast Independent School District, 1972, p. 974).

Under this constrictive approach to school-censorship authority, school officials would only be responsible for speech on school grounds. Courts that choose to strictly follow this approach consider the United States Supreme Court's student-speech precedents inapplicable to off-campus student speech because of the precedents' on-campus origins. While, as noted in the prior paragraph, the United States Court of Appeals, Fifth Circuit, embraces a constrictive approach, it is not wholly opposed to school censorship of off-campus speech. The court is simply less supportive of school censorship of off-campus speech than other courts. As evident in our discussions in chapters eleven and twelve, when courts with a constrictive approach are not wholly opposed to off-campus censorship, they sometimes interpret the Supreme Court's student-speech precedents as applicable to off-campus speech. Even then, those courts at times highlight their reluctance to expand censorship outside the schoolhouse gate by adjuring parents to exercise vigilance about school encroachment into censorship of off-campus speech. The United States Court of Appeals for the Fifth Circuit, for instance, urged parents to oppose school censorship of

Assessing the Current Jurisprudence

off-campus speech because such censorship would give school officials "suzerainty over their children before and after school, off school grounds, and with regard to their children's rights of expressing their thoughts" (Shanley v. Northeast Independent School District, 1972, p. 964).

Like some of the courts discussed above, the United States District Court for the Western District of Pennsylvania requires schools to confine their censorship authority inside the schoolhouse gate (Flaherty v. Keystone Oaks School District, 2003). This court has, however, gone a step further by requiring schools to modify their discipline policies. The court requires school policies to include a geographical limitation specifically constricting the school's jurisdiction to the school campus or school-related events. The court also authorizes schools to include student transit times to and from school within their censorship authority (as long as the students are in the school's custody during those times).

When the student's off-campus speech is in a digital form, many courts hold that school officials must confine their censorship authority within the schoolhouse gate. One such court is the Thurston County Superior Court in Washington which expressed a representative judicial sentiment that "[s]chools can and will adjust to the new challenges created by … students and the internet, but not at the expense of the First Amendment" (Beidler v. North Thurston School District, 2000, p. 3). Other courts like the United States Court of Appeals for the Second Circuit hold that school-censorship authority reaches outside the schoolhouse gate because digital communication has effectively made geographical boundaries constitutionally insignificant in the student-speech jurisprudence (Doninger v. Niehoff, 2008).

Further, a number of courts share the Supreme Court of Pennsylvania's sentiment that the "advent of the Internet has complicated analysis of restrictions on speech" (J.S. v. Bethlehem Area School District, 2002, p. 863). The ubiquity of the internet has made it very difficult for courts to delimit the geographical boundaries of speech. This difficulty and the imprecision in the off-campus student-speech jurisprudence are further complicated by the limited case law available on the distinction between off-campus and on-campus speech. As the Supreme Court of Pennsylvania keenly observed, "[o]nly a few courts have considered whether the off-campus posting of email or a web site, and the accessing of the mail or site at school, constitutes on-campus or off-campus speech" (p. 864). Besides, cases that have ruled on online off-campus student speech have reached contradictory conclusions, creating confusion for students, school officials, judges, lawyers and legal scholars.

Courts that recognize the off-campus censorship authority of schools typically consider the identity of the speaker as a student, and that of the target as a teacher, administrator or student, sufficient to extend school authority beyond the schoolhouse gate. Some courts, however, require school officials to show a nexus between the off-campus student speech and the school in order to censor the speech. The United States District Court for the District of Maine held accordingly when it ruled that, in off-campus settings, school officials cannot simply rely on the speaker's identity or that of the speech target (Klein v. Smith, 1986). This means that the speech must have a substantive connection to the school beyond the speaker's identity as a student or the target's as a student or school official.

The United States Court of Appeals for the Fifth Circuit, for instance, has found such a nexus when off-campus speech is "directed at the campus" (Porter v. Ascension Parish School Board, 2004, p. 615). Unfortunately, however, the court did not specify the parameters for determining when and whether off-campus speech constitutes speech "directed at the campus." As a result, school officials, counsel and scholars have no way to definitively determine what the court expects. If we rely on the literal interpretation of the phrase, speech "directed at the campus" must have content targeting the school, school officials or student action inside the schoolhouse gate. An example could be if the off-campus speech advocates on-campus action (Boucher v. School Board of School District of Greenfield, 1998).

The court's intended meaning will, however, have to be determined through future litigation. The United States District Court for the Central District of California was the only court we found that authorized school officials to censor off-campus student speech that does not solely target the school, school officials or anyone affiliated with the school (Baker v. Downey City Board of Education, 1969). This court was so deferential to school officials that it warned the judiciary to avoid second-guessing school officials.

Even where speech might impact the campus, courts are sometimes reluctant to give school officials censorship authority over off-campus student speech. For instance, the United States District Court for the Southern District of Texas opined that "it makes little sense to extend the influence of school administration to off-campus activity under the theory that such activity might interfere with the function of education" (Sullivan v. Houston Independent School District, 1969, p. 1340). The court was loath to extending school-censorship authority beyond the schoolhouse gate even where speech has an enduring disruptive impact on other students. Despite its reluctance, as happens in many courts and cases, the district court felt, and succumbed to, judicial peer pressure to grant school officials censorship authority over off-campus speech. We characterize this as judicial peer pressure because these courts rule against their own stated inclinations using the justification that other courts had already granted school officials the censorship authority. The problem with this deference to peer pressure is that, often times, those other courts used unsound reasoning for their decisions to grant off-campus censorship authority. Consequently, whenever a court succumbs to the herd mentality to extend school-censorship authority off-campus without proper reasoning, it simply adds pressure on other courts to similarly extend the authority. These courts follow other courts without critically examining the reasoning of the courts they are following; and often without thoroughly identifying or discussing a sound justification. One of the few courts that chose not to join the herd mentality is the Court of Appeals of Oregon. In fact, the court refused to consider any persuasive or binding precedent involving off-campus speech because it found the precedents factually distinct from its own case (Pangle v. Bend-Lapine School District, 2000). This decision is a reasonable one based on the United States Supreme Court's tendencies in the student-speech jurisprudence. Specifically, in each of its student-speech cases, the Supreme Court has created a new test to account for the factual distinction between the case and its earlier test. Thus, it seems reasonable to assume that, in its first off-campus speech case, the Supreme Court will create another test.

Our research reveals that, in the adjudication of off-campus student speech cases, several courts choose not to distinguish between off-campus speech and on-campus speech. The United States District Court for the Central District of California, for instance, observed that "the substantial weight of authority indicates that geographic boundaries generally carry little weight in the student-speech analysis" (J.C. ex rel. R.C. v. Beverly Hills Unified School District, 2010, p. 1104). The choice not to distinguish off-campus speech from on-campus speech enables courts to blindly extend the United States Supreme Court's student-speech precedents from their on-campus context to the context of off-campus student speech without the need to explain the decision to take the precedents out of their original context. The United States Court of Appeals for the Fifth Circuit aptly described this view that off-campus speech and on-campus speech are legally indistinct: "[r]efusing to differentiate between student speech taking place on-campus and speech taking place off-campus, a number of courts have applied the test in *Tinker* when analyzing off-campus speech brought onto the school campus" (Porter v. Ascension Parish School Board, 2004, p. 615). This was the view used in Beussink v. Woodland R-IV School District (1998) – the first case in the United States to rule on students' free speech rights in an online off-campus forum. In that case, the United States District Court for the Eastern District of Missouri applied the material and substantial disruption test to off-campus online speech without even an intimation of awareness that the

Assessing the Current Jurisprudence

test was created in an on-campus context. This decision to extend the material and substantial disruption test to off-campus speech on the internet, without distinction between the on-campus context of the *Tinker* case and the off-campus context of the *Beussink* case, is a dangerous precedent; particularly because it implies that students' speech as well as the current student-speech tests are borderless. It threatens to leave no safe haven for student speech.

Diverse courts, such as the United States Court of Appeals for the Ninth Circuit and the United States District Court for the Western District of Pennsylvania, view the material and substantial disruption test from Tinker v. Des Moines Independent Community School District (1969) as the default test for student speech (Lavine v. Blaine School District, 2001; Killion v. Franklin Regional School District, 2001). In other words, if student speech does not fall under any of the Supreme Court student-speech precedents, the material and substantial disruption test automatically governs. Accordingly, the material and substantial disruption test governs off-campus speech because off-campus speech does not fit under any of the Supreme Court precedents. A few courts such as the United States District Court for the Western District of Pennsylvania apply the material and substantial disruption test to off-campus student speech without first demanding a nexus between off-campus speech and the school campus (Latour v. Riverside Beaver School District, 2005). At times this is because the material and substantial disruption test itself provides a nexus in that it requires speech to cause disruption at the school. In other cases, courts require no nexus before applying the test because they view a nexus as wholly unnecessary. This often occurs in cases where the court sees no constitutional distinction between off-campus speech and on-campus speech.

In order to further school censorship, courts sometimes authorize school officials to convert off-campus speech into on-campus speech. There are various bases for this conversion. For instance, if the speech is brought on-campus by the student-speaker, the court might convert the speech into on-campus speech. A few courts such as the United States Court of Appeals for the Seventh Circuit have ruled that, if off-campus speech is distributed on-campus by a third party with the knowledge of the speaker, the speech would be converted to on-campus speech (Boucher v. School Board of School District of Greenfield, 1998). This approach effectively views the off-campus creation of the speech as part of a single continuous transaction that includes the on-campus distribution of the speech; making the off-campus speech on-campus speech. The United States District Court for the Western District of Pennsylvania has ruled that school officials can censor off-campus speech brought on-campus by someone other than the student-speaker, even if the person is unknown (Killion v. Franklin Regional School District, 2001). On the other hand, according to the United States District Court for the Northern District of Indiana, off-campus speech cannot be converted to on-campus speech simply because it gets to the school (T.V. ex rel. B.V. v. Smith-Green Community School Corporation, 2011). The speech must be shown to have been brought to the campus by the student-speaker rather than another person (T.V. ex rel. B.V. v. Smith-Green Community School Corporation, 2011). Off-campus speech can also be converted into on-campus speech if the speech is aimed at an audience connected to the school. This is the view of the Supreme Court of Pennsylvania (J.S. v. Bethlehem Area School District, 2002). This court also allows conversion if off-campus speech is reasonably foreseeable to reach the school. Other courts like the United States District Court for the Southern District of Florida hold that off-campus speech is not converted into on-campus speech simply because it is aimed at the school (Evans v. Bayer, 2010). This disparity in approaches further muddles the jurisprudence.

In determining whether to convert off-campus speech into on-campus speech, courts occasionally inquire into whether the student-speaker accessed the speech on school grounds (even if the speaker did not bring the speech on-campus). The approach of the Supreme Court of Pennsylvania effectively encapsulates the multifarious judicial approaches to discerning the role of on-campus access in the conversion of speech. According to the Supreme Court of Pennsylvania, if the student-speaker accesses his online speech on-campus, the speech will be converted into on-campus speech (J.S. v. Bethlehem Area School District, 2002). The off-campus speech can also be converted into on-campus speech if the student-speaker shows the speech to at least one student while at school. The proportion of the speech shown to the student is immaterial; as is the proportion of the speech accessed on-campus. Off-campus speech can also be converted into on-campus speech if school officials access the speech on school grounds (even if no student accessed the speech on-campus). Furthermore, conversion would occur if the student-speaker facilitates on-campus access of the speech, even if the speaker did not actually access the speech on school grounds. While no court in our study entirely followed the Supreme Court of Pennsylvania's approach, each aspect of its approach has been used by various courts. Some courts take a contrary approach, holding that off-campus online speech is not converted to on-campus speech simply because the student-speaker accessed the speech on-campus. A few of these courts, like the United States District Court for the Southern District of Florida, have not foreclosed such conversion, however (Evans v. Bayer, 2010).

Courts sometimes examine whether the student used school resources or school time in the creation of the speech when determining whether to convert off-campus speech into on-campus speech. For instance, in Beidler v. North Thurston School District (2000), the Thurston County Superior Court in Washington ruled that a student's on-campus discussion of his website with classmates during school hours was so de minimis that it did not convert his off-campus speech into on-campus speech. The court also ruled that the student's use of photographs from the school annual was too de minimis to convert the speech to on-campus speech. Courts typically rule that off-campus speech is not converted to on-campus speech simply because the student used some pictures or text from the school's website in his speech (J.S. ex rel. Snyder v. Blue Mountain School District, 2011; Layshock ex rel. Layshock v. Hermitage School District, 2011). The United States District Court for the Central District of California, for example, has ruled that the use of school resource or time for off-campus speech is immaterial (J.C. ex rel. R.C. v. Beverly Hills Unified School District, 2010). Nevertheless, if a student makes large-scale use of school resources, one would expect most courts to sanction a conversion from off-campus speech into on-campus speech because of its inextricably-significant link to the school. None of the cases we found involved a large-scale use of school resources, however. Students would be wise to minimize and even more prudently avoid using school resources or time in their off-campus speech.

In certain situations, courts will sever the on-campus component of the student speech from the off-campus component in order to authorize school censorship. The United States District Court for the Western District of Washington did this in Requa v. Kent School District No. 415 (2007) when it distinguished the on-campus filming of speech from the off-campus editing and off-campus online posting of speech. This distinction enabled school officials to censor the speech. Students can avoid such severance by ensuring that all components of their speech occur outside the schoolhouse gate.

A student could preclude off-campus speech from conversion to on-campus speech if the student takes certain precautionary steps. One such step for offline speech is storage of the speech in a secure off-campus location like a personal closet in the student's home where the speech is not likely to get into the custody of someone who will take the speech to school (Porter v. Ascension Parish School Board, 2004). For online postings, the student needs to use privacy settings to restrict access to the page. If the posting is on Facebook or similar sites, the student should not grant "friend" status to any student or anyone who could take the speech to campus. Access to online postings targeting students, teachers or the school are best restricted to family members because of the level of trust. For offline and online speech, the student must also be prepared to prove that he had no intention of ever bringing the speech to the school (Porter v. Ascension Parish School Board, 2004). Furthermore, the student must be ready to establish that he took no step to "increase the chances" of the speech getting on to school grounds (p. 615).

Students could also avoid conversion of off-campus speech into on-campus speech if the speech does not implore students or others to take action on school grounds (Boucher v. School Board of School District of Greenfield, 1998). Even where the speech does not advocate action on school grounds, courts might still authorize censorship of the speech if the speech gets to the school with the knowledge of the student-speaker. Therefore, it is important for the speaker to take steps to disavow and preclude any on-campus presence of the speech. Use of disclaimers as well as warnings to readers or those with access to the speech might help in this regard. Students could warn their readers not to take the speech to campus and expressly disclaim any responsibility for any eventual on-campus presence of the speech. In our research we discovered that the United States District Court for the Central District of California would not excuse students from censorship simply because of disclaimers or other disavowal of the speech's on-campus presence. According to the district court, even if the student-speaker did not encourage or facilitate the presence of the speech on-campus, off-campus speech brought on-campus by the student-speaker or a third party can be censored (J.C. ex rel. R.C. v. Beverly Hills Unified School District, 2010). School officials can censor such speech as long as it was reasonably foreseeable to the student-speaker that the off-campus speech would reach the school's campus.

When the material and substantial disruption test is applied to off-campus student speech, student-speakers are sometimes able to avoid censorship. A few courts such as the United States District Court for the Southern District of Texas require school officials to discipline the student(s) who materially and substantially disrupted the school rather than censoring the student-speaker; unless the speaker can be directly linked to the disruption (Sullivan v. Houston Independent School District, 1969). Additionally, as mentioned earlier, a speaker might be able to avoid censorship by using disclaimers and warnings. Other courts such as the United States Court of Appeals for the Fifth Circuit hold that school officials can censor the student-speaker through reasonable time, place and manner regulations if they can reasonably forecast that opponents of the speaker's views will cause material and substantial disruption because of the speech (Shanley v. Northeast Independent School District, 1972). This ruling applies even when the student-speaker was not involved in the material and substantial disruption on school grounds.

In the absence of time, place and manner regulations, some courts like the United States District Court for the District of Minnesota authorize school officials to censor off-campus speech even if the student-speaker was not directly responsible for the material and substantial disruption (Bystrom By and Through Bystrom v. Fridley High School, 1987). Furthermore, even if the student-speaker did not encourage or advocate disruption, school officials can censor the speech if there is material and substantial disruption at the school. While courts typically do not hold students accountable for merely being at the scene of off-campus speech creation, the United States Court of Appeals for the First Circuit has (Donovan v. Ritchie, 1995). The court held a student present at the off-campus creation of speech jointly and severally responsible for the material and substantial disruption from the speech. The court attributed preparation of the list to the student even though he was never shown to have created the list.

A number of courts have modified the material and substantial disruption test for purposes of off-campus speech. Some courts, like the United States Court of Appeals for the Second Circuit, hold that school officials can censor off-campus speech under the material and substantial disruption test if the speech was reasonably foreseeable to reach the school (Doninger v. Niehoff, 2008). The speech does not have to actually reach the school. In order to determine if off-campus speech was reasonably foreseeable to reach the school, courts examine the intent of the student-speaker. If the student-speaker intended for his classmates or other members of the school community to view the speech, courts will find that the speech was reasonably likely to get to the school. Additionally, if the subject matter of the speech directly relates to events or functions at the school, the court is likely to rule that the speech was reasonably foreseeable to reach the school. While the United States District Court for the District of Minnesota uses the same modified material and substantial disruption test as the United States Court of Appeals for the Second Circuit, it holds that school officials cannot actively monitor or search for students' off-campus speech to censor unless they have reasonable grounds to believe that the speech involves violent and serious threats that could materially and substantially disrupt the school (R.S. ex rel. S.S. v. Minnewaska Area School District No. 2149, 2012).

The United States District Court for the Southern District of Florida is one of the courts to allow censorship based on a modification of the material and substantial disruption test (Evans v. Bayer, 2010). This modified test authorizes schools to censor off-campus student speech under the material and substantial disruption test if "the speech raises on-campus concerns" (p. 1370). This court is the only one to use this version of modified material and substantial disruption test; and since the court did not define what would raise on-campus concerns under this test, we are left to speculate. We assume that on-campus concerns encompasses material and substantial disruption at the school. If so, there was no need for the court to modify the material and substantial disruption test. The modified test already requires, at minimum, that speech must satisfy the material and substantial disruption test. If material and substantial disruption is a minimum requirement, any on-campus concern of larger magnitude or consequence would necessarily satisfy the material and substantial disruption test. Accordingly, the United States District Court for the Southern District of Florida's modification is pleonastic.

The United States Court of Appeals for the Eighth Circuit uses a different modified material and substantial disruption test from the two modified tests discussed earlier (D.J.M. ex rel. D.M. v. Hannibal Public School District No. 60, 2011). Under this court's modification, school officials can censor off-campus student speech under the material and substantial disruption test if the speech was reasonably foreseeable to come to the attention of school officials. While the United States Court of Appeals for the Second Circuit uses the modified test involving the reasonable foreseeability of speech reaching campus, the court also uses, as an alternative test, the modified test based on speech coming to the attention of school officials (Wisniewski v. Board of Education of the Weedsport Central School District, 2007). Under this modified test, off-campus speech is censorable even if the speech was not reasonably foreseeable to reach the school. For this modified test, the United States Court of Appeals for the Eighth Circuit bars school officials from proactively hunting for or monitoring students' off-campus speech (D.J.M. ex rel. D.M. v. Hannibal Public School District No. 60, 2011). They must wait for the speech to be brought to their attention.

The United States District Court for the Northern District of Mississippi uses a modified material and substantial disruption test that requires proof that the student-speaker intended the speech to reach the school (Bell v. Itawamba County School Board, 2012). Under this modified test, the reasonable foreseeability of speech reaching the school is insufficient; intent is decisive. This test also does not require the speech to actually reach the school. As for the material and substantial disruption part of the modified test, the United States District Court for the Northern District of Mississippi holds that threat-

Assessing the Current Jurisprudence

ening speech that actually reaches the school constitutes material and substantial disruption as a matter of law. Threatening speech also suffices in itself to establish reasonable foreseeability of material and substantial disruption from the speech, even if the speech does not reach the school.

The United States District Court for the Western District of Arkansas uses a unique modification to the material and substantial disruption test for online off-campus speech. The modification is unique because this court is the only one we found that uses the modification. The court requires that school officials establish the following before speech can be censored using the material and substantial disruption test:

1. The speech is on the internet;
2. The speech was created in the student's home or other off-campus locale;
3. No part of the speech was created on school property;
4. The student created the speech outside school hours on the student's time; and
5. The speech is not school sponsored (Neal et al. v. Efurd, 2005).

Under any of the modified material and substantial disruption tests, off-campus speech is not censorable simply because it is reasonably foreseeable to be brought to school attention; or simply because the speech is reasonably foreseeable to reach the school; or because the speaker intended the speech to reach campus (Layshock ex rel. Layshock v. Hermitage School District, 2011). School officials must remember that they also need to establish reasonable forecast of or actual material and substantial disruption at the school. As Judge Smith of the United States Court of Appeals, Third Circuit, stated, a "bare foreseeability standard could be stretched too far, and would risk ensnaring any off-campus expression that happened to discuss school-related matters" (J.S. ex rel. Snyder v. Blue Mountain School District, 2011, p. 940).

While several courts have applied the material and substantial disruption test or a modified version, courts have seldom applied the infringement-of-rights test from Tinker v. Des Moines Independent Community School District (1969). This is because, as discussed earlier in this book, the test is very obscure. Given that the United States Supreme Court itself has never applied the test since it alluded to it in the *Tinker* case, many courts do not even acknowledge the existence of the test. Indeed, in 2013, the United States Court of Appeals for the Fifth Circuit conceded that "[f]ew circuit cases address the 'invasion of the rights of others' prong of *Tinker*" (Wynar v. Douglas County School District, p. 1071). One court that has applied the infringement-of-rights test to off-campus speech is the United States District Court for the District of Oregon. The court ruled that, under the infringement-of-rights test, harassing student speech that occurs outside the school's premises, but on the route that students regularly travel to and from school, can be censored as an impingement of the rights of other students (C.R. ex rel. Rainville v. Eugene School District 4J, 2013). The United States Court of Appeals for the Third Circuit rightly cautions against expanding the infringement-of-rights test because it could endanger students' free speech rights: "if that portion of *Tinker* [i.e. the infringement-of-rights test] is broadly construed, an assertion of virtually any 'rights' could transcend and eviscerate the protections of the First Amendment" (J.S. ex rel. Snyder v. Blue Mountain School District, p. 931). This is because the test is so amorphous and could be read so expansively as to render all the other student-speech tests redundant.

In the rare case, a court such as the United States District Court for the Western District of Pennsylvania allows school officials to censor students' off-campus speech simply based on its lewd or obscene nature (Killion v. Franklin Regional School District, 2001). The court, however, requires school officials to show "exceptional circumstances" justifying such censorship (p. 457). This requirement was imposed because the censorship of the lewd or obscene speech is based on content and irrespective of whether the speech causes material and substantial disruption. This limitation is important in protecting students' off-campus speech rights because it holds school officials accountable to a more stringent test than the *Bethel* test. The court, however, failed students by not defining what constitutes exceptional circumstances. There is no indication in the case regarding the court's intended meaning. Without this definition, schools are at liberty to operate in the gray area until willing students bring lawsuits challenging school censorship of their off-campus speech.

There is very limited record of any court using the *Morse* test in an off-campus speech case. This is likely because the United States Supreme Court only created the test in 2007. The United States Court of Appeals for the Fifth Circuit was the only court we found that had extended the *Morse* test from its on-campus speech context to off-campus speech (Ponce v. Socorro Independent School District, 2007). According to the court, the *Morse* test empowers school officials to censor any student speech that advocates a dangerous activity because of the school's compelling interest in preventing such an activity. The court chose not to use the material and substantial disruption test because it felt that the test is too constricting for schools trying to censor student speech advocating illegal drug use or speech advocating other danger to the physical safety of students. The material and substantial disruption test is too constricting because the test requires proving material and substantial disruption; whereas the *Morse* test is a per se rule.

When speech threatens harm to students, most courts use either the material and substantial disruption test or the true-threat doctrine rather than the *Morse* test. Even when courts consider the home to be a sacred place for speech, they understandably exclude true threats from such sanctity. For instance, the United States Court of Appeals for the Eighth Circuit is emphatic that schools have "no business telling an individual what he may read or view in the privacy of his own home" (Doe v. Pulaski County Special School District, 2002, p. 624). Nonetheless, this court excepted speech threatening violence in order to protect people from harm. The United States Court of Appeals for the Fifth Circuit shares this view, holding that school officials should be able to censor off-campus student speech that threatens student and school safety (Wynar v. Douglas County School District, 2013).

Courts use one of two approaches in determining whether student speech constitutes a true threat:

1. The reasonable-speaker view; and
2. The reasonable-recipient view.

Under the reasonable-recipient view, courts examine "whether an objectively reasonable recipient would view the message as a threat" (United States v. J.H.H., 1994, pp. 827-28). The reasonable-speaker view, on the other hand, involves examining whether "a reasonable person would foresee that the statement would be interpreted by those to whom the maker communicates the statement as a serious expression of intent to harm or assault" (United States v. Orozco–Santillan, 1990, p. 1265). While the reasonable-speaker view focuses on the perspective of the speaker and the reasonable-recipient view on the listener, both views lead to the same conclusion: true threats are unprotected under the First Amendment. Accordingly, school officials can censor true threats regardless of locale. A few courts, such as the United States Court of Appeals for the Second Circuit, refuse to apply the true-threat doctrine to school censorship of student speech because they believe the doctrine is limited to cases involving criminal speech (Wisniewski v. Board of Education of the Weedsport Central School District, 2007). As discussed in chapters two and twelve, there is reasonable justification for this: the context of the first United States Supreme Court decision on true threats – Watts v. United States (1969) – involved censorship of criminal speech. As the

Assessing the Current Jurisprudence

United States Court of Appeals for the Second Circuit observed, that case involved criminalized speech outside the schoolhouse gate, in the jurisdiction of law enforcement as opposed to schools (Wisniewski v. Board of Education of the Weedsport Central School District, 2007).

The above background on the off-campus student-speech jurisprudence is important to understanding the jurisprudence. It is, however, also important to determine if there are any trends in the jurisprudence that could inform decision making in schools, families as well as in the judicial and policy halls. We review the trends next.

The Judicial Trends in the Off-Campus Student-Speech Jurisprudence

In this section, we present data, through several tables, on the judicial trends in the off-campus student-speech jurisprudence in the fifty-one cases in this study. As we have emphasized throughout the book, full clarity will not emerge in the jurisprudence until the United States Supreme Court considers and rules on an off-campus student speech case. We hope, however, that the data in this section will provide some measure of clarity on the jurisprudence to school officials, students, lawyers, judges, scholars, policymakers and others interested in the free speech rights of students.

The fifty-one cases covered were discovered through our extensive search of the legal research databases. There are certainly many more situations where school officials censored students' off-campus speech. After all, free speech and the discipline of students are ongoing daily, and hour-to-hour, occurrences at schools. With the emergence of digital technology, it is impossible to keep up with the number of free speech incidents that occur in schools on a daily basis. An internet search reveals so many stories of school censorship of student speech. However, for purposes of our analysis which focuses on the judicial views of off-campus student speech, we needed to review published cases. We have no access to cases that were resolved through settlements. Furthermore, censorship incidents that students failed to challenge through the judicial system are of no import to our analysis because of the absence of adjudication and a written opinion discussing the First Amendment rights of students to off-campus speech. Even when students challenge school censorship, the judicial opinion might not be released to the public because it is not sufficiently significant or is overly brief, inter alia. Since we had no access to such cases and cannot even ascertain their existence, we cannot include those in this analysis.

Application of the United States Supreme Court's Student-Speech Tests to Off-Campus Speech

As evident in Table 1, forty of the fifty-one cases (78.4% of the cases) in our study applied one of the tests that the United States Supreme Court created in its student-speech cases – Tinker v. Des Moines Independent Community School District (1969), Bethel School District No. 403 v. Fraser (1986), Hazelwood v. Kuhlmeier (1988) and Morse v. Frederick (2007). Thirty-eight of the forty cases (95%) applied the material and substantial disruption test from Tinker v. Des Moines Independent Community School District (1969). This is not surprising given that the material and substantial disruption test is the most versatile of the Supreme Court's student-speech tests. It is versatile in the sense that it is not moored to a specific speech category unlike the *Morse* test (advocacy of illegal drug use); the *Bethel* test (vulgar, lewd, obscene or plainly-offensive speech); and the *Hazelwood* test (school-sponsored speech). Consequent to its versatility, when student speech does not fit on all fours with the other student-speech tests,

Table 1. Compilation of cases applying the United States Supreme Court student-speech tests

	Application of the United States Supreme Court's Student-Speech Tests			
		Tests		
Case	*Tinker*	*Bethel*	*Hazelwood*	*Morse*
Hatter v. Los Angeles City High School District	X			
Klein v. Smith	X			
Killion v. Franklin Regional School District	X	X		
Ponce v. Socorro Independent School District				X
Lavine v. Blaine School District	X			
Riggan v. Midland Independent School District	X			
Burch v. Barker	X			
Latour v. Riverside Beaver School District	X			
Boucher v. School Board of School District of Greenfield	X			
Baker v. Downey City Board of Education	X			
C.R. ex rel. Rainville v. Eugene School District 4J	X			
Sullivan v. Houston Independent School District (1969)	X			
Sullivan v. Houston Independent School District (1973)	X			
Shanley v. Northeast Independent School District	X	X		
Beussink v. Woodland R-IV School District	X			
Requa v. Kent School District No. 415	X	X		
J.C. ex rel. R.C. v. Beverly Hills Unified School District	X			
O.Z. v. Board of Trustees of Long Beach Unified School District	X			
Emmett v. Kent School District No. 415	X			
J.S. ex rel. Snyder v. Blue Mountain School District	X	X		
Doninger v. Niehoff	X			
Wisniewski v. Board of Education of the Weedsport Central School District	X			
J.S. v. Bethlehem Area School District	X			
Beidler v. North Thurston School District	X			
Coy ex rel. Coy v. Board of Education of North Canton City Schools	X			
Mahaffey ex rel. Mahaffey v. Aldrich	X			
T.V. ex rel. B.V. v. Smith-Green Community School Corporation	X			
Layshock ex rel. Layshock v. Hermitage School District		X		
S.J.W. v. Lee's Summit R–7 School District	X			
D.J.M. ex rel. D.M. v. Hannibal Public School District No. 60	X			
Evans v. Bayer	X			
Wynar v. Douglas County School District	X			
Kowalski v. Berkeley County Schools	X			
Roasio v. Clark County School District	X			
R.S. ex rel. S.S. v. Minnewaska Area School District No. 2149	X			
Flaherty v. Keystone Oaks School District	X			
Neal et al. v. Efurd	X			

continued on following page

Assessing the Current Jurisprudence

Table 1. Continued

Application of the United States Supreme Court's Student-Speech Tests					
	Tests			
Case	*Tinker*	*Bethel*	*Hazelwood*	*Morse*
Bystrom By and Through Bystrom v. Fridley High School	X	X		
Pangle v. Bend-Lapine School District	X	X		
Bell v. Itawamba County School Board	X			

courts resort to the material and substantial disruption test. Only six of the forty cases (15%) applied the infringement-of-rights test. As we mentioned in an earlier chapter, most courts do not even acknowledge the existence of this test. Furthermore, a majority of those that acknowledge the test fail to apply it; and those courts appear befuddled by the meaning and scope of the test since the Supreme Court itself has never applied the test.

Seven of the forty cases (17.5%) applied the *Bethel* test. This low percentage is reasonable in light of Justice Brennan's statement in his concurrence in Bethel School District No. 403 v. Fraser (1986). In the *Bethel* case, Matthew Fraser delivered an obscene, lewd, plainly-offensive and vulgar speech at a school assembly. In his concurrence in the case, Justice Brennan wrote that if Fraser had "given the same speech outside of the school environment, he could not have been penalized" (Bethel School District No. 403 v. Fraser, p. 688). The United States Supreme Court subsequently endorsed this statement when it stated that, "[h]ad [Matthew] Fraser delivered the same speech in a public forum outside the school context, it would have been protected" (Morse v. Frederick, 2007, p. 405). These statements effectively precluded or at least limited the applicability of the *Bethel* test to off-campus speech. As evident in our analysis of the censorship cases in chapters eleven and twelve, many lower courts recognize these statements as rules precluding applicability of the *Bethel* test to off-campus speech; prompting them to shy away from using the test in off-campus contexts. This is evidence of how the Supreme Court's voice on student speech can dictate the action of lower courts. It indicates that even some hint from the Supreme Court about its views on off-campus speech could begin clearing up the haziness of the jurisprudence. It could help nudge or push courts to cease or minimize misapplication of current student-speech tests.

None of the cases in our study applied the *Hazelwood* test. This is understandable because that test focuses on censorship of school-sponsored student speech. While it is unquestionably possible for school-sponsored student speech to occur off-campus, we found no case implicating students' off-campus speech rights where this happened. School-sponsored speech would be implicated in an off-campus speech case if, for instance, a student staff-member of an official school newspaper did some of the work for the newspaper at home. Even if such a case had arisen, the school's ownership of the speech would preclude a censorship challenge by the student because of the *Hazelwood* test which authorizes censorship of school-sponsored speech in order to serve pedagogical concerns.

Only one of the forty cases (2.5%) applied the *Morse* test. Morse v. Frederick (2007) is the closest that the United States Supreme Court has come to considering off-campus speech as that case was delivered outside school grounds. Even though the speech occurred across the street from the school, the Supreme Court considered it as on-campus speech. Accordingly, the lower courts might view the

Morse test as providing guidance only for on-campus speech. This view could spur the lower courts to resort to the material and substantial disruption test which has historically gained traction in several courts as the test for off-campus student speech. This view could explain the low percentage of cases applying the *Morse* test. A more likely reason stems from Justice Alito's controlling opinion in the case which expressly limited the *Morse* test to censorship of speech advocating illegal drug use. Given that courts have rarely ruled on cases involving student advocacy of illegal drug use in off-campus settings, there has hardly been reason or opportunity to apply the *Morse* test. Another possible reason for the low usage of the *Morse* test is that the test was decided in 2007 whereas several of the off-campus speech cases preceded that date. The one case to apply the *Morse* test Ponce v. Socorro Independent School District was decided in 2007. Several cases such as Kowalski v. Berkeley County Schools (2011), R.S. ex rel. S.S. v. Minnewaska Area School District No. 2149 (2012) and C.R. ex rel. Rainville v. Eugene School District 4J (2013) were decided after the *Morse* case; yet, they did not apply the *Morse* test. It is impossible to know the precise reason for the low usage of the *Morse* test because lower courts rarely mention the test or mention it only incidentally.

Tinker Material and Substantial Disruption Test

As evident in Table 2, the school district won in seventeen of thirty-eight cases (44.7%) when the material and substantial disruption test was applied. The student won in twenty-one of thirty-eight cases (55.3%). This is encouraging for students only in so far as it indicates that students are more likely than not to win in cases where courts apply the material and substantial disruption test. However, with school districts winning seventeen cases and students twenty-one, it appears that courts are just as likely to rule for school districts as students when the material and substantial disruption test is applied. Thus, neither party can feel confident when a court chooses to use this test in an off-campus speech case.

Tinker Infringement-of-Rights Test

When the infringement-of-rights test was applied, as shown in Table 3, the student won in two of six cases (33.3%). The school district won in four of the six cases (66.7%). This disproportionality is not surprising due to the amorphous nature of the infringement-of-rights test. Given that the test provides that school officials can censor student speech that impinges on the rights of others, a willing court could use this elastic test to find student speech to be an impingement of some right of another student. This makes it even more imperative for the judiciary to heed the warning of the United States Court of Appeals for the Third Circuit against expanded use of the infringement-of-rights test: "if that portion of *Tinker* [i.e. the infringement-of-rights test] is broadly construed, an assertion of virtually any 'rights' could transcend and eviscerate the protections of the First Amendment" (J.S. ex rel. Snyder v. Blue Mountain School District, 2010, p. 931). Accordingly, in their First Amendment challenges, students should urge courts not to apply this test because it is unclear and thus threatening to students' free speech rights. The unfortunate reality is that nothing, and no one but the United States Supreme Court, can stop a court from using the infringement-of-rights test if it so chooses.

Assessing the Current Jurisprudence

Table 2. Cases applying the material and substantial disruption test

Tinker Test (Material and Substantial Disruption Test)		
	Winning Party	
Case	**School District**	**Student**
Hatter v. Los Angeles City High School District		X
Klein v. Smith		X
Killion v. Franklin Regional School District		X
Lavine v. Blaine School District	X	
Riggan v. Midland Independent School District		X
Burch v. Barker		X
Latour v. Riverside Beaver School District		X
Boucher v. School Board of School District of Greenfield	X	
Baker v. Downey City Board of Education	X	
Shanley v. Northeast Independent School District		X
Beussink v. Woodland R-IV School District		X
Requa v. Kent School District No. 415	X	
J.C. ex rel. R.C. v. Beverly Hills Unified School District		X
O.Z. v. Board of Trustees of Long Beach Unified School District	X	
Emmett v. Kent School District No. 415		X
J.S. ex rel. Snyder v. Blue Mountain School District		X
Doninger v. Niehoff	X	
Wisniewski v. Board of Education of the Weedsport Central School District	X	
J.S. v. Bethlehem Area School District	X	
Beidler v. North Thurston School District		X
Coy ex rel. Coy v. Board of Education of North Canton City Schools		X
Mahaffey ex rel. Mahaffey v. Aldrich		X
T.V. ex rel. B.V. v. Smith-Green Community School Corporation		X
S.J.W. v. Lee's Summit R-7 School District	X	
D.J.M. ex rel. D.M. v. Hannibal Public School District No. 60	X	
Evans v. Bayer		X
Wynar v. Douglas County School District	X	
Kowalski v. Berkeley County Schools	X	
Roasio v. Clark County School District		X
R.S. ex rel. S.S. v. Minnewaska Area School District No. 2149		X
Flaherty v. Keystone Oaks School District		X
Neal et al. v. Efurd		X
C.R. ex rel. Rainville v. Eugene School District 4J	X	
Sullivan v. Houston Independent School District (1969)		X
Sullivan v. Houston Independent School District (1973)	X	
Pangle v. Bend-Lapine School District	X	
Bystrom By and Through Bystrom v. Fridley High School	X	
Bell v. Itawamba County School Board	X	

Table 3. Cases applying the infringement-of-rights test

Tinker Test (Infringement-of-Rights Test)		
	Winning Party	
Case	School District	Student
Pangle v. Bend-Lapine School District	X	
C.R. ex rel. Rainville v. Eugene School District 4J	X	
J.S. ex rel. Snyder v. Blue Mountain School District		X
Wynar v. Douglas County School District	X	
J.C. ex rel. R.C. v. Beverly Hills Unified School District		X
Kowalski v. Berkeley County Schools	X	

Bethel Test

As evident in Table 4, when the *Bethel* test was applied, school districts emerged victorious in three of seven cases (42.9%) while students were victorious in four cases (57.1%). It is a positive omen for students that the seldom-applied *Bethel* test is not disproportionately used to censor student speech. The fact that the *Bethel* test allows censorship of vulgar, plainly-offensive, lewd or obscene speech makes the test a particular threat to off-campus student speech. As we noted earlier in this book, this test is quite generous to schools as it allows censorship of any vulgar speech in order to maintain civility. Authorizing schools to extend this test to off-campus speech would envelope almost any vulgar student speech and stifle colorful student expression even in students' homes. As a result, it is refreshing that courts do not use this test often; and that when they do, students are just as likely to win as the school district.

Hazelwood Test

We included Table 5 to symbolically and visually show that no court has applied the *Hazelwood* test. Thus, there are no winners or losers. This table is likely to remain blank for years to come because the *Hazelwood* test only governs school-sponsored speech which appears settled, irrespective of the location, as the purview of school officials.

Table 4. Cases applying the Bethel test

Bethel Test		
	Winning Party	
Case	School District	Student
Killion v. Franklin Regional School District		X
Shanley v. Northeast Independent School District		X
Requa v. Kent School District No. 415	X	
J.S. ex rel. Snyder v. Blue Mountain School District		X
Layshock ex rel. Layshock v. Hermitage School District		X
Bystrom By and Through Bystrom v. Fridley High School	X	
Pangle v. Bend-Lapine School District	X	

Table 5. Cases applying the Hazelwood test

Hazelwood Test		
	Winning Party	
Case	School District	Student
No case found		

Table 6. Cases applying the Morse test

Morse Test		
	Winning Party	
Case	School District	Student
Ponce v. Socorro Independent School District	X	

Morse Test

The only case to apply the *Morse* test favored the school district (see Table 6). This favorable ruling was not shocking because the United States Court of Appeals for the Fifth Circuit went to great lengths to extend the test from its specific focus on advocacy of illegal drug use to a generic advocacy of a dangerous activity (Ponce v. Socorro Independent School District, 2007). The court reasoned that, since the United States Supreme Court discussed the dangerous nature of drug use to students in its creation of the *Morse* test, it is logical to extend the same rationale to speech advocating any dangerous activity. The court's decision to so extend the *Morse* test, in spite of the availability of the material and substantial disruption test, signaled that a ruling for the school district was inevitable. If a court extends the *Morse* test beyond the on-campus illegal drug advocacy context involved in Morse v. Frederick (2007) to off-campus speech, it is likely an indicator of the court's willingness to empower school censorship over off-campus speech. There is no sound reason otherwise particularly since the material and substantial disruption test suffices for censorship of speech advocating dangerous activities. The *Morse* test is a categorical rule that allows *per se* censorship of speech advocating illegal drug use while the material and substantial disruption test is a balancing test. As a balancing test that burdens schools with proving actual or reasonable forecast of material and substantial disruption, the material and substantial disruption test is a more stringent standard than the *Morse* test. Consequently, attempts to use the *Morse* test for off-campus speech is an invitation to further censorship.

True-Threat Doctrine

Ten of the fifty-one cases (19.6%) in our study applied the true-threat doctrine to off-campus student speech. The low percentage might be attributable to the fact that the United States Supreme Court has never applied this doctrine to student speech. Thus, lower courts are often unsure that the doctrine even applies to student speech. Moreover, the fact that the Supreme Court created the doctrine in the context of a criminal case makes courts reticent to extend it to the civil context of school censorship. Additionally, the material and substantial disruption test can be used to censor threatening speech; thus, courts likely see no need to resort to the true-threat doctrine.

Table 7. Cases applying the true-threat doctrine

	True Threat	
	Winning Party	
Case	**School District**	**Student**
Sherrell ex rel. Sherrell v. Northern Community School Corporation of Tipton County	X	
Ponce v. Socorro Independent School District	X	
Doe v. Pulaski County Special School District	X	
Latour v. Riverside Beaver School District		X
Porter v. Ascension Parish School Board		X
J.S. v. Bethlehem Area School District		X
Mahaffey ex rel. Mahaffey v. Aldrich		X
D.J.M. ex rel. D.M. v. Hannibal Public School District No. 60	X	
R.S. ex rel. S.S. v. Minnewaska Area School District No. 2149		X
Neal et al. v. Efurd		X

When the true-threat doctrine was used, the student won in six of ten cases (60%) (see Table 7). The school district won in four of the ten cases (40%). The fact that students have been more successful than school districts under this doctrine is not unexpected because the true-threat doctrine is very difficult to satisfy under either the reasonable-recipient or reasonable-speaker views. As we discussed in chapter two, the doctrine requires proof of intent to cause harm as well as a number of other factors, making it difficult for school districts to successfully defend censorship under this doctrine.

Fighting-Words Doctrine

Since the fighting-words doctrine is more typically associated with censorship by law enforcement, it is rarely employed in cases of school censorship of student speech. Only six of fifty-one cases (11.8%) reviewed off-campus student speech using the fighting-words doctrine. The school district won in only one of the six cases on the issue of whether the student speech constituted a fighting word (16.7%) (see Table 8). The student won in five of the six cases (83.3%). This high rate of student success is due to the fact that the fighting-words doctrine, which traditionally governs censorship for the community at large outside the schoolhouse gate, is relatively more exacting than the tests traditionally associated with school censorship of student speech. The exacting nature of the fighting-words doctrine often helps protect citizens from criminal prosecution. With school districts having to meet the same standard as law enforcement in order to deem speech unprotected under the fighting-words doctrine, school districts find it difficult to use the doctrine to censor student speech. Besides student speech is more mundane than criminal. This is good news for students because speech constituting fighting words is constitutionally unprotected and thus vulnerable to school district muzzle without First Amendment recourse.

Miller-Test Approach to Obscenity

As displayed in Table 9, only five of the fifty-one cases (9.8%) in our study reviewed off-campus student speech using the *Miller*-test approach to obscenity (as opposed to the *Bethel*-test approach). Even when the court did not explicitly apply each factor of the *Miller* test, it was evident in the five cases that the

Assessing the Current Jurisprudence

Table 8. Cases applying the fighting-words doctrine

Fighting Words		
	Winning Party	
Case	School District	Student
Klein v. Smith		X
Neal et al. v. Efurd		X
Shanley v. Northeast Independent School District		X
Fenton v. Stear	X	
Sullivan v. Houston Independent School District (1969)		X
Beidler v. North Thurston School District		X

court was reviewing the student speech under the *Miller*-test approach to obscenity. Recall that in Miller v. California (1973), the United States Supreme Court created the *Miller* test for determining whether speech is obscene. Under this test, courts examine the following factors:

1. "Whether the average person, applying contemporary community standards, would find that the work, taken as a whole, appeals to the prurient interest";
2. "Whether the work depicts or describes, in a patently offensive way, sexual conduct specifically defined by the applicable state law"; and
3. "Whether the work, taken as a whole, lacks serious literary, artistic, political, or scientific value" (p. 24).

Speech that is determined to be obscene is constitutionally unprotected, giving the censored student no First Amendment recourse. The *Miller* test traditionally governs government censorship of the speech of all citizens (adult and children) outside the schoolhouse gate. The decision of some lower courts to apply the *Miller* test to off-campus student speech is encouraging for students because it means that school officials have to satisfy the *Miller* test rather than the less stringent *Bethel* test. It could also be interpreted as an acknowledgment by the courts that students have coterminous speech rights with adults outside the schoolhouse gate. In spite of the relative stringency of the *Miller* test, both school districts and students had good success under the test. When the court used a *Miller*-test approach to an off-campus speech case, school districts won in two of five cases (40%). Students won in three of five cases (60%).

Table 9. Cases applying the Miller-test approach to obscenity

Miller-Test Approach to Obscenity		
	Winning Party	
Case	School District	Student
Roasio v. Clark County School District	X	
Neal et al. v. Efurd		X
Sullivan v. Houston Independent School District (1969)		X
Fenton v. Stear	X	
Coy ex rel. Coy v. Board of Education of North Canton City Schools		X

Defamation

Eight of fifty-one off-campus student speech cases (15.7%) ruled on whether the speech constituted defamatory speech. School districts won only three of the cases (37.5%) (see Table 10). The student won in five cases (62.5%). Students had more success because the rules for defamation are difficult to satisfy. These rules are justifiably difficult because once speech is determined to be defamatory, it has no First Amendment refuge. The same standard that governs defamatory adult speech governs defamatory student speech. Given that the constitution regards not only adult speech but citizen (including children) speech as sacred, it is reasonable to make it cumbersome to classify speech as defamation.

Distinguishing On-Campus and Off-Campus Speech Antecedent to Application of the United States Supreme Court's Student-Speech Precedents

Recall that the United States Supreme Court has decided only four student-speech cases. These precedents – Tinker v. Des Moines Independent Community School District (1969), Bethel School District No. 403 v. Fraser (1986), Hazelwood v. Kuhlmeier (1988) and Morse v. Frederick (2007) – involved on-campus speech. Consequently, when confronted with off-campus speech, lower courts sometimes struggle with whether the Supreme Court precedents should apply to off-campus speech. In order to resolve this dilemma, some courts distinguish on-campus speech from off-campus speech. Other courts choose to indiscriminately apply the precedents without distinguishing between off-campus speech and on-campus speech. Those cases generally tend to treat on-campus speech and off-campus speech as legally indistinct. Forty cases in our study applied the Supreme Court's student-speech precedents. Only twenty-three of the forty cases (57.5%) distinguished between on-campus speech and off-campus speech before applying the precedents (see Table 11). Eighteen of the forty cases (45%) did not distinguish on-campus speech from off-campus speech before applying the Supreme Court's student-speech precedents. Students were victorious in thirteen of the twenty-three cases (56.5%) that distinguished off-campus speech from on-campus speech. School districts emerged victorious in ten of twenty-three cases (43.5%). On the other hand, school districts were victorious in eight of eighteen cases (44.4%) that failed to distinguish off-campus speech from on-campus speech. Students were victorious in ten of the eighteen cases (55.6%).

Table 10. Cases reviewing off-campus student speech as defamation

Defamation		
	Winning Party	
Case	School District	Student
Beidler v. North Thurston School District		X
J.S. ex rel. Snyder v. Blue Mountain School District		X
Evans v. Bayer		X
Neal et al. v. Efurd		X
Sullivan v. Houston Independent School District (1969)		X
J.C. ex rel. R.C. v. Beverly Hills Unified School District	X	
Kowalski v. Berkeley County Schools	X	
Fenton v. Stear	X	

Assessing the Current Jurisprudence

Table 11. Cases that distinguished between on-campus and off-campus speech before applying the United States Supreme Court's student-speech precedents

	On-Campus/Off-Campus Distinction?		Winning Party	
Case	Yes	No	School District	Student
Beussink v. Woodland R-IV School District		X		X
Flaherty v. Keystone Oaks School District		X		X
Requa v. Kent School District No. 415	X		X	
J.C. ex rel. R.C. v. Beverly Hills Unified School District		X		X
Lavine v. Blaine School District		X	X	
Shanley v. Northeast Independent School District		X		X
Boucher v. School Board of School District of Greenfield		X	X	
Killion v. Franklin Regional School District		X		X
Coy ex rel. Coy v. Board of Education of North Canton City Schools	X			X
Mahaffey ex rel. Mahaffey v. Aldrich	X			X
T.V. ex rel. B.V. v. Smith-Green Community School Corporation	X			X
Emmett v. Kent School District No. 415	X			X
O.Z. v. Board of Trustees of Long Beach Unified School District		X	X	
J.S. ex rel. Snyder v. Blue Mountain School District	X (for *Bethel*)	X (for *Tinker*)		X
Doninger v. Niehoff	X		X	
Wisniewski v. Board of Education of the Weedsport Central School District	X		X	
J.S. v. Bethlehem Area School District	X		X	
Beidler v. North Thurston School District	X			X
Layshock ex rel. Layshock v. Hermitage School District	X			X
S.J.W. v. Lee's Summit R–7 School District	X		X	
D.J.M. ex rel. D.M. v. Hannibal Public School District No. 60	X		X	
Evans v. Bayer	X			X
Wynar v. Douglas County School District	X		X	
Kowalski v. Berkeley County Schools	X		X	
Roasio v. Clark County School District	X			X
R.S. ex rel. S.S. v. Minnewaska Area School District No. 2149	X			X
Bell v. Itawamba County School Board	X		X	
Neal et al. v. Efurd	X			X
Bystrom By and Through Bystrom v. Fridley High School		X		X
Pangle v. Bend-Lapine School District		X	X	
Hatter v. Los Angeles City High School District		X	X	
Klein v. Smith	X			X

continued on following page

Table 11. Continued

	Did the Court Distinguish between On-Campus and Off-Campus Speech before Applying the United States Supreme Court's Student-Speech Precedents?			
	On-Campus/Off-Campus Distinction?		Winning Party	
Case	Yes	No	School District	Student
Burch v. Barker		X		X
Sullivan v. Houston Independent School District (1969)	X			X
Sullivan v. Houston Independent School District (1973)		X	X	
Riggan v. Midland Independent School District		X		X
C.R. ex rel. Rainville v. Eugene School District 4J	X		X	
Ponce v. Socorro Independent School District		X	X	
Latour v. Riverside Beaver School District		X		X
Baker v. Downey City Board of Education		X	X	

One of the forty cases that applied the Supreme Court's student-speech precedents to off-campus speech took a unique approach to the distinction between on-campus and off-campus speech. The case – J.S. ex rel. Snyder v. Blue Mountain School District (2010) – recognized a distinction between on-campus speech and off-campus speech for purposes of the *Bethel* test but not for the material and substantial disruption test. Justice Brennan's statement in Bethel School District No. 403 v. Fraser (1986) explains the United States Court of Appeals, Third Circuit, decision in J.S. ex rel. Snyder v. Blue Mountain School District to distinguish off-campus speech from on-campus speech for purposes of the *Bethel* test. Recall that in his concurrence in Bethel School District No. 403 v. Fraser, Justice Brennan wrote that, had the student in the case "given the same [vulgar, lewd, plainly-offensive or obscene] speech outside of the school environment, he could not have been penalized" (p. 688). The Supreme Court affirmed this statement in Hazelwood v. Kuhlmeier (1988). Since no Supreme Court Justice has ever made a similar statement in relation to the material and substantial disruption test, the United States Court of Appeals, Third Circuit, was justified in failing to distinguish off-campus speech from on-campus speech for purposes of the material and substantial disruption test. It is, however, curious that the court chose to recognize a distinction between off-campus speech and on-campus speech for one purpose but not the other. Both the *Bethel* test and the material and substantial disruption test arose in on-campus contexts; and so the court should have treated them similarly, irrespective of Justice Brennan's statement which was made in an on-campus speech context (as was the Supreme Court's subsequent endorsement of Justice Brennan's statement).

Distinguishing On-Campus and Off-Campus Speech Even When Not Applying the United States Supreme Court's Student-Speech Precedents

Eleven of the fifty-one cases (21.6%) in our study did not apply any of the United States Supreme Court's student-speech precedents. There is roughly an even split in the number of the cases recognizing a distinction between on-campus speech and off-campus speech. Five of the eleven cases (45.5%) that did not apply the Supreme Court's student-speech precedents acknowledged a distinction between off-campus

Assessing the Current Jurisprudence

Table 12. Cases that distinguished between on-campus and off-campus speech even though they did not apply the United States Supreme Court's student-speech precedents

Even Though the Court Did Not Apply the United States Supreme Court's Student-Speech Precedents, Did It Distinguish between On-Campus And Off-Campus Speech?				
	On-Campus/Off-Campus Distinction?		Winning Party	
Case	Yes	No	School District	Student
Barnett ex rel. Barnett v. Tipton County Board of Education		X	X	
Thomas v. Board of Education, Granville Central School District	X			X
A.B. v. State		X	X	
Fenton v. Stear	X		X	
Lander v. Seaver	X		X	
Porter v. Ascension Parish School Board	X			X
Schwartz v. Schuker		X	X	
Sherrell ex rel. Sherrell v. Northern Community School Corporation of Tipton County		X	X	
Donovan v. Ritchie		X	X	
Doe v. Pulaski County Special School District		X	X	
K.G.S. v. Kemp	X		X	

and on-campus speech (see Table 12). Six of the eleven cases (54.5%) failed to acknowledge such a distinction. The school district was victorious in all six cases (100%) in which the courts failed to recognize a distinction between off-campus speech and on-campus speech. This is not surprising because the unwillingness to recognize the distinction is a convenient excuse to extend school-censorship authority outside the schoolhouse gate. The school district was also victorious in three of the five cases (60%) in which the courts recognized a distinction between off-campus and on-campus speech. The student was victorious in two of the five cases (40%).

De Minimis Use or No Use of School Resource or Time

As evident in Table 13, forty-seven cases out of the fifty-one cases (92.2%) in our study involved either de minimis use or no use of school resource or time in the student's creation or distribution of the off-campus speech. The school district won twenty-five of the forty-seven cases (53.2%) while the student won twenty-two of the forty-seven cases (46.8%). These numbers are counterintuitive since one would expect students to typically win when they make negligible or no use of school time or school resource. The broader lesson, however, is that when students' off-campus speech involves insignificant or no use of school resource or time, courts rely on other factors in determining whether speech can be censored. Such factors, as discussed in this book, include the material and substantial disruptiveness of the speech or the threatening or obscene nature of the speech.

Assessing the Current Jurisprudence

Table 13. Cases involving de minimis use or no use of school resource or time

Case	Winning Party — School District	Winning Party — Student
Lander v. Seaver	X	
Fenton v. Stear	X	
Sherrell ex rel. Sherrell v. Northern Community School Corporation of Tipton County	X	
K.G.S. v. Kemp	X	
Hatter v. Los Angeles City High School District	X	
Klein v. Smith		X
Killion v. Franklin Regional School District		X
Lavine v. Blaine School District	X	
Donovan v. Ritchie	X	
Ponce v. Socorro Independent School District	X	
Doe v. Pulaski County Special School District	X	
Riggan v. Midland Independent School District		X
Burch v. Barker		X
Latour v. Riverside Beaver School District		X
Porter v. Ascension Parish School Board		X
Schwartz v. Schuker	X	
Boucher v. School Board of School District of Greenfield	X	
Baker v. Downey City Board of Education	X	
Thomas v. Board of Education, Granville Central School District		X
C.R. ex rel. Rainville v. Eugene School District 4J	X	
Sullivan v. Houston Independent School District (1969)		X
Sullivan v. Houston Independent School District (1973)	X	
Shanley v. Northeast Independent School District		X
Beussink v. Woodland R-IV School District		X
J.C. ex rel. R.C. v. Beverly Hills Unified School District		X
O.Z. v. Board of Trustees of Long Beach Unified School District	X	
Emmett v. Kent School District No. 415		X
J.S. ex rel. Snyder v. Blue Mountain School District		X
Doninger v. Niehoff	X	
Wisniewski v. Board of Education of the Weedsport Central School District	X	
J.S. v. Bethlehem Area School District	X	
Beidler v. North Thurston School District		X
Coy ex rel. Coy v. Board of Education of North Canton City Schools		X
Mahaffey ex rel. Mahaffey v. Aldrich		X
T.V. ex rel. B.V. v. Smith-Green Community School Corporation		X
A.B. v. State	X	
Layshock ex rel. Layshock v. Hermitage School District		X

continued on following page

Assessing the Current Jurisprudence

Table 13. Continued

De Minimis Use or No Use of School Resource or Time		
	Winning Party	
Case	School District	Student
D.J.M. ex rel. D.M. v. Hannibal Public School District No. 60	X	
Evans v. Bayer		X
Wynar v. Douglas County School District	X	
Kowalski v. Berkeley County Schools	X	
Roasio v. Clark County School District		X
R.S. ex rel. S.S. v. Minnewaska Area School District No. 2149		X
Bell v. Itawamba County School Board	X	
Neal et al. v. Efurd		X
Bystrom By and Through Bystrom v. Fridley High School	X	
Pangle v. Bend-Lapine School District	X	

Material Use of School Resource or Time

Four of the fifty-one cases (7.8%) reviewed involved off-campus student speech that made material use of school resource or school time. As evident in Table 14, the school district won three of the four cases (75%) while the student won one of the four cases (25%). This finding is intuitive since material use of school resource or time closely associates speech with the school. This association could tempt some courts to view the speech as on-campus speech. Thus, it is important that students avoid using school time or school resource for their off-campus speech.

Brought to School Attention by Third Party

Forty of the fifty-one cases (78.4%) reviewed involved off-campus student speech that was brought to school attention by a person other than the student-speaker. Table 15 shows that the student-speaker won in twenty-one of the forty cases (52.5%). The school district won in nineteen of the forty cases (47.5%). This suggests that the student is just as likely to win or lose an off-campus censorship case as the school district when speech is brought to the school's attention through a third party (as opposed to the student-speaker).

Table 14. Cases involving material use of school resources or time

Material Use of School Resources and/or Time		
	Winning Party	
Case	School District	Student
Requa v. Kent School District No. 415	X	
Flaherty v. Keystone Oaks School District		X
Barnett ex rel. Barnett v. Tipton County Board of Education	X	
S.J.W. v. Lee's Summit R–7 School District	X	

Table 15. Cases involving speech brought to school attention by third party

Brought to School Attention by Third Party		
	Winning Party	
Case	School District	Student
Sherrell ex rel. Sherrell v. Northern Community School Corporation of Tipton County	X	
K.G.S. v. Kemp	X	
Killion v. Franklin Regional School District		X
Ponce v. Socorro Independent School District	X	
Doe v. Pulaski County Special School District	X	
Riggan v. Midland Independent School District		X
Latour v. Riverside Beaver School District		X
Porter v. Ascension Parish School Board		X
Boucher v. School Board of School District of Greenfield	X	
Thomas v. Board of Education, Granville Central School District		X
C.R. ex rel. Rainville v. Eugene School District 4J	X	
Sullivan v. Houston Independent School District (1969)		X
Shanley v. Northeast Independent School District		X
Beussink v. Woodland R-IV School District		X
Flaherty v. Keystone Oaks School District		X
Requa v. Kent School District No. 415	X	
J.C. ex rel. R.C. v. Beverly Hills Unified School District		X
O.Z. v. Board of Trustees of Long Beach Unified School District	X	
Emmett v. Kent School District No. 415		X
J.S. ex rel. Snyder v. Blue Mountain School District		X
Doninger v. Niehoff	X	
Wisniewski v. Board of Education of the Weedsport Central School District	X	
J.S. v. Bethlehem Area School District	X	
Barnett ex rel. Barnett v. Tipton County Board of Education	X	
Beidler v. North Thurston School District		X
Coy ex rel. Coy v. Board of Education of North Canton City Schools		X
Mahaffey ex rel. Mahaffey v. Aldrich		X
T.V. ex rel. B.V. v. Smith-Green Community School Corporation		X
A.B. v. State	X	
Layshock ex rel. Layshock v. Hermitage School District		X
S.J.W. v. Lee's Summit R–7 School District	X	
D.J.M. ex rel. D.M. v. Hannibal Public School District No. 60	X	
Evans v. Bayer		X
Wynar v. Douglas County School District	X	
Kowalski v. Berkeley County Schools	X	
Roasio v. Clark County School District		X
R.S. ex rel. S.S. v. Minnewaska Area School District No. 2149		X

continued on following page

Table 15. Continued

Brought to School Attention by Third Party		
	Winning Party	
Case	School District	Student
Bell v. Itawamba County School Board	X	
Neal et al. v. Efurd		X
Bystrom By and Through Bystrom v. Fridley High School	X	

Brought to School Attention by or Through Student-Speaker

Eleven of the fifty-one cases (21.6%) reviewed involved off-campus student speech that was brought to school attention by or through the student-speaker. When compared to the data on cases (78.4%) where off-campus speech was brought to school attention by a third party, it is apparent that most censorship at schools starts after a third party brings the speech to school attention. In other words, student-speakers are more discreet with school officials but maybe not as much with other parties. As displayed in Table 16, the school district won in nine of the eleven cases (81.8%) in which off-campus student speech was brought to school attention by or through the student-speaker. The student won in two of the eleven cases (18.2%). This suggests that school districts are clearly more likely to be victorious in cases where school officials learn of the off-campus speech by or through the student-speaker.

Table 16. Cases involving speech brought to school attention by or through the student-speaker

Brought to School Attention by or through Student-Speaker		
	Winning Party	
Case	School District	Student
Lander v. Seaver	X	
Fenton v. Stear	X	
Hatter v. Los Angeles City High School District	X	
Klein v. Smith		X
Lavine v. Blaine School District	X	
Donovan v. Ritchie	X	
Burch v. Barker		X
Schwartz v. Schuker	X	
Baker v. Downey City Board of Education	X	
Sullivan v. Houston Independent School District (1973)	X	
Pangle v. Bend-Lapine School District	X	

Table 17. Cases involving speech accessed at school by speech-creator

Speech Accessed at School by Speech-Creator		
	Winning Party	
Case	School District	Student
Killion v. Franklin Regional School District		X
Lavine v. Blaine School District	X	
Ponce v. Socorro Independent School District	X	
Schwartz v. Schuker	X	
Thomas v. Board of Education, Granville Central School District		X
Flaherty v. Keystone Oaks School District		X
J.S. v. Bethlehem Area School District	X	
Barnett ex rel. Barnett v. Tipton County Board of Education	X	
Coy ex rel. Coy v. Board of Education of North Canton City Schools		X
Layshock ex rel. Layshock v. Hermitage School District		X
S.J.W. v. Lee's Summit R–7 School District	X	
Bystrom By and Through Bystrom v. Fridley High School	X	
Pangle v. Bend-Lapine School District	X	

Speech Accessed at School by Speech-Creator

Thirteen of the fifty-one cases (25.5%) reviewed involved off-campus student speech accessed at school by the creator of the speech. School districts won eight of the thirteen cases (61.5%) while students won five of the thirteen cases (38.5%) (see Table 17). These numbers are not surprising. Courts tend to favor the school district when the student accesses his speech on-campus. As discussed earlier, courts are inclined to treat off-campus speech that the speech-creator accesses at school as on-campus speech.

Offline Off-Campus Speech: Speech Directed at or against School Officials or the School

As evident in Table 18, eighteen of the fifty-one cases (35.3%) in our study involved offline off-campus student speech that was directed at or against the school or school officials. The school district was victorious in ten of the eighteen cases (55.6%). The student was victorious in eight of the eighteen cases (44.4%). Comparatively, it is apparent that students have lost more often than school districts in First Amendment cases challenging censorship of speech directed at the school or school officials. However, the difference in victories is not sufficiently substantial to create an expectation of either party winning in a given case.

Offline Off-Campus Speech: Speech Directed At or Against Students

Six of the fifty-one cases (11.8%) in our study involved offline off-campus student speech that was directed at or against other students. When this data is compared to data on the number of cases (35.3%) involving offline speech directed at or against school officials or the school, it is evident that courts

Assessing the Current Jurisprudence

Table 18. Cases involving offline off-campus speech: speech directed at or against school officials or the school

Offline Off-Campus Speech: Speech Directed at or against School Officials or the School		
	Winning Party	
Case	School District	Student
Lander v. Seaver	X	
Fenton v. Stear	X	
K.G.S. v. Kemp	X	
Hatter v. Los Angeles City High School District	X	
Klein v. Smith		X
Killion v. Franklin Regional School District		X
Lavine v. Blaine School District	X	
Riggan v. Midland Independent School District		X
Burch v. Barker		X
Porter v. Ascension Parish School Board		X
Schwartz v. Schuker	X	
Boucher v. School Board of School District of Greenfield	X	
Thomas v. Board of Education, Granville Central School District		X
Sullivan v. Houston Independent School District (1969)		X
Sullivan v. Houston Independent School District (1973)	X	
Shanley v. Northeast Independent School District		X
Bystrom By and Through Bystrom v. Fridley High School	X	
Pangle v. Bend-Lapine School District	X	

have ruled on more cases involving speech directed at or against school officials or the school than they have on cases where speech targeted other students. This could be because school officials tend to censor speech more often when they are targeted than when students are targeted. In five of the six cases (83.3%) involving offline off-campus speech directed at or against other students, the school district was victorious (see Table 19). A student won only one of the six cases (16.7%).

Table 19. Cases involving offline off-campus speech: speech directed at or against students

Offline Off-Campus Speech: Speech Directed at or against Students		
	Winning Party	
Case	School District	Student
Sherrell ex rel. Sherrell v. Northern Community School Corporation of Tipton County	X	
Donovan v. Ritchie	X	
Doe v. Pulaski County Special School District	X	
Ponce v. Socorro Independent School District	X	
Latour v. Riverside Beaver School District		X
C.R. ex rel. Rainville v. Eugene School District 4J	X	

Table 20. Cases involving offline off-campus hybrid speech: speech directed at or against school officials as well as non-school entities

Offline Off-Campus Hybrid Speech: Speech Directed at or against School Officials as Well as Non-School Entities		
	Winning Party	
Case	School District	Student
Baker v. Downey City Board of Education	X	

Offline Off-Campus Hybrid Speech: Speech Directed at or against School Officials as Well as Non-School Entities

As displayed in Table 20, we only found one case that involved censorship of hybrid speech, defined for our purposes as speech directed at or against school officials as well as at an entity unaffiliated with the school. In that offline off-campus case, the school district was victorious because the court took a very deferential approach to school censorship. In fact, the court cautioned the judiciary against interfering with school decisions. The court's deferential posture strongly suggests that the school district would have won a hundred percent of the time in this case irrespective of the target of the speech.

Online Off-Campus Speech: Speech Directed at or against School Officials or the School

Seventeen of the fifty-one cases (33.3%) in our study involved online off-campus student speech that was directed at or against the school or school officials. In eight of the seventeen cases (47.1%), the school district was victorious (see Table 21). In nine of the seventeen cases (52.9%), the student was victorious. It is apparent from this data that students have won more cases challenging censorship of speech directed at the school or school officials than school districts. This could be positive news for students inclined to use digital communication to target their school or school officials. However, students need to be wary because the difference in the number of cases students have won relative to those won by school districts is not considerable.

Online Off-Campus Speech: Speech Directed At or Against Students

As evident in Table 22, seven of the fifty-one cases (13.7%) in our study involved online off-campus student speech that was directed at or against other students. A comparison of this data to that on the number of cases (33.3%) involving online speech directed at or against school officials or the school reveals that courts have ruled on more cases involving speech directed at or against school officials or the school than they have on cases where speech targeted other students. As in the case of offline speech directed at or against other students, this disparity (13.7% versus 33.3%) could be due to the fact that sensitive school officials tend to censor speech attacking them than they do speech attacking students.

Students won only three of the seven cases (42.9%) of online off-campus student speech directed at or against students. School districts won four of the seven cases (57.1%). While school districts have won more than students, the difference in victories is not sizeable. This is reassuring news for students in the current age of pervasive digital student communications.

334

Assessing the Current Jurisprudence

Table 21. Cases involving online off-campus speech: speech directed at or against school officials or the school

Online Off-Campus Speech: Speech Directed at or against School Officials or the School		
	Winning Party	
Case	School District	Student
Beussink v. Woodland R-IV School District		X
Requa v. Kent School District No. 415	X	
O.Z. v. Board of Trustees of Long Beach Unified School District	X	
J.S. ex rel. Snyder v. Blue Mountain School District		X
Doninger v. Niehoff	X	
Wisniewski v. Board of Education of the Weedsport Central School District	X	
J.S. v. Bethlehem Area School District	X	
Barnett ex rel. Barnett v. Tipton County Board of Education	X	
Beidler v. North Thurston School District		X
Mahaffey ex rel. Mahaffey v. Aldrich		X
A.B. v. State	X	
Layshock ex rel. Layshock v. Hermitage School District		X
Evans v. Bayer		X
Roasio v. Clark County School District		X
R.S. ex rel. S.S. v. Minnewaska Area School District No. 2149		X
Bell v. Itawamba County School Board	X	
Neal et al. v. Efurd		X

Table 22. Cases involving online off-campus speech: speech directed at or against students

Online Off-Campus Speech: Speech Directed at or against Students		
	Winning Party	
Case	School District	Student
Flaherty v. Keystone Oaks School District		X
J.C. ex rel. R.C. v. Beverly Hills Unified School District		X
Emmett v. Kent School District No. 415		X
Coy ex rel. Coy v. Board of Education of North Canton City Schools		X
D.J.M. ex rel. D.M. v. Hannibal Public School District No. 60	X	
Wynar v. Douglas County School District	X	
Kowalski v. Berkeley County Schools	X	

Table 23. Cases that required reasonable foreseeability that the off-campus speech will reach campus

Reasonable Foreseeability Speech Will Reach Campus (Even if It Does Not Reach Campus)		
	Winning Party	
Case	School District	Student
Boucher v. School Board of School District of Greenfield	X	
Baker v. Downey City Board of Education	X	
J.C. ex rel. R.C. v. Beverly Hills Unified School District		X
Doninger v. Niehoff	X	
Wisniewski v. Board of Education of the Weedsport Central School District	X	
O.Z. v. Board of Trustees of Long Beach Unified School District	X	
J.S. v. Bethlehem Area School District	X	
Mahaffey ex rel. Mahaffey v. Aldrich		X
Kowalski v. Berkeley County Schools	X	
Roasio v. Clark County School District		X
R.S. ex rel. S.S. v. Minnewaska Area School District No. 2149		X

Reasonable Foreseeability Speech Will Reach Campus (Even if It Does Not Reach Campus)

As discussed earlier, some cases imposed an antecedent requirement that off-campus speech must be reasonably foreseeable to reach campus before school officials can censor the speech. Under this requirement, the speech does not have to reach the school's campus. Eleven of the fifty-one cases (21.6%) in our study imposed such a requirement. The school district won in seven of the eleven cases (63.6%) (see Table 23). The student won in four of the eleven cases (36.4%). It seems sensible that school districts have won a majority of the cases with the reasonable-foreseeability requirement. This is because this requirement makes it easier for school districts to censor off-campus speech by not requiring the speech to actually reach school grounds.

Reasonable Foreseeability Speech Would Be Brought to the Attention of School Officials (Even if It Does Not Reach Campus)

Some cases adopted a different reasonable-foreseeability requirement from reasonable foreseeability of speech reaching campus. These cases instead require school officials to prove that, prior to the censorship, it was reasonably foreseeable that the off-campus speech would be brought to the attention of school officials. This is a recent requirement that first appeared in Wisniewski v. Board of Education of the Weedsport Central School District (2007). The United States Court of Appeals for the Second Circuit was divided in this case over whether speech had to actually reach school grounds or whether reasonable foreseeability of reaching school grounds should suffice. Amidst this division, the panel of judges apparently chose the compromise of reasonable foreseeability that speech would be brought to the attention of school officials. As evident in Table 24, only four of the fifty-one cases (7.8%) in our study used this reasonable-foreseeability requirement. The low usage is likely attributable to the recency of the test. School districts won all four of the cases (100%) with this requirement. This is not astonishing

Assessing the Current Jurisprudence

Table 24. Cases that required reasonable foreseeability speech will brought to attention of the school (even if it does not reach campus)

Reasonable Foreseeability Speech Will Be Brought to Attention of School Officials (Even if It Does Not Reach Campus)		
	Winning Party	
Case	School District	Student
Wisniewski v. Board of Education of the Weedsport Central School District	X	
D.J.M. ex rel. D.M. v. Hannibal Public School District No. 60	X	
S.J.W. v. Lee's Summit R–7 School District	X	
Bell v. Itawamba County School Board	X	

because reasonable foreseeability that speech would be brought to the attention of school officials is a relatively lenient standard to meet (relative to reasonable foreseeability of speech reaching campus); especially with the omnipresent nature of the internet. This is borne out in the fact that all four cases that have used this requirement involved online speech.

List of State Courts and Cases

Six of the fifty-one cases (11.8%) studied were adjudicated in a state court (see Table 25). This low percentage could indicate that students are averse to bringing their First Amendment challenges to school censorship in state court. Two of the six cases (33.3%) were in Indiana. Four of the six cases (66.7%) were in Washington, Vermont, Oregon and Pennsylvania.

Winning Party in State Court Cases

Table 26 reveals that the school district won in five of the six cases (83.3%) adjudicated in a state court. The student won in only one of the six cases (16.7%). It is possible that students choose not to bring their First Amendment cases in state courts because of a belief that school districts are more likely to win in such cases. We have no reason to believe that is the case; other than the fact that school districts have predominantly won in the state court cases. It is also possible that more cases are brought in federal court because the First Amendment right to free speech is a federal constitutional right (even though state courts can also adjudicate First Amendment issues).

Table 25. List of state courts and cases

Case	State Court
Lander v. Seaver	Supreme Court of Vermont
Sherrell ex rel. Sherrell v. Northern Community School Corporation of Tipton County	Court of Appeals of Indiana
J.S. v. Bethlehem Area School District	Supreme Court of Pennsylvania
Beidler v. North Thurston School District	Thurston County Superior Court in Washington
A.B. v. State	Supreme Court of Indiana
Pangle v. Bend-Lapine School District	Court of Appeals of Oregon

Table 26. Winning party in state court cases

Winning Party in State Court Cases		
	Winning Party	
Case	School District	Student
Lander v. Seaver	X	
Sherrell ex rel. Sherrell v. Northern Community School Corporation of Tipton County	X	
J.S. v. Bethlehem Area School District	X	
Beidler v. North Thurston School District		X
A.B. v. State	X	
Pangle v. Bend-Lapine School District	X	

List of Federal Courts and Cases

Forty-five of the fifty-one cases (88.2%) studied were adjudicated in a federal court (see Table 27). This ostensibly indicates that students prefer to bring their First Amendment free speech cases in federal court. The next table will present information that might indicate that this is not necessarily a winning decision for students.

Table 27. List of federal courts and cases

Case	Federal Court
Fenton v. Stear	United States District Court for the Western District of Pennsylvania (Third Circuit)
K.G.S. v. Kemp	United States District Court for the Northern District of Texas (Fifth Circuit)
Hatter v. Los Angeles City High School District	United States Court of Appeals for the Ninth Circuit
Klein v. Smith	United States District Court for the District of Maine (First Circuit)
Killion v. Franklin Regional School District	United States District Court for the Western District of Pennsylvania (Third Circuit)
Lavine v. Blaine School District	United States Court of Appeals for the Ninth Circuit
Donovan v. Ritchie	United States Court of Appeals for the First Circuit
Ponce v. Socorro Independent School District	United States Court of Appeals for the Fifth Circuit
Doe v. Pulaski County Special School District	United States Court of Appeals for the Eighth Circuit
Riggan v. Midland Independent School District	United States District Court for the Western District of Texas (Fifth Circuit)
Burch v. Barker	United States Court of Appeals for the Ninth Circuit
Latour v. Riverside Beaver School District	United States District Court for the Western District of Pennsylvania (Third Circuit)
Porter v. Ascension Parish School Board	United States Court of Appeals for the Fifth Circuit
Schwartz v. Schuker	United States District Court for the Eastern District of New York (Second Circuit)
Boucher v. School Board of School District of Greenfield	United States Court of Appeals for the Seventh Circuit
Baker v. Downey City Board of Education	United States District Court for the Central District of California (Ninth Circuit)
Thomas v. Board of Education, Granville Central School District	United States Court of Appeals for the Second Circuit

continued on following page

Assessing the Current Jurisprudence

Table 27. Continued

Case	Federal Court
C.R. ex rel. Rainville v. Eugene School District 4J	United States District Court for the District of Oregon (Ninth Circuit)
Sullivan v. Houston Independent School District (1969)	United States District Court for the Southern District of Texas (Fifth Circuit)
Sullivan v. Houston Independent School District (1973)	United States Court of Appeals for the Fifth Circuit
Shanley v. Northeast Independent School District	United States Court of Appeals for the Fifth Circuit
Beussink v. Woodland R-IV School District	United States District Court for the Eastern District of Missouri (Eighth Circuit)
Flaherty v. Keystone Oaks School District	United States District Court for the Western District of Pennsylvania (Third Circuit)
Requa v. Kent School District No. 415	United States District Court for the Western District of Washington (Ninth Circuit)
J.C. ex rel. R.C. v. Beverly Hills Unified School District	United States District Court for the Central District of California (Ninth Circuit)
Barnett ex rel. Barnett v. Tipton County Board of Education	United States District Court for the Western District of Tennessee (Sixth Circuit)
Doninger v. Niehoff	United States Court of Appeals for the Second Circuit
Coy ex rel. Coy v. Board of Education of North Canton City Schools	United States District Court for the Northern District of Ohio (Sixth Circuit)
T.V. ex rel. B.V. v. Smith-Green Community School Corporation	United States District Court for the Northern District of Indiana (Seventh Circuit)
S.J.W. v. Lee's Summit R–7 School District	United States Court of Appeals for the Eighth Circuit
Evans v. Bayer	United States District Court for the Southern District of Florida (Eleventh Circuit)
Wynar v. Douglas County School District	United States Court of Appeals for the Ninth Circuit
Kowalski v. Berkeley County Schools	United States Court of Appeals for the Fourth Circuit
J.S. ex rel. Snyder v. Blue Mountain School District	United States Court of Appeals for the Third Circuit
O.Z. v. Board of Trustees of Long Beach Unified School District	United States District Court for the Central District of California (Ninth Circuit)
Emmett v. Kent School District No. 415	United States District Court for the Western District of Washington (Ninth Circuit)
Wisniewski v. Board of Education of the Weedsport Central School District	United States Court of Appeals for the Second Circuit
Mahaffey ex rel. Mahaffey v. Aldrich	United States District Court for the Eastern District of Michigan (Sixth Circuit)
Layshock ex rel. Layshock v. Hermitage School District	United States Court of Appeals for the Third Circuit
D.J.M. ex rel. D.M. v. Hannibal Public School District No. 60	United States Court of Appeals for the Eighth Circuit
Roasio v. Clark County School District	United States District Court for the District of Nevada (Ninth Circuit)
R.S. ex rel. S.S. v. Minnewaska Area School District No. 2149	United States District Court for the District of Minnesota (Eighth Circuit)
Bell v. Itawamba County School Board	United States District Court for the Northern District of Mississippi (Fifth Circuit)
Neal et al. v. Efurd	United States District Court for the Western District of Arkansas (Eighth Circuit)
Bystrom By and Through Bystrom v. Fridley High School	United States District Court for the District of Minnesota (Eighth Circuit)

Winning Party in Federal Court Cases

School districts won in twenty-three of the forty-five (51.1%) federal court cases while students won in twenty-two cases (48.9%) (see Table 28). This suggests that school districts are just as likely as students to win in federal court. Thus, if students angle for federal lawsuits instead of state lawsuits because of the belief that they are more likely than school districts to win in federal court, they need to know that the data does not necessarily support such a belief.

Table 28. Winning party in federal court cases

Winning Party in Federal Court Cases		
	Winning Party	
Case	**School District**	**Student**
Fenton v. Stear	X	
K.G.S. v. Kemp	X	
Hatter v. Los Angeles City High School District	X	
Klein v. Smith		X
Killion v. Franklin Regional School District		X
Lavine v. Blaine School District	X	
Donovan v. Ritchie	X	
Ponce v. Socorro Independent School District	X	
Doe v. Pulaski County Special School District	X	
Riggan v. Midland Independent School District		X
Burch v. Barker		X
Latour v. Riverside Beaver School District		X
Porter v. Ascension Parish School Board		X
Schwartz v. Schuker	X	
Boucher v. School Board of School District of Greenfield	X	
Baker v. Downey City Board of Education	X	
Thomas v. Board of Education, Granville Central School District		X
C.R. ex rel. Rainville v. Eugene School District 4J	X	
Sullivan v. Houston Independent School District (1969)		X
Sullivan v. Houston Independent School District (1973)	X	
Shanley v. Northeast Independent School District		X
Beussink v. Woodland R-IV School District		X
Flaherty v. Keystone Oaks School District		X
Requa v. Kent School District No. 415	X	
J.C. ex rel. R.C. v. Beverly Hills Unified School District		X
Barnett ex rel. Barnett v. Tipton County Board of Education	X	
Doninger v. Niehoff	X	
Coy ex rel. Coy v. Board of Education of North Canton City Schools		X

continued on following page

Assessing the Current Jurisprudence

Table 28. Continued

Winning Party in Federal Court Cases		
	Winning Party	
Case	**School District**	**Student**
T.V. ex rel. B.V. v. Smith-Green Community School Corporation		X
S.J.W. v. Lee's Summit R–7 School District	X	
Evans v. Bayer		X
Wynar v. Douglas County School District	X	
Kowalski v. Berkeley County Schools	X	
J.S. ex rel. Snyder v. Blue Mountain School District		X
O.Z. v. Board of Trustees of Long Beach Unified School District	X	
Emmett v. Kent School District No. 415		X
Wisniewski v. Board of Education of the Weedsport Central School District	X	
Mahaffey ex rel. Mahaffey v. Aldrich		X
Layshock ex rel. Layshock v. Hermitage School District		X
D.J.M. ex rel. D.M. v. Hannibal Public School District No. 60	X	
Roasio v. Clark County School District		X
R.S. ex rel. S.S. v. Minnewaska Area School District No. 2149		X
Bell v. Itawamba County School Board	X	
Neal et al. v. Efurd		X
Bystrom By and Through Bystrom v. Fridley High School	X	

Winning Party in Cases Adjudicated within the Jurisdiction of the United States Court of Appeals for the First Circuit

As displayed in Table 29, two of the fifty-one cases (3.9%) reviewed in our study were adjudicated within the jurisdiction of the United States Court of Appeals for the First Circuit. The school district won one case (50%) and the student won one case (50%). 4.4% of the 45 federal court cases occurred within the jurisdiction of this court of appeals. This is ranked seventh among the federal circuit courts of appeals.

Table 29. Winning party in cases adjudicated within the United States Court of Appeals for the First Circuit

Winning Party in Cases Adjudicated within the Jurisdiction of the United States Court Of Appeals for the First Circuit		
	Winning Party	
Case	**School District**	**Student**
Klein v. Smith		X
Donovan v. Ritchie	X	

Table 30. Winning party in cases adjudicated within the United States Court of Appeals for the Second Circuit

Winning Party in Cases Adjudicated within the Jurisdiction of the United States Court Of Appeals for the Second Circuit		
	Winning Party	
Case	School District	Student
Schwartz v. Schuker	X	
Thomas v. Board of Education, Granville Central School District		X
Doninger v. Niehoff	X	
Wisniewski v. Board of Education of the Weedsport Central School District	X	

Winning Party in Cases Adjudicated within the Jurisdiction of the United States Court of Appeals for the Second Circuit

As evident in Table 30, four of the fifty-one cases (7.8%) reviewed in our study were adjudicated within the jurisdiction of the United States Court of Appeals for the Second Circuit. The school district was victorious in three of the four cases (75%). Only one case was decided in favor of a student (25%). 8.9% of the 45 federal court cases were decided within this appellate court's jurisdiction. This is ranked fifth among the federal circuit courts of appeals.

Winning Party in Cases Adjudicated within the Jurisdiction of the United States Court of Appeals for the Third Circuit

Six of the fifty-one cases (11.8%) in our study were adjudicated within the jurisdiction of the United States Court of Appeals for the Third Circuit. Of the six cases, the school district won just one case (16.7%) while the student won in five cases (83.3%) (see Table 31). This is favorable news for students within the jurisdiction of this court of appeals. This court of appeals accounted for 13.3% of the 45 federal court cases in our study. This is ranked fourth among the federal circuit courts of appeals.

Table 31. Winning party in cases adjudicated within the United States Court of Appeals for the Third Circuit

Winning Party in Cases Adjudicated within the Jurisdiction of the United States Court of Appeals for the Third Circuit		
	Winning Party	
Case	School District	Student
Fenton v. Stear	X	
Killion v. Franklin Regional School District		X
Latour v. Riverside Beaver School District		X
Flaherty v. Keystone Oaks School District		X
J.S. ex rel. Snyder v. Blue Mountain School District		X
Layshock ex rel. Layshock v. Hermitage School District		X

Assessing the Current Jurisprudence

Table 32. Winning party in cases adjudicated within the United States Court of Appeals for the Fourth Circuit

Winning Party in Cases Adjudicated within the Jurisdiction of the United States Court of Appeals for the Fourth Circuit		
	Winning Party	
Case	School District	Student
Kowalski v. Berkeley County Schools	X	

Winning Party in Cases Adjudicated within the Jurisdiction of the United States Court of Appeals for the Fourth Circuit

As evident in Table 32, only one of the fifty-one cases (2%) in our study was adjudicated within the United States Court of Appeals for the Fourth Circuit. The school district emerged victorious in the case. This court of appeals accounted for just 2.2% of the 45 federal court cases in our study.

Winning Party in Cases Adjudicated within the Jurisdiction of the United States Court of Appeals for the Fifth Circuit

Eight of the fifty-one cases (15.7%) reviewed were adjudicated in the jurisdiction of the United States Court of Appeals for the Fifth Circuit. School districts won four of the eight cases (50%) within the jurisdiction of this court of appeals (see Table 33). Students also won four of the eight cases (50%). This court of appeals accounted for 17.7% of the 45 federal court cases – the second highest of the federal circuit courts of appeals.

Table 33. Winning party in cases adjudicated within the United States Court of Appeals for the Fifth Circuit

Winning Party in Cases Adjudicated within the Jurisdiction of the United States Court of Appeals for the Fifth Circuit		
	Winning Party	
Case	School District	Student
K.G.S. v. Kemp	X	
Ponce v. Socorro Independent School District	X	
Riggan v. Midland Independent School District		X
Porter v. Ascension Parish School Board		X
Sullivan v. Houston Independent School District (1969)		X
Sullivan v. Houston Independent School District (1973)	X	
Shanley v. Northeast Independent School District		X
Bell v. Itawamba County School Board	X	

Table 34. Winning party in cases adjudicated within the United States Court of Appeals for the Sixth Circuit

Winning Party in Cases Adjudicated within the Jurisdiction of the United States Court of Appeals for the Sixth Circuit		
	\multicolumn{2}{c}{Winning Party}	
Case	School District	Student
Barnett ex rel. Barnett v. Tipton County Board of Education	X	
Coy ex rel. Coy v. Board of Education of North Canton City Schools		X
Mahaffey ex rel. Mahaffey v. Aldrich		X

Winning Party in Cases Adjudicated Within the Jurisdiction of the United States Court of Appeals for the Sixth Circuit

Three of the fifty-one cases (5.9%) reviewed were adjudicated within the United States Court of Appeals for the Sixth Circuit. The school district won only one of the three cases (33.3%). Students won two of the three cases (66.7%) (see Table 34). This court of appeals accounted for 6.7% of the 45 cases adjudicated in a federal court. This is ranked sixth among the federal circuit courts of appeals.

Winning Party in Cases Adjudicated within the Jurisdiction of the United States Court of Appeals for the Seventh Circuit

As displayed in Table 35, two of the fifty-one cases (3.9%) reviewed were adjudicated within the United States Court of Appeals for the Seventh Circuit. This is tied with the number of cases within the United States Court of Appeals for the First Circuit. The school district won one of the two cases (50%). A student won a case (50%) as well. This court of appeals accounted for 4.4% of the 45 cases adjudicated in a federal court. This is ranked seventh among the federal circuit courts of appeals.

Winning Party in Cases Adjudicated within the Jurisdiction of the United States Court of Appeals for the Eighth Circuit

Seven of the fifty-one cases (13.7%) reviewed were adjudicated within the United States Court of Appeals for the Eighth Circuit. The school district won in four of the cases (57.1%) (see Table 36). The student won in three of the seven cases (42.9%). This court of appeals accounted for 15.6% of the 45 federal court cases. This is ranked third among the federal circuit courts of appeals.

Table 35. Winning party in cases adjudicated within the United States Court of Appeals for the Seventh Circuit

Winning Party in Cases Adjudicated within the Jurisdiction of the United States Court of Appeals for the Seventh Circuit		
	\multicolumn{2}{c}{Winning Party}	
Case	School District	Student
Boucher v. School Board of School District of Greenfield	X	
T.V. ex rel. B.V. v. Smith-Green Community School Corporation		X

Assessing the Current Jurisprudence

Table 36. Winning party in cases adjudicated within the United States Court of Appeals for the Eighth Circuit

Winning Party in Cases Adjudicated within the Jurisdiction of the United States Court of Appeals for the Eighth Circuit		
	Winning Party	
Case	**School District**	**Student**
Doe v. Pulaski County Special School District	X	
Beussink v. Woodland R-IV School District		X
S.J.W. v. Lee's Summit R–7 School District	X	
D.J.M. ex rel. D.M. v. Hannibal Public School District No. 60	X	
R.S. ex rel. S.S. v. Minnewaska Area School District No. 2149		X
Neal et al. v. Efurd		X
Bystrom By and Through Bystrom v. Fridley High School	X	

Winning Party in Cases Adjudicated within the Jurisdiction of the United States Court of Appeals for the Ninth Circuit

Eleven of the fifty-one cases (21.6%) studied were adjudicated within the United States Court of Appeals for the Ninth Circuit. The school district won in seven of the eleven cases (63.6%) (see Table 37). The student won in four of the eleven cases (36.4%). The relatively low success rate for students within the jurisdiction of this court of appeals is discouraging for students. It is even more discouraging because this court of appeals accounted for 24.4% of the 45 federal court cases – the highest of the federal circuit courts of appeals.

Table 37. Winning party in cases adjudicated within the United States Court of Appeals for the Ninth Circuit

Winning Party in Cases Adjudicated within the Jurisdiction of the United States Court of Appeals for the Ninth Circuit		
	Winning Party	
Case	**School District**	**Student**
Hatter v. Los Angeles City High School District	X	
Lavine v. Blaine School District	X	
Burch v. Barker		X
Baker v. Downey City Board of Education	X	
C.R. ex rel. Rainville v. Eugene School District 4J	X	
Requa v. Kent School District No. 415	X	
J.C. ex rel. R.C. v. Beverly Hills Unified School District		X
Wynar v. Douglas County School District	X	
O.Z. v. Board of Trustees of Long Beach Unified School District	X	
Emmett v. Kent School District No. 415		X
Roasio v. Clark County School District		X

Table 38. Winning party in cases adjudicated within the United States Court of Appeals for the Tenth Circuit

Winning Party in Cases Adjudicated within the Jurisdiction of the United States Court of Appeals for the Tenth Circuit		
	Winning Party	
Case	School District	Student
No case found		

Table 39. Winning party in cases adjudicated within the United States Court of Appeals for the Eleventh Circuit

Winning Party in Cases Adjudicated within the Jurisdiction of the United States Court of Appeals for the Eleventh Circuit		
	Winning Party	
Case	School District	Student
Evans v. Bayer		X

Winning Party in Cases Adjudicated within the Jurisdiction of the United States Court of Appeals for the Tenth Circuit

Table 38 symbolically represents the fact that none of the fifty-one off-campus student speech cases (0%) was adjudicated within the United States Court of Appeals for the Tenth Circuit.

Winning Party in Cases Adjudicated within the Jurisdiction of the United States Court of Appeals for the Eleventh Circuit

As displayed in Table 39, only one of the fifty-one cases (2%) reviewed was adjudicated within the United States Court of Appeals for the Eleventh Circuit. This is tied with the number of cases within the United States Court of Appeals for the Eleventh Circuit. The student won the lone case decided within the United States Court of Appeals for the Eleventh Circuit. This court of appeals accounted for 2.2% of the 45 federal court cases.

CONCLUSION

This chapter analyzed and outlined the state of the off-campus student-speech jurisprudence. In order to determine how often the United States Supreme Court's student-speech tests are applied to off-campus speech, we tabulated information on the lower courts' application of the tests. We also included data on whether the student or the school district emerged a winner when the tests were applied. We presented examples of lower court approaches to school-censorship authority in off-campus settings. While some lower courts restrict school censorship to the boundaries of the schoolhouse gate, others allow school censorship of off-campus speech if certain conditions are met: the speaker is a student; the target of the speech is a teacher, administrator or student; the material and substantial disruption test (or a modified

Assessing the Current Jurisprudence

version) is satisfied; the *Bethel* test is met; the speech complies with the *Morse* test; or the speech constitutes a true threat, fighting words, defamation or obscenity.

Our research revealed that some courts avoid confronting the difference in contexts between the United States Supreme Court student-speech precedents and off-campus speech by ignoring the distinction between off-campus speech and on-campus speech. This decision unburdens the court of having to give a rationale for extending the Supreme Court precedent(s) beyond their on-campus contexts. It further enables schools to censor off-campus speech under the Supreme Court precedents as they would on-campus speech. Alternatively, some courts convert off-campus speech into on-campus speech in order to pave the way for application of the Supreme Court precedents to the student speech. This decision likewise allows courts to evade responsibility to provide transparency on the off-campus versus on-campus speech distinction and clarity on the off-campus student-speech jurisprudence.

Additionally, we presented data on which party emerged victorious in cases where student use of school resource or time for the speech was material and cases where it was de minimis or nil. Furthermore, we identified the victorious party in cases that considered the student-speaker's role or a third party's role in bringing off-campus speech to the school's attention. Additionally, we presented data for cases where the student-speaker accessed the speech on-campus. We also reported data on the winning party in cases where speech targeted students as well as those where school officials were targeted. Data was also reported on the number of cases adjudicated in federal courts and state courts with a discussion of what the data could mean for students. The diverse data presented in the chapter are designed to inform educators, students and school administrators of the prevailing trends in the off-campus student-speech jurisprudence.

Despite the fact that numerous courts have reviewed off-campus student speech and used the variety of approaches discussed in this chapter (as well as others), they have all missed an interesting yet unspoken dynamic with respect to the speech of the students in Tinker v. Des Moines Independent Community School District (1969), Bethel School District No. 403 v. Fraser (1986) and Morse v. Frederick (2007). Every court, as well as our discussions heretofore, has analyzed these Supreme Court cases as on-campus speech cases because the United States Supreme Court itself approached those cases as on-campus speech cases. However, we challenge our readers to consider that those Supreme Court cases might actually have involved a form of off-campus student speech. After all, the armbands worn by Mary Beth, Christopher and John in Tinker v. Des Moines Independent Community School District were created outside the schoolhouse gate and then brought on-campus. Matthew Fraser's obscene speech at the assembly was likely composed off-campus and then brought on-campus for the assembly (Bethel School District No. 403 v. Fraser, 1986).

In Morse v. Frederick (2007), Joseph Frederick never took his banner "BONG HiTS 4 JESUS" on school grounds. In fact, he arrived late that morning and immediately joined his friends across the street from the school where he unfurled the 14-foot banner in front of the Olympic Relay cameras and torchbearers. The banner that Joseph and his friends used was created off-campus. Joseph stated that the words on the banner came from his girlfriend who showed him a snowboard sticker with the words "Bong Hits For Jesus" for his "free speech experiment" (Moss, 2011, p. 1429). Therefore, in Morse v. Frederick, we had speech created outside the school premises that remained outside the school premises. Even though the student-speaker did not take the banner on to school grounds, the Supreme Court chose to view the speech as on-campus speech. The only Supreme Court student-speech precedent that did not originate off-campus was that in Hazelwood v. Kuhlmeier (1988) since it involved a school-sponsored publication that was part of a journalism lab class.

The fact that the Supreme Court viewed the students' speeches in Tinker v. Des Moines Independent Community School District (1969), Bethel School District No. 403 v. Fraser (1986) and Morse v. Frederick (2007) as on-campus speeches, despite their on-campus origins, could portend bad news for students' First Amendment right to off-campus speech. In Tinker v. Des Moines Independent Community School District and Bethel School District No. 403 v. Fraser, the student-speakers brought their speeches on-campus and the Supreme Court treated their speeches as on-campus speeches. In Morse v. Frederick (2007), the student-speaker did not bring his speech inside the school; yet the Supreme Court still regarded it as on-campus speech because it was speech at a school-sanctioned event in the presence of other students and school officials. While these Supreme Court cases do not apply to student speech that wholly stays off-campus, they could be applicable to off-campus student speech brought on-campus; or to off-campus speech delivered at an off-campus location, in the presence of other students and school officials, during a school-sanctioned event. Thus, maybe scholars and the judiciary need to take a new look at how they have traditionally viewed the Supreme Court's student speech precedents. Maybe the Supreme Court has actually ruled on off-campus speech and we simply have not realized it until now.

REFERENCES

Baker v. Downey City Board of Education (1969). 307 F.Supp. 517.

Barnett ex rel. Barnett v. Tipton County Board of Education (2009). 601 F.Supp.2d 980.

Beidler v. North Thurston School District (2000). No. 99-2-00236-6.

Bell v. Itawamba County School Board (2012). 859 F.Supp.2d 834.

Bethel School District No. 403 v. Fraser (1986). 478 U.S. 675.

Beussink v. Woodland R-IV School District (1998). 30 F. Supp. 2d 1175.

Boucher v. School Board of School District of Greenfield (1998). 134 F.3d 821.

Burch v. Barker (1988). 861 F.2d 1149.

Bystrom By and Through Bystrom v. Fridley High School (1987). 686 F.Supp. 1387.

Coy ex rel. Coy v. Board of Education of North Canton City Schools (2002). 205 F.Supp.2d 791.

C.R. ex rel. Rainville v. Eugene School District 4J (2013). 2013 WL 5102848.

D.J.M. ex rel. D.M. v. Hannibal Public School District No. 60 (2011). 647 F.3d 754.

Doe v. Pulaski County Special School District (2002). 306 F.3d 616.

Doninger v. Niehoff (2008). 527 F.3d 41.

Donovan v. Ritchie (1995). 68 F.3d 14.

Emmett v. Kent School District No. 415 (2000). 92 F.Supp.2d 1088.

Evans v. Bayer (2010). 684 F. Supp. 2d 1365.

Assessing the Current Jurisprudence

Fenton v. Stear (1976). 423 F. Supp. 767.

Flaherty v. Keystone Oaks School District (2003). 247 F.Supp.2d 698.

Hatter v. Los Angeles City High School District (1971). 452 F.2d 673.

Hazelwood v. Kuhlmeier (1988). 484 U.S. 260.

J.C. ex rel. R.C. v. Beverly Hills Unified School District (2010). 711 F.Supp.2d 1094.

J.S. ex rel. Snyder v. Blue Mountain School District (2011). 650 F.3d 915.

J.S. v. Bethlehem Area School District (2002). 807 A.2d 847.

K.G.S. v. Kemp (2011). 2011 WL 4635002.

Killion v. Franklin Regional School District (2001). 136 F.Supp.2d 446.

Klein v. Smith (1986). 635 F. Supp. 1440.

Kowalski v. Berkeley County Schools (2011). 652 F.3d 565.

Lander v. Seaver (1859). 32 Vt. 114.

Latour v. Riverside Beaver School District (2005). 2005 WL 2106562.

Lavine v. Blaine School District (2001). 257 F.3d 981.

Layshock ex rel. Layshock v. Hermitage School District (2011). 650 F.3d 205.

Mahaffey ex rel. Mahaffey v. Aldrich (2002). 236 F.Supp.2d 779.

Miller v. California (1973). 413 U.S. 15.

Morse v. Frederick (2007). 551 U.S. 393.

Moss, S. A. (2011). The overhyped path from Tinker to Morse: How the student speech cases show the limits of Supreme Court decisions–for the law and for the litigants. *Florida Law Review, 63*, 1407–1457.

Neal et al. v. Efurd (2005). No. 04-2195.

O.Z. v. Board of Trustees of Long Beach Unified School District (2008). 2008 WL 4396895.

Pangle v. Bend-Lapine School District (2000). 10 P.3d 275.

Ponce v. Socorro Independent School District (2007). 508 F.3d 765.

Porter v. Ascension Parish School Board (2004). 393 F.3d 608.

Requa v. Kent School District No. 415 (2007). 492 F.Supp.2d 1272.

Riggan v. Midland Independent School District (2000). 86 F.Supp.2d 647.

Roasio v. Clark County School District (2013). 2013 WL 3679375.

R.S. ex rel. S.S. v. Minnewaska Area School District No. 2149 (2012). 894 F.Supp.2d 1128.

Schwartz v. Schuker (1969). 298 F.Supp. 238.

Shanley v. Northeast Independent School District (1972). 462 F.2d 960.

Sherrell ex rel. Sherrell v. Northern Community School Corporation of Tipton County (2004). 801 N.E.2d 693.

S.J.W. v. Lee's Summit R–7 School District (2012). 696 F.3d 771.

State, A.B. v. (2008). 885 N.E. 2d 1223.

Sullivan v. Houston Independent School District (1969). 307 F.Supp. 1328.

Sullivan v. Houston Independent School District (1973). 475 F.2d 1071.

Thomas v. Board of Education, Granville Central School District (1979). 607 F.2d 1043.

Tinker v. Des Moines Independent Community School District (1969). 393 U.S. 503.

T.V. ex rel. B.V. v. Smith-Green Community School Corporation (2011). 807 F.Supp.2d 767.

United States v. J.H.H. (1994). 22 F.3d 821.

United States v. Orozco–Santillan (1990). 903 F.2d 1262.

Watts v. United States (1969). 394 U.S. 705.

Wisniewski v. Board of Education of the Weedsport Central School District (2007). 494 F.3d 34.

Wynar v. Douglas County School District (2013). 728 F.3d 1062.

KEY TERMS AND DEFINITIONS

Bethel **Test:** This is the test the United States Supreme Court created in Bethel School District No. 403 v. Fraser (1986) that authorizes school officials to censor student speech that is vulgar, lewd, plainly offensive or obscene.

Fighting Words: Speech which inflicts injury simply from being uttered or speech with the tendency to incite a disturbance.

Hazelwood **Test:** This is the test the United States Supreme Court created in Hazelwood v. Kuhlmeier (1988) that authorizes school officials to censor student speech that is sponsored by the school as long as the censorship has a legitimate pedagogical purpose. The test is also sometimes referred to as the *Kuhlmeier* test.

Hybrid Speech: Speech that is directed at or against school officials as well as at an entity unaffiliated with the school.

Infringement-of-Rights Test: The judicial standard that conditions censorship of student speech on whether the speech impinges the rights of other students.

Material and Substantial Disruption Test: The judicial standard that conditions censorship of student speech on whether the speech is reasonably foreseeable to cause or actually caused material and substantial disruption to the school.

Assessing the Current Jurisprudence

Miller **Test:** The three-part test the United States Supreme Court created in Miller v. California (1973) for determining whether the government can censor speech as obscenity. Under this test, courts inquire into: (a) whether, under contemporary community standards, the average person would deem the speech as a whole as appealing to a prurient interest; (b) whether the speech describes or shows sexual conduct defined by state law in a manifestly offensive way; and (c) whether the speech as a whole has no serious political, scientific, literary or artistic value (Miller v. California, 1973).

Morse **Test:** This is the test the United States Supreme Court created in Morse v. Frederick (2007) that authorizes school officials to censor student speech that advocates illegal drug use.

Student-Speech Tests: This refers to the four tests that the United States Supreme Court created for reviewing student-speech cases. These are the *Tinker* tests (the material and substantial disruption test as well as the infringement-of-rights test); the *Bethel* test; *Hazelwood* test; and the *Morse* test. These tests were created in the context of on-campus speech.

True-Threat Doctrine: The free speech doctrine that provides that speech which expresses a genuine intent to cause harm is unprotected speech under the First Amendment.

Chapter 14
Acceptable Use Policies

ABSTRACT

This chapter examines critical state and federal requirements for the development of acceptable use policies. It also reviews the role of acceptable use policies in shaping the approach of schools toward student off-campus speech. It highlights components that should be included in acceptable use policies. It also reveals that school districts are increasingly adopting responsible use policies in order to address the student use of personal electronic devices. Acceptable use policies and responsible use policies are viable avenues for school officials to minimize violations of students' First Amendment right to free speech since they are designed to inform and seek student as well as parent consent regarding use of technology-based devices at the school.

INTRODUCTION

An acceptable use policy (AUP) is a "written agreement signed by students, their parents/caregivers, and their teachers…[that] outlines the terms and conditions for using technology-based devices maintained by schools and personal technology-based devices used during school hours on school property" (Virginia Department of Education, 2012). The AUP provides assurance to parents and educators that schools are protecting students from inappropriate, violent, or obscene words or images while they are online (Education World, n.d.). The AUP is one of the most important documents that a school district will create (Education World, n.d.). Particularly because it is designed for student safety and invokes parent and student consent regarding acceptable use of technology. In order to focus their policies on ethical and responsible use of student electronic devices, school districts are now implementing responsible use policies (RUPs) in lieu of AUPs (which were originally designed to exclude student electronic devices from schools). This chapter presents a model district RUP that other districts can follow in transitioning from AUPs to RUPs.

DOI: 10.4018/978-1-4666-9519-1.ch014

Acceptable Use Policies

MAIN FOCUS OF THE CHAPTER

This chapter provides an overview of important legal and policy guidelines of AUPs. The first part discusses important state and federal requirements in developing AUPS. The second part identifies the components that all AUPs should possess. The final part discusses how school districts have recently begun to move away from AUPs toward RUPs to address the use of personally-owned mobile devices on school grounds.

State and Federal Requirements

According to the National Conference of State Legislatures (2014), twenty-four states have enacted internet filtering legislation that public libraries or schools must follow. Most of these states "simply require school boards or public libraries or schools to adopt internet use policies to prevent minors from gaining access to sexually explicit, obscene or harmful materials" (National Conference of State Legislatures, 2014). Some states also require public schools and libraries to install filtering software.

The federal statute that imposes AUP requirements on schools is the Children's Internet Protection Act (CIPA) (2014). Congress passed CIPA in 2000 to protect minors from exposure to obscene materials in public libraries and schools. CIPA provides discounted funding for internet access and connections through the E-rate program. To qualify for E-rate funding, schools and libraries must certify that they have adopted an internet safety policy that incorporates technology protection measures (Federal Communications Commission, 2013). The protection measures must block or filter visual depictions that are obscene, child pornography, or harmful to minors. Before adopting the safety policy, the school or library "must provide reasonable notice and hold at least one public hearing or meeting to address the proposal" (p. 1).

CIPA imposes two additional requirements on participating schools (Federal Communications Commission, 2013). First, schools must certify that their internet safety policies include monitoring of the online activities of minors. Second, in accordance with the Protecting Children in the 21st Century Act, schools must educate minors about appropriate online conduct, such as interactions on social networking websites and chat rooms, "and cyberbullying awareness and response" (p. 1).

Schools and libraries that are subject to CIPA must adopt an internet safety policy that addresses the following:

1. Access by minors to inappropriate matter on the internet;
2. The safety and security of minors when using electronic mail, chat rooms and other forms of direct electronic communications;
3. Unauthorized access, including so-called "hacking," and other unlawful activities by minors online;
4. Unauthorized disclosure, use, and dissemination of personal information regarding minors; and
5. Measures designed to restrict minors' access to material harmful to minors (Federal Communications Commission, 2013, p. 1).

In United States v. American Library Association (2003), the United States Supreme Court held that CIPA did not violate the First Amendment. In this case, a group of library associations, patrons, and website publishers alleged that CIPA violated the First Amendment. The plaintiffs claimed that the public libraries had created a public forum by providing access to the internet. Thus, CIPA was a content-based restriction that was subject to strict scrutiny. The plaintiffs further asserted that filtering software was not narrowly tailored in that it blocked material that was protected by the First Amendment. The Supreme Court rejected this argument. A plurality of the Court found that public libraries had not created a public forum by providing internet access. Libraries did not acquire internet terminals to express opinions. Instead, libraries acquired internet terminals to help patrons with research, learning, and recreational activity.

In Parents, Families and Friends of Lesbians and Gays, Inc. v. Camdenton R-III School District (2012), a New Jersey school district cited CIPA as a justification for installing internet software that blocked access to websites that supported lesbian, gay bisexual and transgender (LGBT) individuals. A group of plaintiffs, including a student in the school district, alleged in federal district court that the software restriction constituted viewpoint discrimination.

The district court granted a preliminary injunction to the plaintiffs, which enjoined the school district from blocking access to the websites (Parents, Families and Friends of Lesbians and Gays, Inc. v. Camdenton R-III School District, 2012). The court found that the filtering software policy could be analyzed in two ways. First, the software could be analyzed under the public forum doctrine. The court found that the school district had created a nonpublic or closed forum. Nevertheless, the district's blocking of content that expressed a positive viewpoint toward LGBT students constituted viewpoint discrimination. As the court observed, "[c]ontrol over access to a nonpublic forum can be based on subject matter and speaker identity so long as the distinctions drawn are reasonable in light of the purpose served by the forum and viewpoint neutral" (p. 899, citing Cornelius v. NAACP Legal Defense and Educational Fund, Inc., 1985, p. 806). In addition, the court ruled that regulations designed to impose "differential burdens upon speech because of its content" must be subjected to strict scrutiny (Parents, Families and Friends of Lesbians and Gays, Inc. v. Camdenton R-III School District, p. 899, citing Turner Broadcasting System Inc. v. Federal Communications Commission, 1994, p. 642). Thus, the screening software was invalid unless the district could show that it was narrowly tailored to achieve a compelling governmental interest.

In the alternative, the district court noted that the screening software could be analyzed under Board of Education, Island Trees Union Free School District No. 26 v. Pico (1982) (Parents, Families and Friends of Lesbians and Gays, Inc. v. Camdenton R-III School District, 2012). In *Pico*, a plurality of the Supreme Court ruled that school districts had broad discretion in determining the content of their libraries (Board of Education, Island Trees Union Free School District No. 26 v. Pico, 1982). Nevertheless, as the district court ruled, even under *Pico*, the viewpoint discrimination could not be based on a disagreement with the subject matter (Parents, Families and Friends of Lesbians and Gays, Inc. v. Camdenton R-III School District, 2012). Rather, the screening software could be justified only under the *Tinker* material and substantial disruption standard (see chapter seven for more on the material and substantial disruption standard).

The court went on to find that the plaintiffs would succeed under public forum analysis or *Pico* (Parents, Families and Friends of Lesbians and Gays, Inc. v. Camdenton R-III School District, 2012). Under forum analysis, the court assumed that the school district had a compelling interest in complying with CIPA. However, the court held that the filtering software was not narrowly tailored to achieve that compelling interest under the strict scrutiny standard of review. The evidence showed that the software employed by the district failed to block 30% of the material prohibited by CIPA, and that the district had used the software to block websites that portrayed LGBT in a positive light. Further, the court concluded that the blocking software failed the narrow tailoring prong because it imposed a differential burden on

Acceptable Use Policies

the LGBT speech because of its content, thus stigmatizing the speech. When using filtering software to block particular content, in order to successfully use CIPA as justification, school districts must comply with the public forum doctrine (see chapter nine for extensive discussion of the doctrine).

The district court also found that the internet filtering software also violated *Pico* (Friends of Lesbians and Gays, Inc. v. Camdenton R-III School District, 2012). By engaging in viewpoint discrimination, the school district sought "to prescribe what shall be orthodox in matters of opinion" (p. 901). The lesson is that school districts must not engage in viewpoint discrimination when using internet blocking software or other software blocking use of any electronic device.

Components of Acceptable Use Policies

According to the National Education Association, an acceptable use policy (AUP) should have six components:

- A preamble,
- A definition section,
- A policy statement,
- An acceptable uses section,
- An unacceptable uses section, and
- A violations/sanctions section (Education World, n.d.)

The preamble should explain the need for the AUP, the policy's goals, and the process for developing it. The preamble should also state that the school's code of conduct applies to student online activity (Education World, n.d.).

The definition section should define key terms that are necessary for parents and students to understand the policy. These terms include, but are not limited to "internet," "computer network," and "education purpose" (Education World, n.d.).

The policy statement should identify the computer services that the AUP covers, "and the circumstances under which students can use computer services" (Education World, n.d.). For instance, to ensure understanding of AUP rules, schools may allow students to access computer services upon completion of a "computer responsibility class" (Education World, n.d.).

The acceptable uses section should explain how students can appropriately use the computer network. For instance, the policy may limit student use to educational purposes, which the policy then defines. By contrast, the unacceptable uses section should provide "clear, specific examples of what constitutes student use" (Education World, n.d.).

The violations/sanction section should explain to students "how to report violations of the policy or whom to question about its application" (Education World, n.d.). The AUP may stipulate that violations will be addressed according to the student disciplinary code.

In addition to the six components mentioned above, the AUP should include a section for students and parents to sign the document, "in acknowledgment that they are aware of students' restrictions to network access and releasing the school district of the responsibility for students who choose to break those restrictions" (Education World, n.d.).

Responsible Use Policies

Most school districts developed their AUPs before the rise of mobile technologies (Bosco & Krueger, 2011). Generally, AUPs banned students from bringing their mobile devices to school (Bosco & Krueger, 2011). Several analysts have criticized this approach, arguing that schools are the best place to teach students how to behave responsibly in an online environment (Consortium for School Networking, 2012). Another critique of highly restrictive mobile device policies is that they provide a false sense of security for protecting students (Bosco & Krueger, 2011). Further, highly restrictive policies might attract students to illicit websites (Bosco & Krueger, 2011; Chaplin, 2012).

The Consortium for School Networking (CoSN) (2012) observes that many school districts are dropping their traditional AUP approaches, and replacing them with "responsible use policies" (RUPs). RUPs are different from traditional AUPs in that they "*treat[] the student as a person responsible for ethical and healthy use of the Internet and mobile devices*" (p. 6).

Chaplin (2012) cites Katy Independent School District (ISD) as an example of a district that has changed its AUP to adopt the tenets of RUP policies. Katy ISD's guidelines for the use of personally-owned communication devices are provided below:

- Internet access is filtered by the District on personal telecommunication devices in the same manner as District-owned equipment. If network access is needed, connection to the filtered, wireless network provided by the District is required.
- These devices are the sole responsibility of the student owner. The campus or District assumes no responsibility for personal telecommunication devices if they are lost, loaned, damaged or stolen and only limited time or resources will be spent trying to locate stolen or lost items.
- These devices have educational and monetary value. Students are prohibited from trading or selling these items to other students on District property, including school buses.
- Each student is responsible for his/her own device: set-up, maintenance, charging, and security. Staff members will not store student devices at any time, nor will any District staff diagnose, repair, or work on a student's personal telecommunication device.
- Telecommunication devices will not be used as a factor in grading or assessing student work.
- Students who do not have access to personal telecommunication devices will be provided with comparable District-owned equipment or given similar assignments that do not require access to electronic devices.
- Telecommunication devices are only to be used for educational purposes at the direction of a classroom teacher or as stated for specific age groups.
- Campus administrators and staff members have the right to prohibit use of devices at certain times or during designated activities (i.e. campus presentations, theatrical performances, or guest speakers) that occur during the school day.
- An appropriately-trained administrator may examine a student's personal telecommunication device and search its contents, in accordance with disciplinary guidelines (Katy Independent School District, 2011).

CONCLUSION

This chapter has provided an overview of acceptable use policies (AUPs), which *Education World* (n.d.) has identified as one of the most important documents that a school district will develop. School districts should be aware of CIPA as well as state requirements. Also, as the *Parents, Families and Friends of Lesbians and Gays, Inc.* case demonstrates, school districts should not use CIPA as an excuse to filter content that they disagree with. Further, school districts should take special care to ensure that their AUPs contain the elements discussed above. Finally, in order to diminish the risk of encroaching students' First Amendment rights, school districts should seriously consider whether to adopt responsible-use policies (RUPs) for personally-owned mobile devices on school grounds. By adopting such policies, school districts will be able to educate students on the ethical and responsible use of devices and digital communication, potentially leading to less censorship incidents.

REFERENCES

Board of Education, Island Trees Union Free School District No. 26 v. Pico (1982). 457 U.S. 853.

Bosco, J., & Krueger, K. (2011). *Moving from "acceptable" to "responsible" use in a Web 2.0 world*. Retrieved July 14, 2014 from http://www.edweek.org/ew/articles/2011/07/20/37bosco.h30.html

Chaplin, H. (2012). *Welcoming mobile: More districts are rewriting acceptable use policies, embracing smartphones and social media in schools*. Retrieved July 14, 2014 from http://spotlight.macfound.org/featured-stories/entry/welcoming-mobile-rewriting-acceptable-use-smartphones-and-social-media

Children's Internet Protection Act, 42 U.S.C. §§ 254(h)(5)(b), (l) (2014).

Consortium for School Networking. (2012). *Making progress: Rethinking state and school district policies concerning mobile technologies and social media*. Retrieved July 14, 2014 from http://www.splc.org/pdf/making_progress_2012.pdf

Cornelius v. NAACP Legal Defense and Educational Fund, Inc. (1985). 473 U.S. 788, 806.

Education World. (n.d.). *Getting started on the internet: Developing an acceptable use policy (AUP)*. Retrieved July 14, 2014 from http://www.educationworld.com/a_curr/curr093.shtml

Federal Communications Commission. (2013). *Children's Internet Protection Act (CIPA)*. Retrieved July 14, 2014 from http://transition.fcc.gov/cgb/consumerfacts/cipa.pdf

Katy Independent School District. (2011). *Student responsible use guidelines for technology*. Retrieved July 14, 2014 from http://www.katyisd.org/parents/Documents/Forms%20and%20Guidelines/AcceptableUse.pdf

National Conference of State Legislatures. (2014). *Laws relating to filtering, blocking and usage policies in schools and libraries*. Retrieved July 14, 2014 from http://www.ncsl.org/research/telecommunications-and-information-technology/state-internet-filtering-laws.aspx

Parents, Families and Friends of Lesbians and Gays, Inc. v. Camdenton R-III School District (2012). 853 F.Supp.2d 888.

Turner Broadcasting System Inc. v. Federal Communications Commission (1994). 512 U.S. 622, 642.

United States v. American Library Association (2003). 539 U.S. 194.

Virginia Department of Education. (2012). *Acceptable use internet policy*. Retrieved July 14, 2014 from http://www.doe.virginia.gov/support/safety_crisis_management/internet_safety/acceptable_use_policy.shtml

KEY TERMS AND DEFINITIONS

Acceptable Use Policies: School policies that represent an agreement between students, parents and schools regarding student use of electronic devices and digital communications in the school.

Child Pornography: Visual of a minor in a nude or partially nude state designed to appeal to prurient interests.

Closed Forum: This is a government-owned forum that has not been made a traditional public forum either by historical traditional or government designation. This forum is also referred to as a reserved forum or a non-public forum.

Cyberbullying: Bullying that occurs in cyberspace.

***Miller* Test:** The three-part test the United States Supreme Court created in Miller v. California (1973) for determining whether the government can censor speech as obscenity. Under this test, courts inquire into: (a) whether, under contemporary community standards, the average person would deem the speech as a whole as appealing to a prurient interest; (b) whether the speech describes or shows sexual conduct defined by state law in a manifestly offensive way; and (c) whether the speech as a whole has no serious political, scientific, literary or artistic value (Miller v. California, 1973).

Obscene Speech: Speech that satisfies the three-part *Miller* test, consequently qualifying as obscene under the First Amendment.

Off-Campus Speech: Speech that occurs in any locale outside the borders or premises of a school and outside school hours. It includes student speech away from the school bus and school-sponsored events such as school trips.

Online Speech: Speech in online communication forums, including Twitter, Facebook, Myspace, Friendster, IM (Instant Messaging), YouTube and Instagram.

Responsible Use Policies: School policies that represent an agreement between students, parents and schools designed to teach students responsible and ethical uses of electronic devices and digital communications.

Viewpoint Discrimination: Discrimination against speech based on the view expressed in the speech.

Chapter 15
State Anti-Bullying Statutes and Student Speech

ABSTRACT

This chapter highlights the role of state anti-bullying statutes in censorship of student off-campus speech. It examines the details of a representative and comprehensive anti-bullying statute – the New Jersey anti-bullying law. This chapter also explores the definition of harassment, intimidation and bullying under the anti-bullying statute. It discusses the various responsibilities under the law for regulating harassing, intimidating and bullying speech and conduct. It then discusses the relationship of the law to off-campus speech.

INTRODUCTION

Various states have enacted statutes designed to regulate student speech that constitutes harassment, intimidation and bullying. These laws are a political and legislative response to the increase in student-bullying incidents and to public outcry against bullying. Some states also have enacted cyberstalking laws to protect students from stalking on electronic devices. These diverse laws often reach beyond the confines of the school, allowing school officials to censor off-campus student speech. In some cases, students could face criminal sanctions for violating those laws. A table of state statutes governing off-campus student speech is presented in Appendix B. Since the state statutes are very similar to each other and generally repetitive of language found in other states' statutes, the chapter per the authors focuses on one of the statutes. Specifically, it discusses New Jersey's anti-bullying statute as a representative state statute governing off-campus speech (unless otherwise specified as school days, the timelines referenced in the New Jersey law are calendar days). New Jersey is a leader in a comprehensive approach to anti-bullying legislation; and its statute includes features evident in large part or whole in other states' statutes. The chapter also presents a few features from other states' anti-bullying legislation not present in New Jersey's. It discusses how the anti-bullying legislation could impact off-campus student speech.

DOI: 10.4018/978-1-4666-9519-1.ch015

MAIN FOCUS OF THE CHAPTER

This chapter examines the role of anti-bullying statutes in the censorship of off-campus speech. These laws, known as harassment, bullying or intimidation laws (or cyberbullying laws when specific to the internet) are designed to promote student safety and empower censorship of off-campus speech that qualifies as harassing, intimidating or bullying speech. Using New Jersey's anti-bullying law as a framework, the chapter per the authors presents the customary statutory definition of harassment, intimidation and bullying. It identifies the acts that qualify as harassment, intimidation and bullying and the statutorily-required motivation necessary for those acts. It also discusses the role of the material and substantial disruption test as well as the infringement-of-rights test in school censorship of student speech under the anti-bullying laws. It presents the obligations of various school officials to report and train various constituencies on the various requirements of the law. It also discusses the statutory requirements for school policies as well as the role of the school safety team in the investigation of harassment, bullying and intimidation. These statutory mandates are detailed in order to ensure that students are protected from harassment, intimidation and bullying without compromising student speech rights. Finally, it examines various parts of the law with direct impact on off-campus speech.

New Jersey's Harassment, Intimidation, or Bullying (HIB) Law

New Jersey enacted its anti-bullying law known as the Harassment, Intimidation or Bullying (HIB) in 2002 in order to curb the burgeoning deviancy in schools and to support positive school climate. This law was a forerunner for the national movement against bullying in schools. Despite its stringency, it was amended in November 2010 to ensure even greater stringency as a response to the suicide of Tyler Clementi (a Rutgers University student) in September 2010. Tyler committed suicide after being harassed by his roommate and another student on account of his sexual orientation. The students recorded Tyler's sexual encounter on a webcam and sought to broadcast it to others. Hurt by the harassment, intimidation and bullying, Tyler leaped to his death from the George Washington Bridge on September 22, 2010. Following the national outrage about the harassment, intimidation and bullying, in November 2010, New Jersey legislators unanimously amended the state's anti-bullying law into an anti-bullying bill of rights. Governor Christie signed the bill into law in January 2011, making the New Jersey law one of the most stringent regulations of harassment, intimidation and bullying in the United States. Under amended law, HIB is grounds for suspension or expulsion of students (New Jersey Statutes Annotated § 18A:37-2(k), 2011). In order to strengthen the education of students about the negative consequences of harassment, bullying and intimidation and to foster a climate of tolerance, the law now requires every school to annually observe the week that begins with the first Monday in October as a "Week of Respect" (New Jersey Statutes Annotated § 18A:37-29, 2011). During that entire week, each school must provide students with age-appropriate instruction for preventing HIB. We discuss the various components of the law next.

A. What Constitutes Harassment, Intimidation, or Bullying?

Harassment, Intimidation or Bullying (HIB) is generally defined as a certain incident or series of incidents targeting a victim and motivated by an actual or perceived characteristic of the victim that substantially disrupts the school (New Jersey Statutes Annotated § 18A:37-14, 2011). The incident could be a verbal, written or physical act or an electronic communication; any of these could constitute speech. As shown

State Anti-Bullying Statutes and Student Speech

in our discussions in sections (A)(I) through (A)(V) below, HIB's comprehensive definition includes a jurisdictional element; the distinguishing characteristic of the victim that motivates the HIB; the impact of the HIB incident; and the material and substantial disruption test from Tinker v. Des Moines Independent Community School District (1969), included to ensure school compliance with the First Amendment test for censoring student speech. As discussed in chapters seven, eleven and twelve, the material and substantial disruption test arose in the context of on-campus student speech. Consequently, it is unclear that the United States Supreme Court would find the test applicable to off-campus student speech. Nonetheless, it is the primary test used in the lower courts for censoring off-campus student speech. Accordingly, it is reasonable that states chose to include this test in their HIB laws; at least until the United States Supreme Court specifically rules on a case involving off-campus student speech, providing clarity on the authority of schools to censor off-campus student speech.

(I) What Acts Qualify as HIB?

HIB could take the form of any gesture, verbal act, physical act, written act or electronic communication. Figure 1 lays out these acts which could either be a single incident or a series of incidents. If the incident (or series of incidents) qualifies under any of the items listed in(i) through (v) of Figure 1, school officials must then ask the questions that we laid out in sections (A)(II) through (A)(V) below: what is the motivation?; does the school have jurisdiction over the HIB incident?; does the HIB substantially disrupt or interfere with the school's orderly operation or the rights of other students?; and what is the effect of the incident? The conditions in sections (A)(II) through (A)(V) below must be satisfied in order for a student to make a successful HIB claim.

Figure 1. Acts constituting harassment, intimidation, and bullying

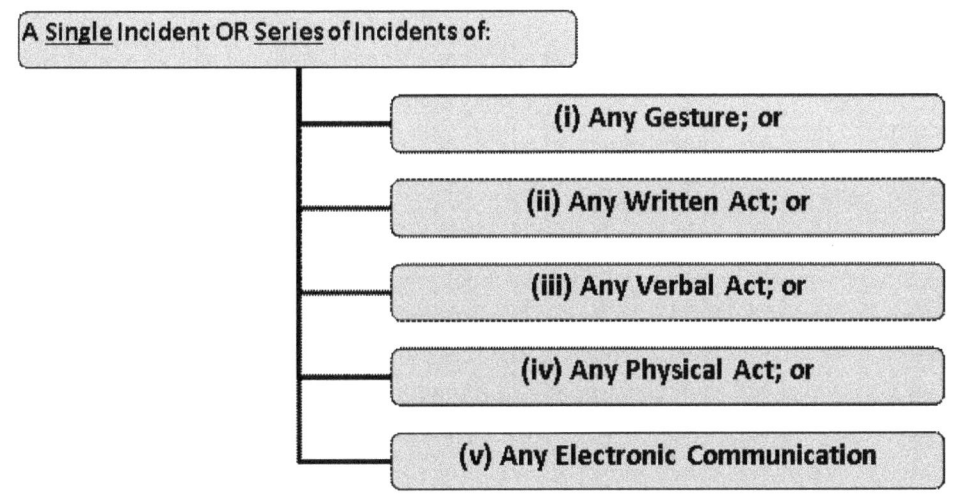

A Single Incident OR Series of Incidents of:
- (i) Any Gesture; or
- (ii) Any Written Act; or
- (iii) Any Verbal Act; or
- (iv) Any Physical Act; or
- (v) Any Electronic Communication

(II) What Is the Motivation?

Once it is established that the incident is a gesture, written act, verbal act, physical act or electronic communication, it must then be established that the gesture, written act, verbal act, physical act or electronic communication is reasonably perceived as motivated by:

1. Any actual characteristic such as race; color; ancestry; national origin; gender; sexual orientation; gender identity and expression; religion; or a mental, physical or sensory disability; or
2. Any perceived characteristic such as race; color; ancestry; national origin; gender; sexual orientation; gender identity and expression; religion; or a mental, physical or sensory disability. The statutory term "perceived" is intended to convey that, even if the victim of the harassment, intimidation or bullying does not actually have the characteristic the bully thought he had, the incident could still constitute HIB (assuming the other parts of the HIB definition are satisfied). For instance, if the bully thinks the student is Hispanic (even though he is not) and on that basis harasses, intimidates or bullies him for being Hispanic, the perceived characteristic is the victim's race; or
3. Any other distinguishing characteristic. This would include a distinguishing characteristic such as a birthmark; a disfiguring characteristic; an accent; height; weight; speech impediment; or socioeconomic status (SES). It could also include the student's grade level – as in the case of a fifth grader taunted by ninth graders for being a fifth grader, for instance. Neither the legislature nor judiciary has clearly delineated what constitutes a distinguishing characteristic; accordingly, this determination will have to be based on the subjective judgments of school officials until there are definitive and limpid guidelines from the judiciary and/or the legislature.

(III) Does the School Have Jurisdiction over the HIB Incident?

School officials can regulate HIB at the following locations:

1. School property;
2. School-sponsored event;
3. School bus; and
4. Off-campus.

Figure 2 sets forth these jurisdictions.

The HIB statute authorizes school censorship of harassment, intimidation and bullying that happens outside the school premises "in cases in which a school employee is made aware of such actions" (New Jersey Statutes Annotated § 18A:37-15.3, 2011). Consequently, school officials do not have go on a fishing expedition for HIB incidents. However, the scope of the law allows a broad exercise of school-censorship authority over off-campus harassing, intimidating or bullying speech once a school official has knowledge of it; as long as all parts of the HIB definition in sections (A)(I) through (A)(V) are also satisfied.

(IV) Does the HIB Substantially Disrupt or Interfere with the School's Orderly Operation or the Rights of Other Students?

Even if the incident meets the above requirements, school officials must still establish that the incident substantially disrupts or interferes with:

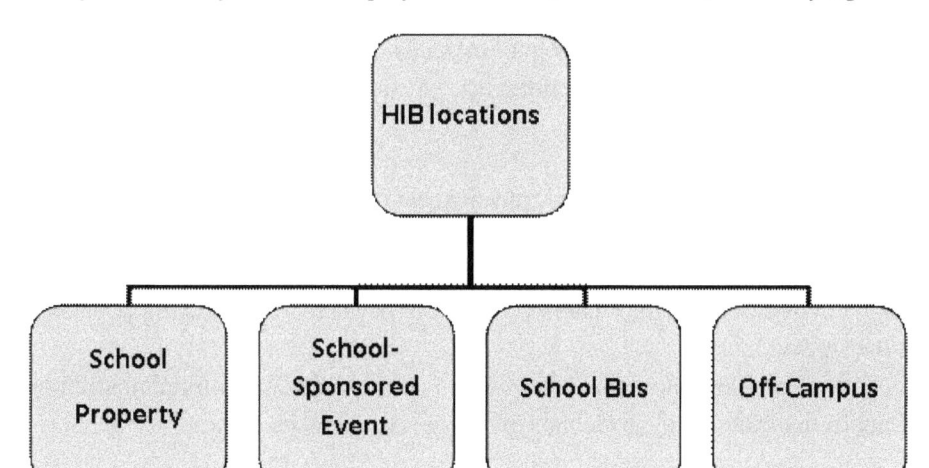

Figure 2. School jurisdiction for censorship of harassment, intimidation, and bullying

```
                    ┌─────────────┐
                    │HIB locations│
                    └──────┬──────┘
         ┌────────────┬────┴─────┬────────────┐
    ┌────┴────┐  ┌────┴────┐ ┌───┴────┐  ┌────┴────┐
    │ School  │  │ School- │ │ School │  │  Off-   │
    │Property │  │Sponsored│ │  Bus   │  │ Campus  │
    │         │  │  Event  │ │        │  │         │
    └─────────┘  └─────────┘ └────────┘  └─────────┘
```

1. The orderly operation of the school; or
2. The rights of other students.

The language used in these two requirements is from the United States Supreme Court decision in Tinker v. Des Moines Independent Community School District (1969) which created the material and substantial disruption test as well as the infringement-of-rights test. Recall, the material and substantial disruption test allows school officials to censor student speech that actually materially and substantially disrupts the school; or is reasonably forecast to cause material and substantial disruption. Given that the Supreme Court has never applied the infringement-of-rights test since its first mention in the *Tinker* case, the meaning of the test is relatively elusive. Nonetheless, the appellation of the test suggests that the test effectively authorizes school officials to censor student speech if the speech impinges on the rights of other students.

A subtle difference between the material and substantial disruption test and the express language of the HIB statute lies in the "reasonable forecast" language: While the Supreme Court ruled in the *Tinker* case that reasonable forecast of material and substantial disruption would suffice for school censorship of student speech, the HIB statute does not include the "reasonable forecast" language. Nonetheless, since the legislature was trying to comply with Supreme Court precedent by including the material and substantial disruption test in the HIB definition, we could presume that the statute includes an implied reasonably-forecast element as in the *Tinker* test.

When applied to off-campus speech, the "substantial disruption" language in the HIB statute provides the nexus between the off-campus speech and the school because of its focus on the disruption of the school. Similarly, with its focus on the student, the infringement-of-rights language of the statute, creates a nexus, albeit nebulous, to the school. It is nebulous because a mere reliance on the impact on students' rights could be stretched too broadly that, irrespective of locale, it leaves little constraint on school authority over students.

(V) What Is the Effect of the Incident?

Once the above requirements are satisfied, school officials must ask themselves the following questions about the effect of the gesture, written act, verbal act, physical act or electronic communication (Figure 3 illustrates these key questions):

1. Does the gesture, written act, verbal act, physical act or electronic communication create a hostile educational environment for the student by interfering with the student's education?; or
2. Does the gesture, written act, verbal act, physical act or electronic communication create a hostile educational environment for the student by severely or pervasively causing physical or emotional harm to the student?; or
3. Does the gesture, written act, verbal act, physical act or electronic communication have the effect of insulting or demeaning any student or group of students?; or

Figure 3. Key questions regarding the effect of the HIB incident

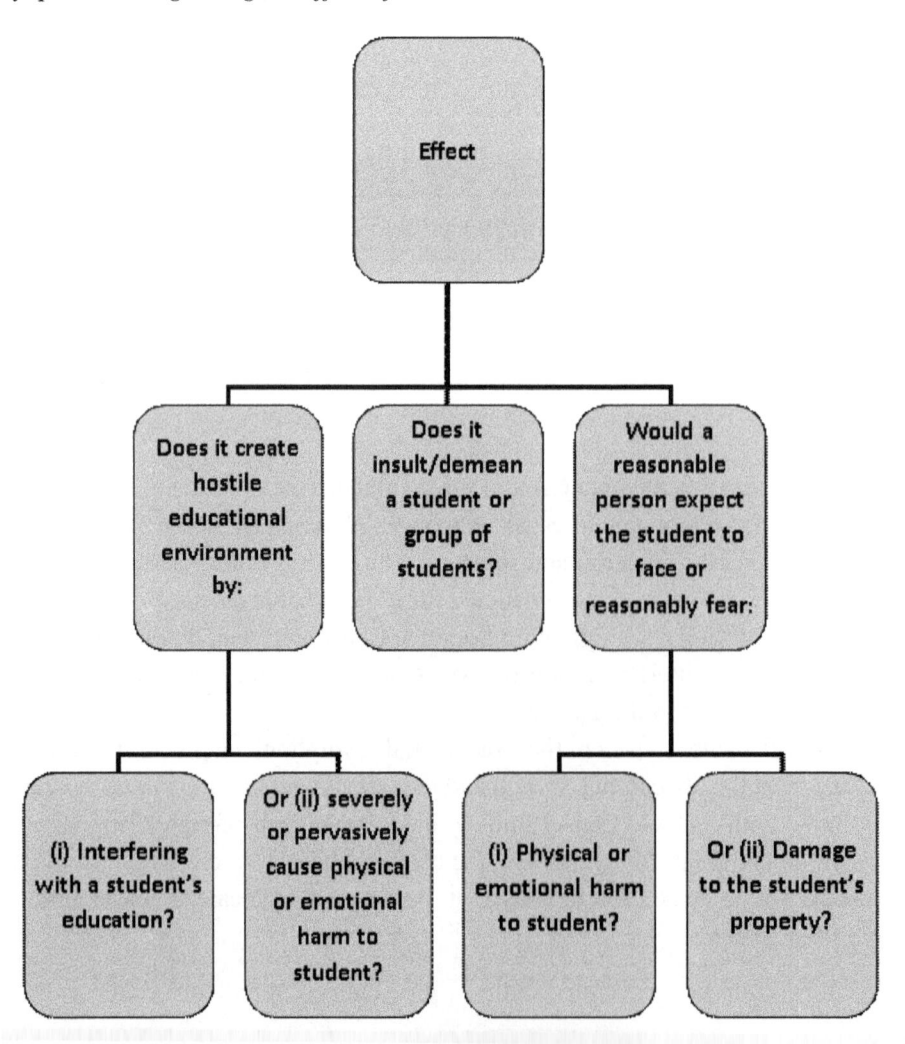

4. Should a reasonable person, under the circumstances, know that the gesture, written act, verbal act, physical act or electronic communication would physically or emotionally harm the student?; or
5. Should a reasonable person, under the circumstances, know that the gesture, written act, verbal act, physical act or electronic communication would damage the student's property?; or
6. Should a reasonable person, under the circumstances, know that the gesture, written act, verbal act, physical act or electronic communication would place the student in reasonable fear of physical or emotional harm to his person?; or
7. Should a reasonable person, under the circumstances, know that the gesture, written act, verbal act, physical act or electronic communication would place the student in reasonable fear of damage to his property?

As evident in the above questions, the HIB definition includes emotional harm. This is important in order to account for the fact that harassing, intimidating or bullying speech or actions could harm students even in the absence of physical injury.

B. What Is the Scope of the Duty to Report HIB?

School-related personnel have a statutory duty to report HIB incidents. They are, however, not required to disclose any information protected from public disclosure under any confidentiality law (New Jersey Statutes Annotated § 18A:17-46, 2011). The statutory directives about the duties to report are so detailed in order to promote accountability and to ensure that harassing, intimidation and bullying incidents are promptly and systematically addressed, precluding continued victimization of the target and protecting the accused from false allegations. The detailed nature of the duties to report is also designed to help limit censorship of speech that does not constitute HIB. We present the duties to report by various school-related personnel below.

1. **All School Employees:** All school employees must report HIB if they either:
   a. Observe HIB;
   b. Have direct knowledge of HIB from a participant or victim; or
   c. Have reliable information that a student has faced HIB.

Employees must make verbal and written reports. However, the law takes a different approach to verbal reports versus written reports. Verbal reports are governed by a same-day rule while written reports are governed by a two-day rule. Verbal Report and the Same-Day Rule: Employees are statutorily required to verbally notify the school's principal of the HIB incident the very same day the employee witnesses the HIB or gets information about the HIB (New Jersey Statutes Annotated § 18A:37-15, 2011).

Written Report and the Two-School-Day Rule: In addition to the verbal report, a written report of the HIB must be filed with the principal within two school days of the employee witnessing the HIB or receiving the information on the HIB. The report must clearly describe the incident (New Jersey Statutes Annotated § 18A:37-15, 2011; New Jersey Statutes Annotated § 18A:17-46, 2011). Additionally, school employees must immediately report the HIB to the school official designated to receive reports of HIB in the district's policy.

2. **The Principal:** The principal must promptly commence the district's HIB procedures once he is aware of an HIB incident (New Jersey Statutes Annotated § 18A:37-16(b), 2011). Within one school day of the report of the HIB incident, the principal must initiate the investigation of the HIB incident (New Jersey Statutes Annotated § 18A:37-15(b)(6)(a), 2011). The principal must also immediately forward the information to the school safety team (described below) and to the school anti-bullying specialist who must conduct the investigation (New Jersey Statutes Annotated § 18A:37-15(b)(6)(a); New Jersey Statutes Annotated § 18A:37-21(c), 2011).

The principal must inform the superintendent of the HIB information he receives and any action that has been taken to address the situation (New Jersey Statutes Annotated § 8A:17-46, 2011). A written copy of any HIB reports received by the principal must be sent to the superintendent. The results of any HIB investigation must be reported to the superintendent within two school days of the completion of the investigation (New Jersey Statutes Annotated § 18A:37-15(b)(6), 2011). The principal must also inform the parents of all students involved in the harassment, bullying or intimidation of the incident. The principal is not expected to wait for the investigation before notifying the parents about the incident (New Jersey Statutes Annotated § 18A:37-15(b)(5), 2011). While the law does not specify a timeline for notifying parents, to comply with due process, the principal would be wise to inform them the very same day he learns of the incident or immediately after it is determined that the information is reliable. The law gives principals discretion to decide whether to also inform the parents of any counseling or other intervention services available for the students involved (New Jersey Statutes Annotated § 18A:37-15(b)(5), 2011).

Even though the anti-bullying specialist is identified in the statute as the primary person responsible for school HIB investigations, the statute also indicates that the principal or other school administrator (as opposed to the anti-bullying specialist) will face discipline for the failure to properly address HIB at the school (New Jersey Statutes Annotated § 18A:37-16(d), 2011). Continuous, seamless and deliberate communication between the school anti-bullying specialist and the principal is therefore extremely important. The principal needs to hold the specialist accountable to ensure that the HIB process is appropriately implemented.

3. **The Superintendent:** There are two reporting periods for the superintendent during each school year. Once during each reporting period, at a public hearing, the superintendent must inform the school board of HIB incidents that happened during the immediately preceding reporting period. The two reporting periods are: (a) between September 1 and January 1; and (b) between January 1 and June 30. The superintendent's report to the board must include all of the following:
    a. The nature of the bullying based on any actual or perceived characteristic such as race; color;
    b. Ancestry; national origin; gender; sexual orientation; gender identity and expression; religion; or a mental, physical or sensory disability; or any other distinguishing characteristic; and
    c. The number of HIBs reported in the district during the preceding reporting period; and
    d. The status of all investigations; and
    e. The names of all investigators; and
    f. The nature and type of discipline imposed on the student who committed the HIB; and
    g. The measures imposed or programs implemented in the district and its schools to reduce HIB; and

h. Training implemented to reduce HIB in the district and its schools (New Jersey Statutes Annotated § 18A:17-46, 2011). In addition to the above reporting periods and requirements, the superintendent must report the results of each HIB investigation, as it is completed, to the board. This report must be provided to the school board no later than the date of the board meeting that immediately follows the completion of the investigation. The report to the school board must include information on any

i. Intervention services provided;
j. Counseling ordered as a result of the investigation's findings;
k. Training programs created to reduce HIB and improve school climate;
l. Discipline imposed; and
m. Any other appropriate action taken or recommended by the superintendent for dealing with those involved in the HIB (New Jersey Statutes Annotated § 18A:37-15(b)(6), 2011).

4. **The Superintendent, School Board, and the District Anti-Bullying Coordinator:** The very same information provided by the superintendent to the school board in section (B)(3) above must be reported to the state department of education at least once during each of the following reporting periods: (a) once between September 1 and January 1; and (b) once between January 1 and June 30. This report to the state department of education must break down the data on HIB according to:

a. Each school in the district; and
b. Actual or perceived characteristic such as race, color, ancestry, national origin, gender,
c. Sexual orientation, gender identity and expression, religion or a mental, physical or sensory disability or any other distinguishing characteristic; and
d. District-wide data (New Jersey Statutes Annotated § 8A:17-46, 2011; New Jersey Statutes Annotated § 18A:37-14, 2011).

The state department of education uses the report to grade each school as well as each school district's efforts to address HIB (New Jersey Statutes Annotated § 8A:17-46, 2011). The district's grade will be the average grade of all its schools. The superintendent and board are expected to work with the district anti-bullying coordinator to gather and submit the necessary HIB data to the state department (New Jersey Statutes Annotated § 18A:37-20(b), 2011).

5. **School Board Members:** Any school board member who either: (a) witnesses HIB; or (b) has reliable information that a student has faced HIB must immediately report it to any of the following persons:
a. Any school administrator; or
b. The school official designated to receive such reports in the district's HIB policy; or
c. The safe schools resource officer (New Jersey Statutes Annotated § 18A:37-16(b), 2011).

6. **Students:** Any student who either (a) witnesses HIB; or (b) has reliable information that a student has faced HIB must immediately report it to any of the following persons:
a. Any school administrator; or
b. The school official designated to receive such reports in the district's HIB policy; or
c. The safe schools resource officer (New Jersey Statutes Annotated § 18A:37-16(b), 2011).

7. **Volunteers or Contracted Service Provider:** Any provider contracted to provide services in the district or any volunteer who either: (a) witnesses HIB; or (b) has reliable information that a student has faced HIB must immediately report it to the same persons to whom students must report (New Jersey Statutes Annotated § 18A:37-16(b), 2011).

Any official designated in the district's policy to receive reports of HIB incidents and any school administrator or safe schools resource officer who receives a report of an HIB incident is required to immediately pass the information to the school safety team. The person must also initiate the district's procedures for addressing the HIB incident.

C. School Safety Team

School districts are required to establish a school safety team at each school in the district (New Jersey Statutes Annotated § 18A:37-21, 2011). While the safety team could be created by either the principal or the superintendent, the principal is responsible for appointing members of his school's safety team. The team must be comprised of:

1. The principal or his designee. If the principal is appointing a designee, that designee must be a senior administrator employed at the school unless this is impossible;
2. At least one teacher employed at the school;
3. The school's anti-bullying specialist (this person serves as chair of the school safety team);
4. At least one parent of a student at the school; and
5. Other persons the principal chooses to name to the team. The school safety team is obligated to meet at least twice each school year (New Jersey Statutes Annotated § 18A:37-21).

The responsibilities of the school safety team are quite broad and designed to foster an environment in which harassment, intimidation and bullying are not prevalent. These responsibilities include:

1. Studying the school's systemic practices and processes to determine how a positive school climate could be created, nurtured and sustained;
2. Addressing issues with the school's climate such as HIB;
3. Receiving any HIB complaints that have been reported to the principal;
4. Identifying and addressing HIB patterns at the school;
5. Receiving copies of all reports prepared after any HIB investigation. Even though the school safety team is responsible for receiving the reports, the school anti-bullying specialist is responsible for leading and conducting the investigation into HIB incidents;
6. Reviewing and strengthening the school's policies so as to prevent and address HIB at the school;
7. Working with the district anti-bullying coordinator to collect district-wide data on HIB;
8. Collaborating with the district anti-bullying coordinator to create district policies that would prevent and address HIB;
9. Educating the community on HIB so as to prevent, identify and address HIB effectively.
10. Participating in professional development opportunities on the effective practices of successful school climate programs or school climate approaches;

State Anti-Bullying Statutes and Student Speech

11. Participating in training on how to prevent, identify and address HIB and any other training the district anti-bullying coordinator or principal requests of the members; and
12. Performing any other responsibilities related to HIB requested by the principal or the district anti-bullying coordinator (New Jersey Statutes Annotated § 18A:37-21, 2011).

In order to protect student confidentiality, the parent member(s) on the school safety team must not participate in any of the following responsibilities of the team:

1. Receiving any of the HIB complaints that have been reported to the principal;
2. Identifying and addressing HIB patterns at the school;
3. Receiving copies of any report prepared after any HIB investigation; and
4. Any other activities of the team that may compromise student confidentiality (New Jersey Statutes Annotated § 18A:37-21, 2011).

While the law only explicitly applies these requirements to parent members of the school safety team, the principal and the safety team must ensure that any non-school employee added to the safety team complies with the same requirements as parents in order to protect student confidentiality.

D. What Are the Training Requirements?

The HIB law requires schools to train various constituents, including school employees, students, and volunteers who have significant student contact. These training requirements, designed to ensure proper handling of harassing, intimidation and bullying incidents, are described next.

1. **All School Employees and Volunteers with Significant Student Contact:** The school district is obligated to provide its HIB policy to all its employees. The district must also train all employees as well as all volunteers with significant student contact on the district's HIB policies. The training must, at a minimum, include instruction on any actual or perceived characteristic such as race, color, ancestry, national origin, gender, sexual orientation, gender identity and expression, religion or a mental, physical or sensory disability or any other distinguishing characteristic that could incite discrimination or HIB (New Jersey Statutes Annotated § 18A:37-17, 2011).
2. **Students:** The school district must create a process for educating and discussing with students its HIB policy (New Jersey Statutes Annotated § 18A: 37-17(b)(3), 2011). It must also educate its students on identification and prevention of HIB. Additionally, throughout the school year, the district must provide ongoing age-appropriate HIB instruction to its students (New Jersey Statutes Annotated § 18A:37-29, 2011).
3. **Additional Training Information:** The law requires the state department of education to offer online HIB tutorials. In order to take advantage of these tutorials, school districts would be smart to require their district anti-bullying coordinator and individual school anti-bullying specialists to regularly check the department's website or contact the department to find out about the latest HIB tutorials offered. Alternatively, this responsibility could be assigned to the school safety team particularly because the law assigns the school safety team the responsibility for educating the community on HIB prevention, identification and solutions (New Jersey Statutes Annotated § 18A:37-21, 2011). The district should require the school safety team to work together with the

professional development committee to plan HIB professional development opportunities at the school in order to ensure consistent training is provided. Principals should follow up with the school safety team and the professional development committee to hold them accountable. The principal should give them specific timelines for reporting back to him each school year on HIB training opportunities discovered, planned and implemented at the school.

E. Bullying Prevention Initiatives

Every year, each school and school district must create bullying prevention initiatives. The initiatives must be implemented, evaluated and documented every year. It does not appear under the statutory language that schools and districts have to use the same initiative each year; they simply have to ensure that they have initiatives in place annually. The bullying prevention initiatives must be designed to establish and promote positive school climate and school-wide conditions that would help prevent and address HIB. School districts must involve parents, school staff, administrators, volunteers, community members and law enforcement in the initiatives (New Jersey Statutes Annotated § 18A:37-17, 2011).

F. What Must Be Included in School Districts' HIB Policies?

Each school district is required to adopt and annually re-evaluate its HIB policies to ensure compliance with the requirements of the law. Furthermore, notice of the district's HIB policy must be included in student handbooks as well as any district publication that sets forth the comprehensive procedures, rules and standards of conduct for the district's schools so as to create broad student awareness of the speech and actions subject to discipline. Parents, school employees, students, administrators, volunteers and community representatives must be enlisted in the process for adopting the policy.

Elements of District HIB Policies

School districts are obligated to include certain elements as minimums in their HIB policies. These elements are designed to protect not only the rights of the victim but also those of the accused. While districts could add other elements beyond the mandatory elements identified below, those additions must not conflict with the required elements. Moreover, the law specifically authorizes school districts to adopt HIB policies with more stringent elements than those required as minimums in the statute (New Jersey Statutes Annotated § 18A:37-15(f), 2011).

The district policy must, at minimum, include all of the following elements:

1. An explicit statement prohibiting HIB of a student;
2. A prohibition of HIB on school properties;
3. A prohibition of HIB at school-sponsored functions;
4. A prohibition of HIB on school buses;
5. A definition of HIB that is not less inclusive than the following statutory definition: "Harassment, intimidation or bullying" means any gesture, any written, verbal or physical act, or any electronic communication, whether it be a single incident or a series of incidents, that is reasonably perceived as being motivated either by any actual or perceived characteristic, such as race, color, religion, ancestry, national origin, gender, sexual orientation, gender identity and expression, or a mental,

physical or sensory disability, or by any other distinguishing characteristic, that takes place on school property, at any school-sponsored function, on a school bus, or off school grounds as provided for in section 16 of P.L.2010, c.122 (C.18A:37-15.3), that substantially disrupts or interferes with the orderly operation of the school or the rights of other students and that:

   a. A reasonable person should know, under the circumstances, will have the effect of physically or emotionally harming a student or damaging the student's property, or placing a student in reasonable fear of physical or emotional harm to his person or damage to his property;
   b. Has the effect of insulting or demeaning any student or group of students; or
   c. Creates a hostile educational environment for the student by interfering with a student's education or by severely or pervasively causing physical or emotional harm to the student (New Jersey Statutes Annotated § 18A:37-14).

6. A description of the type of behavior expected from each student;
7. Consequences for any person who commits HIB;
8. Remedial action for any person who commits HIB;
9. A procedure for reporting HIB;
10. Provision for anonymous reporting of HIB. This anonymous reporting procedure is
11. Not a substitute for the regular procedure that must be implemented for reporting HIB. Indeed, the law strikes a cautionary tone against sole reliance on an anonymous tip as the basis for formal disciplinary action against a student who commits HIB;
12. Same-day rule: a requirement that, on the very same day they witness HIB or receive
13. Information about an HIB, all employees and contracted service providers must verbally report the HIB to the principal;
14. Two-school-day rule: a requirement that, within two school days of witnessing HIB or receiving information about an HIB, all employees and contracted service providers must file a written report of the HIB incident with the principal;
15. A requirement that the principal must inform parents of all students involved in
16. The HIB about the HIB incident;
17. Discretion for the principal to share information, as appropriate, with the parents of students involved in the HIB incident about the availability of counseling and other intervention services;
18. An enumeration of the various ways a school would respond once an HIB incident is
19. Identified. These ways must include an appropriate combination of intervention services, counseling, support services and other programs, as defined by the Commissioner of Education. The principal must work with the anti-bullying specialist in order to determine the range of ways to respond;
20. A statement prohibiting reprisal or retaliation against any person who reports an HIB;
21. A statement identifying the consequences for any person who engages in reprisal or retaliation against anyone who reports an HIB;
22. A statement identifying the appropriate remedial actions for any person who engages in reprisal or retaliation against anyone who reports an HIB;
23. A statement that prohibits false accusations of any person as a means of retaliation or the false accusation of any person as a means of harassing, intimidating or bullying the person;
24. A statement identifying the consequences for any person determined to have falsely accused any person as an act of retaliation or as an act of HIB;
25. A statement identifying the remedial actions for any person found to have falsely accused any person as an act of retaliation or as an act of HIB;

26. A statement on how the district's HIB policy would be publicized;
27. Clear notification that the HIB policy applies to school-sponsored functions. While not explicitly stated in the law, it is also prudent for districts to include notice that the policy would apply to off-campus HIB. The policy should state that off-campus HIB could be disciplined if it substantially and materially disrupts the school or interferes with the rights of other students. Additionally, the policy should state that the off-campus HIB incident is subject to discipline only if it is brought to the attention of the school. Such notice would enable students to know that their off-campus speech or actions related to HIB could be censored;
28. A requirement that a link to the policy must be prominently posted on the district's website;
29. A requirement that the policy must be annually distributed to parents who have children enrolled in a school in the district;
30. A requirement that the name and contact information for the district anti-bullying *coordinator* must be listed on the homepage of the district website as well as that of each school in the district;
31. A requirement that the name and contact information for the school anti-bullying *specialist* must be listed on the homepage of each school in the district; and
32. A procedure for promptly investigating HIB complaints and for promptly investigating violations of the district's HIB policy (New Jersey Statutes Annotated § 18A:37-15, 2011). We discuss this procedure next, in the "Due Process and the Investigation Procedure" section.

Due Process and the Investigation Procedure

In order to ensure due process for the victim and the accused, the district HIB policy must, at the very least, include all of the following with respect to the procedure for investigating HIB complaints and investigating violations of the district's HIB policy:

1. **One-School-Day Rule:** A requirement that the principal (or the principal's designee) begin the investigation within one school day of the report of the HIB. While the law does not explicitly state whether the investigation should begin within one school day of the verbal report of the HIB or within one school day of the written report of the HIB, in order to ensure prompt investigation in compliance with the spirit of the law, school districts would be wise to require, in their policies, that the investigation begin within one school day of the verbal report of the HIB;
2. A provision that the investigation must be conducted by a school anti-bullying specialist;
3. A provision that the principal may appoint additional personnel who are not school anti-bullying specialists to assist in the investigation;
4. **Ten-School-Day Rule:** A requirement that the investigation must be completed as soon as possible but not later than ten school days from the date of the written report of the HIB. This is a reference to the written report to the principal under the two-school-day rule required in the HIB policy as indicated in section (B)(1) of this chapter above;
5. A provision that the school anti-bullying specialist could amend the original report of the investigation results after the ten school days if information relevant to the investigation is received. This provision only applies to information that was expected but not received by the end of the ten-day window for the investigation;
6. A requirement that the results of the investigation must be reported to the superintendent within two school days of the completion of the investigation;

7. A statement that the superintendent, upon receipt of the investigation results, could take any of the following actions:
   a. Provide intervention services;
   b. Order counseling as a result of the investigation's findings;
   c. Create training programs to reduce HIB and improve school climate;
   d. Impose discipline; or
   e. Recommend or take other appropriate action;
8. A provision requiring that the results of each investigation must be reported to the school board no later than the date of the board meeting that immediately follows the completion of the investigation. The policy must also include a statement that the report to the school board must include information on any:
   a. Intervention services provided;
   b. Counseling ordered as a result of the investigation's findings;
   c. Training programs created to reduce HIB and improve school climate;
   d. Discipline imposed; and
   e. Other appropriate action taken or recommended by the superintendent for dealing with those involved in the HIB;
9. A provision requiring that, at the next board meeting following the board's receipt of the investigation results, the board shall issue a written decision affirming, rejecting or modifying the superintendent's decision;
10. **90-Day Rule:** A statement that the board's decision may be appealed to the state commissioner of education, in accordance with the procedures set forth in law and regulation, no later than 90 days after the board issues its decision;
11. **180-Day Rule:** A statement that a parent, student or organization could file a complaint with the Division on Civil Rights within 180 school days of the occurrence of an HIB incident that is based on the student's membership in a protected group;
12. A statement informing parents of students who are parties to the investigation that they are entitled to receive information about the investigation. Some of the information these parents or guardians are entitled to receive include:
    a. The nature of the investigation;
    b. Whether the district found evidence of HIB;
    c. Whether and what discipline was imposed; and
    d. Whether services (e.g., intervention services, counseling, support services, etc.) were provided to address the HIB.

Parents of students who are parties to the investigation must be given a written notice of these four items within five school days after the results of the HIB investigation are reported to the school board. The parent is also entitled to request a hearing before the school board after receiving the information. The law does not specify a time frame for the parent or guardian to request the hearing. It does, however, provide that the hearing must be held within 10 days after the parent makes the request for the hearing. The board is obligated to meet in executive session to consider the parent's request so as to protect student confidentiality. The district HIB policy must mandate this executive session (New Jersey Statutes Annotated § 18A:37-15, 2011).

While the law does not specify whether the parent's request for a hearing must be in writing or verbal, it is critical to hold the hearing within ten days after the request is made (even if the request was made verbally) so as to avert any possibility of violating the law. It is important to also document the date when the parent request is made, particularly if it is made verbally. In terms of whether parents in the district must provide verbal or written request for hearings, a court might allow the district to rely on its already well-publicized existing policy on protocols for parental requests for hearings. If there is no explicit policy requiring written requests, or the district has an established practice of allowing verbal requests for hearings, a court might find that a verbal request suffices. In the case of verbal requests, school districts should think of assigning one person the prime responsibility of receiving the verbal requests so as to ensure accountability through a clear chain-of-command for information flow. All parents in the district must be provided the name, district phone number, district physical address and district email address of that person. The availability of that person, the means of contacting the person and the protocol must also be properly publicized (including on the homepages of the district and school websites). School districts should document their due diligence in publicizing this information. It is advisable to send home, to all parents, information about the contact person along with the district HIB policy. Parents should be required to sign and return to the school, within a specified timeline, a carefully-worded document that acknowledges receipt of the document and the understanding that it is their responsibility to read and familiarize themselves with all aspects of the policy and procedures. This should be done at least annually.

G. Prohibition of Retaliation, Reprisals, and False Accusations

The law prohibits school board members, school employees, volunteers and students from making false HIB accusations against HIB victims, HIB witnesses or anyone with reliable information about an HIB incident (New Jersey Statutes Annotated § 18A:37-16, 2011). The law also forbids retaliatory actions and reprisals against HIB victims, HIB witnesses or anyone with reliable information about an HIB incident. These rules are designed to encourage honest reports of HIB while discouraging false reports. This is critical to protecting students' First Amendment rights because false reports threaten the constitutionally-protected speech.

H. Immunity from Lawsuit for Damages

If certain conditions are satisfied, school employees and school board members will be immune from monetary damages lawsuits that arise from the failure to remedy a reported HIB incident. Specifically, the board member or school employee seeking immunity must show that:

1. He promptly reported the HIB;
2. The HIB was reported to the official designated in district policy to receive reports or to any school administrator or safe schools resource officer; and
3. The report was made in compliance with procedures identified in the district policy (New Jersey Statutes Annotated § 18A:37-16(c), 2011).

I. Discipline of Administrators

Notwithstanding the provision for immunity, school administrators could face discipline under certain circumstances. In order for an administrator to be disciplined under the law, he must fall under either (A)(i) and (A)(ii) or (B)(i) and (B)(ii) below. It must be shown that the administrator:

(A)(i) Received a report of an HIB incident from a district employee; and
(A)(ii) Failed to initiate or conduct an investigation into the HIB; or
(B)(i) Should have known of an HIB incident; and
(B)(ii) Failed to take sufficient action to minimize or eliminate the HIB incident (New Jersey Statutes Annotated § 18A:37-16(d), 2011).

Miscellaneous Harassment, Intimidation, and Bullying Law Features

Some states have a few additional features besides those in the New Jersey anti-bullying statute. One such feature is the inclusion of school employees within the ambit of the harassment, bullying and intimidation law. While this feature is not in the New Jersey statute, it is in New Jersey's administrative code (New Jersey Administrative Code 6A:16-7.7, 2014). Fourteen states have this feature. New Jersey, New York and South Dakota, for instance, protect students from harassment, intimidation and bullying by school employees (New Jersey Administrative Code 6A:16-7.7, 2014; McKinney's Education Law § 12, 2013; South Dakota Codified Laws § 13-32-19, 2014). Arkansas, California and Oklahoma protect employees from student harassment, intimidation and bullying (Arkansas Code Annotated § 6-18-514, 2013; California Code § 48900.4, 2003; 70 Oklahoma Statutes Annotated § 24-100.4(A)(1), 2013). In the eight other states, the law protects both employees and students from harassment, intimidation and bullying by students and employees. These states are Florida, Iowa, Kansas, Massachusetts, Mississippi, Nevada, North Carolina and Utah (Florida Statutes Annotated § 1006.147, 2013; Iowa Code Annotated § 280.28, 2007; Kansas Statutes Annotated 72-8256, 2007; Massachusetts General Laws Annotated 71 § 37O, 2014; Mississippi Code Annotated § 37-11-67, 2010; Nevada Revised Statutes Annotated 200.900, 2013; North Carolina General Statutes Annotated § 115C-407.15, 2009; Utah Code Annotated 1953 § 53A-11a-201, 2011).

We also discovered that four states apply their harassment, bullying and intimidation laws to parents. Kansas explicitly protects both students and parents from harassment, intimidation and bullying by parents and students (Kansas Statutes Annotated 72-8256, 2007). South Dakota prohibits third parties from harassing, intimidating or bullying students (South Dakota Codified Laws § 13-32-19, 2014). The South Dakota law's reference to third parties encompasses parents. Iowa protects students from harassment, intimidation and bullying by school volunteers (this includes parents) (Iowa Code Annotated § 280.28, 2007). Nevada's statute is broadly worded to protect a person from bullying by another person; consequently, parents are comprehended within the law (Nevada Revised Statutes Annotated 200.900, 2013; Nevada Revised Statutes Annotated 388.122, 2013).

A few states exclude speech such as horseplay and teasing from being censored as HIB in order to give students room to express themselves at their level of maturity. Virginia, for example, specifically excludes "ordinary teasing, horseplay, argument, or peer conflict" from its definition of bullying (Virginia Code Annotated § 22.1-276.01, 2014). When horseplay or teasing becomes malicious it is censorable (Louisiana Administrative Code tit. 28, pt. CXV, § 1303, 2013). Florida takes a different approach, including ordinary teasing, within its bullying definition (Florida Statutes Annotated § 1006.147, 2013); the teasing, however, has to involve systematic or chronic infliction of physical or psychological harm in order to constitute bullying (Florida Statutes Annotated § 1006.147, 2013).

Off-Campus Student Speech and Harassment, Intimidation, and Bullying Laws

As noted earlier, school officials are often empowered within state statutes to censor student speech. Table 1 identifies states with laws that school officials can use to censor off-campus student speech. For Oregon, we say the law partly applies off-campus because it merely allows off-campus school-censorship reach over areas adjacent to the school. For South Carolina, we use the term "partly" because the law merely allows off-campus school censorship in locales where the school is responsible for the student.

Table 1. Table of states with statutes that allows censorship of off-campus speech

State	Covers Off-Campus Speech	Does Not Cover Off-Campus Speech
Alabama		X
Alaska	X	
Arizona		X
Arkansas	X	
California	X	
Colorado		X
Connecticut	X	
Delaware	X	
Florida	X	
Georgia		X
Hawaii		X
Idaho	X	
Illinois		X
Indiana	X	
Iowa		X
Kansas		X
Kentucky	X	
Louisiana	X	
Maine	X	
Maryland	X	
Massachusetts	X	
Michigan		X
Minnesota	X	
Mississippi		X
Missouri	X	

continued on following page

Table 1. Continued

State	Harassment, Intimidation, and Bullying Statutes	
	Covers Off-Campus Speech	Does Not Cover Off-Campus Speech
Montana	X	
Nebraska		X
Nevada		X
New Hampshire	X	
New Jersey	X	
New Mexico	X	
New York	X	
North Carolina	X	
North Dakota	X	
Ohio		X
Oklahoma	X	
Oregon	Partly	
Pennsylvania	X	
Rhode Island	X	
South Carolina	Partly	
South Dakota	X	
Tennessee	X	
Texas		X
Utah	X	
Vermont	X	
Virginia		X
Washington	X	
West Virginia		X
Wisconsin		X
Wyoming	X	
Washington D.C.	X	

These laws can be used to censor off-campus student speech that harasses, hazes, intimidates, bullies or stalks another student in electronic and non-electronic contexts. Some states, such as Arkansas and Louisiana, have laws specifically devoted to cyberbullying (Arkansas Code Annotated § 5-71-217, 2013; Louisiana Statutes Annotated-Revised Statutes § 14:40.7, 2010). Even when states do not have specific cyberbullying statutes, their harassment, intimidation and bullying laws can be applied to cyberspace.

State harassment, intimidation and bullying laws generally require school officials to satisfy one of the two tests from Tinker v. Des Moines Independent Community School District (1969): the material and substantial disruption test; or the infringement-of-rights test. For instance, New Jersey's statute provides:

"Harassment, intimidation or bullying" means any gesture, any written, verbal or physical act, or any electronic communication, whether it be a single incident or a series of incidents, that is reasonably per-

ceived as being motivated either by any actual or perceived characteristic, such as race, color, religion, ancestry, national origin, gender, sexual orientation, gender identity and expression, or a mental, physical or sensory disability, or by any other distinguishing characteristic, that takes place on school property, at any school-sponsored function, on a school bus, or off school grounds as provided for in section 16 of P.L. 2010, c. 122 (C.18A:37-15.3), that substantially disrupts or interferes with the orderly operation of the school or the rights of other students ... (New Jersey Statutes Annotated § 18A:37-14, 2011).

It appears that the material and substantial disruption test and the infringement-of-rights test were included in the various state laws to ensure that schools establish a nexus between the school and the speech before censoring the off-campus speech. This is particularly so with the material and substantial disruption test which requires student speech to cause, or be reasonable forecast to cause, material and substantial disruption of the school before school officials can censor the speech. The requirement of an impact on student rights in the infringement-of-rights test also ensures some nexus to the school since students are associated with the school. While the infringement-of-rights test does not provide as strong a nexus as the material and substantial disruption test, both tests provide a nexus to the school for off-campus speech. Otherwise, the power of school officials over off-campus speech would be overly broad. State legislatures apparently understand that, without a nexus to the school, the laws could be subject to successful First Amendment challenge as occurred in some of the cases challenging school censorship policies and practices discussed in chapters eleven, twelve and thirteen.

New York is unique in imposing reasonable foreseeability as an additional nexus requirement. This requirement is the same reasonable-foreseeability standard for censorship of off-campus speech created in various precedents discussed earlier in this book (J.C. ex rel. R.C. v. Beverly Hills Unified School District, 2010; O.Z. v. Board of Trustees of Long Beach Unified School District, 2008; Wisniewski v. Board of Education of the Weedsport Central School District, 2007). Specifically, in New York, before censoring off-campus speech, school officials must also establish that the harassing, intimidating or bullying speech was reasonably foreseeable to reach the school (McKinney's Education Law § 11(7), 2013).

States generally empower school officials to censor off-campus HIB speech without regard to parental authority. Louisiana, however, takes a different approach. Louisiana law expressly protects as sacred the rights of parents, declaring that its bullying law must not interfere with the rights of parents:

Nothing herein shall be deemed to interfere with the authority and the responsibility that a parent or legal guardian has for the student at all times, but particularly when the student is not on the school premises [emphasis added], is not engaged in a school-sponsored function or school-sponsored activity, and is not being transported by school-sponsored means of transportation (Louisiana Statutes Annotated-Revised Statutes § 17:416.13(E), 2013).

This Louisiana HIB provision is an important model for other states since it decidedly recognizes parental authority and responsibility for off-campus speech. Without statutory protection of parental authority, the right of parents to direct the upbringing of their children especially after school hours, and outside the schoolhouse gate, would be threatened. The Louisiana statutory language effectively subjugates school-censorship authority to parental authority, particularly in off-campus settings. Such a legislative limitation might restrain the inclination of some school officials to abuse their censorship authority through overly-aggressive censorship of off-campus speech even in students' homes. Oklahoma takes a contra approach to Louisiana's, giving teachers the same authority as parents over students outside school grounds while students are in transit to and from school; as well as during transit to and from off-campus school-authorized functions (70 Oklahoma Statutes Annotated § 24-100.4(C), 2013). While this Oklahoma grant of authority to teachers is not different in its end result – censorship authority over off-campus speech – from other states' harassment, intimidation and bullying laws, it is nonetheless unique. This is because this Oklahoma law took the additional step of expressly elevating teacher authority to the status of parental authority. This particular grant of authority is curious because another provision of the state's HIB law already allowed school censorship of off-campus harassing, intimidating and bullying speech without regard to whether the speech occurred during student transit times:

Threatening behavior, harassment, intimidation, and bullying by electronic communication is prohibited whether or not such communication originated at school, or with school equipment, if the communication is specifically directed at students or school personnel and concerns harassment, intimidation, or bullying at school (Oklahoma Administrative Code 210:10-1-20(b)(5), 2013).

The state's decision to amplify this broad censorship authority with the elevation of teacher authority to parental status is a strong statement that off-campus speech rights are not viewed as sacred from school censorship.

CONCLUSION

As we noted in this chapter, states have authorized schools to censor off-campus student speech that constitutes harassment, bullying and intimidation through their anti-bullying statutes. An example is the New Jersey anti-bullying law which we discussed in detail because it is a representative and comprehensive HIB statute. Even though the details are designed to provide structure to guide school-censorship authority while also protecting student rights, the enactment of such laws inevitably expands school-censorship authority into and over another category of speech – harassing, intimidating and bullying speech. Although we fully acknowledge and wholly support the vital need to protect students from harassment, bullying and intimidation, we also believe that, rather than encouraging more censorship, state HIB laws should seek to encourage education of students.

Various states already require age-appropriate instruction for students about harassment, intimidation and bullying as in the New Jersey law set forth above. They could, however, go even further by providing a relatively more specific outline of topics for an age-appropriate instructional program such as in Illinois' statute:

Each school may adopt an age-appropriate curriculum for Internet safety instruction of students in grades kindergarten through 12. However, beginning with the 2009-2010 school year, a school district must incorporate into the school curriculum a component on Internet safety to be taught at least once each school year to students in grades 3 through 12. The school board shall determine the scope and duration of this unit of instruction. The age-appropriate unit of instruction may be incorporated into the current courses of study regularly taught in the district's schools, as determined by the school board, and it is recommended that the unit of instruction include the following topics:

- *Safe and responsible use of social networking websites, chat rooms, electronic mail, bulletin boards, instant messaging, and other means of communication on the Internet.*
- *Recognizing, avoiding, and reporting online solicitations of students, their classmates, and their friends by sexual predators.*
- *Risks of transmitting personal information on the Internet.*
- *Recognizing and avoiding unsolicited or deceptive communications received online.*
- *Recognizing and reporting online harassment and cyber-bullying.*
- *Reporting illegal activities and communications on the Internet.*
- *Copyright laws on written materials, photographs, music, and video (105 Illinois Compiled Statutes Annotated 5/27-13.3(c), 2009).*

These topics are designed to ensure informed student decisions and student safety in their use of digital media, without the aggressive posture of censorship.

School employees should likewise be provided strong professional development to support efforts at reducing incidences of harassment, bullying and intimidation. Massachusetts's statute which includes a more detailed professional development plan than in the New Jersey law is a good model to follow as it identifies concrete areas for educating school officials and all school employees:

The plan for a school district, charter school, approved private day or residential school and collaborative school shall include a provision for ongoing professional development to build the skills of all staff members, including, but not limited to, educators, administrators, school nurses, cafeteria workers, custodians, bus drivers, athletic coaches, advisors to extracurricular activities and paraprofessionals, to prevent, identify and respond to bullying. The content of such professional development shall include, but not be limited to: (i) developmentally appropriate strategies to prevent bullying incidents; (ii) developmentally appropriate strategies for immediate, effective interventions to stop bullying incidents; (iii) information regarding the complex interaction and power differential that can take place between and among a perpetrator, victim and witnesses to the bullying; (iv) research findings on bullying, including information about students who have been shown to be particularly at risk for bullying in the school environment; (v) information on the incidence and nature of cyber-bullying; and (vi) internet safety issues as they relate to cyber-bullying. The department [of elementary and secondary education] shall identify and offer information on alternative methods for fulfilling the professional development requirements of this section, at least 1 of these alternative methods shall be available at no cost to school districts, charter schools, approved private day or residential schools and collaborative schools (Massachusetts General Laws Annotated 71 § 37O(d)(4), 2014).

Besides listing specific content for professional development, the Massachusetts law extends the professional development requirement beyond the faculty and administrators (Massachusetts General Laws Annotated 71 § 37O(d)(4), 2014). It also encompasses custodians, cafeteria employees, nurses, bus drivers, paraprofessionals, inter alia, as they interact with students on a regular basis. This is a recognition that faculty and administrators are not the only role models for students. School employees set the example of civil or uncivil speech that students might emulate on-campus as well as off-campus. Two states – Tennessee and West Virginia – explicitly recognize this and adjure school administrators, school employees and volunteers to model exemplary behavior for students by not engaging in harassment, intimidation and bullying (Tennessee Code Annotated § 49-6-4501(3), 2011; West Virginia Code,

§ 18-2C-1, 2011). If school officials intend to censor off-campus harassing, intimidating and bullying speech, they should avoid the hypocrisy of engaging in such speech on and off school grounds. Other states should adopt the Tennessee and West Virginia approach; and even go further by imposing sanctions on school administrators, school employees and volunteers who fail to model exemplary behavior for students with respect to harassment, intimidation and bullying. Parents should also be enlisted in a home-school partnership that provides parent workshops on ways parents can model appropriate speech for students. Massachusetts does this in its statute by requiring schools to provide parents information on HIB-prevention curricular so that parents can augment, at home, school efforts to promote civil speech and actions (Massachusetts General Laws Annotated 71 § 37O(d)(5), 2014). Partnership between parents and the school might lead to less school censorship as school officials honor parental authority and students engage in less off-campus HIB speech as a result of the collaborative education on appropriate speech received from home and school. After all, as the African proverb states, it takes a village to raise a child.

REFERENCES

Arkansas Code Annotated § 5-71-217 (West 2013).

Arkansas Code Annotated § 6-18-514 (West 2013).

California Code § 48900.4 (West 2003).

Florida Statutes Annotated § 1006.147 (West 2013).

105 Illinois Compiled Statutes Annotated 5/27-13.3(c) (West 2009).

Iowa Code Annotated § 280.28 (West 2007).

J.C. ex rel. R.C. v. Beverly Hills Unified School District (2010). 711 F.Supp.2d 1094, 1108.

Kansas Statutes Annotated 72-8256 (West 2007).

Louisiana Administrative Code tit. 28, pt. CXV, § 1303 (West 2013).

Louisiana Statutes Annotated-Revised Statutes § 14:40.7 (West 2010).

Louisiana Statutes Annotated-Revised Statutes § 17:416.13(E) (West 2013).

Massachusetts General Laws Annotated 71 § 37O (West 2014).

McKinney's Education Law § 11(7) (West 2013).

McKinney's Education Law § 12 (West 2013).

Mississippi Code Annotated § 37-11-67 (West 2010).

Nevada Revised Statutes Annotated 200.900 (West 2013).

Nevada Revised Statutes Annotated 388.122 (West 2013).

New Jersey Administrative Code 6A:16-7.7 (West 2014).

New Jersey Statutes Annotated § 18A:17-46 (West 2011).

New Jersey Statutes Annotated § 18A:37-14 (West 2011).

New Jersey Statutes Annotated § 18A:37-15 (West 2011).

New Jersey Statutes Annotated § 18A:37-16 (West 2011).

New Jersey Statutes Annotated § 18A:37-17 (West 2011).

New Jersey Statutes Annotated § 18A:37-21 (West 2011).

New Jersey Statutes Annotated § 18A:37-29 (West 2011).

New Jersey Statutes Annotated § 18A:37-2(k) (West 2011).

North Carolina General Statutes Annotated § 115C-407.15 (West 2009).

Oklahoma Administrative Code 210:10-1-20(b)(5) (West 2013).

70 Oklahoma Statutes Annotated § 24-100.4(A)(1) (West 2013).

70 Oklahoma Statutes Annotated § 24-100.4(C) (West 2013).

O.Z. v. Board of Trustees of Long Beach Unified School District (2008). 2008 WL 4396895.

South Dakota Codified Laws § 13-32-19 (West 2014).

Tennessee Code Annotated § 49-6-4501(3) (West 2011).

Tinker v. Des Moines Independent Community School District (1969). 393 U.S. 503.

Utah Code Annotated 1953 § 53A-11a-201 (West 2011).

Virginia Code Annotated § 22.1-276.01(A) (West 2014).

West Virginia Code, § 18-2C-1 (West 2011).

Wisniewski v. Board of Education of the Weedsport Central School District (2007). 494 F.3d 34, 37.

KEY TERMS AND DEFINITIONS

Anti-Bullying Specialist: The person who chairs the school safety team and leads the overall harassment, bullying and intimidation efforts at each school.

Anti-Bullying Coordinator: The person responsible for directing the district-wide anti-bullying initiatives. This person oversees the responsibilities of the anti-bullying specialists.

Harassment, Intimidation, or Bullying (HIB): A certain incident or series of incidents targeting a victim and motivated by an actual or perceived characteristic of the victim that substantially disrupts the school.

Infringement-of-Rights Test: The judicial standard that conditions censorship of student speech on whether the speech impinges the rights of students.

Material and Substantial Disruption Test: The judicial standard that conditions censorship of student speech on whether the speech is reasonably foreseeable to cause or actually caused material and substantial disruption to the school.

Off-Campus Speech: Speech that occurs in any locale outside the borders or premises of a school and outside school hours. It includes student speech away from the school bus and school-sponsored events such as school trips.

School Safety Team: The team tasked with the responsibilities of investigating harassment, intimidation and bullying and promoting positive climate at the school in order to reduce harassment, intimidation and bullying incidences. The team is comprised of the anti-bullying specialist, at least one teacher, at least one parent and any appointee(s) of the principal.

APPENDIX: HARASSMENT, INTIMIDATION, AND BULLYING STATUTES

ALABAMA

Student Harassment Prevention Act. Alabama Code 1975 § 16-28B, et seq. (West 2009)

Alabama Code 1975 § 16-28B-2

§ 16-28B-2. Legislative intent.

It is the intent of the Legislature to provide for the adoption of policies in public school systems to prevent the harassment of students. It is the further intent of the Legislature that this chapter apply only to student against student harassment, intimidation, violence, and threats of violence in the public schools of Alabama, grades prekindergarten through 12, and that the State Department of Education develop, and each local board of education adopt procedural policies to manage and possibly prevent these acts against any student by another student or students based on the characteristics of a student.

Additionally, it is the intent of the Legislature that the filing of a complaint of harassment be in writing and submitted by the affected student, or the parent or guardian of the affected student, and not by an education employee on behalf of an affected student or his or her parent or guardian.

Alabama Code 1975 § 16-28B-3

§ 16-28B-3. Definitions.

The following terms have the following meanings:

(2) Harassment. A continuous pattern of intentional behavior that takes place on school property, on a school bus, or at a school-sponsored function including, but not limited to, written, electronic, verbal, or physical acts that are reasonably perceived as being motivated by any characteristic of a student, or by the association of a student with an individual who has a particular characteristic, if the characteristic falls into one of the categories of personal characteristics contained in the model policy adopted by the department or by a local board. To constitute harassment, a pattern of behavior may do any of the following:
Place a student in reasonable fear of harm to his or her person or damage to his or her property.
Have the effect of substantially interfering with the educational performance, opportunities, or benefits of a student.
Have the effect of substantially disrupting or interfering with the orderly operation of the school.
Have the effect of creating a hostile environment in the school, on school property, on a school bus, or at a school-sponsored function.
Have the effect of being sufficiently severe, persistent, or pervasive enough to create an intimidating, threatening, or abusive educational environment for a student.

(3) Hostile environment. The perception by an affected student or victim that the conduct of another student constitutes a threat of violence or harassment and that the conduct is objectively severe or pervasive enough that a reasonable person, under the circumstances, would agree that the conduct constitutes harassment, threat of assault, or assault.

Alabama Code 1975 § 16-28B-4

§ 16-28B-4. Prohibited behavior; complaints; school plans or programs.

(a) No student shall engage in or be subjected to harassment, intimidation, violence, or threats of violence on school property, on a school bus, or at any school-sponsored function by any other student in his or her school system.
(b) No person shall engage in reprisal, retaliation, or false accusation against a victim, witness, or other person who has reliable information about an act of harassment, violence, or threat of violence.
(c) Any student, or parent or guardian of the student, who is the object of harassment may file a complaint outlining the details of the harassment, on a form authorized by the local board, and submit the form to the official designated by the local board to receive complaints at the school.
(d) Each school shall develop plans or programs, including, but not limited to, peer mediation teams, in an effort to encourage students to report and address incidents of harassment, violence, or threats of violence.

Alabama Code 1975 § 16-28B-5

§ 16-28B-5. Model policy.

The department [of education] shall develop a model policy prohibiting harassment, violence, and threats of violence on school property, on a school bus, or at any school-sponsored function. The model policy, at a minimum, shall contain all of the following components:

(1) A statement prohibiting harassment, violence, and threats of violence.
(2) Definitions of the terms harassment, as provided in subdivision (2) of Section 16-28B-3, intimidation, and threats of violence.
(3) A description of the behavior expected of each student.
(4) A series of graduated consequences for any student who commits an act of intimidation, harassment, violence, or threats of violence. Punishment shall conform with applicable federal and state disability, antidiscrimination, and education laws and school discipline policies.
(5) A procedure for reporting an act of intimidation, threat of suicide, harassment, violence, or threat of violence. An anonymous report may not be the basis for imposing formal disciplinary action against a student.
(6) A procedure for the prompt investigation of reports of serious violations and complaints, specifying that the principal, or his or her designee, is the person responsible for the investigation.
(7) A response procedure for a school to follow upon confirmation of an incident of intimidation, harassment, violence, or threats of violence.

(8) A statement prohibiting reprisal or retaliation against any person who reports an act of intimidation, violence, threat of violence, or harassment, including the consequences of and any appropriate remedial action that may be taken against a person who engages in such reprisal or retaliation.

(9) A statement of the consequences of and appropriate remedial action that may be taken against a person who has deliberately and recklessly falsely accused another.

(10) A procedure for publicizing local board policy, including providing notice that the policy applies to participation in school-sponsored functions.

(11) A clearly defined procedure for students to use in reporting harassment, including, but not limited to, written reports on local board approved complaint forms and written reports of instances of harassment, intimidation, violence, and threats of violence based on the personal characteristics of a student. The complaint form may be served in person or by mail on the principal, or his or her designee, or his or her office. The procedures shall be made known and be readily available to each student, employee, and the parent or guardian of each student. It is the sole responsibility of the affected student, or the parent or guardian of the affected student, to report incidences of harassment to the principal, or his or her designee.

(12) A procedure for promulgating rules to implement this chapter, including the development of a model student complaint form. The department shall seek public input in developing and revising the model policy, model complaint form, and any other necessary forms.

(13) A procedure for the development of a nonexhaustive list of the specific personal characteristics of a student which may often lead to harassment. Based upon experience, a local board of education may add, but not remove, characteristics from the list. The additional characteristics or perceived characteristics that cause harassment shall be identified by the local board on a case-by-case basis and added to the local board policy. The list shall be included in the code of conduct policy of each local board.

Alabama Code 1975 § 16-28B-6

§ 16-28B-6. Duties of schools

Each school shall do all of the following:

1. Develop and implement evidence-based practices to promote a school environment that is free of harassment, intimidation, violence, and threats of violence.
2. Develop and implement evidence-based practices to prevent harassment, intimidation, violence, and threats of violence based, as a minimum, on the criteria established by this chapter and local board policy, and to intervene when such incidents occur.
3. Incorporate into civility, citizenship, and character education curricula awareness of and sensitivity to the prohibitions of this chapter and local board policy against harassment, intimidation, violence, and threats of violence.
4. Report statistics to the local board of actual violence, submitted reports of threats of violence, and harassment. The local board shall provide the statistics of the school system and each school in the

school system to the department for posting on the department website. The posted statistics shall be available to the public and any state or federal agency requiring the information. The identity of each student involved shall be protected and may not be posted on the department website.

Alabama Code 1975 § 16-28B-8

§ 16-28B-8. Implementation of standards and policies.

To the extent that the Legislature shall appropriate funds, or to the extent that any local board may provide funds from other sources, each school system shall implement the following standards and policies for programs in an effort to prevent student suicide:
***

(11) Provide training for school employees and volunteers who have significant contact with students on the local board policies to prevent harassment, intimidation, violence, and threats of violence.
(12) Develop a process for discussing with students local board policies relating to the prevention of student suicide and to the prevention of harassment, intimidation, violence, and threats of violence.

ALASKA

Alaska Statutes Annotated § 14.33.200, et seq. (West 2006)

Alaska Statutes Annotated § 14.33.200

§ 14.33.200. Harassment, intimidation, and bullying policy

(a) By July 1, 2007, each school district shall adopt a policy that prohibits the harassment, intimidation, or bullying of any student. Each school district shall share this policy with parents or guardians, students, volunteers, and school employees.
(b) The policy must be adopted through the standard policy-making procedure for each district that includes the opportunity for participation by parents or guardians, school employees, volunteers, students, administrators, and community representatives. The policy must emphasize positive character traits and values, including the importance of civil and respectful speech and conduct, and the responsibility of students to comply with the district's policy prohibiting harassment, intimidation, or bullying. The policy must also include provisions for an appropriate punishment schedule up to and including expulsion and reporting of criminal activity to local law enforcement authorities. School employees, volunteers, students, and administrators shall adhere to this policy.
(c) By January 1, 2007, the department [of education and early development], in consultation with representatives of parents or guardians, school personnel, and other interested parties, may provide to school districts a model harassment, intimidation, and bullying prevention policy and training materials on the components that should be included in a district policy. Training materials may be

disseminated in a variety of ways, including workshops and other staff developmental activities, and through the Internet website of the department. Materials included on the Internet website must include the model policy and recommended training and instructional materials. The department may provide a link to the school district's Internet website for further information.

Alaska Statutes Annotated § 14.33.210

§ 14.33.210. Reporting of incidents of harassment, intimidation, or bullying

(a) Beginning with the 2007--2008 school year, each school district shall report to the department by November 30 all incidents resulting in suspension or expulsion for harassment, intimidation, or bullying on school premises or on transportation systems used by schools in the school year preceding the report. The department shall compile the data and report it to the appropriate committees of the Alaska House of Representatives and the Senate.

Alaska Statutes Annotated § 14.33.220

§ 14.33.220. Reporting; no reprisals

(a) A school employee, student, or volunteer may not engage in reprisal, retaliation, or false accusation against a victim, witness, or person with reliable information about an act of harassment, intimidation, or bullying.
(b) A school employee, student, or volunteer who has witnessed, or has reliable information that a student has been subjected to, harassment, intimidation, or bullying, whether verbal or physical, shall report the incident to an appropriate school official.
(c) This section does not prohibit discipline or other adverse action taken in compliance with school district policies against a person who falsely and in bad faith accuses a person of engaging in harassment, intimidation, or bullying or who intentionally provides false information in connection with an investigation of an alleged incident of harassment, intimidation, or bullying.

Alaska Statutes Annotated § 14.33.250

§ 14.33.250. Definitions

(2) "harassment, intimidation, or bullying" means an intentional written, oral, or physical act, when the act is undertaken with the intent of threatening, intimidating, harassing, or frightening the student, and
    (A) physically harms the student or damages the student's property;
    (B) has the effect of substantially interfering with the student's education;
    (C) is so severe, persistent, or pervasive that it creates an intimidating or threatening educational environment; or
    (D) has the effect of substantially disrupting the orderly operation of the school.

Harassment. Alaska Statutes Annotated § 11.61.120 (West 2011)

Alaska Statutes Annotated § 11.61.120

§ 11.61.120. Harassment in the second degree

(a) A person commits the crime of harassment in the second degree if, with intent to harass or annoy another person, that person
  (1) insults, taunts, or challenges another person in a manner likely to provoke an immediate violent response;
  (2) telephones another and fails to terminate the connection with intent to impair the ability of that person to place or receive telephone calls;
  (3) makes repeated telephone calls at extremely inconvenient hours;
  (4) makes an anonymous or obscene telephone call, an obscene electronic communication, or a telephone call or electronic communication that threatens physical injury or sexual contact;
  (5) subjects another person to offensive physical contact; or
  (6) except as provided in [Alaska Statutes Annotated] 11.61.116, publishes or distributes electronic or printed photographs, pictures, or films that show the genitals, anus, or female breast of the other person or show that person engaged in a sexual act.
(b) Harassment in the second degree is a class B misdemeanor.

ARIZONA

Arizona Revised Statutes Annotated § 15-341 (West 2013)

Arizona Revised Statutes Annotated § 15-341

§ 15-341. General powers and duties; immunity; delegation

A. The governing board [of the local school district] shall:
  37. Prescribe and enforce policies and procedures to prohibit pupils from harassing, intimidating and bullying other pupils on school grounds, on school property, on school buses, at school bus stops, at school-sponsored events and activities and through the use of electronic technology or electronic communication on school computers, networks, forums and mailing lists that include the following components:
    (a) A procedure for pupils, parents and school district employees to confidentially report to school officials incidents of harassment, intimidation or bullying. The school shall make available written forms designed to provide a full and detailed description of the incident and any other relevant information about the incident.

(b) A requirement that school district employees report in writing suspected incidents of harassment, intimidation or bullying to the appropriate school official and a description of appropriate disciplinary procedures for employees who fail to report suspected incidents that are known to the employee.

(c) A requirement that, at the beginning of each school year, school officials provide all pupils with a written copy of the rights, protections and support services available to a pupil who is an alleged victim of an incident reported pursuant to this paragraph.

(d) If an incident is reported pursuant to this paragraph, a requirement that school officials provide a pupil who is an alleged victim of the incident with a written copy of the rights, protections and support services available to that pupil.

(e) A formal process for the documentation of reported incidents of harassment, intimidation or bullying and for the confidentiality, maintenance and disposition of this documentation. School districts shall maintain documentation of all incidents reported pursuant to this paragraph for at least six years. The school shall not use that documentation to impose disciplinary action unless the appropriate school official has investigated and determined that the reported incidents of harassment, intimidation or bullying occurred. If a school provides documentation of reported incidents to persons other than school officials or law enforcement, all individually identifiable information shall be redacted.

(f) A formal process for the investigation by the appropriate school officials of suspected incidents of harassment, intimidation or bullying, including procedures for notifying the alleged victim on completion and disposition of the investigation.

(g) Disciplinary procedures for pupils who have admitted or been found to have committed incidents of harassment, intimidation or bullying.

(h) A procedure that sets forth consequences for submitting false reports of incidents of harassment, intimidation or bullying.

(i) Procedures designed to protect the health and safety of pupils who are physically harmed as the result of incidents of harassment, intimidation and bullying, including, if appropriate, procedures to contact emergency medical services or law enforcement agencies, or both.

(j) Definitions of harassment, intimidation and bullying.

Minor's Use of Electronic Communication Devices. Arizona Revised Statutes Annotated § 8-309 (West 2010)

Arizona Revised Statutes Annotated § 8-309

§ 8-309. Unlawful use of an electronic communication device by a minor; classification

A. It is unlawful for a juvenile to intentionally or knowingly use an electronic communication device to transmit or display a visual depiction of a minor that depicts explicit sexual material.

B. It is unlawful for a juvenile to intentionally or knowingly possess a visual depiction of a minor that depicts explicit sexual material and that was transmitted to the juvenile through the use of an electronic communication device.
C. It is not a violation of subsection B of this section if all of the following apply:
   1. The juvenile did not solicit the visual depiction.
   2. The juvenile took reasonable steps to destroy or eliminate the visual depiction or report the visual depiction to the juvenile's parent, guardian, school official or law enforcement official.
D. A violation of subsection A of this section is a petty offense if the juvenile transmits or displays the visual depiction to one other person. A violation of subsection A of this section is a class 3 misdemeanor if the juvenile transmits or displays the visual depiction to more than one other person.
E. A violation of subsection B of this section is a petty offense.
F. Any violation of this section that occurs after adjudication for a prior violation of this section or after completion of a diversion program as a result of a referral or petition charging a violation of this section is a class 2 misdemeanor.
G. For the purposes of this section:
   1. "Electronic communication device" has the same meaning prescribed in § 13-3560.
   2. "Explicit sexual material" means material that depicts human genitalia or that depicts nudity, sexual activity, sexual conduct, sexual excitement or sadomasochistic abuse as defined in § 13-3501.
   3. "Visual depiction" has the same meaning prescribed in § 13-3551.

Sexual Exploitation of Children. Arizona Revised Statutes Annotated § 13-3551 (West 2009)

Arizona Revised Statutes Annotated § 13-3551

§ 13-3551. Definitions

11. "Visual depiction" includes each visual image that is contained in an undeveloped film, videotape or photograph or data stored in any form and that is capable of conversion into a visual image.

Arizona Revised Statutes Annotated § 13-3560

§ 13-3560. Definitions

E. For the purposes of this section:
   1. "Electronic communication device" means any electronic device that is capable of transmitting visual depictions and includes any of the following:
      (a) A computer, computer system or network as defined in § 13-2301.
      (b) A cellular or wireless telephone as defined in § 13-4801.
   2. "Harmful to minors" has the same meaning prescribed in § 13-3501.

ARKANSAS

Antibullying Policies. Arkansas Code Annotated § 6-18-514 (West 2013)

Arkansas Code Annotated § 6-18-514

§ 6-18-514. Antibullying policies

(a) The General Assembly finds that every public school student in this state has the right to receive his or her public education in a public school educational environment that is reasonably free from substantial intimidation, harassment, or harm or threat of harm by another student.

(b) As used in this section:
   (1) "Attribute" means an actual or perceived personal characteristic including without limitation race, color, religion, ancestry, national origin, socioeconomic status, academic status, disability, gender, gender identity, physical appearance, health condition, or sexual orientation;
   (2) "Bullying" means the intentional harassment, intimidation, humiliation, ridicule, defamation, or threat or incitement of violence by a student against another student or public school employee by a written, verbal, electronic, or physical act that may address an attribute of the other student, public school employee, or person with whom the other student or public school employee is associated and that causes or creates actual or reasonably foreseeable:
      (A) Physical harm to a public school employee or student or damage to the public school employee's or student's property;
      (B) Substantial interference with a student's education or with a public school employee's role in education;
      (C) A hostile educational environment for one (1) or more students or public school employees due to the severity, persistence, or pervasiveness of the act; or
      (D) Substantial disruption of the orderly operation of the school or educational environment;
   (3) "Electronic act" means without limitation a communication or image transmitted by means of an electronic device, including without limitation a telephone, wireless phone or other wireless communications device, computer, or pager;
   (4) "Harassment" means a pattern of unwelcome verbal or physical conduct relating to another person's constitutionally or statutorily protected status that causes, or reasonably should be expected to cause, substantial interference with the other's performance in the school environment; and
   (5) "Substantial disruption" means without limitation that any one (1) or more of the following occur as a result of the bullying:
      (A) Necessary cessation of instruction or educational activities;
      (B) Inability of students or educational staff to focus on learning or function as an educational unit because of a hostile environment;
      (C) Severe or repetitive disciplinary measures are needed in the classroom or during educational activities; or
      (D) Exhibition of other behaviors by students or educational staff that substantially interfere with the learning environment.

(c) Bullying of a public school student or a public school employee is prohibited.

(d) A school principal or his or her designee who receives a credible report or complaint of bullying shall promptly investigate the complaint or report and make a record of the investigation and any action taken as a result of the investigation.

(e)(1) The board of directors of every school district shall adopt policies to prevent bullying.

    (2) The policies shall:

(A)(i) Clearly define conduct that constitutes bullying.

    (ii) The definition shall include without limitation the definition contained in subsection (b) of this section;

(B) Prohibit bullying:

    (i) While in school, on school equipment or property, in school vehicles, on school buses, at designated school bus stops, at school-sponsored activities, at school-sanctioned events; or

    (ii)(a) By an electronic act that results in the substantial disruption of the orderly operation of the school or educational environment.

    (b) This section shall apply to an electronic act whether or not the electronic act originated on school property or with school equipment, if the electronic act is directed specifically at students or school personnel and maliciously intended for the purpose of disrupting school and has a high likelihood of succeeding in that purpose;

(C) State the consequences for engaging in the prohibited conduct, which may vary depending on the age or grade of the student involved;

(D) Require that a school employee who has witnessed or has reliable information that a pupil has been a victim of bullying as defined by the district shall report the incident to the principal;

(E) Require that the person or persons who file a complaint will not be subject to retaliation or reprisal in any form;

(F) Require that notice of what constitutes bullying, that bullying is prohibited, and that the consequences of engaging in bullying be conspicuously posted in every classroom, cafeteria, restroom, gymnasium, auditorium, and school bus in the district; and

(G) Require that copies of the notice of what constitutes bullying, that bullying is prohibited, and that the consequences of engaging in bullying be provided to parents, students, school volunteers, and employees. Each policy shall require that a full copy of the policy be made available upon request.

(f) A school district shall provide training on compliance with the antibullying policies to all public school district employees responsible for reporting or investigating bullying under this section.

(g) A school employee who has reported violations under the school district's policy shall be immune from any tort liability that may arise from the failure to remedy the reported incident.

(h) The board of directors of a school district may provide opportunities for school employees to participate in programs or other activities designed to develop the knowledge and skills to prevent and respond to acts covered by this policy.

(i) The school district shall provide the Department of Education with the website address at which a copy of the policies adopted in compliance with this section may be found.

(j) This section is not intended to:

(1) Restrict a public school district from adopting and implementing policies against bullying or school violence or policies to promote civility and student dignity that are more inclusive than the antibullying policies required under this section; or

(2) Unconstitutionally restrict protected rights of freedom of speech, freedom of religious exercise, or freedom of assembly.

Electronic Communication and Bullying. Arkansas Code Annotated § 5-71-217 (West 2013)

Arkansas Code Annotated § 5-71-217

§ 5-71-217. Cyberbullying

(a) As used in this section:
   (1) "Communication" means the electronic communication of information of a person's choosing between or among points specified by the person without change in the form or content of the information as sent and received; and
   (2) "Electronic means" means any textual, visual, written, or oral communication of any kind made through the use of a computer online service, Internet service, telephone, or any other means of electronic communication, including without limitation to a local bulletin board service, an Internet chat room, electronic mail, a social networking site, or an online messaging service.

(b) A person commits the offense of cyberbullying if:
   (1) He or she transmits, sends, or posts a communication by electronic means with the purpose to frighten, coerce, intimidate, threaten, abuse, or harass, another person; and
   (2) The transmission was in furtherance of severe, repeated, or hostile behavior toward the other person.

(c) The offense of cyberbullying may be prosecuted in the county where the defendant was located when he or she transmitted, sent, or posted a communication by electronic means, in the county where the communication by electronic means was received by the person, or in the county where the person targeted by the electronic communications resides.

(d)(1) Cyberbullying is a Class B misdemeanor.

(2)(A) Cyberbullying of a school employee is a Class A misdemeanor.
   (B) As used in this subdivision (d)(2), "school employee" means a person who is employed full time or part time at a school that serves students in any of kindergarten through grade twelve (K-12), including without limitation a:
   (i) Public school operated by a school district;
   (ii) Public school operated by a state agency or institution of higher education;
   (iii) Public charter school; or
   (iv) Private school.

Safe School Initiative Act. Arkansas Code Annotated § 6-15-1303 (West 2013)

Arkansas Code Annotated § 6-15-1303

§ 6-15-1303. Safe Schools Initiative training

(2)(C) The Safe Schools Initiative training also may include without limitation the training and education needed to assist a public school in: …
  (ii) Delivering education to students and faculty on public safety and legal topics such as drugs and alcohol abuse, sexual assault, bullying and cyberbullying, gangs, preventing the possession of weapons by minors, and responding to the threat of weapons at school.

CALIFORNIA

Safe Place to Learn Act. California Code § 234.1, et seq. (West 2013)

California Code § 234.1

§ 234.1. Monitoring, review, and assessment of antidiscrimination, antiharassment, anti-intimidation, and antibullying requirements

The department, pursuant to subdivision (b) of Section 64001, shall monitor adherence to the requirements of Chapter 5.3 (commencing with Section 4900) of Division 1 of Title 5 of the California Code of Regulations and Chapter 2 (commencing with Section 200) of this part as part of its regular monitoring and review of local educational agencies, commonly known as the Categorical Program Monitoring process. The department shall assess whether local educational agencies have done all of the following:

(a) Adopted a policy that prohibits discrimination, harassment, intimidation, and bullying based on the actual or perceived characteristics set forth in Section 422.55 of the Penal Code and Section 220 of this code, and disability, gender, gender identity, gender expression, nationality, race or ethnicity, religion, sexual orientation, or association with a person or group with one or more of these actual or perceived characteristics. The policy shall include a statement that the policy applies to all acts related to school activity or school attendance occurring within a school under the jurisdiction of the superintendent of the school district.

(b) Adopted a process for receiving and investigating complaints of discrimination, harassment, intimidation, and bullying based on any of the actual or perceived characteristics set forth in Section 422.55 of the Penal Code and Section 220 of this code, and disability, gender, gender identity, gender expression, nationality, race or ethnicity, religion, sexual orientation, or association with a person or group with one or more of these actual or perceived characteristics. The complaint process shall include, but not be limited to, all of the following:

(1) A requirement that, if school personnel witness an act of discrimination, harassment, intimidation, or bullying, they shall take immediate steps to intervene when safe to do so.
(2) A timeline to investigate and resolve complaints of discrimination, harassment, intimidation, or bullying that shall be followed by all schools under the jurisdiction of the school district.
(3) An appeal process afforded to the complainant should he or she disagree with the resolution of a complaint filed pursuant to this section.
(4) All forms developed pursuant to this process shall be translated pursuant to Section 48985.

(c) Publicized antidiscrimination, antiharassment, anti-intimidation, and antibullying policies adopted pursuant to subdivision (a), including information about the manner in which to file a complaint, to pupils, parents, employees, agents of the governing board, and the general public. The information shall be translated pursuant to Section 48985.
(d) Posted the policy established pursuant to subdivision (a) in all schools and offices, including staff lounges and pupil government meeting rooms.
(e) Maintained documentation of complaints and their resolution for a minimum of one review cycle.
(f) Ensured that complainants are protected from retaliation and that the identity of a complainant alleging discrimination, harassment, intimidation, or bullying remains confidential, as appropriate.
(g) Identified a responsible local educational agency officer for ensuring school district or county office of education compliance with the requirements of Chapter 5.3 (commencing with Section 4900) of Division 1 of Title 5 of the California Code of Regulations and Chapter 2 (commencing with Section 200) of this part.

California Code § 234.2

§ 234.2. Display and posting of bias-related discrimination, harassment, intimidation

The department shall display current information, and periodically update information, on curricula and other resources that specifically address bias-related discrimination, harassment, intimidation, and bullying based on any of the actual or perceived characteristics set forth in Section 422.55 of the Penal Code and Section 220 on the California Healthy Kids Resource Center Internet Web site and other appropriate department Internet Web sites where information about discrimination, harassment, intimidation, and bullying is posted.

California Code § 234.3

§ 234.3. Rights, obligations, and policies on bias-related discrimination, harassment, intimidation, and bullying in schools; model handout

The department shall develop a model handout describing the rights and obligations set forth in Sections 200, 201, and 220 and the policies addressing bias-related discrimination, harassment, intimidation, and bullying in schools. This model handout shall be posted on appropriate department Internet Web sites.

Interagency School Safety Demonstration Act of 1985. California Code § 32261 (West 2012)

California Code § 32261

§ 32261. Legislative findings, declarations, and intent; definitions

(d) It is the intent of the Legislature in enacting this chapter to encourage school districts, county offices of education, law enforcement agencies, and agencies serving youth to develop and implement interagency strategies, in-service training programs, and activities that will improve school attendance and reduce school crime and violence, including vandalism, drug and alcohol abuse, gang membership, gang violence, hate crimes, bullying, including bullying committed personally or by means of an electronic act, teen relationship violence, and discrimination and harassment, including, but not limited to, sexual harassment.

Interdistrict Attendance. California Code § 46600 (West 2012)

California Code § 46600

§ 46600. Agreements for interdistrict attendance; terms and conditions; victims of bullying

(b) A pupil who has been determined by personnel of either the district of residence or the district of proposed enrollment to have been the victim of an act of bullying, as defined in subdivision (r) of Section 48900, committed by a pupil of the district of residence shall, at the request of the person having legal custody of the pupil, be given priority for interdistrict attendance under any existing interdistrict attendance agreement or, in the absence of an agreement, be given additional consideration for the creation of an interdistrict attendance agreement.

Discipline. California Code § 48900 (West 2014)

California Code § 48900

§ 48900. Grounds for suspension or expulsion; legislative intent

A pupil shall not be suspended from school or recommended for expulsion, unless the superintendent of the school district or the principal of the school in which the pupil is enrolled determines that the pupil has committed an act as defined pursuant to any of subdivisions (a) to (r), inclusive:

(r) Engaged in an act of bullying. For purposes of this subdivision, the following terms have the following meanings:

(1) "Bullying" means any severe or pervasive physical or verbal act or conduct, including communications made in writing or by means of an electronic act, and including one or more acts committed

by a pupil or group of pupils as defined in Section 48900.2, 48900.3, or 48900.4, directed toward one or more pupils that has or can be reasonably predicted to have the effect of one or more of the following:

(A) Placing a reasonable pupil or pupils in fear of harm to that pupil's or those pupils' person or property.

(B) Causing a reasonable pupil to experience a substantially detrimental effect on his or her physical or mental health.

(C) Causing a reasonable pupil to experience substantial interference with his or her academic performance.

(D) Causing a reasonable pupil to experience substantial interference with his or her ability to participate in or benefit from the services, activities, or privileges provided by a school.

    (2)(A) "Electronic act" means the creation and transmission originated on or off the schoolsite, by means of an electronic device, including, but not limited to, a telephone, wireless telephone, or other wireless communication device, computer, or pager, of a communication, including, but not limited to, any of the following:

(i) A message, text, sound, or image.

(ii) A post on a social network Internet Web site, including, but not limited to:

(I) Posting to or creating a burn page. "Burn page" means an Internet Web site created for the purpose of having one or more of the effects listed in paragraph (1).

(II) Creating a credible impersonation of another actual pupil for the purpose of having one or more of the effects listed in paragraph (1). "Credible impersonation" means to knowingly and without consent impersonate a pupil for the purpose of bullying the pupil and such that another pupil would reasonably believe, or has reasonably believed, that the pupil was or is the pupil who was impersonated.

(III) Creating a false profile for the purpose of having one or more of the effects listed in paragraph (1). "False profile" means a profile of a fictitious pupil or a profile using the likeness or attributes of an actual pupil other than the pupil who created the false profile.

(B) Notwithstanding paragraph (1) and subparagraph (A), an electronic act shall not constitute pervasive conduct solely on the basis that it has been transmitted on the Internet or is currently posted on the Internet.

(3) "Reasonable pupil" means a pupil, including, but not limited to, an exceptional needs pupil, who exercises average care, skill, and judgment in conduct for a person of his or her age, or for a person of his or her age with his or her exceptional needs.

California Code § 48900.4 (West 2003)

§ 48900.4. Additional grounds for suspension or expulsion; harassment, threats, or intimidation

In addition to the grounds specified in Sections 48900 and 48900.2, a pupil enrolled in any of grades 4 to 12, inclusive, may be suspended from school or recommended for expulsion if the superintendent or the principal of the school in which the pupil is enrolled determines that the pupil has intentionally engaged in harassment, threats, or intimidation, directed against school district personnel or pupils, that is sufficiently severe or pervasive to have the actual and reasonably expected effect of materially disrupting classwork, creating substantial disorder, and invading the rights of either school personnel or pupils by creating an intimidating or hostile educational environment.

California Administrative Code tit. 5, § 4630 (West 2013)

§ 4630. Filing a Local Complaint; Procedures, Time Lines

(a) Except for complaints under sections 4680-4687 regarding instructional materials, emergency or urgent facilities conditions that pose a threat to the health or safety of pupils or staff, and teacher vacancies or misassignments, and complaints that allege discrimination, harassment, intimidation or bullying and complaints regarding pupil fees, any individual, public agency or organization may file a written complaint with the district superintendent or his or her designee alleging a matter which, if true, would constitute a violation by that LEA [local educational agency] of federal or state law or regulation governing a program listed in section 4610(b) of this chapter.

(b) An investigation of alleged unlawful discrimination, harassment, intimidation or bullying shall be initiated by filing a complaint not later than six months from the date the alleged discrimination, harassment, intimidation or bullying occurred, or the date the complainant first obtained knowledge of the facts of the alleged discrimination, harassment, intimidation or bullying unless the time for filing is extended by the district superintendent or his or her designee, upon written request by the complainant setting forth the reasons for the extension. Such extension by the district superintendent or his or her designee shall be made in writing. The period for filing may be extended by the district superintendent or his or her designee for good cause for a period not to exceed 90 days following the expiration of the six month time period. The district superintendent shall respond immediately upon a receipt of a request for extension.

   (1) The complaint shall be filed by one who alleges that he or she has personally suffered unlawful discrimination, harassment, intimidation or bullying, or by one who believes an individual or any specific class of individuals has been subjected to discrimination, harassment, intimidation or bullying prohibited by this part.

   (2) The complaint shall be filed with the LEA in accordance with the complaint procedures of the LEA.

   (3) An investigation of a discrimination, harassment, intimidation or bullying complaint shall be conducted in a manner that protects confidentiality of the parties and maintains the integrity of the process.

   (c)(1) Pupil fee complaints may be filed with the principal of the school.

   (2) Pupil fee complaints shall be filed not later than one year from the date the alleged violation occurred.

   (3) Pupil fee complaints may be filed anonymously if the complaint provides evidence or information leading to evidence to support an allegation of noncompliance with Education Code sections 49010 and 49011 regarding pupil fees.

COLORADO

School Bullying Prevention and Education Grant Program. Colorado Revised Statutes Annotated § 22-93-106 (West 2011)

Colorado Revised Statutes Annotated § 22-93-106

§ 22-93-106. School bullying prevention and education–availability of best practices and other resources

(1) On or before November 1, 2011, the department shall create a page on its public web site at which the department shall continuously make publicly available evidence-based best practices and other resources for educators and other professionals engaged in bullying prevention and education.

(2) The department shall solicit evidence-based best practices and other resources from the school safety resource center created in section 24-33.5-1803, C.R.S.; from school districts; from the state charter school institute established in section 22-30.5-503; and from other state and federal agencies that are concerned with school bullying prevention and education. The department shall review materials that it receives and, as may be appropriate, make such materials available to the public on the web site described in subsection (1) of this section.

Charter School Act. Colorado Revised Statutes Annotated § 22-30.5-116 (West 2012)

Colorado Revised Statutes Annotated § 22-30.5-116

§ 22-30.5-116. Charter schools–school bullying policies required

1) On or before October 1, 2011, each charter school shall adopt and implement a policy concerning bullying prevention and education. Each charter school's policy, at a minimum, shall set forth appropriate disciplinary consequences for students who bully other students and for any person who takes any retaliatory action against a student who reports in good faith an incident of bullying, which consequences shall comply with all applicable state and federal laws.

(2) For the purposes of this section, "bullying" shall have the same meaning as set forth in section 22-32-109.1(1)(b).

(3) Each charter school is encouraged to ensure that its policy, at a minimum, incorporates the biennial administration of surveys of students' impressions of the severity of bullying in their schools, as described in section 22-93-104(1)(c); includes character building; and includes the designation of a team of persons at each school of the school district who advise the school administration concerning the severity and frequency of bullying incidents that occur in the school, which team may include, but need not be limited to, law enforcement officials, social workers, prosecutors, health professionals, mental health professionals, counselors, teachers, administrators, parents, and students.

State Anti-Bullying Statutes and Student Speech

School District Boards—Powers and Duties. Colorado Revised Statutes Annotated § 22-32-109.1 (West 2013)

Colorado Revised Statutes Annotated § 22-32-109.1

§ 22-32-109.1. Definitions and board of education duties

(1) Definitions. As used in this section, unless the context otherwise requires: ...
   (b) "Bullying" means any written or verbal expression, or physical or electronic act or gesture, or a pattern thereof, that is intended to coerce, intimidate, or cause any physical, mental, or emotional harm to any student. Bullying is prohibited against any student for any reason, including but not limited to any such behavior that is directed toward a student on the basis of his or her academic performance or against whom federal and state laws prohibit discrimination upon any of the bases described in section 22-32-109(1)(*ll*)(I). This definition is not intended to infringe upon any right guaranteed to any person by the first amendment to the United States constitution or to prevent the expression of any religious, political, or philosophical views.
(2) Safe school plan. In order to provide a learning environment that is safe, conducive to the learning process, and free from unnecessary disruption, following consultation with the school district accountability committee and school accountability committees, parents, teachers, administrators, students, student councils where available, and, where appropriate, the community at large, each school district board of education shall adopt and implement a safe school plan, or review and revise, as necessary in response to any relevant data collected by the school district, any existing plans or policies already in effect. In addition to the aforementioned parties, each school district board of education, in adopting and implementing its safe school plan, may consult with victims advocacy organizations, school psychologists, local law enforcement agencies, and community partners. The plan, at a minimum, shall include the following:
   (a) Conduct and discipline code. (I) A concisely written conduct and discipline code that shall be enforced uniformly, fairly, and consistently for all students. Copies of the code shall be provided to each student upon enrollment at the elementary, middle, and high school levels and shall be posted or kept on file at each public school in the school district. The school district shall take reasonable measures to ensure that each student of each public school in the school district is familiar with the code. The code shall include, but need not be limited to: ....
      (K) On and after August 8, 2001, a specific policy concerning bullying prevention and education. Each school district is encouraged to ensure that its policy, at a minimum, incorporates the biennial administration of surveys of students' impressions of the severity of bullying in their schools, as described in section 22-93-104(1)(c); character building; and the designation of a team of persons at each school of the school district who advise the school administration concerning the severity and frequency of bullying incidents that occur in the school, which team may include, but need not be limited to, law enforcement officials, social workers, prosecutors, health professionals, mental health professionals, school psychologists, counselors, teachers, administrators, parents, and students. Each school district's policy shall set forth appropriate disciplinary consequences for students

who bully other students and for any person who takes any retaliatory action against a student who reports in good faith an incident of bullying, which consequences shall comply with all applicable state and federal laws.
(b) Safe school reporting requirements. A policy whereby the principal of each public school in a school district shall submit annually, in a manner and by a date specified by rule of the state board, a written report to the board of education of such school district concerning the learning environment in the school during that school year. The board of education of the school district annually shall compile the reports from every school in the district and shall submit the compiled report to the department of education in a format specified by rule of the state board. The compiled report shall be made available to the general public. Such report shall include, but need not be limited to, the following specific information for the preceding school year: …
(IV) The number of conduct and discipline code violations, each of which violations shall be reported only in the most serious category that is applicable to that violation, including but not limited to specific information identifying the number of, and the action taken with respect to, each of the following types of violations: …
(G) Behavior on school grounds, in a school vehicle, or at a school activity or sanctioned event that is detrimental to the welfare or safety of other students or of school personnel, including but not limited to incidents of bullying and other behavior that creates a threat of physical harm to the student or to other students.

***

(VIII) The school's policy concerning bullying prevention and education, including information related to the development and implementation of any bullying prevention programs.
(C) Recognition and avoidance of on-line bullying.

Safe2tell Act. Colorado Revised Statutes Annotated § 24-31-601, et seq. (West 2014)

Colorado Revised Statutes Annotated § 24-31-602

§ 24-31-602. Legislative declaration

(1) The general assembly hereby finds and declares that:
    (a) The purpose of this part 6 is to empower students and the community by offering a comprehensive program of education, awareness, and training and a readily accessible tool that allows students and the community to easily provide anonymous information about unsafe, potentially harmful, dangerous, violent, or criminal activities in schools, or the threat of these activities, to appropriate law enforcement and public safety agencies and school officials; and
    (b) The ability to anonymously report information about unsafe, potentially harmful, dangerous, violent, or criminal activities in schools before or after they have occurred is critical in reducing, responding to, and recovering from these types of events in schools.

(2) The general assembly therefore finds that it is appropriate and necessary to provide for the anonymity of a person who provides information to law enforcement and public safety agencies and school officials and to provide for the confidentiality of associated materials.

Colorado Revised Statutes Annotated § 24-31-606

§ 24-31-606. Safe2tell program—creation—duties

(1) There is created, within the department, the safe2tell program.
(2) The program must:
    (a) Establish and maintain methods of anonymous reporting concerning unsafe, potentially harmful, dangerous, violent, or criminal activities in schools or the threat of those activities;
    (b) Establish methods and procedures to ensure that the identity of the reporting parties remains unknown to all persons and entities, including law enforcement officers and employees operating the program;
    (c) Establish methods and procedures so that information obtained from a reporting party who voluntarily discloses his or her identity and verifies that he or she is willing to be identified may be shared with law enforcement officers, employees operating the program, and with school officials;
    (d) Establish methods and procedures to ensure that a reporting party's identity that becomes known through any means other than voluntary disclosure is not further disclosed;
    (e) Promptly forward information received by the program to the appropriate law enforcement or public safety agency or school officials;
    (f) Train law enforcement dispatch centers, school districts, individual schools, and other entities determined by the attorney general on appropriate awareness and response to safe2tell tips; and
    (g) Provide safe2tell awareness and education materials to participating schools and school districts.

Institute Charter Schools. Colorado Revised Statutes Annotated § 22-30.5-521 (2011)

Colorado Revised Statutes Annotated § 22-30.5-521

§ 22-30.5-521. Institute charter schools—school bullying policies required

On or before October 1, 2011, each institute charter school shall implement the policy of the institute concerning bullying prevention and education, which policy is adopted by the institute pursuant to section 22-30.5-505(19).

Colorado Revised Statutes Annotated § 22-30.5-505

§ 22-30.5-505. State charter school institute—institute board—appointment—powers and duties—rules

(19)(a) Pursuant to section 22-30.5-521, on or before October 1, 2011, the institute shall adopt and implement a policy concerning bullying prevention and education. The policy, at a minimum, shall set forth appropriate disciplinary consequences for students who bully other students and for any person who takes any retaliatory action against a student who reports in good faith an incident of bullying, which consequences shall comply with all applicable state and federal laws.

(b) The institute is encouraged to include in the policy it adopts and implements pursuant to paragraph (a) of this subsection (19) the biennial administration of surveys of students' impressions of the severity of bullying in their schools, as described in section 22-93-104(1)(c); character building; and the designation of a team of persons at each institute charter school who advise the school administration concerning the severity and frequency of bullying incidents that occur in the school, which team may include, but need not be limited to, law enforcement officials, social workers, prosecutors, health professionals, mental health professionals, counselors, teachers, administrators, parents, and students.

CONNECTICUT

Education and School Culture. Connecticut General Statutes Annotated § 10-222d (West 2011)

Connecticut General Statutes Annotated § 10-222d

§ 10-222d. Safe school climate plans. Definitions. School climate assessments

(a) As used in this section ...:
  (1) "Bullying" means (A) the repeated use by one or more students of a written, oral or electronic communication, such as cyberbullying, directed at or referring to another student attending school in the same school district, or (B) a physical act or gesture by one or more students repeatedly directed at another student attending school in the same school district, that: (i) Causes physical or emotional harm to such student or damage to such student's property, (ii) places such student in reasonable fear of harm to himself or herself, or of damage to his or her property, (iii) creates a hostile environment at school for such student, (iv) infringes on the rights of such student at school, or (v) substantially disrupts the education process or the orderly operation of a school. "Bullying" shall include, but not be limited to, a written, oral or electronic communication or physical act or gesture based on any actual or perceived differentiating characteristic, such as race, color, religion, ancestry, national origin, gender, sexual orientation, gender identity or expression, socioeconomic status, academic status, physical appearance, or mental, physical, developmental or sensory disability, or by association with an individual or group who has or is perceived to have one or more of such characteristics;
  (2) "Cyberbullying" means any act of bullying through the use of the Internet, interactive and digital technologies, cellular mobile telephone or other mobile electronic devices or any electronic communications;

(3) "Mobile electronic device" means any hand-held or other portable electronic equipment capable of providing data communication between two or more individuals, including, but not limited to, a text messaging device, a paging device, a personal digital assistant, a laptop computer, equipment that is capable of playing a video game or a digital video disk, or equipment on which digital images are taken or transmitted;

(4) "Electronic communication" means any transfer of signs, signals, writing, images, sounds, data or intelligence of any nature transmitted in whole or in part by a wire, radio, electromagnetic, photoelectronic or photo-optical system;

(5) "Hostile environment" means a situation in which bullying among students is sufficiently severe or pervasive to alter the conditions of the school climate;

(6) "Outside of the school setting" means at a location, activity or program that is not school related, or through the use of an electronic device or a mobile electronic device that is not owned, leased or used by a local or regional board of education;

(7) "School employee" means (A) a teacher, substitute teacher, school administrator, school superintendent, guidance counselor, psychologist, social worker, nurse, physician, school paraprofessional or coach employed by a local or regional board of education or working in a public elementary, middle or high school; or (B) any other individual who, in the performance of his or her duties, has regular contact with students and who provides services to or on behalf of students enrolled in a public elementary, middle or high school, pursuant to a contract with the local or regional board of education; and

(8) "School climate" means the quality and character of school life with a particular focus on the quality of the relationships within the school community between and among students and adults.

(b) Each local and regional board of education shall develop and implement a safe school climate plan to address the existence of bullying in its schools. Such plan shall:

(1) Enable students to anonymously report acts of bullying to school employees and require students and the parents or guardians of students to be notified annually of the process by which students may make such reports, (2) enable the parents or guardians of students to file written reports of suspected bullying, (3) require school employees who witness acts of bullying or receive reports of bullying to orally notify the safe school climate specialist, described in section 10-222k, or another school administrator if the safe school climate specialist is unavailable, not later than one school day after such school employee witnesses or receives a report of bullying, and to file a written report not later than two school days after making such oral report, (4) require the safe school climate specialist to investigate or supervise the investigation of all reports of bullying and ensure that such investigation is completed promptly after receipt of any written reports made under this section, (5) require the safe school climate specialist to review any anonymous reports, except that no disciplinary action shall be taken solely on the basis of an anonymous report, (6) include a prevention and intervention strategy, as defined by section 10-222g, for school employees to deal with bullying, (7) provide for the inclusion of language in student codes of conduct concerning bullying, (8) require each school to notify the parents or guardians of students who commit any verified acts of bullying and the parents or guardians of students against whom such acts were directed not later than forty-eight hours after the completion of the investigation described in subdivision (4) of this subsection, (9)

require each school to invite the parents or guardians of a student who commits any verified act of bullying and the parents or guardians of the student against whom such act was directed to a meeting to communicate to such parents or guardians the measures being taken by the school to ensure the safety of the student against whom such act was directed and to prevent further acts of bullying, (10) establish a procedure for each school to document and maintain records relating to reports and investigations of bullying in such school and to maintain a list of the number of verified acts of bullying in such school and make such list available for public inspection, and annually report such number to the Department of Education, and in such manner as prescribed by the Commissioner of Education, (11) direct the development of case-by-case interventions for addressing repeated incidents of bullying against a single individual or recurrently perpetrated bullying incidents by the same individual that may include both counseling and discipline, (12) prohibit discrimination and retaliation against an individual who reports or assists in the investigation of an act of bullying, (13) direct the development of student safety support plans for students against whom an act of bullying was directed that address safety measures the school will take to protect such students against further acts of bullying, (14) require the principal of a school, or the principal's designee, to notify the appropriate local law enforcement agency when such principal, or the principal's designee, believes that any acts of bullying constitute criminal conduct, (15) prohibit bullying (A) on school grounds, at a school-sponsored or school-related activity, function or program whether on or off school grounds, at a school bus stop, on a school bus or other vehicle owned, leased or used by a local or regional board of education, or through the use of an electronic device or an electronic mobile device owned, leased or used by the local or regional board of education, and (B) outside of the school setting if such bullying (i) creates a hostile environment at school for the student against whom such bullying was directed, (ii) infringes on the rights of the student against whom such bullying was directed at school, or (iii) substantially disrupts the education process or the orderly operation of a school, (16) require, at the beginning of each school year, each school to provide all school employees with a written or electronic copy of the school district's safe school climate plan, and (17) require that all school employees annually complete the training described in section 10-220a or section 10-222j. The notification required pursuant to subdivision (8) of this subsection and the invitation required pursuant to subdivision (9) of this subsection shall include a description of the response of school employees to such acts and any consequences that may result from the commission of further acts of bullying.

(c) Not later than January 1, 2012, each local and regional board of education shall approve the safe school climate plan developed pursuant to this section and submit such plan to the Department of Education. Not later than thirty calendar days after approval of such plan by the local or regional board of education, the board shall make such plan available on the board's and each individual school in the school district's Internet web site and ensure that such plan is included in the school district's publication of the rules, procedures and standards of conduct for schools and in all student handbooks.

(d) On and after July 1, 2012, and biennially thereafter, each local and regional board of education shall require each school in the district to complete an assessment using the school climate assessment instruments, including surveys, approved and disseminated by the Department of Education pursuant to section 10-222h. Each local and regional board of education shall collect the school climate assessments for each school in the district and submit such school climate assessments to the department.

Connecticut General Statutes Annotated § 10-222g

§ 10-222g. Prevention and intervention strategy for bullying

For the purposes of section 10-222d, the term "prevention and intervention strategy" may include, but is not limited to, (1) implementation of a positive behavioral interventions and supports process or another evidence-based model approach for safe school climate or for the prevention of bullying identified by the Department of Education, (2) school rules prohibiting bullying, harassment and intimidation and establishing appropriate consequences for those who engage in such acts, (3) adequate adult supervision of outdoor areas, hallways, the lunchroom and other specific areas where bullying is likely to occur, (4) inclusion of grade-appropriate bullying education and prevention curricula in kindergarten through high school, (5) individual interventions with the bully, parents and school employees, and interventions with the bullied child, parents and school employees, (6) school-wide training related to safe school climate, (7) student peer training, education and support, and (8) promotion of parent involvement in bullying prevention through individual or team participation in meetings, trainings and individual interventions.

Connecticut General Statutes Annotated § 10-222k (2013)

§ 10-222k. District safe school climate coordinator. Safe school climate specialist. Safe school climate committee

(a) For the school year commencing July 1, 2012, and each school year thereafter, the superintendent of each local or regional board of education shall appoint, from among existing school district staff, a district safe school climate coordinator. The district safe school climate coordinator shall: (1) Be responsible for implementing the district's safe school climate plan, developed pursuant to section 10-222d, (2) collaborate with the safe school climate specialists, described in subsection (b) of this section, the board of education for the district and the superintendent of schools of the school district to prevent, identify and respond to bullying in the schools of the district, (3) provide data and information, in collaboration with the superintendent of schools of the district, to the Department of Education regarding bullying, in accordance with the provisions of subsection (b) of section 10-222d, and subsection (a) of section 10-222h, and (4) meet with the safe school climate specialists at least twice during the school year to discuss issues relating to bullying in the school district and to make recommendations concerning amendments to the district's safe school climate plan.

(b) For the school year commencing July 1, 2012, and each school year thereafter, the principal of each school, or the principal's designee, shall serve as the safe school climate specialist and shall (1) investigate or supervise the investigation of reported acts of bullying in the school in accordance with the district's safe school climate plan, (2) collect and maintain records of reports and investigations of bullying in the school, and (3) act as the primary school official responsible for preventing, identifying and responding to reports of bullying in the school.

(c) (1) For the school year commencing July 1, 2012, and each school year thereafter, the principal of each school shall establish a committee or designate at least one existing committee in the school to be responsible for developing and fostering a safe school climate and addressing issues relating to bullying in the school. Such committee shall include at least one parent or guardian of a student enrolled in the school appointed by the school principal.

(2) Any such committee shall: (A) Receive copies of completed reports following investigations of bullying, (B) identify and address patterns of bullying among students in the school, (C) implement the provisions of the school security and safety plan, developed pursuant to section 10-222m, regarding the collection, evaluation and reporting of information relating to instances of disturbing or threatening behavior that may not meet the definition of bullying, (D) review and amend school policies relating to bullying, (E) review and make recommendations to the district safe school climate coordinator regarding the district's safe school climate plan based on issues and experiences specific to the school, (F) educate students, school employees and parents and guardians of students on issues relating to bullying, (G) collaborate with the district safe school climate coordinator in the collection of data regarding bullying, in accordance with the provisions of subsection (b) of section 10-222d and subsection (a) of section 10-222h, and (H) perform any other duties as determined by the school principal that are related to the prevention, identification and response to school bullying for the school.

(3) Any parent or guardian serving as a member of any such committee shall not participate in the activities described in subparagraphs (A) to (C), inclusive, of subdivision (2) of this subsection or any other activity that may compromise the confidentiality of a student.

DELAWARE

Bullying Prevention. 14 Delaware Code Annotated § 4112D (2012)

14 Delaware Code Annotated § 4112D

§ 4112D. School bullying prevention

(a) Definition of bullying.--As used in this section, "bullying" means any intentional written, electronic, verbal or physical act or actions against another student, school volunteer or school employee that a reasonable person under the circumstances should know will have the effect of:

(1) Placing a student, school volunteer or school employee in reasonable fear of substantial harm to his or her emotional or physical well-being or substantial damages to his or her property; or

(2) Creating a hostile, threatening, humiliating or abusive educational environment due to the pervasiveness or persistence of actions or due to a power differential between the bully and the target; or

(3) Interfering with a student having a safe school environment that is necessary to facilitate educational performance, opportunities or benefits; or

(4) Perpetuating bullying by inciting, soliciting or coercing an individual or group to demean, dehumanize, embarrass or cause emotional, psychological or physical harm to another student, school volunteer or school employee.

(b) Prohibition of bullying.--

(1) Each school district and charter school shall prohibit bullying and reprisal, retaliation or false accusation against a target, witness or one with reliable information about an act of bullying.

(2) Each school district and charter school shall establish a policy which, at a minimum, includes the following components:

   a. A statement prohibiting bullying of any person on school property or at school functions or by use of data or computer software that is accessed through a computer, computer system, computer network or other electronic technology of a school district or charter school from kindergarten through grade 12. For purposes of this section, "school property" and "school functions" have the same definition as in § 4112 of this title.

   b. A definition of bullying no less inclusive than that in subsection (a) of this section.

   c. Direction to develop a school-wide bullying prevention program.

   d. A requirement that each school establish a site-based committee that is responsible for coordinating the school's bully prevention program including the design, approval and monitoring of the program. A majority of the members of the site-based committee shall be members of the school professional staff, of which a majority shall be instructional staff. The committee also shall contain representatives of the administrative staff, support staff, student body (for school enrolling students in grades 7 through 12), parents and staff from the before- or after-school program or programs. These representatives shall be chosen by members of each respective group except that representatives of the nonemployee groups shall be appointed by the school principal. The committee shall operate on a 1-person, 1-vote principle. In the event a site-based school discipline committee has been established pursuant to § 1605(7)a. and b. of this title, that committee shall vote whether or not to accept the aforementioned responsibilities.

   e. A requirement that any school employee that has reliable information that would lead a reasonable person to suspect that a person is a target of bullying shall immediately report it to the administration.

   f. A requirement that each school have a procedure for the administration to promptly investigate in a timely manner and determine whether bullying has occurred, and that such procedure include investigation of such instances, including a determination of whether the target of the bullying was targeted or reports being targeted wholly or in part due to the target's race, age, marital status, creed, religion, color, sex, disability, sexual orientation, gender identity or expression, or national origin. This subsection does not preclude schools from identifying other reasons or criteria why a person is a target of bullying.

g. A requirement that, to the extent that funding is available, each school develop a plan for a system of supervision in nonclassroom areas. The plan shall provide for the review and exchange of information regarding nonclassroom areas.
h. An identification of an appropriate range of consequences for bullying.
i. A procedure for a student and parent, guardian or relative caregiver pursuant to § 202(f) of this title or legal guardian to provide information on bullying activity. However, this paragraph does not permit formal disciplinary action solely based on an anonymous report.
j. A requirement that a parent, guardian or relative caregiver pursuant to § 202(f) of this title or legal guardian of any target of bullying or person who bullies another as defined herein, be notified.
k. A requirement that all reported incidents of bullying, regardless of whether the school could substantiate the incident be reported to the Department of Education within 5 working days pursuant to Department of Education regulations.
l. A statement prohibiting retaliation following a report of bullying.
m. A procedure for communication between school staff members and medical professionals who are involved in treating students for bullying issues.
n. A requirement that the school bullying prevention program be implemented throughout the year, and integrated with the school's discipline policies and § 4112 of this title.

(c) Dissemination of policy and accountability.--
(1) Each school district and charter school shall adopt the policy consistent with subsection (b) of this section and submit a copy to the Delaware Department of Education by January 1, 2008, or by January 1 of a newly approved charter school's first year of operation.
(2) The policy shall appear in the student and staff handbook and if no handbook is available, or it is not practical to reprint new handbooks, a copy of the policy will be distributed annually to all students, parents, faculty and staff. The telephone number of the Department of Justice School Ombudsman shall be provided in writing to parents, students, faculty and staff; and shall be on the website of each school and school district. The contact information shall also be prominently displayed in each school.
(3) The policy shall be submitted to the Delaware Department of Education by January 1 of each subsequent year. Access to the policy via the district or charter school's website will meet the criteria as being submitted. Revision or revisions to an existing district or charter school policy shall be submitted to the Department within 30 days of a district's school board or charter school's board of directors' approval of the revision or revisions. The Department shall review such policy or revision or revisions to policy for compliance with state and federal law and regulations promulgated by the Department of Education.
(4) The Delaware Department of Education shall prepare an annual report, which shall include a summary of all reported and all substantiated incidences of bullying, and shall include a summary of the information gathered pursuant to paragraph (b)(2)f. of this section and the results of audits conducted pursuant to paragraph (d)(4) of this section. This report shall be posted on the Delaware Department of Education's website.

(d) Duties of the Department of Education. --
   (1) The Delaware Department of Education shall collaborate with the Delaware Department of Justice to develop a model policy, that may change from time to time, that is applicable to kindergarten through grade 12, and post this policy, along with the contact information for the School Ombudsman, on their websites in order to assist the school districts and charter schools. In addition, the Department of Education shall promulgate a uniform cyberbullying policy, which shall be based upon a model prepared by the Department of Justice and public comment upon that model. This uniform cyberbullying policy shall be formally adopted as written by each charter school and school district within 90 days of becoming final.
   (2) Distribution of the Comprehensive School Discipline Improvement Program funds to a school district and charter school provided in the General Appropriations Act starting in fiscal year 2009 and thereafter is contingent upon Department of Education approval of the school district's or charter school's bullying prevention policy.
   (3) To the extent that funding is available the State Department of Education will provide for an award system for schools with exemplary programs based on criteria promulgated by the Delaware Department of Education.
   (4) The Department of Education shall conduct random audits of schools to insure compliance with paragraphs (b)(2)i. and (b)(2)k. of this section. The Department shall report the results of these audits annually.
(e) Immunity.--A school employee, school volunteer or student is individually immune from a cause of action for damages arising from reporting bullying in good faith and to the appropriate person or persons using the procedures specified in the school district and charter school's bullying prevention policy, but there shall be no such immunity if the act of reporting constituted gross negligence and/or reckless, wilful or intentional conduct.
(f) Other defenses.--
   (1) The physical location or time of access of a technology-related incident is not a valid defense in any disciplinary action by the school district or charter school initiated under this section provided there is sufficient school nexus.
   (2) This section does not apply to any person who uses data or computer software that is accessed through a computer, computer system, computer network or other electronic technology when acting within the scope of that person's lawful employment or investigation of a violation of this section in accordance with school district or charter school policy.
(g) Relationship to school crime reporting law.--An incident may meet the definition of bullying and also the definition of a particular crime under state or federal law. Nothing in this section or in the policies promulgated as a result thereof shall prevent school officials from fulfilling all of the reporting requirements of § 4112 of this title, or from reporting probable crimes that occur on school property or at a school function which are not required to be reported under that section. Nothing in this section shall abrogate the reporting requirements for child abuse or sexual abuse set forth in Chapter 9 of Title 16, or any other reporting requirement under state or federal law.
(h) Rules and regulations.--Notwithstanding any provision to the contrary, the Delaware Department of Education may promulgate rules and regulations necessary to implement this section.

FLORIDA

Jeffrey Johnston Stand Up for All Students Act. Florida Statutes Annotated § 1006.147 (West 2013)

Florida Statutes Annotated § 1006.147

§ 1006.147. Bullying and harassment prohibited

(1) This section may be cited as the "Jeffrey Johnston Stand Up for All Students Act."
(2) Bullying or harassment of any student or employee of a public K-12 educational institution is prohibited:
   (a) During any education program or activity conducted by a public K-12 educational institution;
   (b) During any school-related or school-sponsored program or activity or on a school bus of a public K-12 educational institution;
   (c) Through the use of data or computer software that is accessed through a computer, computer system, or computer network within the scope of a public K-12 educational institution; or
   (d) Through the use of data or computer software that is accessed at a nonschool-related location, activity, function, or program or through the use of technology or an electronic device that is not owned, leased, or used by a school district or school, if the bullying substantially interferes with or limits the victim's ability to participate in or benefit from the services, activities, or opportunities offered by a school or substantially disrupts the education process or orderly operation of a school. This paragraph does not require a school to staff or monitor any nonschool-related activity, function, or program.
(3) For purposes of this section:
   (a) "Bullying" includes cyberbullying and means systematically and chronically inflicting physical hurt or psychological distress on one or more students and may involve:
      1. Teasing;
      2. Social exclusion;
      3. Threat;
      4. Intimidation;
      5. Stalking;
      6. Physical violence;
      7. Theft;
      8. Sexual, religious, or racial harassment;
      9. Public or private humiliation; or
      10. Destruction of property.
   (b) "Cyberbullying" means bullying through the use of technology or any electronic communication, which includes, but is not limited to, any transfer of signs, signals, writing, images, sounds, data, or intelligence of any nature transmitted in whole or in part by a wire, radio, electromagnetic system, photoelectronic system, or photooptical system, including, but not limited to, electronic mail, Internet communications, instant messages, or facsimile communications. Cyberbullying includes the creation of a webpage or weblog in which the creator

assumes the identity of another person, or the knowing impersonation of another person as the author of posted content or messages, if the creation or impersonation creates any of the conditions enumerated in the definition of bullying. Cyberbullying also includes the distribution by electronic means of a communication to more than one person or the posting of material on an electronic medium that may be accessed by one or more persons, if the distribution or posting creates any of the conditions enumerated in the definition of bullying.

(c) "Harassment" means any threatening, insulting, or dehumanizing gesture, use of data or computer software, or written, verbal, or physical conduct directed against a student or school employee that:
1. Places a student or school employee in reasonable fear of harm to his or her person or damage to his or her property;
2. Has the effect of substantially interfering with a student's educational performance, opportunities, or benefits; or
3. Has the effect of substantially disrupting the orderly operation of a school.

(d) "Within the scope of a public K-12 educational institution" means, regardless of ownership, any computer, computer system, or computer network that is physically located on school property or at a school-related or school-sponsored program or activity.

(e) Definitions in [section] 815.03 and the definition in [section] 784.048(1)(d) relating to stalking are applicable to this section.

(f) The definitions of "bullying" and "harassment" include:
1. Retaliation against a student or school employee by another student or school employee for asserting or alleging an act of bullying or harassment. Reporting an act of bullying or harassment that is not made in good faith is considered retaliation.
2. Perpetuation of conduct listed in paragraph (a), paragraph (b), or paragraph (c) by an individual or group with intent to demean, dehumanize, embarrass, or cause physical harm to a student or school employee by:
  a. Incitement or coercion;
  b. Accessing or knowingly causing or providing access to data or computer software through a computer, computer system, or computer network within the scope of the district school system; or
  c. Acting in a manner that has an effect substantially similar to the effect of bullying or harassment.

(4) By December 1, 2008, each school district shall adopt a policy prohibiting bullying and harassment of any student or employee of a public K-12 educational institution. Each school district's policy shall be in substantial conformity with the Department of Education's model policy mandated in subsection (5). The school district bullying and harassment policy shall afford all students the same protection regardless of their status under the law. The school district may establish separate discrimination policies that include categories of students. The school district shall involve students, parents, teachers, administrators, school staff, school volunteers, community representatives, and local law enforcement agencies in the process of adopting the policy. The school district policy must be implemented in a manner that is ongoing throughout the school year and integrated with a school's curriculum, a school's discipline policies, and other violence prevention efforts. The school district policy must contain, at a minimum, the following components:

(a) A statement prohibiting bullying and harassment.
(b) A definition of bullying and a definition of harassment that include the definitions listed in this section.
(c) A description of the type of behavior expected from each student and employee of a public K-12 educational institution.
(d) The consequences for a student or employee of a public K-12 educational institution who commits an act of bullying or harassment.
(e) The consequences for a student or employee of a public K-12 educational institution who is found to have wrongfully and intentionally accused another of an act of bullying or harassment.
(f) A procedure for reporting an act of bullying or harassment, including provisions that permit a person to anonymously report such an act. However, this paragraph does not permit formal disciplinary action to be based solely on an anonymous report.
(g) A procedure for the prompt investigation of a report of bullying or harassment and the persons responsible for the investigation. The investigation of a reported act of bullying or harassment is deemed to be a school-related activity and begins with a report of such an act. Incidents that require a reasonable investigation when reported to appropriate school authorities shall include alleged incidents of bullying or harassment allegedly committed against a child while the child is en route to school aboard a school bus or at a school bus stop.
(h) A process to investigate whether a reported act of bullying or harassment is within the scope of the district school system and, if not, a process for referral of such an act to the appropriate jurisdiction. Computers without web-filtering software or computers with web-filtering software that is disabled shall be used when complaints of cyberbullying are investigated.
(i) A procedure for providing immediate notification to the parents of a victim of bullying or harassment and the parents of the perpetrator of an act of bullying or harassment, as well as notification to all local agencies where criminal charges may be pursued against the perpetrator.
(j) A procedure to refer victims and perpetrators of bullying or harassment for counseling.
(k) A procedure for including incidents of bullying or harassment in the school's report of data concerning school safety and discipline required under [section] 1006.09(6). The report must include each incident of bullying or harassment and the resulting consequences, including discipline and referrals. The report must include in a separate section each reported incident of bullying or harassment that does not meet the criteria of a prohibited act under this section with recommendations regarding such incidents. The Department of Education shall aggregate information contained in the reports.
(l) A procedure for providing instruction to students, parents, teachers, school administrators, counseling staff, and school volunteers on identifying, preventing, and responding to bullying or harassment, including instruction on recognizing behaviors that lead to bullying and harassment and taking appropriate preventive action based on those observations.
(m) A procedure for regularly reporting to a victim's parents the actions taken to protect the victim.
(n) A procedure for publicizing the policy, which must include its publication in the code of student conduct required under [section] 1006.07(2) and in all employee handbooks.

(5) To assist school districts in developing policies prohibiting bullying and harassment, the Department of Education shall develop a model policy that shall be provided to school districts no later than October 1, 2008.

(6) A school employee, school volunteer, student, or parent who promptly reports in good faith an act of bullying or harassment to the appropriate school official designated in the school district's policy and who makes this report in compliance with the procedures set forth in the policy is immune from a cause of action for damages arising out of the reporting itself or any failure to remedy the reported incident.

(7)(a) The physical location or time of access of a computer-related incident cannot be raised as a defense in any disciplinary action initiated under this section.

(b) This section does not apply to any person who uses data or computer software that is accessed through a computer, computer system, or computer network when acting within the scope of his or her lawful employment or investigating a violation of this section in accordance with school district policy.

(8) Distribution of safe schools funds to a school district provided in the 2009-2010 General Appropriations Act is contingent upon and payable to the school district upon the Department of Education's approval of the school district's bullying and harassment policy. The department's approval of each school district's bullying and harassment policy shall be granted upon certification by the department that the school district's policy has been submitted to the department and is in substantial conformity with the department's model bullying and harassment policy as mandated in subsection (5). Distribution of safe schools funds provided to a school district in fiscal year 2010-2011 and thereafter shall be contingent upon and payable to the school district upon the school district's compliance with all reporting procedures contained in this section.

(9) On or before January 1 of each year, the Commissioner of Education shall report to the Governor, the President of the Senate, and the Speaker of the House of Representatives on the implementation of this section. The report shall include data collected pursuant to paragraph (4)(k).

(10) Nothing in this section shall be construed to abridge the rights of students or school employees that are protected by the First Amendment to the Constitution of the United States.

GEORGIA

Character education program. Georgia Code Annotated § 20-2-145 (West 1997)

Georgia Code Annotated § 20-2-145

§ 20-2-145. Comprehensive character education program

(a) The State Board of Education shall develop by the start of the 1997-1998 school year a comprehensive character education program for levels K-12. This comprehensive character education program shall be known as the "character curriculum" and shall focus on the students' development of the following character traits: courage, patriotism, citizenship, honesty, fairness, respect for others, kindness, cooperation, self-respect, self-control, courtesy, compassion, tolerance, diligence, generosity, punctuality, cleanliness, cheerfulness, school pride, respect for the environment, respect for the creator, patience, creativity, sportsmanship, loyalty, perseverance, and virtue. Such program

shall also address, by the start of the 1999-2000 school year, methods of discouraging bullying and violent acts against fellow students. Local boards shall implement such a program in all grade levels at the beginning of the 2000-2001 school year and shall provide opportunities for parental involvement in establishing expected outcomes of the character education program.
(b) The Department of Education shall develop character education program workshops designed for employees of local school systems.

Discipline. Georgia Code Annotated § 20-2-751.4 (West 2011)

Georgia Code Annotated § 20-2-751.4

§ 20-2-751.4. Policies to prohibit bullying of student by another student

(a) As used in this Code section, the term "bullying" means an act which occurs on school property, on school vehicles, at designated school bus stops, or at school related functions or activities, or by use of data or software that is accessed through a computer, computer system, computer network, or other electronic technology of a local school system, that is:
  (1) Any willful attempt or threat to inflict injury on another person, when accompanied by an apparent present ability to do so;
  (2) Any intentional display of force such as would give the victim reason to fear or expect immediate bodily harm; or
  (3) Any intentional written, verbal, or physical act which a reasonable person would perceive as being intended to threaten, harass, or intimidate, that:
    (A) Causes another person substantial physical harm within the meaning of Code Section 16-5-23.1 or visible bodily harm as such term is defined in Code Section 16-5-23.1;
    (B) Has the effect of substantially interfering with a student's education;
    (C) Is so severe, persistent, or pervasive that it creates an intimidating or threatening educational environment; or
    (D) Has the effect of substantially disrupting the orderly operation of the school.
(b) No later than August 1, 2011:
  (1) Each local board of education shall adopt a policy that prohibits bullying of a student by another student and shall require such prohibition to be included in the student code of conduct for schools in that school system;
  (2) Each local board policy shall require that, upon a finding by the disciplinary hearing officer, panel, or tribunal of school officials provided for in this subpart that a student in grades six through 12 has committed the offense of bullying for the third time in a school year, such student shall be assigned to an alternative school;
  (3) Each local board of education shall establish and publish in its local board policy a method to notify the parent, guardian, or other person who has control or charge of a student upon a finding by a school administrator that such student has committed an offense of bullying or is a victim of bullying; and

(4) Each local board of education shall ensure that students and parents of students are notified of the prohibition against bullying, and the penalties for violating the prohibition, by posting such information at each school and by including such information in student and parent handbooks.

(c) No later than January 1, 2011, the Department of Education shall develop a model policy regarding bullying, that may be revised from time to time, and shall post such policy on its website in order to assist local school systems. Such model policy shall include:

(1) A statement prohibiting bullying;

(2) A requirement that any teacher or other school employee who has reliable information that would lead a reasonable person to suspect that someone is a target of bullying shall immediately report it to the school principal;

(3) A requirement that each school have a procedure for the school administration to promptly investigate in a timely manner and determine whether bullying has occurred;

(4) An age-appropriate range of consequences for bullying which shall include, at minimum and without limitation, disciplinary action or counseling as appropriate under the circumstances;

(5) A procedure for a teacher or other school employee, student, parent, guardian, or other person who has control or charge of a student, either anonymously or in such person's name, at such person's option, to report or otherwise provide information on bullying activity;

(6) A statement prohibiting retaliation following a report of bullying; and

(7) Provisions consistent with the requirements of subsection (b) of this Code section.

(d) The Department of Education shall develop and post on its website a list of entities and their contact information which produce antibullying training programs and materials deemed appropriate by the department for use in local school systems.

(e) Any person who reports an incident of bullying in good faith shall be immune from civil liability for any damages caused by such reporting.

(f) Nothing in this Code section or in the model policy promulgated by the Department of Education shall be construed to require a local board of education to provide transportation to a student transferred to another school as a result of a bullying incident.

(g) Any school system which is not in compliance with the requirements of subsection (b) of this Code section shall be ineligible to receive state funding pursuant to Code Sections 20-2-161 and 20-2-260.

Georgia Code Annotated § 20-2-751.5 (West 2008)

§ 20-2-751.5. Provisions to be included in student codes of conduct; distribution

Each student code of conduct shall contain provisions that address the following conduct of students during school hours, at school related functions, and on the school bus in a manner that is appropriate to the age of the student: …

(15) Bullying as defined by Code Section 20-2-751.4;
- (b)(1) In addition to the requirements contained in subsection (a) of this Code section, each student code of conduct shall include comprehensive and specific provisions prescribing and governing student conduct and safety rules on all public school buses. The specific provisions shall include but not be limited to:
  - (A) Students shall be prohibited from acts of physical violence as defined by Code Section 20-2-751.6, bullying as defined by subsection (a) of Code Section 20-2-751.4, physical assault or battery of other persons on the school bus, verbal assault of other persons on the school bus, disrespectful conduct toward the school bus driver or other persons on the school bus, and other unruly behavior;
- (2) If a student is found to have engaged in physical acts of violence as defined by Code Section 20-2-751.6, the student shall be subject to the penalties set forth in such Code section. If a student is found to have engaged in bullying as defined by subsection (a) of Code Section 20-2-751.4 or in physical assault or battery of another person on the school bus, the local school board policy shall require a meeting of the parent or guardian of the student and appropriate school district officials to form a school bus behavior contract for the student. Such contract shall provide for progressive age-appropriate discipline, penalties, and restrictions for student misconduct on the bus. Contract provisions may include but shall not be not [sic] limited to assigned seating, ongoing parental involvement, and suspension from riding the bus. This subsection is not to be construed to limit the instances when a school code of conduct or local board of education may require use of a student bus behavior contract.

Student Support and Discipline. Georgia Administrative Code 160-4-8-.15 (West 2004)

Georgia Administrative Code 160-4-8-.15

160-4-8-.15. Student Discipline

Each local board of education shall adopt policies designed to improve the student learning environment by improving student behavior and discipline. These policies shall provide for the development of age appropriate student codes of conduct that contain the following, at a minimum: ...

14. Bullying as defined in [Georgia Code Annotated] § 20-2-751.4; ...
16. Each local board of education shall adopt policies, applicable to students in grades 6 through 12 that prohibit bullying of a student by another student and shall require such prohibition to be included in the student code of conduct in that school system. Local board policies shall require that, upon a finding that a student in grades 6 through 12 has committed the offense of bullying for the third time in a school year, such student shall be assigned to an alternative school.

HAWAII

Accountability. Hawaii Revised Statutes Annotated § 302A-1002 (West 1996)

Hawaii Revised Statutes Annotated § 302A-1002.

§ 302A-1002. Reporting of crime-related incidents

The board shall adopt rules pursuant to chapter 91 to:

1) Require a report to appropriate authorities from a teacher, official, or other employee of the department who knows or has reason to believe that an act has been committed or will be committed, which:
   A) Occurred or will occur on school property during school hours or during activities supervised by the school; and
   B) Involves crimes relating to arson, assault, burglary, disorderly conduct, dangerous weapons, dangerous drugs, harmful drugs, extortion, firearms, gambling, harassment, intoxicating drugs, marijuana or marijuana concentrate, murder, attempted murder, sexual offenses, rendering a false alarm, criminal property damage, robbery, terroristic threatening, theft, or trespass;
2) Establish procedures for disposing of any incident reported; and
3) Impose, in addition to any other powers or authority the department may have to discipline school officials, appropriate disciplinary action for failure to report these incidents, including probation, suspension, demotion, and discharge of school officials.

Offenses against Public Order. Hawaii Revised Statutes Annotated § 711-1106 (West 2009)

Hawaii Revised Statutes Annotated § 711-1106.

§ 711-1106. Harassment

1) A person commits the offense of harassment if, with intent to harass, annoy, or alarm any other person, that person:
   a) Strikes, shoves, kicks, or otherwise touches another person in an offensive manner or subjects the other person to offensive physical contact;
   b) Insults, taunts, or challenges another person in a manner likely to provoke an immediate violent response or that would cause the other person to reasonably believe that the actor intends to cause bodily injury to the recipient or another or damage to the property of the recipient or another;
   c) Repeatedly makes telephone calls, facsimile transmissions, or any form of electronic communication as defined in section 711-1111(2), including electronic mail transmissions, without purpose of legitimate communication;
   d) Repeatedly makes a communication anonymously or at an extremely inconvenient hour;

e) Repeatedly makes communications, after being advised by the person to whom the communication is directed that further communication is unwelcome; or

f) Makes a communication using offensively coarse language that would cause the recipient to reasonably believe that the actor intends to cause bodily injury to the recipient or another or damage to the property of the recipient or another.

2) Harassment is a petty misdemeanor.

IDAHO

Crimes and Punishments: Student harassment, intimidation and bullying. Idaho Code Annotated § 18-917A (West 2006)

Idaho Code Annotated § 18-917A

§ 18-917A. Student harassment—Intimidation—Bullying

(1) No student shall intentionally commit, or conspire to commit, an act of harassment, intimidation or bullying against another student.

(2) As used in this section, "harassment, intimidation or bullying" means any intentional gesture, or any intentional written, verbal or physical act or threat by a student that:
   (a) A reasonable person under the circumstances should know will have the effect of:
      (i) Harming a student; or
      (ii) Damaging a student's property; or
      (iii) Placing a student in reasonable fear of harm to his or her person; or
      (iv) Placing a student in reasonable fear of damage to his or her property; or
   (b) Is sufficiently severe, persistent or pervasive that it creates an intimidating, threatening or abusive educational environment for a student.

An act of harassment, intimidation or bullying may also be committed through the use of a land line, car phone or wireless telephone or through the use of data or computer software that is accessed through a computer, computer system, or computer network.

(3) A student who personally violates any provision of this section may be guilty of an infraction.

Attendance at Schools. Idaho Code Annotated § 33-205 (West 2006)

Idaho Code Annotated § 33-205

§ 33-205. Denial of school attendance

The superintendent of any district or the principal of any school may temporarily suspend any pupil for disciplinary reasons, including student harassment, intimidation or bullying, or for other conduct disruptive of good order or of the instructional effectiveness of the school. A temporary suspension by the principal shall not exceed five (5) school days in length; and the school superintendent may extend the temporary suspension an additional ten (10) school days. Provided, that on a finding by the board of trustees that immediate return to school attendance by the temporarily suspended student would be detrimental to other pupils' health, welfare or safety, the board of trustees may extend the temporary suspension for an additional five (5) school days. Prior to suspending any student, the superintendent or principal shall grant an informal hearing on the reasons for the suspension and the opportunity to challenge those reasons. Any pupil who has been suspended may be readmitted to the school by the superintendent or principal who suspended him upon such reasonable conditions as said superintendent or principal may prescribe. The board of trustees shall be notified of any temporary suspensions, the reasons therefor, and the response, if any, thereto.

The board of trustees of each school district shall establish the procedure to be followed by the superintendent and principals under its jurisdiction for the purpose of effecting a temporary suspension, which procedure must conform to the minimal requirements of due process.

ILLINOIS

Courses of Study—Special Instruction. 105 Illinois Compiled Statutes Annotated 5/27-13.3, et seq. (West 2009)

105 Illinois Compiled Statutes Annotated 5/27-13.3

5/27-13.3. Internet safety education curriculum

(a) The purpose of this Section is to inform and protect students from inappropriate or illegal communications and solicitation and to encourage school districts to provide education about Internet threats and risks, including without limitation child predators, fraud, and other dangers.
(b) The General Assembly finds and declares the following:
   (1) it is the policy of this State to protect consumers and Illinois residents from deceptive and unsafe communications that result in harassment, exploitation, or physical harm;
   (2) children have easy access to the Internet at home, school, and public places;
   (3) the Internet is used by sexual predators and other criminals to make initial contact with children and other vulnerable residents in Illinois; and
   (4) education is an effective method for preventing children from falling prey to online predators, identity theft, and other dangers.
(c) Each school may adopt an age-appropriate curriculum for Internet safety instruction of students in grades kindergarten through 12. However, beginning with the 2009-2010 school year, a school district must incorporate into the school curriculum a component on Internet safety to be taught at least once each school year to students in grades 3 through 12. The school board shall determine

the scope and duration of this unit of instruction. The age-appropriate unit of instruction may be incorporated into the current courses of study regularly taught in the district's schools, as determined by the school board, and it is recommended that the unit of instruction include the following topics:
: (1) Safe and responsible use of social networking websites, chat rooms, electronic mail, bulletin boards, instant messaging, and other means of communication on the Internet.
: (2) Recognizing, avoiding, and reporting online solicitations of students, their classmates, and their friends by sexual predators.
: (3) Risks of transmitting personal information on the Internet.
: (4) Recognizing and avoiding unsolicited or deceptive communications received online.
: (5) Recognizing and reporting online harassment and cyber-bullying.
: (6) Reporting illegal activities and communications on the Internet.
: (7) Copyright laws on written materials, photographs, music, and video.

(d) Curricula devised in accordance with subsection (c) of this Section may be submitted for review to the Office of the Illinois Attorney General.

(e) The State Board of Education shall make available resource materials for educating children regarding child online safety and may take into consideration the curriculum on this subject developed by other states, as well as any other curricular materials suggested by education experts, child psychologists, or technology companies that work on child online safety issues. Materials may include without limitation safe online communications, privacy protection, cyber-bullying, viewing inappropriate material, file sharing, and the importance of open communication with responsible adults. The State Board of Education shall make these resource materials available on its Internet website.

105 Illinois Compiled Statutes Annotated 5/27-23.7

5/27-23.7. Bullying prevention

(a) The General Assembly finds that a safe and civil school environment is necessary for students to learn and achieve and that bullying causes physical, psychological, and emotional harm to students and interferes with students' ability to learn and participate in school activities. The General Assembly further finds that bullying has been linked to other forms of antisocial behavior, such as vandalism, shoplifting, skipping and dropping out of school, fighting, using drugs and alcohol, sexual harassment, and sexual violence. Because of the negative outcomes associated with bullying in schools, the General Assembly finds that school districts and non-public, non-sectarian elementary and secondary schools should educate students, parents, and school district or non-public, non-sectarian elementary or secondary school personnel about what behaviors constitute prohibited bullying.

Bullying on the basis of actual or perceived race, color, religion, sex, national origin, ancestry, age, marital status, physical or mental disability, military status, sexual orientation, gender-related identity or expression, unfavorable discharge from military service, association with a person or group with one or more of the aforementioned actual or perceived characteristics, or any other distinguishing characteristic is prohibited in all school districts and non-public, non-sectarian elementary and secondary schools. No student shall be subjected to bullying:

(1) during any school-sponsored education program or activity;
(2) while in school, on school property, on school buses or other school vehicles, at designated school bus stops waiting for the school bus, or at school-sponsored or school-sanctioned events or activities; or
(3) through the transmission of information from a school computer, a school computer network, or other similar electronic school equipment.
    (b)   In this Section:

"Bullying" means any severe or pervasive physical or verbal act or conduct, including communications made in writing or electronically, directed toward a student or students that has or can be reasonably predicted to have the effect of one or more of the following:

(1) placing the student or students in reasonable fear of harm to the student's or students' person or property;
(2) causing a substantially detrimental effect on the student's or students' physical or mental health;
(3) substantially interfering with the student's or students' academic performance; or
(4) substantially interfering with the student's or students' ability to participate in or benefit from the services, activities, or privileges provided by a school.

Bullying, as defined in this subsection (b), may take various forms, including without limitation one or more of the following: harassment, threats, intimidation, stalking, physical violence, sexual harassment, sexual violence, theft, public humiliation, destruction of property, or retaliation for asserting or alleging an act of bullying. This list is meant to be illustrative and non-exhaustive.

(d) Each school district and non-public, non-sectarian elementary or secondary school shall create and maintain a policy on bullying, which policy must be filed with the State Board of Education. Each school district and non-public, non-sectarian elementary or secondary school must communicate its policy on bullying to its students and their parent or guardian on an annual basis. The policy must be updated every 2 years and filed with the State Board of Education after being updated. The State Board of Education shall monitor the implementation of policies created under this subsection (d).
(e) This Section shall not be interpreted to prevent a victim from seeking redress under any other available civil or criminal law. Nothing in this Section is intended to infringe upon any right to exercise free expression or the free exercise of religion or religiously based views protected under the First Amendment to the United States Constitution or under Section 3 or 4 of Article 1 of the Illinois Constitution.

INDIANA

Student Discipline. Indiana Code 20-33-8-0.2, et seq. (West 2013)

Indiana Code 20-33-8-0.2

20-33-8-0.2 "Bullying" defined

Sec. 0.2. (a) As used in this chapter, "bullying" means overt, unwanted, repeated acts or gestures, including verbal or written communications or images transmitted in any manner (including digitally or electronically), physical acts committed, aggression, or any other behaviors, that are committed by a student or group of students against another student with the intent to harass, ridicule, humiliate, intimidate, or harm the targeted student and create for the targeted student an objectively hostile school environment that:

(1) places the targeted student in reasonable fear of harm to the targeted student's person or property;
(2) has a substantially detrimental effect on the targeted student's physical or mental health;
(3) has the effect of substantially interfering with the targeted student's academic performance; or
(4) has the effect of substantially interfering with the targeted student's ability to participate in or benefit from the services, activities, and privileges provided by the school.
   (b) The term may not be interpreted to impose any burden or sanction on, or include in the definition of the term, the following:
   (1) Participating in a religious event.
   (2) Acting in an emergency involving the protection of a person or property from an imminent threat of serious bodily injury or substantial danger.
   (3) Participating in an activity consisting of the exercise of a student's rights protected under the First Amendment to the United States Constitution or Article I, Section 31 of the Constitution of the State of Indiana, or both.
   (4) Participating in an activity conducted by a nonprofit or governmental entity that provides recreation, education, training, or other care under the supervision of one (1) or more adults.
   (5) Participating in an activity undertaken at the prior written direction of the student's parent.
   (6) Engaging in interstate or international travel from a location outside Indiana to another location outside Indiana.

Indiana Code 20-33-8-13.5

20-33-8-13.5 Adoption and application of rules to prohibit bullying, including bullying by use of a computer

Sec. 13.5. (a) Discipline rules adopted by the governing body of a school corporation under section 12 of this chapter must:

(1) prohibit bullying; and
(2) include:

(A) provisions concerning education, parental involvement, and intervention;
(B) a detailed procedure for the expedited investigation of incidents of bullying that includes:
  (i) appropriate responses to bullying behaviors, wherever the behaviors occur;
  (ii) provisions for anonymous and personal reporting of bullying to a teacher or other school staff;
  (iii) timetables for reporting of bullying incidents to the parents of both the targeted student and the bully, in an expedited manner;
  (iv) timetables for reporting of bullying incidents to school counselors, school administrators, the superintendent, or law enforcement, if it is determined that reporting the bullying incident to law enforcement is necessary;
  (v) discipline provisions for teachers, school staff, or school administrators who fail to initiate or conduct an investigation of a bullying incident; and
  (vi) discipline provisions for false reporting of bullying; and
(C) a detailed procedure outlining the use of follow-up services that includes:
  (i) support services for the victim; and
  (ii) bullying education for the bully.
(b) The discipline rules described in subsection (a) may be applied regardless of the physical location in which the bullying behavior occurred, whenever:
  (1) the individual committing the bullying behavior and any of the intended targets of the bullying behavior are students attending a school within a school corporation; and
  (2) disciplinary action is reasonably necessary to avoid substantial interference with school discipline or prevent an unreasonable threat to the rights of others to a safe and peaceful learning environment.
(c) The discipline rules described in subsection (a) must prohibit bullying through the use of data or computer software that is accessed through a:
  (1) computer;
  (2) computer system; or
  (3) computer network.
(d) This section may not be construed to give rise to a cause of action against a person or school corporation based on an allegation of noncompliance with this section. Noncompliance with this section may not be used as evidence against a school corporation in a cause of action.
(e) A record made of an investigation, a disciplinary action, or a follow-up action performed under rules adopted under this section is not a public record under [Indiana Code] 5-14-3.
(f) The department shall periodically review each policy adopted under this section to ensure the policy's compliance with this section.

Mandatory Curriculum. Indiana Code 20-30-5-5.5 (West 2013)

Indiana Code 20-30-5-5.5

20-30-5-5.5 Instruction on bullying prevention

Sec. 5.5. (a) Not later than October 15 of each year, each public school shall provide age appropriate, research based instruction as provided under [Indiana Code] 5-2-10.1-12(d)(1) focusing on bullying prevention for all students in grades 1 through 12.

(b) The department, in consultation with school safety specialists and school counselors, shall prepare outlines or materials for the instruction described in subsection (a) and incorporate the instruction in grades 1 through 12.

(c) Instruction on bullying prevention may be delivered by a school safety specialist, school counselor, or any other person with training and expertise in the area of bullying prevention and intervention.

Student Safety Reporting. Indiana Code 20-34-6-1 (West 2014)

Indiana Code 20-34-6-1

20-34-6-1 Submittal of reports to department and legislative council; deadlines; contents

Sec. 1. (a) By July 1 of each year, each school corporation shall submit a report to the department detailing the following information for the current school year for each school in the school corporation and for the entire school corporation: ...

(8) The number of reported bullying incidents involving a student of the school corporation by category. However, nothing in this subdivision may be construed to require all bullying incidents to be reported to a law enforcement agency.

(b) By August 1 of each year, the department shall submit a report to:
(1) the legislative council;
(2) the education roundtable established by [Indiana Code] 20-19-4-2;
(3) the board for the coordination of programs serving vulnerable individuals established by [Indiana Code] 4-23-30.2-8; and
(4) the criminal justice institute;
(5) providing a summary of the reports submitted to the department under subsection (a). The report to the legislative council must be in an electronic format under [Indiana Code] 5-14-6.

(c) By August 1 of each year, the department must post the reports described in subsections (a) and (b) on the department's Internet web site.

Indiana Safe Schools Fund. Indiana Code 5-2-10.1-2 (West 2013)

Indiana Code 5-2-10.1-2

5-2-10.1-2 Purpose and composition of fund; grant priorities and amounts

Sec. 2. (a) The Indiana safe schools fund is established to do the following: ...

(5) Provide educational outreach and training to school personnel concerning:
(A) the identification of;
(B) the prevention of; and
(C) intervention in;

bullying.

IOWA

Uniform School Requirements: Harassment and bullying.
Iowa Code Annotated § 280.28 (West 2007)

Iowa Code Annotated § 280.28

§ 280.28. Harassment and bullying prohibited--policy--immunity

1. **Purpose--findings--policy.** The state of Iowa is committed to providing all students with a safe and civil school environment in which all members of the school community are treated with dignity and respect. The general assembly finds that a safe and civil school environment is necessary for students to learn and achieve at high academic levels. Harassing and bullying behavior can seriously disrupt the ability of school employees to maintain a safe and civil environment, and the ability of students to learn and succeed. Therefore, it is the policy of the state of Iowa that school employees, volunteers, and students in Iowa schools shall not engage in harassing or bullying behavior.
2. **Definitions.** For purposes of this section, unless the context otherwise requires:
    a. "Electronic" means any communication involving the transmission of information by wire, radio, optical cable, electromagnetic, or other similar means. "Electronic" includes but is not limited to communication via electronic mail, internet-based communications, pager service, cell phones, and electronic text messaging.
    b. "Harassment" and "bullying" shall be construed to mean any electronic, written, verbal, or physical act or conduct toward a student which is based on any actual or perceived trait or characteristic of the student and which creates an objectively hostile school environment that meets one or more of the following conditions:
    (1) Places the student in reasonable fear of harm to the student's person or property.
    (2) Has a substantially detrimental effect on the student's physical or mental health.
    (3) Has the effect of substantially interfering with a student's academic performance.
    (4) Has the effect of substantially interfering with the student's ability to participate in or benefit from the services, activities, or privileges provided by a school.
    c. "Trait or characteristic of the student" includes but is not limited to age, color, creed, national origin, race, religion, marital status, sex, sexual orientation, gender identity, physical attributes, physical or mental ability or disability, ancestry, political party preference, political belief, socioeconomic status, or familial status.
3. **Policy.** On or before September 1, 2007, the board of directors of a school district and the authorities in charge of each accredited nonpublic school shall adopt a policy declaring harassment and bullying in schools, on school property, and at any school function, or school-sponsored activity regardless of its location, in a manner consistent with this section, as against state and school policy. The board and the authorities shall make a copy of the policy available to all school employees, volunteers, students, and parents or guardians and shall take all appropriate steps to bring the policy against harassment and bullying and the responsibilities set forth in the policy to the attention of school employees, volunteers, students, and parents or guardians. Each policy shall, at a minimum, include all of the following components:

a. A statement declaring harassment and bullying to be against state and school policy. The statement shall include but not be limited to the following provisions:
   (1) School employees, volunteers, and students in school, on school property, or at any school function or school-sponsored activity shall not engage in harassing and bullying behavior.
   (2) School employees, volunteers, and students shall not engage in reprisal, retaliation, or false accusation against a victim, witness, or an individual who has reliable information about such an act of harassment or bullying.
b. A definition of harassment and bullying as set forth in this section.
c. A description of the type of behavior expected from school employees, volunteers, parents or guardians, and students relative to prevention measures, reporting, and investigation of harassment or bullying.
d. The consequences and appropriate remedial action for a person who violates the antiharassment and antibullying policy.
e. A procedure for reporting an act of harassment or bullying, including the identification by job title of the school official responsible for ensuring that the policy is implemented, and the identification of the person or persons responsible for receiving reports of harassment or bullying.
f. A procedure for the prompt investigation of complaints, either identifying the school superintendent or the superintendent's designee as the individual responsible for conducting the investigation, including a statement that investigators will consider the totality of circumstances presented in determining whether conduct objectively constitutes harassment or bullying under this section.
g. A statement of the manner in which the policy will be publicized.

4. **Programs encouraged.** The board of directors of a school district and the authorities in charge of each accredited nonpublic school are encouraged to establish programs designed to eliminate harassment and bullying in schools. To the extent that funds are available for these purposes, school districts and accredited nonpublic schools shall do the following:
   a. Provide training on antiharassment and antibullying policies to school employees and volunteers who have significant contact with students.
   b. Develop a process to provide school employees, volunteers, and students with the skills and knowledge to help reduce incidents of harassment and bullying.

5. **Immunity.** A school employee, volunteer, or student, or a student's parent or guardian who promptly, reasonably, and in good faith reports an incident of harassment or bullying, in compliance with the procedures in the policy adopted pursuant to this section, to the appropriate school official designated by the school district or accredited nonpublic school, shall be immune from civil or criminal liability relating to such report and to participation in any administrative or judicial proceeding resulting from or relating to the report.

6. **Collection requirement.** The board of directors of a school district and the authorities in charge of each nonpublic school shall develop and maintain a system to collect harassment and bullying incidence data.

7. **Integration of policy and reporting.** The board of directors of a school district and the authorities in charge of each nonpublic school shall integrate its antiharassment and antibullying policy into

the comprehensive school improvement plan required under section 256.7, subsection 21, and shall report data collected under subsection 6, as specified by the department, to the local community.
8. **Existing remedies not affected.** This section shall not be construed to preclude a victim from seeking administrative or legal remedies under any applicable provision of law.

Administration of Schools. Iowa Administrative Code 281-12.3(256) (West 2014)

Iowa Administrative Code 281-12.3(256)

281-12.3(256) Administration

12.3(13) *Policy declaring harassment and bullying against state and school policy.* The policy adopted by the [local school] board regarding harassment of or by students and staff shall declare harassment and bullying in schools, on school property, and at any school function or school-sponsored activity regardless of its location to be against state and school policy. The board shall make a copy of the policy available to all school employees, volunteers, students, and parents or guardians and shall take all appropriate steps to bring the policy against harassment and bullying and the responsibilities set forth in the policy to the attention of school employees, volunteers, students, and parents or guardians. Each policy shall, at a minimum, include all of the following components:

a. A statement declaring harassment and bullying to be against state and school policy. The statement shall include but not be limited to the following provisions:
   (1) School employees, volunteers, and students in school, on school property, or at any school function or school-sponsored activity shall not engage in harassing and bullying behavior.
   (2) School employees, volunteers, and students shall not engage in reprisal, retaliation, or false accusation against a victim, a witness, or an individual who has reliable information about such an act of harassment or bullying.

b. A definition of harassment and bullying consistent with the following: Harassment and bullying shall be construed to mean any electronic, written, verbal, or physical act or conduct toward a student which is based on the student's actual or perceived age, color, creed, national origin, race, religion, marital status, sex, sexual orientation, gender identity, physical attributes, physical or mental ability or disability, ancestry, political party preference, political belief, socioeconomic status, or familial status, and which creates an objectively hostile school environment that meets one or more of the following conditions:
   (1) Places the student in reasonable fear of harm to the student's person or property.
   (2) Has a substantially detrimental effect on the student's physical or mental health.
   (3) Has the effect of substantially interfering with a student's academic performance.
   (4) Has the effect of substantially interfering with the student's ability to participate in or benefit from the services, activities, or privileges provided by a school.

The local board policy must set forth all 17 of the above-enumerated traits or characteristics, but does not need to be limited to the 17 enumerated traits or characteristics.

c. A description of the type of behavior expected from school employees, volunteers, parents or guardians, and students relative to prevention, reporting, and investigation of harassment or bullying.
d. The consequences and appropriate remedial action for a person who violates the antiharassment and antibullying policy.
e. A procedure for reporting an act of harassment or bullying, including the identification by job title of the school official responsible for ensuring that the policy is implemented, and the identification of the person or persons responsible for receiving reports of harassment or bullying.
f. A procedure for the prompt investigation of complaints, identifying either the school superintendent or the superintendent's designee as the individual responsible for conducting the investigation, including a statement that investigators will consider the totality of circumstances presented in determining whether conduct objectively constitutes harassment or bullying under this subrule.
g. A statement of the manner in which the policy will be publicized.

The board shall integrate its policy into its comprehensive school improvement plan. The board shall develop and maintain a system to collect harassment and bullying incidence data, and report such data, on forms specified by the department [of education], to the local community and to the department.

Crime Control and Criminal Acts. Iowa Code Annotated § 708.7 (West 2009)

Iowa Code Annotated § 708.7

708.7. Harassment

1.a. A person commits harassment when, with intent to intimidate, annoy, or alarm another person, the person does any of the following:
  (1) Communicates with another by telephone, telegraph, writing, or via electronic communication without legitimate purpose and in a manner likely to cause the other person annoyance or harm.
  (2) Places a simulated explosive or simulated incendiary device in or near a building, vehicle, airplane, railroad engine or railroad car, or boat occupied by another person.
  (3) Orders merchandise or services in the name of another, or to be delivered to another, without the other person's knowledge or consent.
  (4) Reports or causes to be reported false information to a law enforcement authority implicating another in some criminal activity, knowing that the information is false, or reports the alleged occurrence of a criminal act, knowing the act did not occur.
    b. A person commits harassment when the person, purposefully and without legitimate purpose, has personal contact with another person, with the intent to threaten, intimidate, or alarm that other person. As used in this section, unless the context otherwise requires, "personal contact" means an encounter in which two or more people are in visual or physical proximity to each other. "Personal contact" does not require a physical touching or oral communication, although it may include these types of contacts.

2. a. A person commits harassment in the first degree when the person commits harassment involving a threat to commit a forcible felony, or commits harassment and has previously been convicted of harassment three or more times under this section or any similar statute during the preceding ten years.
   b. Harassment in the first degree is an aggravated misdemeanor.
3. a. A person commits harassment in the second degree when the person commits harassment involving a threat to commit bodily injury, or commits harassment and has previously been convicted of harassment two times under this section or any similar statute during the preceding ten years.
   b. Harassment in the second degree is a serious misdemeanor.
4. a. Any other act of harassment is harassment in the third degree.
   b. Harassment in the third degree is a simple misdemeanor.
5. For purposes of determining whether or not the person should register as a sex offender pursuant to the provisions of chapter 692A, the fact finder shall make a determination as provided in section 692A.126.

KANSAS

Bullying Policies. Kansas Statutes Annotated 72-8256 (West 2007)

Kansas Statutes Annotated 72-8256

72-8256. Bullying, school district policies

(a) As used in this section:

(1) "Bullying" means:
   (A) Any intentional gesture or any intentional written, verbal, electronic or physical act or threat either by any student, staff member or parent towards a student or by any student, staff member or parent towards a staff member that is sufficiently severe, persistent or pervasive that such gesture, act or threat creates an intimidating, threatening or abusive educational environment that a reasonable person, under the circumstances, knows or should know will have the effect of:
      (i)   Harming a student or staff member, whether physically or mentally;
      (ii) damaging a student's or staff member's property;
      (iii) placing a student or staff member in reasonable fear of harm to the student or staff member; or
      (iv) placing a student or staff member in reasonable fear of damage to the student's or staff member's property;
   (B) cyberbullying; or
   (C) any other form of intimidation or harassment prohibited by the board of education of the school district in policies concerning bullying adopted pursuant to this section or subsection (e) of [Kansas Statutes Annotated] 72-8205, and amendments thereto.

(2) "Cyberbullying" means bullying by use of any electronic communication device through means including, but not limited to, e-mail, instant messaging, text messages, blogs, mobile phones, pagers, online games and websites.

(b) The board of education of each school district shall adopt a policy to prohibit bullying either by any student, staff member or parent towards a student or by a student, staff member or parent towards a staff member on or while utilizing school property, in a school vehicle or at a school-sponsored activity or event.

(c) The board of education of each school district shall adopt and implement a plan to address bullying either by any student, staff member or parent towards a student or by a student, staff member or parent towards a staff member on school property, in a school vehicle or at a school-sponsored activity or event. Such plan shall include provisions for the training and education for staff members and students.

(d) The board of education of each school district may adopt additional policies relating to bullying pursuant to subsection (e) of [Kansas Statutes Annotated] 72-8205, and amendments thereto.

(e) Nothing in this section shall be construed to limit or supersede or in any manner affect or diminish the requirements of compliance by a staff member with the provisions of [Kansas Statutes Annotated] 38-2223 or 38-2226, and amendments thereto.

KENTUCKY

Conduct of Schools. Kentucky Revised Statutes Annotated § 158.148 (West 2014)

Kentucky Revised Statutes Annotated § 158.148

§ 158.148 Student discipline guidelines and model policy; local code of acceptable behavior

(1) In cooperation with the Kentucky Education Association, the Kentucky School Boards Association, the Kentucky Association of School Administrators, the Kentucky Association of Professional Educators, the Kentucky Association of School Superintendents, the Parent-Teachers Association, the Kentucky Chamber of Commerce, the Farm Bureau, members of the Interim Joint Committee on Education, and other interested groups, and in collaboration with the Center for School Safety, the Department of Education shall develop or update as needed and distribute to all districts by August 31 of each even-numbered year, beginning August 31, 2008:

    a) Statewide student discipline guidelines to ensure safe schools, including the definition of serious incident for the reporting purposes as identified in [Kentucky Revised Statutes Annotated] 158.444;

    b) Recommendations designed to improve the learning environment and school climate, parental and community involvement in the schools, and student achievement; and

    c) A model policy to implement the provisions of this section and [Kentucky Revised Statutes Annotated] 158.156, 158.444, 525.070, and 525.080.

2) The department shall obtain statewide data on major discipline problems and reasons why students drop out of school. In addition, the department, in collaboration with the Center for School Safety, shall identify successful strategies currently being used in programs in Kentucky and in other states and shall incorporate those strategies into the statewide guidelines and the recommendations under subsection (1) of this section.

3) Copies of the discipline guidelines shall be distributed to all school districts. The statewide guidelines shall contain broad principles and legal requirements to guide local districts in developing their own discipline code and school councils in the selection of discipline and classroom management techniques under [Kentucky Revised Statutes Annotated] 158.154; and in the development of the district-wide safety plan.

4) Each local board of education shall be responsible for formulating a code of acceptable behavior and discipline to apply to the students in each school operated by the board. The code shall be updated no less frequently than every two (2) years, with the first update being completed by November 30, 2008.

a) The superintendent, or designee, shall be responsible for overall implementation and supervision, and each school principal shall be responsible for administration and implementation within each school. Each school council shall select and implement the appropriate discipline and classroom management techniques necessary to carry out the code. The board shall establish a process for a two-way communication system for teachers and other employees to notify a principal, supervisor, or other administrator of an existing emergency.

b) The code shall contain the type of behavior expected from each student, the consequences of failure to obey the standards, and the importance of the standards to the maintenance of a safe learning environment where orderly learning is possible and encouraged.

c) The code shall contain:
  1. Procedures for identifying, documenting, and reporting incidents of violations of the code and incidents for which reporting is required under [Kentucky Revised Statutes Annotated] 158.156;
  2. Procedures for investigating and responding to a complaint or a report of a violation of the code or of an incident for which reporting is required under [Kentucky Revised Statutes Annotated] 158.156, including reporting incidents to the parents, legal guardians, or other persons exercising custodial control or supervision of the students involved;
  3. A strategy or method of protecting from retaliation a complainant or person reporting a violation of the code or an incident for which reporting is required under [Kentucky Revised Statutes Annotated] 158.156;
  4. A process for informing students, parents, legal guardians, or other persons exercising custodial control or supervision, and school employees of the requirements of the code and the provisions of this section and [Kentucky Revised Statutes Annotated] 158.156, 158.444, 525.070, and 525.080, including training for school employees; and
  5. Information regarding the consequences of violating the code and violations reportable under [Kentucky Revised Statutes Annotated] 158.154, 158.156, or 158.444.

d) The principal of each school shall apply the code of behavior and discipline uniformly and fairly to each student at the school without partiality or discrimination.

e) A copy of the code of behavior and discipline adopted by the board of education shall be posted at each school. Guidance counselors shall be provided copies for discussion with students. The code shall be referenced in all school handbooks. All school employees and parents, legal guardians, or other persons exercising custodial control or supervision shall be provided copies of the code.

Kentucky Revised Statutes Annotated § 158.154

§ 158.154 Principal's duty to report certain acts to local law enforcement agency

When the principal has a reasonable belief that an act has occurred on school property or at a school-sponsored function involving assault resulting in serious physical injury, a sexual offense, kidnapping, assault involving the use of a weapon, possession of a firearm in violation of the law, possession of a controlled substance in violation of the law, or damage to the property, the principal shall immediately report the act to the appropriate local law enforcement agency. For purposes of this section, "school property" means any public school building, bus, public school campus, grounds, recreational area, or athletic field, in the charge of the principal.

Kentucky Revised Statutes Annotated § 158.156

§ 158.156 Reporting of commission of felony [Kentucky Revised Statutes Annotated] Chapter 508 offense against a student; investigation; immunity from liability for reporting; privileges no bar to reporting

1) Any employee of a school or a local board of education who knows or has reasonable cause to believe that a school student has been the victim of a violation of any felony offense specified in [Kentucky Revised Statutes Annotated] Chapter 508 committed by another student while on school premises, on school-sponsored transportation, or at a school-sponsored event shall immediately cause an oral or written report to be made to the principal of the school attended by the victim. The principal shall notify the parents, legal guardians, or other persons exercising custodial control or supervision of the student when the student is involved in an incident reportable under this section. The principal shall file with the local school board and the local law enforcement agency or the Department of Kentucky State Police or the county attorney within forty-eight (48) hours of the original report a written report containing:
a) The names and addresses of the student and his or her parents, legal guardians, or other persons exercising custodial control or supervision;
b) The student's age;
c) The nature and extent of the violation;
d) The name and address of the student allegedly responsible for the violation; and
e) Any other information that the principal making the report believes may be helpful in the furtherance of the purpose of this section.

2) An agency receiving a report under subsection (1) of this section shall investigate the matter referred to it. The school board and school personnel shall participate in the investigation at the request of the agency.

3) Anyone acting upon reasonable cause in the making of a report required under this section in good faith shall have immunity from any liability, civil or criminal, that might otherwise be incurred or imposed. Any such participant shall have the same immunity with respect to participation in any judicial proceeding resulting from such report or action.

4) Neither the husband-wife nor any professional-client/patient privilege, except the attorney-client and clergy-penitent privilege, shall be a ground for refusing to report under this section or for excluding evidence regarding student harassment in any judicial proceedings resulting from a report pursuant to this section. This subsection shall also apply in any criminal proceeding in District or Circuit Court regarding student harassment.

School Safety and School Discipline. Kentucky Revised Statutes Annotated § 158.444 (West 2008)

Kentucky Revised Statutes Annotated § 158.444

§ 158.444 Administrative regulations relating to school safety; role of Department of Education to maintain statewide data collection system; reportable incidents; annual statistical reports; confidentiality

2) The Kentucky Department of Education shall:
   a) Collaborate with the Center for School Safety in carrying out the center's mission;
   b) Establish and maintain a statewide data collection system by which school districts shall report by sex, race, and grade level:
      1. a. All incidents of violence and assault against school employees and students; …
      d. All incidents in which a student has been disciplined by the school for a serious incident, including the nature of the discipline, or charged criminally for conduct constituting a violation of any offense specified in [Kentucky Revised Statutes Annotated] Chapter 508; [Kentucky Revised Statutes Annotated] 525.070 occurring on school premises, on school-sponsored transportation, or at school functions; or [Kentucky Revised Statutes Annotated] 525.080;
      3. The number of suspensions, expulsions, and corporal punishments; and
      4. Data required during the assessment process under [Kentucky Revised Statutes Annotated] 158.445; and
   c) Provide all data collected relating to this subsection to the Center for School Safety according to timelines established by the center.

Riot, Disorderly Conduct, and Related Offenses. Kentucky Revised Statutes Annotated § 525.070, et seq. (West 2008)

Kentucky Revised Statutes Annotated § 525.070.

§ 525.070 Harassment

1) A person is guilty of harassment when, with intent to intimidate, harass, annoy, or alarm another person, he or she:
   a) Strikes, shoves, kicks, or otherwise subjects him to physical contact;
   b) Attempts or threatens to strike, shove, kick, or otherwise subject the person to physical contact;
   c) In a public place, makes an offensively coarse utterance, gesture, or display, or addresses abusive language to any person present;
   d) Follows a person in or about a public place or places;
   e) Engages in a course of conduct or repeatedly commits acts which alarm or seriously annoy such other person and which serve no legitimate purpose; or
   f) Being enrolled as a student in a local school district, and while on school premises, on school-sponsored transportation, or at a school-sponsored event:
      1. Damages or commits a theft of the property of another student;
      2. Substantially disrupts the operation of the school; or
      3. Creates a hostile environment by means of any gestures, written communications, oral statements, or physical acts that a reasonable person under the circumstances should know would cause another student to suffer fear of physical harm, intimidation, humiliation, or embarrassment.
   (a) Except as provided in paragraph (b) of this subsection, harassment is a violation.
   (b) Harassment, as defined in paragraph (a) of subsection (1) of this section, is a Class B misdemeanor.

Kentucky Revised Statutes Annotated § 525.080

§ 525.080 Harassing communications

1) A person is guilty of harassing communications when, with intent to intimidate, harass, annoy, or alarm another person, he or she:
   a) Communicates with a person, anonymously or otherwise, by telephone, telegraph, mail, or any other form of written communication in a manner which causes annoyance or alarm and serves no purpose of legitimate communication;
   b) Makes a telephone call, whether or not conversation ensues, with no purpose of legitimate communication; or
   c) Communicates, while enrolled as a student in a local school district, with or about another school student, anonymously or otherwise, by telephone, the Internet, telegraph, mail, or any other form of electronic or written communication in a manner which a reasonable person

under the circumstances should know would cause the other student to suffer fear of physical harm, intimidation, humiliation, or embarrassment and which serves no purpose of legitimate communication.

2) Harassing communications is a Class B misdemeanor.

LOUISIANA

Student Code of Conduct and Bullying. Louisiana Statutes Annotated-Revised Statutes § 17:416.13 (West 2013)

Louisiana Statutes Annotated-Revised Statutes § 416.13

§ 416.13. Student code of conduct; requirement; bullying; prohibition; notice; reporting; accountability

B. Bullying Policy. (1) The governing authority of each public elementary and secondary school shall adopt, and incorporate into the student code of conduct, a policy prohibiting the bullying of a student by another student, which includes the definition of bullying as provided in Subsection C of this Section. This policy must be implemented in a manner that is ongoing throughout the school year and integrated with a school's curriculum, a school's discipline policies, and other violence prevention efforts.

(2) The governing authority of each public elementary and secondary school shall:
   (a) Conduct a review of the student code of conduct required by this Section and amend the code as may be necessary to assure that the policy prohibiting the bullying of a student by another student specifically addresses the behavior constituting bullying, the effect the behavior has on others, including bystanders, and the disciplinary and criminal consequences, and includes the definition of bullying as provided in Subsection C of this Section.
   (b) Create a program to provide a minimum of four hours of training for new employees who have contact with students and two hours of training each year for all school employees who have contact with students, including bus drivers, with respect to bullying. The training shall specifically include the following:
      (i) How to recognize the behaviors defined as bullying in Subsection C of this Section.
      (ii) How to identify students at each grade level in the employee's school who are most likely to become victims of bullying, while not excluding any student from protection from bullying.
      (iii) How to use appropriate intervention and remediation techniques and procedures.
      (iv) The procedures by which incidents of bullying are to be reported to school officials.
      (v) Information on suicide prevention, including the relationship between suicide risk factors and bullying. This content shall be based on information supported by peer-reviewed research conducted in compliance with accepted scientific methods and recognized as accurate by leading professional organizations and agencies with relevant experience.

C. Definition of Bullying. "Bullying" means:

(1) A pattern of any one or more of the following:
    (a) Gestures, including but not limited to obscene gestures and making faces.
    (b) Written, electronic, or verbal communications, including but not limited to calling names, threatening harm, taunting, malicious teasing, or spreading untrue rumors. Electronic communication includes but is not limited to a communication or image transmitted by email, instant message, text message, blog, or social networking website through the use of a telephone, mobile phone, pager, computer, or other electronic device.
    (c) Physical acts, including but not limited to hitting, kicking, pushing, tripping, choking, damaging personal property, or unauthorized use of personal property.
    (d) Repeatedly and purposefully shunning or excluding from activities.

(2)(a) Where the pattern of behavior as provided in Paragraph (1) of this Subsection is exhibited toward a student, more than once, by another student or group of students and occurs, or is received by, a student while on school property, at a school-sponsored or school-related function or activity, in any school bus or van, at any designated school bus stop, in any other school or private vehicle used to transport students to and from schools, or any school-sponsored activity or event.

  (b) The pattern of behavior as provided in Paragraph (1) of this Subsection must have the effect of physically harming a student, placing the student in reasonable fear of physical harm, damaging a student's property, placing the student in reasonable fear of damage to the student's property, or must be sufficiently severe, persistent, and pervasive enough to either create an intimidating or threatening educational environment, have the effect of substantially interfering with a student's performance in school, or have the effect of substantially disrupting the orderly operation of the school.

D. The State Board of Elementary and Secondary Education, in collaboration with the state Department of Education, shall develop and adopt rules and regulations to implement the provisions of this Section relative to the procedures and processes to be used to report and investigate bullying and which shall include but not be limited to:

(1) **Notice to Students and Parents.** The governing authority of each public elementary and secondary school shall inform each student, orally and in writing at the orientation required under [Louisiana Statutes Annotated-Revised Statutes] 17:416.20, of the prohibition against bullying of a student by another student, the nature and consequences of such actions, including the potential criminal consequences and loss of driver's license as provided in [Louisiana Statutes Annotated-Revised Statutes] 17:416.1, and the proper process and procedure for reporting any incidents involving such prohibited actions. A copy of the written notice shall also be delivered to each student's parent or legal guardian.

(2) **Reporting. (a)** The governing authority of each public elementary and secondary school shall develop a procedure for the reporting of incidents of bullying. This shall include a form for the purposes of bullying reports. The form shall include an affirmation of truth of statement. Any bullying report submitted regardless of recipient shall use this form, but additional information may be provided. The form shall be available on the Department of Education's website.

(b) **Students and parents.** Any student who believes that he has been, or is currently, the victim of bullying, or any student, or any parent or guardian, who witnesses bullying or has good reason to believe bullying is taking place, may report the situation to a school official. A student, or parent or guardian, may also report concerns regarding bullying to a teacher, counselor, other school employee, or to any parent chaperoning or supervising a school function or activity. Any report of bullying shall remain confidential.

(c) **School personnel.** Any teacher, counselor, bus driver, or other school employee, whether full or part time, and any parent chaperoning or supervising a school function or activity, who witnesses bullying or who learns of bullying from a student pursuant to Subparagraph (b) of this Paragraph, shall report the incident to a school official. A verbal report shall be submitted by the school employee or the parent on the same day as the employee or parent witnessed or otherwise learned of the bullying incident and a written report shall be filed no later than two days thereafter.

(d) **Retaliation.** Retaliation against any person who reports bullying in good faith, who is thought to have reported bullying, who files a complaint, or who otherwise participates in an investigation or inquiry concerning allegations of bullying is prohibited conduct and subject to discipline. School and district resources shall not be used to prohibit or dissuade any person who meets the specifications of this Subparagraph.

(e) **False Reports.** Intentionally making false reports about bullying to school officials is prohibited conduct and will result in the appropriate disciplinary measures as determined by the governing authority of the school in accordance with the rules and regulations of the State Board of Elementary and Secondary Education.

(3) Investigation Procedure. The State Board of Elementary and Secondary Education shall develop and adopt a procedure for the investigation of reports of bullying of a student by another student. The procedure shall include the following:

(a) **Scope of investigation.** An investigation shall include an interview of the reporter, the victim, the alleged bully, and any witnesses, and shall include obtaining copies or photographs of any audio-visual evidence.

(b) **Timing.** The school shall begin an investigation of any complaint that is properly reported and that alleges conduct prohibited in this Section the next business day during which school is in session after the report is received by the school official. The investigation shall be completed not later than ten school days after the date the written report of the incident is submitted to the appropriate school official. If additional information is received after the end of the ten-day period, the school principal or his designee shall amend all documents and reports required by this Section to reflect such information.

(c) **Appeal.** (i) If the school official does not take timely and effective action pursuant to this Section, the student, parent, or school employee may report the bullying incident to the city, parish, or other local school board or local school governing authority. The school board or school governing authority shall begin an investigation of any complaint that is properly reported and that alleges conduct prohibited in this Section the next business day during which school is in session after the report is received by a school board or governing authority official.

(ii) If the school board does not take timely and effective action, the student, parent, or other school employee may report the bullying incident to the state Department of Education.

The department shall track the number of reports, shall notify in writing the superintendent and the president of the school's governing authority, and shall publish the number of reports by school district or governing authority on its website. The department shall provide both the number of actual reports received and the number of reports received by affected student.

(d) Parental Notification.
   (i) Upon receiving a report of bullying, the school official shall notify the student's parent or legal guardian according to the definition of notice created by the state Department of Education.
   (ii) Under no circumstances shall the delivery of the notice to the parent or legal guardian, which is required by this Subsection, be the responsibility of an involved student. Delivery of the notice by an involved student shall not constitute notice as is required pursuant to this Subsection.
   (iii) Before any student under the age of eighteen is interviewed, his parent or legal guardian shall be notified by the school official of the allegations made and shall have the opportunity to attend any interviews with his child conducted as part of the investigation. If, after three attempts in a forty-eight-hour period, the parents or legal guardians of a student cannot be reached or do not respond, the student may be interviewed.
   (iv) The State Board of Elementary and Secondary Education, in collaboration with the state Department of Education, shall develop a procedure for meetings with the parent or legal guardian of the victim and the parent or legal guardian of the alleged perpetrator. This procedure shall include:
   (aa) Separate meetings with the parents or legal guardians of the victim and the parents or legal guardians of the alleged perpetrator.
   (bb) Notification of parents or legal guardians of the victim and of the alleged perpetrator of the available potential consequences, penalties, and counseling options.
   (cc) In any case where a teacher, principal, or other school employee is authorized in this Section to require the parent or legal guardian of a student who is under the age of eighteen and not judicially emancipated or emancipated by marriage to attend a conference or meeting regarding the student's behavior and, after notice, the parent, tutor, or legal guardian willfully refuses to attend, that the principal or his designee shall file a complaint with a court exercising juvenile jurisdiction, pursuant to Children's Code Article 730(8) and 731. The principal may file a complaint pursuant to Children's Code Article 730(1) or any other applicable ground when, in his judgment, doing so is in the best interests of the student.

(e) **Disciplinary Action.** If the school has received a report of bullying, has determined that an act of bullying has occurred, and after meeting with the parent or legal guardian of the students involved, the school official shall:
   (i) Take prompt and appropriate disciplinary action, pursuant to [Louisiana Statutes Annotated-Revised Statutes] 17:416 and 416.1, against the student that the school official determines has engaged in conduct which constitutes bullying, if appropriate.
   (ii) Report criminal conduct to law enforcement, if appropriate.

(f) **Parental Relief.** (i) If a parent, legal guardian, teacher, or other school official has made four or more reports of separate instances of bullying, as provided in Paragraph (2) of this Subsection, and no investigation pursuant to Paragraph (3) of this Subsection has occurred, the parent or legal guardian with responsibility for decisions regarding the education of the victim about whom the report or reports have been made may exercise an option to have the student enroll in or attend another school operated by the governing authority of the public elementary or secondary school in which the student was enrolled on the dates when at least three of the reports were submitted.

(ii) The parent shall file a request with the superintendent for the transfer of the student to another school under the governing authority's jurisdiction.

(iii) The governing authority of the public elementary or secondary school in which the student is enrolled shall make a seat available at another public elementary or secondary school under its jurisdiction within ten school days of the parent or legal guardian's request for a transfer. If the governing authority has no other school under its jurisdiction serving the grade level of the victim, within fifteen school days of receiving the request, the superintendent or director of the governing authority shall:

(aa) Inform the student and his parent or legal guardian and facilitate the student's enrollment in a statewide virtual school.

(bb) Offer the student a placement in a full-time virtual program or virtual school under the jurisdiction of the school's governing authority.

(cc) Enter into a memorandum of understanding with the superintendent or director of another governing authority to secure a placement and provide for the transfer of the student to a school serving the grade level of the victim under the jurisdiction of the governing authority, pursuant to [Louisiana Statutes Annotated-Revised Statutes] 17:105 and 105.1.

(iv) If no seat or other placement pursuant to Item (iii) of this Subparagraph is made available within thirty calendar days of the receipt by the superintendent of the request, the parent or legal guardian may request a hearing with the school's governing authority, which shall be public or private at the option of the parent or legal guardian. The school's governing authority shall grant the hearing at the next scheduled meeting or within sixty calendar days, whichever is sooner.

(v) At the end of any school year, the parent or legal guardian may make a request to the governing authority of the school at which the student was enrolled when at least three of the reports were filed to transfer the student back to the school. The governing authority shall make a seat available at the school at which the student was originally enrolled. No other schools shall qualify for transfer under this Subparagraph.

(g) **Documentation.** (i) The state Department of Education shall develop a behavior incidence checklist that the governing authority of each public elementary and secondary school shall use to document the details of each reported incident of bullying.

(ii) The governing authority of each public elementary and secondary school shall report all such documented incidences of bullying to the state Department of Education as prescribed in rules adopted by the State Board of Elementary and Secondary Education in accordance with the Administrative Procedure Act and documented incidents in reports received by the local superintendent of schools pursuant to [Louisiana Statutes Annotated-Revised Statutes] 17:415.

(iii) After the investigation and meeting with the parents, pursuant to this Section, a school, local school board or other local school governing authority shall:

(aa) Compose a written document containing the findings of the investigation, including input from the students' parents or legal guardian, and the decision by the school or school system official. The document shall be placed in the school records of both students.

(bb) Promptly notify the complainant of the findings of the investigation and that remedial action has been taken, if such release of information does not violate the law.

(cc) Keep complaints and investigative reports confidential, except as provided in this Section and where disclosure is required to be made pursuant to 20 U.S.C. 1232g or by other applicable federal laws, rules, or regulations or by state law.

(dd) Maintain complaints and investigative reports for three years in the event that disclosure is warranted by law enforcement officials.

(ee) As applicable, provide a copy of any reports and investigative documents to the governing authority of the school in order that the governing authority can comply with the provisions of [Louisiana Statutes Annotated-Revised Statutes] 17:416.1.

(ff) As applicable, provide a copy of any reports and investigative documents to the state Department of Education. Upon receipt, the department shall remove any reports related to the investigative documents from notation on the department's website, but shall maintain a record of those reports for three years.

E. **Parental Responsibilities.** Nothing herein shall be deemed to interfere with the authority and the responsibility that a parent or legal guardian has for the student at all times, but particularly when the student is not on the school premises, is not engaged in a school-sponsored function or school-sponsored activity, and is not being transported by school-sponsored means of transportation.

F. This Section shall not be interpreted to conflict with or supercede the provisions requiring mandatory reporting pursuant to Louisiana Children's Code Article 609 and as enforced through [Louisiana Statutes Annotated-Revised Statutes] 14:403.

G. **Preclusion.** (1) This Section shall not be interpreted to prevent a victim of bullying, or his parent or legal guardian, from seeking redress under any other available law, either civil or criminal.

(2) Nothing in this Section is intended to infringe upon the right of a school employee or student to exercise their right of free speech.

H. **Construction; equal protection.** All students subject to the provisions of this Section shall be protected equally and without regard to the subject matter or the motivating animus of the bullying.

Student Discipline. Louisiana Statutes Annotated-Revised Statutes § 17:416 (West 2012)

Louisiana Statutes Annotated-Revised Statutes § 17:416

§ 416. Discipline of students; suspension; expulsion

(ii) In addition to those procedures set forth in [Louisiana Statutes Annotated-Revised Statutes] 17:416.13 regarding bullying, disciplinary action may include but is not limited to:

(aa) Oral or written reprimands.
(bb) Referral for a counseling session which shall include but shall not be limited to conflict resolution, social responsibility, family responsibility, peer mediation, and stress management.
(cc) Written notification to parents of disruptive or unacceptable behavior, a copy of which shall be provided to the principal.
(dd) Other disciplinary measures approved by the principal and faculty of the school and in compliance with school board policy.
(c)(i) When a student's behavior prevents the orderly instruction of other students or poses an immediate threat to the safety or physical well being of any student or teacher, when a student exhibits disrespectful behavior toward the teacher such as using foul or abusive language or gestures directed at or threatening a student or a teacher, when a student violates the school's code of conduct, or when a student exhibits other disruptive, dangerous, or unruly behavior, including inappropriate physical contact, inappropriate verbal conduct, sexual or other harassment, bullying, throwing objects, inciting other students to misbehave, or destroying property, the teacher may have the student immediately removed from his classroom and placed in the custody of the principal or his designee. A student removed from the classroom pursuant to this Subparagraph shall be assigned school work missed and shall receive either partial or full credit for such work if it is completed satisfactorily and timely as determined by the principal or his designee, upon the recommendation of the student's teacher; however, the teacher shall not be required to interrupt class instruction time to prepare any such assignment.
(ii)(aa) Upon being sent to the principal's office pursuant to the provisions of this Subparagraph, the principal or his designee shall advise the pupil of the particular misconduct of which he is accused as well as the basis for such accusation, and the pupil shall be given an opportunity at that time to explain his version of the facts. The principal or his designee then shall conduct a counseling session with the pupil as may be appropriate to establish a course of action, consistent with school board policy to identify and correct the behavior for which the pupil is being disciplined.
(bb) The principal or his designee shall provide oral or written notification to the parent or legal guardian of any pupil removed from the classroom pursuant to the provisions of this Subparagraph. Such notification shall include a description of any disciplinary action taken.
(cc) The principal or his designee may provide oral or written feedback to teachers initiating the removal of pupils from the classroom. The principal or his designee may provide to such teachers guidance and support on practicing effective classroom management including but not limited to positive behavior supports.
(dd) The principal or designee shall follow all procedures set forth in [Louisiana Statutes Annotated-Revised Statutes] 17:416.13 regarding bullying.

Offenses against the Person. Louisiana Statutes Annotated-Revised Statutes § 14:40.7 (West 2010)

Louisiana Statutes Annotated-Revised Statutes § 14:40.7

§ 14:40.7. Cyberbullying

A. Cyberbullying is the transmission of any electronic textual, visual, written, or oral communication with the malicious and willful intent to coerce, abuse, torment, or intimidate a person under the age of eighteen.
B. For purposes of this Section:
    (1) "Cable operator" means any person or group of persons who provides cable service over a cable system and directly, or through one or more affiliates, owns a significant interest in such cable system, or who otherwise controls or is responsible for, through any arrangement, the management and operation of such a cable system.
    (2) "Electronic textual, visual, written, or oral communication" means any communication of any kind made through the use of a computer online service, Internet service, or any other means of electronic communication, including but not limited to a local bulletin board service, Internet chat room, electronic mail, or online messaging service.
    (3) "Interactive computer service" means any information service, system, or access software provider that provides or enables computer access by multiple users to a computer server, including a service or system that provides access to the Internet and such systems operated or services offered by libraries or educational institutions.
    (4) "Telecommunications service" means the offering of telecommunications for a fee directly to the public, regardless of the facilities used.
C. An offense committed pursuant to the provisions of this Section may be deemed to have been committed where the communication was originally sent, originally received, or originally viewed by any person.
D. (1) Except as provided in Paragraph (2) of this Subsection, whoever commits the crime of cyberbullying shall be fined not more than five hundred dollars, imprisoned for not more than six months, or both.
    (2) When the offender is under the age of seventeen, the disposition of the matter shall be governed exclusively by the provisions of Title VII of the Children's Code.
E. The provisions of this Section shall not apply to a provider of an interactive computer service, provider of a telecommunications service, or a cable operator as defined by the provisions of this Section.
F. The provisions of this Section shall not be construed to prohibit or restrict religious free speech pursuant to Article I, Section 8 of the Constitution of Louisiana.

Student Discipline. Louisiana Administrative Code tit. 28, pt. CXV, § 1303 (West 2013)

Louisiana Administrative Code tit. 28, pt. CXV, § 1303

§ 1303. Bullying

A. Policy. Each LEA [local educational agency] shall develop and adopt a policy that prohibits the bullying of a student by another student.
   1. The bullying policy must be implemented in a manner that is ongoing throughout the year and integrated with a school's curriculum, a school's discipline policies, and other violence prevention efforts.
   2. The policy shall contain the definition of bullying found in this Section and shall address the following:
      a. behavior constituting bullying;
      b. the effect the behavior has on others, including bystanders; and
      c. the disciplinary and criminal consequences of bullying another student.
B. Training for School Personnel. Each LEA shall create a program to provide a minimum of four hours of training each year for new school employees who have contact with students, including bus drivers, with respect to bullying. The training shall be two hours each following year for all school employees who have contact with students and have received the four hour training. The training shall specifically include the following:
   1. how to recognize the behaviors defined as bullying;
   2. how to identify students at each grade level who are most likely to become victims of bullying, while not excluding any student from protection from bullying;
   3. how to use appropriate intervention and remediation techniques and procedures;
   4. the procedures by which incidents of bullying are to be reported to school officials; and
   5. information on suicide prevention, including the relationship between suicide risk factors and bullying.
C. Definition of Bullying
   1. *Bullying* is defined as a pattern of one or more of the following behaviors:
      a. gestures, including but not limited to obscene gestures and making faces;
      b. written, electronic, or verbal communications, including but not limited to calling names, threatening harm, taunting, malicious teasing, or spreading untrue rumors;
      c. physical acts, including but not limited to hitting, kicking, pushing, tripping, choking, damaging personal property, or unauthorized use of personal property; and
      d. repeatedly and purposefully shunning or excluding from activities.
   2. Behavior defined as bullying is exhibited toward a student, more than once, by another student or group of students and occurs, or is received by, a student while on school property, at a school-sponsored or school-related function or activity, in any school bus or van, at any designated school bus stop, in any other school or private vehicle used to transport students to and from schools, or any school-sponsored activity or event.

3. Bullying must have the effect of physically harming a student, placing the student in reasonable fear of physical harm, damaging a student's property, placing the student in reasonable fear of damage to the student's property, or must be sufficiently severe, persistent, and pervasive enough to either create an intimidating or threatening educational environment, have the effect of substantially interfering with a student's performance in school, or have the effect of substantially disrupting the orderly operation of the school.

D. Notice of Bullying Policy to students and parents. The LEA shall inform each student orally and in writing of the prohibition against the bullying of a student by another student, the nature and consequences of such actions, including the potential criminal consequences and loss of driver's license, and the proper process and procedure for reporting any incidents of bullying. A copy of the written notice shall also be delivered to each student's parent or legal guardian.

E. Reporting Incidents of Bullying. The LEA shall develop a procedure for the reporting of incidents of bullying using the bullying report form approved by BESE and available on the DOE website. The procedure shall include the following.
   1. Students and Parents
      a. Any student who believes that he or she is or has been the victim of bullying, or any student or parent or legal guardian, who witnesses bullying or has good reason to believe bullying is taking place, may report the bullying to a school official.
      b. A student, or parent or guardian, may also report concerns regarding bullying to a teacher, counselor, other school employee, or to any parent chaperoning or supervising a school function or activity.
      c. Any report of bullying shall remain confidential.
   2. School Personnel and Chaperones. Any teacher, counselor, bus driver, or other school employee, whether full or part time, and any parent chaperoning or supervising a school function or activity, who witnesses or who learns of bullying of a student, shall report the incident to a school official. A verbal report shall be submitted by the school employee or parent on the same day as the school employee or parent witnessed or otherwise learned of the bullying incident, and a written report must be filed no later than two days thereafter.
   3. Retaliation. Retaliation against any person who reports bullying in good faith, who is thought to have reported bullying, who files a complaint, or who otherwise participates in an investigation or inquiry concerning allegations of bullying is prohibited conduct and subject to disciplinary action.
   4. False Reports. Making false reports about bullying to school officials is prohibited conduct and will result in disciplinary action.

F. Investigation Procedure. When a report of the bullying of a student by another student is received, the school shall conduct an investigation using the following procedure.
   1. Timing. The investigation shall begin the next school day following the day on which the written report was received and shall be completed no later than 10 school days after receipt of the report. If additional information is received after the end of the 10-day period, the school official shall amend all documents and reports to reflect such information.
   2. Parental Notification of Allegation of Bullying
      a. Upon receiving a report of bullying, the school shall notify the parents or legal guardians of the alleged offender and the alleged victim no later than the following school day

b. Under no circumstances shall the delivery of this notice to the parent or legal guardian, be the responsibility of an involved student. Delivery of notice by an involved student shall not constitute notice as is required by this Section.

c. Before any student under the age of 18 is interviewed, his parents or legal guardians shall be notified of the allegations made and shall have the opportunity to attend any interviews conducted with their child as part of the investigation. If, after three attempts in a 48-hour period, the parents or legal guardians of a student cannot be reached or do not respond, the student may be interviewed.

d. All meetings with the parents or legal guardians of an alleged victim or an alleged offender shall be in compliance with the following:

i. separate meetings with the parents or legal guardians of the alleged victim and the alleged offender;

ii. parents or legal guardians of the alleged victim and alleged offender must be notified of the potential consequences, penalties and counseling options.

e. In any case where a school official is authorized to require a parent or legal guardian of a student under the age of 18 to attend a conference or meeting regarding the student's behavior, and after notice willfully refuses to attend, the principal or designee shall file a complaint with a court of competent juvenile jurisdiction, pursuant to *Children's Code* article 730(8) and 731.

f. A principal or designee may file a complaint pursuant to *Children's Code* article 730(1) or any other applicable ground when, in his judgment, doing so is in the best interests of the student.

3. Scope
   a. The investigation shall include documented interviews by the designated school official of the reporter, the alleged victim, the alleged offender, and any witnesses.
   b. The school official shall collect and evaluate all facts using the bullying investigation form approved by BESE [Board of Elementary and Secondary Education] and available on the DOE [Department of Education] website.
   c. The school official shall obtain copies or photographs of any audio-visual evidence.

4. Documentation. At the conclusion of a bullying investigation, and after meeting with the parents or legal guardians, the school official or school board shall:
   a. prepare a written report containing the findings of the investigation, including input from students' parents or legal guardians, and the decision by the school official or school system official. The document shall be placed in the school records of both students. If completed entirely, the bullying investigation form may serve as the report;
   b. promptly notify the reporter/complainant of the findings of the investigation and whether remedial action has been taken, if such release of information does not violate the law;
   c. keep reports/complaints and investigative reports confidential, except where disclosure is required by law;
   d. maintain reports/complaints and investigative reports for three years;
   e. provide a copy of any reports and investigative documents to the LEA, as necessary.

5. Disciplinary Action. If the school official has determined bullying has occurred, and after meeting with the parents or legal guardians of the students involved, the school official shall take prompt and appropriate disciplinary action against the offender and report criminal conduct to law enforcement, if appropriate.
6. LEA Reporting
    a. The LEA shall electronically report all such documented incidences of bullying to the DOE using the DOE behavior report and incidence checklist to document the details of each reported incident of bullying.
7. Appeal
    a. If the school official does not take timely and effective action, the student, parent, or school employee may report the bullying incident to the school board. The school board shall begin an investigation of any properly reported complaint of bullying no later than the next school day after the board receives the report.
    b. If the school board does not take timely and effective action, the student, parent, or other school employee may report the bullying incident to the DOE. The DOE shall track the number of reports, shall notify the superintendent and the president of the LEA, and shall publish the number of reports by school district on its website.
8. Parental Relief. If four or more reports of separate incidents of bullying have been made, and no investigation has occurred, the parent or legal guardian of the alleged victim shall have the option to request that the student be transferred to another school operated by the LEA.
    a. In order to exercise this option, the parent or legal guardian shall file a request with the superintendent of the LEA for the transfer of the student to another school under the LEA's jurisdiction.
    b. The LEA shall make a seat available at another of its schools within 10 school days of receipt of the request for a transfer. If the LEA has no other school serving the grade level of the student, then within 15 school days of receipt of the request, the superintendent of the LEA shall:

i. inform the student and the student's parents or legal guardians and facilitate the student's enrollment in a statewide virtual school;

ii. offer the student placement in a full-time virtual program or virtual school under the jurisdiction of the LEA;

iii. enter into a memorandum of understanding with the superintendent of another LEA to secure a placement and provide for the transfer of the student to a school serving the grade level of the student, pursuant to [Louisiana Statutes Annotated-Revised Statutes] 17:105 and 105.1.

    c. If no seat or other placement is made available within 30 calendar days of the receipt of the request by the superintendent, the parent or legal guardian may request a hearing with the school board, which shall be public or private at the option of the parent or legal guardian. The school board shall grant the hearing at its next scheduled meeting or within 60 calendar days, whichever is sooner.
    d. At the end of any school year, the parent or legal guardian may request that the LEA transfer the student back to the original school. The LEA shall make a seat available at the school.

MAINE

Student Safety. 20-Maine Revised Statutes Annotated § 6554 (West 2012)

20-Maine Revised Statutes Annotated § 6554

§ 6554. Prohibition on bullying in public schools

1. **Findings.** All students have the right to attend public schools that are safe, secure and peaceful environments. The Legislature finds that bullying and cyberbullying have a negative effect on the school environment and student learning and well-being. These behaviors must be addressed to ensure student safety and an inclusive learning environment. Bullying may be motivated by a student's actual or perceived race; color; religion; national origin; ancestry or ethnicity; sexual orientation; socioeconomic status; age; physical, mental, emotional or learning disability; gender; gender identity and expression; physical appearance; weight; family status; or other distinguishing personal characteristics or may be based on association with another person identified with such a characteristic. Nothing in this section may be interpreted as inconsistent with the existing protection, in accordance with the First Amendment of the United States Constitution, for the expression of religious, political and philosophical views in a school setting.

2. **Definitions.** As used in this section, unless the context otherwise indicates, the following terms have the following meanings.

    A. "Alternative discipline" means disciplinary action other than suspension or expulsion from school that is designed to correct and address the root causes of a student's specific misbehavior while retaining the student in class or school, or restorative school practices to repair the harm done to relationships and persons from the student's misbehavior. "Alternative discipline" includes, but is not limited to:

    (1) Meeting with the student and the student's parents;

    (2) Reflective activities, such as requiring the student to write an essay about the student's misbehavior;

    (3) Mediation when there is mutual conflict between peers, rather than one-way negative behavior, and when both parties freely choose to meet;

    (4) Counseling;

    (5) Anger management;

    (6) Health counseling or intervention;

    (7) Mental health counseling;

    (8) Participation in skills building and resolution activities, such as social-emotional cognitive skills building, resolution circles and restorative conferencing;

    (9) Community service; and

    (10) In-school detention or suspension, which may take place during lunchtime, after school or on weekends.

    B. "Bullying" includes, but is not limited to, a written, oral or electronic expression or a physical act or gesture or any combination thereof directed at a student or students that:

(1) Has, or a reasonable person would expect it to have, the effect of:
(a) Physically harming a student or damaging a student's property; or
(b) Placing a student in reasonable fear of physical harm or damage to the student's property;
(2) Interferes with the rights of a student by:
(a) Creating an intimidating or hostile educational environment for the student; or
(b) Interfering with the student's academic performance or ability to participate in or benefit from the services, activities or privileges provided by a school; or
(3) Is based on a student's actual or perceived characteristics identified in Title 5, section 4602 or 4684-A, or is based on a student's association with a person with one or more of these actual or perceived characteristics or any other distinguishing characteristics and that has the effect described in subparagraph (1) or (2).

"Bullying" includes cyberbullying.

C. "Cyberbullying" means bullying through the use of technology or any electronic communication, including, but not limited to, a transfer of signs, signals, writing, images, sounds, data or intelligence of any nature transmitted by the use of any electronic device, including, but not limited to, a computer, telephone, cellular telephone, text messaging device and personal digital assistant.
D. "Retaliation" means an act or gesture against a student for asserting or alleging an act of bullying. "Retaliation" also includes reporting that is not made in good faith on an act of bullying.
E. "School grounds" means a school building; property on which a school building or facility is located; and property that is owned, leased or used by a school for a school-sponsored activity, function, program, instruction or training. "School grounds" also includes school-related transportation vehicles.

3. **Prohibition.** A person may not engage in bullying on school grounds. This section does not modify or eliminate a school's obligation to comply with state and federal constitutional protections and civil rights laws applicable to schools.
4. **Scope.** This section applies to bullying that:
   A. Takes place at school or on school grounds, at any school-sponsored or school-related activity or event or while students are being transported to or from school or school-sponsored activities or events; or
   B. Takes place elsewhere or through the use of technology, but only if the bullying also infringes on the rights of the student at school as set forth in subsection 2, paragraph B.
5. **Adoption of policy.** When revising the policies and procedures it has established to address bullying pursuant to section 1001, subsection 15, paragraph H, a school board shall ensure that its policies and procedures are consistent with the model policy developed or revised by the commissioner pursuant to section 254, subsection 11-A. The policies and procedures must include, but are not limited to:
   A. A provision identifying the responsibility of students and others on school grounds to comply with the policies;
   B. A clear statement that bullying, harassment and sexual harassment and retaliation for reporting incidents of such behavior are prohibited;

State Anti-Bullying Statutes and Student Speech

C. A provision outlining the responsibility of a superintendent to implement and enforce the bullying policies required by this section, including:

(1) A requirement that the superintendent designate a school principal or other school personnel to administer the policies at the school level; and

(2) A procedure for publicly identifying the superintendent's designee or designees for administering the policies at the school level;

D. A requirement that school staff members, coaches and advisors for extracurricular and cocurricular activities report incidents of bullying to the school principal or other school personnel designated by the superintendent pursuant to paragraph C;

E. Procedures for students, school staff members, parents and others to report incidents of bullying. The procedures must permit reports of bullying to be made anonymously;

F. A procedure for promptly investigating and responding to incidents of bullying, including written documentation of reported incidents and the outcome of the investigations;

G. A clear statement that any person who engages in bullying, who is determined to have knowingly and falsely accused another of bullying or who engages in acts of retaliation against a person who reports a suspected incident of bullying is subject to disciplinary actions, which actions may include but are not limited to imposing a series of graduated consequences that include alternative discipline;

H. A procedure for a person to appeal a decision of a school principal or a superintendent's designee related to taking or not taking disciplinary action in accordance with the policies adopted pursuant to this subsection. The appeals procedure must be consistent with other appeals procedures established by the school board and may include an appeal to the superintendent;

I. A procedure to remediate any substantiated incident of bullying to counter the negative impact of the bullying and reduce the risk of future bullying incidents, which may include referring the victim, perpetrator or other involved persons to counseling or other appropriate services;

J. A process for the school to communicate to the parent of a student who has been bullied the measures being taken to ensure the safety of the student who has been bullied and to prevent further acts of bullying; and

K. A procedure for communicating with a local or state law enforcement agency if the school principal or the superintendent's designee believes that the pursuit of criminal charges or a civil action under the Maine Civil Rights Act is appropriate.

School boards may combine the policies and procedures required by this subsection with nondiscrimination, harassment and sexual harassment policies and grievance procedures.

6. **Dissemination of policy.** Each school board shall annually provide the written policies and procedures adopted pursuant to subsection 5 to students, parents, volunteers, administrators, teachers and school staff. The policies and procedures must be posted on the school administrative unit's publicly accessible website. Each school board shall include in its student handbook a section that addresses in detail the policies and procedures adopted pursuant to subsection 5.

7. **Application.** A superintendent or the superintendent's designee shall ensure that every substantiated incident of bullying is addressed.

A. The prohibition on bullying and retaliation and the attendant consequences apply to any student, school employee, contractor, visitor or volunteer who engages in conduct that constitutes bullying or retaliation.
B. Any contractor, visitor or volunteer who engages in bullying must be barred from school grounds until the superintendent is assured that the person will comply with this section and the policies of the school board.
C. Any organization affiliated with the school that authorizes or engages in bullying or retaliation forfeits permission for that organization to operate on school grounds or receive any other benefit of affiliation with the school.

8. **Transparency and monitoring.** Each school administrative unit shall file its policies to address bullying and cyberbullying with the department [of education].
9. **Staff training.** A school administrative unit shall provide professional development and staff training in the best approaches to implementing this section.

Model Policy. 20-Maine Revised Statutes Annotated § 254 (West 2012)

20-Maine Revised Statutes Annotated § 254

§ 254. Educational duties

11-A. Model policy; reporting. By January 1, 2013, the commissioner shall develop a model policy to address bullying and cyberbullying for use by school administrative units pursuant to section 6554. A copy of the model policy must be sent to each school administrative unit in the State and posted on the publicly accessible portion of the department's website along with any training and instructional materials related to the policy that the commissioner determines necessary.

A. The commissioner shall create a procedure by which school administrative units report substantiated incidents of bullying and cyberbullying to the department on at least an annual basis. These reports may not contain personally identifying information about students or other involved persons, but must delineate the specific nature of the incidents, the consequences and the actions taken.
B. The commissioner may update or revise the model policy and shall post the update or revision on the publicly accessible portion of the department's website and send a copy of the update or revision to each school administrative unit.

Student Safety. 20-Maine Revised Statutes Annotated § 6553 (West 1999)

20-Maine Revised Statutes Annotated § 6553

§ 6553. Prohibition of hazing

1. **Definitions.** As used in this section, unless the context otherwise indicates, the following terms have the following meanings.

A. "Injurious hazing" means any action or situation, including harassing behavior, that recklessly or intentionally endangers the mental or physical health of any school personnel or a student enrolled in a public school.

B. "Violator" means any person or any organization which engages in injurious hazing.

2. **Adoption of policy.** The school board shall adopt a policy which establishes that "injurious hazing," either on or off school property, by any student, staff member, group or organization affiliated with the public school is prohibited.

3. **Penalties.** The school board shall establish penalties for violation of the rules established in subsection 2. The penalties shall include, but not be limited to, provisions for:

    A. In the case of a person not associated with the public school, the ejection of the violator from school property;

    B. In the case of a student, administrator or staff violator, the individual's suspension, expulsion or other appropriate disciplinary action; and

    C. In the case of an organization affiliated with the public school which authorizes hazing, rescission of permission for that organization to operate on school property or receive any other benefit of affiliation with the public school.

These penalties shall be in addition to any other civil or criminal penalty to which the violator or organization may be subject.

4. **Administrative responsibility.** The school board shall assign responsibility for administering the policy to the superintendent of schools and establish procedures for appealing the action or lack of action of the superintendent.

5. **Dissemination.** The school board shall clearly set forth the policy and penalties adopted and shall distribute copies of them to all students enrolled in the public school.

MARYLAND

Health and Safety of Students. Maryland Code, Education, § 7-424, et seq. (West 2008)

Maryland Code, Education, § 7-424

§ 7-424. Reports relating to bullying, harassment and intimidation of students

Definitions

(a) (1) In this section the following words have the meanings indicated.

   (2) "Bullying, harassment, or intimidation" means intentional conduct, including verbal, physical, or written conduct, or an intentional electronic communication, that:

(i) Creates a hostile educational environment by substantially interfering with a student's educational benefits, opportunities, or performance, or with a student's physical or psychological well-being and is:
1. Motivated by an actual or a perceived personal characteristic including race, national origin, marital status, sex, sexual orientation, gender identity, religion, ancestry, physical attributes, socioeconomic status, familial status, or physical or mental ability or disability; or
2. Threatening or seriously intimidating; and
    (ii) 1. Occurs on school property, at a school activity or event, or on a school bus; or
        2. Substantially disrupts the orderly operation of a school.
(3) "Electronic communication" means a communication transmitted by means of an electronic device, including a telephone, cellular phone, computer, or pager.

Mandatory reporting of bullying, harassment, or intimidation of students

(b) (1) The Department shall require a county board to report incidents of bullying, harassment, or intimidation against students attending a public school under the jurisdiction of the county board.

  (2) An incident of bullying, harassment, or intimidation may be reported by:
    (i) A student;
    (ii) The parent, guardian, or close adult relative of a student; or
    (iii) A school staff member.

Standard report form

(c) (1) The Department shall create a standard victim of bullying, harassment, or intimidation report form.

  (2) Each victim of bullying, harassment, or intimidation report form shall:
    (i) Identify the victim and the alleged perpetrator, if known;
    (ii) Indicate the age of the victim and alleged perpetrator;
    (iii) Describe the incident, including alleged statements made by the alleged perpetrator;
    (iv) Indicate the location of the incident;
    (v) Identify any physical injury suffered by the victim and describe the seriousness and any permanent effects of the injury;
    (vi) Indicate the number of days a student is absent from school, if any, as a result of the incident;
    (vii) Identify any request for psychological services initiated by the victim or the victim's family due to psychological injuries suffered; and
    (viii) Include instructions on how to fill out the form and the mailing address to where the form shall be sent.
  (3) A county board shall distribute copies of the victim of bullying, harassment, or intimidation report form to each public school under the county board's jurisdiction.

State Anti-Bullying Statutes and Student Speech

Report form summaries

(d) (1) Each county board shall submit summaries of report forms filed with the county board to the State Board on or before January 31 each year.

(2) A county board shall delete any information that identifies an individual.

Confidentiality of information contained in report form

(e) The information contained in a victim of bullying, harassment, or intimidation report form in accordance with subsection (c) of this section:

(1) Is confidential and may not be redisclosed except as otherwise provided under the Family Educational Rights and Privacy Act or this section; and
(2) May not be made a part of a student's permanent educational record.

Reporting requirements

(f)(1) The Department [of Education] shall submit a report on or before March 31 each year to the Senate Education, Health, and Environmental Affairs Committee and the House Ways and Means Committee, in accordance with § 2-1246 of the State Government Article, consisting of a summary of the information included in the victim of bullying, harassment, or intimidation report forms filed with the county boards the previous year.

(2) The report submitted by the Department shall include, to the extent feasible:
 (i) A description of the act constituting the bullying, harassment, or intimidation;
 (ii) The age of the victim and alleged perpetrator;
 (iii) The allegation of the alleged perpetrator's motive;
 (iv) A description of the investigation of the complaint and any corrective action taken by the appropriate school authorities;
 (v) The number of days a student is absent from school, if any, as a result of the incident; and
 (vi) The number of false allegations reported.

Maryland Code, Education, § 7-424.1

§ 7-424.1. Model policy prohibiting bullying, harassment, or intimidation

Definitions

(a) (1) In this section the following words have the meanings indicated.
 (2) "Bullying, harassment, or intimidation" means intentional conduct, including verbal, physical, or written conduct, or an intentional electronic communication, that:

(i) Creates a hostile educational environment by substantially interfering with a student's educational benefits, opportunities, or performance, or with a student's physical or psychological well-being and is:
1. Motivated by an actual or a perceived personal characteristic including race, national origin, marital status, sex, sexual orientation, gender identity, religion, ancestry, physical attribute, socioeconomic status, familial status, or physical or mental ability or disability; or
2. Threatening or seriously intimidating; and
(ii) 1. Occurs on school property, at a school activity or event, or on a school bus; or
2. Substantially disrupts the orderly operation of a school.
(3) "Electronic communication" means a communication transmitted by means of an electronic device, including a telephone, cellular phone, computer, or pager.

Model policy prohibiting bullying, harassment, and intimidation

(b) (1) By March 31, 2009, the State Board, after consultation with and input from local school systems, shall develop a model policy prohibiting bullying, harassment, or intimidation in schools.
(2) The model policy developed under paragraph (1) of this subsection shall include:
(i) A statement prohibiting bullying, harassment, and intimidation in schools;
(ii) A statement prohibiting reprisal or retaliation against individuals who report acts of bullying, harassment, or intimidation;
(iii) A definition of bullying, harassment, or intimidation that is either the same as set forth in subsection (a)(2) of this section or a definition that is not less inclusive than that definition;
(iv) Standard consequences and remedial actions for persons committing acts of bullying, harassment, or intimidation and for persons engaged in reprisal or retaliation;
(v) Standard consequences and remedial actions for persons found to have made false accusations;
(vi) Model procedures for reporting acts of bullying, harassment, and intimidation;
(vii) Model procedures for the prompt investigation of acts of bullying, harassment, and intimidation;
(viii) Information about the types of support services available to the student bully, victim, and any bystanders; and
(ix) Information regarding the availability and use of the bullying, harassment, or intimidation form under § 7-424 of this subtitle.

Policies established by county boards based on model policy

(c) (1) Each county board shall establish a policy prohibiting bullying, harassment, or intimidation at school based on the model policy.
(2) The policy shall address the components of the model policy specified in subsection (b)(2) of this section.
(3) A county board shall develop the policy in consultation with representatives of the following groups:

State Anti-Bullying Statutes and Student Speech

        (i)   Parents or guardians of students;
        (ii)   School employees and administrators;
        (iii) School volunteers;
        (iv) Students; and
        (v)   Members of the community.

Publication of policy

(d)   Each county board shall publicize its policy in student handbooks, school system websites, and any other location or venue the county board determines is necessary or appropriate.

Procedure for reporting incidents

(e)   Each county board policy shall include information on the procedure for reporting incidents of bullying, harassment, or intimidation, including:

(1)   A chain of command in the reporting process; and
(2)   The name and contact information for an employee of the Department, designated by the Department, who is familiar with the reporting and investigation procedures in the applicable school system.

Submission of county board policies to State Superintendent

(f)   Each county board shall submit its policy to the State Superintendent by July 1, 2009.

Educational programs

(g)   Each county board shall develop the following educational programs in its efforts to prevent bullying, harassment, and intimidation in schools:

    (1)   An educational bullying, harassment, and intimidation prevention program for students, staff, volunteers, and parents; and
    (2)   A teacher and administrator development program that trains teachers and administrators to implement the policy.

Immunity of school employees

(h) (1) A school employee who reports an act of bullying, harassment, or intimidation under this section in accordance with the county board's policy established under subsection (c) of this section is not civilly liable for any act or omission in reporting or failing to report an act of bullying, harassment, or intimidation under this section.

    (2)   The provisions of this section may not be construed to limit the legal rights of a victim of bullying, harassment, or intimidation.

Maryland Code, Education, § 7-424.3

§ 7-424.3. School polices prohibiting bullying, harassment, and intimidation

Definitions

(a) (1) In this section the following words have the meanings indicated.

    (2) "Bullying, harassment, and intimidation" means any intentional written, verbal, or physical act, including an electronic communication, that:
        (i) 1. Physically harms an individual;
            2. Damages an individual's property;
            3. Substantially interferes with an individual's education or learning environment; or
            4. Places an individual in reasonable fear of harm to the individual's person or property; and
        (ii) 1. Occurs on school property, at a school activity or event, or on a school bus; or
            2. Substantially disrupts the orderly operation of a school.
    (3) "Electronic communication" means a communication transmitted by means of an electronic device, including a telephone, cellular phone, computer, or pager.
    (4) "Nonpublic school" means a nonpublic school that participates in State-funded education programs.

Policies required by nonpublic schools

(b) By March 31, 2012, each nonpublic school shall adopt a policy prohibiting bullying, harassment, and intimidation.

Policy requirements

(c) The policy adopted under subsection (b) of this section shall include:

(1) A statement prohibiting bullying, harassment, and intimidation in the school;
(2) A statement prohibiting reprisal or retaliation against individuals who report acts of bullying, harassment, or intimidation;
(3) A definition of bullying, harassment, and intimidation that is either the same as set forth in subsection (a) of this section or a definition that is not less inclusive than that definition;
(4) Standard consequences and remedial actions for persons committing acts of bullying, harassment, or intimidation and for persons engaged in reprisal or retaliation, including:
    (i) Specific penalties for persons who repeatedly commit acts of bullying, harassment, or intimidation; and
    (ii) A requirement that persons who commit acts of bullying, harassment, or intimidation receive educational and therapeutic services concerning bullying prevention;
(5) Standard consequences and remedial actions for persons found to have made false accusations;

State Anti-Bullying Statutes and Student Speech

(6) Standard procedures for reporting acts of bullying, harassment, or intimidation, including a chain of command in the reporting process;

(7) Standard procedures for the prompt investigation of acts of bullying, harassment, or intimidation;

(8) Standard procedures for protecting victims of bullying, harassment, or intimidation from additional acts of bullying, harassment, or intimidation, and from retaliation; and

(9) Information about the types of support services available to a student bully or victim and any bystanders.

Nonpublic schools encouraged to consult with parent, school, and student groups

(d) A nonpublic school is encouraged to develop the policy adopted under subsection (b) of this section in consultation with the following groups:

(1) Parents or guardians of students;
(2) School employees and administrators;
(3) School volunteers; and
(4) Students.

Publication of policy

(e) A nonpublic school is encouraged to publicize the policy adopted under subsection (b) of this section in student handbooks, on the school's Web site, and any other location or venue the school determines is necessary or appropriate.

Educational programs encouraged for nonpublic schools

(f) A nonpublic school is encouraged to develop the following educational programs in its efforts to prevent bullying, harassment, and intimidation:

(1) An educational bullying, harassment, and intimidation prevention program for students, staff, volunteers, and parents; and
(2) A teacher and administrator development program that trains teachers and administrators to implement the policy adopted under subsection (b) of this section.

Immunity of nonpublic school employees

(g) An employee of a nonpublic school who reports an act of bullying, harassment, or intimidation in accordance with the nonpublic school's policy adopted under subsection (b) of this section is not civilly liable for any act or omission in reporting or failing to report an act of bullying, harassment, or intimidation in accordance with the policy.

Construction of section

(h) The provisions of this section may not be construed to:

(1) Limit the legal rights of a victim of bullying, harassment, or intimidation; or
(2) Require a statewide policy in nonpublic schools relating to bullying, harassment, and intimidation.

MASSACHUSETTS

Conduct of Teachers or Students. Massachusetts General Laws Annotated 71 § 37H (West 2014)

Massachusetts General Laws Annotated 71 § 37H

§ 37H. Policies relative to conduct of teachers or students; student handbooks

The superintendent of every school district shall publish the district's policies pertaining to the conduct of teachers and students. ... The policies shall also prohibit bullying as defined in section 37O and shall include the student-related sections of the bullying prevention and intervention plan required by said section 37O. Copies of these policies shall be provided to any person upon request and without cost by the principal of every school within the district.

***

The student handbook shall include an age-appropriate summary of the student-related sections of the bullying prevention and intervention plan required by section 37O. The school council shall review the student handbook each spring to consider changes in disciplinary policy to take effect in September of the following school year, but may consider policy changes at any time. The annual review shall cover all areas of student conduct, including but not limited to those outlined in this section.

Notwithstanding any general or special law to the contrary, all student handbooks shall contain the following provisions:

(a) Any student who is found on school premises or at school-sponsored or school-related events, including athletic games, in possession of a dangerous weapon, including, but not limited to, a gun or a knife; or a controlled substance as defined in chapter ninety-four C, including, but not limited to, marijuana, cocaine, and heroin, may be subject to expulsion from the school or school district by the principal.

(b) Any student who assaults a principal, assistant principal, teacher, teacher's aide or other educational staff on school premises or at school-sponsored or school-related events, including athletic games, may be subject to expulsion from the school or school district by the principal.

School Bullying and Prevention Plan. Massachusetts General Laws Annotated 71 § 37O (West 2014)

§ 37O. School bullying prohibited; bullying prevention plans

(a) As used in this section the following words shall, unless the context clearly requires otherwise, have the following meaning:

"Bullying", the repeated use by one or more students or by a member of a school staff including, but not limited to, an educator, administrator, school nurse, cafeteria worker, custodian, bus driver, athletic coach, advisor to an extracurricular activity or paraprofessional of a written, verbal or electronic expression or a physical act or gesture or any combination thereof, directed at a victim that: (i) causes physical or emotional harm to the victim or damage to the victim's property; (ii) places the victim in reasonable fear of harm to himself or of damage to his property; (iii) creates a hostile environment at school for the victim; (iv) infringes on the rights of the victim at school; or (v) materially and substantially disrupts the education process or the orderly operation of a school. For the purposes of this section, bullying shall include cyber-bullying.

"Cyber-bullying", bullying through the use of technology or any electronic communication, which shall include, but shall not be limited to, any transfer of signs, signals, writing, images, sounds, data or intelligence of any nature transmitted in whole or in part by a wire, radio, electromagnetic, photo electronic or photo optical system, including, but not limited to, electronic mail, internet communications, instant messages or facsimile communications. Cyber-bullying shall also include (i) the creation of a web page or blog in which the creator assumes the identity of another person or (ii) the knowing impersonation of another person as the author of posted content or messages, if the creation or impersonation creates any of the conditions enumerated in clauses (i) to (v), inclusive, of the definition of bullying. Cyber-bullying shall also include the distribution by electronic means of a communication to more than one person or the posting of material on an electronic medium that may be accessed by one or more persons, if the distribution or posting creates any of the conditions enumerated in clauses (i) to (v), inclusive, of the definition of bullying.

"Hostile environment", a situation in which bullying causes the school environment to be permeated with intimidation, ridicule or insult that is sufficiently severe or pervasive to alter the conditions of the student's education.

"Perpetrator", a student or a member of a school staff including, but not limited to, an educator, administrator, school nurse, cafeteria worker, custodian, bus driver, athletic coach, advisor to an extracurricular activity or paraprofessional who engages in bullying or retaliation.

"School grounds", property on which a school building or facility is located or property that is owned, leased or used by a school district, charter school, non-public school, approved private day or residential school, or collaborative school for a school-sponsored activity, function, program, instruction or training.

"Victim", a student against whom bullying or retaliation has been perpetrated.

(b) Bullying shall be prohibited: (i) on school grounds, property immediately adjacent to school grounds, at a school-sponsored or school-related activity, function or program whether on or off school grounds, at a school bus stop, on a school bus or other vehicle owned, leased or used by a school district or school, or through the use of technology or an electronic device owned, leased or used by a school district or school and (ii) at a location, activity, function or program that is not school-related, or through the use of technology or an electronic device that is not owned, leased or used by a school district or school, if the bullying creates a hostile environment at school for the victim, infringes on the rights of the victim at school or materially and substantially disrupts the education process or the orderly operation of a school. Nothing contained herein shall require schools to staff any non-school related activities, functions, or programs.

Retaliation against a person who reports bullying, provides information during an investigation of bullying, or witnesses or has reliable information about bullying shall be prohibited.

(c) Each school district, charter school, approved private day or residential school and collaborative school shall provide age-appropriate instruction on bullying prevention in each grade that is incorporated into the curriculum of the school district or school. The curriculum shall be evidence-based.

(d)(1) Each school district, charter school, non-public school, approved private day or residential school and collaborative school shall develop, adhere to and update a plan to address bullying prevention and intervention in consultation with teachers, school staff, professional support personnel, school volunteers, administrators, community representatives, local law enforcement agencies, students, parents and guardians. The plan shall apply to students and members of a school staff, including, but not limited to, educators, administrators, school nurses, cafeteria workers, custodians, bus drivers, athletic coaches, advisors to an extracurricular activity and paraprofessionals. The consultation shall include, but not be limited to, notice and a public comment period; provided, however, that a non-public school shall only be required to give notice to and provide a comment period for families that have a child attending the school. The plan shall be updated at least biennially.

(2) Each plan shall include, but not be limited to: (i) descriptions of and statements prohibiting bullying, cyber-bullying and retaliation, including procedures for collecting, maintaining and reporting bullying incident data required under subsection (k); (ii) clear procedures for students, staff, parents, guardians and others to report bullying or retaliation; (iii) a provision that reports of bullying or retaliation may be made anonymously; provided, however, that no disciplinary action shall be taken against a student solely on the basis of an anonymous report; (iv) clear procedures for promptly responding to and investigating reports of bullying or retaliation; (v) the range of disciplinary actions that may be taken against a perpetrator for bullying or retaliation; provided, however, that the disciplinary actions shall balance the need for accountability with the need to teach appropriate behavior; (vi) clear procedures for restoring a sense of safety for a victim and assessing that victim's needs for protection; (vii) strategies for protecting from bullying or retaliation a person who reports bullying, provides information during an investigation of bullying or witnesses or has reliable information about an act of bullying; (viii) procedures consistent with state and federal law for promptly notifying the parents or guardians of a victim and a perpetrator; provided, that the parents or guardians of a victim shall also be notified of the action taken to prevent any further acts of bullying or retaliation; and provided, further, that the procedures shall provide for immediate notification pursuant to regulations promulgated under this subsection by the principal or person who holds a comparable role to the local law enforcement agency when criminal charges may be pursued against the perpetrator; (ix) a provision that a student who knowingly makes a false accusation of bullying or retaliation shall be subject to disciplinary action; and (x) a strategy for providing counseling or referral to appropriate services for perpetrators and victims and for appropriate family members of said students. The plan shall afford all students the same protection regardless of their status under the law.

(3) Each plan shall recognize that certain students may be more vulnerable to becoming a target of bullying or harassment based on actual or perceived differentiating characteristics, including race, color, religion, ancestry, national origin, sex, socioeconomic status, homelessness, academic status

gender identity or expression, physical appearance, pregnant or parenting status, sexual orientation, mental, physical, developmental or sensory disability or by association with a person who has or is perceived to have 1 or more of these characteristics. The plan shall include the specific steps that each school district, charter school, non-public school, approved private day or residential school and collaborative school shall take to support vulnerable students and to provide all students with the skills, knowledge and strategies needed to prevent or respond to bullying or harassment. A school district, charter school, non-public school, approved private day or residential school or collaborative school may establish separate discrimination or harassment policies that include additional categories of students. Nothing in this section shall alter the obligations of a school district, charter school, non-public school, approved private day or residential school or collaborative school to remediate any discrimination or harassment based on a person's membership in a legally protected category under local, state or federal law.

(4) The plan for a school district, charter school, approved private day or residential school and collaborative school shall include a provision for ongoing professional development to build the skills of all staff members, including, but not limited to, educators, administrators, school nurses, cafeteria workers, custodians, bus drivers, athletic coaches, advisors to extracurricular activities and paraprofessionals, to prevent, identify and respond to bullying. The content of such professional development shall include, but not be limited to: (i) developmentally appropriate strategies to prevent bullying incidents; (ii) developmentally appropriate strategies for immediate, effective interventions to stop bullying incidents; (iii) information regarding the complex interaction and power differential that can take place between and among a perpetrator, victim and witnesses to the bullying; (iv) research findings on bullying, including information about students who have been shown to be particularly at risk for bullying in the school environment; (v) information on the incidence and nature of cyber-bullying; and (vi) internet safety issues as they relate to cyber-bullying. The department [of elementary and secondary education] shall identify and offer information on alternative methods for fulfilling the professional development requirements of this section, at least 1 of these alternative methods shall be available at no cost to school districts, charter schools, approved private day or residential schools and collaborative schools.

(5) The plan shall include provisions for informing parents and guardians about the bullying prevention curriculum of the school district or school and shall include, but not be limited to: (i) how parents and guardians can reinforce the curriculum at home and support the school district or school plan; (ii) the dynamics of bullying; and (iii) online safety and cyber-bullying.

(6) The department [of elementary and secondary education] shall promulgate rules and regulations on the requirements related to a principal's duties under clause (viii) of the second paragraph of this subsection; provided, however, that school districts, charter schools, approved private day or residential schools and collaborative schools shall be subject to the regulations. A non-public school shall develop procedures for immediate notification by the principal or person who holds a comparable role to the local law enforcement agency when criminal charges may be pursued against the perpetrator.

(e)(1) Each school district, charter school, non-public school, approved private day or residential school and collaborative school shall provide to students and parents or guardians, in age-appropriate terms and in the languages which are most prevalent among the students, parents or guardians, annual written notice of the relevant student-related sections of the plan.

(2) Each school district, charter school, non-public school, approved private day or residential school and collaborative school shall provide to all school staff annual written notice of the plan. The faculty and staff at each school shall be trained annually on the plan applicable to the school. Relevant sections of the plan relating to the duties of faculty and staff shall be included in a school district or school employee handbook.

(3) The plan shall be posted on the website of each school district, charter school, non-public school, approved private day or residential school and collaborative school.

(f) Each school principal or the person who holds a comparable position shall be responsible for the implementation and oversight of the plan at his school.

(g) A member of a school staff, including, but not limited to, an educator, administrator, school nurse, cafeteria worker, custodian, bus driver, athletic coach, advisor to an extracurricular activity or paraprofessional, shall immediately report any instance of bullying or retaliation the staff member has witnessed or become aware of to the principal or to the school official identified in the plan as responsible for receiving such reports or both. Upon receipt of such a report, the school principal or a designee shall promptly conduct an investigation. If the school principal or a designee determines that bullying or retaliation has occurred, the school principal or designee shall (i) notify the local law enforcement agency if the school principal or designee believes that criminal charges may be pursued against a perpetrator; (ii) take appropriate disciplinary action; (iii) notify the parents or guardians of a perpetrator; (iv) notify the parents or guardians of the victim, and to the extent consistent with state and federal law, notify them of the action taken to prevent any further acts of bullying or retaliation; and (v) inform the parents or guardians of the victim about the department's problem resolution system and the process for seeking assistance or filing a claim through the problem resolution system.

(h) If an incident of bullying or retaliation involves students from more than one school district, charter school, non-public school, approved private day or residential school or collaborative school, the school district or school first informed of the bullying or retaliation shall, consistent with state and federal law, promptly notify the appropriate administrator of the other school district or school so that both may take appropriate action. If an incident of bullying or retaliation occurs on school grounds and involves a former student under the age of 21 who is no longer enrolled in a local school district, charter school, non-public school, approved private day or residential school or collaborative school, the school district or school informed of the bullying or retaliation shall contact law enforcement consistent with the provisions of clause (viii) of the second paragraph of subsection (d).

(i) Nothing in this section shall supersede or replace existing rights or remedies under any other general or special law, nor shall this section create a private right of action.

(j) The department, after consultation with the department of public health, the department of mental health, the attorney general, the Massachusetts District Attorneys Association and experts on bullying shall: (i) publish a model plan for school districts and schools to consider when creating their plans; and (ii) compile a list of bullying prevention and intervention resources, evidence-based curricula, best practices and academic-based research that shall be made available to schools. The model plan shall be consistent with the behavioral health and public schools framework developed by the department in accordance with section 19 of chapter 321 of the acts of 2008. The resources may include, but shall not be limited to, print, audio, video or digital media; subscription based online services; and on-site or technology-enabled professional development and training sessions. The department shall biennially update the model plan and the list of the resources, curricula, best practices and research and shall post them on its website.

(k) Each school district, charter school, approved private day or residential school and collaborative school shall annually report bullying incident data to the department. The data shall include, but not be limited to: (i) the number of reported allegations of bullying or retaliation; (ii) the number and nature of substantiated incidents of bullying or retaliation; (iii) the number of students disciplined for engaging in bullying or retaliation; and (iv) any other information required by the department. Said incident data shall be reported in the form and manner established by the department, in consultation with the attorney general; provided, that the department shall minimize the costs and resources needed to comply with said reporting requirements; and provided further, that the department may use existing data collection and reporting mechanisms to collect the information from school districts. The department shall analyze the bullying incident data and shall publish an annual report containing aggregate statewide information on the frequency and nature of bullying in schools. The department shall file the annual report with the attorney general and with the clerks of the senate and the house of representatives who shall forward the same to the chairs of the joint committee on education, the joint committee on the judiciary and the house and senate committees on ways and means.

(l) The department shall develop a student survey to assess school climate and the prevalence, nature and severity of bullying in schools. The survey shall be administered by each school district, charter school, approved private day or residential school and collaborative school at least once every 4 years. The survey shall be designed to protect student privacy and allow for anonymous participation by students.

The school official identified in the plan as responsible for receiving reports of bullying or retaliation shall verify the completion of the student surveys. All completed surveys shall be forwarded to the department. The department shall use the survey results to help assess the effectiveness of bullying prevention curricula and instruction developed and administered under subsection (c). The department shall collect and analyze the student survey data in order to: compare the survey results with the bullying incident data reported under subsection (k); identify long-term trends and areas of improvement; and monitor bullying prevention efforts in schools over time. The department shall make its findings available to the school official.

(m) Each school district, charter school, approved private day or residential school or collaborative school may adopt an anti-bullying seal to represent the district or school's commitment to bullying prevention and intervention.

(n) The department may investigate certain alleged incidents of bullying. If, upon completion of investigation by the department, a school district, charter school, approved private day or residential school or collaborative school is found to not have properly implemented its prevention plan as outlined in subsection (d), the department may require that school district, charter school, approved private day or residential school or collaborative school to properly implement the plan or take other actions to address the findings of the investigation.

Notification of Bullying or Retaliation. 603 Code of Massachusetts Regulations 49.00, et seq. (West 2010)

603 Code of Massachusetts Regulations 49.01

49.01: Authority

603 CMR 49.00 is promulgated by the Board of Elementary and Secondary Education pursuant to [Massachusetts General Laws Annotated] c. 71, § 37O, as added by St. 2010, c. 92.

603 Code of Massachusetts Regulations 49.02

49.02: Scope and Purpose

603 [Code of Massachusetts Regulations] 49.00 governs the requirements related to the duty of the principal or leader of a public school, approved private day or residential school, collaborative school, or charter school to notify the parents or guardians of a target and an aggressor when there is an incident of bullying or retaliation, and to notify the local law enforcement agency when criminal charges may be pursued against the aggressor. 603 [Code of Massachusetts Regulations] 49.00 also address confidentiality of student record information related to notification of bullying and retaliation.

603 Code of Massachusetts Regulations 49.03

49.03: Definitions and Terms

Aggressor means perpetrator of bullying or retaliation as defined in [Massachusetts General Laws Annotated] c. 71, § 37O.

Bullying, pursuant to [Massachusetts General Laws Annotated] c. 71, § 37O, means the repeated use by one or more students of a written, verbal or electronic expression or a physical act or gesture or any combination thereof, directed at a target that:

(a) causes physical or emotional harm to the target or damage to the target's property;
(b) places the target in reasonable fear of harm to himself or herself or damage to his or her property;
(c) creates a hostile environment at school for the target;
(d) infringes on the rights of the target at school; or
(e) materially and substantially disrupts the education process or the orderly operation of a school. Bullying shall include cyberbullying.

Cyberbullying, pursuant to [Massachusetts General Laws Annotated] c. 71, § 37O, means bullying through the use of technology or any electronic communication, which shall include, but not be limited to, any transfer of signs, signals, writing, images, sounds, data or intelligence of any nature transmitted in whole or in part by a wire, radio, electromagnetic, photo electronic or photo optical system, including, but not limited to, electronic mail, internet communications, instant messages or facsimile communications. Cyberbullying shall also include:

State Anti-Bullying Statutes and Student Speech

(a) the creation of a web page or blog in which the creator assumes the identity of another person; or

(b) the knowing impersonation of another person as the author of posted content or messages, if the creation or impersonation creates any of the conditions in 603 [Code of Massachusetts Regulations] 49.03: *Bullying*(a) through (e). Cyberbullying shall also include the distribution by electronic means of a communication to more than one person or the posting of material on an electronic medium that may be accessed by one or more persons, if the distribution or posting creates any of the conditions in 603 [Code of Massachusetts Regulations] 49.03: *Bullying*(a) through (e).

Hostile Environment, pursuant to [Massachusetts General Laws Annotated] c. 71, § 37O, means a situation in which bullying causes the school environment to be permeated with intimidation, ridicule or insult that is sufficiently severe or pervasive to alter the conditions of the student's education.

Retaliation means any form of intimidation, reprisal or harassment directed against a person who reports bullying, provides information during an investigation about bullying, or witnesses or has reliable information about bullying.

Student Record has the meaning set forth in the Massachusetts Student Records Regulations, 603 [Code of Massachusetts Regulations] 23.02.

Target means a student victim of bullying or retaliation as defined in [Code of Massachusetts Regulations] c. 71, § 37O.

603 Code of Massachusetts Regulations 49.04

49.04: Bullying and Retaliation Prohibited

(1) Bullying of a student is prohibited as provided in [Massachusetts General Laws Annotated] c. 71, § 37O. Retaliation is also prohibited.

(2) Bullying shall be prohibited on school grounds, property immediately adjacent to school grounds, at a school-sponsored or school-related activity, function or program whether on or off school grounds, at a school bus stop, on a school bus or other vehicle owned, leased or used by a school district or school, or through the use of technology or an electronic device owned, leased or used by a school district or school. Bullying at a location, activity, function or program that is not school-related, or through the use of technology or an electronic device that is not owned, leased or used by a school district or school, shall be prohibited if the bullying:

(a) creates a hostile environment at school for the target;

(b) infringes on the rights of the target at school; or

(c) materially and substantially disrupts the education process or the orderly operation of a school.

(3) Each school district and school shall have procedures for receiving reports of bullying or retaliation; promptly responding to and investigating such reports, and determining whether bullying or retaliation has occurred; responding to incidents of bullying or retaliation; and reporting to parents and law enforcement as set forth in 603 [Code of Massachusetts Regulations] 49.05 and 49.06.

603 Code of Massachusetts Regulations 49.05

49.05: Notice to Parents

(1) Upon investigation and determination that bullying or retaliation has occurred, the principal shall promptly notify the parents of the target and the aggressor of the determination and the school district or school's procedures for responding to the bullying or retaliation. The principal shall inform the target's parent of actions that school officials will take to prevent further acts of bullying or retaliation. Nothing in 603 [Code of Massachusetts Regulations] 49.05(1) prohibits the principal from contacting a parent of a target or aggressor about a report of bullying or retaliation prior to a determination that bullying or retaliation has occurred.

(2) Notice required by 603 [Code of Massachusetts Regulations] 49.05 shall be provided in the primary language of the home.

(3) Each school district and school shall include the requirements and procedures for communicating with the parents of the aggressor and target of bullying or retaliation in the local plan.

(4) A principal's notification to a parent about an incident or a report of bullying or retaliation must comply with confidentiality requirements of the Massachusetts Student Records Regulations, 603 [Code of Massachusetts Regulations] 23.00, and the Federal Family Educational Rights and Privacy Act Regulations, 34 [Code of Federal Regulations] Part 99, as set forth in 603 [Code of Massachusetts Regulations] 49.07.

603 Code of Massachusetts Regulations 49.06

49.06: Notice to Law Enforcement Agency

(1) Before the first day of each school year, the superintendent or designee of a school district and the school leader or designee of an approved private day or residential school, collaborative school, or charter school shall communicate with the chief of police or designee of the local police department about the implementation of 603 [Code of Massachusetts Regulations] 49.06. Such communication may include agreeing on a method for notification, a process for informal communication, updates of prior written agreements, or any other subject appropriate to the implementation of 603 [Code of Massachusetts Regulations] 49.06.

(2) At any point after receipt of a report of bullying or retaliation, including after an investigation, the principal shall notify the local law enforcement agency if the principal has a reasonable basis to believe that criminal charges may be pursued against the aggressor. Notice shall be consistent with the requirements of 603 [Code of Massachusetts Regulations] 49.00 and established agreements with the local law enforcement agency. The principal shall document the reasons for his or her decision to notify law enforcement. Nothing in 603 [Code of Massachusetts Regulations] 49.06 shall be interpreted to require reporting to a law enforcement agency in situations in which bullying and retaliation can be handled appropriately within the school district or school.

  (a) In making the determination whether notification to law enforcement is appropriate, the principal may consult with the school resource officer and any other individuals the principal deems appropriate.

  (b) Nothing in 603 [Code of Massachusetts Regulations] 49.06 shall prevent the principal from taking appropriate disciplinary or other action pursuant to school district or school policy and state law, provided that disciplinary actions balance the need for accountability with the need to teach appropriate behavior.

(c) The principal shall respond to the incident as set forth in relevant provisions of the local plan consistent with 603 [Code of Massachusetts Regulations] 49.06.

(3) If an incident of bullying or retaliation occurs on school grounds and involves a former student under the age of 21 who is no longer enrolled in the school district or school, the principal of the school informed of the bullying or retaliation shall notify the local law enforcement agency if the principal has a reasonable basis to believe that criminal charges may be pursued against the aggressor.

(4) Each school district and school shall include the requirements and procedures for communicating with the local law enforcement agency in the local plan.

603 Code of Massachusetts Regulations 49.07

49.07: Confidentiality of Records

(1) A principal may not disclose information from a student record of a target or aggressor to a parent unless the information is about the parent's own child.

(2) A principal may disclose a determination of bullying or retaliation to a local law enforcement agency under 603 [Code of Massachusetts Regulations] 49.06 without the consent of a student or his or her parent. The principal shall communicate with law enforcement officials in a manner that protects the privacy of targets, student witnesses, and aggressors to the extent practicable under the circumstances.

(3) A principal may disclose student record information about a target or aggressor to appropriate parties in addition to law enforcement in connection with a health or safety emergency if knowledge of the information is necessary to protect the health or safety of the student or other individuals as provided in 603 [Code of Massachusetts Regulations] 23.07(4)(e) and 34 [Code of Federal Regulations] 99.31(a)(10) and 99.36. 603 [Code of Massachusetts Regulations] 49.07(3) is limited to instances in which the principal has determined there is an immediate and significant threat to the health or safety of the student or other individuals. It is limited to the period of emergency and does not allow for blanket disclosure of student record information. The principal must document the disclosures and the reasons that the principal determined that a health or safety emergency exists.

MICHIGAN

Matt's Safe School Law. Michigan Compiled Laws Annotated 380.1310b (West 2011)

Michigan Compiled Laws Annotated 380.1310b

380.1310b. Matt's Safe School Law; bullying policies; adoption and implementation

Sec. 1310b. (1) Subject to subsection (3), not later than 6 months after the effective date of this section, the board of a school district or intermediate school district or board of directors of a public school academy shall adopt and implement a policy prohibiting bullying at school, as defined in this section.

(2) Subject to subsection (3), before adopting the policy required under subsection (1), the board or board of directors shall hold at least 1 public hearing on the proposed policy. This public hearing may be held as part of a regular board meeting. Subject to subsection (3), not later than 30 days after adopting the policy, the board or board of directors shall submit a copy of its policy to the department.

(3) If, as of the effective date of this section, a school district, intermediate school district, or public school academy has already adopted and implemented an existing policy prohibiting bullying at school and that policy is in compliance with subsection (5), the board of the school district or intermediate school district or board of directors of the public school academy is not required to adopt and implement a new policy under subsection (1). However, this subsection applies to a school district, intermediate school district, or public school academy described in this subsection only if the board or board of directors submits a copy of its policy to the department [of education] not later than 60 days after the effective date of this section.

(4) Not later than 1 year after the deadline under subsection (2) for districts and public school academies to submit copies of their policies to the department, the department shall submit a report to the senate and house standing committees on education summarizing the status of the implementation of policies under this section.

(5) A policy adopted pursuant to subsection (1) shall include at least all of the following:
 (a) A statement prohibiting bullying of a pupil.
 (b) A statement prohibiting retaliation or false accusation against a target of bullying, a witness, or another person with reliable information about an act of bullying.
 (c) A provision indicating that all pupils are protected under the policy and that bullying is equally prohibited without regard to its subject matter or motivating animus.
 (d) The identification by job title of school officials responsible for ensuring that the policy is implemented.
 (e) A statement describing how the policy is to be publicized.
 (f) A procedure for providing notification to the parent or legal guardian of a victim of bullying and the parent or legal guardian of a perpetrator of the bullying.
 (g) A procedure for reporting an act of bullying.
 (h) A procedure for prompt investigation of a report of violation of the policy or a related complaint, identifying either the principal or the principal's designee as the person responsible for the investigation.
 (i) A procedure for each public school to document any prohibited incident that is reported and a procedure to report all verified incidents of bullying and the resulting consequences, including discipline and referrals, to the board of the school district or intermediate school district or board of directors of the public school academy on an annual basis.

(6) The legislature encourages a board or board of directors to include all of the following in the policy required under this section:
 (a) Provisions to form bullying prevention task forces, programs, teen courts, and other initiatives involving school staff, pupils, school clubs or other student groups, administrators, volunteers, parents, law enforcement, community members, and other stakeholders.

(b) A requirement for annual training for administrators, school employees, and volunteers who have significant contact with pupils on preventing, identifying, responding to, and reporting incidents of bullying.

(c) A requirement for educational programs for pupils and parents on preventing, identifying, responding to, and reporting incidents of bullying and cyberbullying.

(7) A school employee, school volunteer, pupil, or parent or guardian who promptly reports in good faith an act of bullying to the appropriate school official designated in the school district's or public school academy's policy and who makes this report in compliance with the procedures set forth in the policy is immune from a cause of action for damages arising out of the reporting itself or any failure to remedy the reported incident. However, this immunity does not apply to a school official who is designated under subsection (5)(d), or who is responsible for remedying the bullying, when acting in that capacity.

(8) As used in this section:

(a) "At school" means in a classroom, elsewhere on school premises, on a school bus or other school-related vehicle, or at a school-sponsored activity or event whether or not it is held on school premises. "At school" includes conduct using a telecommunications access device or telecommunications service provider that occurs off school premises if the telecommunications access device or the telecommunications service provider is owned by or under the control of the school district or public school academy.

(b) "Bullying" means any written, verbal, or physical act, or any electronic communication, that is intended or that a reasonable person would know is likely to harm 1 or more pupils either directly or indirectly by doing any of the following:

(i) Substantially interfering with educational opportunities, benefits, or programs of 1 or more pupils.

(ii) Adversely affecting the ability of a pupil to participate in or benefit from the school district's or public school's educational programs or activities by placing the pupil in reasonable fear of physical harm or by causing substantial emotional distress.

(iii) Having an actual and substantial detrimental effect on a pupil's physical or mental health.

(iv) Causing substantial disruption in, or substantial interference with, the orderly operation of the school.

(c) "Telecommunications access device" and "telecommunications service provider" mean those terms as defined in section 219a of the Michigan penal code, 1931 PA 328, [Michigan Compiled Laws Annotated] 750.219a.

(9) This section shall be known as "Matt's Safe School Law".

MINNESOTA

Student Rights, Responsibilities, and Behavior Discrimination; Harassment; Violence. Minnesota Statutes Annotated § 121A.031 (West 2014)

Minnesota Statutes Annotated § 121A.031

§ 121A.031. School student bullying policy

Subdivision 1. Student bullying policy; scope and application. (a) This section applies to bullying by a student against another student enrolled in a public school and which occurs:

(1) on the school premises, at the school functions or activities, or on the school transportation;
(2) by use of electronic technology and communications on the school premises, during the school functions or activities, on the school transportation, or on the school computers, networks, forums, and mailing lists; or
(3) by use of electronic technology and communications off the school premises to the extent such use substantially and materially disrupts student learning or the school environment.
   (b) A nonpublic school under section 123B.41, subdivision 9, consistent with its school accreditation cycle, is encouraged to electronically transmit to the commissioner its antibullying policy, if any, and any summary data on its bullying incidents.
   (c) This section does not apply to a home school under sections 120A.22, subdivision 4, and 120A.24, or a nonpublic school under section 123B.41, subdivision 9.
   (d) A school-aged child who voluntarily participates in a public school activity such as a co-curricular or extra-curricular activity, is subject to the same student bullying policy provisions applicable to the public school students participating in the activity.

Subdivision 2. Definitions. (a) For purposes of this section, the following terms have the meanings given them. ...

(e) "Bullying" means intimidating, threatening, abusive, or harming conduct that is objectively offensive and:
   (1) there is an actual or perceived imbalance of power between the student engaging in prohibited conduct and the target of the behavior and the conduct is repeated or forms a pattern; or
   (2) materially and substantially interferes with a student's educational opportunities or performance or ability to participate in school functions or activities or receive school benefits, services, or privileges.
(f) "Cyberbullying" means bullying using technology or other electronic communication, including, but not limited to, a transfer of a sign, signal, writing, image, sound, or data, including a post on a social network Internet Web site or forum, transmitted through a computer, cell phone, or other electronic device.
(g) Intimidating, threatening, abusive, or harming conduct may involve, but is not limited to, conduct that causes physical harm to a student or a student's property or causes a student to be in reasonable fear of harm to person or property; under Minnesota common law, violates a student's reasonable expectation of privacy, defames a student, or constitutes intentional infliction of emotional distress against a student; is directed at any student or students, including those based on a person's actual or perceived race, ethnicity, color, creed, religion, national origin, immigration status, sex, marital status, familial status, socioeconomic status, physical appearance, sexual orientation, including gender identity and expression, academic status related to student performance, disability, or status with regard to public assistance, age, or any additional characteristic defined in chapter 363A. However, prohibited conduct need not be based on any particular characteristic defined in this paragraph or chapter 363A.

(h) "Prohibited conduct" means bullying or cyberbullying as defined under this subdivision or retaliation for asserting, alleging, reporting, or providing information about such conduct or knowingly making a false report about bullying.

(i) "Remedial response" means a measure to stop and correct prohibited conduct, prevent prohibited conduct from recurring, and protect, support, and intervene on behalf of the student who is the target of the prohibited conduct. Districts and schools may seek the assistance of the school safety technical assistance center under section 127A.052 to develop and implement remedial responses on behalf of a student who is the target of prohibited conduct, to stop and correct a student engaging in prohibited conduct, and for use with students and adults in the school community.

Subdivision 3. Local district and school policy. (a) Districts and schools, in consultation with students, parents, and community organizations, to the extent practicable, shall adopt, implement, and, on a cycle consistent with other district policies, review, and revise where appropriate, a written policy to prevent and prohibit student bullying consistent with this section. The policy must conform with sections 121A.41 to 121A.56. A district or school must adopt and implement a local policy under subdivisions 3 to 5 or comply with the provisions of the state model policy in subdivision 6.

(b) Each local district and school policy must establish research-based, developmentally appropriate best practices that include preventive and remedial measures and effective discipline for deterring policy violations; apply throughout the school or district; and foster active student, parent, and community participation. A district or school may request assistance from the school safety technical assistance center under section 127A.052 in complying with local policy requirements. The policy shall:

(1) define the roles and responsibilities of students, school personnel, and volunteers under the policy;
(2) specifically list the characteristics contained in subdivision 2, paragraph (g);
(3) emphasize remedial responses;
(4) be conspicuously posted in the administrative offices of the school and school district in summary form;
(5) be given to each school employee and independent contractor, if a contractor regularly interacts with students, at the time of employment with the district or school;
(6) be included in the student handbook on school policies; and
(7) be available to all parents and other school community members in an electronic format in the languages appearing on the district or school Web site, consistent with the district policies and practices.

(c) Consistent with its applicable policies and practices, Each district and school under this subdivision must discuss its policy with students, school personnel, and volunteers and provide appropriate training for all school personnel to prevent, identify, and respond to prohibited conduct. Districts and schools must establish a training cycle, not to exceed a period of three school years, for school personnel under this paragraph. Newly employed school personnel must receive the training within the first year of their employment with the district or school. A district or school administrator may accelerate the training cycle or provide additional training based on a particular need or circumstance.

(d) Each district and school under this subdivision must submit an electronic copy of its prohibited conduct policy to the commissioner.

Subdivision 4. Local policy components. (a) Each district and school policy implemented under this section must, at a minimum:

(1) designate a staff member as the primary contact person in the school building to receive reports of prohibited conduct under clause (3), ensure the policy and its procedures including restorative practices, consequences, and sanctions are fairly and fully implemented, and serve as the primary contact on policy and procedural matters implicating both the district or school and the department;
(2) require school employees who witness prohibited conduct or possess reliable information that would lead a reasonable person to suspect that a student is a target of prohibited conduct to make reasonable efforts to address and resolve the prohibited conduct;
(3) provide a procedure to begin to investigate reports of prohibited conduct within three school days of the report, and make the primary contact person responsible for the investigation and any resulting record and for keeping and regulating access to any record;
(4) indicate how a school will respond to an identified incident of prohibited conduct, including immediately intervening to protect the target of the prohibited conduct; at the school administrator's discretion and consistent with state and federal data practices law governing access to data, including section 13.02, subdivision 8, a presumption that a district or school official will notify the parent of the reported target of the prohibited conduct and the parent of the actor engaged in the prohibited conduct; providing other remedial responses to the prohibited conduct; and ensuring that remedial responses are tailored to the particular incident and nature of the conduct and the student's developmental age and behavioral history;
(5) prohibit reprisals or retaliation against any person who asserts, alleges, or reports prohibited conduct or provides information about such conduct and establish appropriate consequences for a person who engages in reprisal or retaliation;
(6) allow anonymous reporting but do not rely solely on an anonymous report to determine discipline;
(7) provide information about available community resources to the target, actor, and other affected individuals, as appropriate;
(8) where appropriate for a child with a disability to prevent or respond to prohibited conduct, allow the child's individualized education program or section 504 plan to address the skills and proficiencies the child needs to respond to or not engage in prohibited conduct;
(9) use new employee training materials, the school publication on school rules, procedures, and standards of conduct, and the student handbook on school policies to publicize the policy;
(10) require ongoing professional development, consistent with section 122A.60, to build the skills of all school personnel who regularly interact with students, including, but not limited to, educators, administrators, school counselors, social workers, psychologists, other school mental health professionals, school nurses, cafeteria workers, custodians, bus drivers, athletic coaches, extracurricular activities advisors, and paraprofessionals to identify, prevent, and appropriately address prohibited conduct;
(11) allow the alleged actor in an investigation of prohibited conduct to present a defense; and

(12) inform affected students and their parents of their rights under state and federal data practices laws to obtain access to data related to the incident and their right to contest the accuracy or completeness of the data.

(b) Professional development under a local policy includes, but is not limited to, information about:
  (1) developmentally appropriate strategies both to prevent and to immediately and effectively intervene to stop prohibited conduct;
  (2) the complex dynamics affecting an actor, target, and witnesses to prohibited conduct;
  (3) research on prohibited conduct, including specific categories of students at risk for prohibited conduct in school;
  (4) the incidence and nature of cyberbullying; and
  (5) Internet safety and cyberbullying.

Subdivision 5. Safe and supportive schools programming. (a) Districts and schools are encouraged to provide developmentally appropriate programmatic instruction to help students identify, prevent, and reduce prohibited conduct; value diversity in school and society; develop and improve students' knowledge and skills for solving problems, managing conflict, engaging in civil discourse, and recognizing, responding to, and reporting prohibited conduct; and make effective prevention and intervention programs available to students. Upon request, the school safety technical assistance center under section 127A.052 must assist a district or school in helping students understand social media and cyberbullying. Districts and schools must establish strategies for creating a positive school climate and use evidence-based social-emotional learning to prevent and reduce discrimination and other improper conduct.

(b) Districts and schools are encouraged to:

  (1) engage all students in creating a safe and supportive school environment;
  (2) partner with parents and other community members to develop and implement prevention and intervention programs;
  (3) engage all students and adults in integrating education, intervention, and other remedial responses into the school environment;
  (4) train student bystanders to intervene in and report incidents of prohibited conduct to the school's primary contact person;
  (5) teach students to advocate for themselves and others;
  (6) prevent inappropriate referrals to special education of students who may engage in prohibited conduct; and
  (7) foster student collaborations that foster a safe and supportive school climate.

Subdivision 6. State model policy. (a) The commissioner, in consultation with the commissioner of human rights, shall develop and maintain a state model policy. A district or school that does not adopt and implement a local policy under subdivisions 3 to 5 must implement and may supplement the provisions of the state model policy. The commissioner must assist districts and schools under this subdivision to implement the state policy. The state model policy must:

(1) define prohibited conduct, consistent with this section;

(2) apply the prohibited conduct policy components in this section;

(3) for a child with a disability, whenever an evaluation by an individualized education program team or a section 504 team indicates that the child's disability affects the child's social skills development or the child is vulnerable to prohibited conduct because of the child's disability, the child's individualized education program or section 504 plan may address the skills and proficiencies the child needs to not engage in and respond to such conduct; and

(4) encourage violence prevention and character development education programs under section 120B.232, subdivision 1.

    (b) The commissioner shall develop and post departmental procedures for:

        (1) periodically reviewing district and school programs and policies for compliance with this section;

        (2) investigating, reporting, and responding to noncompliance with this section, which may include an annual review of plans to improve and provide a safe and supportive school climate; and

        (3) allowing students, parents, and educators to file a complaint about noncompliance with the commissioner.

    (c) The commissioner must post on the department's Web site information indicating that when districts and schools allow noncurriculum-related student groups access to school facilities, the district or school must give all student groups equal access to the school facilities regardless of the content of the group members' speech.

Subdivision 7. Relation to existing law. This section does not:

(1) establish any private right of action;

(2) limit rights currently available to an individual under other civil or criminal law, including, but not limited to, chapter 363A; or

(3) interfere with a person's rights of religious expression and free speech and expression under the First Amendment of the Unites States Constitution.

MISSISSIPPI

Bullying Prohibition and Policy. Mississippi Code Annotated § 37-11-67, et seq. (West 2010)

Mississippi Code Annotated § 37-11-67

§ 37-11-67. Bullying; definitions; prohibition; reporting

(1) As used in this section and Section 37-11-69, "bullying or harassing behavior" is any pattern of gestures or written, electronic or verbal communications, or any physical act or any threatening communication, or any act reasonably perceived as being motivated by any actual or perceived differentiating characteristic, that takes place on school property, at any school-sponsored function, or on a school bus, and that:

(a) Places a student or school employee in actual and reasonable fear of harm to his or her person or damage to his or her property; or

(b) Creates or is certain to create a hostile environment by substantially interfering with or impairing a student's educational performance, opportunities or benefits. For purposes of this section, "hostile environment" means that the victim subjectively views the conduct as bullying or harassing behavior and the conduct is objectively severe or pervasive enough that a reasonable person would agree that it is bullying or harassing behavior.

(2) No student or school employee shall be subjected to bullying or harassing behavior by school employees or students.

(3) No person shall engage in any act of reprisal or retaliation against a victim, witness or a person with reliable information about an act of bullying or harassing behavior.

(4) A school employee who has witnessed or has reliable information that a student or school employee has been subject to any act of bullying or harassing behavior shall report the incident to the appropriate school official.

(5) A student or volunteer who has witnessed or has reliable information that a student or school employee has been subject to any act of bullying or harassing behavior should report the incident to the appropriate school official.

Mississippi Code Annotated § 37-11-69

§ 37-11-69. Anti-bullying policy requirement

Before December 31, 2010, each local school district shall include in its personnel policies, discipline policies and code of student conduct a prohibition against bullying or harassing behavior and adopt procedures for reporting, investigating and addressing such behavior. The policies must recognize the fundamental right of every student to take reasonable actions as may be necessary to defend himself or herself from an attack by another student who has evidenced menacing or threatening behavior through bullying or harassing.

MISSOURI

Anti-Bullying Requirements. Vernon's Annotated Missouri Statutes 160.775 (West 2010)

Vernon's Annotated Missouri Statutes 160.775

160.775. Anti-bullying policy required--definition--requirements

1. Every district shall adopt an antibullying policy by September 1, 2007.
2. "Bullying" means intimidation or harassment that causes a reasonable student to fear for his or her physical safety or property. Bullying may consist of physical actions, including gestures, or oral, cyberbullying, electronic, or written communication, and any threat of retaliation for reporting of such acts.

3. Each district's antibullying policy shall be founded on the assumption that all students need a safe learning environment. Policies shall treat students equally and shall not contain specific lists of protected classes of students who are to receive special treatment. Policies may include age-appropriate differences for schools based on the grade levels at the school. Each such policy shall contain a statement of the consequences of bullying.
4. Each district's antibullying policy shall require district employees to report any instance of bullying of which the employee has firsthand knowledge. The district policy shall address training of employees in the requirements of the district policy.

MONTANA

School Policy. Montana Administrative Rule 10.55.719 (West 2013)

Montana Administrative Rule 10.55.719

10.55.719 Student Protection Procedures

(1) A local board of trustees shall adopt a policy designed to deter persistent threatening, insulting, or demeaning gestures or physical conduct, including an intentional written, verbal, or electronic communication or threat directed against a student or students regardless of the underlying reason for such conduct, that:
   (a) causes a student physical or emotional harm, damages a student's property, or places a reasonable fear of harm to the student or the student's property;
   (b) substantially and materially interferes with access to an educational opportunity or benefit; or
   (c) substantially and materially disrupts the orderly operation of the school.
(2) Behavior prohibited under (1) includes retaliation against a victim or witness who reports behavior prohibited under (1).
(3) "Persistent" as used in this rule can consist of repeated acts against a single student or isolated acts directed against a number of different students.
(4) The behavior prohibited in (1) includes but is not limited to conduct:
   (a) in a classroom or other location on school premises;
   (b) during any school-sponsored program, activity, or function where the school is responsible for the student including when the student is traveling to and from school or on a school bus or other school-related vehicle; or
   (c) through the use of electronic communication, as defined in 45-8-213, [Montana Code Annotated], that substantially and materially disrupts the orderly operation of the school or any school-sponsored program, activity, or function where the school is responsible for the student.
(5) Each local board of trustees has discretion and control over the development of its policies and procedures regarding behavior prohibited under (1), but each district's policies and procedures must include at a minimum:

(a) a prohibition on the behavior specified in (1), regardless of the underlying reason or reasons the student has engaged in such behavior;
(b) a procedure for reporting and documenting reported acts of behavior prohibited under (1);
(c) a procedure for investigation of all reports of behavior prohibited under (1)(a) that includes an identification of the persons responsible for the investigation and response;
(d) a procedure for determining whether the reported act is subject to the jurisdiction of the school district or another public agency, including law enforcement, and a procedure for referral to the necessary persons or entity with appropriate jurisdiction;
(e) a procedure for prompt notification, as defined in the district policy, of the alleged victim and the alleged perpetrator, or the parents or guardian of such students when the students are minors;
(f) a procedure to protect any alleged victim of behavior prohibited under (1)(a) from further incidents of such behavior;
(g) a disciplinary procedure establishing the consequences for students found to have committed behavior prohibited under (1); and
(h) a procedure for the use of appropriate intervention and remediation for victims and perpetrators.

School Climate Rules. Montana Administrative Rule 10.55.801 (West 2013)

Montana Administrative Rule 10.55.801

10.55.801 School Climate

(1) The local board of trustees shall:
(a) develop policies, procedures, and rules that respect the rights of all learners, promote an awareness of and concern for the well-being of others, and address bullying, intimidation, and harassment of students and school personnel; ...
(b) offer programs and services which, in content and presentation, endeavor to be free of stereotyping in terms of age, sex, religion, race, national origin, or handicapping condition; ...
(c) encourage students to take responsibility for their education, including preparing for and participating in class and school activities, taking full advantage of learning services provided, helping design their educational goals, and conducting themselves respectfully and appropriately.

NEBRASKA

Bullying Prevention and Education. Nebraska Revised Statutes § 79-2,137 (West 2008)

Nebraska Revised Statutes § 79-2,137

§79-2,137. School district; development and adoption of bullying prevention and education policy; review

(1) The Legislature finds and declares that:
   (a) Bullying disrupts a school's ability to educate students; and
   (b) Bullying threatens public safety by creating an atmosphere in which such behavior can escalate into violence.
(2) For purposes of this section, bullying means any ongoing pattern of physical, verbal, or electronic abuse on school grounds, in a vehicle owned, leased, or contracted by a school being used for a school purpose by a school employee or his or her designee, or at school-sponsored activities or school-sponsored athletic events.
(3) On or before July 1, 2009, each school district as defined in section 79-101 shall develop and adopt a policy concerning bullying prevention and education for all students.
(4) The school district shall review the policy annually.

Student Discipline. Nebraska Revised Statutes § 79-267 (West 2014)

Nebraska Revised Statutes § 79-267

§ 79-267. Student conduct constituting grounds for long-term suspension, expulsion, or mandatory reassignment; enumerated; alternatives for truant or tardy students

The following student conduct shall constitute grounds for long-term suspension, expulsion, or mandatory reassignment, subject to the procedural provisions of the Student Discipline Act, when such activity occurs on school grounds, in a vehicle owned, leased, or contracted by a school being used for a school purpose or in a vehicle being driven for a school purpose by a school employee or by his or her designee, or at a school-sponsored activity or athletic event:

(1) Use of violence, force, coercion, threat, intimidation, or similar conduct in a manner that constitutes a substantial interference with school purposes;

***

(3) Causing or attempting to cause personal injury to a school employee, to a school volunteer, or to any student. Personal injury caused by accident, self-defense, or other action undertaken on the reasonable belief that it was necessary to protect some other person shall not constitute a violation of this subdivision;
(4) Threatening or intimidating any student for the purpose of or with the intent of obtaining money or anything of value from such student;
(5) Knowingly possessing, handling, or transmitting any object or material that is ordinarily or generally considered a weapon;

***

(8) Engaging in bullying as defined in section 79-2,137;

***

(10) Engaging in any other activity forbidden by the laws of the State of Nebraska which activity constitutes a danger to other students or interferes with school purposes; or

(11) A repeated violation of any rules and standards validly established pursuant to section 79-262 if such violations constitute a substantial interference with school purposes.

It is the intent of the Legislature that alternatives to suspension or expulsion be imposed against a student who is truant, tardy, or otherwise absent from required school activities.

NEVADA

Bullying by Use of Electronic Communication Device. Nevada Revised Statutes Annotated 200.900 (West 2013)

Nevada Revised Statutes Annotated 200.900

200.900. Penalties; definitions

1. A minor shall not knowingly and willfully use an electronic communication device to transmit or distribute, or otherwise knowingly and willfully transmit or distribute, an image of bullying committed against a minor to another person with the intent to encourage, further or promote bullying and to cause harm to the minor.
2. A minor who violates subsection 1:
   (a) For the first violation, is a child in need of supervision, as that term is used in title 5 of NRS, and is not a delinquent child; and
   (b) For the second or a subsequent violation, commits a delinquent act, and the court may order the detention of the minor in the same manner as if the minor had committed an act that would have been a misdemeanor if committed by an adult.
3. For the purposes of this section, to determine whether a person who is depicted in an image of bullying is a minor, the court may:
   (a) Inspect the person in question;
   (b) View the image;
   (c) Consider the opinion of a witness to the image regarding the person's age;
   (d) Consider the opinion of a medical expert who viewed the image; or
   (e) Use any other method authorized by the rules of evidence at common law.
4. As used in this section:
   (a) "Bullying" means a willful act which is written, verbal or physical, or a course of conduct on the part of one or more persons which is not otherwise authorized by law and which exposes a person one time or repeatedly and over time to one or more negative actions which is highly offensive to a reasonable person and:

(1) Is intended to cause or actually causes the person to suffer harm or serious emotional distress;
(2) Poses a threat of immediate harm or actually inflicts harm to another person or to the property of another person;
(3) Places the person in reasonable fear of harm or serious emotional distress; or
(4) Creates an environment which is hostile to a pupil by interfering with the education of the pupil.
(b) "Electronic communication device" means any electronic device that is capable of transmitting or distributing an image of bullying, including, without limitation, a cellular telephone, personal digital assistant, computer, computer network and computer system.
(c) "Image of bullying" means any visual depiction, including, without limitation, any photograph or video, of a minor bullying another minor.
(d) "Minor" means a person who is under 18 years of age.

Provision of Safe and Respectful Learning Environment. Nevada Revised Statutes Annotated 388.122, et seq. (West 2013)

Nevada Revised Statutes Annotated 388.122

388.122. "Bullying" defined

"Bullying" means a willful act which is written, verbal or physical, or a course of conduct on the part of one or more persons which is not authorized by law and which exposes a person repeatedly and over time to one or more negative actions which is highly offensive to a reasonable person and:

1. Is intended to cause or actually causes the person to suffer harm or serious emotional distress;
2. Exploits an imbalance in power between the person engaging in the act or conduct and the person who is the subject of the act or conduct;
3. Poses a threat of immediate harm or actually inflicts harm to another person or to the property of another person;
4. Places the person in reasonable fear of harm or serious emotional distress; or
5. Creates an environment which is hostile to a pupil by interfering with the education of the pupil.

Cyber-bullying. Nevada Revised Statutes Annotated 388.123 (West 2011)

Nevada Revised Statutes Annotated 388.123

388.123. "Cyber-bullying" defined

"Cyber-bullying" means bullying through the use of electronic communication. The term includes the use of electronic communication to transmit or distribute a sexual image of a minor. As used in this section, "sexual image" has the meaning ascribed to it in [Nevada Revised Statutes Annotated] 200.737 ["'Sexual image' means any visual depiction, including, without limitation, any photograph or video, of a minor simulating or engaging in sexual conduct or of a minor as the subject of a sexual portrayal"].

System of Accountability. Nevada Revised Statutes Annotated 385.3483 (West 2013)

Nevada Revised Statutes Annotated 385.3483

385.3483. District accountability report: Discipline of pupils

1. The annual report of accountability prepared pursuant to [Nevada Revised Statutes Annotated] 385.347 must include information on the discipline of pupils, including, without limitation: ...
   (e) For each school in the district and the district as a whole, including, without limitation, each charter school sponsored by the district:
      (1) The number of reported violations of [Nevada Revised Statutes Annotated] 388.135 occurring at a school or otherwise involving a pupil enrolled at a school, regardless of the outcome of the investigation conducted pursuant to [Nevada Revised Statutes Annotated] 388.1351;
      (2) The number of incidents determined to be bullying or cyber-bullying after an investigation is conducted pursuant to [Nevada Revised Statutes Annotated] 388.1351;
      (3) The number of incidents resulting in suspension or expulsion for bullying or cyber-bullying; and
      (4) Any actions taken to reduce the number of incidents of bullying or cyber-bullying including, without limitation, training that was offered or other policies, practices and programs that were implemented.

Provision of Safe and Respectful Learning Environment. Nevada Revised Statutes Annotated 388.132, et seq. (West 2013)

Nevada Revised Statutes Annotated 388.132

388.132. Legislative declaration concerning safe and respectful learning environment

The Legislature declares that:

1. A learning environment that is safe and respectful is essential for the pupils enrolled in the public schools in this State to achieve academic success and meet this State's high academic standards;
2. Any form of bullying or cyber-bullying seriously interferes with the ability of teachers to teach in the classroom and the ability of pupils to learn;
3. The use of the Internet by pupils in a manner that is ethical, safe and secure is essential to a safe and respectful learning environment and is essential for the successful use of technology;
4. The intended goal of the Legislature is to ensure that:
   (a) The public schools in this State provide a safe and respectful learning environment in which persons of differing beliefs, characteristics and backgrounds can realize their full academic and personal potential;

(b) All administrators, principals, teachers and other personnel of the school districts and public schools in this State demonstrate appropriate behavior on the premises of any public school by treating other persons, including, without limitation, pupils, with civility and respect and by refusing to tolerate bullying and cyber-bullying; and

(c) All persons in public schools are entitled to maintain their own beliefs and to respectfully disagree without resorting to bullying, cyber-bullying or violence; and

5. By declaring its goal that the public schools in this State provide a safe and respectful learning environment, the Legislature is not advocating or requiring the acceptance of differing beliefs in a manner that would inhibit the freedom of expression, but is requiring that pupils with differing beliefs be free from abuse.

Nevada Revised Statutes Annotated 388.133

388.133. Policy by Department [of Education] concerning safe and respectful learning environment

1. The Department shall, in consultation with the boards of trustees of school districts, educational personnel, local associations and organizations of parents whose children are enrolled in public schools throughout this State, and individual parents and legal guardians whose children are enrolled in public schools throughout this State, prescribe by regulation a policy for all school districts and public schools to provide a safe and respectful learning environment that is free of bullying and cyber-bullying.

2. The policy must include, without limitation:

    (a) Requirements and methods for reporting violations of [Nevada Revised Statutes Annotated] 388.135; and

    (b) A policy for use by school districts to train members of the board of trustees and all administrators, principals, teachers and all other personnel employed by the board of trustees of a school district. The policy must include, without limitation:

    (1) Training in the appropriate methods to facilitate positive human relations among pupils by eliminating the use of bullying and cyber-bullying so that pupils may realize their full academic and personal potential;

    (2) Training in methods to prevent, identify and report incidents of bullying and cyber-bullying;

    (3) Methods to improve the school environment in a manner that will facilitate positive human relations among pupils; and

    (4) Methods to teach skills to pupils so that the pupils are able to replace inappropriate behavior with positive behavior.

Nevada Revised Statutes Annotated 388.135

388.135. Bullying and cyber-bullying prohibited

A member of the board of trustees of a school district, any employee of the board of trustees, including, without limitation, an administrator, principal, teacher or other staff member, a member of a club or organization which uses the facilities of any public school, regardless of whether the club or organization has any connection to the school, or any pupil shall not engage in bullying or cyber-bullying on the premises of any public school, at an activity sponsored by a public school or on any school bus.

Nevada Revised Statutes Annotated 388.1351

388.1351. Staff member required to report violation to principal; written notice of reported violation to parent of each pupil involved; time period for initiation and completion of investigation; authorization for parent to appeal disciplinary decision

1. A teacher or other staff member who witnesses a violation of [Nevada Revised Statutes Annotated] 388.135 or receives information that a violation of [Nevada Revised Statutes Annotated] 388.135 has occurred shall verbally report the violation to the principal or his or her designee on the day on which the teacher or other staff member witnessed the violation or received information regarding the occurrence of a violation.
2. The principal or his or her designee shall initiate an investigation not later than 1 day after receiving notice of the violation pursuant to subsection 1. The principal or the designee shall provide written notice of a reported violation of [Nevada Revised Statutes Annotated] 388.135 to the parent or legal guardian of each pupil involved in the reported violation. The notice must include, without limitation, a statement that the principal or the designee will be conducting an investigation into the reported violation and that the parent or legal guardian may discuss with the principal or the designee any counseling and intervention services that are available to the pupil. The investigation must be completed within 10 days after the date on which the investigation is initiated and, if a violation is found to have occurred, include recommendations concerning the imposition of disciplinary action or other measures to be imposed as a result of the violation, in accordance with the policy governing disciplinary action adopted by the board of trustees of the school district.
3. The parent or legal guardian of a pupil involved in the reported violation of [Nevada Revised Statutes Annotated] 388.135 may appeal a disciplinary decision of the principal or his or her designee, made against the pupil as a result of the violation, in accordance with the policy governing disciplinary action adopted by the board of trustees of the school district.

Nevada Revised Statutes Annotated 388.1352

388.1352. Establishment of policy by school districts for employees to report violations to law enforcement

The board of trustees of each school district, in conjunction with the school police officers of the school district, if any, and the local law enforcement agencies that have jurisdiction over the school district, shall establish a policy for the procedures which must be followed by an employee of the school district when reporting a violation of [Nevada Revised Statutes Annotated] 388.135 to a school police officer or local law enforcement agency.

Nevada Revised Statutes Annotated 388.136

388.136. School officials prohibited from interfering with disclosure of violations

1. A school official shall not directly or indirectly interfere with or prevent the disclosure of information concerning a violation of [Nevada Revised Statutes Annotated] 388.135.
2. As used in this section, "school official" means:
    (a) A member of the board of trustees of a school district; or
    (b) A licensed or unlicensed employee of a school district.

Nevada Revised Statutes Annotated 388.137

388.137. Immunity for reporting of violations; exceptions; recommendation for disciplinary action if person who made report acted with malice, intentional misconduct, gross negligence or violation of law

1. No cause of action may be brought against a pupil or an employee or volunteer of a school who reports a violation of [Nevada Revised Statutes Annotated] 388.135 unless the person who made the report acted with malice, intentional misconduct, gross negligence, or intentional or knowing violation of the law.
2. If a principal determines that a report of a violation of [Nevada Revised Statutes Annotated] 388.135 is false and that the person who made the report acted with malice, intentional misconduct, gross negligence, or intentional or knowing violation of the law, the principal may recommend the imposition of disciplinary action or other measures against the person in accordance with the policy governing disciplinary action adopted by the board of trustees of the school district.

Nevada Revised Statutes Annotated 388.139

388.139. Text of certain provisions required to be included in rules of behavior

Each school district shall include the text of the provisions of [Nevada Revised Statutes Annotated] 388.121 to 388.145, inclusive, and the policies adopted by the board of trustees of the school district pursuant to [Nevada Revised Statutes Annotated] 388.134 under the heading "Bullying and Cyber-Bullying Is Prohibited in Public Schools," within each copy of the rules of behavior for pupils that the school district provides to pupils pursuant to [Nevada Revised Statutes Annotated] 392.463.

Nevada Revised Statutes Annotated 388.145

388.145. Requirements for delivery of information during annual "Week of Respect"

The board of trustees of each school district and the governing body of each charter school shall determine the most effective manner for the delivery of information to the pupils of each public school during the "Week of Respect" proclaimed by the Governor each year pursuant to [Nevada Revised Statutes Annotated] 236.073. The information delivered during the "Week of Respect" must focus on:

1. Methods to prevent, identify and report incidents of bullying and cyber-bullying;
2. Methods to improve the school environment in a manner that will facilitate positive human relations among pupils; and

State Anti-Bullying Statutes and Student Speech

3. Methods to facilitate positive human relations among pupils by eliminating the use of bullying and cyber-bullying.

Pupils and Unlawful Acts. Nevada Revised Statutes Annotated 392.915 (West 2010)

Nevada Revised Statutes Annotated 392.915

392.915. Threatening to cause bodily harm or death to pupil or school employee by means of oral, written or electronic communication; penalties

1. A person shall not, through the use of any means of oral, written or electronic communication, including, without limitation, through the use of cyber-bullying, knowingly threaten to cause bodily harm or death to a pupil or employee of a school district or charter school with the intent to:
   (a) Intimidate, harass, frighten, alarm or distress a pupil or employee of a school district or charter school;
   (b) Cause panic or civil unrest; or
   (c) Interfere with the operation of a public school, including, without limitation, a charter school.
2. Unless a greater penalty is provided by specific statute, a person who violates the provisions of subsection 1 is guilty of:
   (a) A misdemeanor, unless the provisions of paragraph (b) apply to the circumstances.
   (b) A gross misdemeanor, if the threat causes:
      (1) Any pupil or employee of a school district or charter school who is the subject of the threat to be intimidated, harassed, frightened, alarmed or distressed;
      (2) Panic or civil unrest; or
      (3) Interference with the operation of a public school, including, without limitation, a charter school.
3. As used in this section:
   (a) "Cyber-bullying" has the meaning ascribed to it in [Nevada Revised Statutes Annotated] 388.123.
   (b) "Oral, written or electronic communication" includes, without limitation, any of the following:
      (1) A letter, note or any other type of written correspondence.
      (2) An item of mail or a package delivered by any person or postal or delivery service.
      (3) A telegraph or wire service, or any other similar means of communication.
      (4) A telephone, cellular phone, satellite phone, page or facsimile machine, or any other similar means of communication.
      (5) A radio, television, cable, closed-circuit, wire, wireless, satellite or other audio or video broadcast or transmission, or any other similar means of communication.
      (6) An audio or video recording or reproduction, or any other similar means of communication.
      (7) An item of electronic mail, a modem or computer network, or the Internet, or any other similar means of communication.

Notification of Certain Offenses. Nevada Revised Statutes Annotated 62C.400 (West 2013)

Nevada Revised Statutes Annotated 62C.400

Department of juvenile services to provide certain information to juvenile court and school district concerning child who engaged in bullying or cyber-bullying

1. If a department of juvenile services determines that a child who is currently enrolled in school unlawfully engaged in bullying or cyber-bullying, the department shall provide the information specified in subsection 2 to the juvenile court in the judicial district in which the child resides and to the school district in which the child is currently enrolled.
2. The information required to be provided pursuant to subsection 1 must include:
    (a) The name of the child;
    (b) The name of the person who was the subject of the bullying or cyber-bullying; and
    (c) A description of any bullying or cyber-bullying committed by the child against the other person.
3. As used in this section:
    (a) "Bullying" has the meaning ascribed to it in [Nevada Revised Statutes Annotated] 388.122.
    (b) "Cyber-bullying" has the meaning ascribed to it in [Nevada Revised Statutes Annotated] 388.123.

Disposition of Cases by Juvenile Court. Nevada Revised Statutes Annotated 62E.030 (West 2013)

Nevada Revised Statutes Annotated 62E.030

62E.030. Court to provide certain information to school district concerning certain offenses

1. If a court determines that a child who is currently enrolled in school unlawfully caused or attempted to cause serious bodily injury to another person, the court shall provide the information specified in subsection 2 to the school district in which the child is currently enrolled.
2. The information required to be provided pursuant to subsection 1 must include:
    (a) The name of the child;
    (b) A description of any injury sustained by the other person;
    (c) A description of any weapon used by the child; and
    (d) A description of any threats made by the child against the other person before, during or after the incident in which the child injured or attempted to injure the person.
3. If a court determines that a child who is currently enrolled in school unlawfully engaged in bullying or cyber-bullying, the court shall provide the information specified in subsection 4 to the school district in which the child is currently enrolled.
4. The information required to be provided pursuant to subsection 3 must include:
    (a) The name of the child;

(b) The name of the person who was the subject of the bullying or cyber-bullying; and

(c) A description of any bullying or cyber-bullying committed by the child against the other person.

5. As used in this section:

(a) "Bullying" has the meaning ascribed to it in [Nevada Revised Statutes Annotated] 388.122.

(b) "Cyber-bullying" has the meaning ascribed to it in [Nevada Revised Statutes Annotated] 388.123.

NEW HAMPSHIRE

Pupil Safety and Violence Prevention. New Hampshire Revised Statutes § 193-F:2, et seq. (West 2010)

New Hampshire Revised Statutes § 193-F:2

§ 193-F:2 Purpose and Intent

I. All pupils have the right to attend public schools, including chartered public schools, that are safe, secure, and peaceful environments. One of the legislature's highest priorities is to protect our children from physical, emotional, and psychological violence by addressing the harm caused by bullying and cyberbullying in our public schools.

II. Bullying in schools has historically included actions shown to be motivated by a pupil's actual or perceived race, color, religion, national origin, ancestry or ethnicity, sexual orientation, socioeconomic status, age, physical, mental, emotional, or learning disability, gender, gender identity and expression, obesity, or other distinguishing personal characteristics, or based on association with any person identified in any of the above categories.

III. It is the intent of the legislature to protect our children from physical, emotional, and psychological violence by addressing bullying and cyberbullying of any kind in our public schools, for all of the historical reasons set forth in this section, and to prevent the creation of a hostile educational environment.

IV. The sole purpose of this chapter is to protect all children from bullying and cyberbullying, and no other legislative purpose is intended, nor should any other intent be construed from the enactment of this chapter.

New Hampshire Revised Statutes § 193-F:3

193-F:3 Definitions

In this chapter:

I. (a) "Bullying" means a single significant incident or a pattern of incidents involving a written, verbal, or electronic communication, or a physical act or gesture, or any combination thereof, directed at another pupil which:

(1) Physically harms a pupil or damages the pupil's property;
(2) Causes emotional distress to a pupil;
(3) Interferes with a pupil's educational opportunities;
(4) Creates a hostile educational environment; or
(5) Substantially disrupts the orderly operation of the school.
(b) "Bullying" shall include actions motivated by an imbalance of power based on a pupil's actual or perceived personal characteristics, behaviors, or beliefs, or motivated by the pupil's association with another person and based on the other person's characteristics, behaviors, or beliefs.
II. "Cyberbullying" means conduct defined in paragraph I of this section undertaken through the use of electronic devices.
III. "Electronic devices" include, but are not limited to, telephones, cellular phones, computers, pagers, electronic mail, instant messaging, text messaging, and websites.
IV. "Perpetrator" means a pupil who engages in bullying or cyberbullying.
V. "School property" means all real property and all physical plant and equipment used for school purposes, including public or private school buses or vans.
VI. "Victim" means a pupil against whom bullying or cyberbullying has been perpetrated.

New Hampshire Revised Statutes § 193-F:4

193-F:4 Pupil Safety and Violence Prevention

I. Bullying or cyberbullying shall occur when an action or communication as defined in [New Hampshire Revised Statutes] 193-F:3:
   (a) Occurs on, or is delivered to, school property or a school-sponsored activity or event on or off school property; or
   (b) Occurs off of school property or outside of a school-sponsored activity or event, if the conduct interferes with a pupil's educational opportunities or substantially disrupts the orderly operations of the school or school-sponsored activity or event.
II. The school board of each school district and the board of trustees of a chartered public school shall, no later than 6 months after the effective date of this section, adopt a written policy prohibiting bullying and cyberbullying. Such policy shall include the definitions set forth in [New Hampshire Revised Statutes] 193-F:3. The policy shall contain, at a minimum, the following components:
   (a) A statement prohibiting bullying or cyberbullying of a pupil.
   (b) A statement prohibiting retaliation or false accusations against a victim, witness, or anyone else who in good faith provides information about an act of bullying or cyberbullying and, at the time a report is made, a process for developing, as needed, a plan to protect pupils from retaliation.
   (c) A requirement that all pupils are protected regardless of their status under the law.
   (d) A statement that there shall be disciplinary consequences or interventions, or both, for a pupil who commits an act of bullying or cyberbullying, or falsely accuses another of the same as a means of retaliation or reprisal.

(e) A statement indicating how the policy shall be made known to school employees, regular school volunteers, pupils, parents, legal guardians, or employees of a company under contract to a school, school district, or chartered public school. Recommended methods of communication include, but are not limited to, handbooks, websites, newsletters, and workshops.

(f) A procedure for reporting bullying or cyberbullying that identifies all persons to whom a pupil or another person may report bullying or cyberbullying.

(g) A procedure outlining the internal reporting requirements within the school or school district or chartered public school.

(h) A procedure for notification, within 48 hours of the incident report, to the parent or parents or guardian of a victim of bullying or cyberbullying and the parent or parents or guardian of the perpetrator of the bullying or cyberbullying. The content of the notification shall comply with the Family Educational Rights and Privacy Act, 20 U.S.C. 1232g.

(i) A provision that the superintendent or designee may, within the 48-hour period, grant the school principal or designee a waiver from the notification requirement if the superintendent or designee deems such waiver to be in the best interest of the victim or perpetrator. Any such waiver granted shall be in writing. Granting of a waiver shall not negate the school's responsibility to adhere to the remainder of its approved written policy.

(j) A written procedure for investigation of reports, to be initiated within 5 school days of the reported incident, identifying either the principal or the principal's designee as the person responsible for the investigation and the manner and time period in which the results of the investigation shall be documented. The superintendent or designee may grant in writing an extension of the time period for the investigation and documentation of reports for up to an additional 7 school days, if necessary. The superintendent or superintendent's designee shall notify in writing all parties involved of the granting of an extension.

(k) A requirement that the principal or designee develop a response to remediate any substantiated incident of bullying or cyberbullying, including imposing discipline if appropriate, to reduce the risk of future incidents and, where deemed appropriate, to offer assistance to the victim or perpetrator. When indicated, the principal or designee shall recommend a strategy for protecting all pupils from retaliation of any kind.

(l) A requirement that the principal or designee report all substantiated incidents of bullying or cyberbullying to the superintendent or designee.

(m) A written procedure for communication with the parent or parents or guardian of victims and perpetrators regarding the school's remedies and assistance, within the boundaries of applicable state and federal law. This communication shall occur within 10 school days of completion of the investigation.

(n) Identification, by job title, of school officials responsible for ensuring that the policy is implemented.

III. The department of education may develop a model policy in accordance with the requirements set forth in this chapter which may be used by schools, school districts, and chartered public schools as a basis for adopting a local policy.

IV. A school board or board of trustees of a chartered public school shall, to the greatest extent practicable, involve pupils, parents, administrators, school staff, school volunteers, community representatives, and local law enforcement agencies in the process of developing the policy. The policy shall be adopted by all public schools within the school district and, to the extent possible, the policy should be integrated with the school's curriculum, discipline policies, behavior programs, and other violence prevention efforts.

New Hampshire Revised Statutes § 193-F:6

193-F:6 Reporting

I. Each school district and chartered public school shall annually report substantiated incidents of bullying or cyberbullying to the department of education. Pursuant to the Family Educational Rights and Privacy Act, 20 U.S.C. 1232g, such reports shall not contain any personally identifiable information pertaining to any pupil. The department shall develop a form to facilitate the reporting by school districts and chartered public schools. The department shall maintain records of such reports.

II. The department of education shall prepare an annual report of substantiated incidents of bullying or cyberbullying in the schools. The report shall include the number and types of such incidents in the schools and shall be submitted to the president of the senate, the speaker of the house of representatives, and the chairpersons of the house and senate education committees. The department of education shall assist school districts with recommendations for appropriate actions to address identified problems with pupil safety and violence prevention.

NEW JERSEY

Discipline of Pupils. New Jersey Statutes Annotated 18A:37-14 (West 2011)

New Jersey Statutes Annotated 18A:37-14

18A:37-14. Electronic communication, harassment, intimidation or bullying defined

As used in this act:

"Electronic communication" means a communication transmitted by means of an electronic device, including, but not limited to, a telephone, cellular phone, computer, or pager;

"Harassment, intimidation or bullying" means any gesture, any written, verbal or physical act, or any electronic communication, whether it be a single incident or a series of incidents, that is reasonably perceived as being motivated either by any actual or perceived characteristic, such as race, color, religion, ancestry, national origin, gender, sexual orientation, gender identity and expression, or a mental, physical or sensory disability, or by any other distinguishing characteristic, that takes place on school property, at any school-sponsored function, on a school bus, or off school grounds as provided for in section 16 of P.L. 2010, c. 122 (C.18A:37-15.3), that substantially disrupts or interferes with the orderly operation of the school or the rights of other students and that:

a. a reasonable person should know, under the circumstances, will have the effect of physically or emotionally harming a student or damaging the student's property, or placing a student in reasonable fear of physical or emotional harm to his person or damage to his property;
b. has the effect of insulting or demeaning any student or group of students; or
c. creates a hostile educational environment for the student by interfering with a student's education or by severely or pervasively causing physical or emotional harm to the student.

Public School Safety Law. New Jersey Statutes Annotated 18A:17-46 (West 2011)

New Jersey Statutes Annotated 18A:17-46

18A:17-46. Act of violence; report by school employee; notice of action taken; bi-annual reports

Any school employee observing or having direct knowledge from a participant or victim of an act of violence shall, in accordance with standards established by the commissioner, file a report describing the incident to the school principal in a manner prescribed by the commissioner, and copy of same shall be forwarded to the district superintendent.

The principal shall notify the district superintendent of schools of the action taken regarding the incident. Two times each school year, between September 1 and January 1 and between January 1 and June 30, at a public hearing, the superintendent of schools shall report to the board of education all acts of violence, vandalism, and harassment, intimidation, or bullying which occurred during the previous reporting period. The report shall include the number of reports of harassment, intimidation, or bullying, the status of all investigations, the nature of the bullying based on one of the protected categories identified in section 2 of P.L.2002, c. 83 (C.18A:37-14), the names of the investigators, the type and nature of any discipline imposed on any student engaged in harassment, intimidation, or bullying, and any other measures imposed, training conducted, or programs implemented, to reduce harassment, intimidation, or bullying. The information shall also be reported once during each reporting period to the Department of Education. The report must include data broken down by the enumerated categories as listed in section 2 of P.L.2002, c. 83 (C.18A:37-14), and data broken down by each school in the district, in addition to district-wide data. It shall be a violation to improperly release any confidential information not authorized by federal or State law for public release.

The report shall be used to grade each school for the purpose of assessing its effort to implement policies and programs consistent with the provisions of P.L.2002, c. 83 (C.18A:37-13 et seq.). The district shall receive a grade determined by averaging the grades of all the schools in the district. The commissioner shall promulgate guidelines for a program to grade schools for the purposes of this section.

The grade received by a school and the district shall be posted on the homepage of the school's website. The grade for the district and each school of the district shall be posted on the homepage of the district's website. A link to the report shall be available on the district's website. The information shall be posted on the websites within 10 days of the receipt of a grade by the school and district.

Verification of the reports on violence, vandalism, and harassment, intimidation, or bullying shall be part of the State's monitoring of the school district, and the State Board of Education shall adopt regulations that impose a penalty on a school employee who knowingly falsifies the report. A board of education shall provide ongoing staff training, in cooperation with the Department of Education, in fulfilling the reporting requirements pursuant to this section. The majority representative of the school employees shall have access monthly to the number and disposition of all reported acts of school violence, vandalism, and harassment, intimidation, or bullying.

Discipline of Pupils. New Jersey Statutes Annotated 18A:37-2 (West 2011)

New Jersey Statutes Annotated 18A:37-2

18A:37-2. Causes for suspension or expulsion of pupils

Any pupil who is guilty of continued and willful disobedience, or of open defiance of the authority of any teacher or person having authority over him, or of the habitual use of profanity or of obscene language, or who shall cut, deface or otherwise injure any school property, shall be liable to punishment and to suspension or expulsion from school.

Conduct which shall constitute good cause for suspension or expulsion of a pupil guilty of such conduct shall include, but not be limited to, any of the following: …

k. Harassment, intimidation, or bullying.

New Jersey Statutes Annotated 18A:37-13.1

18A:37-13.1. Legislative findings and declarations; harassment, intimidation and bullying in schools

The Legislature finds and declares that:

a. A 2009 study by the United States Departments of Justice and Education, "Indicators of School Crime and Safety," reported that 32% of students aged 12 through 18 were bullied in the previous school year. The study reported that 25% of the responding public schools indicated that bullying was a daily or weekly problem;
b. A 2009 study by the United States Centers for Disease Control and Prevention, "Youth Risk Behavior Surveillance," reported that the percentage of students bullied in New Jersey is 1 percentage point higher than the national median;
c. In 2010, the chronic persistence of school bullying has led to student suicides across the country, including in New Jersey;
d. Significant research has emerged since New Jersey enacted its public school anti-bullying statute in 2002, and since the State amended that law in 2007 to include cyber-bullying and in 2008 to require each school district to post its anti-bullying policy on its website and distribute it annually to parents or guardians of students enrolled in the district;
e. School districts and their students, parents, teachers, principals, other school staff, and board of education members would benefit by the establishment of clearer standards on what constitutes harassment, intimidation, and bullying, and clearer standards on how to prevent, report, investigate, and respond to incidents of harassment, intimidation, and bullying;

State Anti-Bullying Statutes and Student Speech

f. It is the intent of the Legislature in enacting this legislation to strengthen the standards and procedures for preventing, reporting, investigating, and responding to incidents of harassment, intimidation, and bullying of students that occur in school and off school premises;
g. Fiscal responsibility requires New Jersey to take a smarter, clearer approach to fight school bullying by ensuring that existing resources are better managed and used to make our schools safer for students;
h. In keeping with the aforementioned goal of fiscal responsibility and in an effort to minimize any burden placed on schools and school districts, existing personnel and resources shall be utilized in every possible instance to accomplish the goals of increased prevention, reporting, and responsiveness to incidents of harassment, intimidation, or bullying, including in the appointment of school anti-bullying specialists and district anti-bullying coordinators;
i. By strengthening standards for preventing, reporting, investigating, and responding to incidents of bullying this act will help to reduce the risk of suicide among students and avert not only the needless loss of a young life, but also the tragedy that such loss represents to the student's family and the community at large; and
j. Harassment, intimidation, and bullying is also a problem which occurs on the campuses of institutions of higher education in this State, and by requiring the public institutions to include in their student codes of conduct a specific prohibition against bullying, this act will be a significant step in reducing incidents of such activity.

Anti-Bullying Bill of Rights Act. New Jersey Statutes Annotated 18A:37-15, et seq. (West 2012)

New Jersey Statutes Annotated 18A:37-15

18A:37-15. Harassment, intimidation and bullying policy to be adopted by school districts; contents and notice

a. Each school district shall adopt a policy prohibiting harassment, intimidation or bullying on school property, at a school-sponsored function or on a school bus. The school district shall adopt the policy through a process that includes representation of parents or guardians, school employees, volunteers, students, administrators, and community representatives.
b. A school district shall have local control over the content of the policy, except that the policy shall contain, at a minimum, the following components:
    (1) a statement prohibiting harassment, intimidation or bullying of a student;
    (2) a definition of harassment, intimidation or bullying no less inclusive than that set forth in section 2 of P.L.2002, c. 83 (C.18A:37-14);
    (3) a description of the type of behavior expected from each student;
    (4) consequences and appropriate remedial action for a person who commits an act of harassment, intimidation or bullying;
    (5) a procedure for reporting an act of harassment, intimidation or bullying, including a provision that permits a person to report an act of harassment, intimidation or bullying anonymously; however, this shall not be construed to permit formal disciplinary action solely on the basis of an anonymous report.

All acts of harassment, intimidation, or bullying shall be reported verbally to the school principal on the same day when the school employee or contracted service provider witnessed or received reliable information regarding any such incident. The principal shall inform the parents or guardians of all students involved in the alleged incident, and may discuss, as appropriate, the availability of counseling and other intervention services. All acts of harassment, intimidation, or bullying shall be reported in writing to the school principal within two school days of when the school employee or contracted service provider witnessed or received reliable information that a student had been subject to harassment, intimidation, or bullying;

(6) a procedure for prompt investigation of reports of violations and complaints, which procedure shall at a minimum provide that:

(a) the investigation shall be initiated by the principal or the principal's designee within one school day of the report of the incident and shall be conducted by a school anti-bullying specialist. The principal may appoint additional personnel who are not school anti-bullying specialists to assist in the investigation. The investigation shall be completed as soon as possible, but not later than 10 school days from the date of the written report of the incident of harassment, intimidation, or bullying. In the event that there is information relative to the investigation that is anticipated but not yet received by the end of the 10-day period, the school anti-bullying specialist may amend the original report of the results of the investigation to reflect the information;

(b) the results of the investigation shall be reported to the superintendent of schools within two school days of the completion of the investigation, and in accordance with regulations promulgated by the State Board of Education pursuant to the "Administrative Procedure Act," P.L.1968, c. 410 (C.52:14B-1 et seq.), the superintendent may decide to provide intervention services, establish training programs to reduce harassment, intimidation, or bullying and enhance school climate, impose discipline, order counseling as a result of the findings of the investigation, or take or recommend other appropriate action;

(c) the results of each investigation shall be reported to the board of education no later than the date of the board of education meeting next following the completion of the investigation, along with information on any services provided, training established, discipline imposed, or other action taken or recommended by the superintendent;

(d) parents or guardians of the students who are parties to the investigation shall be entitled to receive information about the investigation, in accordance with federal and State law and regulation, including the nature of the investigation, whether the district found evidence of harassment, intimidation, or bullying, or whether discipline was imposed or services provided to address the incident of harassment, intimidation, or bullying. This information shall be provided in writing within 5 school days after the results of the investigation are reported to the board. A parent or guardian may request a hearing before the board after receiving the information, and the hearing shall be held within 10 days of the request. The board shall meet in executive session for the hearing to protect the confidentiality of the students. At the hearing the board may hear from the school anti-bullying specialist about the incident, recommendations for discipline or services, and any programs instituted to reduce such incidents;

(e) at the next board of education meeting following its receipt of the report, the board shall issue a decision, in writing, to affirm, reject, or modify the superintendent's decision. The board's decision may be appealed to the Commissioner of Education, in accordance with the procedures set forth in law and regulation, no later than 90 days after the issuance of the board's decision; and

(f) a parent, student, guardian, or organization may file a complaint with the Division on Civil Rights within 180 days of the occurrence of any incident of harassment, intimidation, or bullying based on membership in a protected group as enumerated in the "Law Against Discrimination," P.L.1945, c. 169 (C.10:5-1 et seq.);

(7) the range of ways in which a school will respond once an incident of harassment, intimidation or bullying is identified, which shall be defined by the principal in conjunction with the school anti-bullying specialist, but shall include an appropriate combination of services that are available within the district such as counseling, support services, intervention services, and other programs, as defined by the commissioner. In the event that the necessary programs and services are not available within the district, the district may apply to the Department of Education for a grant from the "Bullying Prevention Fund" established pursuant to section 25 of P.L.2010, c. 122 (C.18A:37-28) to support the provision of out-of-district programs and services;

(8) a statement that prohibits reprisal or retaliation against any person who reports an act of harassment, intimidation or bullying and the consequence and appropriate remedial action for a person who engages in reprisal or retaliation;

(9) consequences and appropriate remedial action for a person found to have falsely accused another as a means of retaliation or as a means of harassment, intimidation or bullying;

(10) a statement of how the policy is to be publicized, including notice that the policy applies to participation in school-sponsored functions;

(11) a requirement that a link to the policy be prominently posted on the home page of the school district's website and distributed annually to parents and guardians who have children enrolled in a school in the school district; and

(12) a requirement that the name, school phone number, school address and school email address of the district anti-bullying coordinator be listed on the home page of the school district's website and that on the home page of each school's website the name, school phone number, school address and school email address of the school anti-bullying specialist and the district anti-bullying coordinator be listed. The information concerning the district anti-bullying coordinator and the school anti-bullying specialists shall also be maintained on the department's website.

c. A school district shall adopt a policy and transmit a copy of its policy to the appropriate executive county superintendent of schools by September 1, 2003. A school district shall annually conduct a re-evaluation, reassessment, and review of its policy, making any necessary revisions and additions. The board shall include input from the school anti-bullying specialists in conducting its re-evaluation, reassessment, and review. The district shall transmit a copy of the revised policy to the appropriate executive county superintendent of schools within 30 school days of the revision. The first revised policy following the effective date of P. L.2010, c. 122 (C.18A:37-13.1 et al.) shall be transmitted to the executive county superintendent of schools by September 1, 2011.

d. (1) To assist school districts in developing policies for the prevention of harassment, intimidation, or bullying, the Commissioner of Education shall develop a model policy applicable to grades kindergarten through 12. This model policy shall be issued no later than December 1, 2002.
(2) The commissioner shall adopt amendments to the model policy which reflect the provisions of P.L.2010, c. 122 (C.18A:37-13.1 et al.) no later than 90 days after the effective date of that act and shall subsequently update the model policy as the commissioner deems necessary.
e. Notice of the school district's policy shall appear in any publication of the school district that sets forth the comprehensive rules, procedures and standards of conduct for schools within the school district, and in any student handbook.
f. Nothing in this section shall prohibit a school district from adopting a policy that includes components that are more stringent than the components set forth in this section.

Discipline of Pupils. New Jersey Statutes Annotated 18A:37-15.1, et seq. (West 2007)

New Jersey Statutes Annotated 18A:37-15.1

18A:37-15.1. Harassment or bullying by way of electronic communication; incorporation into school district policy

a. A school district's policy on prohibiting harassment, intimidation or bullying adopted pursuant to section 3 of P.L.2002, c. 83 (C.18A:37-15), shall be amended, if necessary, to reflect the provisions of P.L.2007, c. 129 (C.18A:37-15.1 et al.). The district shall transmit a copy of the amended policy to the appropriate county superintendent of schools. Notice of the amended policy shall appear in any publication of the school district that sets forth the comprehensive rules, procedures and standards of conduct for schools within the school district, and in any student handbook.
b. In the event that a school district's policy on prohibiting harassment, intimidation or bullying adopted pursuant to section 3 of P.L.2002, c. 83 (C.18A:37-15) does not accord with the provisions of subsection a. of this section by the 90th day following the effective date of this act, the district's existing policy prohibiting harassment, intimidation or bullying shall be deemed to include an "electronic communication" as defined in section 2 of P.L.2002, c. 83 (C.18A:37-14) as amended by section 1 of P.L.2007, c. 129.

New Jersey Statutes Annotated 18A:37-15.3 (West 2011)

18A:37-15.3. School district policy to include appropriate responses to harassment, intimidation and bullying occurring off school grounds

The policy adopted by each school district pursuant to section 3 of P.L.2002, c. 83 (C.18A:37-15) shall include provisions for appropriate responses to harassment, intimidation, or bullying, as defined in section 2 of P.L.2002, c. 83 (C.18A:37-14), that occurs off school grounds, in cases in which a school employee is made aware of such actions. The responses to harassment, intimidation, or bullying that occurs off school grounds shall be consistent with the board of education's code of student conduct and other provisions of the board's policy on harassment, intimidation, or bullying.

New Jersey Statutes Annotated 18A:37-16 (West 2011)

18A:37-16. Retaliation or false accusation against victim prohibited; mandatory reporting; immunity for failure to remedy

a. A member of a board of education, school employee, student or volunteer shall not engage in reprisal, retaliation or false accusation against a victim, witness or one with reliable information about an act of harassment, intimidation or bullying.
b. A member of a board of education, school employee, contracted service provider, student or volunteer who has witnessed, or has reliable information that a student has been subject to, harassment, intimidation or bullying shall report the incident to the appropriate school official designated by the school district's policy, or to any school administrator or safe schools resource officer, who shall immediately initiate the school district's procedures concerning school bullying.
c. A member of a board of education or a school employee who promptly reports an incident of harassment, intimidation or bullying, to the appropriate school official designated by the school district's policy, or to any school administrator or safe schools resource officer, and who makes this report in compliance with the procedures in the district's policy, is immune from a cause of action for damages arising from any failure to remedy the reported incident.
d. A school administrator who receives a report of harassment, intimidation, or bullying from a district employee, and fails to initiate or conduct an investigation, or who should have known of an incident of harassment, intimidation, or bullying and fails to take sufficient action to minimize or eliminate the harassment, intimidation, or bullying, may be subject to disciplinary action.

New Jersey Statutes Annotated 18A:37-20 (West 2011)

18A:37-20. Anti-bullying specialists; appointment and duties; district anti-bullying coordinator; appointment and duties

a. The principal in each school in a school district shall appoint a school anti-bullying specialist. When a school guidance counselor, school psychologist, or another individual similarly trained is currently employed in the school, the principal shall appoint that individual to be the school anti-bullying specialist. If no individual meeting this criteria is currently employed in the school, the principal shall appoint a school anti-bullying specialist from currently employed school personnel. The school anti-bullying specialist shall:
(1) chair the school safety team as provided in section 18 of P.L.2010, c. 122 (C.18A:37-21);
(2) lead the investigation of incidents of harassment, intimidation, and bullying in the school; and

(3) act as the primary school official responsible for preventing, identifying, and addressing incidents of harassment, intimidation, and bullying in the school.

b. The superintendent of schools shall appoint a district anti-bullying coordinator. The superintendent shall make every effort to appoint an employee of the school district to this position. The district anti-bullying coordinator shall:

(1) be responsible for coordinating and strengthening the school district's policies to prevent, identify, and address harassment, intimidation, and bullying of students;

(2) collaborate with school anti-bullying specialists in the district, the board of education, and the superintendent of schools to prevent, identify, and respond to harassment, intimidation, and bullying of students in the district;

(3) provide data, in collaboration with the superintendent of schools, to the Department of Education regarding harassment, intimidation, and bullying of students; and

(4) execute such other duties related to school harassment, intimidation, and bullying as requested by the superintendent of schools.

c. The district anti-bullying coordinator shall meet at least twice a school year with the school anti-bullying specialists in the district to discuss and strengthen procedures and policies to prevent, identify, and address harassment, intimidation, and bullying in the district.

Definitions. New Jersey Administrative Code 6A:16-1.3 (West 2014)

New Jersey Administrative Code 6A:16-1.3

6A:16–1.3 Definitions

"Electronic communication" means a communication transmitted by means of an electronic device, including, but not limited to, a telephone, cellular phone, computer, or remotely activating paging device.

"Harassment, intimidation, or bullying" means any gesture, any written, verbal, or physical act, or any electronic communication, whether it be a single incident or a series of incidents, in accordance with [New Jersey Statutes Annotated] 18A:37-14, that is reasonably perceived as being motivated either by any actual or perceived characteristic, such as race, color, religion, ancestry, national origin, gender, sexual orientation, gender identity and expression, or a mental, physical or sensory disability, or by any other distinguishing characteristic, that takes place on school property, at any school-sponsored function, on a school bus, or off school grounds as provided for in [New Jersey Statutes Annotated] 18A:37-14 and 15.3, that substantially disrupts or interferes with the orderly operation of the school or the rights of other students and that a reasonable person should know, under the circumstances, will have the effect of physically or emotionally harming a student or damaging the student's property or placing a student in reasonable fear of physical or emotional harm to his or her person or damage to his or her property; has the effect of insulting or demeaning any student or group of students; or creates a hostile educational environment for a student by interfering with the student's education or by severely or pervasively causing physical or emotional harm to the student.

State Anti-Bullying Statutes and Student Speech

Student Conduct. New Jersey Administrative Code 6A:16-7.5, et seq. (West 2014)

New Jersey Administrative Code 6A:16-7.5

6A:16–7.5 Conduct away from school grounds

(a) School authorities have the right to impose a consequence on a student for conduct away from school grounds that is consistent with the district board of education's code of student conduct, pursuant to [New Jersey Administrative Code] 6A:16-7.1.
   1. This authority shall be exercised only when it is reasonably necessary for the student's physical or emotional safety, security and well-being or for reasons relating to the safety, security and well-being of other students, staff or school grounds, pursuant to [New Jersey Statutes Annotated] 18A:25–2 and 18A:37–2.
   2. This authority shall be exercised only when the conduct that is the subject of the proposed consequence materially and substantially interferes with the requirements of appropriate discipline in the operation of the school.
   3. The consequence pursuant to (a) above shall be handled in accordance with the district board of education's approved code of student conduct, pursuant to [New Jersey Administrative Code] 6A:16-7.1, and as appropriate, in accordance with [New Jersey Administrative Code] 6A:16-7.2, 7.3, or 7.4.
(b) School authorities shall respond to harassment, intimidation, or bullying that occurs off school grounds, pursuant to [New Jersey Statutes Annotated] 18A:37-14 and 15.3 and [New Jersey Administrative Code] 6A:16-1.3, 7.1, and 7.7.

New Jersey Administrative Code 6A:16-7.7

6A:16–7.7 Harassment, intimidation, and bullying

(a) Each district board of education shall develop, adopt, and implement a policy prohibiting harassment, intimidation, or bullying on school grounds, pursuant to [New Jersey Statutes Annotated] 18A:37-15.
   1. Each district board of education shall develop the policy in consultation with, at a minimum, parents and other community members, school employees, school volunteers, students, and school administrators.
   2. Each district board of education shall have control over the content of the policy, except that it shall contain, at a minimum, the following components:
      i. A statement prohibiting harassment, intimidation or bullying of a student;
      ii. A definition of harassment, intimidation or bullying no less inclusive than that set forth in the definition at [New Jersey Statutes Annotated] 18A:37–14 and [New Jersey Administrative Code] 6A:16–1.3;
      iii. A description of the type of behavior expected from each student;

iv. Appropriate remedial action for a student who commits an act of harassment, intimidation or bullying that takes into account the nature of the behavior, the developmental age of the student and the student's history of problem behaviors and performance and that may include the following:
(1) A behavioral assessment or evaluation including, but not limited to, a referral to the child study team, as appropriate; and
(2) Supportive interventions and referral services, including those at [New Jersey Administrative Code] 6A:16–8;
v. Consequences for a student who commits an act of harassment, intimidation, or bullying that are:
(1) Varied and graded according to the nature of the behavior, the developmental age of the student and the student's history of problem behaviors and performance; and
(2) Consistent with the provisions of [New Jersey Administrative Code] 6A:16–7, as appropriate;
vi. Appropriate consequences and remedial action for a staff member who commits an act of harassment, intimidation, or bullying;
vii. A procedure for reporting, verbally and in writing, an act of harassment, intimidation, or bullying, including a provision that permits a person to report anonymously consistent with [New Jersey Statutes Annotated] 18A:37-15.b(5);
(1) The district board of education shall not take formal disciplinary action based solely on the anonymous report;
viii. A procedure for prompt investigation of violation and complaint reports consistent with [New Jersey Statutes Annotated] 18A:37-15.b(6)(a) through (f) and 16.d;
ix. A requirement for the principal, in conjunction with the school anti-bullying specialist, to define the range of ways in which a school will respond once an incident of harassment, intimidation, or bullying is identified, consistent with the range of responses adopted by the board of education, pursuant to [New Jersey Statutes Annotated] 18A:37-15.b(7);
(1) The responses, at a minimum, shall include support for victims of harassment, intimidation, or bullying and corrective actions for documented systemic problems related to harassment, intimidation, or bullying;
x. A statement that prohibits a district board of education member, school employee, student, or volunteer from engaging in reprisal, retaliation, or false accusation against a victim, witness, or any person who reports or has reliable information about an act of harassment, intimidation, or bullying.
(1) The statement shall include the consequence(s) and appropriate remedial action(s) for a person who engages in reprisal or retaliation;
xi. Consequences and appropriate remedial action for a person found to have falsely accused another as a means of retaliation or harassment, intimidation, or bullying;
xii. A statement of how the harassment, intimidation, and bullying policy is to be publicized, including notice that the policy applies to participation in school-sponsored functions and on school buses.

(1) Notice of the district board of education's policy shall appear in any publication of the school district that sets forth the code of student conduct, pursuant to [New Jersey Administrative Code] 6A:16-7.1, for schools within the school district;

xiii. A requirement that a link to the harassment, intimidation, and bullying policy be posted prominently on the home page of the school district's and each school's website;

xiv. A requirement that the harassment, intimidation, and bullying policy be distributed annually to all school staff, students, and parents;

xv. A requirement that the name of the school district's anti-bullying coordinator and his or her school phone number, school address, and school e-mail address be listed on the home page of the school district's website;

xvi. A requirement that the name of the school's anti-bullying specialist and his or her school phone number, school address, and school e-mail address be listed on the home page of the school's website; and

xvii. Provisions for appropriate responses to harassment, intimidation, or bullying, as defined in [New Jersey Statutes Annotated] 18A:37-14 and [New Jersey Administrative Code] 6A:16-1.3, that occurs off school grounds in cases in which a school employee is made aware of the actions or a school administrator should have known of an incident of harassment, intimidation, or bullying.

(1) Responses to harassment, intimidation, or bullying that occurs off school grounds shall be consistent with [New Jersey Administrative Code] 6A:16-7.1 and 7.5 and this section.

(b) A district board of education shall not be prohibited from adopting a harassment, intimidation, and bullying policy that includes components more stringent than components set forth in [New Jersey Statutes Annotated] 18A:37-15 and (a) above.

(c) A district board of education member, school employee, contracted service provider, student, or volunteer who has witnessed, or has reliable information that a student has been subject to harassment, intimidation, or bullying shall report the incident to the appropriate school official designated by the district board of education's policy, pursuant to [New Jersey Statutes Annotated] 18A:37-15 and (a)2vii above, or to any school administrator or safe schools resource officer, who shall immediately initiate the school district's procedures concerning harassment, intimidation, and bullying.

1. A district board of education member or school employee who promptly reports an incident of harassment, intimidation, or bullying to the appropriate school official designated by the district board of education's policy, or to any school administrator or safe schools resource officer, and who makes the report in compliance with the district board of education's policy, is immune from a cause of action for damages arising from a failure to remedy the reported incident, as set forth in [New Jersey Statutes Annotated] 18A:37-16.c.

(d) A school administrator who receives from a school district employee a report of harassment, intimidation, or bullying, and fails to initiate or conduct an investigation, or who should have known of an incident of harassment, intimidation, or bullying and fails to take sufficient action to minimize or eliminate the harassment, intimidation, or bullying, may be subject to disciplinary action.

(e) The district board of education shall:

1. Annually review the training needs of school employees and volunteers who have significant contact with students for the effective implementation of the harassment, intimidation, and bullying policies, procedures, programs and initiatives of the district board of education and implement training programs for school employees and volunteers who have significant contact with students, consistent with P.L. 2010, c. 122, the annual review of training needs and the findings of the annual review and update of the code of student conduct, pursuant to [New Jersey Administrative Code] 6A:16-7.1(a)2.
    i. Information regarding the district board of education's policy against harassment, intimidation, and bullying shall be incorporated into the school district's employee training program.
    (1) The program shall be provided to full-and part-time staff, volunteers who have significant contact with students and persons contracted by the school district to provide services to students;
2. Develop a process for annually discussing with students the school district's harassment, intimidation, and bullying policy;
3. Annually conduct a re-evaluation, reassessment and review of its harassment, intimidation, and bullying policy, and make any necessary revisions, consistent with [New Jersey Statutes Annotated] 18A:37-15.c.
    i. The programs or other responses shall be planned in consultation with, at a minimum, parents and other community members, school employees, school volunteers, students, and school administrators;
4. Annually establish, implement, document, and assess bullying-prevention programs or approaches and other initiatives designed to create schoolwide conditions to prevent or intervene in harassment, intimidation, and bullying in schools of the school district.
    i. Programs, approaches, and initiatives shall be planned in consultation with, at a minimum, parents and other community members, school employees, school volunteers, students, and school administrators; and
5. Submit to the executive county superintendent a copy of its approved harassment, intimidation, and bullying policy within 30 days of its adoption.

(f) The principal of each school in the school district shall appoint a school anti-bullying specialist to perform the functions established in [New Jersey Statutes Annotated] 18A:37-20.a and c.

(g) The chief school administrator of the school district shall appoint a district anti-bullying coordinator to perform the functions established in [New Jersey Statutes Annotated] 18A:37-20.b and c.

(h) The district board of education shall form a school safety team in each school in the school district to achieve the purposes and perform the functions established in [New Jersey Statutes Annotated] 18A:37-21.

(i) The requirements are promulgated pursuant to [New Jersey Statutes Annotated] 18A:37-13 through 32 and shall not be interpreted to prevent a victim from seeking redress under any other available civil or criminal law.

NEW MEXICO

Bullying and Cyberbulling. New Mexico Statutes Annotated 1978, § 22-2-21 (West 2013)

New Mexico Statutes Annotated 1978, § 22-2-21

§ 22-2-21. Bullying and cyberbullying prevention programs

A. The department shall establish guidelines for bullying prevention policies to be promulgated by local school boards. Every local school board shall promulgate a bullying prevention policy by August 2011. Every public school shall implement a bullying prevention program by August 2012.
B. Every local school board shall promulgate a specific cyberbullying prevention policy by August 2013. Cyberbullying prevention policies shall require that:
    (1) all licensed school employees complete training on how to recognize signs that a person is being cyberbullied;
    (2) any licensed school employee who has information about or a reasonable suspicion that a person is being cyberbullied report the matter immediately to the school principal or the local superintendent or both;
    (3) any school administrator or local superintendent who receives a report of cyberbullying take immediate steps to ensure prompt investigation of the report; and
    (4) school administrators take prompt disciplinary action in response to cyberbullying confirmed through investigation. Disciplinary action taken pursuant to this subsection must be by the least restrictive means necessary to address a hostile environment on the school campus resulting from the confirmed cyberbullying and may include counseling, mediation and appropriate disciplinary action that is consistent with the legal rights of the involved students.
C. Each local school board shall make any necessary revisions to its disciplinary policies to ensure compliance with the provisions of this section.
D. As used in this section, "cyberbullying" means electronic communication that:
    (1) targets a specific student;
    (2) is published with the intention that the communication be seen by or disclosed to the targeted student;
    (3) is in fact seen by or disclosed to the targeted student; and
    (4) creates or is certain to create a hostile environment on the school campus that is so severe or pervasive as to substantially interfere with the targeted student's educational benefits, opportunities or performance.

Bullying Prevention, Definitions and Requirements. New Mexico Administrative Code 6.12.7, et seq. (West 2014)

New Mexico Administrative Code 6.12.7.6

6.12.7.6. Objective

This rule establishes requirements for local school boards and public schools, including charter schools, to address bullying of students by adopting and implementing policies and prevention programs.

New Mexico Administrative Code 6.12.7.7

6.12.7.7 Definitions

A. "Bullying" means any repeated and pervasive written, verbal or electronic expression, physical act or gesture, or a pattern thereof, that is intended to cause distress upon one or more students in the school, on school grounds, in school vehicles, at a designated bus stop, or at school activities or sanctioned events. Bullying includes, but is not limited to, hazing, harassment, intimidation or menacing acts of a student which may, but need not be based on the student's race, color, sex, ethnicity, national origin, religion, disability, age or sexual orientation.
B. "Cyberbullying" means electronic communication that:
   (1) targets a specific student;
   (2) is published with the intention that the communication be seen by or disclosed to the targeted student;
   (3) is in fact seen by or disclosed to the targeted student; and
   (4) creates or is certain to create a hostile environment on the school campus that is so severe or pervasive as to substantially interfere with the targeted student's educational benefits, opportunities or performance.
C. "Harassment" means knowingly pursuing a pattern of conduct that is intended to annoy, alarm or terrorize another person.

New Mexico Administrative Code 6.12.7.8

6.12.7.8 Requirements

A. This section governs policies and programs to be adopted and implemented by local school boards addressing bullying and cyberbullying. Cyberbullying policies and programs must be in effect beginning with the 2013-2014 school year.
B. Each local school board shall develop and implement a policy that addresses and [sic] cyberbullying. Each local school board shall make any necessary revisions to its disciplinary policies to ensure that cyberbullying is addressed in accordance with the requirements of this rule.

C. The anti-bullying policy shall at least include, but shall not be limited to:
 (1) definitions;
 (2) an absolute prohibition against bullying and cyberbullying;
 (3) a method to ensure initial and annual dissemination of the anti-bullying and anti-cyberbullying policy to all students, parents, teachers, administrators and all other school or district employees;
 (4) procedures for reporting incidents of bullying and cyberbullying which ensure confidentiality to those reporting bullying or cyberbullying incidents and protection from reprisal, retaliation or false accusation against victims, witnesses or others with information regarding a bullying or cyberbullying incident;
 (5) consequences for bullying and cyberbullying which include consideration of compliance with state and federal IDEA requirements;
 (6) consequences for knowingly making false reports pursuant to the anti-bullying policy;
 (7) procedures for investigation by administration of incidents reported pursuant to the anti-bullying policy;
 (8) a requirement that teachers and other school staff report any incidents of bullying and cyberbullying; and
 (9) a requirement that anti-bullying is included as part of the health education curriculum as set forth in 6.30.2.19 [New Mexico Administrative Code] ("content standards - health education").
D. The cyberbullying prevention policy shall require that:
 (1) all licensed school employees complete training on how to recognize signs of cyberbullying;
 (2) any licensed school employee who has information about or a reasonable suspicion of cyberbullying shall report the matter immediately to either or both the school principal and the local superintendent or to the head administrator of a charter school;
 (3) any school administrator or local superintendent who receives a report of cyberbullying take immediate steps to ensure prompt investigation of the report; and
 (4) school administrators take prompt disciplinary action in response to cyberbullying confirmed through investigation; disciplinary action taken pursuant to this subsection must be by the least restrictive means necessary to address a hostile environment on the school campus resulting from the confirmed cyberbullying and may include counseling, mediation and appropriate disciplinary action that is consistent with the legal rights of the involved students.
E. Every public school shall implement a bullying and cyberbullying prevention program.
F. Every local school board shall submit to the department, as directed by the department, assurances of:
 (1) adoption and implementation of a policy addressing bullying and cyberbullying; and
 (2) review and, if necessary, revision of disciplinary polices to ensure that the policies address cyberbullying; and
 (3) implementation of cyberbullying training for all licensed school employees.
G. Every local school board and every charter school shall submit to the department, as directed by the department, assurances of implementation of bullying and cyberbullying prevention programs.

NEW YORK

Dignity for All Students. McKinney's Education Law § 10, et seq. (West 2012)

McKinney's Education Law § 10

§ 10. Legislative intent

The legislature finds that students' ability to learn and to meet high academic standards, and a school's ability to educate its students, are compromised by incidents of discrimination or harassment including bullying, taunting or intimidation. It is hereby declared to be the policy of the state to afford all students in public schools an environment free of discrimination and harassment. The purpose of this article is to foster civility in public schools and to prevent and prohibit conduct which is inconsistent with a school's educational mission.

McKinney's Education Law § 11 (West 2013)

§ 11. Definitions

For the purposes of this article, the following terms shall have the following meanings:

1. "School property" shall mean in or within any building, structure, athletic playing field, playground, parking lot, or land contained within the real property boundary line of a public elementary or secondary school; or in or on a school bus, as defined in section one hundred forty-two of the vehicle and traffic law.
2. "School function" shall mean a school-sponsored extra-curricular event or activity.
...
5. "Sexual orientation" shall mean actual or perceived heterosexuality, homosexuality or bisexuality.
6. "Gender" shall mean actual or perceived sex and shall include a person's gender identity or expression.
7. "Harassment" and "bullying" shall mean the creation of a hostile environment by conduct or by threats, intimidation or abuse, including cyberbullying, that (a) has or would have the effect of unreasonably and substantially interfering with a student's educational performance, opportunities or benefits, or mental, emotional or physical well-being; or (b) reasonably causes or would reasonably be expected to cause a student to fear for his or her physical safety; or (c) reasonably causes or would reasonably be expected to cause physical injury or emotional harm to a student; or (d) occurs off school property and creates or would foreseeably create a risk of substantial disruption within the school environment, where it is foreseeable that the conduct, threats, intimidation or abuse might reach school property. Acts of harassment and bullying shall include, but not be limited to, those acts based on a person's actual or perceived race, color, weight, national origin, ethnic group, religion, religious practice, disability, sexual orientation, gender or sex. For the purposes of this definition the term "threats, intimidation or abuse" shall include verbal and non-verbal actions.

8. "Cyberbullying" shall mean harassment or bullying as defined in subdivision seven of this section, including paragraphs (a), (b), (c) and (d) of such subdivision, where such harassment or bullying occurs through any form of electronic communication.

McKinney's Education Law § 12 (West 2013)

§ 12. Discrimination and harassment prohibited

1. No student shall be subjected to harassment or bullying by employees or students on school property or at a school function; nor shall any student be subjected to discrimination based on a person's actual or perceived race, color, weight, national origin, ethnic group, religion, religious practice, disability, sexual orientation, gender, or sex by school employees or students on school property or at a school function. Nothing in this subdivision shall be construed to prohibit a denial of admission into, or exclusion from, a course of instruction based on a person's gender that would be permissible under section thirty-two hundred one-a or paragraph (a) of subdivision two of section twenty-eight hundred fifty-four of this chapter and title IX of the Education Amendments of 1972 (20 U.S.C. section 1681, et. seq.), or to prohibit, as discrimination based on disability, actions that would be permissible under section 504 of the Rehabilitation Act of 1973.
2. An age-appropriate version of the policy outlined in subdivision one of this section, written in plain-language, shall be included in the code of conduct adopted by boards of education and the trustees or sole trustee pursuant to section twenty-eight hundred one of this chapter and a summary of such policy shall be included in any summaries required by such section twenty-eight hundred one.

McKinney's Education Law § 13

§ 13. Policies and guidelines

The board of education and the trustees or sole trustee of every school district shall create policies, procedures and guidelines that shall include, but not be limited to:

1. Policies and procedures intended to create a school environment that is free from harassment, bullying and discrimination, that include but are not limited to provisions which:
    a. identify the principal, superintendent or the principal's or superintendent's designee as the school employee charged with receiving reports of harassment, bullying and discrimination;
    b. enable students and parents to make an oral or written report of harassment, bullying or discrimination to teachers, administrators and other school personnel that the school district deems appropriate;
    c. require school employees who witness harassment, bullying or discrimination, or receive an oral or written report of harassment, bullying or discrimination, to promptly orally notify the principal, superintendent or the principal's or superintendent's designee not later than one school day after such school employee witnesses or receives a report of harassment, bullying or discrimination, and to file a written report with the principal, superintendent or the principal or superintendent's designee not later than two school days after making such oral report;

d. require the principal, superintendent or the principal's or superintendent's designee to lead or supervise the thorough investigation of all reports of harassment, bullying and discrimination, and to ensure that such investigation is completed promptly after receipt of any written reports made under this section;

e. require the school, when an investigation reveals any such verified harassment, bullying or discrimination, to take prompt actions reasonably calculated to end the harassment, bullying or discrimination, eliminate any hostile environment, create a more positive school culture and climate, prevent recurrence of the behavior, and ensure the safety of the student or students against whom such harassment, bullying or discrimination was directed. Such actions shall be consistent with the guidelines created pursuant to subdivision four of this section;

f. prohibit retaliation against any individual who, in good faith, reports, or assists in the investigation of, harassment, bullying or discrimination;

g. include a school strategy to prevent harassment, bullying and discrimination;

h. require the principal to make a regular report on data and trends related to harassment, bullying and discrimination to the superintendent;

i. require the principal, superintendent or the principal's or superintendent's designee, to notify promptly the appropriate local law enforcement agency when such principal, superintendent or the principal's or superintendent's designee, believes that any harassment, bullying or discrimination constitutes criminal conduct;

j. include appropriate references to the provisions of the school district's code of conduct adopted pursuant to section twenty-eight hundred one of this chapter that are relevant to harassment, bullying and discrimination;

k. require each school, at least once during each school year, to provide all school employees, students and parents with a written or electronic copy of the school district's policies created pursuant to this section, or a plain-language summary thereof, including notification of the process by which students, parents and school employees may report harassment, bullying and discrimination. This subdivision shall not be construed to require additional distribution of such policies and guidelines if they are otherwise distributed to school employees, students and parents;

l. maintain current versions of the school district's policies created pursuant to this section on the school district's internet website, if one exists;

2. Guidelines to be used in school training programs to discourage the development of harassment, bullying and discrimination, and to make school employees aware of the effects of harassment, bullying, cyberbullying and discrimination on students and that are designed:

a. to raise the awareness and sensitivity of school employees to potential harassment, bullying and discrimination, and

b. to enable employees to prevent and respond to harassment, bullying and discrimination; and

3. Guidelines relating to the development of nondiscriminatory instructional and counseling methods, and requiring that at least one staff member at every school be thoroughly trained to handle human relations in the areas of race, color, weight, national origin, ethnic group, religion, religious practice, disability, sexual orientation, gender, and sex; and

4. Guidelines relating to the development of measured, balanced and age-appropriate responses to instances of harassment, bullying or discrimination by students, with remedies and procedures

following a progressive model that make appropriate use of intervention, discipline and education, vary in method according to the nature of the behavior, the developmental age of the student and the student's history of problem behaviors, and are consistent with the district's code of conduct; and

5. Training required by this section shall address the social patterns of harassment, bullying and discrimination, as defined in section eleven of this article, including but not limited to those acts based on a person's actual or perceived race, color, weight, national origin, ethnic group, religion, religious practice, disability, sexual orientation, gender or sex, the identification and mitigation of harassment, bullying and discrimination, and strategies for effectively addressing problems of exclusion, bias and aggression in educational settings.

Conduct on School District Property. McKinney's Education Law § 2801-a (West 2000)

McKinney's Education Law § 2801-a. School safety plans

1. The board of education or trustees, as defined in section two of this chapter, of every school district within the state, however created, and every board of cooperative educational services and county vocational education and extension board and the chancellor of the city school district of the city of New York shall adopt and amend a comprehensive district-wide school safety plan and building-level school safety plans regarding crisis intervention, emergency response and management, provided that in the city school district of the city of New York, such plans shall be adopted by the chancellor of the city school district. Such plans shall be developed by a district-wide school safety team and a building-level school safety team established pursuant to subdivision four of this section and shall be in a form developed by the commissioner in consultation with the division of criminal justice services, the superintendent of the state police and any other appropriate state agencies. A school district having only one school building, shall develop a single building-level school safety plan, which shall also fulfill all requirements for development of a district-wide plan.
2. Such comprehensive district-wide safety plan shall be developed by the district-wide school safety team and shall include at a minimum:
    a. policies and procedures for responding to implied or direct threats of violence by students, teachers, other school personnel as well as visitors to the school;
    b. policies and procedures for responding to acts of violence by students, teachers, other school personnel as well as visitors to the school, including consideration of zero-tolerance policies for school violence;
    c. appropriate prevention and intervention strategies such as:
        (i) collaborative arrangements with state and local law enforcement officials, designed to ensure that school safety officers and other security personnel are adequately trained, including being trained to de-escalate potentially violent situations, and are effectively and fairly recruited;
        (ii) non-violent conflict resolution training programs;
        (iii) peer mediation programs and youth courts; and
        (iv) extended day and other school safety programs;

d. policies and procedures for contacting appropriate law enforcement officials in the event of a violent incident;
e. policies and procedures for contacting parents, guardians or persons in parental relation to the students of the district in the event of a violent incident;
f. policies and procedures relating to school building security, including where appropriate the use of school safety officers and/or security devices or procedures;
g. policies and procedures for the dissemination of informative materials regarding the early detection of potentially violent behaviors, including but not limited to the identification of family, community and environmental factors, to teachers, administrators, school personnel, persons in parental relation to students of the district, students and other persons deemed appropriate to receive such information;
h. policies and procedures for annual school safety training for staff and students;
i. protocols for responding to bomb threats, hostage-takings, intrusions and kidnappings;
j. strategies for improving communication among students and between students and staff and reporting of potentially violent incidents, such as the establishment of youth-run programs, peer mediation, conflict resolution, creating a forum or designating a mentor for students concerned with bullying or violence and establishing anonymous reporting mechanisms for school violence; and
k. a description of the duties of hall monitors and any other school safety personnel, the training required of all personnel acting in a school security capacity, and the hiring and screening process for all personnel acting in a school security capacity.

NORTH CAROLINA

Computer-Related Crime. North Carolina General Statutes Annotated § 14-458.1, et seq. (West 2012)

North Carolina General Statutes Annotated § 14-458.1

§ 14-458.1. Cyber-bullying; penalty

(a) Except as otherwise made unlawful by this Article, it shall be unlawful for any person to use a computer or computer network to do any of the following:

(1) With the intent to intimidate or torment a minor:
    a. Build a fake profile or Web site;
    b. Pose as a minor in:
        1. An Internet chat room;
        2. An electronic mail message; or
        3. An instant message;
    c. Follow a minor online or into an Internet chat room; or

d. Post or encourage others to post on the Internet private, personal, or sexual information pertaining to a minor.
(2) With the intent to intimidate or torment a minor or the minor's parent or guardian:
   a. Post a real or doctored image of a minor on the Internet;
   b. Access, alter, or erase any computer network, computer data, computer program, or computer software, including breaking into a password protected account or stealing or otherwise accessing passwords; or
   c. Use a computer system for repeated, continuing, or sustained electronic communications, including electronic mail or other transmissions, to a minor.
(3) Make any statement, whether true or false, intending to immediately provoke, and that is likely to provoke, any third party to stalk or harass a minor.
(4) Copy and disseminate, or cause to be made, an unauthorized copy of any data pertaining to a minor for the purpose of intimidating or tormenting that minor (in any form, including, but not limited to, any printed or electronic form of computer data, computer programs, or computer software residing in, communicated by, or produced by a computer or computer network).
(5) Sign up a minor for a pornographic Internet site with the intent to intimidate or torment the minor.
(6) Without authorization of the minor or the minor's parent or guardian, sign up a minor for electronic mailing lists or to receive junk electronic messages and instant messages, with the intent to intimidate or torment the minor.
(b) Any person who violates this section shall be guilty of cyber-bullying, which offense shall be punishable as a Class 1 misdemeanor if the defendant is 18 years of age or older at the time the offense is committed. If the defendant is under the age of 18 at the time the offense is committed, the offense shall be punishable as a Class 2 misdemeanor.
(c) Whenever any person pleads guilty to or is guilty of an offense under this section, and the offense was committed before the person attained the age of 18 years, the court may, without entering a judgment of guilt and with the consent of the defendant, defer further proceedings and place the defendant on probation upon such reasonable terms and conditions as the court may require. Upon fulfillment of the terms and conditions of the probation provided for in this subsection, the court shall discharge the defendant and dismiss the proceedings against the defendant. Discharge and dismissal under this subsection shall be without court adjudication of guilt and shall not be deemed a conviction for purposes of this section or for purposes of disqualifications or disabilities imposed by law upon conviction of a crime. Upon discharge and dismissal pursuant to this subsection, the person may apply for an order to expunge the complete record of the proceedings resulting in the dismissal and discharge, pursuant to the procedures and requirements set forth in [North Carolina General Statutes Annotated] 15A-146.

North Carolina General Statutes Annotated § 14-458.2

§ 14-458.2. Cyber-bullying of school employee by student; penalty

(a) The following definitions apply in this section: ...
   (2) Student.--A person who has been assigned to a school by a local board of education as provided in [North Carolina General Statutes Annotated] 115C-366 or has enrolled in a charter

school authorized under [North Carolina General Statutes Annotated] 115C-238.29D, a regional school created under [North Carolina General Statutes Annotated] 115C-238.62, or a nonpublic school which has filed intent to operate under Part 1 or Part 2 of Article 39 of Chapter 115C of the General Statutes, or a person who has been suspended or expelled from any of those schools within the last year.

(b) Except as otherwise made unlawful by this Article, it shall be unlawful for any student to use a computer or computer network to do any of the following:
  (1) With the intent to intimidate or torment a school employee, do any of the following:
    a. Build a fake profile or Web site.
    b. Post or encourage others to post on the Internet private, personal, or sexual information pertaining to a school employee.
    c. Post a real or doctored image of the school employee on the Internet.
    d. Access, alter, or erase any computer network, computer data, computer program, or computer software, including breaking into a password-protected account or stealing or otherwise accessing passwords.
    e. Use a computer system for repeated, continuing, or sustained electronic communications, including electronic mail or other transmissions, to a school employee.
  (2) Make any statement, whether true or false, intending to immediately provoke, and that is likely to provoke, any third party to stalk or harass a school employee.
  (3) Copy and disseminate, or cause to be made, an unauthorized copy of any data pertaining to a school employee for the purpose of intimidating or tormenting that school employee (in any form, including, but not limited to, any printed or electronic form of computer data, computer programs, or computer software residing in, communicated by, or produced by a computer or computer network).
  (4) Sign up a school employee for a pornographic Internet site with the intent to intimidate or torment the employee.
  (5) Without authorization of the school employee, sign up a school employee for electronic mailing lists or to receive junk electronic messages and instant messages, with the intent to intimidate or torment the school employee.

(c) Any student who violates this section is guilty of cyber-bullying a school employee, which offense is punishable as a Class 2 misdemeanor.

(d) Whenever any student pleads guilty to or is guilty of an offense under this section, the court may, without entering a judgment of guilt and with the consent of the student, defer further proceedings and place the student on probation upon such reasonable terms and conditions as the court may require. Upon fulfillment of the terms and conditions of the probation provided for in this subsection, the court shall discharge the student and dismiss the proceedings against the student. Discharge and dismissal under this subsection shall be without court adjudication of guilt and shall not be deemed a conviction for purposes of this section or for purposes of disqualifications or disabilities imposed by law upon conviction of a crime. Upon discharge and dismissal pursuant to this subsection, the student may apply for an order to expunge the complete record of the proceedings resulting in the dismissal and discharge, pursuant to the procedures and requirements set forth in [North Carolina General Statutes Annotated] 15A-146.

(e) Whenever a complaint is received pursuant to Article 17 of Chapter 7B of the General Statutes based upon a student's violation of this section, the juvenile may, upon a finding of legal sufficiency pursuant to [North Carolina General Statutes Annotated] 7B-1706, enter into a diversion contract pursuant to [North Carolina General Statutes Annotated] 7B-1706.

North Carolina General Statutes Annotated § 115C-366.4

§ 115C-366.4. Assignment of students convicted of cyber-bullying

A student who is convicted under [North Carolina General Statutes Annotated] 14-458.2 of cyberbullying a school employee shall be transferred to another school within the local school administrative unit. If there is no other appropriate school within the local school administrative unit, the student shall be transferred to a different class or assigned to a teacher who was not involved as a victim of the cyberbullying. Notwithstanding the provisions in this section, the superintendent may modify, in writing, the required transfer of an individual student on a case-by-case basis.

School Violence Prevention. North Carolina General Statutes Annotated § 115C-407.15, et seq. (West 2009)

North Carolina General Statutes Annotated § 115C-407.15

§ 115C-407.15. Bullying and harassing behavior

(a) As used in this Article, "bullying or harassing behavior" is any pattern of gestures or written, electronic, or verbal communications, or any physical act or any threatening communication, that takes place on school property, at any school-sponsored function, or on a school bus, and that:
   (1) Places a student or school employee in actual and reasonable fear of harm to his or her person or damage to his or her property; or
   (2) Creates or is certain to create a hostile environment by substantially interfering with or impairing a student's educational performance, opportunities, or benefits. For purposes of this section, "hostile environment" means that the victim subjectively views the conduct as bullying or harassing behavior and the conduct is objectively severe or pervasive enough that a reasonable person would agree that it is bullying or harassing behavior.

Bullying or harassing behavior includes, but is not limited to, acts reasonably perceived as being motivated by any actual or perceived differentiating characteristic, such as race, color, religion, ancestry, national origin, gender, socioeconomic status, academic status, gender identity, physical appearance, sexual orientation, or mental, physical, developmental, or sensory disability, or by association with a person who has or is perceived to have one or more of these characteristics.

(b) No student or school employee shall be subjected to bullying or harassing behavior by school employees or students.

(c) No person shall engage in any act of reprisal or retaliation against a victim, witness, or a person with reliable information about an act of bullying or harassing behavior.
(d) A school employee who has witnessed or has reliable information that a student or school employee has been subject to any act of bullying or harassing behavior shall report the incident to the appropriate school official.
(e) A student or volunteer who has witnessed or has reliable information that a student or school employee has been subject to any act of bullying or harassing behavior should report the incident to the appropriate school official.

North Carolina General Statutes Annotated § 115C-407.16

§ 115C-407.16. Policy against bullying or harassing behavior

(a) Before December 31, 2009, each local school administrative unit shall adopt a policy prohibiting bullying or harassing behavior.
(b) The policy shall contain, at a minimum, the following components:
  (1) A statement prohibiting bullying or harassing behavior.
  (2) A definition of bullying or harassing behavior no less inclusive than that set forth in this Article.
  (3) A description of the type of behavior expected for each student and school employee.
  (4) Consequences and appropriate remedial action for a person who commits an act of bullying or harassment.
  (5) A procedure for reporting an act of bullying or harassment, including a provision that permits a person to report such an act anonymously. This shall not be construed to permit formal disciplinary action solely on the basis of an anonymous report.
  (6) A procedure for prompt investigation of reports of serious violations and complaints of any act of bullying or harassment, identifying either the principal or the principal's designee as the person responsible for the investigation.
  (7) A statement that prohibits reprisal or retaliation against any person who reports an act of bullying or harassment, and the consequence and appropriate remedial action for a person who engages in reprisal or retaliation.
  (8) A statement of how the policy is to be disseminated and publicized, including notice that the policy applies to participation in school-sponsored functions.
(c) Nothing in this Article shall prohibit a local school administrative unit from adopting a policy that includes components beyond the minimum components provided in this section or that is more inclusive than the requirements of this Article.
(d) Notice of the local policy shall appear in any school unit publication that sets forth the comprehensive rules, procedures, and standards of conduct for schools within the school unit and in any student and school employee handbook.
(e) Information regarding the local policy against bullying or harassing behavior shall be incorporated into a school's employee training program.
(f) To the extent funds are appropriated for these purposes, a local school administrative unit shall, by March 1, 2010, provide training on the local policy to school employees and volunteers who have significant contact with students.

State Anti-Bullying Statutes and Student Speech

North Carolina General Statutes Annotated § 115C-407.17

§ 115C-407.17. Prevention of school violence

Schools shall develop and implement methods and strategies for promoting school environments that are free of bullying or harassing behavior.

NORTH DAKOTA

Students and Safety. North Dakota Century Code Annotated, § 15.1-19-17, et seq. (West 2011)

North Dakota Century Code Annotated, § 15.1-19-17

§ 15.1-19-17. Bullying—Definition

As used in sections 15.1-19-17 through 15.1-19-22:

1. "Bullying" means:
    a. Conduct that occurs in a public school, on school district premises, in a district owned or leased schoolbus or school vehicle, or at any public school or school district sanctioned or sponsored activity or event and which:
        (1) Is so severe, pervasive, or objectively offensive that it substantially interferes with the student's educational opportunities;
        (2) Places the student in actual and reasonable fear of harm;
        (3) Places the student in actual and reasonable fear of damage to property of the student; or
        (4) Substantially disrupts the orderly operation of the public school; or
    b. Conduct that is received by a student while the student is in a public school, on school district premises, in a district owned or leased schoolbus or school vehicle, or at any public school or school district sanctioned or sponsored activity or event and which:
        (1) Is so severe, pervasive, or objectively offensive that it substantially interferes with the student's educational opportunities;
        (2) Places the student in actual and reasonable fear of harm;
        (3) Places the student in actual and reasonable fear of damage to property of the student; or
        (4) Substantially disrupts the orderly operation of the public school.
2. "Conduct" includes the use of technology or other electronic media.

North Dakota Century Code Annotated, § 15.1-19-18

§ 15.1-19-18. Bullying--Prohibition by policy

1. Before July 1, 2012, each school district shall adopt a policy providing that while at a public school, on school district premises, in a district owned or leased schoolbus or school vehicle, or at any public school or school district sanctioned or sponsored activity or event, a student may not:

a. Engage in bullying; or
b. Engage in reprisal or retaliation against:
   (1) A victim of bullying;
   (2) An individual who witnesses an alleged act of bullying;
   (3) An individual who reports an alleged act of bullying; or
   (4) An individual who provides information about an alleged act of bullying.
2. The policy required by this section must:
   a. Include a definition of bullying that at least encompasses the conduct described in section 15.1-19-17;
   b. Establish procedures for reporting and documenting alleged acts of bullying, reprisal, or retaliation, and include procedures for anonymous reporting of such acts;
   c. Establish procedures, including timelines, for school district personnel to follow in investigating reports of alleged bullying, reprisal, or retaliation;
   d. Establish a schedule for the retention of any documents generated while investigating reports of alleged bullying, reprisal, or retaliation;
   e. Set forth the disciplinary measures applicable to an individual who engaged in bullying or who engaged in reprisal or retaliation, as set forth in subsection 1;
   f. Require the notification of law enforcement personnel if an investigation by school district personnel results in a reasonable suspicion that a crime might have occurred;
   g. Establish strategies to protect a victim of bullying, reprisal, or retaliation; and
   h. Establish disciplinary measures to be imposed upon an individual who makes a false accusation, report, or complaint pertaining to bullying, reprisal, or retaliation.
3. In developing the bullying policy required by this section, a school district shall involve parents, school district employees, volunteers, students, school district administrators, law enforcement personnel, domestic violence sexual assault organizations as defined by subsection 3 of section 14-07.1-01, and community representatives.
4. Upon completion of the policy required by this section, a school district shall:
   a. Ensure that the policy is explained to and discussed with its students;
   b. File a copy of the policy with the superintendent of public instruction; and
   c. Make the policy available in student and personnel handbooks.
5. Each school district shall review and revise its policy as it determines necessary and shall file a copy of the revised policy with the superintendent of public instruction.

North Dakota Century Code Annotated, § 15.1-19-20

§ 15.1-19-20. Bullying prevention programs

Each school district shall provide bullying prevention programs to all students from kindergarten through grade twelve.

OHIO

Hazing. Ohio Revised Code Annotated § 2903.31 (West 2014)

Ohio Revised Code Annotated § 2903.31

§ 2903.31 Hazing; recklessly participating or permitting

(A) As used in this section, "hazing" means doing any act or coercing another, including the victim, to do any act of initiation into any student or other organization that causes or creates a substantial risk of causing mental or physical harm to any person.

(B) (1) No person shall recklessly participate in the hazing of another.
    (2) No administrator, employee, or faculty member of any primary, secondary, or post-secondary school or of any other educational institution, public or private, shall recklessly permit the hazing of any person.

(C) Whoever violates this section is guilty of hazing, a misdemeanor of the fourth degree.

Model Policy. Ohio Revised Code Annotated § 3301.22 (West 2007)

Ohio Revised Code Annotated § 3301.22

§ 3301.22 Model policy to prohibit harassment, intimidation, or bullying

The state board of education shall develop a model policy to prohibit harassment, intimidation, or bullying in order to assist school districts in developing their own policies under section 3313.666 of the Revised Code. The board shall issue the model policy within six months after the effective date of this section.

Municipal School Districts and Bullying. Ohio Revised Code Annotated § 3311.742 (West 2012)

Ohio Revised Code Annotated § 3311.742

§ 3311.742 Student advisory committees

(B) The board of education of each municipal school district and the governing authority of each partnering community school shall require each of its schools offering grades nine to twelve to establish a student advisory committee to make recommendations as prescribed in this division. The principal of the school and, if applicable, representatives of the teachers' labor organization who are employed in the school shall determine the composition of the committee and the process for selecting committee members, which shall allow for all students enrolled in the school to be informed about, and involved in, member selection.

The committee shall make regular recommendations, but at least semiannually, regarding the following: …

(4) Ways in which students may improve the behavior of other students and reduce incidents of bullying and other disruptive conduct;

Bullying Policy and Immunity. Ohio Revised Code Annotated § 3313.666, et seq. (West 2012)

Ohio Revised Code Annotated § 3313.666

§ 3313.666 Policy prohibiting harassment, intimidation, or bullying; immunity for reporting

(A) As used in this section:
  (1) "Electronic act" means an act committed through the use of a cellular telephone, computer, pager, personal communication device, or other electronic communication device.
  (2) "Harassment, intimidation, or bullying" means either of the following:
    (a) Any intentional written, verbal, electronic, or physical act that a student has exhibited toward another particular student more than once and the behavior both:
  (i) Causes mental or physical harm to the other student;
  (ii) Is sufficiently severe, persistent, or pervasive that it creates an intimidating, threatening, or abusive educational environment for the other student.
    (b) Violence within a dating relationship.
(B) The board of education of each city, local, exempted village, and joint vocational school district shall establish a policy prohibiting harassment, intimidation, or bullying. The policy shall be developed in consultation with parents, school employees, school volunteers, students, and community members. The policy shall include the following:
  (1) A statement prohibiting harassment, intimidation, or bullying of any student on school property, on a school bus, or at school-sponsored events and expressly providing for the possibility of suspension of a student found responsible for harassment, intimidation, or bullying by an electronic act;
  (2) A definition of harassment, intimidation, or bullying that includes the definition in division (A) of this section;
  (3) A procedure for reporting prohibited incidents;
  (4) A requirement that school personnel report prohibited incidents of which they are aware to the school principal or other administrator designated by the principal;
  (5) A requirement that the custodial parent or guardian of any student involved in a prohibited incident be notified and, to the extent permitted by section 3319.321 of the Revised Code and the "Family Educational Rights and Privacy Act of 1974," 88 Stat. 571, 20 U.S.C. 1232g, as amended, have access to any written reports pertaining to the prohibited incident;
  (6) A procedure for documenting any prohibited incident that is reported;
  (7) A procedure for responding to and investigating any reported incident;
  (8) A strategy for protecting a victim or other person from new or additional harassment, intimidation, or bullying, and from retaliation following a report, including a means by which a person may report an incident anonymously;

(9) A disciplinary procedure for any student guilty of harassment, intimidation, or bullying, which shall not infringe on any student's rights under the first amendment to the Constitution of the United States;

(10) A statement prohibiting students from deliberately making false reports of harassment, intimidation, or bullying and a disciplinary procedure for any student responsible for deliberately making a false report of that nature;

(11) A requirement that the district administration semiannually provide the president of the district board a written summary of all reported incidents and post the summary on its web site, if the district has a web site, to the extent permitted by section 3319.321 of the Revised Code and the "Family Educational Rights and Privacy Act of 1974," 88 Stat. 571, 20 U.S.C. 1232g, as amended.

(C) Each board's policy shall appear in any student handbooks, and in any of the publications that set forth the comprehensive rules, procedures, and standards of conduct for schools and students in the district. The policy and an explanation of the seriousness of bullying by electronic means shall be made available to students in the district and to their custodial parents or guardians. Information regarding the policy shall be incorporated into employee training materials.

(D) (1) To the extent that state or federal funds are appropriated for this purpose, each board shall require that all students enrolled in the district annually be provided with age-appropriate instruction, as determined by the board, on the board's policy, including a written or verbal discussion of the consequences for violations of the policy.

(2) Each board shall require that once each school year a written statement describing the policy and the consequences for violations of the policy be sent to each student's custodial parent or guardian. The statement may be sent with regular student report cards or may be delivered electronically.

(E) A school district employee, student, or volunteer shall be individually immune from liability in a civil action for damages arising from reporting an incident in accordance with a policy adopted pursuant to this section if that person reports an incident of harassment, intimidation, or bullying promptly in good faith and in compliance with the procedures as specified in the policy.

(F) Except as provided in division (E) of this section, nothing in this section prohibits a victim from seeking redress under any other provision of the Revised Code or common law that may apply.

(G) This section does not create a new cause of action or a substantive legal right for any person.

(H) Each board shall update the policy adopted under this section to include violence within a dating relationship and harassment, intimidation, or bullying by electronic means.

Ohio Revised Code Annotated § 3313.667

§ 3313.667 Bullying prevention task forces, programs, and initiatives

(A) Any school district may form bullying prevention task forces, programs, and other initiatives involving volunteers, parents, law enforcement, and community members.

(B) To the extent that state or federal funds are appropriated for these purposes, each school district shall provide training, workshops, or courses on the district's harassment, intimidation, or bullying policy adopted pursuant to section 3313.666 of the Revised Code to school employees and volunteers who have direct contact with students and are not subject to section 3319.073 of the Revised Code. Time spent by school employees in the training, workshops, or courses shall apply towards any state- or district-mandated continuing education requirements.

(C) This section does not create a new cause of action or a substantive legal right for any person.

OKLAHOMA

School Safety and Bullying Prevention Act. 70 Oklahoma Statutes Annotated § 24-100.2, et seq. (West 2013)

70 Oklahoma Statutes Annotated § 24-100.2

§ 24-100.2. Short title--School Safety and Bullying Prevention Act

Sections 24-100.2 through 24-100.5 of this title shall be known and may be cited as the "School Safety and Bullying Prevention Act".

70 Oklahoma Statutes Annotated § 24-100.3

§ 24-100.3. Definitions

A. As used in the School Safety and Bullying Prevention Act:
   1. "Bullying" means any pattern of harassment, intimidation, threatening behavior, physical acts, verbal or electronic communication directed toward a student or group of students that results in or is reasonably perceived as being done with the intent to cause negative educational or physical results for the targeted individual or group and is communicated in such a way as to disrupt or interfere with the school's educational mission or the education of any student;
   2. "At school" means on school grounds, in school vehicles, at school-sponsored activities, or at school-sanctioned events;
   3. "Electronic communication" means the communication of any written, verbal, pictorial information or video content by means of an electronic device, including, but not limited to, a telephone, a mobile or cellular telephone or other wireless telecommunication device, or a computer; and
   4. "Threatening behavior" means any pattern of behavior or isolated action, whether or not it is directed at another person, that a reasonable person would believe indicates potential for future harm to students, school personnel, or school property.
B. Nothing in this act shall be construed to impose a specific liability on any school district.

State Anti-Bullying Statutes and Student Speech

70 Oklahoma Statutes Annotated § 24-100.4

§ 24-100.4. School Safety and Bullying Prevention Act--Control and discipline of child—Prohibition of bullying at school and online—Policy Requirements

A. Each district board of education shall adopt a policy for the discipline of all children attending public school in that district, and for the investigation of reported incidents of bullying. The policy shall provide options for the discipline of the students and shall define standards of conduct to which students are expected to conform. The policy shall:
  1. Specifically address bullying by students at school and by electronic communication, if the communication is specifically directed at students or school personnel and concerns bullying at school;
  2. Contain a procedure for reporting an act of bullying to a school official, including a provision that permits a person to report an act anonymously. No formal disciplinary action shall be taken solely on the basis of an anonymous report;
  3. Contain a requirement that any school employee that has reliable information that would lead a reasonable person to suspect that a person is a target of bullying shall immediately report it to the principal or a designee of the principal;
  4. Contain a statement of how the policy is to be publicized including a requirement that:
     a. an annual written notice of the policy be provided to parents, guardians, staff, volunteers and students, with age-appropriate language for students,
     b. notice of the policy be posted at various locations within each school site, including but not limited to cafeterias, school bulletin boards, and administration offices,
     c. the policy be posted on the Internet website for the school district and each school site that has an Internet website, and
     d. the policy be included in all student and employee handbooks;
  5. Require that appropriate school district personnel involved in investigating reports of bullying make a determination regarding whether the conduct is actually occurring;
  6. Contain a procedure for providing timely notification to the parents or guardians of a victim of documented and verified bullying and to the parents or guardians of the perpetrator of the documented and verified bullying;
  7. Identify by job title the school official responsible for enforcing the policy;
  8. Contain procedures for reporting to law enforcement all documented and verified acts of bullying which may constitute criminal activity or reasonably have the potential to endanger school safety;
  9. Require annual training for administrators and school employees as developed and provided by the State Department of Education in preventing, identifying, responding to and reporting incidents of bullying;
  10. Provide for an educational program as designed and developed by the State Department of Education for students and parents in preventing, identifying, responding to and reporting incidents of bullying;
  11. Address prevention by providing:
     a. consequences and remedial action for a person who commits an act of bullying,

  b. consequences and remedial action for a student found to have falsely accused another as a means of retaliation, reprisal or as a means of bullying, and
  c. a strategy for providing counseling or referral to appropriate services, including guidance, academic intervention, and other protection for students, both targets and perpetrators, and family members affected by bullying, as necessary;
12. Establish a procedure for:
  a. the investigation, determination and documentation of all incidents of bullying reported to school officials,
  b. identifying the principal or a designee of the principal as the person responsible for investigating incidents of bullying,
  c. reporting the number of incidents of bullying, and
  d. determining the severity of the incidents and their potential to result in future violence;
13. Establish a procedure whereby, upon completing an investigation of bullying, a school may recommend that available community mental health care, substance abuse or other counseling options be provided to the student, if appropriate; and
14. Establish a procedure whereby a school may request the disclosure of any information concerning students who have received mental health, substance abuse, or other care pursuant to paragraph 13 of this subsection that indicates an explicit threat to the safety of students or school personnel, provided the disclosure of the information does not violate the requirements and provisions of the Family Educational Rights and Privacy Act of 1974, the Health Insurance Portability and Accountability Act of 1996, Section 2503 of Title 12 of the Oklahoma Statutes, Section 1376 of Title 59 of the Oklahoma Statutes, or any other state or federal laws regarding the disclosure of confidential information.

B. In developing the policy, the district board of education shall make an effort to involve the teachers, parents, administrators, school staff, school volunteers, community representatives, local law enforcement agencies and students. The students, teachers, and parents or guardian of every child residing within a school district shall be notified by the district board of education of its adoption of the policy and shall receive a copy upon request. The school district policy shall be implemented in a manner that is ongoing throughout the school year and is integrated with other violence prevention efforts.

C. The teacher of a child attending a public school shall have the same right as a parent or guardian to control and discipline such child according to district policies during the time the child is in attendance or in transit to or from the school or any other school function authorized by the school district or classroom presided over by the teacher.

D. Except concerning students on individualized education plans (IEP) pursuant to the Individuals with Disabilities Education Act (IDEA), P.L. No. 101-476, the State Board of Education shall not have authority to prescribe student disciplinary policies for school districts or to proscribe corporal punishment in the public schools. The State Board of Education shall not have authority to require school districts to file student disciplinary action reports more often than once each year and shall not use disciplinary action reports in determining a school district's or school site's eligibility for program assistance including competitive grants.

E. The board of education of each school district in this state shall have the option of adopting a dress code for students enrolled in the school district. The board of education of a school district shall also have the option of adopting a dress code which includes school uniforms.
F. The State Board of Education shall:
1. Promulgate rules for periodically monitoring school districts for compliance with this section and providing sanctions for noncompliance with this section;
2. Establish and maintain a central repository for the collection of information regarding documented and verified incidents of bullying; and
3. Publish a report annually on the State Department of Education website regarding the number of documented and verified incidents of bullying in the public schools in the state.

70 Oklahoma Statutes Annotated § 24-100.5

§ 24-100.5. School Safety and Bullying Prevention Act--Safe School Committees--Model policy

A. Every year each public school site shall establish a Safe School Committee to be composed of at least seven (7) members. The Safe School Committee shall be composed of teachers, parents of enrolled students, students, and a school official who participates in the investigation of reports of bullying as required by subsection A of Section 24-100.4 of this title. The Committee may include administrators, school staff, school volunteers, community representatives, and local law enforcement agencies. The Committee shall assist the school board in promoting a positive school climate through planning, implementing and evaluating effective prevention, readiness and response strategies, including the policy required by Section 24-100.4 of this title.
B. The Safe School Committee shall study and make recommendations to the principal regarding:
1. Unsafe conditions, possible strategies for students, faculty and staff to avoid physical and emotional harm at school, student victimization, crime prevention, school violence, and other issues which prohibit the maintenance of a safe school;
2. Student bullying as defined in Section 24-100.3 of this title;
3. Professional development needs of faculty and staff to recognize and implement methods to decrease student bullying; and
4. Methods to encourage the involvement of the community and students, the development of individual relationships between students and school staff, and use of problem-solving teams and resources that include counselors and other behavioral health resources within or outside the school system.

In its considerations, the Safe School Committee shall review the district policy for the prevention of bullying and the list of research-based programs appropriate for the prevention of bullying of students at school compiled by the State Department of Education. In addition, the Committee may review traditional and accepted bullying prevention programs utilized by other states, state agencies, or school districts.

C. The State Department of Education shall:
1. Develop a model policy and deliver training materials to all school districts on the components that should be included in a school district policy for the prevention of bullying; and

2. Compile and distribute to each public school site, prominently display on the State Department of Education website and annually publicize in print media a list of research-based programs appropriate for the prevention of bullying of students. If a school district implements a commercial bullying prevention program, it shall use a program listed by the State Department of Education.

D. The provisions of this section shall not apply to technology center schools.

Harassment, Intimidation, and Bullying. Oklahoma Administrative Code 210:10-1-20 (West 2013)

Oklahoma Administrative Code 210:10-1-20

210:10-1-20. Implementation of policies prohibiting harassment, intimidation, and bullying

(a) **Purpose.** Bullying has a negative effect on the social environment of schools, creates a climate of fear among students, inhibits the ability to learn, and leads to other antisocial behavior. Other detrimental effects of bullying include impact on school safety, student engagement, and the overall school environment. Successful school programs recognize, prevent, effectively identify, and intervene in incidents involving harassment, intimidation and bullying behavior. Schools that implement these programs have improved safety and create a more inclusive learning environment. The purpose of the Oklahoma School Bullying Prevention Act, 70 [Oklahoma Statutes Annotated] § 24-100.2, et seq., is to provide a comprehensive approach for public schools to create an environment free of unnecessary disruption which is conducive to the learning process by implementing policies for the prevention of harassment, intimidation and bullying.

(b) **Definitions.** The following words and terms, when used in this subchapter, shall have the following meaning:

(1) **"Harassment, Intimidation, and Bullying"** means any gesture, written or verbal expression, electronic communication, or physical act that a reasonable person should know will:
  (A) Harm another student;
  (B) Damage another student's property;
  (C) Place another student in reasonable fear of harm to the student's person or damage to the student's property; or
  (D) Insult or demean any student or group of students,

(2) **"Applicability"** means the aforementioned conduct constitutes harassment, intimidation, and bullying if conducted in such a way as to disrupt or interfere with the school's educational mission or the education of any student. This includes, but is not limited to gestures, written, verbal, or physical acts, or electronic communications.

(3) **"Electronic Communication"** means the communication of any written, verbal, or pictorial information by means of an electronic device, including, but not limited to, a telephone, a cellular telephone or other wireless telecommunication device, or computer.

(4) **"Threatening Behavior"** means any pattern of behavior or isolated action, whether or not it is directed at another person, that a reasonable person would believe indicates potential for future harm to students, school personnel, or school property.

(5) **Scope.** Threatening behavior, harassment, intimidation, and bullying is prohibited on school grounds, in school vehicles, at designated bus stops, at school-sponsored activities, or at school-sanctioned events. Threatening behavior, harassment, intimidation, and bullying by electronic communication is prohibited whether or not such communication originated at school, or with school equipment, if the communication is specifically directed at students or school personnel and concerns harassment, intimidation, or bullying at school.

(c) **Implementation.** Each district board of education shall adopt a policy for the control and discipline of all children attending public school in that district. Such policy shall set forth investigative procedures of reported incidents of harassment, intimidation, bullying or threatening behavior. Such policy shall provide options for the methods of control and discipline of the students and shall define standards of conduct to which students are expected to conform, which may include a detailed description of a graduated range of consequences and sanctions for bullying. The policy adopted by each district board of education shall include and/or establish the following:

(1) Specifically prohibit threatening behavior, harassment, intimidation, and bullying by students at school and by electronic communication. Electronic communication shall be prohibited whether or not such communication originated at school or with school equipment, if the communication is specifically directed at students or school personnel and concerns harassment, intimidation, or bullying at school.

(2) Address prevention of and education about threatening behavior, harassment, intimidation, and bullying.

(3) A procedure for the investigation of harassment, intimidation, bullying or threatening behavior reported to school officials for the purpose of determining the severity of the incidents and their potential to result in future violence.

(4) A procedure which provides, upon the completion of an investigation, that a school may recommend that available community mental health care options be provide to the student, if appropriate. This may include information about the types of support services available to the student bully, victim, and any other students affected by the prohibited behavior.

(5) A procedure whereby a school may request the disclosure of any information concerning students who have received mental health care pursuant to sub-section (4) of this rule that indicates an explicit threat to the safety of students or school personnel provided, the disclosure of information does not violate the provisions or requirements of the Family Educational Rights and Privacy Act of 1974, the Health Insurance Portability and Accountability Act of 1996, Section 2503 of Title 12 of the Oklahoma Statutes, Section 1376 of Title 59 of Oklahoma Statutes, or any other state or federal laws relating to the disclosure of confidential information.

(d) **Policy Adoption.** The policy adopted by the local school board pursuant to 70 [Oklahoma Statutes Annotated] § 24-100.4 shall include the statutorily required sections outlined in section (c) of this rule. Failure to include such items shall result in action pursuant to section (f) of this rule.

(e) **Policy Development.** In developing a district policy, each district board of education shall make an effort to involve teachers, parents, and students. The students, teachers, and parents or guardian of every child residing within a school district shall be notified by the district board of education of the adoption of the policy and shall receive a copy upon request.

(f) **Monitoring and Compliance.** The State Board of Education shall monitor school districts for compliance with 70 [Oklahoma Statutes Annotated] § 24-100.4 and section (c) of this rule.
   (1) To assist the State Department of Education with compliance efforts pursuant to this section, each school district shall identify a Bullying Coordinator who will serve as the district contact responsible for providing information to the State Board of Education. The Bullying Coordinator shall maintain on file with the Department of Education updated contact information. Each school district shall notify the State Department of Education within fifteen (15) business days of the appointment of a new Bullying Coordinator.
   (2) Beginning with the 2012-2013 school year, and for each school year following, each school district shall submit to the State Board of Education a copy of the district's bullying policy. The bullying policy shall be submitted to the State Department of Education by December 10th of each school year, and shall be submitted as a part of the school's Annual Performance Report.
   (3) Beginning with the 2012-2013 school year, and for each school year following, the State Department of Education shall conduct a comprehensive review of each school district's bullying policy to ensure compliance with 70 [Oklahoma Statutes Annotated] § 24-100.4. School districts that do not comply with the statutory requirements of the statute shall be notified in writing, and be required to make necessary changes to comply with state law.
   (4) State Department of Education staff shall monitor school districts for compliance with 70 [Oklahoma Statutes Annotated] § 24-100.4 and section (c) of this rule. The State Department of Education may initiate a compliance review upon receipt of evidence which indicates noncompliance with 70 [Oklahoma Statutes Annotated] § 24-100.4. Evidence of potential noncompliance shall be based on the nature or frequency of confirmed complaints of noncompliance received by the State Department of Education. The scope of a compliance review initiated pursuant to sub-section (f) of this rule shall be limited to determining whether a school district has implemented policies required by 70 [Oklahoma Statutes Annotated] § 24-100.4.
   (5) Records indicating substantial noncompliance with sub-sections (3) or (4) of this rule shall be submitted to the school district's Regional Accreditation Officer (RAO) for review and consideration during the district's accreditation process. Record of a school district's failure to comply with 70 [Oklahoma Statutes Annotated] § 24-100.4, including the number of confirmed complaints of non-compliance involving the district shall be documented in the district's compliance report and be considered for purposes of accreditation.
(g) **Federal Applicability.** Harassment, intimidation, and bullying behavior may also result in discriminatory harassment, prohibited by Title VI of the Civil Rights Act of 1964 (Title VI), which prohibits discrimination on the basis of race, color, or national origin; Title IX of the Education Amendments of 1972 (Title IX), which prohibits discrimination on the basis of sex; Section 504 of the Rehabilitation Act of 1973 (Section 504); and Title II of the Americans with Disabilities Act of 1990 (Title II). Section 504 and Title II prohibit discrimination on the basis of disability. Each school district shall take necessary steps to ensure compliance with federal law.

OREGON

Harassment, Intimidation and Bullying. Oregon Revised Statutes Annotated § 339.351, et seq. (West 2009)

Oregon Revised Statutes Annotated § 339.351

339.351. Definitions

(1) "Cyberbullying" means the use of any electronic communication device to harass, intimidate or bully.
(2) "Harassment, intimidation or bullying" means any act that:
 (a) Substantially interferes with a student's educational benefits, opportunities or performance;
 (b) Takes place on or immediately adjacent to school grounds, at any school-sponsored activity, on school-provided transportation or at any official school bus stop;
 (c) Has the effect of:
  (A) Physically harming a student or damaging a student's property;
  (B) Knowingly placing a student in reasonable fear of physical harm to the student or damage to the student's property; or
  (C) Creating a hostile educational environment, including interfering with the psychological well-being of a student; and
 (d) May be based on, but not be limited to, the protected class status of a person.
(3) "Protected class" means a group of persons distinguished, or perceived to be distinguished, by race, color, religion, sex, sexual orientation, national origin, marital status, familial status, source of income or disability.

Oregon Revised Statutes Annotated § 339.353 (West 2007)

339.353. Legislative findings

(1) The Legislative Assembly finds that:
 (a) A safe and civil environment is necessary for students to learn and achieve high academic standards.
 (b) Harassment, intimidation or bullying and cyberbullying, like other disruptive or violent behavior, are conduct that disrupts a student's ability to learn and a school's ability to educate its students in a safe environment.
 (c) Students learn by example.
(2) The Legislative Assembly commends school administrators, faculty, staff and volunteers for demonstrating appropriate behavior, treating others with civility and respect, refusing to tolerate harassment, intimidation or bullying and refusing to tolerate cyberbullying.

Oregon Revised Statutes Annotated § 339.356

339.356. Mandatory policy on harassment, intimidation and bullying

(1) Each school district shall adopt a policy prohibiting harassment, intimidation or bullying and prohibiting cyberbullying. School districts shall develop the policy after consultation with parents, guardians, school employees, volunteers, students, administrators and community representatives.
(2) School districts must include in the policy:
   (a) A statement prohibiting harassment, intimidation or bullying and prohibiting cyberbullying.
   (b) Definitions of "harassment," "intimidation" or "bullying" and of "cyberbullying" that are consistent with [Oregon Revised Statutes Annotated] 339.351.
   (c) Definitions of "protected class" that are consistent with [Oregon Revised Statutes Annotated] 174.100 and 339.351.
   (d) A statement of the scope of the policy, including a notice that the policy applies to behavior at school-sponsored activities, on school-provided transportation and at any official school bus stop.
   (e) A description of the type of behavior expected from each student.
   (f) A procedure that is uniform throughout the school district for reporting an act of harassment, intimidation or bullying or an act of cyberbullying. A procedure established under this paragraph shall:
      (A) Identify by job title the school officials responsible for receiving such a report at a school.
      (B) Require a school employee to report an act of harassment, intimidation or bullying or an act of cyberbullying to a person identified under subparagraph (A) of this paragraph.
      (C) Identify any remedial action that may be imposed on a school employee for failure to make a report as required by subparagraph (B) of this paragraph.
      (D) Allow a student or volunteer to report an act of harassment, intimidation or bullying or an act of cyberbullying voluntarily and anonymously to a person identified under subparagraph (A) of this paragraph. Nothing in this subparagraph may be construed to permit remedial action solely on the basis of an anonymous report.
   (g) A procedure that is uniform throughout the school district for prompt investigation of a report of an act of harassment, intimidation or bullying or an act of cyberbullying. A procedure established under this paragraph shall identify by job title the school officials responsible for investigating such a report.
   (h) A procedure by which a person may request a school district to review the actions of a school in responding to a report of an act of harassment, intimidation or bullying or an act of cyberbullying or investigating such a report.
   (i) A statement of the manner in which a school and a school district will respond after an act of harassment, intimidation or bullying or an act of cyberbullying is reported, investigated and confirmed.
   (j) A statement of the consequences and appropriate remedial action for a person found to have committed an act of harassment, intimidation or bullying or an act of cyberbullying.
   (k) A statement prohibiting reprisal or retaliation against any person who reports an act of harassment, intimidation or bullying or an act of cyberbullying and stating the consequences and appropriate remedial action for a person who engages in such reprisal or retaliation.

(L) A statement of the consequences and appropriate remedial action for a person found to have falsely accused another of having committed an act of harassment, intimidation or bullying or an act of cyberbullying as a means of reprisal or retaliation, as a means of harassment, intimidation or bullying or as a means of cyberbullying.

(m) A statement of how the policy is to be publicized within the district. At a minimum, a school district shall make the policy:

(A) Annually available to parents, guardians, school employees and students in a student or employee handbook; and

(B) Readily available to parents, guardians, school employees, volunteers, students, administrators and community representatives at each school office or at the school district office and, if available, on the website for a school or the school district.

(n) The identification by job title of school officials and school district officials responsible for ensuring that the policy is implemented.

(3) A school district that does not comply with the requirements of this section is considered nonstandard under [Oregon Revised Statutes Annotated] 327.103.

Oregon Revised Statutes Annotated § 339.362 (West 2012)

339.362. Retaliation prohibited; required and encouraged reporting; employee immunity

(1) A school employee, student or volunteer may not engage in reprisal or retaliation against a victim of, witness to or person with reliable information about an act of harassment, intimidation or bullying or an act of cyberbullying.

(2) (a) A school employee who witnesses or has reliable information that a student has been subjected to an act of harassment, intimidation or bullying or an act of cyberbullying must report the act to the appropriate school official designated by the school district's policy.

(b) A student or volunteer who witnesses or has reliable information that a student has been subjected to an act of harassment, intimidation or bullying or an act of cyberbullying is encouraged to report the act to the appropriate school official designated by the school district's policy.

(3) A school employee who promptly reports an act of harassment, intimidation or bullying or an act of cyberbullying to the appropriate school official in compliance with the procedures set forth in the school district's policy is immune from a cause of action for damages arising from any failure to remedy the reported act.

Administration Standards for Public Elementary and Secondary Schools. Oregon Administrative Rule 581-022-1140 (West 2008)

Oregon Administrative Rule 581-022-1140

581-022-1140 Equal Educational Opportunities

(2) Each district school board shall adopt a policy in accordance with [Oregon Revised Statutes Annotated] 339.356 prohibiting harassment, intimidation or bullying and prohibiting cyberbullying. School districts are encouraged to develop the policy after consultation with parents and guardians, school employees, volunteers, students, administrators and community representatives.

PENNSYLVANIA

Offenses Involving Danger to the Person. 18 Pennsylvania Statutes and Consolidated Statutes § 2709 (West 2014)

18 Pennsylvania Statutes and Consolidated Statutes § 2709

§ 2709. Harassment.

(a) **Offense defined.**--A person commits the crime of harassment when, with intent to harass, annoy or alarm another, the person:
  (1) strikes, shoves, kicks or otherwise subjects the other person to physical contact, or attempts or threatens to do the same;
  (2) follows the other person in or about a public place or places;
  (3) engages in a course of conduct or repeatedly commits acts which serve no legitimate purpose;
  (4) communicates to or about such other person any lewd, lascivious, threatening or obscene words, language, drawings or caricatures;
  (5) communicates repeatedly in an anonymous manner;
  (6) communicates repeatedly at extremely inconvenient hours; or
  (7) communicates repeatedly in a manner other than specified in paragraphs (4), (5) and (6).

(b.1) **Venue.**--
  (1) An offense committed under this section may be deemed to have been committed at either the place at which the communication or communications were made or at the place where the communication or communications were received.
  (2) Acts indicating a course of conduct which occur in more than one jurisdiction may be used by any other jurisdiction in which an act occurred as evidence of a continuing pattern of conduct or a course of conduct.

(c) **Grading.**--
  (1) Except as provided under paragraph (3), an offense under subsection (a)(1), (2) or (3) shall constitute a summary offense.
  (2) An offense under subsection (a)(4), (5), (6) or (7) shall constitute a misdemeanor of the third degree.
  (3) The grading of an offense under subsection (a)(1), (2) or (3) shall be enhanced one degree if the person has previously violated an order issued under 23 Pennsylvania Statutes and Consolidated Statutes § 6108 (relating to relief) involving the same victim, family or household member.

(d) **False reports.**--A person who knowingly gives false information to any law enforcement officer with the intent to implicate another under this section commits an offense under section 4906 (relating to false reports to law enforcement authorities).

(e) **Application of section.**--This section shall not apply to conduct by a party to a labor dispute as defined in the act of June 2, 1937 (P.L. 1198, No. 308), known as the Labor Anti-Injunction Act, or to any constitutionally protected activity.

(f) **Definitions.--**As used in this section, the following words and phrases shall have the meanings given to them in this subsection:

"Communicates." Conveys a message without intent of legitimate communication or address by oral, nonverbal, written or electronic means, including telephone, electronic mail, Internet, facsimile, telex, wireless communication or similar transmission.

"Course of conduct." A pattern of actions composed of more than one act over a period of time, however short, evidencing a continuity of conduct. Acts indicating a course of conduct which occur in more than one jurisdiction may be used by any other jurisdiction in which an act occurred as evidence of a continuing pattern of conduct or a course of conduct.

"Family or household member." Spouses or persons who have been spouses, persons living as spouses or who lived as spouses, parents and children, other persons related by consanguinity or affinity, current or former sexual or intimate partners or persons who share biological parenthood.

Safe Schools. 24 Pennsylvania Statutes and Consolidated Statutes § 13-1303.1-A (West 2008)

24 Pennsylvania Statutes and Consolidated Statutes § 13-1303.1-A

§ 13-1303.1-A. Policy relating to bullying

(a) No later than January 1, 2009, each school entity shall adopt a policy or amend its existing policy relating to bullying and incorporate the policy into the school entity's code of student conduct required under 22 [Pennsylvania Administrative Code] § 12.3(c) (relating to school rules). The policy shall delineate disciplinary consequences for bullying and may provide for prevention, intervention and education programs, provided that no school entity shall be required to establish a new policy under this section if one currently exists and reasonably fulfills the requirements of this section. The policy shall identify the appropriate school staff person to receive reports of incidents of alleged bullying.

(b) Each school entity shall make the policy available on its publicly accessible Internet website, if available, and in every classroom. Each school entity shall post the policy at a prominent location within each school building where such notices are usually posted. Each school entity shall ensure that the policy and procedures for reporting bullying incidents are reviewed with students within ninety (90) days after their adoption and thereafter at least once each school year.

(c) Each school entity shall review its policy every three (3) years and annually provide the office with a copy of its policy relating to bullying, including information related to the development and implementation of any bullying prevention, intervention and education programs. The information required under this subsection shall be attached to or made part of the annual report required under section 1303-A(b).

(d) In its policy relating to bullying adopted or maintained under subsection (a), a school entity shall not be prohibited from defining bullying in such a way as to encompass acts that occur outside a school setting if those acts meet the requirements contained in subsection (e)(1), (3) and (4). If a school entity reports acts of bullying to the office in accordance with section 1303-A(b), it shall report all incidents that qualify as bullying under the entity's adopted definition of that term.

(e) For purposes of this article, "bullying" shall mean an intentional electronic, written, verbal or physical act, or a series of acts:
  (1) directed at another student or students;
  (2) which occurs in a school setting;
  (3) that is severe, persistent or pervasive; and
  (4) that has the effect of doing any of the following:
      (i) substantially interfering with a student's education;
      (ii) creating a threatening environment; or
      (iii) substantially disrupting the orderly operation of the school; and
      (iv) "school setting" shall mean in the school, on school grounds, in school vehicles, at a designated bus stop or at any activity sponsored, supervised or sanctioned by the school.

RHODE ISLAND

Computer Crime. Rhode Island Statute § 11-52-4.2 (West 2013)

Rhode Island Statute § 11-52-4.2

§ 11-52-4.2. Cyberstalking and cyberharassment prohibited

(a) Whoever transmits any communication by computer or other electronic device to any person or causes any person to be contacted for the sole purpose of harassing that person or his or her family is guilty of a misdemeanor, and shall be punished by a fine of not more than five hundred dollars ($500), by imprisonment for not more than one year, or both. For the purpose of this section, "harassing" means any knowing and willful course of conduct directed at a specific person which seriously alarms, annoys, or bothers the person, and which serves no legitimate purpose. The course of conduct must be of a kind that would cause a reasonable person to suffer substantial emotional distress, or be in fear of bodily injury. "Course of conduct" means a pattern of conduct composed of a series of acts over a period of time, evidencing a continuity of purpose. Constitutionally protected activity is not included within the meaning of "course of conduct".

(b) A second or subsequent conviction under subsection (a) of this section shall be deemed a felony punishable by imprisonment for not more than two (2) years, by a fine of not more than six thousand dollars ($6,000), or both.

State Anti-Bullying Statutes and Student Speech

Health and Safety of Pupils. Rhode Island Statute § 16-21-33, et seq. (West 2011)

Rhode Island Statute § 16-21-33

§ 16-21-33. Safe Schools Act

(a) **Definitions.** As used in this chapter:
   (1) "Bullying" means the use by one or more students of a written, verbal or electronic expression or a physical act or gesture or any combination thereof directed at a student that:
      (i) Causes physical or emotional harm to the student or damage to the student's property;
      (ii) Places the student in reasonable fear of harm to himself/herself or of damage to his/her property;
      (iii) Creates an intimidating, threatening, hostile, or abusive educational environment for the student;
      (iv) Infringes on the rights of the student to participate in school activities; or
      (v) Materially and substantially disrupts the education process or the orderly operation of a school. The expression, physical act or gesture may include, but is not limited to, an incident or incidents that may be reasonably perceived as being motivated by characteristics such as race, color, religion, ancestry, national origin, gender, sexual orientation, gender identity and expression or mental, physical, or sensory disability, intellectual ability or by any other distinguishing characteristic.
   (2) "Cyber-bullying" means bullying through the use of technology or any electronic communication, which shall include, but shall not be limited to, any transfer of signs, signals, writing, images, sounds, data, texting or intelligence of any nature transmitted in whole or in part by a wire, radio, electromagnetic, photo electronic or photo optical system, including, but not limited to, electronic mail, Internet communications, instant messages or facsimile communications. For purposes of this section, cyber-bullying shall also include:
      (i) The creation of a web page or blog in which the creator assumes the identity of another person;
      (ii) The knowing impersonation of another person as the author of posted content or messages; or
      (iii) The distribution by electronic means of a communication to more than one person or the posting of materials on an electronic medium that may be accessed by one or more persons, if the creation, impersonation, or distribution results in any of the conditions enumerated in clauses (i) to (v) of the definition of bullying herein.
   (3) "At school" means on school premises, at any school-sponsored activity or event whether or not it is held on school premises, on a school-transportation vehicle, at an official school bus stop, using property or equipment provided by the school, or creates a material and substantial disruption of the education process or the orderly operation of the school.

Rhode Island Statute § 16-21-34

§ 16-21-34. Statewide bullying policy implemented

(a) The Rhode Island department of education shall prescribe by regulation a statewide bullying policy, ensuring a consistent and unified, statewide approach to the prohibition of bullying at school. The statewide policy shall apply to all schools that are approved for the purpose of § 16-9-1 and shall contain the following:
  (1) Descriptions of and statements prohibiting bullying, cyber-bullying and retaliation of school;
  (2) Clear requirements and procedures for students, staff, parents, guardians and others to report bullying or retaliation;
  (3) A provision that reports of bullying or retaliation may be made anonymously; provided, however, that no disciplinary action shall be taken against a student solely on the basis of an anonymous report;
  (4) Clear procedures for promptly responding to and investigating reports of bullying or retaliation;
  (5) The range of disciplinary actions that may be taken against a perpetrator for bullying or retaliation; provided, however, that the disciplinary actions shall balance the need for accountability with the need to teach appropriate behavior; and provided, further:
    (i) A parental engagement strategy; and
    (ii) A provision that states punishments for violations of the bullying policy shall be determined by the school's appropriate authority; however, no student shall be suspended from school unless it is deemed a necessary consequence of the violations;
  (6) Clear procedures for restoring a sense of safety for a victim and assessing that victim's needs for protection;
  (7) Strategies for protecting from bullying or retaliation a person who reports bullying, provides information during an investigation of bullying or witnesses or has reliable information about an act of bullying;
  (8) Procedures for promptly notifying the parents or guardians of a victim and a perpetrator; provided, further, that the parents or guardians of a victim shall also be notified of the action taken to prevent any further acts of bullying or retaliation; and provided, further, that the procedures shall provide for immediate notification of the local law enforcement agency when criminal charges may be pursued against the perpetrator;
  (9) A provision that a student who knowingly makes a false accusation of bullying or retaliation shall be subject to disciplinary action;
  (10) A strategy for providing counseling or referral to appropriate services currently being offered by schools or communities for perpetrators and victims and for appropriate family members of said students. The plan shall afford all students the same protection regardless of their status under the law;
  (11) A provision that requires a principal or designee to be responsible for the implementation and oversight of the bullying policy;
  (12) Provisions for informing parents and guardians about the bullying policy of the school district or school shall include, but not be limited to:

(i) A link to the policy prominently posted on the home page of the school district's website and distributed annually to parents and guardians of students;

(ii) A provision for notification, within twenty-four (24) hours, of the incident report, to the parents or guardians of the victim of bullying and parents or guardians of the alleged perpetrator of the bullying;

(13) A school employee, school volunteer, student, parent, legal guardian, or relative caregiver who promptly reports, in good faith, an act of bullying to the appropriate school official designated in the school's policy is immune from a cause of action for damages arising from reporting bullying;

(14) This section does not prevent a victim from seeking redress under any other available law, either civil or criminal. This section does not create or alter any tort liability;

(15) Students shall be prohibited from accessing social networking sites at school, except for educational or instructional purposes and with the prior approval from school administration. Nothing in this act shall prohibit students from using school department or school websites for educational purposes. School districts and schools are encouraged to provide in-service training on Internet safety for students, faculty and staff; and

(16) All school districts, charter schools, career and technical schools, approved private day or residential schools and collaborative schools shall be subject to the requirements of this section. School districts and schools must adopt the statewide bullying policy promulgated pursuant to this section by June 30, 2012.

SOUTH CAROLINA

Safe School Climate Act. Code 1976 § 59-63-120, et seq. (West 2006)

Code 1976 § 59-63-120

§ 59-63-120. Definitions.

(1) "Harassment, intimidation, or bullying" means a gesture, an electronic communication, or a written, verbal, physical, or sexual act that is reasonably perceived to have the effect of:
 (a) harming a student physically or emotionally or damaging a student's property, or placing a student in reasonable fear of personal harm or property damage; or
 (b) insulting or demeaning a student or group of students causing substantial disruption in, or substantial interference with, the orderly operation of the school.

(2) "School" means in a classroom, on school premises, on a school bus or other school-related vehicle, at an official school bus stop, at a school-sponsored activity or event whether or not it is held on school premises, or at another program or function where the school is responsible for the child.

Code 1976 § 59-63-130

§ 59-63-130. Prohibited conduct; reports by witnesses.

(A) A person may not engage in:
    (1) harassment, intimidation, or bullying; or
    (2) reprisal, retaliation, or false accusation against a victim, witness, or one with reliable information about an act of harassment, intimidation, or bullying.
(B) A school employee, student, or volunteer who witnesses, or has reliable information that a student has been subject to harassment, intimidation, or bullying shall report the incident to the appropriate school official.

Code 1976 § 59-63-140

§ 59-63-140. Local school districts to adopt policies prohibiting harassment; required components; model policies by State Board of Education; bullying prevention programs.

(A) Before January 1, 2007, each local school district shall adopt a policy prohibiting harassment, intimidation, or bullying at school. The school district shall involve parents and guardians, school employees, volunteers, students, administrators, and community representatives in the process of creating the policy.
(B) The policy must include, but not be limited to, the following components:
    (1) a statement prohibiting harassment, intimidation, or bullying of a student;
    (2) a definition of harassment, intimidation, or bullying no less inclusive than the definition in Section 59-63-120;
    (3) a description of appropriate student behavior;
    (4) consequences and appropriate remedial actions for persons committing acts of harassment, intimidation, or bullying, and for persons engaging in reprisal or retaliation;
    (5) procedures for reporting acts of harassment, intimidation, or bullying, to include a provision for reporting anonymously. However, formal disciplinary action must not be taken solely on the basis of an anonymous report. The procedures must identify the appropriate school personnel responsible for taking the report and investigating the complaint;
    (6) procedures for prompt investigation of reports of serious violations and complaints;
    (7) a statement that prohibits reprisal or retaliation against a person who reports an act of harassment, intimidation, or bullying;
    (8) consequences and appropriate remedial action for persons found to have falsely accused another;
    (9) a process for discussing the district's harassment, intimidation, or bullying policy with students; and
    (10) a statement of how the policy is to be publicized, including notice that the policy applies to participation in school-sponsored functions.
(C) To assist local school districts in developing policies for the prevention of harassment, intimidation, or bullying, the State Board of Education shall develop model policies applicable to grades kindergarten through twelve. Additionally, the State Board of Education shall develop teacher preparation program standards on the identification and prevention of bullying. The model policies and standards must be developed no later than September 1, 2006.

(D) The local school board shall ensure that the school district's policy developed pursuant to this article is included in the school district's publication of the comprehensive rules, procedures, and standards of conduct for schools and in the student's handbook.

(E) Information regarding a local school district policy against harassment, intimidation, or bullying must be incorporated into a school's employee training program. Training also should be provided to school volunteers who have significant contact with students.

(F) Schools and school districts are encouraged to establish bullying prevention programs and other initiatives involving school staff, students, administrators, volunteers, parents, law enforcement, and community members.

SOUTH DAKOTA

Supervision of Students and Conduct of School. South Dakota Codified Laws § 13-32-14, et seq. (West 2014)

South Dakota Codified Laws § 13-32-14

§ 13-32-14. Adoption of bullying policy

If a school district does not have a bullying policy, the school district shall follow the model bullying policy in § 13-32-19 until such time as the school district adopts its own bullying policy. Nothing in §§ 13-32-14 to 13-32-19, inclusive, supplants or preempts an existing school district policy, except that no school district policy prohibiting bullying, whether it is existing or adopted pursuant to §§ 13-32-14 to 13-32-19, inclusive, may contain any protected classes of students.

South Dakota Codified Laws § 13-32-15

§ 13-32-15. Bullying defined

Bullying is a pattern of repeated conduct that causes physical hurt or psychological distress on one or more students that may include threats, intimidation, stalking as defined in chapter 22-19A, physical violence, theft, destruction of property, any threatening use of data or computer software, written or verbal communication, or conduct directed against a student that:

(1) Places a student in reasonable fear of harm to his or her person or damage to his or her property; and either
(2) Substantially interferes with a student's educational performance; or
(3) Substantially disrupts the orderly operation of a school.

For the purposes of §§ 13-32-14 to 13-32-19, inclusive, bullying also includes retaliation against a student for asserting or alleging an act of bullying.

South Dakota Codified Laws § 13-32-16

§ 13-32-16. Bullying policy requirements

Each school district policy developed pursuant to §§ 13-32-14 to 13-32-19, inclusive, shall contain the following provisions:

(1) A statement prohibiting bullying and a definition of bullying that includes the definition listed in § 13-32-15;
(2) A description of the type of behavior expected from each student of the school district, and the consequences for a student of the school district who commits an act of bullying;
(3) A procedure for reporting an act of bullying, including provisions that permit a person to anonymously report such an act, although formal disciplinary action may not be based solely on an anonymous report; and
(4) A procedure for the prompt investigation and response to any report of bullying, including a requirement that an investigation be conducted on any alleged incident of bullying committed against a child while the child is aboard a school bus, at a school bus stop, or at a school-sponsored event.

South Dakota Codified Laws § 13-32-18

§ 13-32-18. Incidents involving electronic devices

Neither the physical location nor the time of day of any incident involving the use of computers or other electronic devices is a defense to any disciplinary action taken by a school district for conduct determined to meet the definition of bullying in § 13-32-15.

South Dakota Codified Laws § 13-32-19

§ 13-32-19. Model bullying policy

The model bullying policy pursuant to §§ 13-32-14 to 13-32-18, inclusive, is as follows:

PROHIBITION OF HARASSMENT, INTIMIDATION, AND BULLYING

The School District is committed to maintaining a constructive, safe school climate that is conducive to student learning and fostering an environment in which all students are treated with respect and dignity.

Persistent bullying can severely inhibit a student's ability to learn and may have lasting negative effects on a student's life. The bullying of students by students, staff, or third parties is strictly prohibited and will not be tolerated.

Bullying consists of repeated physical, verbal, non-verbal, written, electronic, or any conduct directed toward a student that is so pervasive, severe, and objectively offensive that it:

State Anti-Bullying Statutes and Student Speech

(1) Has the purpose of creating or resulting in an intimidating, hostile, or offensive academic environment; or
(2) Has the purpose or effect of substantially or unreasonably interfering with a student's academic performance which deprives the student access to educational opportunities.

Any staff member observing or suspecting bullying toward another individual is required to report the issue to his or her building supervisor.

This policy is in effect while students are on property within the jurisdiction of the School Board; while students are in school-owned or school-operated vehicles; and while students are attending or engaged in school-sponsored activities.

The District will act to investigate all complaints (formal or informal, verbal or written) of bullying. A formal complaint may be submitted to the building principal. Any student engaging in an act of bullying is subject to discipline pursuant to the District's student discipline procedure.

This policy may not be interpreted to prohibit civil exchange of opinions or debate protected under the state or federal constitutions if the opinion expressed does not otherwise materially or substantially disrupt the education process or intrude upon the rights of others.

TENNESSEE

Schools Against Violence in Education (Save) Act.
Tennessee Code Annotated § 49-6-812 (West 2013)

Tennessee Code Annotated § 49-6-812

§ 49-6-812. Harassment and bullying policy compliance

Each LEA [local educational agency] shall ensure that the district-wide safety plans and building-level emergency response plans required by this part are developed in such a manner as to be consistent with the district's harassment and bullying policies developed pursuant to § 49-6-4503.

Harassment, Intimidation, Bullying and Cyber-Bullying.
Tennessee Code Annotated § 49-6-4501, et seq. (West 2011)

Tennessee Code Annotated § 49-6-4501

§ 49-6-4501. Legislative findings

The general assembly finds and declares that:

(1) A safe and civil environment is necessary for students to learn and achieve high academic standards;
(2) Harassment, intimidation, bullying or cyber-bullying, like other disruptive or violent behavior, is conduct that disrupts a student's ability to learn and a school's ability to educate its students in a safe environment;

(3) Students learn by example. School administrators, faculty, staff and volunteers who demonstrate appropriate behavior, treating others with civility and respect and refusing to tolerate harassment, intimidation, bullying or cyber-bullying, encourage others to do so as well; and

(4) The use of telephones, cellular phones or other wireless telecommunication devices, personal digital assistants (PDAs), computers, electronic mail, instant messaging, text messaging, and web sites by students in a manner that is safe and secure is essential to a safe and civil learning environment and is necessary for students to successfully use technology.

Tennessee Code Annotated § 49-6-4502 (West 2013)

§ 49-6-4502. Definitions

(1) "Cyber-bullying" means bullying undertaken through the use of electronic devices;
(2) "Electronic devices" include, but are not limited to, telephones, cellular phones or other wireless telecommunication devices, personal digital assistants (PDAs), computers, electronic mail, instant messaging, text messaging, and web sites;
(3) "Harassment, intimidation or bullying" means any act that substantially interferes with a student's educational benefits, opportunities or performance; and:
 (A) If the act takes place on school grounds, at any school-sponsored activity, on school-provided equipment or transportation or at any official school bus stop, the act has the effect of:
  (i) Physically harming a student or damaging a student's property;
  (ii) Knowingly placing a student or students in reasonable fear of physical harm to the student or damage to the student's property;
  (iii) Causing emotional distress to a student or students; or
  (iv) Creating a hostile educational environment; or
 (B) If the act takes place off school property or outside of a school-sponsored activity, it is directed specifically at a student or students and has the effect of creating a hostile educational environment or otherwise creating a substantial disruption to the education environment or learning process.

Tennessee Code Annotated § 49-6-4503

§ 49-6-4503. School district policies

(a) Each school district shall adopt a policy prohibiting harassment, intimidation, bullying or cyber-bullying. School districts are encouraged to develop the policy after consultation with parents and guardians, school employees, volunteers, students, administrators and community representatives.
(b) School districts shall include in the policies:
 (1) A statement prohibiting harassment, intimidation, bullying or cyber-bullying;
 (2) A definition of harassment, intimidation, bullying or cyber-bullying;
 (3) A description of the type of behavior expected from each student;
 (4) A statement of the consequences and appropriate remedial action for a person who commits an act of harassment, intimidation, bullying or cyber bullying;

(5) A procedure for reporting an act of harassment, intimidation, bullying or cyber-bullying, including a provision that permits a person to report an act of harassment, intimidation, bullying or cyber-bullying anonymously. Nothing in this section may be construed to permit formal disciplinary action solely on the basis of an anonymous report;

(6) A procedure for prompt investigation of a report of an act of harassment, intimidation, bullying or cyber-bullying;

(7) A statement of the manner in which a school district shall respond after an act of harassment, intimidation, bullying or cyber-bullying is reported, investigated and confirmed;

(8) A statement of the consequences and appropriate remedial action for a person found to have committed an act of harassment, intimidation, bullying or cyber-bullying;

(9) A statement prohibiting reprisal or retaliation against any person who reports an act of harassment, intimidation, bullying or cyber-bullying and stating the consequences and appropriate remedial action for a person who engages in such reprisal or retaliation;

(10) A statement of the consequences and appropriate remedial action for a person found to have falsely accused another of having committed an act of harassment, intimidation, bullying or cyber-bullying as a means of reprisal or retaliation or as a means of harassment, intimidation, bullying or cyber-bullying;

(11) A statement of how the policy is to be publicized within the district, including a notice that the policy applies to behavior at school-sponsored activities;

(12) The identification by job title of school officials responsible for ensuring that the policy is implemented; and

(13) A procedure for discouraging and reporting conduct aimed at defining a student in a sexual manner or conduct impugning the character of a student based on allegations of sexual promiscuity.

(c)(1) Each LEA [local educational agency] shall, at the beginning of each school year, provide teachers and school counselors a copy of the policy along with information on the policy's implementation, bullying prevention and strategies to address bullying and harassment when it happens. In addition, each LEA shall provide training to teachers and counselors regarding the policy and appropriate procedures relative to implementation of the policy. The department of education shall provide guidelines for such training and provide recommendations of appropriate, available and free bullying and harassment prevention resources.

(2) Each LEA shall also:

(A) At the beginning of the school year, make available to students and parents information relative to bullying prevention programs to promote awareness of the harmful effects of bullying and to permit discussion with respect to prevention policies and strategies;

(B) Beginning August 1, 2013, and annually thereafter, prepare and provide to the department of education a report concerning the number of bullying cases brought to the attention of school officials during the preceding year and the manner in which they were resolved or the reason they are still pending.

(3) The department shall annually submit a report to the education committees of the house of the representatives and the senate updating membership on the number of bullying cases reported statewide, the number of LEAs implementing this part and any other information relating to the subject of bullying and harassment as will be helpful to the committee in establishing policy in this area.

(d)(1) The principal of a middle school, junior high school, or high school, or the principal's designee, shall investigate harassment, intimidation, bullying or cyber-bullying when a student reports to any principal, teacher or guidance counselor that physical harm or a threat of physical harm to such student's person or property has occurred.

(2) Following any investigation required by this part, the principal or such principal's designee shall report the findings, along with any disciplinary action taken, to the director of schools and the chair of the local board of education.

Tennessee Code Annotated § 49-6-4504

§ 49-6-4504. LEA [Local Educational Agency] policies

Each LEA shall adopt a policy prohibiting harassment, intimidation, bullying or cyber-bullying and transmit a copy of the policy to the commissioner of education by January 1, 2006.

Tennessee Code Annotated § 49-6-4505

§ 49-6-4505. Retaliation and reporting

(a) A school employee, student or volunteer may not engage in reprisal or retaliation against a victim of, witness to, or person with reliable information about an act of harassment, intimidation, bullying or cyber-bullying.

(b) A school employee, student or volunteer who witnesses or has reliable information that a student has been subjected to an act of harassment, intimidation, bullying or cyber-bullying is encouraged to report the act to the appropriate school official designated by the school district's policy.

(c) A school employee who promptly reports an act of harassment, intimidation, bullying or cyber-bullying to the appropriate school official in compliance with the procedures set forth in the school district's policy is immune from a cause of action for damages arising from any failure to remedy the reported act.

(d) Notwithstanding subsections (b) and (c), a school employee, student or volunteer who witnesses or possesses reliable information that a student has transmitted by an electronic device any communication containing a credible threat to cause bodily injury or death to another student or school employee, as prohibited by § 49-6-4216, shall report such information to the appropriate school official designated by the policy of the school district. Such school official shall make a determination regarding the administration of the report.

State Anti-Bullying Statutes and Student Speech

Tennessee Code Annotated § 49-6-4506

§ 49-6-4506. Prevention initiatives

School districts are encouraged to form harassment, intimidation, bullying or cyber-bullying prevention task forces, programs and other initiatives involving school employees, students, administrators, volunteers, parents, guardians, law enforcement and community representatives.

TEXAS

Admission, Transfer, and Attendance. Vernon's Texas Statutes and Codes Annotated, Education Code § 25.0342 (West 2011)

Vernon's Texas Statutes and Codes Annotated, Education Code § 25.0342

§ 25.0342. Transfer of Students Who Are Victims of or Have Engaged In Bullying

(a) In this section, "bullying" has the meaning assigned by Section 37.0832.
(b) On the request of a parent or other person with authority to act on behalf of a student who is a victim of bullying, the board of trustees of a school district or the board's designee shall transfer the victim to:
  (1) another classroom at the campus to which the victim was assigned at the time the bullying occurred; or
  (2) a campus in the school district other than the campus to which the victim was assigned at the time the bullying occurred.
(b-1) The board of trustees of a school district may transfer the student who engaged in bullying to:
  (1) another classroom at the campus to which the victim was assigned at the time the bullying occurred; or
  (2) a campus in the district other than the campus to which the victim was assigned at the time the bullying occurred, in consultation with a parent or other person with authority to act on behalf of the student who engaged in bullying.
(b-2) Section 37.004 applies to a transfer under Subsection (b-1) of a student with a disability who receives special education services.
(c) The board of trustees or the board's designee shall verify that a student has been a victim of bullying before transferring the student under this section.
(d) The board of trustees or the board's designee may consider past student behavior when identifying a bully.
(e) The determination by the board of trustees or the board's designee is final and may not be appealed.
(f) A school district is not required to provide transportation to a student who transfers to another campus under Subsection (b)(2).
(g) Section 25.034 does not apply to a transfer under this section.

Discipline; Law and Order. Vernon's Texas Statutes and Codes Annotated, Education Code, Education Code § 37.001 (West 2013)

Vernon's Texas Statutes and Codes Annotated, Education Code, Education Code § 37.001

§ 37.001. Student Code of Conduct

(a) The board of trustees of an independent school district shall, with the advice of its district-level committee established under Subchapter F, Chapter 11, adopt a student code of conduct for the district. The student code of conduct must be posted and prominently displayed at each school campus or made available for review at the office of the campus principal. In addition to establishing standards for student conduct, the student code of conduct must:

...

(7) prohibit bullying, harassment, and making hit lists and ensure that district employees enforce those prohibitions; and
(8) provide, as appropriate for students at each grade level, methods, including options, for:
    (A) managing students in the classroom, on school grounds, and on a vehicle owned or operated by the district;
    (B) disciplining students; and
    (C) preventing and intervening in student discipline problems, including bullying, harassment, and making hit lists.
(b) In this section:
(1) "Bullying" has the meaning assigned by Section 37.0832.
(2) "Harassment" means threatening to cause harm or bodily injury to another student, engaging in sexually intimidating conduct, causing physical damage to the property of another student, subjecting another student to physical confinement or restraint, or maliciously taking any action that substantially harms another student's physical or emotional health or safety.

Vernon's Texas Statutes and Codes Annotated, Education Code § 37.0832 (West 2011).

§ 37.0832. Bullying Prevention Policies and Procedures

(a) In this section, "bullying" means, subject to Subsection (b), engaging in written or verbal expression, expression through electronic means, or physical conduct that occurs on school property, at a school-sponsored or school-related activity, or in a vehicle operated by the district and that:
    (1) has the effect or will have the effect of physically harming a student, damaging a student's property, or placing a student in reasonable fear of harm to the student's person or of damage to the student's property; or
    (2) is sufficiently severe, persistent, and pervasive enough that the action or threat creates an intimidating, threatening, or abusive educational environment for a student.
(b) Conduct described by Subsection (a) is considered bullying if that conduct:

(1) exploits an imbalance of power between the student perpetrator and the student victim through written or verbal expression or physical conduct; and
(2) interferes with a student's education or substantially disrupts the operation of a school.
(c) The board of trustees of each school district shall adopt a policy, including any necessary procedures, concerning bullying that:
(1) prohibits the bullying of a student;
(2) prohibits retaliation against any person, including a victim, a witness, or another person, who in good faith provides information concerning an incident of bullying;
(3) establishes a procedure for providing notice of an incident of bullying to a parent or guardian of the victim and a parent or guardian of the bully within a reasonable amount of time after the incident;
(4) establishes the actions a student should take to obtain assistance and intervention in response to bullying;
(5) sets out the available counseling options for a student who is a victim of or a witness to bullying or who engages in bullying;
(6) establishes procedures for reporting an incident of bullying, investigating a reported incident of bullying, and determining whether the reported incident of bullying occurred;
(7) prohibits the imposition of a disciplinary measure on a student who, after an investigation, is found to be a victim of bullying, on the basis of that student's use of reasonable self-defense in response to the bullying; and
(8) requires that discipline for bullying of a student with disabilities comply with applicable requirements under federal law, including the Individuals with Disabilities Education Act (20 U.S.C. Section 1400 et seq.).
(d) The policy and any necessary procedures adopted under Subsection (c) must be included:
(1) annually, in the student and employee school district handbooks; and
(2) in the district improvement plan under Section 11.252.
(e) The procedure for reporting bullying established under Subsection (c) must be posted on the district's Internet website to the extent practicable.

UTAH

Bullying and Hazing. Utah Code Annotated 1953 § 53A-11a-102, et seq. (West 2011)

Utah Code Annotated 1953 § 53A-11a-102

§ 53A-11a-102. Definitions

(1)(a) "Bullying" means intentionally or knowingly committing an act that:
　(i)(A) endangers the physical health or safety of a school employee or student;

(B) involves any brutality of a physical nature such as whipping, beating, branding, calisthenics, bruising, electric shocking, placing of a harmful substance on the body, or exposure to the elements;
(C) involves consumption of any food, liquor, drug, or other substance;
(D) involves other physical activity that endangers the physical health and safety of a school employee or student; or
(E) involves physically obstructing a school employee's or student's freedom to move; and
(ii) is done for the purpose of placing a school employee or student in fear of:
(A) physical harm to the school employee or student; or
(B) harm to property of the school employee or student.
(b) The conduct described in Subsection (1)(a) constitutes bullying, regardless of whether the person against whom the conduct is committed directed, consented to, or acquiesced in, the conduct.
(2) "Communication" means the conveyance of a message, whether verbal, written, or electronic.
(3) "Cyber-bullying" means using the Internet, a cell phone, or another device to send or post text, video, or an image with the intent or knowledge, or with reckless disregard, that the text, video, or image will hurt, embarrass, or threaten an individual, regardless of whether the individual directed, consented to, or acquiesced in the conduct, or voluntarily accessed the electronic communication.
(4) "Harassment" means repeatedly communicating to another individual, in an objectively demeaning or disparaging manner, statements that contribute to a hostile learning or work environment for the individual.
(5)(a) "Hazing" means intentionally or knowingly committing an act that:
(i)(A) endangers the physical health or safety of a school employee or student;
(B) involves any brutality of a physical nature such as whipping, beating, branding, calisthenics, bruising, electric shocking, placing of a harmful substance on the body, or exposure to the elements;
(C) involves consumption of any food, liquor, drug, or other substance;
(D) involves other physical activity that endangers the physical health and safety of a school employee or student; or
(E) involves physically obstructing a school employee's or student's freedom to move; and
(ii)(A) is done for the purpose of initiation or admission into, affiliation with, holding office in, or as a condition for, membership or acceptance, or continued membership or acceptance, in any school or school sponsored team, organization, program, or event; or
(B) if the person committing the act against a school employee or student knew that the school employee or student is a member of, or candidate for, membership with a school, or school sponsored team, organization, program, or event to which the person committing the act belongs to or participates in.
(b) The conduct described in Subsection (5)(a) constitutes hazing, regardless of whether the person against whom the conduct is committed directed, consented to, or acquiesced in, the conduct.
(6) "Policy" means a bullying and hazing policy described in Section 53A-11a-301.
(7) "Retaliate" means an act or communication intended:
(a) as retribution against a person for reporting bullying or hazing; or
(b) to improperly influence the investigation of, or the response to, a report of bullying or hazing.

Utah Code Annotated 1953 § 53A-11a-201

§ 53A-11a-201. Bullying, cyber-bullying, harassment, hazing, sexual battery, and sexual exposure prohibited

(1) No school employee or student may engage in bullying or harassing a school employee or student:
   (a) on school property;
   (b) at a school related or sponsored event;
   (c) on a school bus;
   (d) at a school bus stop; or
   (e) while the school employee or student is traveling to or from a location or event described in Subsections (1)(a) through (d).
(2) No school employee or student may engage in hazing or cyber-bullying a school employee or student at any time or in any location.

Utah Code Annotated 1953 § 53A-11a-202

§ 53A-11a-202. Retaliation and making false allegation prohibited

(1) No school employee or student may engage in retaliation against:
   (a) a school employee;
   (b) a student; or
   (c) an investigator for, or a witness of, an alleged incident of bullying, cyber-bullying, harassment, hazing, or retaliation.
(2) No school employee or student may make a false allegation of bullying, cyber-bullying, harassment, hazing, or retaliation against a school employee or student.

Utah Code Annotated 1953 § 53A-11a-203 (West 2013)

§ 53A-11a-203. Parental notification of certain incidents and threats required.

(1) For purposes of this section, "parent" includes a student's guardian.
(2) A school shall:
   (a) notify a parent if the parent's student threatens to commit suicide; or
   (b) notify the parents of each student involved in an incident of bullying, cyber-bullying, harassment, hazing, or retaliation, of the incident involving each parent's student.

Utah Code Annotated 1953 § 53A-11a-301 (West 2013)

§ 53A-11a-301. Bullying, cyber-bullying, harassment, hazing, and retaliation policy

(1) On or before September 1, 2013, each school board shall update the school board's bullying, cyber-bullying, harassment, hazing, and retaliation policy consistent with this chapter.

(2) The policy shall:
  (a) be developed only with input from:
    (i) students;
    (ii) parents;
    (iii) teachers;
    (iv) school administrators;
    (v) school staff; or
    (vi) local law enforcement agencies; and
  (b) provide protection to a student, regardless of the student's legal status.
(3) The policy shall include the following components:
  (a) definitions of bullying, cyber-bullying, harassment, and hazing that are consistent with this chapter;
  (b) language prohibiting bullying, cyber-bullying, harassment, and hazing;
  (c) language prohibiting retaliation against an individual who reports conduct that is prohibited under this chapter;
  (d) language prohibiting making a false report of bullying, cyber-bullying, harassment, hazing, or retaliation; and
  (e) as required in Section 53A-11a-203, parental notification of:
    (i) a student's threat to commit suicide; and
    (ii) an incident of bullying, cyber-bullying, harassment, hazing, or retaliation involving the parent's student.
(4) A copy of the policy shall be included in student conduct handbooks and employee handbooks.
(5) A policy may not permit formal disciplinary action that is based solely on an anonymous report of bullying, cyber-bullying, harassment, hazing, or retaliation.
(6) Nothing in this chapter is intended to infringe upon the right of a school employee or student to exercise their right of free speech.

Utah Code Annotated 1953 § 53A-11a-401 (West 2011)

§ 53A-11a-401. Training, education, and prevention

(1) A school board shall include in the training of a school employee, training regarding bullying, cyber-bullying, harassment, hazing, and retaliation.
(2) To the extent that state or federal funding is available for this purpose, school boards are encouraged to implement programs or initiatives, in addition to the training described in Subsection (1), to provide for training and education regarding, and the prevention of, bullying, hazing, and retaliation.
(3) The programs or initiatives described in Subsection (2) may involve:
  (a) the establishment of a bullying task force; or
  (b) the involvement of school employees, students, or law enforcement.

State Anti-Bullying Statutes and Student Speech

School Policy and Electronic Devices. Utah Administrative Code R277-495, et seq. (West 2013)

Utah Administrative Code R277-495

R277-495. Required Policies for Electronic Devices in Public Schools.

B. "Electronic device" means a privately owned device that is used for audio, video, or text communication or any other type of computer or computer-like instrument.

Utah Administrative Code R277-495-3

R277-495-3. Local Board and Charter School Responsibilities.

A. LEAs [Local Educational Agencies] shall require all schools under their supervision to have a policy or policies for students, employees and, where appropriate, for invitees, governing the use of electronic devices on school premises and at school sponsored activities.
B. LEAs shall review and approve policies regularly.
C. LEAs shall encourage schools to involve teachers, parents, students, school employees and community members in developing local policies; school community councils could provide helpful information and guidance within various school communities and neighborhoods.
D. LEAs shall provide copies of their policies or clear electronic links to policies at LEA offices, in schools and on the LEA website.
E. LEAs and schools within LEAs shall work together to ensure that all policies within a school or school district are consistent and understandable for parents.
F. LEAs shall provide reasonable public notice and at least one public hearing or meeting to address a proposed or revised Internet safety policy. LEAs shall retain documentation of the policy review and adoption actions.

Utah Administrative Code R277-495-4

R277-495-4. Policy Requirements.

A. Local policies shall address the following minimum components:
    (1) definitions of devices covered by policy;
    (2) prohibitions on the use of electronic devices in ways that bully, humiliate, harass, or intimidate school-related individuals, including students, employees, and invitees, consistent with R277-609 and R277-613, or violate local, state, or federal laws; and
    (3) the prohibition of access by students, LEA [local educational agency] employees and invitees to inappropriate matter on the Internet and World Wide Web while using LEA equipment, services or connectivity whether on school property or while using school-owned or issued devices;

(4) the safety and security of students when using electronic mail, chat rooms, and other forms of direct electronic communications (including instant messaging);

(5) unauthorized access, including hacking and other unlawful activities by LEA electronic device users; and

(6) unauthorized disclosure, use and dissemination of personal student information under the Family Educational Rights and Privacy Act, 34 CFR, Part 99.

B. Additional requirements for student policies—In addition to the provisions of R277-495-4A, policies for student use of electronic devices shall include:

(1) prohibitions against use of electronic devices during standardized assessments unless specifically allowed by statute, regulation, student IEP, or assessment directions;

(2) provisions that inform students that there may be administrative and criminal penalties for misuse of electronic devices and that local law enforcement officers may be notified if school employees believe that a student has misused an electronic device in violation of the law;

(3) provisions that inform students that violation of LEA acceptable use policies may result in confiscation of LEA-owned devices which may result in missed assignments, inability to participate in required assessments and possible loss of credit or academic grade consequences;

(4) provisions that inform students that they are personally responsible for devices assigned or provided to them by the LEA, both for loss or damage of devices and use of devices consistent with LEA directives;

(5) provisions that inform students and parents that use of electronic devices in violation of LEA or teacher instructional policies may result in the confiscation of personal devices for a designated period; and

(6) provisions that inform students that use of privately-owned electronic devices to bully or harass other students or employees and result in disruption at school or school-sponsored activities may justify administrative penalties, including expulsion from school and notification to law enforcement.

C. Additional requirements for employee policies—In addition to the provisions of R277-495-4A, policies for employee use of electronic devices shall include:

(1) notice that use of electronic devices to access inappropriate or pornographic images on school premises is illegal, may have both criminal and employment consequences, and where appropriate, shall be reported to law enforcement;

(2) notice that employees are responsible for LEA-issued devices at all times and misuse of devices may have employment consequences, regardless of the user; and

(3) notice that employees may use privately-owned electronic devices on school premises or at school sponsored activities when the employee has supervisory duties only as directed by the employing LEA; and

(4) required staff responsibilities in educating minors on appropriate online activities and in supervising such activities.

D. Local policies may also include the following:

(1) prohibitions or restrictions on unauthorized audio recordings, capture of images, transmissions of recordings or images, or invasions of reasonable expectations of student and employee privacy;

(2) procedures to report the misuse of electronic devices;

(3) potential disciplinary actions toward students or employees or both for violation of local policies regarding the use of electronic devices;
(4) exceptions to the policy for special circumstances, health-related reasons and emergencies, if any; and
(5) strategies for use of technology that enhance instruction.

Utah Administrative Code R277-613

R277-613. LEA [Local Educational Agency] Bullying, Cyber-bullying, Hazing and Harassment Policies and Training.

B. "Bullying" means intentionally or knowingly committing an act that:
(1)(a) endangers the physical health or safety of a school employee or student;
 (b) involves any brutality of a physical nature such as whipping, beating, branding, calisthenics, bruising, electric shocking, placing of a harmful substance on the body, or exposure to the elements;
 (c) involves consumption of any food, liquor, drug, or other substance;
 (d) involves other physical activity that endangers the physical health and safety of a school employee or student; or
 (e) involves physically obstructing a school employee's or student's freedom to move; and
(2) is done for the purpose of placing a school employee or student in fear of:
(a) physical harm to the school employee or student; or
(b) harm to property of the school employee or student.
(3) The conduct described in R277-613-1B constitutes bullying, regardless of whether the person against whom the conduct is committed directed, consented to, or acquiesced in, the conduct.
(4) Bullying is commonly understood as aggressive behavior that:
(a) is intended to cause distress and harm;
(b) exists in a relationship in which there is an imbalance of power and strength; and
(c) is repeated over time.
C. "Civil rights violations," for purposes of this rule, means bullying, cyber-bullying, hazing or harassing that is targeted at a federally protected class.
D. "Cyber-bullying" means using the Internet, a cell phone, or another device to send or post text, video, or an image with the intent or knowledge, or with reckless disregard, that the text, video, or image will hurt, embarrass, or threaten an individual, regardless of whether the individual directed, consented to, or acquiesced in the conduct, or voluntarily accessed the electronic communication.
E. "Federally protected class" means any group protected from discrimination under the following federal laws:
(1) Title VI of the Civil Rights Act of 1964 prohibits discrimination on the basis of race, color, or national origin;
(2) Title IX of the Education Amendments of 1972 prohibits discrimination on the basis of sex;
(3) Section 504 of the Rehabilitation Act of 1973 and Title II of the Americans with Disabilities Act of 1990 prohibits discrimination on the basis of disability; and

(4) Other areas included under these acts prohibit discrimination on the basis of religion, gender identity, and sexual orientation.

F. "Harassment" means repeatedly communicating to another individual, in an objectively demeaning or disparaging manner, statements that contribute to a hostile learning or work environment for the individual.

G. "Hazing" means intentionally or knowingly committing an act that:

(1)(a) endangers the physical health or safety of a school employee or student;

(b) involves any brutality of a physical nature such as whipping, beating, branding, calisthenics, bruising, electric shocking, placing of a harmful substance on the body, or exposure to the elements;

(c) involves consumption of any food, liquor, drug, or other substance;

(d) involves other physical activity that endangers the physical health and safety of a school employee or student; or

(e) involves physically obstructing a school employee's or student's freedom to move; and

(f)(i) is done for the purpose of initiation or admission into, affiliation with, holding office in, or as a condition for, membership or acceptance, or continued membership or acceptance, in any school or school sponsored team, organization, program, or event; or

(ii) if the person committing the act against a school employee or student knew that the school employee or student is a member of, or candidate for, membership with a school, or school sponsored team, organization, program, or event to which the person committing the act belongs to or participates in.

(2) The conduct described in R277-613-1G constitutes hazing, regardless of whether the person against whom the conduct is committed, directed, consented to, or acquiesced in, the conduct.

...

L. "Retaliate or retaliation" means an act or communication intended:

(1) as retribution against a person for reporting bullying, cyber-bullying, hazing and harassment; or

(2) to improperly influence the investigation of, or the response to, a report of bullying, cyber-bullying, hazing and harassment.

Utah Administrative Code R277-613-2

R277-613-2. Authority and Purpose.

B. The purpose of the rule is to require LEAs to implement bullying, cyber-bullying, hazing and harassment policies district and school wide; to provide for regular and meaningful training of school employees and students; to provide for enforcement of the policies in schools, at the state level and in public school athletic programs; to require LEAs to notify parents of specific bullying, cyber-bullying, hazing, harassment and suicide threat incidents; and to require LEAs to maintain documentation as required by law.

State Anti-Bullying Statutes and Student Speech

Utah Administrative Code R277-613-4

R277-613-4. LEA Responsibility to Create Bullying Policies.

A. Each LEA shall implement an updated policy prohibiting bullying, cyber-bullying, hazing, harassment and retaliation, and making a false report, consistent with Section 53A-11a-301.
...
C. The policy shall include parental notification of:
    (2) an incident of bullying, cyber-bullying, hazing, harassment or retaliation involving the parent's student.
    (3) This part of the policy shall also include:
        (a) timely parent notification;
        (b) designation of the appropriate school employee(s) to provide parent notification;
        (c) designation of the format in which notification shall be provided to parents and maintained by the LEA;
        (d) directives for secure maintenance of the notification record as required under Section 53A-11a-203(1);
        (e) a retention period and destruction process for the notification; and
        (f) an LEA definition of parent(s) consistent with Section 53A-11-203 and this rule.
D. The policy shall provide for student assessment of the prevalence of bullying, cyber-bullying, hazing and harassment in LEAs and schools, specifically locations where students are unsafe and additional adult supervision may be required, such as playgrounds, hallways, and lunch areas.
E. The policy shall include required strong responsive action against retaliation, including assistance to harassed students and their parents in reporting subsequent problems and new incidents.
F. The policy shall provide that students, staff, and volunteers receive training on bullying, cyber-bullying, hazing and harassment from individuals qualified to provide such training. The LEA shall determine how often training shall be provided.
    (1) The training should be specific to:
        (a) overt aggression that may include physical fighting such as punching, shoving, kicking, and verbal threatening behavior, such as name calling, or both physical and verbal aggression or threatening behavior;
        (b) relational aggression or indirect, covert, or social aggression, including rumor spreading, intimidation, enlisting a friend to assault a child, and social isolation;
        (c) sexual aggression or acts of a sexual nature or with sexual overtones;
        (d) cyber-bullying, including use of email, web pages, text messaging, instant messaging, three-way calling or messaging or any other electronic means for aggression inside or outside of school; and
        (e) civil rights violations, appropriate reporting and investigative procedures. This includes bullying, cyber-bullying, hazing and harassment based upon the students' actual or perceived identities and conformance or failure to conform with stereotypes.

(2) Training should also include awareness and intervention skills such as social skills training for students and staff, including aides, custodians, kitchen and lunchroom workers, secretaries, paraprofessionals, and coaches.
(3) Training on bullying, cyber-bullying, hazing and harassment required of LEA policies under the rule should complement the suicide prevention program required for students under R277-620 and the suicide prevention training required for licensed educators consistent with Section 53A-1-603(9).

G. Policies shall also complement existing safe and drug free school policies and school discipline plans. Consistent with R277-609, the discipline plan shall provide direction for dealing with bullying, cyber-bullying, hazing, harassment and disruptive students. This part of the plan shall:
 (1) direct schools to determine the range of behaviors and establish the continuum of administrative procedures that may be used by school personnel to address the behavior of habitually disruptive students;
 (2) provide for identification, by position(s), of individual(s) designated to issue notices of disruptive student and bullying, cyber-bullying, hazing and harassment behavior;
 (3) designate to whom notices shall be provided;
 (4) provide for documentation of disruptive student behavior prior to referral of disruptive students to juvenile court;
 (5) include strategies to provide for necessary adult supervision;
 (6) be clearly written and consistently enforced;
 (7) include administration, instruction and support staff, students, parents, community council and other community members in policy development, training and prevention implementation so as to create a community sense of participation, ownership, support and responsibility; and
 (8) provide notice to employees that violation(s) of this rule may result in employment discipline or action.

Utah Administrative Code R277-613-5

R277-613-5. Training by LEAs [Local Educational Agencies] Specific to Participants in Public School Athletic Programs and School Clubs.

A. Prior to any student, employee or volunteer coach participating in a public school sponsored athletic program, both curricular and extracurricular, or extracurricular club or activity, the student, employee or coach shall participate in bullying, cyber-bullying, hazing and harassment prevention training. This training shall be offered to new participants on an annual basis and to all participants at least once every three years.
B. LEAs may collaborate with the Utah High School Activities Association to develop and provide training.
C. Student athletes and extracurricular club members shall be informed of prohibited activities under this rule and notified of potential consequences for violation of the law and the rule.

VERMONT

Harassment, Hazing, and Bullying. 16 Vermont Statutes Annotated § 570, et seq. (West 2014)

16 Vermont Statutes Annotated § 570

§ 570. Harassment, hazing, and bullying prevention policies

(a) State policy. It is the policy of the state of Vermont that all Vermont educational institutions provide safe, orderly, civil, and positive learning environments. Harassment, hazing, and bullying have no place and will not be tolerated in Vermont schools. No Vermont student should feel threatened or be discriminated against while enrolled in a Vermont school.

(b) Prevention policies. Each school board shall develop, adopt, ensure the enforcement of, and make available in the manner described under subdivision 563(1) of this title harassment, hazing, and bullying prevention policies that shall be at least as stringent as model policies developed by the Secretary. Any school board that fails to adopt one or more of these policies shall be presumed to have adopted the most current model policy or policies published by the Secretary.

(c) Notice. Annually, prior to the commencement of curricular and cocurricular activities, the school board shall provide notice of the policy and procedures developed under this subchapter to students, custodial parents or guardians of students, and staff members, including reference to the consequences of misbehavior contained in the plan required by section 1161a of this title. Notice to students shall be in age-appropriate language and should include examples of harassment, hazing, and bullying. At a minimum, this notice shall appear in any publication that sets forth the comprehensive rules, procedures, and standards of conduct for the school. The school board shall use its discretion in developing and initiating age-appropriate programs to inform students about the substance of the policy and procedures in order to help prevent harassment, hazing, and bullying. School boards are encouraged to foster opportunities for conversations between and among students regarding tolerance and respect.

(d) Duties of the Secretary. The Secretary shall:
  (1) develop and, from time to time, update model harassment, hazing, and bullying prevention policies; and
  (2) establish an advisory council to review and coordinate school and statewide activities relating to the prevention of and response to harassment, hazing, and bullying. The council shall report annually in January to the State Board and the House and Senate Committees on Education. The council shall include:
      (A) the executive director of the Vermont Principals' Association or designee;
      (B) the executive director of the Vermont School Boards Association or designee;
      (C) the executive director of the Vermont Superintendents Association or designee;
      (D) the president of the Vermont-National Education Association or designee;
      (E) the executive director of the Vermont Human Rights Commission or designee;
      (F) the executive director of the Vermont Independent Schools Association or designee; and

(G) other members selected by the Secretary, at least one of whom shall be a current secondary student who has witnessed or experienced harassment, hazing, or bullying in the school environment.
(e) Definitions. In this subchapter:
  (1) "Educational institution" and "school" mean a public school or an approved or recognized independent school as defined in section 11 of this title.
  (2) "Organization," "pledging," and "student" have the same meanings as in section 570i of this title.
  (3) "Harassment," "hazing," and "bullying" have the same meanings as in subdivisions 11(a)(26), (30), and (32) of this title.
  (4) "School board" means the board of directors or other governing body of an educational institution when referring to an independent school.

16 Vermont Statutes Annotated § 570b

§ 570b. Hazing

The hazing prevention policy required by section 570 of this title and its plan for implementation shall include:

(1) A statement that hazing, as defined in subdivision 11(a)(30) of this title, is prohibited and may be subject to civil penalties pursuant to article 3 of this subchapter 5.
(2) A procedure that directs students, staff, parents, and guardians how to report violations and file complaints.
(3) A procedure for investigating reports of violations and complaints.
(4) A description of the circumstances under which hazing may be reported to a law enforcement agency.
(5) Appropriate penalties or sanctions or both for organizations that or individuals who engage in hazing and revocation or suspension of an organization's permission to operate or exist within the institution's purview if that organization knowingly permits, authorizes, or condones hazing.
(6) A description of how the school board will ensure that teachers and other staff members receive training in preventing, recognizing, and responding to hazing.
(7) Annual designation of two or more people at each school campus to receive complaints and a procedure for publicizing those people's availability.

16 Vermont Statutes Annotated § 570c

§ 570c. Bullying

The bullying prevention policy required by section 570 of this title and its plan for implementation shall include:

(1) A statement that bullying, as defined in subdivision 11(a)(32) of this title, is prohibited

(2) A procedure that directs students, staff, parents, and guardians how to report violations and file complaints.
(3) A procedure for investigating reports of violations and complaints.
(4) A description of the circumstances under which bullying may be reported to a law enforcement agency.
(5) Consequences and appropriate remedial action for students who commit bullying.
(6) A description of how the school board will ensure that teachers and other staff members receive training in preventing, recognizing, and responding to bullying.
(7) Annual designation of two or more people at each school campus to receive complaints and a procedure both for publicizing the availability of those people and clarifying that their designation does not preclude a student from bringing a complaint to any adult in the building.

16 Vermont Statutes Annotated § 570f

§ 570f. Harassment; notice and response

(a)(1) An educational institution that receives actual notice of alleged conduct that may constitute harassment shall promptly investigate to determine whether harassment occurred. After receiving notice of the alleged conduct, the school shall provide a copy of its harassment policy, including its harassment investigation procedure, to the alleged victim and the alleged perpetrator. If either the alleged victim or the alleged perpetrator is a minor, the copy of the policy shall be provided to the person's parent or guardian. Nothing in this section shall be construed to prohibit educational institutions from investigating and imposing disciplinary consequences upon students for misconduct. Elementary and secondary school officials shall strive to implement the plan developed in accordance with subdivision 1161a(a)(6) of this title in order to prevent misconduct from escalating to the level of harassment.
(2) If, after notice, the educational institution finds that the alleged conduct occurred and that it constitutes harassment, the educational institution shall take prompt and appropriate remedial action reasonably calculated to stop the harassment.
(b) A claim may be brought under the Fair Housing and Public Accommodations Act pursuant to 9 [Vermont Statutes Annotated] chapter 139 only after the administrative remedies available to the claimant under the policy adopted by the educational institution pursuant to subsection 166(e) or section 570 of this title or pursuant to the harassment policy of a postsecondary school have been exhausted. Such a showing shall not be necessary where the claimant demonstrates that:
(1) the educational institution does not maintain such a policy;
(2) a determination has not been rendered within the time limits established under section 570a of this title;
(3) the health or safety of the complainant would be jeopardized otherwise;
(4) exhaustion would be futile; or
(5) requiring exhaustion would subject the student to substantial and imminent retaliation.
(c) To prevail in an action alleging unlawful harassment filed pursuant to this section and 9 [Vermont Statutes Annotated] chapter 139, the plaintiff shall prove both of the following:

(1) The student was subjected to unwelcome conduct based on the student's or the student's family member's actual or perceived membership in a category protected by law by 9 [Vermont Statutes Annotated] § 4502.
(2) The conduct was either:
   (A) for multiple instances of conduct, so pervasive that when viewed from an objective standard of a similarly situated reasonable person, it substantially and adversely affected the targeted student's equal access to educational opportunities or benefits provided by the educational institution; or
   (B) for a single instance of conduct, so severe that when viewed from an objective standard of a similarly situated reasonable person, it substantially and adversely affected the targeted student's equal access to educational opportunities or benefits provided by the educational institution.
(d) As used in this article:
   (1) "Designated employee" means an employee who has been designated by an educational institution to receive complaints of harassment pursuant to section 570a of this title or in accordance with the harassment policy of a postsecondary school.
   (2) "Educational institution" means a Vermont public or independent school or a postsecondary school that offers or operates a program of college or professional education for credit or degree in Vermont.
   (3) "Notice" means a written complaint or oral information that harassment may have occurred which has been provided to a designated employee from another employee, the student allegedly subjected to the harassment, another student, a parent or guardian, or any other individual who has reasonable cause to believe the alleged conduct may have occurred. If the complaint is oral, the designated employee shall promptly reduce the complaint to writing, including the time, place, and nature of the conduct, and the identity of the participants and complainant.

General Provisions. 16 Vermont Statutes Annotated § 11 (West 2014)

16 Vermont Statutes Annotated § 11

§ 11 Classifications and definitions

(26)(A) "Harassment" means an incident or incidents of verbal, written, visual, or physical conduct, including any incident conducted by electronic means, based on or motivated by a student's or a student's family member's actual or perceived race, creed, color, national origin, marital status, sex, sexual orientation, gender identity, or disability that has the purpose or effect of objectively and substantially undermining and detracting from or interfering with a student's educational performance or access to school resources or creating an objectively intimidating, hostile, or offensive environment.
   (B) "Harassment" includes conduct which violates subdivision (A) of this subdivision (26) and constitutes one or more of the following:

(i) Sexual harassment, which means conduct that includes unwelcome sexual advances, requests for sexual favors and other verbal, written, visual, or physical conduct of a sexual nature when one or both of the following occur:

(I) Submission to that conduct is made either explicitly or implicitly a term or condition of a student's education.

(II) Submission to or rejection of such conduct by a student is used as a component of the basis for decisions affecting that student.

(ii) Racial harassment, which means conduct directed at the characteristics of a student's or a student's family member's actual or perceived race or color, and includes the use of epithets, stereotypes, racial slurs, comments, insults, derogatory remarks, gestures, threats, graffiti, display, or circulation of written or visual material, and taunts on manner of speech and negative references to racial customs.

(iii) Harassment of members of other protected categories, which means conduct directed at the characteristics of a student's or a student's family member's actual or perceived creed, national origin, marital status, sex, sexual orientation, gender identity, or disability and includes the use of epithets, stereotypes, slurs, comments, insults, derogatory remarks, gestures, threats, graffiti, display, or circulation of written or visual material, taunts on manner of speech, and negative references to customs related to any of these protected categories.

***

(30)(A) "Hazing" means any act committed by a person, whether individually or in concert with others, against a student in connection with pledging, being initiated into, affiliating with, holding office in, or maintaining membership in any organization which is affiliated with an educational institution; and which is intended to have the effect of, or should reasonably be expected to have the effect of, humiliating, intimidating or demeaning the student or endangering the mental or physical health of a student. Hazing also includes soliciting, directing, aiding, or otherwise participating actively or passively in the above acts. Hazing may occur on or off the campus of an educational institution. Hazing shall not include any activity or conduct that furthers legitimate curricular, extracurricular, or military training program goals, provided that:
(i) the goals are approved by the educational institution; and
(ii) the activity or conduct furthers the goals in a manner that is appropriate, contemplated by the educational institution, and normal and customary for similar programs at other educational institutions.

***

(32) "Bullying" means any overt act or combination of acts, including an act conducted by electronic means, directed against a student by another student or group of students and which:

(A) is repeated over time;
(B) is intended to ridicule, humiliate, or intimidate the student; and

(C) (i) occurs during the school day on school property, on a school bus, or at a school-sponsored activity, or before or after the school day on a school bus or at a school-sponsored activity; or

(ii) does not occur during the school day on school property, on a school bus, or at a school-sponsored activity and can be shown to pose a clear and substantial interference with another student's right to access educational programs.

Attendance and Discipline. 16 Vermont Statutes Annotated § 1161a, et seq. (West 2014)

16 Vermont Statutes Annotated § 1161a

§ 1161a. Discipline

(a) Each public and each approved independent school shall adopt and implement a comprehensive plan for responding to student misbehavior. To the extent appropriate, the plan shall promote the positive development of youth. The plan shall include:

(1) the school's approach to classroom management and response to disruptive behavior, including the use of alternative educational settings;
(2) the manner in which the school will provide information and training to students in methods of conflict resolution, peer mediation and anger management;
(3) procedures for informing parents of the school's discipline policies, for notifying parents of student misconduct, and for working with parents to improve student behavior;
(4) the school's response to significant disruptions, such as threats or use of bombs or weapons;
(5) a description of how the school will ensure that all staff and contractors who routinely have unsupervised contact with students periodically receive training on the maintenance of a safe, orderly, civil and positive learning environment. The training shall be appropriate to the role of the staff member being trained and shall teach classroom and behavior management, enforcement of the school's discipline policies and positive youth development models;
(6) a description of behaviors on and off school grounds which constitute misconduct, including harassment, bullying, and hazing, particularly those behaviors which may be grounds for expulsion. The plan shall include a description of misconduct as listed in subdivisions 11(a)(26)(A)-(C) and (32) of this title which, although serious, does not rise to the level of harassment or bullying as those terms are defined therein; and
(7) standard due process procedures for suspension and expulsion of a student.

16 Vermont Statutes Annotated § 1162

§ 1162. Suspension or expulsion of students

(a) A superintendent or principal may, pursuant to policies adopted by the school board that are consistent with state board rules, suspend a student for up to 10 school days or, with the approval of the board of the school district, expel a student for up to the remainder of the school year or up to 90 school days, whichever is longer, for misconduct:

(1) on school property, on a school bus, or at a school-sponsored activity when the misconduct makes the continued presence of the student harmful to the welfare of the school;

(2) not on school property, on a school bus, or at a school-sponsored activity where direct harm to the welfare of the school can be demonstrated; or

(3) not on school property, on a school bus, or at a school-sponsored activity where the misconduct can be shown to pose a clear and substantial interference with another student's equal access to educational programs.

(b) Nothing contained in this section shall prevent a superintendent or principal, subject to subsequent due process procedures, from removing immediately from a school a student who poses a continuing danger to persons or property or an ongoing threat of disrupting the academic process of the school, or from expelling a student who brings a weapon to school pursuant to section 1166 of this title.

(c) Principals, superintendents, and school boards are authorized and encouraged to provide alternative education services or programs to students during any period of suspension or expulsion authorized under this section.

VIRGINIA

Discipline. Virginia Code Annotated § 22.1-276.01, et seq. (West 2014)

Virginia Code Annotated § 22.1-276.01

§ 22.1-276.01. Definitions

A. For the purposes of this article, unless the context requires a different meaning:

"Bullying" means any aggressive and unwanted behavior that is intended to harm, intimidate, or humiliate the victim; involves a real or perceived power imbalance between the aggressor or aggressors and victim; and is repeated over time or causes severe emotional trauma. "Bullying" includes cyber bullying. "Bullying" does not include ordinary teasing, horseplay, argument, or peer conflict.

Virginia Code Annotated § 22.1-279.6

§ 22.1-279.6. Board of Education guidelines and model policies for codes of student conduct; school board regulations

Be it enacted by the General Assembly of Virginia:

1. That § 22.1-279.6 of the Code of Virginia is amended and reenacted ... as follows:

A. The Board of Education shall establish guidelines and develop model policies for codes of student conduct to aid local school boards in the implementation of such policies. The guidelines and model policies shall include, but not be limited to, (i) criteria for the removal of a student from a class, the use of suspension, expulsion, and exclusion as disciplinary measures, the grounds for suspension and expulsion and exclusion, and the procedures to be followed in such cases, including proceedings for such suspension, expulsion, and exclusion decisions and all applicable appeals processes; (ii) standards, consistent with state, federal and case laws, for school board policies on alcohol and drugs, gang-related activity, hazing, vandalism, trespassing, threats, search and seizure, disciplining of students with disabilities, intentional injury of others, self-defense, bullying, the use of electronic means for purposes of bullying, harassment, and intimidation, and dissemination of such policies to students, their parents, and school personnel; and (iii) standards for in-service training of school personnel in and examples of the appropriate management of student conduct and student offenses in violation of school board policies.

***

C. Each school board shall include in its code of student conduct prohibitions against hazing and profane or obscene language or conduct. School boards shall also cite in their codes of student conduct the provisions of § 18.2-56, which defines and prohibits hazing and imposes a Class 1 misdemeanor penalty for violations, that is, confinement in jail for not more than 12 months and a fine of not more than $2,500, either or both.

D. Each school board shall include in its code of student conduct, by July 1, 2014, policies and procedures that include a prohibition against bullying. Such policies and procedures shall be consistent with the standards for school board policies on bullying and the use of electronic means for purposes of bullying developed by the Board pursuant to subsection A.

Such policies and procedures shall not be interpreted to infringe upon the First Amendment rights of students and are not intended to prohibit expression of religious, philosophical, or political views, provided that such expression does not cause an actual, material disruption of the work of the school.

E. A school board may regulate the use or possession of beepers or other portable communications devices and laser pointers by students on school property or attending school functions or activities and establish disciplinary procedures pursuant to this article to which students violating such regulations will be subject.

***

This subsection shall not be construed to diminish the authority of the Board of Education or to diminish the Governor's authority to coordinate and provide policy direction on official communications between the Commonwealth and the United States government.

***

2. That each school board shall update its policies and code of student conduct to comply with the provisions of this act by July 1, 2015.

Virginia Code Annotated § 18.2-56

§ 18.2-56. Hazing unlawful; civil and criminal liability; duty of school, etc., officials; penalty.

Be it enacted by the General Assembly of Virginia:

1. That § 18.2-56 of the Code of Virginia is amended and reenacted as follows:

§ 18.2-56. Hazing unlawful; civil and criminal liability; duty of school, etc., officials; penalty.
It shall be unlawful to haze so as to cause bodily injury, any student at any school, college, or university. Any person found guilty thereof shall be guilty of a Class 1 misdemeanor.
Any person receiving bodily injury by hazing shall have a right to sue, civilly, the person or persons guilty thereof, whether adults or infants.
The president or other presiding official of any school, college or university receiving appropriations from the state treasury shall, upon satisfactory proof of the guilt of any student hazing another student, sanction and discipline such student in accordance with the institution's policies and procedures. The institution's policies and procedures shall provide for expulsions or other appropriate discipline based on the facts and circumstances of each case and shall be consistent with the model policies established by the Department of Education or the State Council of Higher Education for Virginia, as applicable. The president or other presiding official of any school, college or university receiving appropriations from the state treasury shall report hazing which causes bodily injury to the attorney for the Commonwealth of the county or city in which such school, college or university is, who shall take such action as he deems appropriate.
For the purposes of this section, "hazing" means to recklessly or intentionally endanger the health or safety of a student or students or to inflict bodily injury on a student or students in connection with or for the purpose of initiation, admission into or affiliation with or as a condition for continued membership in a club, organization, association, fraternity, sorority, or student body regardless of whether the student or students so endangered or injured participated voluntarily in the relevant activity.

2. That the Department of Education and the State Council of Higher Education for Virginia, with the Department of Criminal Justice Services, shall establish model policies regarding the prevention of and appropriate disciplinary action for hazing as defined in § 18.2-56 of the Code of Virginia.

Virginia Code Annotated § 22.1-279.3:1

§ 22.1-279.3:1. Reports of certain acts to school authorities.

A. Reports shall be made to the division superintendent and to the principal or his designee on all incidents involving (i) the assault or assault and battery, without bodily injury, of any person on a school bus, on school property, or at a school-sponsored activity; (ii) the assault and battery that results in bodily injury, sexual assault, death, shooting, stabbing, cutting, or wounding of any person, or stalking of any person as described in § 18.2-60.3, on a school bus, on school property, or at a school-sponsored activity; (iii) any conduct involving alcohol, marijuana, a controlled substance, imitation controlled substance, or an anabolic steroid on a school bus, on school property, or at a school-sponsored activity, including the theft or attempted theft of student prescription medications; (iv) any threats against school personnel while on a school bus, on school property or at a school-sponsored activity; (v) the illegal carrying of a firearm, as defined in § 22.1-277.07, onto school property; (vi) any illegal conduct involving firebombs, explosive materials or devices, or hoax explosive devices, as defined in § 18.2-85, or explosive or incendiary devices, as defined in § 18.2-433.1, or chemical bombs, as described in § 18.2-87.1, on a school bus, on school property, or at a school-sponsored activity; (vii) any threats or false threats to bomb, as described in § 18.2-83, made against school personnel or involving school property or school buses; or (viii) the arrest of any student for an incident occurring on a school bus, on school property, or at a school-sponsored activity, including the charge therefor.

B. Notwithstanding the provisions of Article 12 (§ 16.1-299 et seq.) of Chapter 11 of Title 16.1, local law-enforcement authorities shall report, and the principal or his designee and the division superintendent shall receive such reports, on offenses, wherever committed, by students enrolled at the school if the offense would be a felony if committed by an adult or would be a violation of the Drug Control Act (§ 54.1-3400 et seq.) and occurred on a school bus, on school property, or at a school-sponsored activity, or would be an adult misdemeanor involving any incidents described in clauses (i) through (viii) of subsection A, and whether the student is released to the custody of his parent or, if 18 years of age or more, is released on bond. As part of any report concerning an offense that would be an adult misdemeanor involving an incident described in clauses (i) through (viii) of subsection A, local law-enforcement authorities and attorneys for the Commonwealth shall be authorized to disclose information regarding terms of release from detention, court dates, and terms of any disposition orders entered by the court, to the superintendent of such student's school division, upon request by the superintendent, if, in the determination of the law-enforcement authority or attorney for the Commonwealth, such disclosure would not jeopardize the investigation or prosecution of the case. No disclosures shall be made pursuant to this section in violation of the confidentiality provisions of subsection A of § 16.1-300 or the record retention and redisclosure provisions of § 22.1-288.2. Further, any school superintendent who receives notification that a juvenile has committed an act that would be a crime if committed by an adult pursuant to subsection G of § 16.1-260 shall report such information to the principal of the school in which the juvenile is enrolled.

C. The principal or his designee shall submit a report of all incidents required to be reported pursuant to this section to the superintendent of the school division. The division superintendent shall annually report all such incidents to the Department of Education for the purpose of recording the frequency of such incidents on forms that shall be provided by the Department and shall make such information available to the public.

In submitting reports of such incidents, principals and division superintendents shall accurately indicate any offenses, arrests, or charges as recorded by law enforcement authorities and required to be reported by such authorities pursuant to subsection B.

A division superintendent who knowingly fails to comply or secure compliance with the reporting requirements of this subsection shall be subject to the sanctions authorized in § 22.1-65. A principal who knowingly fails to comply or secure compliance with the reporting requirements of this section shall be subject to sanctions prescribed by the local school board, which may include, but need not be limited to, demotion or dismissal.

The principal or his designee shall also notify the parent of any student involved in an incident required pursuant to this section to be reported, regardless of whether disciplinary action is taken against such student or the nature of the disciplinary action. Such notice shall relate to only the relevant student's involvement and shall not include information concerning other students.

Whenever any student commits any reportable incident as set forth in this section, such student shall be required to participate in such prevention and intervention activities as deemed appropriate by the superintendent or his designee. Prevention and intervention activities shall be identified in the local school division's drug and violence prevention plans developed pursuant to the federal Improving America's Schools Act of 1994 (Title IV - Safe and Drug-Free Schools and Communities Act).

D. Except as may otherwise be required by federal law, regulation, or jurisprudence, the principal shall immediately report to the local law-enforcement agency any act enumerated in clauses (ii) through (vii) of subsection A that may constitute a criminal offense and may report to the local law-enforcement agency any incident described in clause (i) of subsection A. Nothing in this section shall require delinquency charges to be filed or prevent schools from dealing with school-based offenses through graduated sanctions or educational programming before a delinquency charge is filed with the juvenile court.

Further, except as may be prohibited by federal law, regulation, or jurisprudence, the principal shall also immediately report any act enumerated in clauses (ii) through (v) of subsection A that may constitute a criminal offense to the parents of any minor student who is the specific object of such act. Further, the principal shall report that the incident has been reported to local law enforcement as required by law and that the parents may contact local law enforcement for further information, if they so desire.

E. A statement providing a procedure and the purpose for the requirements of this section shall be included in school board policies required by § 22.1-253.13:7.

The Board of Education shall promulgate regulations to implement this section, including, but not limited to, establishing reporting dates and report formats.

F. For the purposes of this section, "parent" or "parents" means any parent, guardian or other person having control or charge of a child.
G. This section shall not be construed to diminish the authority of the Board of Education or to diminish the Governor's authority to coordinate and provide policy direction on official communications between the Commonwealth and the United States government.

Programs and Courses of Instruction Generally. Virginia Code Annotated § 22.1-208.01 (West 2013)

Virginia Code Annotated § 22.1-208.01

§ 22.1-208.01. Character education required

A. Each school board shall establish, within its existing programs or as a separate program, a character education program in its schools, which may occur during the regular school year, during the summer in a youth development academy offered by the school division, or both. The Department of Education shall develop curricular guidelines for school divisions to use in establishing a character education program through a summer youth development academy. The purpose of the character education program shall be to instill in students civic virtues and personal character traits so as to improve the learning environment, promote student achievement, reduce disciplinary problems, and develop civic-minded students of high character. The components of each program shall be developed in cooperation with the students, their parents, and the community at large. The basic character traits taught may include (i) trustworthiness, including honesty, integrity, reliability, and loyalty; (ii) respect, including the precepts of the Golden Rule, tolerance, and courtesy; (iii) responsibility, including hard work, economic self-reliance, accountability, diligence, perseverance, and self-control; (iv) fairness, including justice, consequences of bad behavior, principles of nondiscrimination, and freedom from prejudice; (v) caring, including kindness, empathy, compassion, consideration, generosity, and charity; and (vi) citizenship, including patriotism, the Pledge of Allegiance, respect for the American flag, concern for the common good, respect for authority and the law, and community-mindedness.

Classroom instruction may be used to supplement a character education program; however, each program shall be interwoven into the school procedures and environment and structured to instruct primarily through example, illustration, and participation, in such a way as to complement the Standards of Learning. The program shall also address the inappropriateness of bullying, as defined in § 22.1-276.01.

This provision is intended to educate students regarding those core civic values and virtues that are efficacious to civilized society and are common to the diverse social, cultural, and religious groups of the Commonwealth. Consistent with this purpose, Virginia's civic values, which are the principles articulated in the Bill of Rights (Article I) of the Constitution of Virginia and the ideals reflected in the seal of the Commonwealth, as described in § 1-500, may be taught as representative of such civic values. Nothing herein shall be construed as requiring or authorizing the indoctrination in any particular religious or political belief.

B. The Board of Education shall establish criteria for character education programs consistent with the provisions of this section. The Department of Education shall assist school divisions in implementing character education programs and practices that are designed to promote the development of personal qualities as set forth in this section and the Standards of Quality and that will improve family and community involvement in the public schools. With such funds as are made available for this purpose, the Department of Education shall provide resources and technical assistance to school divisions regarding successful character education programs and shall (i) identify and analyze effective character education programs and practices and (ii) collect and disseminate among school divisions information regarding such programs and practices and potential funding and support sources. The Department of Education may also provide resources supporting professional development for administrators and teachers in the delivery of any character education programs.

C. The Department of Education shall award, with such funds as are appropriated for this purpose, grants to school boards for the implementation of innovative character education programs, including a summer youth development academy.

WASHINGTON

Harassment, Intimidation, and Bullying. Revised Code of Washington Annotated 28A.300.285, et seq. (West 2013)

Revised Code of Washington Annotated 28A.300.285

28A.300.285. Harassment, intimidation, and bullying prevention policies and procedures—Model policy and procedure—Training materials—Posting on web site—Rules—Advisory Committee

(1) By August 1, 2011, each school district shall adopt or amend if necessary a policy and procedure that at a minimum incorporates the revised model policy and procedure provided under subsection (4) of this section that prohibits the harassment, intimidation, or bullying of any student. It is the responsibility of each school district to share this policy with parents or guardians, students, volunteers, and school employees in accordance with rules adopted by the superintendent of public instruction. Each school district shall designate one person in the district as the primary contact regarding the antiharassment, intimidation, or bullying policy. The primary contact shall receive copies of all formal and informal complaints, have responsibility for assuring the implementation of the policy and procedure, and serve as the primary contact on the policy and procedures between the school district, the office of the education ombuds, and the office of the superintendent of public instruction.

(2) "Harassment, intimidation, or bullying" means any intentional electronic, written, verbal, or physical act, including but not limited to one shown to be motivated by any characteristic in [Revised Code of Washington Annotated] 9A.36.080(3), or other distinguishing characteristics, when the intentional electronic, written, verbal, or physical act:

(a) Physically harms a student or damages the student's property; or
(b) Has the effect of substantially interfering with a student's education; or
(c) Is so severe, persistent, or pervasive that it creates an intimidating or threatening educational environment; or
(d) Has the effect of substantially disrupting the orderly operation of the school.

Nothing in this section requires the affected student to actually possess a characteristic that is a basis for the harassment, intimidation, or bullying.

(3) The policy and procedure should be adopted or amended through a process that includes representation of parents or guardians, school employees, volunteers, students, administrators, and community representatives. It is recommended that each such policy emphasize positive character traits and values, including the importance of civil and respectful speech and conduct, and the responsibility of students to comply with the district's policy prohibiting harassment, intimidation, or bullying.

(4) (a) By August 1, 2010, the superintendent of public instruction, in consultation with representatives of parents, school personnel, the office of the education ombuds, the Washington state school directors' association, and other interested parties, shall provide to the education committees of the legislature a revised and updated model harassment, intimidation, and bullying prevention policy and procedure. The superintendent of public instruction shall publish on its web site, with a link to the safety center web page, the revised and updated model harassment, intimidation, and bullying prevention policy and procedure, along with training and instructional materials on the components that shall be included in any district policy and procedure. The superintendent shall adopt rules regarding school districts' communication of the policy and procedure to parents, students, employees, and volunteers.

(b) The office of the superintendent of public instruction has the authority to update with new technologies access to this information in the safety center, to the extent resources are made available.

(c) Each school district shall by August 15, 2011, provide to the superintendent of public instruction a brief summary of its policies, procedures, programs, partnerships, vendors, and instructional and training materials to be posted on the school safety center web site, and shall also provide the superintendent with a link to the school district's web site for further information. The district's primary contact for bullying and harassment issues shall annually by August 15th verify posted information and links and notify the school safety center of any updates or changes.

(5) The Washington state school directors' association, with the assistance of the office of the superintendent of public instruction, shall convene an advisory committee to develop a model policy prohibiting acts of harassment, intimidation, or bullying that are conducted via electronic means by a student while on school grounds and during the school day. The policy shall include a requirement that materials meant to educate parents and students about the seriousness of cyberbullying be disseminated to parents or made available on the school district's web site. The school directors' association and the advisory committee shall develop sample materials for school districts to disseminate, which shall also include information on responsible and safe internet use as well as what options are available if a student is being bullied via electronic means including, but not limited to, reporting threats to local police and when to involve school officials, the internet service provider, or phone service provider. The school directors' association shall submit the model policy and sample materials, along with a recommendation for local adoption, to the governor and the legislature and shall post the model policy and sample materials on its web site by January 1, 2008. Each school district board of directors shall establish its own policy by August 1, 2008.

(6) As used in this section, "electronic" or "electronic means" means any communication where there is the transmission of information by wire, radio, optical cable, electromagnetic, or other similar means.

State Anti-Bullying Statutes and Student Speech

Revised Code of Washington Annotated 28A.300.2851

28A.300.2851. School bullying and harassment--Work group

(1) The office of the superintendent of public instruction and the office of the education ombuds shall convene a work group on school bullying and harassment prevention to develop, recommend, and implement strategies to improve school climate and create respectful learning environments in all public schools in Washington. The superintendent of public instruction or a designee shall serve as the chair of the work group.

(2) The work group shall:
   (a) Consider whether additional disaggregated data should be collected regarding incidents of bullying and harassment or disciplinary actions and make recommendations to the office of the superintendent of public instruction for collection of such data;
   (b) Examine possible procedures for anonymous reporting of incidents of bullying and harassment;
   (c) Identify curriculum and best practices for school districts to improve school climate, create respectful learning environments, and train staff and students in de-escalation and intervention techniques;
   (d) Identify curriculum and best practices for incorporating instruction about mental health, youth suicide prevention, and prevention of bullying and harassment;
   (e) Recommend best practices for informing parents about the harassment, intimidation, and bullying prevention policy and procedure under RCW 28A.300. 285 and involving parents in improving school climate;
   (f) Recommend training for district personnel who are designated as the primary contact regarding the policy and procedure and for school resource officers and other school security personnel;
   (g) Recommend educator preparation and certification requirements in harassment, intimidation, and bullying prevention and de-escalation and intervention techniques for teachers, educational staff associates, and school administrators;
   (h) Examine and recommend policies for discipline of students and staff who harass, intimidate, or bully; and
   (i) In collaboration with the state board for community and technical colleges, examine and recommend policies to protect K-12 students attending community and technical colleges from harassment, intimidation, and bullying.

(3) The work group must include representatives from the state board of education, the Washington state parent teacher association, the Washington state association of school psychologists, school directors, school administrators, principals, teachers, school counselors, classified school staff, youth, community organizations, and parents.

(4) The work group shall submit a biennial progress and status report to the governor and the education committees of the legislature, beginning December 1, 2011, with additional reports by December 1, 2013, and December 1, 2015.

(5) The work group is terminated effective January 1, 2016.

Revised Code of Washington Annotated 28A.600.480

28A.600.480. Reporting of harassment, intimidation, or bullying--Retaliation prohibited—Immunity

(1) No school employee, student, or volunteer may engage in reprisal, retaliation, or false accusation against a victim, witness, or one with reliable information about an act of harassment, intimidation, or bullying.
(2) A school employee, student, or volunteer who has witnessed, or has reliable information that a student has been subjected to, harassment, intimidation, or bullying, whether verbal or physical, is encouraged to report such incident to an appropriate school official.
(3) A school employee, student, or volunteer who promptly reports an incident of harassment, intimidation, or bullying to an appropriate school official, and who makes this report in compliance with the procedures in the district's policy prohibiting bullying, harassment, or intimidation, is immune from a cause of action for damages arising from any failure to remedy the reported incident.

Crimes and Punishments. Revised Code of Washington Annotated 9.61.260 (West 2004)

Revised Code of Washington Annotated 9.61.260

9.61.260. Cyberstalking

(1) A person is guilty of cyberstalking if he or she, with intent to harass, intimidate, torment, or embarrass any other person, and under circumstances not constituting telephone harassment, makes an electronic communication to such other person or a third party:
  (a) Using any lewd, lascivious, indecent, or obscene words, images, or language, or suggesting the commission of any lewd or lascivious act;
  (b) Anonymously or repeatedly whether or not conversation occurs; or
  (c) Threatening to inflict injury on the person or property of the person called or any member of his or her family or household.
(2) Cyberstalking is a gross misdemeanor, except as provided in subsection (3) of this section.
(3) Cyberstalking is a class C felony if either of the following applies:
  (a) The perpetrator has previously been convicted of the crime of harassment, as defined in [Revised Code of Washington Annotated] 9A.46.060, with the same victim or a member of the victim's family or household or any person specifically named in a no-contact order or no-harassment order in this or any other state; or
  (b) The perpetrator engages in the behavior prohibited under subsection (1)(c) of this section by threatening to kill the person threatened or any other person.
(4) Any offense committed under this section may be deemed to have been committed either at the place from which the communication was made or at the place where the communication was received.

(5) For purposes of this section, "electronic communication" means the transmission of information by wire, radio, optical cable, electromagnetic, or other similar means. "Electronic communication" includes, but is not limited to, electronic mail, internet-based communications, pager service, and electronic text messaging.

Washington State School for the Deaf Student Conduct Code. Washington Administrative Code 148-120-100 (West 1994)

Washington Administrative Code 148-120-100

148-120-100. Conduct violations.

A student who, either as actor, aider, abettor, or accomplice, violates any provision of this chapter shall be subject to the disciplinary actions herein adopted. A student may be an accomplice, or found to have aided and abetted in the commission of a violation of the student conduct code if he or she knowingly associates with the wrongful purpose, undertaking or activity; encourages, promotes, or counsels another student in the commission of an offense, or participates in it as in something he or she desires to bring about, and seeks by his or her action to make it succeed.

The following offenses are prohibited:

***

(19) Harassment, intimidation or bullying based on actual or perceived race, color, religion, ancestry, national origin, gender, gender identity, disability, socio-economic status, physical appearance, or other distinguishing characteristic. For purposes of this rule, harassment, intimidation, and bullying includes any intentionally written message or image, including those that are electronically transmitted including, but not limited to, sexting, which constitutes any threat of or act of physical, verbal, or emotional abuse, or attacks on the property of another, which has the effect of materially interfering with a student's education; is so severe, pervasive, or persistent, and objectively offensive as to threaten an individual or limit the individual's ability to work, study or participate in the activities of WSD [Washington School for the Deaf], creates an intimidating or threatening education or residential environment, or has the effect of materially disrupting the orderly operation of the school or residential program.

The term 'sexting' as used in this rule means the sending, possession, displaying, or distribution of text messages and picture of an explicit sexual nature. Intentional acts refer to the individual's choice to engage in the act rather than the ultimate impact of the action(s).

Harassment, intimidation, and bullying may include, but is not limited to, taunts, sexting, slurs, rumors, jokes, innuendos, demeaning comments, drawings, cartoons, pranks, gestures, ostracism, extortion of money, physical attacks, threats or other written, oral, physical or electronically transmitted messages or images.

Harassment, intimidation, and bullying are often carried out through acts of misconduct, which are addressed and prohibited under other rules in this chapter.

This rule does not prohibit the civil, respectful expression of religious or political views, provided that the expression does not materially disrupt the education environment.

Harassment, Intimidation, and Bullying. Washington Administrative Code 392-190-059 (West 2011)

Washington Administrative Code 392-190-059

392-190-059. Harassment, intimidation, and bullying prevention policy and procedure- Adoption date

(1) By August 1, 2011, each school district must adopt or amend if necessary a harassment, intimidation, and bullying prevention policy and procedure as provided for in [Revised Code of Washington Annotated] 28A.300.285.

(2) When monitoring school districts' compliance with this chapter pursuant to [Washington Administrative Code] 392-190-076, the office of superintendent of public instruction will review such policies and procedures to ensure that they provide that students will not be harassed, intimidated, or bullied because of their sex, race, creed, religion, color, national origin, sexual orientation including gender expression or identity, the presence of any sensory, mental, or physical disability, or the use of a trained dog guide or service animal.

(3) This section is not intended to limit the scope of [Revised Code of Washington Annotated] 28A.300.285.

Pupils and Bullying Policies and Procedures. Washington Administrative Code 392-400-226 (West 2011)

Washington Administrative Code 392-400-226

392-400-226. School district rules defining harassment, intimidation and bullying prevention policies and procedures-Distribution of rules

A district's harassment, intimidation and bullying policy and procedure shall be published and made available to all parents or guardians, students, employees, and volunteers on an annual basis. The district will publish, at a minimum, the following materials: Policy and procedure, an incident reporting form and current contact information for the district's harassment, intimidation and bullying compliance officer. If a school district chooses not to distribute such rules to all parents or guardians, students, employees, and volunteers, then notice which describes the contents of such rules and specifies the person(s) to contact for a copy shall be provided to students and parents on an annual basis in a manner reasonably calculated to come to their attention.

WEST VIRGINIA

Harassment, Intimidation or Bullying Prohibition. West Virginia Code, § 18-2C-1, et seq. (West 2011)

West Virginia Code, § 18-2C-1

§ 18-2C-1. Legislative findings

The Legislature finds that a safe and civil environment in school is necessary for students to learn and achieve high academic standards. The Legislature finds that harassment, intimidation or bullying, like other disruptive or violent behavior, is conduct that disrupts both a student's ability to learn and a school's ability to educate its students in a safe, nonthreatening environment.

The legislature further finds that students learn by example. The legislature charges school administrators, faculty, staff and volunteers with demonstrating appropriate behavior, treating others with civility and respect, and refusing to tolerate harassment, intimidation or bullying.

West Virginia Code, § 18-2C-2

§ 18-2C-2. Definitions

(a) As used in this article, "harassment, intimidation or bullying" means any intentional gesture, or any intentional electronic, written, verbal or physical act, communication, transmission or threat that:
  (1) A reasonable person under the circumstances should know will have the effect of any one or more of the following:
      (A) Physically harming a student;
      (B) Damaging a student's property;
      (C) Placing a student in reasonable fear of harm to his or her person; or
      (D) Placing a student in reasonable fear of damage to his or her property;
  (2) Is sufficiently severe, persistent or pervasive that it creates an intimidating, threatening or emotionally abusive educational environment for a student; or
  (3) Disrupts or interferes with the orderly operation of the school.
(b) As used in this article, an electronic act, communication, transmission or threat includes but is not limited to one which is administered via telephone, wireless phone, computer, pager or any electronic or wireless device whatsoever, and includes but is not limited to transmission of any image or voice, email or text message using any such device.

West Virginia Code, § 18-2C-3

§ 18-2C-3. Policy prohibiting harassment, intimidation or bullying

(a) Each county board shall establish a policy prohibiting harassment, intimidation or bullying. Each county board has control over the content of its policy as long as the policy contains, at a minimum,

the requirements of subdivision (b) of this section. The policy shall be adopted through a process that includes representation of parents or guardians, school employees, school volunteers, students and community members.
(b) Each county board policy shall, at a minimum, include the following components:
   (1) A statement prohibiting harassment, intimidation or bullying of any student on school property, a school bus, at a school bus stop or at school sponsored events;
   (2) A definition of harassment, intimidation or bullying no less inclusive than that in section two of this article;
   (3) A procedure for reporting prohibited incidents;
   (4) A requirement that school personnel report prohibited incidents of which they are aware;
   (5) A requirement that parents or guardians of any student involved in an incident prohibited pursuant to this article be notified;
   (6) A procedure for documenting any prohibited incident that is reported;
   (7) A procedure for responding to and investigating any reported incident;
   (8) A strategy for protecting a victim from additional harassment, intimidation or bullying, and from retaliation following a report;
   (9) A disciplinary procedure for any student guilty of harassment, intimidation or bullying;
   (10) A requirement that any information relating to a reported incident is confidential, and exempt from disclosure under the provisions of chapter twenty-nine-b of this code; and
   (11) A requirement that each county board shall input into the uniform integrated regional computer information system (commonly known as the West Virginia Education Information System) described in section twenty-six, article two of this chapter, and compile an annual report regarding the means of harassment, intimidation or bullying that have been reported to them, and the reasons therefor, if known. The West Virginia Department of Education shall compile the information and report it annually beginning July 1, 2012, to the Legislative Oversight Committee on Education Accountability.
(c) Each county board shall adopt the policy and submit a copy to the State Superintendent of Schools by December 1, 2011.
(d) To assist county boards in developing their policies, the West Virginia Department of Education shall develop a model policy applicable to grades kindergarten through twelfth. The model policy shall be issued by September 1, 2011.
(e) Notice of the county board's policy shall appear in any student handbook, and in any county board publication that sets forth the comprehensive rules, procedures and standards of conduct for the school.

West Virginia Code, § 18-2C-4

§ 18-2C-4. Immunity

A school employee, student or volunteer is individually immune from a cause of action for damages arising from reporting said incident, if that person:

(1) In good faith promptly reports an incident of harassment, intimidation or bullying;

(2) Makes the report to the appropriate school official as designated by policy; and
(3) Makes the report in compliance with the procedures as specified in policy.

Educational Purpose and Acceptable Use of Electronic Resources, Technologies and the Internet. West Virginia Administrative Code § 126-41-6 (West 2014)

West Virginia Administrative Code § 126-41-6

§ 126-41-6. Use of Electronic Resources, Technology and the Internet.

6.1. Overview of Use:
- 6.1.a. Unauthorized or unacceptable use of the Internet or any safety violations as part of an educational program by students, educators or staff may result in suspension or revocation of such use.
- 6.1.b. Each student who will access the Internet will be provided acceptable use training and shall have an acceptable use form, signed by a parent or legal guardian, on file at the county/school.
- 6.1.c. The WVDE provides the network system, e-mail accounts and Internet access as tools for education and administration in support of the WVBE's [West Virginia Board of Education] mission, including student mastery of rigorous subject matter content and acquisition of global skills. Therefore, users should have no expectation of privacy; and the WVDE [West Virginia Department of Education] reserves the right to monitor, inspect, investigate, copy, review and store, without prior notice, information about the content and usage of:
  - 6.1.c.1. The network and system files;
  - 6.1.c.2. User files and disk space utilization;
  - 6.1.c.3. User applications and bandwidth utilization;
  - 6.1.c.4. User document files, folders and electronic communications;
  - 6.1.c.5. E-mail;
  - 6.1.c.6. Internet access; and
  - 6.1.c.7. Any and all information transmitted or received in connection with networks, e-mail use and web-based tools.
- 6.1.d. No student or staff user should have any expectation of privacy when using the district's network. The WVDE reserves the right to disclose any electronic message, files, media, etc., to law enforcement officials or third parties as appropriate.
- 6.1.e. No temporary accounts will be issued, nor will a student use an Internet account not specifically created for him or her that allows anonymous posting. Based upon the acceptable use and safety guidelines outlined in this document, WVDE, State Superintendent of Schools and providers) system administrators will determine what appropriate use is, and their decision is final.
- 6.1.f. The system administrator and/or local teachers may deny users access for inappropriate use. Additionally, violation of use policies could result in loss of access, personal payment

of fees incurred, employment discipline, licensure revocation and/or prosecution. Otlier [sic] violations may also be found in Policy 4373.

6.1.g. The WVDE's administrative information systems, including the West Virginia Education Information System (WVEIS), are to be used exclusively for the business of the respective state, district (county) and school organizations. All information system data are records of the respective organizations. The WVDE reserves the right to access and disclose all data sent over its information systems for any purposes. All staff must maintain the confidentiality of student data in accordance with The Family Educational Rights and Privacy Act (FERPA) (20 U.S.C. § 1232g; 34 CFR Part 99).

6.1.h. For reasons of privacy, employees may not attempt to gain access to another employee's files in the WVDE's information systems. However, the WVDE reserves the right to enter an employee's information system files whenever there is a business need to do so.

6.1.i Any of these guidelines are to be cognizant of and superseded by FERPA and other appropriate federal and state laws.

6.2. Acceptable Use:

6.2.a. The use of the electronic resources, technologies and the Internet must be in support of education and consistent with the educational goals, objectives and priorities of the WVBE. Use of other networks or computing resources must comply with the rules appropriate for that network and for copyright compliance. Users must also be in compliance with the rules and regulations of the network provider(s) serving West Virginia counties and schools.

6.2.b. The use of telecommunications and/or access to the Internet is an extension of the students' responsibility in the classroom and must follow all federal and state laws as well as state and local policies.

6.2.c. State, district and school-owned technology is to be used to enhance learning and teaching as well as improve the operation of the district and school.

6.2.d. Safety measures must be enforced to carry out policies at the state, RESA, county, and school to implement the intent of CIPA [Children's Internet Protection Act], COPPA [Children's Online Privacy Protection], E-rate guidelines, FERPA [Family Educational Rights and Privacy Act], and any other applicable state and federal statute and policy. (See also Policy 4373 and West Virginia Code § 18-2C-2.)

6.2.e. Acceptable network use by students and staff includes the following:

6.2.e.1. Creation of files, projects, videos, web pages and podcasts using network resources in support of student personalized academic learning and educational administration;

6.2.e.2. Appropriate participation in school-sponsored blogs, wikis, web 2.0 tools, social networking sites and online groups;

6.2.e.3. With parental permission, the online publication of original educational material, curriculum related materials and student work. Sources outside the classroom or school must be cited appropriately;

6.2.e.4. Staff use of the network for incidental personal use in accordance with all district/school policies and guidelines.

6.2.f. At no time should a student be given administrative responsibilities for a server with a wide area network or Internet connection.

6.3. Unacceptable Use:
- 6.3.a. Inappropriate use or transmission of any material in violation of any U.S. or state law or regulation is prohibited. This includes, but is not limited to, copyrighted material, threatening, abusive, or obscene material, or material protected by trade secrets.
- 6.3.b. Use for commercial activities by for-profit institutions is not acceptable.
- 6.3.c. Use for product advertisement or political lobbying is also prohibited.
- 6.3.d. Illegal activities and privacy and safety violations of COPPA, CIPA and FERPA are strictly prohibited.
- 6.3.e. Specific examples of unacceptable and/or unauthorized use include, but are not limited to:
    - 6.3.e.1. Viewing, creating, accessing, uploading, downloading, storing, sending, or distributing obscene, pornographic or sexually explicit material.
    - 6.3.e.2. Downloading, uploading and/or executing viruses, worms, Trojan horses, time bombs, bots, malware, spyware, SPAM, etc., and changes to tools used to filter content or monitor hardware and software.
    - 6.3.e.3. Using e-mail and other electronic user IDs/passwords other than one's own. Passwords are the first level of security for a user account. E-mail and system logins and accounts are to be used only by the authorized owner of the account, for authorized purposes. Students and staff are responsible for all activity on their account and must not share their account IDs and passwords.
    - 6.3.e.4. Illegally accessing or attempting to access another person's data or personal system files or unauthorized access to other state/district/school computers, networks and information systems.
    - 6.3.e.5. Supplying your password and user information to any electronic request or sharing them with others via any other communications.
    - 6.3.e.6. Storing passwords in a file without encryption.
    - 6.3.e.7. Using the "remember password" feature of Internet browsers and e-mail clients.
    - 6.3.e.8. Leaving the computer without locking the screen or logging off.
    - 6.3.e.9. Corrupting, destroying, deleting, or manipulating system data with malicious intent.
    - 6.3.e.10. Requesting that inappropriate material be transferred.
    - 6.3.e.11. Violating safety and/or security measures when using e-mail, chat rooms, blogs, wikis, social networking sites, Web 2.0 tools and other forms of electronic communications.
    - 6.3.e.12. Hacking, cracking, vandalizing or any other unlawful online activities.
    - 6.3.e.13. Disclosing, using, or disseminating personal information regarding students.
    - 6.3.e.14. Cyber bullying, hate mail, defamation, harassment of any kind, discriminatory jokes and remarks and other unauthorized uses as referenced in WVBE policies or other policies and laws.
    - 6.3.e.15. Personal gain, commercial solicitation and compensation of any kind.
    - 6.3.e.16. Any activity which results in liability or cost incurred by the district.
    - 6.3.e.17. Downloading, installing and/or executing non-educational gaming, audio files, video files or other applications (including shareware or freeware) without permission or approval.

6.3.e.18. Support or opposition for ballot measures, candidates and any other political activity.

6.3.e.19. Information posted, sent or stored online that could endanger others (e.g., bomb construction, drug manufacture, etc.).

6.3.e.20. Plagiarism or reproducing/repurposing audio/video without permission/consent.

6.3.e.21. Attaching unauthorized equipment to the district or school networks. Any such equipment may be confiscated and turned over to law enforcement officers for a potential violation of West Virginia Code § 61-3C-5, Unauthorized Access To Computer Services.

6.3.e.22. Attaching unauthorized equipment or making unauthorized changes to the state backbone network. Unauthorized equipment may be confiscated and may turned over to law enforcement officers for a potential violation of West Virginia Code § 61-3C-5, Unauthorized Access To Computer Services. Only WVDE network personnel may authorize changes which affect the state backbone network.

6.3.e.23. Vandalizing technology equipment or data. Vandalism is defined as any attempt to harm or destroy data of another user or to intentionally damage equipment or any connections that are part of the Internet. This includes, but is not limited to, uploading, downloading or creating computer viruses. Vandalism will result in revocation of user privileges.

6.3.e.24. Uses related to or in support of illegal activities will be reported to authorities.

Regulations for Education Programs. West Virginia Administrative Code § 126-42-7 (West 2014)

West Virginia Administrative Code § 126-42-7

§ 126-42-7. County Board of Education Responsibilities.

7.1. The county board of education shall establish policies and implement written procedures to provide high quality delivery of its education program. In meeting this responsibility the county board shall address the components of a high quality program listed below. ....

7.3.k. A student code of conduct policy that requires public schools to respond immediately and consistently to incidents of harassment, intimidation, bullying, substance abuse and/or violence or other student code of conduct violations in a manner that effectively deters future incidents and affirms respect for individuals as outlined in West Virginia. 126CSR99, WVBE Policy 4373, Expected Behaviors in Safe and Supportive Schools.

WISCONSIN

Model Policy Requirement. Wisconsin Statutes Annotated 118.46 (West 2010)

Wisconsin Statutes Annotated 118.46

118.46. Policy on bullying

(1) By March 1, 2010, the department [Wisconsin Department of Public Instruction] shall do all of the following:
  (a) Develop a model school policy on bullying by pupils. The policy shall include all of the following:
    1. A definition of bullying.
    2. A prohibition on bullying.
    3. A procedure for reporting bullying that allows reports to be made confidentially.
    4. A prohibition against a pupil retaliating against another pupil for reporting an incident of bullying.
    5. A procedure for investigating reports of bullying. The procedure shall identify the school district employee in each school who is responsible for conducting the investigation and require that the parent or guardian of each pupil involved in a bullying incident be notified.
    6. A requirement that school district officials and employees report incidents of bullying and identify the persons to whom the reports must be made.
    7. A list of disciplinary alternatives for pupils that engage in bullying or who retaliate against a pupil who reports an incident of bullying.
    8. An identification of the school-related events at which the policy applies.
    9. An identification of the property owned, leased, or used by the school district on which the policy applies.
    10. An identification of the vehicles used for pupil transportation on which the policy applies.
  (b) Develop a model education and awareness program on bullying.
  (c) Post the model policy under par. (a) and the model program under par. (b) on its Internet site.
(2) By August 15, 2010, each school board shall adopt a policy prohibiting bullying by pupils. The school board may adopt the model policy under sub. (1)(a). The school board shall provide a copy of the policy to any person who requests it. Annually, the school board shall distribute the policy to all pupils enrolled in the school district and to their parents or guardians.

Crimes against Public Peace, Order and Other Interests.
Wisconsin Statutes Annotated 947.0125 (West 2013)

Wisconsin Statutes Annotated 947.0125

947.0125. Unlawful use of computerized communication systems

(1) In this section, "message" means any transfer of signs, signals, writing, images, sounds, data or intelligence of any nature, or any transfer of a computer program, as defined in [section] 943.70(1)(c).
(2) Whoever does any of the following is guilty of a Class B misdemeanor:
  (a) With intent to frighten, intimidate, threaten, abuse or harass another person, sends a message to the person on an electronic mail or other computerized communication system and in that message threatens to inflict injury or physical harm to any person or the property of any person.

(b) With intent to frighten, intimidate, threaten, abuse or harass another person, sends a message on an electronic mail or other computerized communication system with the reasonable expectation that the person will receive the message and in that message threatens to inflict injury or physical harm to any person or the property of any person.

(c) With intent to frighten, intimidate, threaten or abuse another person, sends a message to the person on an electronic mail or other computerized communication system and in that message uses any obscene, lewd or profane language or suggests any lewd or lascivious act.

(d) With intent to frighten, intimidate, threaten or abuse another person, sends a message on an electronic mail or other computerized communication system with the reasonable expectation that the person will receive the message and in that message uses any obscene, lewd or profane language or suggests any lewd or lascivious act.

(e) With intent to frighten, intimidate, threaten or abuse another person, sends a message to the person on an electronic mail or other computerized communication system while intentionally preventing or attempting to prevent the disclosure of his or her own identity.

(f) While intentionally preventing or attempting to prevent the disclosure of his or her identity and with intent to frighten, intimidate, threaten or abuse another person, sends a message on an electronic mail or other computerized communication system with the reasonable expectation that the person will receive the message.

(3) Whoever does any of the following is subject to a Class B forfeiture:

(a) With intent to harass, annoy or offend another person, sends a message to the person on an electronic mail or other computerized communication system and in that message uses any obscene, lewd or profane language or suggests any lewd or lascivious act.

(b) With intent to harass, annoy or offend another person, sends a message on an electronic mail or other computerized communication system with the reasonable expectation that the person will receive the message and in that message uses any obscene, lewd or profane language or suggests any lewd or lascivious act.

(c) With intent solely to harass another person, sends repeated messages to the person on an electronic mail or other computerized communication system.

(d) With intent solely to harass another person, sends repeated messages on an electronic mail or other computerized communication system with the reasonable expectation that the person will receive the messages.

(e) With intent to harass or annoy another person, sends a message to the person on an electronic mail or other computerized communication system while intentionally preventing or attempting to prevent the disclosure of his or her own identity.

(f) While intentionally preventing or attempting to prevent the disclosure of his or her identity and with intent to harass or annoy another person, sends a message on an electronic mail or other computerized communication system with the reasonable expectation that the person will receive the message.

(g) Knowingly permits or directs another person to send a message prohibited by this section from any computer terminal or other device that is used to send messages on an electronic mail or other computerized communication system and that is under his or her control.

Crimes against Reputation, Privacy and Civil Liberties. Wisconsin Statutes Annotated 942.01 (West 2014)

Wisconsin Statutes Annotated 942.01

942.01. Defamation

(1) Whoever with intent to defame communicates any defamatory matter to a 3rd person without the consent of the person defamed is guilty of a Class A misdemeanor.
(2) Defamatory matter is anything which exposes the other to hatred, contempt, ridicule, degradation or disgrace in society or injury in the other's business or occupation.
(3) This section does not apply if the defamatory matter was true and was communicated with good motives and for justifiable ends or if the communication was otherwise privileged.
(4) No person shall be convicted on the basis of an oral communication of defamatory matter except upon the testimony of 2 other persons that they heard and understood the oral statement as defamatory or upon a plea of guilty or no contest.

WYOMING

Harassment, Intimidation or Bullying. Wyoming Statutes Annotated 1977 § 21-4-313 (West 2009)

Wyoming Statutes Annotated 1977 § 21-4-312

§ 21-4-312. Definitions

(a) As used in this act:

  (i) "Harassment, intimidation or bullying" means any intentional gesture, any intentional electronic communication or any intentional written, verbal or physical act initiated, occurring or received at school that a reasonable person under the circumstances should know will have the effect of:
     (A) Harming a student physically or emotionally, damaging a student's property or placing a student in reasonable fear of personal harm or property damage;
     (B) Insulting or demeaning a student or group of students causing substantial disruption in, or substantial interference with, the orderly operation of the school; or
     (C) Creating an intimidating, threatening or abusive educational environment for a student or group of students through sufficiently severe, persistent or pervasive behavior.
  (ii) "School" includes a classroom or other location on school premises, a school bus or other school-related vehicle, a school bus stop, an activity or event sponsored by a school, whether or not it is held on school premises, and any other program or function where the school is responsible for the child;
  (iii) "This act" means [Wyoming Statutes Annotated] 21-4-311 through 21-4-315.

Wyoming Statutes Annotated 1977 § 21-4-313

§ 21-4-313. Prohibition against harassment, intimidation or bullying; reporting to school officials

(a) No person shall engage in:

   (i) Harassment, intimidation or bullying; or
   (ii) Reprisal or retaliation against a victim, witness or person who reports information about an act of harassment, intimidation or bullying.

Wyoming Statutes Annotated 1977 § 21-4-314

§ 21-4-314. School district implementation; state policies, training and technical assistance

(a) Not later than December 31, 2009, each school district shall adopt a policy prohibiting harassment, intimidation or bullying at school. The school district shall involve parents and guardians, school employees, volunteers, students, administrators and community representatives in the process of creating the policy. Policies created under this section shall be continuously reviewed and may be revised as necessary.

(b) The policy prohibiting harassment, intimidation or bullying shall include, without limitation:

   (i) A statement prohibiting harassment, intimidation or bullying of a student;
   (ii) A definition of "harassment, intimidation or bullying" which includes at minimum the definition as provided in [Wyoming Statutes Annotated] 21-4-312(a)(i);
   (iii) Consequences and appropriate remedial actions for persons committing acts of harassment, intimidation or bullying or engaging in reprisal or retaliation;
   (iv) Procedures for reporting and documenting acts of harassment, intimidation or bullying, including a provision for reporting anonymously. However, formal disciplinary action shall not be taken solely on the basis of an anonymous report. The procedures shall identify the appropriate school personnel responsible for receiving a report and investigating a complaint;
   (v) Procedures for prompt investigation of reports or complaints of serious violations;
   (vi) A statement that prohibits reprisal or retaliation against a person who reports or makes a complaint of harassment, intimidation or bullying;
   (vii) A strategy for protecting a victim from additional harassment, intimidation or bullying, and from retaliation following a report;
   (viii) Consequences and appropriate remedial action for a person who is found to have made a false accusation, report or complaint;
   (ix) A process for discussing the district's harassment, intimidation or bullying policy with students; and
   (x) A statement of how the policy is to be publicized, including notice that the policy applies to participation in functions sponsored by the school.

(c) To assist local school districts in developing a policy under subsection (b) of this section, the department of education shall not later than September 1, 2009, develop model policies applicable to grades kindergarten through twelve (12) and teacher preparation program standards on the identification and prevention of bullying. In addition, the department shall provide necessary training programs and technical assistance to districts in carrying out this act.

(d) Each local school board shall include the policy adopted by a school district pursuant to this section in a publication of the comprehensive rules, procedures and standards of conduct for schools of a school district and in each school's student's handbook.

(e) Information regarding the school district's policy against harassment, intimidation or bullying shall be incorporated into each district's professional development programs and shall be provided to volunteers and other noncertified employees of the district who have significant contact with students.

(f) School districts may establish bullying prevention programs or other initiatives and may involve school staff, students, administrators, volunteers, parents, law enforcement and community members.

WASHINGTON D.C.

Youth Bullying Prevention. District of Columbia Statute § 2-1535.01, et seq. (West 2012)

District of Columbia Statute § 2-1535.01

§ 2-1535.01. Definitions.

For the purposes of this subchapter, the term:

(1) "Agency" means a District government entity that provides services, activities, or privileges to youth, including the:
  (A) Office of the State Superintendent of Education;
  (B) Department of Parks and Recreation;
  (C) District of Columbia Public Library; and
  (D) University of the District of Columbia.
(2)(A) "Bullying" means any severe, pervasive, or persistent act or conduct, whether physical, electronic, or verbal that:
  (i) May be based on a youth's actual or perceived race, color, ethnicity, religion, national origin, sex, age, marital status, personal appearance, sexual orientation, gender identity or expression, intellectual ability, familial status, family responsibilities, matriculation, political affiliation, genetic information, disability, source of income, status as a victim of an intrafamily offense, place of residence or business, or any other distinguishing characteristic, or on a youth's association with a person, or group with any person, with one or more of the actual or perceived foregoing characteristics; and
  (ii) Can be reasonably predicted to:
    (I) Place the youth in reasonable fear of physical harm to his or her person or property;
    (II) Cause a substantial detrimental effect on the youth's physical or mental health;

(III) Substantially interfere with the youth's academic performance or attendance; or
(IV) Substantially interfere with the youth's ability to participate in or benefit from the services, activities, or privileges provided by an agency, educational institution, or grantee.
(B) For the purposes of this paragraph, the terms "familial status," "family responsibilities," "gender identity or expression," "genetic information," "intrafamily offense," "marital status," "matriculation," "personal appearance," "political affiliation," "sexual orientation," and "source of income" shall have the same meaning as provided in § 2-1401.02.
(3) "Educational institution" means any local education agency that receives funds from the District of Columbia.
(4) "Electronic communication" means a communication transmitted by means of an electronic device, including a telephone, cellular phone, computer, tablet, pager, or video or audio recording.
(5) "Employee" means an individual who performs a function for the District government for an agency, educational institution, or grantee who receives compensation for the performance of that function.
(6) "Grantee" means an entity or a contractor of an entity that, on behalf of the District government or through District funding, provides services, activities, or privileges to youth.
(7) "Human Rights Act" means Chapter 14 of this title.
(8) "Party" means a person accused of bullying, a target of bullying, or a parent or guardian of either a person accused of bullying or a target of bullying.
(9) "Youth," depending on the context, means:
(A) An individual of 21 years of age or less who is enrolled in an educational institution or who accesses the services or programs provided by an agency or grantee, or an individual of 22 years of age or less who is receiving special education services from an educational institution; or
(B) Individuals as described in subparagraph (A) of this paragraph considered as a group.

District of Columbia Statute § 2-1535.02

§ 2-1535.02. Bullying prevention task force.

(a) Within 90 days of September 14, 2012, the Mayor shall establish a bullying prevention task force.
(b)(1) The task force shall consist of representatives from a diversity of the educational institutions and agencies that will be affected by this subchapter, as well as community representatives, including:
(A) Teachers;
(B) Administrators from educational institutions and agencies;
(C) School mental health professionals;
(D) Parents, and legal guardians;
(E) Youth;
(F) Direct service providers; and
(G) Advocates.
(2) In constituting this task force, the Mayor shall consider geographic and socioeconomic diversity as well as other forms of diversity.
(c) The task force shall:
(1) Provide guidance to the Mayor on the implementation of this subchapter;

(2) Within 180 days of September 14, 2012, publicize a model policy, which shall contain each of the components required in § 2-1535.03(b);
(3) Assist educational institutions and agencies with developing policies in accordance with § 2-1535.03;
(4) Compile, and make available to each agency, educational institution, and grantee, a list of free or low-cost methods for establishing the bullying prevention programs authorized in § 2-1535.06;
(5) Within 180 days of receipt of the bullying prevention policies submitted pursuant to § 2-1535.03(c), review each adopted policy for compliance with the requirements of § 2-1535.03(b); and
(6) Promulgate guidelines to assist the Mayor in evaluating the effectiveness of the bullying prevention policies that have been established.
(d) The task force shall disband 2 years after its initial meeting; provided, that at the discretion of the Mayor, a one-year extension may be granted by the Mayor.

District of Columbia Statute § 2-1535.03

§ 2-1535.03. Bullying prevention policy.

(a) Within 365 days of September 14, 2012, in coordination with the task force established pursuant to § 2-1535.02, each agency, educational institution, and grantee shall adopt a bullying prevention policy to be enforced:
  (1) On its property, including electronic communication on, or with, its property;
  (2) At sponsored functions;
  (3) On its transportation, or transportation sponsored by it; and
  (4) Through electronic communication to the extent that it is directed at a youth and it substantially interferes with the youth's ability to participate in or benefit from the services, activities, or privileges provided by the agency, education institution, or grantee.
(b) Each agency, educational institution, and grantee shall control the content of its policy; provided, that each policy includes:
  (1) The definition of bullying set forth in § 2-1535.01(2);
  (2) A statement prohibiting bullying;
  (3) A statement that the policy applies to participation in functions sponsored by the agency, educational institution, or grantee;
  (4) The expected code of conduct;
  (5) A list of the consequences that can result from an identified incident of bullying, which are designed to;
    (A) Appropriately correct the bullying behavior;
    (B) Prevent another occurrence of bullying or retaliation;
    (C) Protect the target of the bullying;
    (D) Be flexible so that in application they can be unique to the individual incident and varied in method and severity based on the:

(i) Nature of the incident;
(ii) Developmental age of the person bullying; and
(iii) Any history of problem behavior from the person bullying;
(6) A procedure for reporting bullying or retaliation for reporting an act of bullying, including for reporting bullying anonymously; provided, that no formal response shall be taken solely on the basis of an anonymous report;
(7) A procedure for prompt investigation of reports of violations of its policy and of complaints of bullying or retaliation, including the name and contact information of the person responsible for investigating reports;
(8) An appeal process, in accordance with § 2-1535.04, for a person accused of bullying or a person who is the target of bullying who is not satisfied with the outcome of the initial investigation; and
(9) A statement that prohibits retaliation against any person who reports bullying, including the possible consequences for a person who engages in retaliatory behavior.
(c) Within 365 days of September 14, 2012, each agency, educational institution, and grantee shall submit a copy of its adopted policy to the task force, pursuant to § 2-1535.02(c)(5).
(d) The requirements of this subchapter and any policy adopted pursuant to this subchapter shall be deemed to constitute health and safety requirements for educational institutions.
(e) Information on the bullying prevention policy shall be incorporated into new employee training.
(f) Each agency, educational institution, and grantee shall develop a plan for how the policy is to be publicized, including the plan for:
(1) Discussing its bullying policy with youth; and
(2) Publicizing that the policy applies to participation in functions sponsored by an agency, educational institution, or grantee.

District of Columbia Statute § 2-1535.04

§ 2-1535.04. Secondary investigation appeal.

(a)(1) A party who is not satisfied with the outcome of the initial investigation conducted pursuant to § 2-1535.03(b)(7) may request a secondary investigation by submitting a written appeal to the higher-level authority in the agency, educational institution, or grantee designated to hear appeals within 30 days of the conclusion of the investigation conducted pursuant to § 2-1535.03(b)(7).
(2) The secondary investigation shall be completed within 30 days of receipt of the appeal, unless:
(A) Circumstances require additional time to complete a thorough investigation;
(B) The higher-level authority sets forth those circumstances in writing; and
(C) The additional time does not exceed 15 days.
(b)(1) When an appeal for a secondary investigation is submitted, the agency, educational institution, or grantee shall inform the party about his or her ability to seek further redress under Chapter 14 of this title.
(2) This section shall not be construed to limit the right of a person to assert or seek redress for a claim arising under Chapter 14 of this title.

District of Columbia Statute § 2-1535.05

§ 2-1535.05. Retaliation.

(a) An employee, volunteer, or youth shall not retaliate against a victim or witness of bullying or a person who reports bullying.
(b) An employee or volunteer who has witnessed bullying in violation of a bullying prevention policy that is consistent with § 2-1535.03(a), or has reliable information that a person has been subject to bullying in violation of a bullying prevention policy that is consistent with § 2-1535.03(a), shall report the incident or information to the person designated by the agency, educational institution, or grantee, in accordance with § 2-1535.03(b)(7), as responsible for investigating the reports.
(c) An employee, volunteer, or youth who promptly and in good faith reports an incident of, or information on, bullying in compliance with the policy of the agency, educational institution, or grantee shall be immune from a cause of action for damages arising from the making of such report.

District of Columbia Statute § 2-1535.06

§ 2-1535.06. Bullying prevention programs.

Following the adoption of a bullying prevention policy, as required by § 2-1535.03, each agency, educational institution, and grantee may:

(1) Establish an annual bullying prevention program for youth, which for each educational institution should align with established health-education standards;
(2) Inform youth about their right to be free from discrimination in public accommodations and education, and of the redress available for a violation of their rights under Chapter 14 of this title; and
(3) Provide training on bullying prevention to all employees and volunteers who have significant contact with youth.

District of Columbia Statute § 2-1535.07

§ 2-1535.07. Reporting requirement.

(a) Each educational institution shall provide to the Mayor, by a date determined by the Mayor, an annual report regarding the aggregate incidents of bullying, and any other information that the Mayor determines is necessary or appropriate.
(b) By September 1, 2014, and biennially thereafter, the Mayor shall:
   (1) Review the programs, activities, services, and policies established pursuant to this subchapter of each agency, educational institution, or grantee to determine their effectiveness and whether the agency, educational institution, or grantee is in compliance with this subchapter; and
   (2) Report the findings to the Council by December 31 of each year that a report is due, along with an assessment of the current level and nature of bullying in agencies, educational institutions, and grantees and recommendations for appropriate actions to address identified problems.

Chapter 16
Forging the Path Forward from Censorship

ABSTRACT

This chapter presents the conclusions to the book. It discusses ideas for the future of the off-campus student-speech jurisprudence. This discussion includes guidance for school officials and students on how to navigate the jurisprudence. The discussion urges school officials to exercise censorship restraint when confronted with off-campus student speech unless the speech constitutes a true threat. It also implores school officials and lower courts to treat students as citizens entitled to the right to free speech under the United States Constitution. Consonantly, the chapter recommends that school officials leave censorship of off-campus speech to law enforcement as well as the civil and criminal judicial processes as obtains for the citizenry at large. The goal of the chapter is to recommend ideas that students, school officials and lower courts can consider in order to minimize the abridgement of students' right to speech in off-campus settings.

INTRODUCTION

This chapter concludes the book's examination of the off-campus student speech jurisprudence. As evident in the analysis in prior chapters, the jurisprudence is in disarray because the United States Supreme Court has thus far chosen silence rather than a clear and conclusive articulation of the First Amendment right of students to speak off-campus. Lower courts have tried to fill the void through inconsistent and conflicting decisions as highlighted in chapters eleven, twelve and thirteen. The lower courts have based their decisions on application of the material and substantial disruption test, the infringement-of-rights test, the *Bethel* test and the *Morse* test from their on-campus context to the context of off-campus speech. Some courts have also relied upon the true-threat doctrine, the *Miller* test, the fighting-words doctrine and defamation law. The variety of tests and doctrines used by different courts has created contrariant interpretations of the scope of students' off-campus speech rights and a clouded jurisprudence. Amidst the incongruent jurisprudence, school officials have a prime opportunity to censor as much off-campus speech as possible without imperative and decisive judicial pushback. This chapter proposes that school

DOI: 10.4018/978-1-4666-9519-1.ch016

Forging the Path Forward from Censorship

officials not censor off-campus student speech despite this opportunity. It presents ideas for lower courts, school officials and students to ensure that students enjoy the citizenship right to free speech as guaranteed under the First Amendment. Ultimately, it proposes that lower courts and school officials should confine school-censorship authority inside the schoolhouse gate unless a true threat is present.

MAIN FOCUS OF THE CHAPTER

This chapter is designed to provide recommendations for navigating the off-campus student-speech jurisprudence. It argues that school officials should not censor off-campus student speech if the speech does not constitute a true threat. Additionally, censorship of off-campus student speech should be left to the jurisdiction of law enforcement, parents and the judiciary. The chapter also argues that lower courts should arrest the current jurisprudence's inclination toward censorship in order to preserve the opportunity for students to develop as active participants in our constitutional democracy. Further, it argues that, once students exit the schoolhouse gate, they should be treated as part of the citizenry entitled to First Amendment protection under the United States Constitution. It also argues that, in light of the unsettled and inconsistent nature of the off-campus student-speech jurisprudence, school officials should be precluded from making censorship decisions about off-campus speech since they are not schooled in First Amendment niceties. Instead, schools should educate students on the civil use of speech and adopt policies that are protective of students' rights to speak off-campus. The chapter also discusses the Erase Bill in California as an opportunity for students to avoid school censorship.

The Extant Fragmented Off-Campus Student-Speech Jurisprudence

As shown in this book, the current off-campus student-speech jurisprudence is unsettled and fragmented. This is evident in the motley of approaches that courts have taken to off-campus student speech in both online and offline settings. The uncertainty in the jurisprudence arises from the fact that the United States Supreme Court has never ruled on an off-campus student speech case. While a number of courts believe that the material and substantial disruption test from Tinker v. Des Moines Independent Community School District (1969) is applicable to off-campus speech, others believe this test is inapplicable because this test was created in the context of on-campus speech. Further, while a few courts have recognized an infringement-of-rights test, based on the Supreme Court's language in the *Tinker* case, most courts have never recognized the test. Even when courts recognize the infringement-of-rights test, most choose simply to acknowledge the test without defining or applying it. Besides, the Supreme Court itself has never applied this test or explicitly recognized it as a test. This further muddles the jurisprudence.

An exiguous number of courts have applied the *Bethel* test to off-campus speech. Many courts have, however, declined to extend this test off-campus because of the on-campus context of the Bethel School District No. 403 v. Fraser (1986) case. The perplexing thing is that a few of these courts inconsistently used context as rationale. Specifically, these courts relied on context in rejecting the application of the *Bethel* test to off-campus speech. Yet these same courts disregarded the on-campus context of Tinker v. Des Moines Independent Community School District (1969) when deciding to extend the material and substantial disruption test to off-campus speech. This is quite bewildering as it says context matters until it does not matter. Some other courts declined to apply the *Bethel* test to off-campus speech because of

Justice Brennan's concurrence in Bethel School District No. 403 v. Fraser which stated that if the vulgar, lewd or plainly-offensive student speech in that case had been delivered off-campus, school officials could not censor the speech. The Supreme Court has endorsed this statement, in obiter, in both Hazelwood v. Kuhlmeier (1988) and Morse v. Frederick (2007), even though both cases involved on-campus speech. As for the other two Supreme Court student-speech tests, we found that only one court has chosen the *Morse* test as the governing test for off-campus speech while no court has used the *Hazelwood* test.

Some courts have chosen to use doctrines that traditionally govern citizen speech in the community at large; despite the fact that the United States Supreme Court has never applied these doctrines to school censorship of student speech. These doctrines include the true-threat doctrine, the *Miller* test, the fighting-words doctrine and defamation law. Speech that satisfies any of these doctrines is unprotected speech under the First Amendment, thus giving schools leeway to reach off-campus to censor such speech. Several other courts have yet to apply these doctrines to off-campus speech. The unsystematic use of the Supreme Court's student-speech precedents and these doctrines will continue until the Supreme Court accepts and rules on a case involving off-campus student speech.

Calls for Censorship Restraint in the Off-Campus Student-Speech Jurisprudence

Rather than capitalize on the unsettled, fragmented and incohesive nature of the current jurisprudence, school officials need to exercise censorship restraint. Further, simply because the material and substantial disruption test provides an entry point to censorship of off-campus student speech does not mean school officials should take advantage of it. School officials should instead heed the admonition of the United States Court of Appeals for the Fifth Circuit to respect and celebrate students' right to free speech:

Tinker's dam to school board absolutism does not leave dry the fields of school discipline. This court has gone a considerable distance with the school boards to uphold its disciplinary fiats where reasonable. ... Tinker simply irrigates, rather than floods, the fields of school discipline. It sets canals and channels through which school discipline might flow with the least possible damage to the nation's priceless topsoil of the First Amendment. Perhaps it would be well if those entrusted to administer the teaching of American history and government to our students began their efforts by practicing the document on which that history and government are based. Our eighteen-year-olds can now vote, serve on juries, and be drafted; yet the board fears the 'awakening' of their intellects without reasoned concern for its effect upon school discipline (Shanley v. Northeast Independent School District, 1972, p. 978).

It is treacherous to extend the material and substantial disruption test off-campus as it could take our nation down a path that weakens the speech rights of adults as well. The United States Supreme Court created the material and substantial disruption test specifically to address student speech in a school setting. This test was created so school officials did not have to comply with the stringent censorship requirements that govern speech of the community at large off-campus. Thus, taking this less stringent test and applying it to students when they are in their citizen status, as other citizens off-campus, is setting a dangerous precedent that could eventually impact the speech rights of all citizens. Judge Smith warned of this danger in J.S. ex rel. Snyder v. Blue Mountain School District (2011):

[I]f Tinker were applied to off-campus speech, there would be little reason to prevent school officials from regulating adult speech uttered in the community.... Adults often say things that give rise to disruptions in public schools. Those who championed desegregation in the 1950s and 60s caused more than a minor disturbance in the southern schools (J.S. ex rel. Snyder v. Blue Mountain School District, 2011, p. 940).

As Judge Smith observed, the very thought of using the material and substantial disruption test to censor adults is presently "absurd" (J.S. ex rel. Snyder v. Blue Mountain School District, p. 940). Nonetheless it is a real possibility if we continue on this expansive path of whittling and usurping off-campus student speech rights through the material and substantial disruption test.

The United States Supreme Court appeared to limit school-censorship authority to the confines of the school setting when it defined the primary function of schools as follows: "The principal use to which the schools are dedicated is to accommodate students during prescribed hours for the purpose of certain types of activities" (Tinker v. Des Moines Independent Community School District, 1969, p. 512). This indicates that school authority is limited to student actions during the hours that students are inside the schoolhouse gate. Furthermore, the Supreme Court has ruled that the government has no business telling citizens what they can watch or read, and clearly concomitantly write, within their houses (Stanley v. Georgia, 1969, p. 565). School officials need to respect these limitations on their censorship authority.

We believe that the most prudent approach for courts to use in reviewing censorship of off-campus student speech is that articulated by the United States District Court for the Southern District of Texas:

[I]t makes little sense to extend the influence of school administration to off-campus activity under the theory that such activity might interfere with the function of education. School officials may not judge a student's behavior while he is in his home with his family nor does it seem to this court that they should have jurisdiction over his acts on a public street corner. A student is subject to the same criminal laws and owes the same civil duties as other citizens, and his status as a student should not alter his obligations to others during his private life away from the campus (Sullivan v. Houston Independent School District, 1969, pp. 1340-41).

This approach recognizes students as citizens outside the schoolhouse gate and recognizes their free speech rights as coextensive with those of the community at large. It recognizes that students have rights and obligations under both criminal and civil laws off-campus. It recognizes that the language of the First Amendment does not subjugate children to a different class than adults. It does not assign them second-class citizenship status. Moreover, as the United States Supreme Court has iterated, "[s]tudents in school as well as out of school are 'persons' under our Constitution. They are possessed of fundamental rights which the State must respect, just as they themselves must respect their obligations to the State" (Tinker v. Des Moines Independent Community School District, 1969, p. 511). Consequently, efforts to subject students to additional censorship through the medium of schools diminish their status as citizens and treat them as non-equivalents to other citizens.

If school officials can discipline students for off-campus speech, students would be subjected to more laws than the typical citizen. They would be subjected to "two sets of punishments: liability in court for civil or criminal violations and school discipline" (Caplan, 2003, p. 143). In essence, school censorship of off-campus speech subjects students to "too many sovereigns once they leave school: they answer to local law enforcement and to school administrators" (p. 143). This teaches students at an early age that they are not truly fully citizens or persons. School censorship of off-campus speech also misses a fundamental point: when on school grounds, children are merely in an "occupational status" as students, analogous to the occupational status on a job (Calvert, 2001, p. 276). Thus, when students are outside the school, they should be treated as citizens the same way children and adults are treated under the law when they are away from their jobs. Just because students are on school grounds for about forty-five hours of their weekday does not make them vassals in a fiefdom school system. As the United States Supreme Court has ruled, "[s]chool officials do not possess absolute authority over their students" (Tinker v. Des Moines Independent Community School District, p. 511).

Students could find navigation of their legal liability confusing when concurrently subjected to the lenient censorship standard applicable to schools and the more stringent standards applicable to law enforcement and other government entities off-campus. Students might not know how to abide by each standard without violating the requirements of the other. Since students are less mature than adults, they might also find it difficult to even process the intricacies of the many standards governing their speech. This could chill their speech as they might avoid speaking rather than risk the consequences of speaking under the cloud of an uncertain jurisprudence. This disengagement is not healthy for students' appreciation of the First Amendment. We agree with the United States Court of Appeals for the Fifth Circuit that "[i]t is most important that our young become convinced that our Constitution is a living reality, not parchment preserved under glass" (Shanley v. Northeast Independent School District, 1972, pp. 972-73).

Amidst the uncertainty in the off-campus student-speech jurisprudence, school officials have a unique opportunity to model appropriate restraint in order to convey to students that the First Amendment is not a hollow promise. Student speech off-campus should be left to the purview of law enforcement unless the student-speaker brings the speech to school or accesses the speech on-campus in which case school officials can treat the speech as on-campus speech. It weakens the force of the First Amendment to allow censorship of a student-speaker when the speaker had no role in bringing the speech to campus. Recall that in some cases, courts have authorized school censorship based on school officials bringing the speech on-campus or requiring another student to bring the speech on-campus. A censorship jurisprudence founded upon on-campus access of speech by someone other than the student-speaker is tomfoolery as highlighted in the following example:

Imagine a student who writes a letter to the editor of the local newspaper, criticizing the principal in language sufficiently vulgar to justify punishment under Bethel if the letter had been read aloud at a school assembly. The school could not punish the student for expressing her views in the free press. This would be true even if the school library subscribes to the paper, the student knows about the subscription, and she tells friends where to find it in the school library's copy (Caplan, 2003, p. 143).

If school officials cannot censor a student's letter to the editor simply because of an on-campus presence created by someone other than the student-speaker, they should similarly not be able to censor off-campus student speech in offline or online settings under such circumstances.

Tuneski (2003) analogizes broadcast speech to online speech in a way that further illustrates the absurdity of using the on-campus access of speech by someone other than the student-speaker as the basis for censoring a student-speaker:

[I]t may be useful to consider speech on a website as being analogous to a television program broadcast over the airwaves to a general audience. While both the internet and television broadcast information so that anyone in the general population may access it, only a small segment of the population may be

interested in turning on their televisions or web browsers to receive the information. Clearly, a student expressing his opinions on a television program would be considered an off-campus speaker; it is inconceivable that the student would become an on-campus speaker merely because another student turned on a television in a school classroom and viewed the broadcast. Like a student speaking on television, a student web page publisher does not speak on-campus merely because his expression may be accessible there (p. 164).

In spite of the fact that some courts have empowered school officials to censor speech where the student-speaker was not responsible for bringing or accessing the speech on school grounds, school officials should opt against doing so. It is quite disingenuous and manipulative to censor a student-speaker by circumventing the speaker. It is easy to find a proxy to access speech on-campus and then use that on-campus access as the basis for censoring the speaker who had no role in the on-campus access. Even if the on-campus presence of the speech is attributable to a reporting parent or student, school officials should exercise censorship restraint because it circumvents the student-speaker. The exception should be when the speech expresses a serious intent to do harm.

Recommendations and Guidance for Navigating the Off-Campus Student-Speech Jurisprudence

When off-campus student speech expresses a serious intent to do harm, a zero tolerance policy for true threats is justifiable; particularly in this age of increased school violence. School officials must be careful, however, not to use such policies to silence cries for help. When students make threatening statements, they are sometimes merely calling attention to their insecurities and reaching out for help (Hils, 2001). "Speech may serve as a non-violent and passive method of blowing off steam" (Calvert, 2001, p. 282). Speech provides a safe outlet for students and a safeguard for society: "If societies are not to explode from festering tensions, there must be valves through which citizens may blow off steam. Openness fosters resiliency; peaceful protest displaces more violence than it triggers; free debate dissipates more hate than it stirs" (Calvert, p. 282, citing Smolla, 1992, p. 13).

Zero tolerance policies for student expression could make the student reach inward and recoil from the public. This could then build up resentment and consequent violence as release for the pent-up emotions. It is naïve to think that simply muzzling a student would automatically prevent the student from doing harm. In other words, free speech might actually be more critical to protecting schools from violence than the protection, if any, that censorship can provide schools. As Calvert (2001) noted, we should be grateful when a student uses speech rather than a gun to emote. A balanced approach, rather than a zero tolerance policy, is key. Under a balanced approach, students who make threatening statements would be required to undergo some form of counseling or psychological evaluation in order to better understand the nature of the threat. If the threat is deemed to be genuine, school officials would then promptly notify law enforcement in order to protect students and staff, given that law enforcement is best equipped to address such threats.

If the speech is, however, deemed to be merely boorish, school officials should respect the purview of parents and their right to deal with the off-campus speech. Parents understand the import of their children's use of digital communication. In a survey of 935 parents and their children between the ages 12 and 17, the Pew Research Center's Internet and American Life Project found that parents do monitor their children's digital communications (Macgill, 2007). Sixty-nine percent of parents regulate how much time their children spend online while sixty-eight percent regulate the content their children view online (Macgill, 2007). Sixty-five percent of parents review the online communications of their children once they are offline (Macgill, 2007). The Pew Research study found that "[i]n most families, internet use is a subject of family rule-making and discussion" (p. 2). In essence, parents are more than capable of directing the upbringing of their children outside the schoolhouse gate without school intervention.

Even when off-campus speech is obscene, and thus unprotected, school officials should not censor the speech. Certainly, it would be silly for school officials to "consign a student to a segregated study hall because he and a classmate watched an X-rated film on his living room cable television" (Thomas v. Board of Education, Granville Central School District, 1979, p. 1051). Disciplinary decisions for obscene as well as defamatory speech should be left to parents, law enforcement and the judicial system. School policy as well as student and teacher handbooks should clearly state that, with the exception of true threats, school officials will not censor student speech that originates off-campus unless the student-speaker had a proactive role in the speech's presence or dissemination on school grounds. When speech outside these parameters comes to the attention of school officials, they should promptly notify the parents who should retain the prerogative to discipline their child for the speech. As Justice Alito warned in the most recent Supreme Court student-speech case, "[i]t is a dangerous fiction to pretend that parents simply delegate their authority—including their authority to determine what their children may say and hear—to public school authorities" (Morse v. Frederick, 2007, p. 424). Thus, schools need to exercise censorship self-control.

One school that did not exercise censorship restraint, thus blunting the First Amendment, was Dowell Middle School in Texas (Lewin, 1998). Thirteen-year old student Aaron Smith drew an image which his friend thought represented the killing of a Chihuahua. This image, created in the school computer lab, became the subject of Aaron's classmates' wisecracks; inspiring Aaron to create a website based on the image. Aaron created the website called "C.H.O.W" (Chihuahua Haters of the World) after school hours in the privacy of his home on his personal computer. The site was designed to "share tidbits like the tale of the seven-foot boa constrictor that ate a Chihuahua" (p. 1). One posting stated: "Today in the California region a 7-ft. boa constrictor was caught devouring a chihuahua. I have repeatedly called the snake's home to tell him what a great job our operatives are doing out there, but he won't answer the phone. If anyone can relay this information to him C.H.O.W. would be grateful" (p. 1). The site included several facetious comments about Chihuahuas. It also stated that the idea for the website originated while Aaron was in the school computer lab.

An adult Chihuahua breeder who discovered the website expressed anger to school officials (Lewin, 1998). She threatened an animal-rights protest if school officials failed to discipline Aaron. The superintendent received about fifty emails protesting the website. Aaron was suspended from school for the website, removed from his computer lab class and required to apologize and delete the website. The American Civil Liberties Union (ACLU) intervened and successfully secured a settlement of the case, allowing Aaron to return to his computer lab class and avoid a disciplinary record of the website. This was clearly a case of off-campus speech with an on-campus connection since the idea for the website originated on school grounds. Nevertheless, the website for which Aaron was suspended was created off-campus. The only connection on the website to the school was the mention of the fact that the idea originated in the school computer lab. However, as we discussed in earlier chapters, courts have generally considered such minor use of a school resource as constitutionally de minimis. Consequently, it is not surprising that the ACLU had success in getting Aaron back to school with a clean disciplinary record.

Forging the Path Forward from Censorship

This censorship incident at Dowell Middle School illustrates how school officials can overreact to speech simply because someone finds the off-campus speech offensive. It also shows how an offended party can pressure school officials to censor speech that the offended could not get law enforcement to censor. Whether the site was created by an adult or a child, the Chihuahua breeder had no censorship recourse for such a site in law enforcement. Thus, the school was a convenient target and alternative medium for the breeder to execute her censorship design. The school took the bait, clearly ignoring the United States Supreme Court's warning in Tinker v. Des Moines Independent Community School District (1969): "In order for the State in the person of school officials to justify prohibition of a particular expression of opinion, it must be able to show that its action was caused by something more than a mere desire to avoid the discomfort and unpleasantness that always accompany an unpopular viewpoint" (p. 509).

Dowell Middle School essentially taught and modeled for students that it is appropriate to "discount important principles of our government as mere platitudes" (West Virginia State Board of Education v. Barnette, 1943, p. 637). The school also caused irreparable harm to Aaron's free speech rights. As the United States District Court for the Northern District of Oklahoma aptly stated, "any time the movant's First Amendment rights are violated, it constitutes irreparable harm, regardless of the punishment" (D.G. v. Independent School District No. 11 of Tulsa County, Oklahoma, 2000, p. 16). This is a very prudent rule that all courts and school officials should adhere to in order to protect the development of students as thoughtful citizens. School officials' respect of students' free speech rights is instrumental to proper student development as it teaches them the value of self-governance and self-autonomy as well as the role of speech in holding government accountable (Qasir, 2013; Papandrea, 2008).

Certainly, schools' exercise of censorship self-control will enable some students to engage in thoughtless off-campus student speech. That is a necessary risk we must embrace in order to protect the multitude of other thoughtful expressions that are critical to helping students embrace the First Amendment, and the free speech rights that the First Amendment guarantees to them through adulthood. The liberty to experiment with offensive and non-offensive speech is the essence of the First Amendment. United States Supreme Court Justice Oliver Holmes, Jr. eloquently articulated this essence when he declared that "the ultimate good desired is better reached by free trade in ideas–that the best test of truth is the power of the thought to get itself accepted in the competition of the market. ... That at any rate is the theory of our Constitution" (Abrams v. United States, 1919, p. 630). The Supreme Court has similarly accentuated the concernment of free speech, and of the tolerance of offensive speech, to preservation of the First Amendment:

*To many, the immediate consequence of this freedom [free speech] may often appear to be only verbal tumult, discord, and even offensive utterance. These are, however, within established limits, in truth necessary side effects of the broader enduring values which the process of open debate permits us to achieve. That the air may at times seem filled with verbal cacophony is, in this sense not a sign of weakness but of strength. We cannot lose sight of the fact that, in what otherwise might seem a trifling and annoying instance of individual distasteful abuse of a privilege, these fundamental societal values are truly implicated. That is why '[w]holly neutral futilities * * * come under the protection of free speech as fully as do Keats' poems or Donne's sermons' ... and why so long as the means are peaceful, the communication need not meet standards of acceptability' (Cohen v. California, 1971, pp. 24-25).*

Free speech helps promote the bedrocks of pluralism and individuality. In a nation as diverse as ours, individuals as well as collectives forge a unique identity that finds expression through speech. Students are part of their own collectives at school as well as outside of school. Students also have their own individual identities which they yearn to express through speech. The United States Supreme Court has emphasized the importance of speech to pluralism and individuality:

The constitutional right of free expression is powerful medicine in a society as diverse and populous as ours. It is designed and intended to remove governmental restraints from the arena of public discussion, putting the decision as to what views shall be voiced largely into the hands of each of us, in the hope that use of such freedom will ultimately produce a more capable citizenry and more perfect polity and in the belief that no other approach would comport with the premise of individual dignity and choice upon which our political system rests (Cohen v. California, 1971, p. 24).

School officials and the lower courts should take note of this Supreme Court declaration when trying to encroach on the off-campus speech rights of students. Off-campus speech is the opportunity for students to practice use of the precious right to free speech like other citizens; and to express their individual and collective identities that help affirm the diversity of our nation. We must remember that students "need access to information and ideas, not indoctrination and ignorance of controversy, precisely because they are in the process of identity formation" (Garfield, 2005, p. 580, citing Heins, 2001, p. 258). Furthermore, "[t]hey are also in the process of becoming functioning adults in a democratic society and, as the Supreme Court has pointed out, this is not so easy to do if they are shielded from dangerous or disturbing ideas until they are 18" (Garfield, pp. 580-81, citing Heins, p. 258).

The only clear inclination we have from the United States Supreme Court of its view on off-campus student speech was expressed in Hazelwood v. Kuhlmeier (1988) and iterated in Morse v. Frederick (2007). In these cases, the Supreme Court indicated an aversion to school censorship of off-campus vulgar, lewd, obscene or plainly-offensive speech (or at least school censorship of the speech featured in Bethel School District No. 403 v. Fraser (1986)). This suggests that the Supreme Court is willing to protect off-campus speech more than it does on-campus speech. Unfortunately, as evident in various chapters of this book, school officials and lower courts continue to censor students' off-campus speech similarly as on-campus speech, eroding off-campus speech rights. The Supreme Court needs to speak clearly on the off-campus student-speech jurisprudence by ruling on an off-campus speech case. In order to affirm students as citizens rather than mere subjects of the school or second-class citizens, the Supreme Court should hold that the same rules governing the speech of the community-at-large governs off-campus student speech. As it did in Cohen v. California (1971), the Supreme Court needs to declare to school officials and students alike that they have "no right to cleanse public debate to the point where it is grammatically palatable to the most squeamish among us" (p. 25).

The Supreme Court has been quite tolerant of citizen use of language such as the four-letter word in off-campus settings. For instance, in Cohen v. California (1971), the Court declared that "while the particular four-letter word ... is perhaps more distasteful than most others of its genre, it is nevertheless often true that one man's vulgarity is another's lyric. Indeed, we think it is largely because governmental officials cannot make principled distinctions in this area that the Constitution leaves matters of taste and style so largely to the individual" (p. 25). The Supreme Court should affirm this same right for students in the context of school censorship of off-campus speech. The Court has also recognized First Amendment protection for emotive delivery of speech; thus, even if offensive speech is passionately conveyed online or offline, it is still entitled to First Amendment protection (Cohen v. California, 1971). The Court should clearly declare this same right for students in the context of school censorship of off-campus speech. Moreover, in the context of an off-campus school censorship case, the Supreme Court must remind school officials and the lower courts that "[i]t is rare that a regulation restricting speech because of its content will ever be permissible" (United States v. Playboy Entertainment Group, Inc., 2000, p. 818). As the Court has stated, "were we to give the Government the benefit of the doubt when it attempted to restrict speech, we would risk leaving regulations in place that sought to shape our unique personalities or to silence dissenting ideas" (p. 818).

School officials need to develop a thick skin against student criticism of their policies and persons. In light of the fact that the United States Supreme Court has opposed censorship of citizen speech critical of government officials, school officials should similarly not have the authority to censor critical student speech. It is disappointing that none of the off-campus student speech cases we found highlighted a vital Supreme Court ruling on the right to criticize officials: "[o]ne of the prerogatives of American citizenship is the right to criticize public men and measures—and that means not only informed and responsible criticism but the freedom to speak foolishly and without moderation" (Cohen v. California, 1971, p. 26, citing Baumgartner v. United States, 1944, pp. 673-74). Perhaps, some lower courts would have been more inclined to protect students' right to criticize school officials in off-campus settings if they had been aware of this Supreme Court ruling. Unfortunately, however, the current off-campus speech jurisprudence is prejudicial to students' First Amendment rights, "preventing students from developing a capacity to be critical of higher authority, which is an important aspect of living in a democratic society where individuals retain political sovereignty" (Li, 2005, p. 89).

Judge Merritt of the United States Court of Appeals, Sixth Circuit asked a great question that educators, policymakers and judges alike need to answer about the educational impact of the current censorship regime: "If the school administration can silence a student criticizing it for being narrow minded and authoritarian, how can students engage in political dialogue with their educators about their education" in a society like ours that cherishes speech and democratic values? (Poling v. Murphy, 1989, p. 766). It is time we recognize that "[t]he First Amendment protection of freedom of expression may not be made a casualty of the effort to force-feed good manners to the ruffians among us" (Klein v. Smith, 1986, p. 1442). As the Supreme Court has ruled, school officials should not use their authority to impose and enforce orthodoxy in speech or other arenas of individual decisions (West Virginia State Board of Education v. Barnette, 1943).

School officials should not be allowed to censor off-campus student speech simply because the speech was related to or directed at the school or students. Students spend about forty-five hours of their weekday at school, so it is fair to expect their off-campus speech to be intertwined with or related to the school. Allowing school officials to censor such speech would greatly undermine students' First Amendment rights. As Caplan (2003) acutely pointed out, "[i]f talk about school is treated as talk in school, there is no logical stopping point. Even discussions around the family dinner table could become subject to school discipline" (p. 161).

If school officials feel that a student's off-campus speech is unacceptable, they should pursue criminal or civil remedies through the judicial process just like any other law enforcement agency or citizen would. School officials should not be able to exploit the privilege of teaching our youth to muzzle them; especially not to pacify overly-sensitive school officials. Besides, school officials are not so schooled in the punctilios of the First Amendment as to make constitutional judgments about the complicated and unsettled issues involved with protected and unprotected off-campus speech. That role is best left to law enforcement and the judiciary who have established credibility and competence in this area. As evident in this book, even the judiciary struggles to grasp and interpret the nuances of the jurisprudence.

Online speech has even further complicated the off-campus speech jurisprudence by making it difficult to define geographical boundaries. Judge Jordan of the United States Court of Appeals, Third Circuit, poignantly explained this complication:

For better or worse, wireless internet access, smart phones, tablet computers, social networking services like Facebook, and stream-of-consciousness communications via Twitter give an omnipresence to speech that makes any effort to trace First Amendment boundaries along the physical boundaries of a school campus a recipe for serious problems in our public schools (Layshock ex rel. Layshock v. Hermitage School District, 2011, pp. 220-21).

As we have shown in this book, judges find it challenging to define the geographical boundaries for online speech. Given this reality and the risk of deprivation through inappropriate boundary definitions, school officials should be precluded from making such determinations.

In spite of the lower courts' struggles with online speech, they must not lose sight of the fact that the United States Supreme Court has been quite clear about the impact of technology on First Amendment rights. Specifically, the Supreme Court has ruled that technology does not dilute First Amendment rights even for students:

When a student first encounters our free speech jurisprudence, he or she might think it is influenced by the philosophy that one idea is as good as any other, and that in art and literature objective standards of style, taste, decorum, beauty, and esthetics are deemed by the Constitution to be inappropriate, indeed unattainable. Quite the opposite is true. The Constitution no more enforces a relativistic philosophy or moral nihilism than it does any other point of view. The Constitution exists precisely so that opinions and judgments, including esthetic and moral judgments about art and literature, can be formed, tested, and expressed. What the Constitution says is that these judgments are for the individual to make, not for the Government to decree, even with the mandate or approval of a majority. Technology expands the capacity to choose; and it denies the potential of this revolution if we assume the Government is best positioned to make these choices for us (United States v. Playboy Entertainment Group, Inc., 2000, p. 818).

Regrettably, none of the cases in our study acknowledged this Supreme Court ruling. It is possible that the lower courts would have minimized the abridgement of students' rights in online settings if they had found this ruling; after all, the ruling shows that the Supreme Court values technology as expansive rather than contractive of free speech. Hopefully, legal scholars, counsel and the judiciary will become aware of this ruling through this book. Courts and school officials need to reverse the burgeoning trend that threatens to vitiate the off-campus speech rights of students by acknowledging what the Supreme Court has recognized: the opportunities for digital speech should be celebrated, not censored.

Rather than expending energy to censor students, school officials should create curriculum to educate students on the proper use of speech in online and offline settings so that they can develop into responsible adults who make optimal use of speech. In lieu of censorship, students should be taught from an early age not to treat online forums as the "wild west with incivility and brutality as the norm" (Citron, 2009, p. 105). Besides, school officials should recuse themselves from censoring off-campus student speech because they are not the best arbiters of speech in which they have a vested interest. As the United States Court of Appeals for the Second Circuit solemnly counseled, "when those charged with evaluating expression have a vested interest in its regulation, the temptation to expand the other-

Forging the Path Forward from Censorship

wise precise and narrow boundaries of punishable speech may prove irresistible" (Thomas v. Board of Education, Granville Central School District, 1979, p. 1048). This may further chill speech because the "cautious expositor of controversy may well choose silence over expression if he knows that his words will be judged by a decisionmaker predisposed to rule against him" (p. 1048).

Given that school officials are disposed to censor off-campus student speech, anonymity might be the best mode for student communications, particularly in online settings. As University of Oxford Professor Jonathan Zittrain observed, the internet involves "a cat and mouse game of forensics, and if people don't go to some effort to stay anonymous, it's frequently possible to figure out who they are" (Efrati, 2008, p. 1). Accordingly, students would be wise not to identify themselves or their schools in off-campus communications so as to leave very few trackable fingerprints. Instead, students should use fictitious identifiers to further their anonymity. As Li (2005) noted, anonymity protects student-speakers from ostracization, invasion of privacy and retaliation by schools. For these reasons, anonymous speech could be a healthy outlet for students even when the content of such speech upsets certain readers who feel depowered to confront the speaker.

Additionally, anonymous online speech might provide a relatively healthier forum than non-anonymous speech for students to "experiment and learn the uses and abuses of language than in the offline world" (Caplan, 2003, p. 193). Unfortunately, students who resort to anonymous speech might be unable to build an online profile based on their true identities in benefit of their lifelong academic and career pursuits; particularly because they spend most of their time building their anonymous profile and identity. Students forced to rely on anonymous speech are also being denied an opportunity to participate fully in speech on a level playing field with other speakers in the marketplace of ideas. Aside from using anonymous speech, students could also limit the judicial success of school censorship by using disclaimers within their speech. These disclaimers should alert readers, in large bold print, that the content of the speech is merely facetious. Disclaimers could protect student speech from censorship as true threats, materially and substantially disruptive speech, or defamatory speech (Calvert, 2001).

If schools want to minimize on-campus access of anonymous speech or preclude disclaimers from impacting their ability and authority to censor speech that gets on-campus, they should invest in filtering software for their computers and wireless networks. Filtering software can be configured to restrict access based on content, time, computer user or other customized basis (American Civil Liberties Union v. Gonzales, 2007, pp. 789-96). The software should be configured to block student access of non-school-sponsored or non-school-sanctioned speech. School officials should have students and their parents sign acceptable use policies that clearly limit student use of school computers and wireless networks to school-sponsored and school-sanctioned speech. School officials should notify students that communications on school computers and wireless networks are neither private nor confidential. They should also inform students that communications on school computers and wireless networks constitute school records and will be subject to monitoring. Pop-up screens should reiterate these notices when students log on to school computers or wireless networks, with students required to click an "OK" button consenting to the terms of the notices before they are allowed to use or access school computers or wireless networks.

School officials should provide students with several school-sponsored and school-sanctioned outlets to express their views and concerns safely so that they do not feel the need to resort to non-school-sponsored or non-school-sanctioned speech. School officials should also implement policies that restrict when students can possess or use personal electronic devices on school grounds. These policies could ban all student possession of electronic devices on school grounds or restrict possession to certain areas of the school or times during the school day. Alternatively, the policies could allow possession of electronic devices but ban or restrict student use of those devices. For policies regulating possession or use, it is important to make an exception for emergencies as students might sometimes need to communicate with their families if there is an emergency. Students should be informed of the legal and school consequences of inappropriate uses of electronic devices. The faculty and administrators should be educated on the First Amendment rights of students and on school policies governing student speech so that they can make wise and constitutional decisions when confronted with student speech. School officials should not wait until they are sued and found liable, or forced to waste taxpayer funds paying settlements or damages, before they begin implementing changes designed to avoid overreaching into protected off-campus speech.

In September 2013, California became a national trailblazer in the protection of students in online settings when Governor Jerry Brown signed into law the Erase Bill. The law which became effective January 1, 2015, empowers residents under eighteen years old to delete their own online communications unless one of the following is satisfied:

1. The website operator makes the communication anonymous;
2. The communication was posted by a third party;
3. Federal or state law mandates the website operator to retain the communication;
4. The minor was paid to post the communication; or
5. The minor failed to comply with the website operator's directions for deleting the communication (West's Annotated California Business and Professions Code § 22581, 2015).

Under this law, operators of digital platforms must allow their minor users to remove or request the removal of the user's postings. They must also notify minor users of this right to erase digital footprints and provide clear directions to minors on how to exercise this right. Furthermore, operators of digital platforms must make it clear to minors that, even if they delete their postings, those postings do not necessarily entirely disappear. We would encourage students to take advantage of this law to delete any of their postings that could trigger school censorship. While this law is a step in the right direction, its protective scope is limited because minors have no right to delete or request deletion of postings made by third parties. Even though concededly the free exchange of ideas online is important, students should be empowered to delete abusive postings by other users. When abusive messages are posted in off-campus settings, the targeted students, rather than school officials, should be authorized to delete or request deletion of the postings. Just like adults cannot simply delete the postings of other adults, school officials as adults should not be allowed to delete student speech simply because they find it critical.

If school officials insist on censoring off-campus student speech, students might find refuge in the new mobile photo-sharing application Snapchat. "Snapchat is a mobile app which lets users share images or videos that disappear after a few seconds ... they vanish forever in the time it takes you to read a tweet" (Gross, 2013). This application which boasts millions of users provides a detailed tutorial for creating and posting snaps as well as stories (Snapchat, 2014). In June, 2014, Apple announced that it would also start offering disappearing text messages and pictures to users of its iMessage application in order to compete with Snapchat (Whitehouse, 2014). Also in 2014, Facebook founder Mark Zuckerberg purchased WhatsApp – another application that allows users to send disappearing pictures and text messages (Whitehouse, 2014). These forums might be the new trend for students to explore since they leave no records of the off-campus speech for schools to use in censorship. Students should, however, exercise prudence in using Snapchat, iMessage and WhatsApp. They should not regard the opportunity to use these new applications as a license to abuse speech. Schools should also teach students about the civil use of Snapchat, iMessage and WhatsApp without any design on off-campus speech censorship.

CONCLUSION

The United States Court of Appeals for the Second Circuit once stated that "our willingness to grant school officials substantial autonomy within their academic domain rests in part on the confinement of that power within the metes and bounds of the school itself" (Thomas v. Board of Education, Granville Central School District, 1979, p. 1052). This is an important statement because it restricts school authority to the confines of the school. Courts must make this statement an axiom and mantra of the student-speech jurisprudence in order to reverse the ongoing enervation of students' off-campus First Amendment free speech rights. Students already sacrifice their free speech rights within the schoolhouse gate; they should not have to do the same outside the schoolhouse gate. School officials should recognize and appreciate this sacrifice which enables them substantial autonomy inside the schoolhouse gate. They should cease abusing this sacrifice through expansive censorship outside the schoolhouse gate that sometimes even reaches into students' homes. If school officials will not do this on their own, courts must rein them in. The judiciary must make it clear to school officials that their substantial autonomy inside the schoolhouse gate is conditional on keeping that authority inside the borders of the school. If the lower courts will not do it, the United States Supreme Court must rein in the lower courts.

REFERENCES

Abrams v. United States (1919). 250 U.S. 616.

American Civil Liberties Union v. Gonzales (2007). 478 F.Supp.2d 775.

Baumgartner v. United States (1944). 322 U.S. 665.

Bethel School District No. 403 v. Fraser (1986). 478 U.S. 675.

Calvert, C. (2001). Off-campus speech, on-campus punishment: Censorship of the emerging internet underground. *Boston University Journal of Science and Technology Law, 7*, 243–287.

Caplan, A. H. (2003). Public school discipline for creating uncensored anonymous internet forums. *Willamette Law Review, 39*, 93–194.

Citron, D. K. (2009). Cyber civil rights. *Boston University Law Review. Boston University. School of Law, 89*, 61–125.

Cohen v. California (1971). 403 U.S. 15.

D.G. vs. Independent School District No. 11 of Tulsa County, Oklahoma (2000). 2000 U.S. Dist. LEXIS 12197 *1-15.

Efrati (2008). Subpoenas allowed in autoadmit suit. *The Wall Street Journal Law Blog Times*. Retrieved May 24, 2014, from http://blogs.wsj.com/law/2008/01/30/subpoena-allowed-in-autoadmit-suit/

Garfield, A. E. (2005). Protecting children from speech. *Florida Law Review*, *57*, 565–651.

Gross, D. (2013). Snapchat: Sexting tool, or the next Instagram? *CNN*. Retrieved May 24, 2014, from http://www.cnn.com/2013/01/03/tech/mobile/snapchat/index.html

Hazelwood v. Kuhlmeier (1988). 484 U.S. 260.

Heins, M. (2001). *Not in front of the children: "Indecency," censorship, and the innocence of youth*. New York: Hill and Wang.

Hils, L. (2001). "Zero tolerance" for free speech. *Journal of Law and Education*, *30*, 365–373.

Klein v. Smith (1986). 635 F. Supp. 1440.

Layshock ex rel. Layshock v. Hermitage School District (2011). 650 F.3d 205.

Lewin, T. (1998, March 8). Schools challenge students' internet talk. *NY Times*. Retrieved May 12, 2014, from http://www.nytimes.com/1998/03/08/us/schools-challenge-students-internet-talk.html

Li, S. (2005). The need for a new, uniform standard: The continued threat to internet-related student speech. *Loyola of Los Angeles Entertainment Law Review*, *26*, 65–106.

Macgill, A. (2007). *Parent and teen internet use*. Pew Internet & American Life Project. Washington, DC: Pew Research Center. Retrieved May 18, 2014, from http://www.pewinternet.org/files/old-media//Files/Reports/2007/PIP_Teen_Parents_data_memo_Oct2007.pdf.pdf

Morse v. Frederick (2007). 551 U.S. 393.

New Jersey Statutes Annotated § 18A:17-46 (West 2011).

Papandrea, M. (2008). Student speech rights in the digital age. *Florida Law Review*, *60*, 1027–1102.

Poling v. Murphy (1989). 872 F.2d 757.

Qasir, S. (2013). Anonymity in cyberspace: Judicial and legislative regulations. *Fordham Law Review*, *81*, 3652–3691.

Shanley v. Northeast Independent School District (1972). 462 F.2d 960.

Smolla, R. (1992). *Free speech in an open society*. New York: Alfred A. Knopf.

Snapchat. (2014). Retrieved May 24, 2014, from http://www.snapchat.com/

Stanley v. Georgia (1969). 394 U.S. 557.

Thomas v. Board of Education, Granville Central School District (1979). 607 F.2d 1043, 1057.

Tinker v. Des Moines Independent Community School District (1969). 393 U.S. 503.

Tuneski. (2003). Online, not on grounds: Protecting student internet speech. *Virginia Law Review*, *89*, 139-87.

United States v. Playboy Entertainment Group, Inc. (2000). 529 U.S. 803.

West Virginia State Board of Education v. Barnette (1943). 319 U.S. 624.

West's Annotated California Business and Professions Code § 22581 (2015).

Whitehouse, K. (1998, March 8). Apple is taking on rival Snapchat with disappearing messages. *NY Post*. Retrieved June 4, 2014, from http://nypost.com/2014/06/02/apple-is-taking-on-rival-snapchat-with-disappearing-messages/

KEY TERMS AND DEFINITIONS

Bethel **Test:** This is the test the United States Supreme Court created in Bethel School District No. 403 v. Fraser (1986) that authorizes school officials to censor student speech that is vulgar, lewd, plainly offensive or obscene.

Erase Bill: A California law which requires website operators to allow minors to delete their own postings on websites. The law became effective January 1, 2015.

Hazelwood **Test:** This is the test the United States Supreme Court created in Hazelwood v. Kuhlmeier (1988) that authorizes school officials to censor student speech that is sponsored by the school as long as the censorship has a legitimate pedagogical purpose. The test is also sometimes referred to as the *Kuhlmeier* test.

Infringement-of-Rights Test: The judicial standard that conditions censorship of student speech on whether the speech impinges the rights of other students.

Jurisprudence: The body of case law governing a particular area of American life.

Material and Substantial Disruption Test: The judicial standard that conditions censorship of student speech on whether the speech is reasonably foreseeable to cause or actually caused material and substantial disruption to the school.

Morse **Test:** This is the test the United States Supreme Court created in Morse v. Frederick (2007) that authorizes school officials to censor student speech that advocates illegal drug use.

Off-Campus: Any locale outside the borders or premises of a school.

On-Campus: Any area inside the school or on school premises.

True Threat: Speech that expresses a genuine intent to cause harm.

Compilation of References

105 Illinois Compiled Statutes Annotated 5/27-13.3(c) (West 2009).

70 Oklahoma Statutes Annotated § 24-100.4(A)(1) (West 2013).

70 Oklahoma Statutes Annotated § 24-100.4(C) (West 2013).

A Book Named "John Cleland's Memoirs of a Woman of Pleasure" v. Attorney General of Massachusetts (1966). 383 U.S. 413.

Abrams v. United States (1919). 250 U.S. 616, 630.

Abrams v. United States (1919). 250 U.S. 616.

Administrative Office of the United States Courts. (2013). United States Courts: Court Locator. *Administrative Office of the United States Courts*. Retrieved December 18, 2013, from http://www.uscourts.gov/court_locator.aspx

American Amusement Machine Association v. Kendrick (2001). 244 F.3d 572.

American Civil Liberties Union v. Gonzales (2007). 478 F.Supp.2d 775.

Arkansas Code Annotated § 5-71-217 (West 2013).

Arkansas Code Annotated § 6-18-514 (West 2013).

Ashcroft v. Free Speech Coalition (2002). 535 U.S. 234.

Baker v. Downey City Board of Education (1969). 307 F.Supp. 517.

Barnett ex rel. Barnett v. Tipton County Board of Education (2009). 601 F.Supp.2d 980, 983.

Barnett ex rel. Barnett v. Tipton County Board of Education (2009). 601 F.Supp.2d 980.

Baumgartner v. United States (1944). 322 U.S. 665.

Beidler v. North Thurston School District (2000). No. 99-2-00236-6.

Bell v. Itawamba County School Board (2012). 859 F.Supp.2d 834.

Bethel School District No. 403 v. Fraser (1986). 478 U.S. 675

Bethel School District No. 403 v. Fraser (1986). 478 U.S. 675, 682.

Bethel School District No. 403 v. Fraser (1986). 478 U.S. 675.

Beussink v. Woodland R-IV School District (1998). 30 F. Supp. 2d 1175.

Compilation of References

Beussink v. Woodland R-IV School District (1998). 30 F.Supp. 2d 1175.

Board of Education of Westside Community School v. Mergens (1990). 496 U.S. 226, 250.

Board of Education v. Pico (1982). 457 U.S. 853.

Board of Education, Island Trees Union Free School District No. 26 v. Pico (1982). 457 U.S. 853.

Board of School Trustees of the Muncie Community School v. Barnell (1997). 678 N.E.2d 799, 802.

Boim v. Fulton County School District (2007). 494 F.3d 978.

Borkoski, K. (2013). Tinker v. Des Moines Independent Community School District: Kelly Shackelford on symbolic speech. *SCOTUSblog*. Retrieved December 22, 2013, from http://www.scotusblog.com/2013/11/tinker-v-des-moines-independent-community-school-district-kelly-shackelford-on-symbolic-speech/

Bosco, J., & Krueger, K. (2011). *Moving from "acceptable" to "responsible" use in a Web 2.0 world*. Retrieved July 14, 2014 from http://www.edweek.org/ew/articles/2011/07/20/37bosco.h30.html

Boucher v. School Board of School District of Greenfield (1998). 134 F.3d 821.

Brandenburg v. Ohio (1969). 395 U.S. 444.

Brenton, K. W. (2008). Bonghits4jesus.com? Scrutinizing public school authority over student cyberspeech through the lens of personal jurisdiction. *Minnesota Law Review*, *92*, 1206–1245.

Broadrick v. Oklahoma (1973). 413 U.S. 601.

Burch v. Barker (1988). 861 F.2d 1149.

Burke, M. (2011). Cracks in the armor?: The future of the Communications Decency Act and potential challenges to the protections of Section 230 to gossip web sites. *Boston University Journal of Science and Technology Law*, *17*, 232–257.

Bush By and Through Bush v. Dassel-Cokato Board of Education (1990). 745 F.Supp. 562.

Bystrom By and Through Bystrom v. Fridley High School (1987). 686 F.Supp. 1387.

C.R. ex rel. Rainville v. Eugene School District 4J (2013). 2013 WL 5102848.

California Code § 48900.4 (West 2003).

Calvert, C. (2001). Off-campus speech, on-campus punishment: Censorship of the emerging internet underground. *Boston University Journal of Science and Technology Law*, *7*, 243–287.

Calvert, C. (2010). Fighting words in the era of texts, IM's and e-mails: Can a disparaged doctrine be resuscitated to punish cyber-bullies? *DePaul Journal of Art, Technology, and Intellectual Property Law*, *21*, 1–48.

Caplan, A. H. (2003). Public school discipline for creating uncensored anonymous internet forums. *Willamette Law Review*, *39*, 93–194.

Carvin, A. (2006). *Is MySpace your space as well?* Retrieved December 12, 2013, from http://www.pbs.org/teachers/learning.now/2006/10/is_myspace_your_space_as_well.html

Centers for Disease Control and Prevention. (2006). Youth risk behavior surveillance—United States, 2005: Surveillance summaries (No. SS-5). *Morbidity and Mortality Weekly Report*, *55*, 19. Retrieved from http://www.cdc.gov/mmwr/PDF/SS/ss5505.pdf

Centers for Disease Control and Prevention. (2012). Understanding school violence: Fact sheet. *CDC*. Retrieved November 29, 2013, from http://www.cdc.gov/ViolencePrevention/pdf/SchoolViolence_FactSheet-a.pdf

Chaplin, H. (2012). *Welcoming mobile: More districts are rewriting acceptable use policies, embracing smartphones and social media in schools*. Retrieved July 14, 2014 from http://spotlight.macfound.org/featured-stories/entry/welcoming-mobile-rewriting-acceptable-use-smartphones-and-social-media

Chaplinsky v. New Hampshire (1942). 315 U.S. 568, 572.

Chaplinsky v. New Hampshire (1942). 315 U.S. 568.

Children's Internet Protection Act, 42 U.S.C. §§ 254(h)(5)(b), (l) (2014).

Citron, D. K. (2009). Cyber civil rights. *Boston University Law Review. Boston University. School of Law*, *89*, 61–125.

City of Houston v. Hill (1987). 482 U.S. 450.

Clements by Clements v. Board of Education of Decatur Public School District No. 61 (1985). 478 N.E.2d 1209.

CNN. (2012, March 10). Minnesota girl alleges school privacy invasion. *CNN*. Retrieved November 29, 2013, from http://www.cnn.com/2012/03/10/us/minnesota-student-privacy/index.html

Cohen v. California (1971). 403 U.S. 15.

Cohen v. California (1971). 403 U.S. 16.

Communications Decency Act of 1996, Section 230(c)(1) (2014).

Consortium for School Networking. (2012). *Making progress: Rethinking state and school district policies concerning mobile technologies and social media*. Retrieved July 14, 2014 from http://www.splc.org/pdf/making_progress_2012.pdf

Cooper v. McJunkin (1853) 4 Ind. 290, 291.

Cornelius v. NAACP Legal Defense and Educational Fund, Inc. (1985). 473 U.S. 788, 802.

Cornelius v. NAACP Legal Defense and Educational Fund, Inc. (1985). 473 U.S. 788, 806.

Coy ex rel. Coy v. Board of Education of North Canton City Schools (2002). 205 F.Supp.2d 791.

Crowther, J. (Ed.). (2005). No Fear Macbeth. *SparkNotes*. Retrieved January 5, 2014, from http://nfs.sparknotes.com/macbeth/page_202.html

Cukor, G., & Fleming, V. (Directors). (1939). *Gone with the wind*. [Motion Picture]. United States: Warner Bros.

Curtis Publishing Co. v. Butts (1967). 388 U.S. 130.

D.G. v. Independent School District No. 11 of Tulsa County, Oklahoma (2000). 2000 U.S. Dist. LEXIS 12197 *1-15.

D.G. vs. Independent School District No. 11 of Tulsa County, Oklahoma (2000). 2000 U.S. Dist. LEXIS 12197 *1-15.

D.J.M. ex rel. D.M. v. Hannibal Public School District No. 60 (2011). 647 F.3d 754, 759.

D.J.M. ex rel. D.M. v. Hannibal Public School District No. 60 (2011). 647 F.3d 754.

Denning, B. P., & Taylor, M. C. (2008). Morse v. Frederick and the regulation of student cyberspeech. *Hastings Constitutional Law Quarterly*, *35*, 835–896.

Doe v. Pulaski County Special School District (2002). 306 F.3d 616.

Compilation of References

Doninger v. Niehoff (2007). 514 F.Supp.2d 199.

Doninger v. Niehoff (2008). 527 F.3d 41.

Doninger v. Niehoff (2009). 594 F.Supp.2d 211 (affirmed in part, reversed in part on other grounds by Doninger v. Niehoff (2011) 642 F.3d 334).

Doninger v. Niehoff (2011). 642 F.3d 334, 347.

Donovan v. Ritchie (1995). 68 F.3d 14.

Draker v. Schreiber (2008). 271 S.W.3d 318.

Dritt v. Snodgrass (1877). 66 Mo. 286.

Education World. (n.d.). *Getting started on the internet: Developing an acceptable use policy (AUP)*. Retrieved July 14, 2014 from http://www.educationworld.com/a_curr/curr093.shtml

Efrati (2008). Subpoenas allowed in autoadmit suit. *The Wall Street Journal Law Blog Times*. Retrieved May 24, 2014, from http://blogs.wsj.com/law/2008/01/30/subpoena-allowed-in-autoadmit-suit/

Elonis v. United States (2015). 135 S.Ct. 2001.

Elrod v. Burns (1976). 427 U.S. 347, 373.

Emerson, G. B., & Potter, A. (1843). *The School and the Schoolmaster: A Manual*. New York: Harper & Brothers Publishers.

Emerson, T. I. (1970). *The System of Freedom of Expression*. New York: Random House.

Emmett v. Kent School District No. 415 (2000). 92 F.Supp.2d 1088.

Emrick, T. (2009). When Myspace crosses the school gates: The implications of cyberspeech on students' free-speech rights. *University of Toledo Law Review. University of Toledo. College of Law*, *40*, 785–818.

Engel v. Vitale (1962). 370 U.S. 421.

Epperson v. Arkansas (1968). 393 U.S. 97, 104.

Erb, T. D. (2008). A case for strengthening school district jurisdiction to punish off-campus incidents of cyberbullying. *Arizona State Law Journal*, *40*, 257–287.

Evans v. Bayer (2010). 684 F. Supp. 2d 1365, 1368, 1371–72.

Evans v. Bayer (2010). 684 F. Supp. 2d 1365.

Federal Communications Commission v. Pacifica Foundation (1978). 438 U.S. 726.

Federal Communications Commission. (2013). *Children's Internet Protection Act (CIPA)*. Retrieved July 14, 2014 from http://transition.fcc.gov/cgb/consumerfacts/cipa.pdf

Felton v. Fayette School District (1989). 875 F.2d 191.

Fenton v. Stear (1976). 423 F. Supp. 767.

Flaherty v. Keystone Oaks School District (2003). 247 F.Supp.2d 698.

Florida Statutes Annotated § 1006.147 (West 2013).

Frederick v. Morse (2006). 439 F.3d 1114.

Frederick, D. D. (2007). Restricting student speech that invades others' rights: A novel interpretation of student speech jurisprudence in Harper v. Poway Unified School District. *University of Hawaii Law Review, 29*, 479-500.

Garfield, A. E. (2005). Protecting children from speech. *Florida Law Review, 57*, 565–651.

Garrison v. Louisiana (1964). 379 U.S. 64.

Gay, Lesbian & Straight Education Network (2013). Info + Resources. *Glsen Day of Silence*. Retrieved December 27, 2013, from http://www.dayofsilence.org/resources/

Gertz v. Robert Welch, Inc. (1974). 418 U.S. 323.

Ginsberg v. New York (1968). 390 U.S. 629, 639.

Ginsberg v. New York (1968). 390 U.S. 629.

Ginsberg v. United States (1968). 390 U.S. 629.

Gitlow v. New York (1925). 268 U.S. 652.

Gooding v. Wilson (1972). 405 U.S. 518.

Gross, D. (2013). Snapchat: Sexting tool, or the next Instagram? *CNN*. Retrieved May 24, 2014, from http://www.cnn.com/2013/01/03/tech/mobile/snapchat/index.html

Harpaz, L. (2000). Internet speech and the First Amendment rights of public school students. *Brigham Young University Education and Law Journal, 123*, 142–143.

Harper ex rel. Harper v. Poway Unified School District (2007). 549 U.S. 1262.

Harper v. Poway Unified School District (2006). 445 F.3d 1166 (vacated by Harper ex rel. Harper v. Poway Unified School District (2007), 549 U.S. 1262 and dismissed as moot in Harper ex rel. Harper v. Poway Unified School District (2007), 485 F.3d 1052).

Harvard Law Review Association. (2007). Recent Cases: Constitutional Law—Freedom of Speech—Ninth Circuit Upholds Public School's Prohibition of Anti-Gay T-Shirts – Harper v. Poway Unified School District. *Harvard Law Review, 120*(1691), 1694-95.

Hatter v. Los Angeles City High School District (1971). 452 F.2d 673.

Hazelwood v. Kuhlmeier (1988). 484 U.S. 260, 265-66, 271-73, 289.

Hazelwood v. Kuhlmeier (1988). 484 U.S. 260.

Hedges v. Wauconda Community Unit No. 118 (1993). 9 F.3d 1295, 1299.

Heins, M. (2001). *Not in front of the children: "Indecency," censorship, and the innocence of youth*. New York: Hill and Wang.

Hils, L. (2001). "Zero tolerance" for free speech. *Journal of Law and Education, 30*, 365–373.

Hobbs v. Germany (1909). 49 So. 515.

Holloman ex rel. Holloman v. Harland (2004). 370 F.3d 1252.

Compilation of References

Hudson, D. (2001). Matthew Fraser speaks out on 15-year-old Supreme Court free-speech decision. *First Amendment Center*. Retrieved January 5, 2014, from http://www.firstamendmentcenter.org/matthew-fraser-speaks-out-on-15-year-old-supreme-court-free-speech-decision

Hudson, D. L., Jr. (2002). Underground papers and off-campus speech. *First Amendment Center*. Retrieved November 29, 2013, from http://www.firstamendmentcenter.org/underground-papers-off-campus-speech

Hudson, D. L. Jr. (2000). Censorship of student internet speech: The effect of diminishing student rights, fear of the internet and columbine. *Law Review of Michigan State University Detroit College of Law*, *2000*, 199–222.

Hustler Magazine, Inc. v. Falwell (1988). 485 U.S. 46.

I.M.L. v. State (2002). 61 P.3d 1038.

Iowa Code Annotated § 280.28 (West 2007).

J.C. ex rel. R.C. v. Beverly Hills Unified School District (2010). 711 F.Supp.2d 1094, 1108.

J.C. ex rel. R.C. v. Beverly Hills Unified School District (2010). 711 F.Supp.2d 1094.

J.S. ex rel. H.S. v. Bethlehem (2002). 807 A.2d 847, 865.

J.S. ex rel. Snyder v. Blue Mountain School District (2011). 650 F.3d 915.

J.S. v. Bethlehem Area School District (2002). 807 A.2d 847, 857-58.

J.S. v. Bethlehem Area School District (2002). 807 A.2d 847.

Jacobellis v. Ohio (1964). 378 U.S. 184.

K.G.S. v. Kemp (2011). 2011 WL 4635002.

Kansas Statutes Annotated 72-8256 (West 2007).

Katy Independent School District. (2011). *Student responsible use guidelines for technology*. Retrieved July 14, 2014 from http://www.katyisd.org/parents/Documents/Forms%20and%20Guidelines/AcceptableUse.pdf

Keyishian v. Board of Regents (1967). 385 U.S. 589, 603.

Killion v. Franklin Regional School District (2001). 136 F.Supp.2d 446, 449.

Killion v. Franklin Regional School District (2001). 136 F.Supp.2d 446.

Klein v. Smith (1986). 635 F. Supp. 1440.

Klein, R. (2013). California district hires company to monitor students' online activity. *Huffington Post*. Retrieved November 29, 2013, from http://legalclips.nsba.org/2013/08/29/california-district-hires-company-to-monitor-students-online-activity/#sthash.4iCISc7b.dpuf

Kowalski v. Berkeley County Schools (2011). 652 F.3d 565, 573.

Kowalski v. Berkeley County Schools (2011). 652 F.3d 565.

Kuhlmeier v. Hazelwood School District (1986). 795 F.2d 1368.

Lamb's Chapel v. Center Moriches Union Free School District (1993). 508 U.S. 384.

Lander v. Seaver (1859). 32 Vt. 114, 115.

Lander v. Seaver (1859). 32 Vt. 114.

Latour v. Riverside Beaver School District (2005). 2005 WL 2106562.

Lavine v. Blaine School District (2001). 257 F.3d 981.

Layshock ex rel. Layshock v. Hermitage School District (2010). 593 F.3d 249 (rehearing en banc, opinion vacated by Layshock ex rel. Layshock v. Hermitage School District (2010) 650 F.3d 205).

Layshock ex rel. Layshock v. Hermitage School District (2011). 650 F.3d 205, 210.

Layshock ex rel. Layshock v. Hermitage School District (2011). 650 F.3d 205.

Layshock v. Hermitage School District (2007). 496 F.Supp.2d 587.

Lewin, T. (1998, March 8). Schools challenge students' internet talk. *NY Times*. Retrieved May 12, 2014, from http://www.nytimes.com/1998/03/08/us/schools-challenge-students-internet-talk.html

Lewis v. City of New Orleans (1974). 415 U.S. 123.

Li, S. (2005). The need for a new, uniform standard: The continued threat to internet-related student speech. *Loyola of Los Angeles Entertainment Law Review, 26*, 65–106.

Louisiana Administrative Code tit. 28, pt. CXV, § 1303 (West 2013).

Louisiana Statutes Annotated-Revised Statutes § 14:40.7 (West 2010).

Louisiana Statutes Annotated-Revised Statutes § 17:416.13(E) (West 2013).

Lovell By and Through Lovell v. Poway Unified School District (1996). 90 F.3d 367.

Macgill, A. (2007). *Parent and teen internet use*. Pew Internet & American Life Project. Washington, DC: Pew Research Center. Retrieved May 18, 2014, from http://www.pewinternet.org/files/old-media//Files/Reports/2007/PIP_Teen_Parents_data_memo_Oct2007.pdf.pdf

Madden, M., et al. (2013). *Teens, Social Media, and Privacy*. Pew Internet and American Life Project. Washington, DC: Pew Research Center. Retrieved November 29, 2013, from pewinternet.org/~/media//Files/Reports/2013/PIP_TeensSocialMediaandPrivacy.pdf.

Mahaffey ex rel. Mahaffey v. Aldrich (2002). 236 F.Supp.2d 779, 785.

Mahaffey ex rel. Mahaffey v. Aldrich (2002). 236 F.Supp.2d 779.

Massachusetts General Laws Annotated 71 § 37O (West 2014).

McKinney's Education Law § 11(7) (West 2013).

McKinney's Education Law § 12 (West 2013).

Miller v. California (1973). 413 U.S. 15.

Mississippi Code Annotated § 37-11-67 (West 2010).

Morse v. Frederick (2007). 551 U.S. 393.

Moss, S. A. (2011). The overhyped path from Tinker to Morse: How the student speech cases show the limits of Supreme Court decisions–for the law and for the litigants. *Florida Law Review, 63*, 1407–1457.

Compilation of References

NAACP v. Claiborne Hardware Company (1982). 458 U.S. 886.

National Conference of State Legislatures. (2014). *Laws relating to filtering, blocking and usage policies in schools and libraries.* Retrieved July 14, 2014 from http://www.ncsl.org/research/telecommunications-and-information-technology/state-internet-filtering-laws.aspx

National School Boards Association. (2012a). Indiana legislature considers proposal that would allow schools to discipline students for off-campus behavior, including online speech. *Legal Clips.* Retrieved November 29, 2013, from http://legalclips.nsba.org/2012/02/08/indiana-legislature-considers-proposal-that-would-allow-schools-to-discipline-students-for-off-campus-behavior-including-online-speech/#sthash.Lt2bSJtr.dpuf

National School Boards Association. (2012b). Supreme Court declines to hear student internet speech cases. *Legal Clips.* Retrieved November 29, 2013, from http://legalclips.nsba.org/2012/01/19/breaking-news-supreme-court-denies-cert-in-student-internet-speech-cases/

Neal et al. v. Efurd (2005). No. 04-2195.

Nevada Revised Statutes Annotated 200.900 (West 2013).

Nevada Revised Statutes Annotated 388.122 (West 2013).

New Jersey Administrative Code 6A:16-7.7 (West 2014).

New Jersey Statutes Annotated § 18A:17-46 (West 2011).

New Jersey Statutes Annotated § 18A:37-14 (West 2011).

New Jersey Statutes Annotated § 18A:37-15 (West 2011).

New Jersey Statutes Annotated § 18A:37-16 (West 2011).

New Jersey Statutes Annotated § 18A:37-17 (West 2011).

New Jersey Statutes Annotated § 18A:37-2(k) (West 2011).

New Jersey Statutes Annotated § 18A:37-21 (West 2011).

New Jersey Statutes Annotated § 18A:37-29 (West 2011).

New Jersey v. T.L.O. (1985). 469 U.S. 325.

New York Times Co. v. Sullivan (1964). 376 U.S. 254.

New York Times v. Sullivan (1964). 376 U.S. 254.

New York v. Ferber (1982). 458 U.S. 747.

Nixon v. Northern Local School District Board of Education (2005). 383 F.Supp.2d 965.

North Carolina General Statutes Annotated § 115C-407.15 (West 2009).

Nuxoll ex rel. Nuxoll v. Indian Prairie School District #204 (2008). 523 F.3d 668.

O.Z. v. Board of Trustees of Long Beach Unified School District (2008). 2008 WL 4396895.

O'toole, M. E., ... (1999). The School Shooter: A Threat Assessment Perspective. *Federal Bureau of Investigation Office of the Attorney General.* Retrieved November 29, 2013, from http://www.fbi.gov/stats-services/publications/school-shooter

Ohio Revised Code Annotated § 2907.01 (West 2002).

Oklahoma Administrative Code 210:10-1-20(b)(5) (West 2013).

Oluwole, J., Green, P., & Stackpole, M. (2013). *SextEd: Obscenity versus free speech in our schools*. Santa Barbara, CA: Praeger Publishers.

Osborne v. Ohio (1990). 495 U.S. 103.

Pangle v. Bend-Lapine School District (2000). 10 P.3d 275.

Papandrea, M. (2008). Student speech rights in the digital age. *Florida Law Review, 60*, 1027–1102.

Parents, Families and Friends of Lesbians and Gays, Inc. v. Camdenton R-III School District (2012). 853 F.Supp.2d 888.

Perry Education Association v. Perry Local Educators' Association (1983). 460 U.S. 37.

Pike, K. R. (2008). Locating the mislaid gate: Revitalizing tinker by repairing judicial overgeneralizations of technologically enabled student speech. *Brigham Young University Law Review, 2008*, 990.

Pisciotta, L.M. (2000). Beyond sticks & stones: A First Amendment framework for educators who seek to punish student threats. *Seton Hall Law Review, 30*, 635, 662.

Pisciotta, L. M. (2000). Beyond sticks & stones: A First Amendment framework for educators who seek to punish student threats. *Seton Hall Law Review, 30*, 635–670.

Pisciotta, L. M. (2000). Beyond sticks and stones: A First Amendment framework for educators who seek to punish student threats. *Seton Hall Law Review, 30*, 635–670.

Planned Parenthood Association v. Chicago Transit Authority (1985). 767 F.2d 1225, 1229.

Planned Parenthood of the Columbia/Willamette, Inc. v. American Coalition of Life Activists (2002). 290 F.3d 1058, 1075.

Poling v. Murphy (1989). 872 F.2d 757.

Ponce v. Socorro Independent School District (2007). 508 F.3d 765.

Popkin, A. S. H. (2013, October 6). Careful what you tweet: Police, schools tap social media to track behavior. *NBC News*. Retrieved November 29, 2013, from http://www.nbcnews.com/technology/careful-what-you-tweet-police-schools-tap-social-media-track-4B11215908

Porter ex rel. LeBlanc v. Ascension Parish School Board (2004). 301 F.Supp.2d 576.

Porter v. Ascension Parish School Board (2004). 393 F.3d 608.

Qasir, S. (2013). Anonymity in cyberspace: Judicial and legislative regulations. *Fordham Law Review, 81*, 3652–3691.

R. R. v. Board of Education of the Shore Regional High School District (1970). 263 A.2d 180.

R.A.V. v. City of St. Paul (1992). 505 U.S. 377.

R.A.V. v. City of St. Paul, Minnesota (1992). 505 U.S. 377, 382–90.

R.A.V. v. City of St. Paul, Minnesota (1992). 505 U.S. 377.

R.S. ex rel. S.S. v. Minnewaska Area School District No. 2149 (2012). 894 F.Supp.2d 1128.

Regina v. Hicklin (1868). L.R. 3 Q.B. 360.

Compilation of References

Reno v. American Civil Liberties Union (1997). 521 U.S. 844.

Requa v. Kent School District No. 415 (2007). 492 F.Supp.2d 1272, 1275, 1282.

Requa v. Kent School District No. 415 (2007). 492 F.Supp.2d 1272.

Retzlaff v. de la Viña (2009). 606 F.Supp.2d 654.

Riggan v. Midland Independent School District (2000). 86 F.Supp.2d 647, 656.

Riggan v. Midland Independent School District (2000). 86 F.Supp.2d 647.

Roasio v. Clark County School District (2013). 2013 WL 3679375.

Roberts, C. E. (2008). Is Myspace their space? Protecting student cyberspeech in a post-Morse v. Frederick world. *UMKC Law Review*, *76*, 1177–1192.

Roberts, C. E. (2008). Is Myspace their space?: Protecting student cyberspeech in a post-Morse v. Frederick world. *UMKC Law Review*, *76*, 1177–1192.

Rogers, T. (n.d.). Faculty advisers increasingly face the ax for not censoring high school papers. *About.com*. Retrieved December 7, 2013, from http://journalism.about.com/od/schoolsinternships/a/studentcensorship.htm

Rosenberger v. Rector and Visitors of University of Virginia (1995). 515 U.S. 819.

Rosenbloom v. Metromedia, Inc. (1971). 403 U.S. 29.

Roth v. United States (1957). 354 U.S. 476.

Rothman, J. E. (2001). Freedom of speech and true threats. *Harvard Journal of Law & Public Policy*, *25*, 283–367.

Roy v. United States (1969). 416 F.2d 874, 877-78.

Russo, C. J. (2006). Legal research: The "traditional" method. In S. Permuth & R. D. Mawdsley (Eds.), *Research methods for studying legal issues in education* (pp. 5–24). Dayton, OH: Education Law Association.

S.J.W. v. Lee's Summit R–7 School District (2012). 696 F.3d 771.

Salgado, R. (2005). Protecting student speech rights while increasing school safety: School jurisdiction and the search for warning signs in a post-Columbine/Red Lake environment. *Brigham Young University Law Review*, *2005*, 1371–1414.

Saxe v. State College Area School District (2001). 240 F.3d 200, 217.

Saxe v. State College Area School District (2001). 240 F.3d 200.

Schenck v. United States (1919). 249 U.S. 47, 52.

Schimmel, D., Stellman, L., & Fischer, L. (2010). Teachers and the law (8th ed.). Academic Press.

Schwartz v. Schuker (1969). 298 F.Supp. 238.

Shanley v. Northeast Independent School District (1972). 462 F.2d 960.

Sherrell ex rel. Sherrell v. Northern Community School Corporation of Tipton County (2004). 801 N.E.2d 693.

Simonich, M. (2002, December 2). Newsmaker: Jack Flaherty Jr. / Teen fought school district in court, won. *Pittsburgh Post-Gazette*. Retrieved March 11, 2014, from http://old.post-gazette.com/localnews/20021202newsmakerreg5p5.asp

Slotterback v. Interboro School District (1991). 766 F.Supp. 280, 289.

Smolla, R. (1992). *Free speech in an open society*. New York: Alfred A. Knopf.

Snapchat. (2014). Retrieved May 24, 2014, from http://www.snapchat.com/

South Dakota Codified Laws § 13-32-19 (West 2014).

Stanley v. Georgia (1969). 394 U.S. 557.

State v. Drahota (2011). 788 N.W.2d 796.

State v. Perkins (2001). 626 N.W.2d 762.

State, A.B. v. (2008). 885 N.*E. 2d*1223.

Student Press Law Center. (2001). District pays $62,000 in damages after losing suit filed by student suspended for web site. *SPLC.org*. Retrieved November 29, 2013, from http://www.splc.org/news/report_detail.asp?id=673&edition=18

Sullivan v. Houston Independent School District (1969). 307 F.Supp. 1328.

Sullivan v. Houston Independent School District (1973). 475 F.2d 1071.

Swartz, J. K. (2000). Beyond the schoolhouse gates: Do students shed their constitutional rights when communicating to a cyber-audience? *Drake Law Review*, *48*, 587–604.

T.V. ex rel. B.V. v. Smith-Green Community School Corporation (2011). 807 F.Supp.2d 767, 773-74.

T.V. ex rel. B.V. v. Smith-Green Community School Corporation (2011). 807 F.Supp.2d 767.

Tennessee Code Annotated § 49-6-4501(3) (West 2011).

Terminiello v. City of Chicago (1948). 337 U.S. 1.

Terminiello v. City of Chicago (1949). 337 U.S. 1.

Texas v. Johnson (1989). 491 U.S. 397.

Thomas v. Board of Education, Granville Central School District (1979). 607 F.2d 1043, 1057.

Thomas v. Board of Education, Granville Central School District (1979). 607 F.2d 1043.

Thomas v. Collins (1945). 323 U.S. 516, 545.

Tinker v. Des Moines Independent Community School District (1969). 393 U.S. 503.

Tuneski (2003). Online, not on grounds: Protecting student internet speech. *Virginia Law Review*, *89*, 139-87.

Tuneski (2003). Online, not on grounds: Protecting student internet speech. *Virginia Law Review*, *89*, 139–87.

Tuneski. (2003). Online, not on grounds: Protecting student internet speech. *Virginia Law Review*, *89*, 139-87.

Turner Broadcasting System Inc. v. Federal Communications Commission (1994). 512 U.S. 622, 642.

United States Constitution Amendment I. (n.d.). Retrieved online May 1, 2015, from https://www.law.cornell.edu/constitution/overview

United States Constitution Amendment XIV. (n.d.). Retrieved online May 1, 2015, from https://www.law.cornell.edu/constitution/overview

United States v. Adams (1999). 73 F. Supp. 2d 2, 3.

Compilation of References

United States v. American Library Association (2003). 539 U.S. 194.

United States v. Callahan (1983). 702 F.2d 964, 965.

United States v. Cassel (2005). 408 F.3d 622, 633.

United States v. Daugenbaugh (1995). 49 F.3d 171, 173-74.

United States v. Dinwiddie (1996). 76 F.3d 913, 925.

United States v. Elonis (2013). 730 F.3d 321.

United States v. Fulmer (1997). 108 F.3d 1486.

United States v. Glover (1988). 846 F.2d 339, 344.

United States v. Hart (2000). 212 F.3d 1067, 1071.

United States v. J.H.H. (1994). 22 F.3d 821, 827-28.

United States v. J.H.H. (1994). 22 F.3d 821.

United States v. Kelner (1976). 534 F.2d 1020, 1027.

United States v. Khorrami (1990). 895 F.2d 1186, 1192.

United States v. Lincoln (1972). 462 F.2d 1368.

United States v. Lineberry (2001). 7 Fed.Appx. 520.

United States v. Malik (1994). 16 F.3d 45, 49.

United States v. Orozco–Santillan (1990). 903 F.2d 1262, 1265.

United States v. Orozco-Santillan (1990). 903 F.2d 1262.

United States v. Orozco–Santillan (1990). 903 F.2d 1262.

United States v. Playboy Entertainment Group, Inc. (2000). 529 U.S. 803.

United States v. Roberts (1990). 915 F.2d 889, 891.

United States v. Schneider (1990). 910 F.2d 1569, 1570.

United States v. Viefhaus (1999). 168 F.3d 392, 396.

Utah Code Annotated 1953 § 53A-11a-201 (West 2011).

Verga, R. J. (2007). Policing their space: The First Amendment parameters of school discipline of student cyberspeech. *Santa Clara Computer and High-Technology Law Journal, 23*, 727–748.

Vernonia School Dist. 47J v. Acton (1995). 515 U.S. 646.

Virginia Code Annotated § 22.1-276.01(A) (West 2014).

Virginia Department of Education. (2012). *Acceptable use internet policy*. Retrieved July 14, 2014 from http://www.doe.virginia.gov/support/safety_crisis_management/internet_safety/acceptable_use_policy.shtml

Virginia v. Black (2003). 538 U.S. 343.

Wagner v. Miskin (2003). 660 N.W.2d 593.

Waldman, E. G. (2008). A Post–Morse Framework for Students' Potentially Hurtful Speech (Religious and Otherwise). *Journal of Law and Education, 37*, 463–503.

Waldman, E. G. (2008a). Returning to Hazelwood's core: A new approach to restrictions on school-sponsored speech. *Florida Law Review, 60*, 63–123.

Watts v. United States (1969). 394 U.S. 705.

West Virginia Code, § 18-2C-1 (West 2011).

West Virginia State Board of Education v. Barnette (1943). 319 U.S. 624.

West's Annotated California Business and Professions Code § 22581 (2015).

West, S. R. (2008). Sanctionable conduct: How the Supreme Court stealthily opened the schoolhouse gate. *Lewis and Clark Law Review, 12*, 27–44.

Wheeler, T. E. II. (2004). Slamming in cyberspace: The boundaries of student First Amendment rights. *Res Gestae, 47*, 24–32.

Whitehouse, K. (1998, March 8). Apple is taking on rival Snapchat with disappearing messages. *NY Post*. Retrieved June 4, 2014, from http://nypost.com/2014/06/02/apple-is-taking-on-rival-snapchat-with-disappearing-messages/

Whitney v. California (1927). 274 U.S. 357, 377.

Wisniewski v. Board of Education of the Weedsport Central School District (2007). 494 F.3d 34, 37.

Wisniewski v. Board of Education of the Weedsport Central School District (2007). 494 F.3d 34.

Wynar v. Douglas County School District (2013). 728 F.3d 1062, 1068.

Wynar v. Douglas County School District (2013). 728 F.3d 1062, 1071-72.

Wynar v. Douglas County School District (2013). 728 F.3d 1062.

Zamecnik v. Indian Prairie School District No. 204 (2011). 636 F.3d 874, 877.

Zeran v. American Online, Inc. (1997). 129 F.3d 227.

About the Authors

Joseph O. Oluwole, J.D., Ph.D., is a professor of education law at Montclair State University. His scholarly interests include the constitutional and statutory rights and responsibilities of students, teachers, and public school districts. In addition to being a scholar, he is an attorney-at-law and has served as an Assistant Attorney General for the State of Ohio. Dr. Oluwole has published several articles analyzing laws and policies affecting education and presented at various venues nationally including the University Council for Educational Administration, the Education Law Association, University of Iowa College of Law, Stanford Law School, and the American Education Research Association. He has been recognized in Marquis' Who's Who in America, Marquis' Who's Who in American Law, and Cambridge's Who's Who Registry among Executives and Professionals. He was the 2006 recipient of the Emerging Scholar Award from the American Educational Research Association, Law and Education Special Interest Group.

Preston C. Green III, J.D., Ed.D., is the John and Carla Klein Professor of Urban Education and professor of Educational Leadership and Law at the University of Connecticut. Previously, he was the Harry Lawrence Batschelet II Chair Professor of Educational Administration and Professor of Education and Law at The Pennsylvania State University. He is a foremost national expert on education law whose extensive published works include the following books: *Charter Schools and the Law: Establishing New Legal Relationships*; *The Legal and Policy Implications of Value-Added Teacher Assessment Policies*; *SextEd: Obscenity versus Free Speech in our Schools*; and *Financing Education Systems*. He is the leading authority on charter school law. His expertise has been featured in newspapers and radio. He consistently presents at national forums and provides expert support for cases. Dr. Green holds a juris doctorate from Columbia Law School and an Educational Administration doctorate from Columbia University, Teachers College.

Index

A

Acceptable Use Policies 352, 355, 357-358, 601
anonymous 139, 601
anti-bullying 359-360, 366-367, 375, 379, 382-383, 477, 495, 499
Anti-Bullying Coordinator 367, 382, 499
Anti-Bullying Specialist 366, 382-383

C

Chaplinsky v. New Hampshire 13, 36-37, 91
characteristic 75, 118, 187, 360-361, 378, 382, 423, 454, 456, 492, 500, 515, 569
Child Pornography 13, 55-60, 144, 353, 358
Child Pornography Prevention Act 57
Children's Internet Protection Act 353
Closed Forum 101-103, 354, 358
Closed Public Forum 97, 101-102, 106
Common Law 51, 54
Communications Decency Act (CDA) 44
compelling 40, 43, 56-57, 60, 63, 101, 129, 186, 188, 197, 314, 354
Compelling Interest 40, 43, 56-57, 60, 186, 314, 354
constitutional rights 4, 31, 62, 66-68, 86, 90-91, 103, 114, 121, 141, 193, 197, 205, 238, 242
Contemporary Community Standards 51-52, 54, 60, 96, 200, 257, 302, 351, 358
conviction 37-39, 41, 51-52, 56-57, 90, 144, 238
coordinator 247, 367, 382, 407, 499
Cyberbullying 353, 358, 360, 377, 394, 444, 450, 452, 466, 475, 505

D

Defamation 13, 44-49, 77, 80, 144, 218, 245, 251, 268, 274, 305, 324, 347, 583, 590, 592
defamatory 44, 46-48, 127, 131, 153-154, 158, 217, 244-245, 251, 274, 276, 297, 324, 596, 601
de minimis 168, 218, 234, 244, 248-249, 280-281, 310, 327, 347, 596
De Minimus 56, 60, 127
Dicta 67, 73, 82, 286
distributing 55-56, 58-59, 131, 137, 142, 152, 164
drugs 9, 47, 109, 115, 118-119, 134, 217, 247, 295-296
due process 4, 121, 366, 372, 421

E

Erase Bill 591, 602, 605

F

Facebook 6, 8, 18, 43, 49, 58, 249-251, 258-259, 261-262, 284-286, 302, 310, 358, 600, 602
Ferber 13, 55-58
Fighting Words 13, 36-38, 40-43, 78, 127-128, 130-131, 144, 153, 158-159, 200, 268, 322, 347, 350
fighting-words doctrine 36-42, 123, 198, 217-218, 274, 305, 322, 590, 592
Fighting-Words Jurisprudence 36, 43
filtering 102, 353-355, 601
Fourteenth Amendment 1, 4, 114, 121, 204, 207
Fourth Amendment 114, 121
Free Speech Clause 1, 4, 18, 20, 28, 35, 62-64, 66, 68, 84-85, 93-94, 96-97, 108-109, 115, 131, 134

G

Ginsberg v. New York 51-52, 56, 88

H

Harassment, Intimidation, or Bullying (HIB) 359-370, 372-375, 377-383, 420, 494-495, 498, 529 530, 574

Index

I

Injunction 66, 74, 86, 99, 106, 127-129, 137, 141, 161, 164, 186, 213, 265, 354

J

Justice Alito 79-80, 117-118, 173, 187-189, 242-243, 256, 295, 318, 596
Justice Brennan 80, 87-88, 93-94, 105, 114, 155, 158, 165, 184-185, 196, 221-222, 232, 245, 260, 282, 286, 299, 317, 326, 592
Justice Breyer 80, 118-119
Justice Stevens 80, 86, 88, 94, 113, 119
Justice Thomas 115-117

L

Libel 40, 44-47, 49, 77
Libelous Per Se 45, 49
Limited Public Forum 97, 101-102, 106
Lower Court 1, 18, 38, 40, 46-48, 56, 73, 79-80, 118, 123-124, 129, 200, 208, 299, 302, 346

M

Malice 45, 47-49, 486
Miller Test 43, 52-54, 60, 87-90, 95-96, 99, 144-145, 158, 166, 169, 184, 200, 245, 257-258, 268, 278, 302, 322-323, 351, 358, 590, 592
Miller-test approach 305, 322-323
Miller v. California 13, 50, 52-54, 56, 60, 87-89, 96, 144, 158, 166, 184, 200, 278, 302, 323, 351, 358
minors 42, 51-52, 56-57, 110, 353, 602, 605
modified 151, 230-231, 234, 251, 258, 260, 262, 291-293, 297-299, 311-313, 346
Monetary Damages 11, 86, 99, 106, 110, 127, 154, 161, 164, 181, 217, 230, 233, 247, 265, 271, 285, 289, 294, 374
Morse Test 108-109, 115, 117-118, 121, 134, 186-189, 222, 254, 280, 302, 314-315, 318, 321, 347, 351, 590, 592, 605
motivation 360-362
Myspace 6, 18, 40, 43, 48-49, 58, 212-215, 239-241, 244, 246-247, 252-253, 255-256, 284-286, 293, 302, 358

N

Narrowly Tailored 13, 40, 43, 354

O

Objective Standard 24, 35, 193
Obscene Speech 6, 43, 50, 54, 60, 84, 87, 89, 91-92, 94-96, 127, 145, 158, 162, 165-166, 251-252, 257, 268, 273, 313, 320, 347, 358
Off-Campus Offline Student-Speech Jurisprudence 124, 200
off-campus student-speech jurisprudence 136, 142, 151, 185, 243, 259, 299, 304, 306-307, 315, 346-347, 590-592, 594-595, 598
Offline Speech 7, 18, 123-124, 178, 198, 280, 286, 310, 332, 334
oral 31, 44, 49, 59, 487, 533, 573
ordinance 37-40, 218
overbreadth 38, 56, 58, 218
Overbroad 38-39, 43, 45, 48, 56-58, 60

P

parent 2, 118, 125, 215-216, 228, 236, 264, 284, 287, 289, 293, 352, 369, 373-374, 378, 381, 383-384, 407, 442, 459, 485, 567, 595
peace 37-38, 40-41, 118, 127, 148, 160, 201, 205-206, 581
pedagogical 98, 100, 103-106, 121, 197, 317, 350, 605
plainly offensive 75, 79, 84-86, 88-90, 92, 94, 96, 115, 121, 185, 200, 214, 219, 224, 286, 301, 350, 605
possession 52, 57, 134, 176, 190, 278, 434, 573, 601-602
prurient 51-52, 54, 56, 60, 96, 200, 257, 302, 351, 358
Public Figures 45-46, 48-49
Public Official 45-46, 49

R

reasonable forecast 71, 129, 153, 159, 165, 174, 211, 215, 227, 231, 244, 268, 275, 283, 288, 296, 313, 321, 363, 378
Reasonable-Recipient View 24-26, 31-32, 35, 136, 193-194, 224-225, 260, 266, 291, 314
Reasonable-Speaker View 24-26, 29, 31-32, 35, 190, 193, 224, 255, 314
Responsible Use Policies 352, 356, 358
restraint 24, 38-39, 128, 130, 132-133, 167, 179, 590, 592, 594-596
Rosario 50, 53
Roth Test 51, 54

S

School Safety Team 360, 368-369, 382-383
School-Sanctioned Speech 108, 121, 601
School-Sponsored Student Speech 97-98, 100, 103-105, 107, 134, 317
Scienter 56, 60
Sexual Material 52, 54
Slander 44, 49, 77
Snapchat 602-603
specialist 278, 281, 366, 382-383, 407
Stanley v. Georgia 52, 57, 88, 593
statute 37-38, 40-41, 45, 47-48, 51-52, 57-59, 218, 278, 353, 359, 362-363, 366, 370, 375, 377, 379-381, 534-536, 585-589
Student-Speech Tests 119, 151, 177, 188, 242, 304-305, 309, 313, 315, 317, 346, 351, 592
Subjective Standard 23, 35

T

technology 8, 57, 218-219, 247, 278, 281, 315, 352-353, 461, 466, 577, 600
third party 136, 142, 194, 274, 291, 305, 309, 311, 329, 331, 347
Tinker Tests 64, 83, 89, 99-100, 102, 104, 107, 157-158, 164-165, 184, 214, 221, 253-255, 265, 277, 351

Totality of the Circumstances 26, 32, 35, 162, 223, 225
Traditional-Obscenity Jurisprudence 85, 87, 96
Traditional Public Forum 97, 101, 106-107, 358
Trier of Fact 26, 35
truth 13, 45, 49, 51, 73, 78, 299, 597
tweet 53, 257, 602
Twitter 6, 18, 43, 49, 256, 285, 302, 358, 600
unaffiliated 23, 123, 125, 200, 268, 334, 350

U

Underinclusive 56, 60
United States Constitution 1, 3-4, 12, 18, 34-35, 54, 63, 67-68, 82, 90-91, 96, 106, 121, 128, 131, 143, 161, 200, 205, 590-591

V

Viewpoint Discrimination 40, 70, 77, 113, 121, 354-355, 358
vulgar, lewd 79, 84-85, 88-89, 91-96, 114, 121, 162, 184-185, 196, 200, 251, 273, 299, 301, 315, 326, 350, 592, 598, 605

Y

YouTube 6, 18, 43, 49, 212-214, 226, 261, 263, 271, 274, 302, 358

IRMA Information Resources Management Association

Become an IRMA Member

Members of the **Information Resources Management Association (IRMA)** understand the importance of community within their field of study. The Information Resources Management Association is an ideal venue through which professionals, students, and academicians can convene and share the latest industry innovations and scholarly research that is changing the field of information science and technology. Become a member today and enjoy the benefits of membership as well as the opportunity to collaborate and network with fellow experts in the field.

IRMA Membership Benefits:

- **One FREE Journal Subscription**
- **30% Off Additional Journal Subscriptions**
- **20% Off Book Purchases**
- Updates on the latest events and research on Information Resources Management through the IRMA-L listserv.
- Updates on new open access and downloadable content added to Research IRM.
- A copy of the Information Technology Management Newsletter twice a year.
- A certificate of membership.

IRMA Membership $195

Scan code to visit irma-international.org and begin by selecting your free journal subscription.

Membership is good for one full year.

www.irma-international.org